THE EXPEDIENCY
of CULTURE

Uses of Culture in the Global Era

GEORGE YÚDICE

DUKE UNIVERSITY PRESS

Durham and London 2003

2nd printing, 2005

© 2003 Duke University Press

All rights reserved

Printed in the United States of
America on acid-free paper ∞

Designed by Amy Ruth Buchanan

Typeset in Quadraat by Tseng
Information Systems, Inc.

Library of Congress Cataloging-
in-Publication Data appear on
the last printed page of this book.

Chapter 3 was originally published
in *Cultures of Politics, Politics of
Cultures: Re-Visioning Latin American
Social Movements*, edited by Sonia
E. Alvarez, Evelina Dagnino, and
Arturo Escobar. Boulder, CO:
Westview Press, 1998.

THE EXPEDIENCY OF CULTURE

POST-CONTEMPORARY

INTERVENTIONS

Series Editors:

Stanley Fish and

Fredric Jameson

CONTENTS

Acknowledgments, vii

Introduction, 1

1 The Expediency of Culture, 9

2 The Social Imperative to Perform, 40

3 The Globalization of Culture and
the New Civil Society, 82

4 The Funkification of Rio, 109

5 Parlaying Culture into Social Justice, 133

6 Consumption and Citizenship?, 160

7 The Globalization of Latin America:
Miami, 192

8 Free Trade and Culture, 214

9 Producing the Cultural Economy:
The Collaborative Art of inSITE, 287

Conclusion, 338

Notes, 363
Works Cited, 391
Index, 453

ACKNOWLEDGMENTS

This book could not have been written without the myriad discussions and debates with friends and colleagues. Some of these go back decades and inform my everyday views of the world. Sohnya Sayres, Juan Flores, Jean Franco, Néstor García Canclini, Daniel Mato, Toby Miller, Andrew Ross, Randy Martin, Doris Sommer, Silviano Santiago, Heloísa Buarque de Hollanda, Beatriz Resende, Alberto Moreiras, Idelber Avelar, John Kraniauskas, Mirta Antonelli, and many others are part of this transnational interpretive community. I am particularly appreciative of the time and effort that Toby Miller, Andrew Ross, Larry Grossberg, Alberto Moreiras, Luis Cárcamo, Micol Seigel, Sonia Alvarez, Arturo Escobar, and Ana María Ochoa dedicated to reading and making specific comments on one or more chapters. Néstor García Canclini's review of the Spanish version, as well as Gabriela Ventureira's excellent translation, added significant and highly appreciated insights. I am also indebted to my editor at Duke University Press, Ken Wissoker, and to the various institutions that have given me support to conduct research on this book over the years: the PSC-CUNY Research Award for research in Brazil; the U.S.-Mexico Fund for Culture, for a grant to study how diversity is construed differentially in Mexico and the United States; the Rockefeller Foundation's Post-Doctoral Humanities Fellowship Program, which enabled me to coordinate research on cultural policy as part of the Privatization of Culture Project at New York University; and New York University's various forms of support. To these individuals and institutions, as well as to the many others mentioned in the pages that follow, I give my heartfelt thanks.

INTRODUCTION

At a recent international meeting of cultural policy specialists, a UNESCO official lamented that culture is invoked to solve problems that previously were the province of economics and politics. Yet, she continued, the only way to convince government and business leaders that it is worth supporting cultural activity is to argue that it will reduce social conflicts and lead to economic development (Yúdice 2000b: 10). This book aims to provide an understanding, and a series of illustrations, of how culture as an expedient gained legitimacy and displaced or absorbed other understandings of culture. Permit me to stress at the outset that I am not reprising Adorno and Horkheimer's critique of the commodity and its instrumentalization. As I explain in chapter 1, *culture-as-resource* is much more than commodity; it is the lynchpin of a new epistemic framework in which ideology and much of what Foucault called disciplinary society (i.e., the inculcation of norms in such institutions as education, medicine, and psychiatry) are absorbed into an economic or ecological rationality, such that management, conservation, access, distribution, and investment— in "culture" and the outcomes thereof—take priority.

Culture-as-resource can be compared with nature-as-resource, particularly as both trade on the currency of diversity. Think of biodiversity,[1] including traditional and scientific knowledge thereof, which, according to the "Convention on Biological Diversity," must be fostered and conserved to "[maintain] its potential to meet the needs and aspirations of present and future generations" ("Convention" 1992:5). Taking into consideration the proclivity of private enterprise to seek profit at all costs, the tendency of developed nations to have an advantage over developing countries, the greater legitimacy of scientific over traditional knowledge, ever increasing pollution, and so on, the major issue at hand becomes management of resources, knowledges, technologies, and the risks entailed thereof, defined in myriad ways.

Culture, for most people, does not evoke the same sense of life-threatening urgency, although it is true that many lament the ravages that tourism, fast food, and the global entertainment industries have on traditional ways of life. More recently, however, the very managers of global resources have "discovered culture," at least paying lip service to notions of cultural maintenance and cultural investment. On the one hand, it has become common sense that to preserve biodiversity, cultural traditions also need be maintained. On the other hand, it is argued — if not really believed — that (gender- and race-sensitive) investment in culture will strengthen the fiber of civil society, which in turn serves as the ideal host for political and economic development.

It is not always easy to make both — sociopolitical and economic — aspects of cultural management jibe without problems or contradictions. Consider, for example, that in accepting Western forms of law in order to protect their technologies (e.g., engineering of seed varieties) and cultural practices (e.g., aboriginal dream paintings), non-Western peoples may undergo even more rapid transformation. If a particular technology or ritual is not currently included as a form of protectable property, the recourse to Western law to ensure that others do not make profits therefrom almost certainly entails the acceptance of the property principle. What will it mean when non-Western forms of knowledge, technology, and cultural practices are incorporated into intellectual property and copyright law? Will the sale of "inalienable" culture become something akin to the sale of pollution permits in the United States, whereby companies that reduce their air emissions can sell the rights to emit those air pollutants? Increasingly, in cultural as in natural resources, management is the name of the game.

Although I obviously identify villains and heroes in this book, most of the situations I examine are more complex. Some readers of the manuscript wondered if I wasn't pessimistic about the prospects of grassroots movements. One anonymous reader remarked that "cautionary conclusions outweigh the grass-roots politics of cultural work." I am, to be sure, sounding a note of caution regarding the celebration of cultural agency, so prevalent in cultural studies work. But this caution does not ensue from a desire to be a killjoy; rather, it follows from a different understanding of agency. For some, the relatively "powerless" can draw strength from their culture to face the onslaught of the powerful. For others, the content of culture itself is almost irrelevant; what matters is that it buttresses a politics for change. Although these views can be quite compelling, it is also the case that cultural expression by itself is not enough. It helps to engage in a struggle when you have a good knowledge of the complex machinations involved in seeing an agenda through a range of multiscale, intermediary instances populated with others' similar, overlapping, or differing agendas. Cultural studies scholars often see cultural agency in a more circumscribed manner, as if a particular individual or group expression or identity in itself leads to change. But as Iris Marion Young points out, "We find ourselves positioned in relations of class, gender, race, nationality, religion, and so on, [within a 'given history of sedimented meanings and material landscape, and interaction with others in the social field'] which are sources of both possibilities of action and constraint" (2000: 100).

The black activists in the Grupo Cultural Afro Reggae, whose cultural activism I examine in chapter 5, do not simply get their way without negotiating with certified social activists, community elders, church officials, journalists, lawyers, academics, businessmen, philanthropists, the music and entertainment industries, international solidarity groups, and foundation officers. They have to work, sometimes with differing strategies, on many fronts. And each of the actors they encounter at a given instance must also negotiate at several levels. The local Ford Foundation officer in the Rio office, for example, must communicate with the office director and the foundation officers in New York before funding that may advance a particular agenda is approved.

Working at these different levels, a phenomenon ever more familiar as transnational actors become involved in the "local," nudges "agency" more in the direction of performativity, the topic of chapter 2. As the negotiation of cultural agency straddles more numerous instances, the "care of the [individual or collective] self" becomes performative. As I argue toward the end of chapter 1, on expediency, there is a compatibility between the Foucauldian notion of the care of the self and performativity; Foucault's ethics entail a reflexive practice of self-management vis-à-vis models (or what Bakhtin called "voices" and "perspectives") imposed by a given society or cultural formation. Bakhtin's notion of the author may serve as a prototype of Foucault's performative ethics, because he or she is an orchestration of others' "voices," an appropriation that consists of "populating those 'voices' with his or her own intentions, with his or her own accent" (1981: 293). One who practices care of the self must also forge one's freedom by working through the "models that he finds in his culture and are proposed, suggested, imposed upon him by his culture, his society, and his social group" (Foucault 1997a: 291).

In chapter 1, I review the ways culture is invested in, distributed in the most inclusive ways, used as an attraction for capital development and tourism, as the prime motor of the culture industries and as an inexhaustible kindling for new industries dependent on intellectual property. Consequently, the concept of resource absorbs and cancels out hitherto prevailing distinctions among high culture, anthropological, and mass culture definitions. High culture becomes a resource for urban development in the contemporary museum (e.g., the Bilbao Guggenheim). Rituals, everyday aesthetic practices such as songs, folktales, cuisine, customs, and other symbolic practices, are also mobilized as resources in tourism and in the promotion of the heritage industries. Mass culture industries, in particular the entertainment and copyright industries that have increasingly integrated vertically music, film, video, television, magazines, satellite, and cable diffusion, constitute the United States' major contributor to the GNP.

The notion of culture as a resource entails its management, a view that was not characteristic of either high culture or everyday culture in the anthropological sense. And to further complicate matters, culture as a resource circulates globally, with ever increasing velocity. Consequently, its management, which for a half-century was administrated on a national scale in most countries of Europe, Latin America, and North America—in the United States local cultural administration has predominated over the national scale, even in the heyday of the National Endowment for the Arts—is now coordinated both locally and supranationally, by corporations and the international nongovernmental sector (e.g., UNESCO, foundations, nongovernmental organizations). Despite this global circulation, or perhaps because of it, there has emerged a new international division of cultural labor that imbricates local difference with transnational administration and investment. This does not mean that the effects of this increasingly transnational culture, evident in the entertainment industries *and* in the so-called global civil society of NGOs, is homogenized. National and regional differences, understood as the differently structured fields of force that shape the meaning of any phenomenon, from a pop song to environmental and antiracist activism, are functional to global trade and global activism.

In chapter 2, I examine how these structured fields of force are understood as sets of performative injunctions relating to the interactional pacts, interpretive frameworks, and institutional conditionings of comportment and knowledge production. The synergy produced by the relations among the institutions of the state and civil society, the judiciary, the police, schools and universities, the media, and consumer markets, shapes understanding and behavior. This performative force is exemplified by an analysis of the U.S. "culture wars," which I argue are a societal fantasy whereby the normative and the nonnormative are in a head-on clash. On the one hand, the culture wars brought us the ravings of Jesse Helms and other conservatives; on the other, many cultural leftists were more than happy to push all the right buttons and in the process gain the visibility that comes with self-righteousness and in-your-face spectacle. The notion of fantasy is used in a psychoanalytic sense to refer to the projective character of this cultural standoff.

One of the most significant aspects of the cultural activism of identity groups is that it has been in part facilitated by legislation and due process. Although critical race theorists find that the rule of law is "composed essentially of choices made for and against people, and imposed through violence" (T. Ross 2000), agreeing with Foucault's (1997b) view of law as the violent imperative of a "society that defends itself," law is nevertheless a fundamental principle for action. Indeed, law is also a given in everyday performativity in U.S. society, as Judith Butler has argued. Perhaps the greatest discrepancy between the United States and the other countries of the Americas has to do with the performative force of law. It is widely recognized throughout the Americas that law is permeated by favor, hierarchy, and other personalist biases, even in the postdictatorship years in which human rights legislation accompanied much of the activism in the region. Law, therefore, does not have in all societies the same projective fantasies that impinge on questions of identity. An examination of the culture of favor in Brazil brings out this difference.

Chapter 3 explores how the transdisciplinary field of cultural studies might deal with cultural changes wrought by globalization processes. I am particularly interested in how these processes have generated discussions on the role of civil society as the medium through which the conventional compromise between the state and the diverse sectors of the nation—the E pluribus unum— is renegotiated. This revision is often brought to the fore by localities that have the most to gain or the most to lose from the vicissitudes wrought by globalization. Civil society has become the concept of choice as many movements for reform and revolution have been chastened by the eviction of socialism as a political alternative, at least for the near future. The current dominance of neoliberalism—the set of policies that include trade liberalization, privatization, the reduction (and, in some cases, near elimination) of state-subsidized social services such as health care and education, the lowering of wages, and the evisceration of labor rights—has contributed to the left's shift in political attention from the takeover of state power (which in many cases has not resolved the question of sovereignty) to issues of civil and human rights and quality of life. Conventional and even progressive political parties have succeeded in doing very little to counter these policies, both because the institutionalized political process is largely dysfunctional in responding to social needs and because enormous pressures from international financial interests not only have discouraged reform but have actually worsened conditions, such as the ever increasing gap in income distribution. Consequently, the most innovative actors in setting agendas for political and social policies are grassroots movements and the national and international NGOs that support them. These actors have put a premium on culture, defined in myriad ways, a resource already targeted for exploitation by capital (e.g., in the media, consumerism, and tourism), and a foundation for resistance against the ravages of that very same economic system.

Chapters 4 and 5 together constitute a case study of the transformation of social strife, particularly racist exclusion and criminalization in the *favelas* of Rio de Janeiro, into a resource that "NGOized" cultural groups can mobilize to seek empowerment. Chapter 4 narrates the denigration of mostly black youth from the favelas and their preferred music, especially funk, which has been associated with violence, much like rap in the United States in the 1980s. It is significant that the turn to funk departs from the traditional adherence to samba, "music of the people." In fact, *funkeiros* sought to counter the performance of "the popular," subordinated yet accepted by elites, with a music that challenged this accommodation. Funk, and other black diasporic musics such as rap and reggae, contested the place of black people in Brazil, their controlled access to privatized public space.

As the race-based claims made on behalf of funk and rap gained greater recognition, especially from local and international NGOs and such U.S. foundations as the Rockefeller Foundation, "cultural groups" were able to open up a space for empowerment. In chapter 5, I review a youth cultural network and a citizen action initiative, both of which bear out the insight that culture has become the terrain on which new legitimation narratives have been forged to naturalize the neoliberal desideratum to purge the social from government. Neoliberalism reintroduces the expectation that "institutions of assistance" will be situated in civil society rather than in government. This opens up new spaces for activism that enable certain kinds of empowerment at the same time that they make available new forms of social management. As Foucault has argued, "Civil society is the concrete ensemble within which these abstract points, economic men, need to be positioned in order to be made adequately manageable" (1979). The network structure adopted by the groups I examine here also disseminates the phenomenon of agency; it is layered across differently positioned social actors: the activist cultural groups, the community in whose name the activism is carried out, funding sources that range from local government agencies and foundations to transnational corporations and NGOs, even the World Bank and the Inter-American Development Bank. The discourses of these groups are largely overdetermined by this network of collaborators and intermediaries.

Chapter 6 is a further exploration of the ways consumerism has made inroads into how people negotiate identity, status, and political leverage. In this chapter, I assess the degree to which it is feasible to envision civil society not as the Habermasian space of free debate and opinion shaping, but as a handmaiden to neoliberal policies that reduce and privatize the social and the cultural. Even political activity can take place through "point-of-purchase" sites, as well as socially conscious credit cards. One can literally do politics by shopping or sartorially displaying one's favorite political slogans. Cultural studies scholars pressed the case of such consumerist politics in the 1980s and 1990s, claiming that, to the degree that identity is bolstered by consumerism, it is better equipped to make demands in the neoliberal institutional sphere. Such a politics has yet to be put fully to the test, particularly as it is riddled by the contradictions of antiglobalization protestors who nevertheless consume music and other entertainment produced by the most globalizing of industries: the entertainment conglomerates.

Chapter 7 examines a cultural-economic "bridge" or "corridor" that straddles the United States and all of Latin America. Miami is exemplary of the creative economies that have been touted in recent years for their use of culture and innovation as engines of economic growth. In Miami, the culture industries, especially music, television, Internet portals, fashion photography, and arts institutions, play this role. Initially located there to take advantage of both Latin American markets and U.S. Latino markets, these industries also amass cohorts of cultural workers who have taken an interest in Miami itself and have begun to transform the city. I argue that this transformation is part of an internationalization that renders Miami a post-Cuban and post-Caribbean city. But this is a problematic internationalization, for the enthusiastic fusion of U.S. multiculturalism and Latin American *mestizaje*, though more encompassing than the traditional U.S. racial order, nevertheless intensifies historical inequalities, especially of black immigrants. In this chapter, I also examine the claim that racialized immigrants are exploited contributors to the cultural economy; they "give life" to a city, as Castells argues, not only through their labor in the service industries but also in their cultural impact through music, dance, food, and festivals. This is an underrecognized contribution in the international division of cultural labor.

Chapter 8 examines the international property regimes that enable conglomerates to maintain their hold on such a large share of cultural production, and above all its distribution, and the profits generated therefrom. The very notion of innovation as an engine of capital accumulation is often identified with culture; in this chapter, we see how the strategies of global trade are rearticulating all conceptions of culture, even to the point that some of the most economically profitable products and services, say, computer software and Internet sites, are treated, respectively, as cultural forms of intellectual property and cultural "content." Also examined are strategies for cultural integration in Latin America that, even as they counter the inordinate influence of U.S. and transnational entertainment culture, also increasingly rely on partnerships with private capital and neoliberal policies. Special attention is given to the cultural complements of the North American Free Trade Agreement and the Common Market of the South (MERCOSUR). Cultural diversity, for example, is incorporated and to some degree neutralized in these venues as part of the international division of cultural labor.

Chapter 9 is an extrapolation of chapter 8 into a case study of a triennial program of art events, inSITE, held in the San Diego–Tijuana corridor that crosses the U.S.-Mexico border. Although the event departs significantly from trade-related issues, much of the division of cultural labor that characterizes trade relations is evident here as well. This division is found in the financing of the event, in the relations between artists and publics, and in the expectations of and from "communities." The chapter considers the political and cultural economy of a vast and increasingly influential art event. Central to this examination is the fact of labor, not only in the asymmetry that cuts across the border, but also in the very notion of collaboration, an important concept for advocates of empowerment through community-based art programs. Something akin to industrial maquiladoras takes place here, allowing one to speak of cultural maquiladoras.

The conclusion considers, briefly, whether the phenomena examined in the preceding chapters holds in a world characterized by crisis, such as that generated by the September 11 attacks, in contrast to the stability assumed by those who make expedient claims for culture. Does culture have the power to remake community when the world is thrown into crisis?

The Expediency of Culture

But it is culture—not raw technology alone—that will determine whether the United States retains its status as the pre-eminent Internet nation.
—Sever Lohr, "Welcome to the Internet, the First Global Colony"

Culture as Resource

I argue in this book that the role of culture has expanded in an unprecedented way into the political and economic at the same time that conventional notions of culture largely have been emptied out. I do not focus on the content of culture—that is, the model of uplift (following Schiller or Arnold) or distinction (following Bourdieu) that it offered in its traditional acceptations, or more recently its anthropologization as a whole way of life (Williams), according to which it is recognized that everyone's culture has value. Instead, I approach the question of culture in our period, characterized as one of accelerated globalization, as a *resource*. Allow me to bracket for the moment the requisite reference to Heidegger's discussion of resource as *standing reserve (Bestand)* and to the myriad discussions of globalization. I will return to these questions, but the point I would like to stress at the outset is that culture is increasingly wielded as a resource for both sociopolitical and economic amelioration, that is, for increasing participation in this era of waning political involvement, conflicts over citizenship (Young 2000: 81–120), and the rise of what Jeremy Rifkin (2000) has called "cultural capitalism." The immaterialization characteristic of many new sources of economic growth (e.g., intellectual property rights as defined by the General Agreement on Tariffs and Trade [GATT] and the World Trade Organization) and the increasing share of the world trade by symbolic goods (movies, TV programs, music, tourism, etc.) have given the cultural sphere greater protagonism than at any other moment in the history of modernity. It could be argued that culture has simply become a pretext for sociopolitical amelioration and economic growth, but even if that were the case, the proliferation of such arguments, in those fora provided by local culture and development projects as well as by UNESCO, the World Bank, and the so-called globalized civil society of international foundations and NGOs, has operated a transformation in what we understand by the notion of culture and what we do in its name.

The relation between cultural and political spheres or cultural and economic spheres is not new. On the one hand, culture is the medium in which the public sphere emerges in the eighteenth century; as Foucauldian and cultural studies scholars have argued, it became a means to internalize social control (i.e., via discipline and governmentality) throughout the nineteenth and twentieth centuries. Tony Bennett (1995), for example, has demonstrated that culture provided not only ideological uplift, according to which people were gauged to have human worth, but also a material inscription in forms of behavior: people's behavior was transformed by the physical requirements involved in moving through schools and museums (ways of walking, dressing, talking, etc.). Also well studied are the political uses of culture to promote a particular ideology, for clientelist purposes or for currying favor in foreign relations, as evidenced in the advancement of proletarian culture by the Soviet Commissariat of Enlightenment (Fitzpatrick 1992), the clientelist sponsorship of muralism by the Mexican state in the 1920s and 1930s (Folgarait 1998), or the currying of influence in foreign relations, as in the United States' Good Neighbor (Yúdice 2000a) and cold war cultural policies (Saunders 1999).

Also on the economic front, nineteenth-century Europe saw the increasing subjection of the artist and the writer to the commercial imperative. In this context, and with the emergence of new technologies such as lithography, photography, film, and sound recording, some theorists and critics came to define art in contradistinction to the commercial. In his famous 1938 essay, "On the Fetish-Character in Music and the Regression of Listening," Theodor Adorno rejected the political-economic basis of the new mass media, which turned the engagement with art away from its use-value and toward the "fetish character of commodities" ([1938] 1978: 278–279; 1984: 25). In the first half of the twentieth century, Adorno could define art as the process through which the individual gains freedom by externalizing himself, in contrast to the philistine "who craves art for what he can get out of it" (1984: 25). Today it is nearly impossible to find public statements that do not recruit instrumentalized art and culture, whether to better social conditions, as in the creation of multicultural tolerance and civic participation though UNESCO-like advocacy for cultural citizenship and cultural rights, or to spur economic growth through urban cultural development projects and the concomitant proliferation of museums for cultural tourism, epitomized by the increasing number of Guggenheim franchises.

To illustrate the extent to which this is the case, consider *American Canvas*, a 1997 report of the National Endowment for the Arts (NEA) on the place of arts and culture in U.S. society:

> No longer restricted solely to the sanctioned arenas of culture, the arts would be literally suffused throughout the civic structure, finding a home in a variety of community service and economic development activities–from youth programs and crime prevention to job training and race relations–far afield from the traditional aesthetic functions of the arts. This extended role for culture can also be seen in the many new partners that arts organizations have taken on in recent years, with school districts, parks and recreation departments, convention and visitor bureaus, chambers of commerce, and a host of social welfare agencies all serving to highlight the utilitarian aspects of the arts in contemporary society. (Larson 1997: 127–128)

This expanded role for culture is due in part to the reduction of direct subvention of all social services, culture included, by the state, thus requiring a new legitimation strategy in the post-Fordist and the post–civil rights era in the United States. Advocacy for the centrality of culture in solving social problems is not new, but it took different forms in the past, such as the ideological (re)production of proper citizens (whether bourgeois, proletarian, or national). Although there have long been art therapy programs for the mentally ill and for the incarcerated, culture more generally was not regarded as a proper therapy for such social dysfunctions as racism and genocide. Nor was it considered, historically, an incentive for economic growth. Why the turn to a legitimation based on utility?

There are, I think, two main reasons. Globalization has pluralized the contacts among diverse peoples and facilitated migrations, thus problematizing the use of culture as a national expedient. Additionally, in the United States, the end of the cold war pulled the legitimizing rug out from under a belief in artistic freedom, and with it unconditional support for the arts, as a major marker of difference with respect to the Soviet Union. Of course, this politically motivated sponsorship of freedom was fundamental in giving certain artistic styles (jazz, modern dance, abstract expressionism) the shot in the arm needed for "New York to steal the idea of modern art" from Paris, according to Serge Guilbaut (1983).

Without cold war legitimation, there is no holding back utilitarian arguments in the United States. Art has completely folded into an expanded conception of culture that can solve problems, including job creation. Its purpose is to lend a hand in the reduction of expenditures and at the same time help maintain the level of state intervention for the stability of capitalism.

Because almost all actors in the cultural sphere have latched onto this strategy, culture is no longer experienced, valued, or understood as transcendent. And insofar as this is the case, appeals to culture are no longer tied to this strategy. The culture wars, for example, take the form they do in a context in which art and culture are seen as fundamentally interested—so much so that they set in motion a particular performative force, on which I elaborate in chapter 2, "The Social Imperative to Perform." Conservatives and liberals are not willing to give each other the benefit of the doubt that art is beyond interest. (Of course, most leftists, following Marx and Gramsci, already believed that culture is political struggle.) As conservatives began to exercise more influence in the 1980s and 1990s, this basic belief in the interested character of art and culture was expressed by eliminating entitlements and redistributive programs bequeathed by Johnson's Great Society and the civil rights legacy, which benefit marginalized groups. Many of these programs were legitimized by claims that the needs of these groups were premised on cultural difference, which had to be taken as a deciding factor in the distribution of recognition and resources. Conservatives, on the other hand, saw these differences as incapacities or moral flaws (e.g., the "culture of poverty" attributed to racial minorities or the libertinism of gay and lesbian sexual preferences and practices) that rendered these groups ineligible for public resources (see chapter 2).

But this move to reduce state expenditures, which might seem like the death knell of the nonprofit arts and cultural activities, is actually their condition of continued possibility. The arts and culture sector is now claiming that it can solve the United States' problems: enhance education, salve racial strife, help reverse urban blight through cultural tourism, create jobs, reduce crime, and perhaps even make a profit. This reorientation of the arts is being brought about by arts administrators. Much as in classic cases of governmentality, in which there is total subordination of technicians to administrators (Castel 1991: 293), artists are being channeled to manage the social (see chapter 9).

The academy has turned to "managerial professionals," who bridge traditional liberal professions ("a technical body of knowledge, advanced education . . . professional associations and journals, codes of ethics") and corporate middle management in the business of producing students, research, outreach, institutional development, and so on (Rhoades and Slaughter 1997: 23). So also has the art and culture sector burgeoned into an enormous network of arts administrators who mediate between funding sources and artists and/or communities. Like their counterparts in the university and the business world, they must produce and distribute the producers of art and culture, who in turn deliver communities or consumers.

Cultural Development

This view is not exclusive to the United States. One important policymaker from the European Task Force on Culture and Development attributes multipurposes to art and culture: it is useful in fostering social cohesion in divisive polities and, because it is a labor-intensive sector, it helps reduce unemployment (E. Delgado 1998). Indeed, as powerful institutions like the European Union, the World Bank, the Inter-American Development Bank (IADB), and the major international foundations begin to understand culture as a crucial sphere for investment, it is increasingly treated like any other resource. James D. Wolfensohn, president of the World Bank, in his keynote address at the international conference "Culture Counts: Financing, Resources, and the Economics of Culture in Sustainable Development" (October 1999), folds culture into the Bank's policies as an instrument for human development. He stresses a "holistic view of development" that focuses on community empowerment of the poor so that they may hold onto—sustain—those assets that enable them to cope with "trauma and loss," stave off "social disconnectedness," "maintain self-esteem," and also provide material resources. He writes, "There are development dimensions of culture. Physical and expressive culture is an undervalued resource in developing countries. It can earn income, through tourism, crafts, and other cultural enterprises" (World Bank 1999b: 11). "Heritage gives value. Part of our joint challenge is to analyze the local and national returns on investments which restore and draw value from cultural heritage—whether it is built or living cultural expression, such as indigenous music, theater, crafts" (13).

Now consider the lending strategy of the IADB in the cultural sphere. According to one bank official, "Given economic orthodoxy throughout the world, the old model of state public support for culture is dead. The new models consist of partnerships with the public sector and with international financial institutions, particularly the Multilateral Development Banks (MDBs) like the World Bank and the Inter-American Development Bank" (Santana 1999). The turn to cultural capital is part of the history of recognition of shortcomings in investment for physical capital in the 1960s, human capital in the 1980s, and social capital in the 1990s. Each new notion of capital was devised as a way of ameliorating some of the failures of development according to the preceding framework. The concept of social capital was operationalized in the MDBs, taking the social fabric into consideration in their development projects. This concept also ensued from the recognition that although economic returns have been substantial in the 1990s, inequality has increased exponentially. The trickle-down premise of neoliberal economic theory has not been confirmed. Consequently, there has been a turn to investment in civil society, and culture as its prime animator.

According to Santana (1999), empirical examples suggest that there is force to this argument. For example, Villa El Salvador in Peru showed an impressive increase in social indicators in its near thirty years of existence. In 1971, homeless people invaded Lima and the government relocated them to a semidesert-like area. Twenty years later they comprised a city of eighty-one hundred people with some of the best social indicators in the country. Illiteracy declined from an index of 5.8 to 3.8, infant mortality was reduced to a lower than average rate of 67 per 1,000, and registration in basic education grew to a better than average 98 percent. The variable that explains this, according to Santana, is culture, which enables the consolidation of citizenship founded on active participation of the population. The majority of the people came from the highlands of Peru and maintained their indigenous cultural customs, communal work, and solidarity, which provided those characteristics that lead to development. Santana compared these characteristics to the civic and cultural traditions that, according to Robert Putnam (1993), enabled a northern Italian region to prosper. Consequently, if it could be shown, he added, that culture produces the patterns of trust, cooperation, and social interaction that result in a more vigorous economy, more democratic and effective government, and fewer social problems, then MDBs will be likely to invest in cultural development projects.

There are, of course, tens of thousands of cultural projects in any given country. How does a funder like the IADB decide on which to invest? Mechanisms of compensation and incentive need to be designed, argued Santana (1999), to generate confidence that there will be a return to investors. These mechanisms would function as an alternative to price. What kind of rationality can economic agents rely on for investment in culture? What kind of structure of incentives will get results? Incentives, he added, can provide a stable environment for private investment in culture, rather than the episodic character of private investment in culture. Moreover, the cultural funding model must be limited to specific segments of culture because the demand for resources is great and because only those likely to produce returns will be funded. In this scenario, Santana cautioned, "culture for culture's sake," whatever that may be, will never be funded, unless it provides an indirect form of return.

The different kinds of return are fiscal incentives, institutional marketing or publicity value, and the conversion of nonmarket activity to market activity. MDBs prioritize cultural funding projects that bear some relation to the traditional areas of these banks and must have an instrumental outcome, for example, in health, education, the formation of social capital, or the support and reinforcement of civil society. Because the meeting at which Santana made this presentation was for cultural organizations who were seeking new funding partners, a range of scenarios were discussed. One of the projects considered likely for funding is the annual cultural festival CREA in Colombia (Ochoa Gautier 2001). Music competitions were held in every municipality in the country, and a number of finalists were selected to compete in state-level festivals, which in turn made a selection of finalists to compete in a federal-level festival. The musicians came from all parts of the country, including those controlled by guerrillas and paramilitary groups. It was argued that the festivals were the only activity that guerrillas and paramilitaries permitted their residents to engage in. That is, the festivals were the only forum in which there was contact and exchange among adversaries and different parts of the country. Consequently, the case could be made that there would be a higher likelihood of return, as these festivals contribute to the peace process and so create a safer environment for investment.

However, to get financing there have to be quantitative data for the technical staff of the bank to evaluate the impact of the festivals and measure the benefit in terms of a safer environment for investment and return. The measurement instruments have to go beyond intuitions and opinions. It is for this reason that most cultural projects funded by MDBs piggyback on other projects in education or urban renewal. This piggybacking mode of entry has to do with the difficulty that banks have in dealing with culture. Without hard data (e.g., indicators), it is difficult to justify investing in a project. And, of course, there are methodological difficulties in developing indicators for culture. The concept is modeled after economic indicators, which enable economists to determine the "health" of the economy and to predict what kinds of interventions will strengthen it. Of course, there are different approaches to the design of indicators, depending on which criteria are foregrounded: economic (How many jobs will be produced?), professional (Are mainstream arts institutions viable?), or social justice (Are the cultural values and preferences of community residents understood and honored when resources are earmarked for cultural support?; M. Jackson 1998: 2, 33). To be sure, there are important differences here, and the democratic ethos of the third option is certainly to be applauded. Yet the "bottom line" is that cultural institutions and funders are increasingly turning to the measurement of utility because there is no other accepted legitimation for social investment. In this context, the idea that the experience of *jouissance*, the unconcealment of truth, or deconstructive critique might be admissible criteria for investment in culture comes off as a conceit perhaps worthy of a Kafkaesque performance skit.

The Cultural Economy

The notion of culture has mutated enough, however, to meet the requirements of the bottom line. Artistic trends such as multiculturalism that emphasize social justice (perhaps understood no more broadly than equal visual representation in public spheres) and initiatives to promote sociopolitical and economic utility have been fused into the notion of what I call the "cultural economy" and what Blair's New Labourite rhetoric dubbed the "creative economy." Also marketed at home and to the world as "Cool Britannia," this creative economy includes both a sociopolitical agenda, particularly the protagonism of multiculturalism as embodied in the work of the so-called young British artists, as well as an economic agenda, that is, the belief that the creativity provided by this new generation transformed London into "the creative hub for trends in music, fashion, art and design" (Mercer 1999–2000: 52). Applying the logic that a creative environment begets innovation (Castells 2000), hip London culture was touted as the foundation for the so-called new economy based on "content provision," which is supposed to be the engine of accumulation. This premise is quite widespread, with U.S. rhetoric of a "new economy" and British hype about the "creative economy" echoed in New Zealand's "HOT Nation," Scotland's "Create in Scotland," and Canada's "A Sense of Place, a Sense of Being" (Volkerling 2001: 10). Similar projects have been developed in a spate of Latin American cities: Buenos Aires' Puerto Madero (Berríos and Abarca 2001) and Palermo Viejo (Oropeza 2001), Fortaleza's Puerto Digital (Berríos and Abarca

2001), and Valparaíso. This last has contracted the team that renovated Barcelona's port for the 1992 Olympics and which is now to be the first host for the Universal Forum of Cultures, one of whose principal aims is to explore and celebrate the ways the "creativity of all nations" can be harnessed for development, inclusion of diversity, and peaceful coexistence (Yúdice 2001b; Universal Forum of Cultures–Barcelona 2004).

It should be evident from the foregoing examples, and the many more reviewed in this book, that the understanding and practice of culture is quite complex, located at the intersection of economic and social justice agendas. Culture is increasingly being invoked not only as an engine of capital development, as evidenced by the ad nauseam repetition that the audiovisual industry is second only to the aerospace industry in the United States. Some have even argued that culture has transformed into the very logic of contemporary capitalism, a transformation that "already is challenging many of our most basic assumptions about what constitutes human society" (Rifkin 2000: 10–11). This culturalization of the economy has not occurred naturally, of course; it has been carefully coordinated via agreements on trade and intellectual property, such as GATT and the WTO, laws controlling the movement of mental and manual labor (i.e., immigration laws), and so on. In other words, the new phase of economic growth, the cultural economy, is also political economy. As Thomas Streeter argues, "property creation" — that is, the transformation of, say, signal transmission into something that can be bought and sold, which is fundamental to profit in the electronic media — does not just happen in the "absence of political or social control" but "involves an ongoing, collective effort of . . . turning social activities into property" (1996: 164).

Property creation and the infrastructural and legal conditions to make it profitable are not, of course, new. Take, for example, the U.S. film industry, which, since its flight from unionized New York to Los Angeles in the 1920s, established a close relationship with finance capital and U.S. government offices in charge of trade. As the industry transformed itself in the post–World War II period due to the challenge of television and the antitrust suits that forced it to divest itself of movie theaters, Hollywood began to leverage the risk of investment in its capital-intensive products through outsourcing to networks of independent production companies providing services in scripting, casting, set design, cinematography, costuming, sound mixing and mastering, editing, film processing, and so on. Indeed, the film industry has been characterized as the model of post-Fordist flexible specialization (Storper 1989: 277; Yúdice 1999b). It can also be seen as the harbinger of what Manuel Castells

(1996) has called the "network society." Moreover, a range of pressures, particularly the displacement of studio production by cheaper location production, led to vertical disintegration and the recomposition of the entertainment-industrial complex (Storper 1989: 289). Part of this story is Hollywood's move overseas, first its acquisition of theaters abroad to supplement its waning profits domestically, and ultimately to capitalize on the internationalization of production services, that is, of the division of labor. Today, a film or an arts festival or biennial are as much international composites as the clothes we wear or the cars we drive, with parts made from steel produced in one country, electronics in another, leather and plastic in still others, and finally assembled in yet other countries.

U.S. citizens are largely oblivious to the potential threat of the internationalization of the division of cultural labor. Some may be aware of the potential loss of audiovisual production jobs to Canada or Australia, but culturally there appears to be no threat because it is "our culture" that is exported. However, the question might be asked, and, in fact, has been asked, whether this kind of production makes a symbolic difference when dealing with cultural products like films, music, television shows, and new Internet entertainment. The French, for example, in their bid to have culture exempted from the GATT rounds and WTO negotiations, have long argued that film and music are crucial to cultural identity and should not be subject to the same terms of trade as, say, cars and running shoes. U.S. negotiators have countered that film and TV programs are commodities, subject to the same terms. This debate is indeed important, and one can discern meaning effects due to this mode of flexible production (e.g., Hollywood films specifically tailored to appeal to foreign audiences), but the major effects of this new international division of cultural labor are not limited, for example, to whether more multicultural or more European actors are used. What is more important is that the rights of authorship are increasingly in the hands of producers and distributors, the major entertainment conglomerates that have gradually achieved the terms by which intellectual property is possessed, such that "creators" are now little more than "content providers." Indeed, Hollywood has been the leader in the internationalization of intellectual property law. As Miller, Govil, McMurria, and Maxwell note, "Copyright and the control of intellectual property have underwritten Hollywood's internationalism because they stabilize the market and render it predictable, a crucial factor given the tremendous costs of feature film production" (2001: chap. 4).

Thus, we begin to see the maquiladora model in the film industry and all other industries in which accumulation is based on intellectual property rights and the more diffuse concept of cultural property rights. Profits are made by holding (or, as Storper would say, creating) property rights; those who don't hold these rights or who have lost them due to laws devised in the interest of corporations are relegated to working for hire as service and content providers.

The culturalization of the so-called new economy, based on cultural and mental labor (Terranova 2000) — or better yet, on the expropriation of the value of cultural and mental labor — has, with the aid of new communications and informatics technology, become the basis of a new division of labor. To the degree that communications enable services and independent producers to be located almost anywhere on earth, this is also a new international division of *cultural* labor (Miller 1996), necessary for fostering innovation and creating content. Culturalization is also political economy, for the U.S. government has been a central actor in ensuring that the nation can maintain its domination of the new economy. For example, the report on Intellectual Property and the National Information Infrastructure of the White House Information Infrastructure Task Force (IITF) recommended bolstering copyright regimes so that content provision would ensure U.S. dominance in the new economy: "All the computers, telephones, scanners, printers, switches, routers, wires, cables, networks and satellites in the world," the task force argues, "will not create a successful national information infrastructure (NII) if there is no content. What will drive the NII is the content moving through it": information and entertainment resources; access to the world's cultural resources; new product innovation; greater variety in cultural consumption (U.S. IITF 1995).

More traditional activities such as cultural tourism and arts development are also facilitating the transformation of postindustrial cities. The most sensational example is the Guggenheim Museum in Bilbao, which is serving as a model for the franchising of museums in other parts of the world, such as Rio de Janeiro and Lyons (Iturribarria 1999; J. Rojas 2000). Local political and business leaders, concerned about Bilbao's fraying postindustrial infrastructure as well as the city's reputation for terrorism, sought to revitalize it by investing in cultural infrastructure that would attract tourists and lay the foundation for an economic complex of service, information, and culture industries. By investing in a museum stamped by Frank Gehry's stylistic grandiosity, city leaders provided the magnet that would attract those activities that "give life," to use Manuel Castells's (2000) phrase: "Alongside technological innovation there has mushroomed an extraordinary urban activity . . . fortifying the social fabric of bars, restaurants, chance encounters on the street, etc. that give life to a place." Enhancing the quality of life in this way enables a city to attract and retain the innovators indispensable to the new "creative economy." "Knowledge, culture, art . . . will help catapult Bilbao to the short list of world capitals," according to Alfonso Martínez Cearra, head of Bilbao Metrópoli 30, a network of government officials, businessmen, educators, nonprofit directors, and media executives spearheading the city's development (Jacobs 1997: 14). Another postindustrial city that turned to culture to revive the economy is Peekskill, New York. Reasoning that "artists are a kind of pilot fish for gentrification," the city council created an arts district and offered incentives, such as cheap loft space, so that artists would relocate there from New York City (I. Peterson 1999).

These initiatives also have a downside, for, as in classic instances of gentrification, they tend to displace residents. (Elsewhere, I examine an instance of cultural development that involved the renowned Afro-Brazilian music group Olodum in both the renovation of the Pelourinho, historical site of the slave trade and current centerpiece of the tourism industry, and the ironic displacement of its poor black residents; see Yúdice 2000c.) The turn to the "creative economy" evidently favors the professional-managerial class, even as it trades on the rhetoric of multicultural inclusion. Subordinate or minoritized groups have a place in this scheme as low-level service workers and as providers of "life-giving" ethnic and other cultural experiences, which, according to Rifkin, "represent the new stage of capitalist development" (2000: 265). Economic development thus necessarily entails management of populations to decrease the risk of violence in the buying and selling of experiences. The Bilbao metro system installed surveillance cameras in every station to keep track of travelers' activities (Jacobs 1997: 13–14); Peekskill officials installed them on street corners in an effort to control the drug trade. Many residents, however, interpreted this as a way of reining in black residents, many of whom had been left unemployed by industrial flight to the third world. City leaders were accused of interpreting urban development in racial terms, seeking to attract white professionals and limiting the mobility of minorities (I. Peterson 1999).

Culturalization, then, is also based on the mobilization and management of populations, particularly the "life-enhancing" marginal populations who nourish the innovation of the "creators" (Castells 2000). This means a marriage of culture-as-vernacular practices, notions of community, and economic development. We see this at work in global cities that concentrate command and control headquarters for transnational corporations and a concomitant critical mass of complementary advanced producer services. These services are concentrated in cities, as Castells argues, where innovation results from the synergy of networks of complementary enterprises and from reservoirs of "human talent," much of it composed of intra- and international migrants. To attract such talent, Castells adds, cities must offer a high quality of life, which means that such cities are also major generators of cultural capital and value. The role of culture in capital accumulation, however, is not limited to this ancillary function; it is central to the processes of globalization, which are evident in Miami, the topic of chapter 7. Globalization, in fact, has invigorated the concept of cultural citizenship because political rights most often do not apply to immigrants and undocumented workers. However, the idea that people's different cultures and the needs ensuing therefrom should be recognized is a powerful argument that has found receptivity in many international fora. To the degree that social identity is developed in a collective cultural context, it is argued that democratic inclusion of "communities of difference" should recognize that context and respect the notions of responsibility and rights developed therein (Fierlbeck 1996: 4, 6).

Cultural Citizenship

Cultural rights include the freedom to engage in cultural activity, to speak one's language of choice, to teach one's language and culture to one's children, to identify with the cultural communities of one's choice, to discover the whole range of cultures that constitute world heritage, to gain knowledge of human rights, to have an education, to be free from being represented without consent or from having one's cultural space used for publicity, and to gain public provision to safeguard these rights (Groupe de Fribourg 1996). However, as one commentator puts it, cultural rights are the "Cinderellas of the human rights family" (Filibek 1995: 75) because their definition is still ambiguous: the full range of what is to be included in "culture" is not clear, nor is it easy to reconcile universal applicability with cultural relativism (Niec 1998: 5). Moreover, even though cultural rights refer to collectivities, the individual rights of members of such collectivities have priority, at least in international covenants. Consequently, cultural rights are not universally accepted and in most cases are not justiciable, unlike economic rights, whose status is firmly entrenched in international law (Steiner and Alston 1996: 268). Moreover, even if cultural rights do gain universal validity, it is not a foregone conclusion that in different cultural contexts they will be applied in the same manner. Differing legal systems provide potent or weak contexts in which to secure citizenship rights, whether political or civil/human. This is why I speak of different *fields of force* for the enactment or performance of norms and the critique of norms in chapter 2. Nevertheless, some justiciable rights overlap with cultural rights, as in the case of the right to information. Yet, how that right is exercised is dependent on cultural context (Niec 1998: 8). As Javier Pérez de Cuéllar, president of the World Commission on Culture and Development, observes in his introduction to the UNESCO report *Our Creative Diversity*, "Economic and political rights cannot be realized separately from social and cultural rights" (1996: 11).

In the United States, this legislation of affirmative cultural rights goes back to the juridical and institutional precedents laid down in the civil rights era. This history reveals an interesting dialectic between the devaluation of minority groups — for example, blacks and Puerto Ricans in Moynihan (1965; Glazer and Moynihan 1963) are characterized as lacking, *for cultural reasons*, voluntary associations and other characteristics of a valorized civil society — and the activism of those groups, who turned "culture of poverty" theses on their heads, valorizing precisely that which was disqualified by a dominant culture (e.g., Puerto Rican social clubs and adoption traditions, unrecognized by Glazer and Moynihan as bona fide voluntary associations). Once the norm-bound acculturation implicit in mainstream social science analysis and politics was seen to be unworkable, the cultural practices of minority groups could be understood as communal strategies of survival worthy of affirmation. In contrast to the assimilationist and progressivist assumptions underlying Glazer and Moynihan's thesis, multiculturalists appeal to a pluralist or relativist egalitarian position whereby different cultures are equally constitutive of society and expressive of a humanity.

It is this notion of culture that underpins the concept of cultural citizenship as developed by Renato Rosaldo in the late 1980s (1989; Rosaldo and Flores 1987). At odds with conventional notions of citizenship, which emphasize universal, albeit formal, applicability of political rights to all members of a nation, Rosaldo posited that cultural citizenship entailed that groups of people bound together by shared social, cultural, and/or physical features should not be excluded from participation in the public spheres of a given polity on the basis of those features. In a juridical context that enables litigation against exclusion and a cultural-political ethos that eschews marginalizing the "nonnormative" (considered as such from the perspective of the "mainstream"), culture serves as the ground or warrant for making "claim[s] to rights in the public square" (Rosaldo 1997: 36). Because culture is what "create[s] space where people feel 'safe' and 'at home,' where they feel a sense of belonging and membership," it is, according to this view, a necessary condition for citizenship (Flores and

Benmayor 1997: 15). In chapter 6 I provide an account of the emergence of this new form of citizenship rights and point out that originally, the eligibility requirements for conventional citizenship rights were not based on the cultural relativism of belonging to specific cultures.

Consequently, if democracy is to be fostered, public spheres in which deliberation on questions of the public good is held must be permeable to different cultures. The relativist strain in anthropological theory, according to which "communal culture" as an ensemble of ideas and values provides the individual with identity (Sapir 1924: 401), is mobilized here for political ends. Culture is thus more than an anchoring ensemble of ideas and values. It is, according to Flores and Benmayor, premised on difference, which functions as a *resource* (1997: 5). The content of culture recedes in importance as the *usefulness of the claim to difference* as a warrant gains legitimacy. The result is that *politics* trumps the content of culture. As Iris Marion Young argues, "Claims to cultural recognition usually are means to the end of undermining domination or wrongful deprivation" (2000: 83). Despite recognizing that "people discover themselves with cultural affinities that solidify them into groups by virtue of their encounter with those who are culturally different," culture has no "in itself": it is a resource for politics. "It is important to remember, however, that much of the ground for conflict between culturally differentiated groups is not cultural, but a competition over territory, resources, or jobs" (91).

Young's arguments, which correspond to the new epistemic conjuncture of expediency that I explain below, are quite useful, for they show how the liberal-communitarian debate on universality versus specificity or the "common good" versus the perspective from "situated knowledges" is superseded. Against classic liberal political philosophy identified with John Rawls, Young shows that institutions and other social web-forming entities do matter and there is no such thing as individuals who stand apart from such webs. But contra communitarian views, Young also argues that social structure takes precedence over identitarian structure, rejecting Charles Taylor's position that a politics of recognition of group difference (or culture) is in itself an objective. Instead, a politics of recognition "usually is part of or a means to claims for political and social inclusion or an end to structural inequalities that disadvantage them" (2000: 104–105). Her point is that "most group-based political claims cannot be reduced to such conflicts concerning the expression and preservation of cultural meaning" (104). Evidently, culture is a reductive category for Young. Although I acknowledge the force of Young's arguments, I explain below that governmentality operates in a field of force in which the market, with its techniques of managed difference as a primary resource, largely erodes the idealized Habermasian public sphere that she assumes.

In the following section, I comment on the epochal significance of the transformation of culture into resource. Here I would like to preface that commentary by noting that the rapprochement of culture and community is an expression not only of the pursuit of social justice and citizenship rights; it is also overdetermined by the penetration of capital logic into the as-yet-uncolonized recesses of life. In his definition of postmodernity, Fredric Jameson (1984, 1991) characterizes these as the unconscious and the third world. In a Weberian or Habermasian model, these two would be defined, respectively, as the source of aesthetic-expressive rationality and a form of social organization that is as yet outside the reach of Western regulation. Elaborating on this model, Boaventura de Sousa Santos (1995) explains that aesthetic-expressive rationality and community were overshadowed by the other logics of modern development. On the axis of regulation, the market took precedence over the state and community; on the axis of emancipation, the cognitive-instrumental rationality of science, which wreaked destruction on nature and helped regulate the body and transform it into a commodity via biotechnology, took precedence over moral-practical and aesthetic-expressive rationalities. As "modern emancipation collapsed into modern regulation" under the rule of the market, it "ceased to be the other of regulation" to become its double. Although revolution and "alternative futures" no longer seem to threaten capitalist domination, "a new sense of insecurity stemming from the fear of uncontrollable developments" ensues from the "asymmetry between the capacity to act and the capacity to predict" (8–9).

Santos's projection of a new utopian paradigm is premised (predictably) on the activation of a "community principle" based on solidarity and of an "aesthetic-expressive principle" based on authorship and artifactuality (1995: 478). This in turn should lead to emancipatory alternatives such as the abolishment of the North-South hierarchy (487), knowledge oriented to shared authority (489), new forms of sociability characterized by weak hierarchies, plurality of powers and laws, fluidity of social relations (492–493), and a baroque-like taste for mixture or mestizaje (499). However, what seems to have developed in the rapprochement of the two "unfinished representations of modernity" is an even more pervasive mechanism of control. In the past three decades, progressive activists and theorists who have broken both with the statist and the cognitivist emphases of traditional Marxism and with commodified and counterrational (modernist) inflections of the arts have collapsed aesthetics and community in the formulation of a cultural-political alternative to domination. The anthropological turn in the conceptualization of the arts and society is consistent with what might be called *cultural power*—my term for the extension of biopower in the age of globalization—and is also one of the main reasons *cultural policy* has become a visible factor in rethinking collective arrangements. The very term conjoins what in modernity belonged to emancipation on the one hand, and to regulation on the other. But, as I demonstrate throughout this book, this conjoining is perhaps the clearest expression of the expediency of culture. It is called on to resolve a range of problems *for* community, which seems only to be able to recognize itself in culture, which in turn has lost its specificity. Consequently, culture and community are caught in a circular, tautological reasoning. This problem is recognized by officials of the institution that has done the most to bring it about. As the director of the Division of Creativity, Cultural Industries and Copyright at UNESCO remarked at a recent meeting, culture is being invoked to solve problems that previously were the province of economics and politics (Yúdice 2000b: 10).

As previous understandings of culture—canons of artistic excellence; symbolic patterns that give coherence to and thus endow a group of people or society with human worth—lose force, we see here an iteration of the expediency of culture. In our era, representations of and claims to cultural difference are expedient insofar as they multiply commodities and empower community. Yet, as Virginia R. Domínguez writes, to understand what culture means when it "is invoked to describe, analyze, argue, justify, and theorize," one has to focus on "*what is being accomplished* socially, politically, discursively" (1992: 21). That is the objective of this book.

The Expediency of Culture

There are several senses in which the idea of the expediency of culture as resource might be understood here, but I should make clear at the outset that it is not my purpose to dismiss this strategy as a perversion of culture or as a cynical reduction of patterns of symbols or ways of life to "mere" politics. Such dismissals are often premised on a nostalgic or reactionary desire for the restoration of the high place of culture, presumably discredited by philistines who really don't believe in it anyway. Nor is it right to scapegoat the kind of identity politics that I have briefly described, for it is not alone in making recourse to culture as an expedient, as a resource for other ends. We can find this strategy in many different sectors of contemporary life: the use of high culture (e.g., museums and other high-culture venues) for the purposes of urban development; the promotion of native cultures and national patrimonies to be consumed in tourism; historical sites that are turned into Disneyfied theme parks; the creation of transnational culture industries as complements of supranational integration, whether in the European Union or the Common Market of the South (MERCOSUR; see chapter 8); the redefinition of intellectual property as forms of culture for the purposes of spurring capital accumulation in informatics, communications, pharmaceuticals, and entertainment; and so on. Elsewhere, I have reviewed several expedient projects of this instrumentalist character of cultural policy (Yúdice 1999c).

American Canvas, the NEA report on a series of town hall–like discussions with people from all sectors of society interested in salvaging the support system for the arts, made the following recommendations: "It is time for those who know the power of the arts . . . to become members of the school board, the city and county commission, the planning and zoning commission, the housing authority, the merchants association, the library board . . . The point is not simply to underscore the relevance of the arts to those various civic concerns, but to tap the public funds that flow through these channels, some of which might be used for the arts." Another advocate cited in the report argues, "We must insist that when roads, sewers, prisons, libraries and schools are planned and funded . . . that the arts are also planned and funded. We must find the line items, the budget categories, the dollar signs in all of these local sources" (Larson 1997: 83).

It would indeed be cynical to single out identity politics as an aberration when the expediency of culture is so obviously a feature of contemporary life. Rather than engage in censure, it may be more effective for the purposes of strategic thinking to establish a genealogy of the transformation of culture into resource. What does it signal about our historical period?

Although my understanding of culture as resource is not Heideggerian, a brief reflection on his notion of *standing reserve* will help situate my own argument vis-à-vis modernity and postmodernity. In "The Question Concerning Technology" (1977b) Heidegger identifies technology as a way of understanding in which nature becomes a resource, a means to an end, or a "standing reserve." Everything, including human beings, comes to be regarded as standing ready to be used as resources. In an earlier essay, "The Age of the World Picture" (1977a), not yet speaking of a standing reserve, Heidegger nevertheless characterizes the modern age, defined by representation as a technology, as that which renders the essence of things invisible. Science, technology as an autonomous transformation of praxis, the transmutation of the artwork into the object of "mere subjective experience," the consummation of human life as culture, and the loss of the gods (1977: 116) are the phenomena that bring about the "age of the world picture," when the opacity of the cognitive embodiment of the previous age is rendered invisible. As the processes that, in this order, cast an "invisible shadow around all things," that is, made their essence invisible, Heidegger posited "calculation, planning, and molding of all things" (135). This is precisely Foucault's definition of governmentality to characterize the transition of economy from the home to society at large, when the res publica or things such as climate, wealth, health, disease, industry, finance, and custom had to be arranged, calculated via statistics, and managed through the *savoirs* of discipline (1991: 95–103).

The essence of technology is thus not merely its instrumentality but, Heidegger tells us, a "calling-forth" that assembles and orders (1977:21, 19), an "enframing" (*Ge-Stell*) that "destines" a revealing of ordering and that "drives out every other possibility of revealing" (27), including *poiesis* and art, which, in "The Origin of the Work of Art," Heidegger had characterized as the revealing of truth, of the "undisguised presence of the thing" (1971: 25). This blocking of other kinds of revealing is a danger: "The coming to presence of technology threatens revealing, threatens it with the possibility that all revealing will be consumed in ordering and that everything will present itself only in the unconcealedness of standing-reserve" (1977: 33). Surprisingly, at the end of the essay on technology, Heidegger entertains the possibility that once technology has suffused everything everywhere, "the essence of technology may come to presence in the coming-to-pass of truth." For this to be the case, reflection on technology, he tells us, must happen "in a realm that is, on the one hand, akin to the essence of technology and, on the other, fundamentally different from it." That realm of reflection, he adds, is art. However, if the essence of technology has suffused everything, enjoining us to behold art through the medium of aesthetics, then "the more mysterious the essence of art becomes" (35).

The paradox sounded at the end of this essay offers a possibility, within or at the end of modernity, that is foreclosed for other interpretations of the role of art. For Peter Bürger, for example, as the bourgeoisie expands its domain, even resistances to instrumental reason — or we might substitute ordering — are increasingly ordered via institutionalization, thus cutting off the aesthetic from other spheres of social life. In attempting to rejoin art and life, the avant-garde first aestheticizes life and then institutionalizes that aestheticization (1984: 49). A similar paradox is evident in the rapprochement of culture and community, as Santos characterizes these two "unfinished representations of modernity." They are suffused with a managerial approach that blocks and even makes unfathomable prior understandings of these concepts and modes of practice. Moreover, with the reciprocal permeation of culture and economy, not just as commodity—which would be the equivalent of instrumentality— but as a mode of cognition, social organization, and even attempts at social emancipation, seem to feed back into the system they resist or oppose.

A New Episteme?

It is at this juncture that I would like to propose the notion of *performativity* as the mode, beyond instrumentality, in which the social is increasingly practiced. I only introduce the topic here in anticipation of further development in chapter 2.

The expediency of culture underpins performativity as the fundamental logic of social life today. First, globalization has accelerated the transformation of everything into resource. Second, the specific transformation of culture into resource epitomizes the emergence of a new episteme, in the Foucauldian sense. Third, this transformation should not be understood as a manifestation of "mere politics," against which it is simply necessary to invoke a voluntaristic and politically expedient notion of agency. That would only increase the Antaeus-like power of expediency.

CULTURE AND GLOBALIZATION   It has been argued that under conditions of globalization, difference rather than homogenization infuses the prevailing logic of accumulation. Globalization, a process of economic expansion datable from sixteenth-century European exploration and conquest and of modernization, produces encounters of diverse traditions such that "cultures can no longer be examined as if they were islands in an archipelago" (UNESCO 1998: 16). The recently published *World Culture Report 1998: Culture, Creativity and Markets* attempts to map out the coordinates of this greater cultural complexity and how it might be harnessed, "creatively," for greater development and democracy.

Discourses on globalization, however, have less sanguine precedents. It was not so long ago that the economic and mediatic global reach of the United States and Western Europe was characterized as cultural imperialism. Exponents of this view endeavored to unveil the will to power that subtended the reverence for Western high art, the concealment of power differentials in celebrations of the common humanity shared by all peoples as promoted in much anthropological work, and the brainwashing of the entire globe by Hollywood. Although Roberto Fernández Retamar's *Calibán* ([1971] 1989) and Ariel Dorfman and Armand Mattelart's *How to Read Donald Duck* ([1972] 1975) are perhaps the classic texts of this orientation, a critique of cultural imperialism is already evident in José Carlos Mariátegui's ([1928] 1971) work in the 1920s.

The cultural imperialism argument has been criticized for three main reasons. In the first place, it has overlooked the subordination of internal minorities that takes place within the nationalism of developing countries as they gird themselves to stave off the symbolic aggression of imperial powers. Second, migrations and diasporic movements generated by global processes have complicated the unity presumed to exist in the nation; belonging may be infra- or supranational. Third, and relatedly, the exchange of ideas, information, knowledge, and labor "multiplies the number of permutations and in the process creates new ways of life, new cultures" often premised on elements from one culture sampled into another (Rao 1998: 42–43), such as the rap music that black Brazilian youth incorporate into their own antiracist projects (see chapters 4 and 5). It is no longer viable to argue that such hybrid cultures are inauthentic (García Canclini 1995b).

These arguments suggest that there is an expedient relation between globalization and culture in the sense that there is a *fit* or a *suitability* between them.[1] Globalization involves the (mostly commercial and informatic) dissemination of symbolic processes that increasingly drive economics and politics. Malcolm Waters bases his entire study of globalization on this first sense of expediency: "The theorem that guides the argument of this book is that: *material exchanges localize; political exchanges internationalize; and symbolic exchanges globalize.* It follows that the globalization of human society is contingent on the extent to which cultural arrangements are effective relative to economic and political arrangements. We can expect the economy and the polity to be globalized to the extent that they are culturalized" (1995: 9).

FROM CULTURE AS RESOURCE TO POLITICS As argued above, culture is expedient as a resource for attaining an end. Culture as a resource is a principal component of what might be characterized as a postmodern episteme. In *The Order of Things*, Foucault (1973) sketches out three different and discontinuous modalities of relation between thought and world, or epistemes, that enable the various fields of knowledge in each given era. In each era, knowledge is organized, according to Foucault, by a series of fundamental operative rules. The Renaissance or sixteenth-century episteme is based on resemblance, the mode by which language relates words and the signatures that mark things (32). Knowledge consisted of relating, through interpretation, the different forms of language so as to "restor[e] the great, unbroken plain of words and things" (40). The classical episteme of the seventeenth and eighteenth centuries consisted of the representation and classification of all entities according to the principles of order and measurement (57). It is this episteme that Borges caricatures in his image of the Chinese encyclopedia, cited by Foucault as his inspiration for thinking its obverse, the heteroclite (xv–xix). With the rise of the modern episteme, which Foucault locates at the turn of the eighteenth and nineteenth centuries, representation is no longer adequate for the examination of concerns with life, the organic, and history. This inadequacy in turn implies a *depth* or a "density withdrawn into itself" in which "what matters is no longer identities, distinctive characters, permanent tables with all their possible paths and routes, but great hidden forces developed on the basis of their primitive and inaccessible nucleus, origin, causality, and history" (251). These hidden forces are analogous in Foucualt's account to what remains concealed in Heidegger's account of modern technology. Modern knowledge thus consists of unveiling the primary processes (the infrastructure, the unconscious) that lurk in the depths, beneath the surface: manifestations of ideology, personality, and the social.

If representation is the relation between words and things appropriate to the ordered world of the sovereign, new techniques of government or management, based in disciplinary knowledge, come to occupy that mediatory role between primary processes and the autonomous subject. The law, which was the sovereign's instrument, takes second place to the internalization of norms via discipline. Government, in turn, becomes a way of regulating life and death, what could be calculated and managed between them, extending to climate, disease, industry, finance, custom, and disaster. Biopower or "biological existence [as] reflected in political existence," the means by which the social was produced, "brought life and its mechanisms into the realm of explicit calculations and made knowledge-power an agent of transformation of human life." Bodies were identified with politics because managing them was part of running the country. For Foucault, "a society's 'threshold of modernity' was reached when the life of the species is wagered on its own political strategies" (1991: 97, 92–95; 1984: 143).

I am skeptical of most formulations of postmodernity, particularly those that merely reinterpret modernist fragmentation as something new or locate the new episteme in the crisis of authority of *grands récits*, as if this crisis had never taken place before. However, I would like to extend Foucault's archaeological periodization and propose a fourth episteme based on a relationship between words and world that draws on the previous epistemes — resemblance, representation, and historicity — yet recombines them in a way that accounts for the constitutive force of signs. Some have characterized this constitutive force as simulation, that is, an effect of reality premised on the "precession of the model": "Facts no longer have any trajectory of their own, they arise at the intersection of the models" (Baudrillard 1983: 32). I prefer the term performativity, which refers to the processes by which identities and the entities of social reality are constituted by repeated approximations of models (i.e., the normative) as well as by those "remainders" ("constitutive exclusions") that fall short. As I explained above, to the degree that globalization brings different cultures into contact with each other, it escalates the questioning of norms and thus abets performativity.

As Judith Butler (1993) has observed, power constitutes object domains or fields of intelligibility by taking the material effects of that constitutivity as "material data or primary givens" that seem to operate outside of discourse and power. She credits Foucault with having shown that these material effects are the result of an "investiture of discourse and power," but finds that he did not provide a way of discerning "what constrains the domain of what is materializable" (34–35). Principles of intelligibility inscribe not only what materializes but also zones of unintelligibility that define the above-mentioned "constitutive exclusions." Theories of the unconscious (whether psychoanalytic or political) tend to condense multiple processes into a specific "law" (the Oedipal complex or "paternal law," the "class law" that underlies ideology as false consciousness) that reins in, so to speak, the sundry deviations. Performativity, as Butler elaborates it, suggests that instead of fundamental laws, there are contests of many different principles of constitution and exclusion: "*To supply the character and content to a law that secures the borders between the 'inside' and the 'outside' of symbolic intelligibility is to preempt the specific social and historical analysis that is required, to conflate into 'one' law the effect of a convergence of many, and to preclude the very possibility of a future rearticulation of that boundary which is central to the democratic project that Žižek, Laclau and Mouffe promote*" (206–207).

What Butler invokes here is the interface between the individual subject and society, with an implied recommendation for democratic social change. What connects subject and society are the performative forces that operate both, on the one hand, to "rein in" or make converge the many differences or interpellations that constitute and hail the subject, and on the other, to rearticulate the larger arrangement of the social. Both individuals and societies are fields of force that constellate the multiplicity. For Butler, the tension among these forces or "laws" makes it possible for individuals-as-constellations to mutate, to fail to conform. Yet the contours of the social remain. I can think of two metaphors to make this view of the individual and the social more palpable. One is Bakhtin's account of the novel as myriad speech registers — heteroglossia — which nevertheless hang together as a genre:

> The novel can be defined as a diversity of social speech types (sometimes even diversity of languages) and a diversity of individual voices, artistically organized. The internal stratification of any single national language into social dialects, characteristic group behavior, professional jargons, generic languages, languages of generations and age groups, tendentious languages, languages of the authorities, of various circles and of passing fashions, languages that serve the specific sociopolitical purposes of the day, even of the hour (each day has its own slogan, its own vocabulary, its own emphases) — this internal stratification present in every language at any given moment of its historical existence is the indispensable prerequisite for the novel as a genre. (1984: 263)

What defines the novel for Bakhtin comes close to Derrida's "law of genre," which "is precisely a principle of contamination, a law of impurity, a parasitical economy" (1980: 55). Bakhtin proposes that the novel's effect is an "other consciousness [that] is not inserted into the frame of authorial consciousness, it is revealed from within as something that stands *outside*" (1984: 284). For Derrida, "The trait that marks membership inevitably divides, the boundary of the set comes to form by invagination, an internal pocket larger than the whole; and the outcome of this division and of this abounding remains as singular as it is limitless" (1980: 65). A consciousness that is within yet stands outside and a singular yet limitless invagination are both virtual models or models of the virtuality of what Laclau calls the social. Just as subjects are contradictory yet brought in line by naming, so also is the "impossibility of society," composed of myriad "unstable differences," managed by hegemony. Rearticulation of the arrangement of differences characterizes both Butler's subversive performative subject and Laclau's notion of social change. "Hegemonic relations depend upon the fact that the meaning of each element in a social system is not definitely fixed. If it were fixed, it would be impossible to rearticulate it in a different way, and thus rearticulation could only be thought under such categories as false consciousness" (Laclau 1988: 254).

This flexible system of (re)articulations, which maintains the appearance of an entity and yet is in constant change, is reminiscent of the stochastic systems reviewed by Bateson in *Steps to an Ecology of Mind* ([1972] 1985). To generate something new requires a source of randomness. Some systems (e.g., evolution) have a built-in selective process that reinforces certain random changes so that they become part of the system. There is a "governor," so to speak, that keeps the pieces of the kaleidoscope from dispersing, although the arrangement of the crystals changes with each turn. Similarly, societies maintain their shape, conform to the law of genre, despite rearticulations. In this model, social change is akin to a turn of the kaleidoscope. Such a process may be more characteristic of modern societies than of postmodern ones.

A key premise of modernity is that tradition (safeguarded in the domestic sphere) is eroded by the constant changes of industrialization, new divisions of labor, and concomitant effects such as migration and consumer capitalism. However, recent theories of disorganized capitalism entertain the possibility that the "system" itself gains by the erosion of such traditions, that is, that it can dispense with governmentality. Disorganized capitalism thrives on this erosion, assisted by new technologies that enable, for example, time compression in financial markets, the internationalization of advanced producer services, the dissemination of risk, greater mobility of people, commodities, sounds, and images, the proliferation of styles, and what I characterized above as a new international division of cultural labor. Both these changes and the attempts to recuperate tradition feed the system. Consequently, the failure to repeat normative behavior as the constitutive feature of subversive performativity may actually enhance the system rather than threaten it. The system feeds off of "disorder."

Lash and Urry (1987) argue that instead of increased order, as Marx and Weber predicted, capitalism has moved toward a deconcentration of capital within nation-states; an increased separation of banks, industry, and the state; and a redistribution of productive relations and class-relevant residential patterns. Similarly, we might add, there is a process of degovernmentalization, evident in the withdrawal of the welfare state and its replacement with the heterogeneous and more micro-administered organizations of civil society, where they exist, and their counterparts, the organizations of uncivil society (mafias, guerrillas, militias, racist groups, etc.). The antiglobalization movement that emerged in Seattle in 1999 may be the counter–mirror image of the "disorder" that has taken root in capitalism itself, although it is not yet evident that it feeds the system.

This said, the chapters below demonstrate that Lash and Urry are wrong to assume that "with an ever quickening turnover time, objects as well as cultural artefacts become disposable and depleted of meaning" (1987: 10). To be sure, the buying and selling of experiences that Rifkin (2000) puts at the center of the capital order make it possible to harness not only the labor and desire of producers and consumers (e.g., the tourists and the indigenous persons who perform identity) but even their politics, which easily shade into commodities (see chapter 6). But it is also the case that the same "disorganized" capitalism that spawns myriad networks for the sake of accumulation also makes possible the networking of all kinds of affinity associations working in solidarity and cooperation.

I should point out that although I share Hardt and Negri's skepticism re- garding NGOs dedicated to welfare and rights advocacy as states abandon the Keynesian compromise, it strikes me as too absolutist to relegate them all to the category of the "mendicant orders of Empire" (2000: 36). There are two reasons for my discrepancy, evident in chapter 5 on citizen action initiatives in Brazil. In the first place, Hardt and Negri's view presumes that all such organizations "strive to identify universal needs" and that through their action they "define the enemy as privation . . . and recognize the enemy as sin" (36). Many of the organizations I studied (and some of which I worked with) do indeed "defend human rights," but they do not necessarily do so in a universal manner; and if they do, they may do so strategically, to take the money and run, so to speak. In the second place, many NGOs and the actors working within them are the very ones working to establish the "cooperation, the collective existence, and the communicative networks that are formed and reformed within the multitude" (401–402), the "global citizenship" that Hardt and Negri claim to be consis- tent with the "multitude's power to reappropriate control over space and thus to design the new cartography" (400). Do they think that there aren't lines of connection among NGOs, academics, media organizations, political and soli- darity groups, and movements like the Zapatistas or the Movimento dos Sem Terra or the so-called antiglobalization protests? There is an enormous short- coming in theoretical work that assumes that the categories they criticize do not intersect, contradict, and jump in bed with each other, just as Hardt and Ne- gri claim for their own "incommensurate, parasitic, and misceginated" visions of constituent power (353–389).

Hardt and Negri's understanding of politics is just as absolutist as their dis- missal of NGOs. They claim that "the transcendental fiction of politics can no longer stand up and has no argumentative utility because we all exist entirely within the realm of the social and the political" (2000: 353). This view derives from their belief that globalization and the concomitant society of control have rendered ineffective any political action deriving from a national base. Yet, presumably, activists based in national frameworks are also a part of the "multitude" that has converged in Seattle, Davos, Prague, Washington, Porto Alegre, and Genoa. A significant political project is to delegitimize the basis for global capitalism's regime of accumulation. One of the major reasons for the exploitation of workers outside of the United States, Europe, and Japan (and within as well) is the undemocratic rule of international trade, juridified by the World Bank, the International Monetary Fund (IMF), the WTO, and its predecessors. This inequitable use of the law not only determines the conditions of investment, production, and trade for so-called developing countries, but has led to a major shift in value from productive labor to mental labor, which favors centers of "innovation," most of which are in the North. The emergence of a new (perhaps better characterized as an intensification of the same old geopolitically determined) international division of labor is centered in mental, immaterial, affective, and cultural forms of labor that, at this moment at least, are far from being the condition for a "spontaneous and elementary communism" (294).

This shift is buttressed by intellectual property laws that are criminal, not only because they, for example, determine that HIV+ people in so-called developing countries cannot afford medication due to the exorbitant costs of patents, but more pervasively because they undermine the possibility of establishing a living wage as production takes on the model of the maquiladora, which labor organization is assuming with renewed vigor. The "flexibility" in "flexible capitalism" accounts for the stretching of profits in the North and shrinkage of salaries everywhere. Several chapters in this book examine not only the exploitation of "immaterial" labor (e.g., the "life" that subaltern populations provide the professional-managerial classes and tourists in today's global cities) but also the transformation of artists and intellectuals into managers of that expropriation under the guise of "community-based" work. Chapter 9 examines the contradictions in the labor of networking for community-based art projects that ultimately enhance the value of real estate, foster investment, and so on.

That culture as resource is at the heart of these processes does not mean that capital's assault on workers and others who flout its illegitimate "rule of law" has become merely virtual. It is for this reason that cultural politics, at least as was envisioned in the dominant strain of cultural studies in the United States, is unlikely to make a difference. Indeed, I argue in the next chapter that the "cultural left" is largely enjoined to perform such a cultural politics, as in the so-called culture wars of the 1980s and 1990s. The protection of the cultural resources that global entertainment conglomerates have expropriated involves not only the law but also the use of police and military forces, for example, in the pursuit of piracy, or what the entertainment industry calls the "traffic in music," which is estimated to exceed the volume of narcotraffic (Yúdice 1999b: 149). From the perspective of most forms of cultural politics, at least as they are conceived in some versions of U.S. cultural studies, subversion of the assumptions implicit in dominant media as a way of appropriating them is thought to be a viable option. Although this option can certainly be considered a form of resistance, it is hardly effective vis-à-vis the institutions that produce and distribute "content." From another, also subversive perspective we might imagine the "traffic in music" as a more frontal assault on global cultural capitalism, as it surely is.

However, this strategy encourages the industry to strengthen its juridical and military hold over the people and spaces in which this activity takes place. This is already evident in the U.S. government's targeting of Ciudad del Este on the Triple Border of Paraguay, Argentina, and Brazil, where it is claimed that pirating, drug trafficking, and terrorism are related activities, linking merchants there with Colombian guerrillas and narcotraffickers and Middle Eastern terrorist networks. Most often, there is no concrete proof but vague allegations, as in the case of Ali Khalil Mehri, a naturalized Paraguayan citizen born in Lebanon who "was charged with selling millions of dollars of counterfeit software, the proceeds from which he allegedly funneled to the militant Islamic group Hezbollah in Lebanon." As a result of "rumored links between groups within the city's 12,000-member Arab community and the Sept. 11 attacks," a transnational surveillance network under U.S. leadership has been spying on that community (Mazer 2001). Ann Patterson, U.S. ambassador to Colombia, similarly alleged that the "Revolutionary Army of Colombia (FARC) and bin Laden share the same moral hyprocrisy and lack of ideas. The Afghan Taliban do not represent Islam and the Colombian guerrillas do not seek social justice" (qtd. in Kollmann 2001). The upshot is the intensification of surveillance and militarization in Latin America. The rhetoric and allegations that transnational corporations have generated regarding piracy have served to naturalize and justify using national police forces for the sake of the copyright industries (Yúdice 1999b: 147).

In the aftermath of September 11, such arguments provide greater legitimacy for corporate protection of trade-related intellectual property rights

(TRIPS), a turn of events that has dealt a blow to the antiglobalization move-ment's strategies to break the hold that the World Bank, IMF, and WTO have on the definition and control of value. To cite Mazer (2001) again, "The con-vergence of our economic security and our national security became starkly apparent on Sept. 11. The staggering economic losses to America's copyright and trademark industries—alarming unto themselves—now are compounded by the opportunistic trafficking in IP [intellectual property] products to finance terrorism and other organized criminal endeavors." Yet, countering the global inequalities generated by the advantage that the G-7 have arrogated via these custodians of corporate capital is necessary for global justice and reducing the resentment of countries that get the short end of the stick. Although the with-drawal of a lawsuit by thirty-nine pharmaceutical corporations against South Africa (which by law permits compulsory licensing of medicines without the patent holder's consent and also parallel imports cheaper than those produced by the manufacturer's local subsidiary) and the decision by the Brazilian gov-ernment to violate a patent held by Hoffman la Roche to produce a generic ver-sion of a protease inhibitor do not spell the doom of TRIPS, they nevertheless "force a crowbar into a crack in the dam" ("Health GAP" 2001). This statement, made by a Health GAP Coalition member from ACT UP, also demonstrates that the NGOization of social justice, which otherwise governmentalizes counter-politics (a critique that both Hardt and Negri in *Empire* and I myself make in this book), nevertheless fosters networks of solidarity that include activists (in this case, from Brazil, South Africa, the United States), NGOs, foundations, and other third-sector institutions, government officials in developing coun-tries, and the protestors in the antiglobalization movement. Indeed, such a network has formed to oppose the advance southward of the Free Trade Agree-ment for the Americas, for it includes articles that would jeopardize Brazil's law that requires compulsory licensing of generic drugs (Consumer Project on Technology 2001).

Developed countries touted the trade talks at Doha, Qatar, in November 2001 as a victory for developing countries on a number of issues, among them, exemption to patent rules in the interests of public health, a "concession" due to the need "to get poor countries on-side to get a deal, which could explain why the U.S. was prepared to concede early on the patents issue" (Denny 2001). But as Walden Bello and Anuradha Mittal (2001) explain, developing countries lost not only on this issue but on many others as well. Although there is noth-ing in the TRIPS agreement that prevents developing countries from ignor-ing patents when public health is in question, the wording of the agreement itself was not changed, leaving in place the possibility of future challenges to overriding patents. Moreover, the European Union got its way in maintaining agricultural subsidies, and the United States was able to hold onto textile and garment quotas.

"MERE POLITICS" Expediency in this sense refers to what is, according to the *Oxford English Dictionary*, "merely politic (esp. with regard to self-interest) to the neglect of what is just or right." I would like to modify this understanding of expediency, for it implies that there is a notion of right that exists outside of the play of interests. A performative understanding of the expediency of culture, in contrast, focuses on the strategies implied in any invocation of culture, any invention of tradition, in relation to some purpose or goal. That there is an end is what makes it possible to speak of culture as a resource. For example, the debate over Rigoberta Menchú's (1984) alleged exaggeration, and in some cases fabrication, of the events narrated in her *testimonio* turns on the productive role that culture performs. Those who, like David Stoll (1999), argue that she has distorted the truth for her own ends, for her self-interest, see her testimonio as expedient in the negative sense. Stoll makes the case that Menchú does not exemplify the values of her culture. Those who defend her, like John Beverley (1999), argue that she altered the facts of the events to make her narrative more compelling and thus to be more persuasive in attracting attention to the plight of her people. In both cases, however, there is a calculation of interest being made; and in both cases, culture is being invoked as a resource for determining the value of an action, in this case, a speech act, a testimonio.

Some readers might assume that my brief précis of the Rigoberta Menchú case entails a negative view of the instrumentalization of culture, as if the truth hovered somewhere among the various accounts, attacks, and counterattacks. My own view is that it is not possible not to make recourse to culture as a resource. Consequently, cultural analysis necessarily entails taking a position, even in those cases where the writer seeks objectivity or transcendence. But such a position need not be a normative one, based on right and wrong. Foucault rejected such moralism in the last phase of his work, positing instead an ethical basis for practice. Ethics, Foucault argued, did not entail a teleological foundation, such as is usually attributed to utilitarianism. His notion of the care of the self emphasized the active role of the subject in his or her own process of constitution. There is a compatibility between this notion of the care of the self and performativity, for Foucault's ethics entails a reflexive practice of self-management vis-à-vis models (or what Bakhtin called "voices" and "perspectives") imposed by a given society or cultural formation. Bakhtin's notion of the author may serve as a prototype of Foucault's performative ethics, since the author is an orchestration of others' "voices," an appropriation that consists of "populating those 'voices' with his or her own intentions, with his or her own accent" (1981: 293). He or she who practices care of the self must also forge his or her freedom by working through the "models that he finds in his culture and are proposed, suggested, imposed upon him by his culture, his society, and his social group" (Foucault 1997b: 291).

The next chapter, a companion piece to this one, elaborates on the notion of performative force, meaning the conditionings, elicitations, and pressures exerted by the multidimensional field of social and institutional relations. If in this chapter I have dealt more generally with the notion of culture as resource, in the following I argue that specific struggles around this resource take different shapes depending on the society—or field of force—in which they operate.

※ 2 ※

. Imperative to Perform

Complicit Laughter

In September 1989, I was surprised by my audience, a group of Brazilian graduate students and professors in Rio de Janeiro, in the discussion period after one of my lectures on U.S. cultural studies. On this occasion, I had chosen to illustrate critiques of racialized and gendered representations by discussing Donna Haraway's "A Cyborg Manifesto" and a video of a 1988 lecture by her titled "Apes, Aliens, Cyborgs and Women: The Intersection of Colonial Discourse and Feminist Theory" that was subsequently incorporated into several of her books, especially *Primate Visions* (1989b; see also 1991, 1997). The basic premise of Haraway's slide lecture is that developments in science — whether primatology, immunology, virtuality, or space exploration — as portrayed in popular scientific magazines (e.g., *National Geographic*) and advertising in professional journals constantly invokes the question "What counts as nature?" The question is then answered by rearticulating a set of racialized and gendered myths and narratives generated in colonizing societies as part of their explanation of the world. Such representations collapsed into each other, Haraway explained, the textual, the technic, the mythic, the organic, and the imaginary. The twists and turns resulting from academic, scientific, and technological innovation produced curious new representations that nevertheless replayed old narratives and myths, such as the creation of the world and first contacts, with archaeological research extrapolating representations of the first family (brown and animal-like, to be sure) taking their first steps on volcanic ash. In this way, science not only reprised the nuclear family as portrayed in the story of Adam and Eve, but also echoed, *pre-post-erously*, the first walk on the moon.

As will become evident, the preposterous and racialized collapsing of before and after were significant factors in the reactions of Haraway's audience, which I will describe presently. This chapter augments the first by demonstrating that context conditions expediency: different receptions of cultural work respond to different groundings of expectations in differing fields of performative force. Hence the importance given to Haraway's audience as a way of illustrating this argument.

New scientific and cultural developments produce situations in which, under certain circumstances, woman could represent man and an animal could represent universal humanity. Haraway illustrated this proposition by showing an image of a brown leathery hand (of a gorilla) holding the white hand (of none other than "Jane"; 1989b: 133). Reproducing the first contact narrative, this photograph, from an advertisement in *Natural History Magazine* titled "Understanding is everything," is captioned with text that includes the sentence: "In a spontaneous gesture of trust, a chimpanzee in the wilds of Tanzania folds his leathery hand around that of Jane Goodall—sufficient reward for Dr. Goodall's years of patience." This rearticulation of representation of first contact took place, ironically in Haraway's gloss, precisely when African countries were undergoing decolonization: as these "dependent" nations were headed to sovereignty, new images of creation and contact were being generated in natural history and scientific spheres. This harking back to the origin via the Ur-story of the white-woman-among-the-apes-in-the-jungle, Jane Goodall—recast by Haraway as "Jane" in the Tarzan story, capitalizing on the documentaries and feature stories that call her by her first name—*provoked a report of hilarity from the audience.*

Indeed, Haraway used a number of (in)felicitous coincidences to bring out some of the foundational myths and stories rearticulated in the representations we were viewing. The reference to Goodall as Jane, of course, prompted recollections of *Tarzan among the Apes*, and indeed, in *Primate Visions* that connection is reinforced by a reproduction of the photograph of the happy family: Tarzan, Jane, Boy, and Cheetah (1989b: 155). The real Goodall story, however, dissolved with the waning hierarchy of the nuclear family, but as Haraway quipped, she was not going to deal with the "real" Jane (she flexed the index and middle fingers of each hand to salt her words postmodernly), only representations of her (179). Notwithstanding, she invoked the real Jane in her interpretation of a photograph of Goodall's baby son in the embrace of Princess, a baby orangutan. Haraway's audience broke out in laughter as she ironized the constructed character of both "culture" and "nature," as human and animal exchanged roles in teaching each other what presumably is the province of the other: "The baby human learned language from an Orangutan, who in turn was learning to be wild from Binty's mother."[1] The irony was based on Goodall's work in teaching zoo-raised primates to be wild so they can be returned to (finger-flexed) "nature."

Another instance in which Haraway, with the timing of a standup comedian, brought down the house was the suggestion that an astronaut chimp named Ham, "the first American to go into outer space," was a reference to "Noah's youngest and only black son" (1989b: 137). After admitting that she had led her audience astray—the serendipitous conceit was too good to pass up—Haraway explained that Ham was an acronym for Holloman Aero-Medical base, "the scientific-military institution that launched him" (138). Wired with telemetric devices to monitor his body functions, and thus turned into a cyborg, Ham, Haraway writes, is an "understudy for 'man'" (139).

All of these images were characterized by Haraway as emblematic of "the traffic between nature and culture, represented at the intersection of decolonization, the international questioning of race and gender, multinational capitalism, the apparatus of bodily production, all within postmodern consciousness" (1988). Race and gender are, of course, key to modernity and postmodernity, that is, modernist constructions of progress and primitivism, and self-conscious, postmodernist recognitions of the constructed and engineerable character of our categories of cognition. Haraway, however, is very quick to ironize by association, or by synecdoche, without sufficiently historicizing the concepts she uses, as Michael Schudson (1997: 386) argues in a trenchant critique of another essay, "Teddy Bear Patriarchy," included in *Primate Visions* (1989b: 26–58). She relies on her raised index and middle fingers to do a lot of the work that historicization might do, as is arguably the case in her glosses on Jane Goodall's "life."

But for the purposes of my argument here, I am less interested in her suasive strategies or her postmodern finger flexing than in (what I characterize as) the *ritual irony* of this quasi-deconstruction of the images she presents to her audience. This irony instantiates and corroborates a pact between speaker and listener, writer and reader, performer and audience. Those with whom the pact is established or establishable (the implied audience) are invited to laugh at those (the other, target audience) who are projected into the opposing position of racists, sexists, homophobes, colonialists, civilizationalists whose assumptions are subject to deconstruction. There are thus at least two audiences: the implicit/complicit one that laughs, and the one that is subject to derision. It is this dynamic that I explore by couching Haraway's lecture within the larger performative context of the so-called culture wars of the 1980s and 1990s.

Before delving into this correlation, I would like to point out that my own Rio audience was neither complicit nor the target of the critique; consequently, they did not understand the laughter. Haraway's main political-theoretical intervention, "A Cyborg Manifesto" (1991: 149–181), makes clear that despite references to colonialism, imperialism, the third world, and people of color, the imagined and target audiences presupposed by her discourse are circumscribed within the United States. It is quite understandable, then, that people in my own audience asked me why Haraway's listeners laughed. I gave my talk and showed the Haraway video in other universities on this trip and the reaction was the same: my Brazilian audiences did not laugh during her lecture but they did show puzzlement at the reaction of her U.S. audience. The difference in reaction is certainly not attributable to an inability to understand English, because it was known that I would give part of my talk in that language. Moreover, my own questions to the audience on this point verified that the problem was not linguistic per se. And it is less attributable to a lack of humor on the part of Brazilians; in this land of carnival, on the contrary, derision is not in short supply.

My explanation hinges on the notion of performativity, on the interactional pacts, interpretive frameworks, and institutional conditionings of comportment and, more significant, knowledge production. After mulling over this difference in reception over the years, I am increasingly convinced that it has to do with *performative force* understood and experienced differently in different societies. This difference is not attributable to "national character," an interpretive lens quite common in Latin America from the 1930s to the 1950s, as evidenced in the work of the Argentine Ezequiel Martínez Estrada (1933), the Brazilian Gilberto Freyre (1933), the Cuban Fernando Ortiz ([1940] 1995), and the Mexicans Samuel Ramos (1934) and Octavio Paz (1950). It has to do, rather, with a different field of force generated by differently arranged relations among institutions of the state and civil society, the judiciary, the police, schools and universities, the media, consumer markets, and so on. Given that these institutions are of national scope, the force fields are specific synergistic assemblages of the component vectors. Of course, there is no one performative style, and certainly not *a national* performative style, but there are significant differences across national societies that I will attempt to describe, largely because these differences are constitutive of how culture, the protagonist of this book, is invoked and practiced in different societies, even when it appears that the same process is at work universally. For example, although the notion of *cultural difference* has worldwide currency in making claims to respect, inclusion, participation, and citizenship, it has a different *uptake* in different societies. To be sure, international foundations and NGOs and intergovernmental organizations like UNESCO do provide one of the vectors within the force fields holding in different societies, but how the injunction to attend to difference is exerted will ultimately be channeled in relation to the entire field of force, and to the varying institutions and actors and how they tread upon that field.

In what follows, I segue from this brief reference to Haraway's relationship with her audience to the culture wars as the context in which I explore performativity in the United States. Then I consider how one might conceive of performativity in several Latin American contexts, to highlight the difference with respect to the United States and to each other. Finally, I consider the relationship of performativity to the deployment of culture as a solution to the problems that arise in the examples reviewed. The subsequent chapters are elaborations of what I introduce in this chapter and the preceding chapter on the expediency of culture.

Performativity and the Culture Wars

Haraway's lecture and her writing manifest, on the one hand, a ceaseless unveiling of the racist, sexist, and homophobic norms that underpin representations of social and cognitive progress, and on the other, advocacy for social identities and arrangements that flout or circumvent normativity. Hence her interest in the cyborg and the queer (in both the sexual and general sense of the word). As I suggest above, her audience is largely complicit with these views and values. Her work, along with that of many other "cultural leftists,"[2] represents what is anathema to conservatives (and to many liberals). Indeed, I will highlight those aspects of this kind of work that are performative of cultural war.

Although most of the U.S. populace was largely *not* party to the culture wars, they were played out, performed, in very visible and vocal fora. I argue that the culture wars enact a national fantasy, whereby a national debate was structured by the split between radically normative and nonnormative positions, most conspicuously staged during the NEA arts funding controversies of the late 1980s and 1990s, and in which performance artists—and performativity itself—had a protagonist role. The term fantasy is not meant to belittle "progressive" positions in a struggle that is patently real, although powerfully projective (in the psychoanalytic sense) on all sides. The critique of the compulsoriness of norms, as in Haraway's work, is not only analytical; indeed, it is often more performative than analytical insofar as the critic evokes the norms that presumably underlie the discourse of others. One begins to assume that these norms are operative everywhere.

As captured in the press and other media, one would have thought that the entire country was polarized. However, based on the analysis of twenty years' worth of data drawn from the General Social Survey and the National Election Survey, Paul DiMaggio (2001; DiMaggio and Ostrower 1992; DiMaggio, Unseem, and Brown 1978) and his fellow analysts found that, with the exception of division around abortion, there is no evidence to support the view that "Americans' " opinions on social issues have become more "extreme." [3] They found that Americans were polarized on many issues but not more so from 1972 to 1993. Moreover, "the public actually has become *more unified* in its attitudes toward race, gender, and crime since the 1970s," largely reflecting liberal viewpoints on race and gender, and a harder, conservative line regarding crime. These researchers also found that a second definition of polarization, the differences among groups (blacks and whites, Republicans and Democrats, men and women), had not become greater. In addition, the generation gap characteristic of the 1960s had narrowed, as over-45-year-olds and under-35-year-olds did not have significantly divergent views. Men and women have similar opinions regarding crime and sex education; whites are less overtly racist and black views more heterogeneous with the rise of a sizable middle class; religiously conservative and religiously liberal people "have become *more similar* in their attitudes toward abortion, gender roles, sexual morality, race, sex education and divorce." The last convergence is due to an increase in the level of educational attainment among the religiously conservative, especially evangelists. Only people who strongly identified as Republicans or Democrats showed an increase in divergent views. From all this, DiMaggio developed the research question "How is it that our public politics have become more polarized while our private attitudes and opinions have become more united?" In assessing the disjuncture between these politics and attitudes, DiMaggio discounted two "chronic fallacies": that of *change* (to assume that every notable political event is a trend rather than a blip), and that of *proportionate sampling* (the assumption that "public conflicts mirror private divisions in fixed proportion"). Regarding the latter, DiMaggio argued that vocal minorities can "overshadow and even appear more numerous than . . . reticent majorities." Hence the work of projection.

DiMaggio considered whether something other than attitudes had changed, and came up with the hypothesis that there is a divergence on what is factually true, for example, the divergence in belief between blacks and whites regarding the origins of the AIDS epidemic. However, he found that there were very few art controversies, epitome of the culture wars, like those concerning Mapplethorpe, Serrano, and the NEA Four. Americans' values may be polarized, yet researchers should not simply assume that values translate into compartmentalized beliefs. On the contrary, DiMaggio argues, people are more complex. What does characterize U.S. society is the increase on the part of social movement groups and political organizers to "gain converts not only by changing people's attitudes, but also by changing the political salience of people's various social identities." Institutional uptake of attitudes is what makes them salient: "Attitudes matter most when they become the basis for organizing people into contentious groups." Changes in the media from the 1980s to the 1990s, which included "more conservative views . . . in public debate" — or a greater number of projections by conservatives — have led to the impression of exacerbated social divisions. Another factor producing the impression of greater polarization is that the Republicans used cultural issues to gain salience such that "moral politics increasingly shaped the party identification of both white Evangelical and mainline Protestants in the 1980s."

DiMaggio's explanation for polarization thus hinges on the strategy of Republicans to articulate a rhetorical frame within which it would be possible to "persuade Americans to accept their views on social issues [not on a one-by-one basis but] wedded together into a compelling narrative frame." Culture war is such a frame. In contrast to those (presumably mostly on the left) who understand the culture wars as driven by class and race differences, DiMaggio points to the ideological frame as the means by which are melded "such disparate topics as sex education, family leave, abortion, government subsidies for the arts, and gun control into a coherent and navigable political terrain (while leaving uncharted, and therefore less politically salient, such matters as economic inequality, racial discrimination, or campaign finance reform)." This sounds like Gramsci's notion of hegemony, and indeed, some of the conservatives referred to by DiMaggio actually invoked the concept. In other words, conservatives poached the rhetorical suasion of identity politics and steered it in a more conservative direction.

It is the premise of this section that the arts funding controversies and the culture wars more generally, in which I contextualize the receptivity by Haraway's audience as described above, made ostensible a particularly U.S. style of social relations, what I call performative force. The NEA Four, Senator Helms, and myriad other actors were caught in a very public performance of declarations about social mores and values. This was a situation in which it was not difficult for opponents to "press the right buttons" to get the other side worked into a frenzy. Whether in Boston (where the controversial Mapplethorpe exhibition was shown at the Institute for Contemporary Art), Washington (where it was canceled at the Corcoran Gallery), Cincinnati (where the director of the Contemporary Art Center was arrested for showing it anew), Minneapolis (where Ron Athey, a "scarification" artist with AIDS, generated a similar controversy), or southern California (where the performance project Art Rebate infuriated conservatives and xenophobic nativists when a group of artists gave $10 bills to undocumented workers on the Mexican side of the border to compensate for denial of health and other welfare benefits), the clash of cultural leftists and conservatives fed a national fantasy that lasted for several years.

Performativity is based on the assumption that the maintenance of the status quo (i.e., the reproduction of social hierarchies of race, gender, sexuality) is achieved by repeatedly performing norms. Every day we rehearse the rituals of conformity in the media of dress, gesture, gaze, and verbal interaction within the purview of the workplace, the school, the church, the government office. But repetition is never exact; people, particularly those with a will to dis-identify or "transgress," do not fail to repeat, they just "fail to repeat loyally." It's precisely that failure, Judith Butler (1993) contends in Bodies That Matter, that compels individuals to compensate for it by enacting over and over the models sanctioned by society. Because none of us can embody the model fully, there is always a parallax or discrepancy that can be taken advantage of—played with, dramatized, exaggerated—as a means to assert our will, or, in Butler's terms, our "agency" (220).

Since the emergence of performativity theory—based largely on the Derridean-inspired elaborations of J. L. Austin's account of the performative speech act (e.g., "I do" in a marriage ceremony) by Judith Butler (1990, 1993) and Eve Kosofsky Sedgwick (1990, 1992)—performativity has been characterized predominantly as an act that "produces that which it names" and in the process operates a compulsory exclusion (Butler 1993: 13). Those enjoined to witness the staging of compulsory norms by their presence, particularly if those norms invalidate who they are (or better yet, *what they do*), often engage them in silence or through parody, deflection, and even resistance. Parker and

Sedgwick (1995) give the example of queers who do not attend the weddings of family and friends because *merely* being present without speaking out against the act ("speak now or forever hold your peace") is a self-negation. "The bare, negative, potent but undiscretionary speech act of our physical presence— maybe even *especially* the presence of those people whom the institution of marriage defines itself by excluding—. . . ratifies and recruits the legitimacy of its privilege" (10–11).

This approach to performativity is crucial for understanding the injunctions to identify (in the United States, around the categories of race, gender, and sexuality), and indeed a great deal of work has been done on "alternative" identities.

In the U.S. context, it becomes evident that these alternatives carry their own performative force, which is considerable, based on long-standing, historically constructed norms. Alternatives have been incorporated into a range of governmental (in the Foucauldian sense) mechanisms that provide the compulsoriness of performing them (as a Latino, an African American, gay, etc.). Indeed, these alternatives are most often part of official and informal monitoring practices. As I explain below, since the civil rights struggles of the 1950s and 1960s, the interpellation to which Parker and Sedgwick refer has largely been coordinated around identities. And these have been buttressed by state institutions and media and market projections that shape, respectively, clients and consumers. Moreover, to the degree that the law and legal institutions design or extend rights to such identities, they apply "coherentist assumptions" that exert a powerful force in demographic profiling. Moreover, when rights discourse is oriented to identity, it becomes harder for "groups distinguished by theoretically mutable characteristics—fat people, for instance—to make anti-discrimination claims (why don't they just lose weight?)" (Halley 2000: 66). On the other hand, it is more acceptable that those "imprisoned" in their difference (e.g., skin color) have legitimate claims against denigrations or rejections of that difference.

Another feature of the performative imperative is that it does not come only from above (the state, corporations, philanthropic associations) but also from groups who do advocacy work on behalf of people construed as minorities, and even from group members themselves. Consider graduate programs in ethnic studies in which applicants are presumed to embody or subscribe to coherentist alternatives to the compulsory norms of the larger society. The expectations that candidates for admission into these programs will embody or ratify these alternatives ironically suggests that the performative force or injunction to perform or deflect is equally operative in these spheres as well. This is not to say that applicants to these programs necessarily "believe in their identity in the ways that the critics disdain" (Patton 1995: 181). This fissure in believability opens up a space of contestation, maneuver, negotiation. When U.S. politicians and scholars engage "alternative" identities from other countries, as the Ford Foundation has done regarding Afro-Brazilian movements from an African American imaginary (Penha 2000), the performative injunctions become even more problematic, as we will soon see.

The point of these comments is not to "blame the victims" who wield identity politics; it is, rather, to question the effectiveness of such politics. As Michael Warner writes, "Because the politics of resistance was early defined in the United States along identitarian lines, while many of the most policed sites have been those where sex happens, and not those associated with a distinct identity, the organized lesbian and gay movement has traditionally been reluctant to engage in a principled defense of sexual culture outside the home" (2000: 88). In other words, acceptance of the identitarian ticket to negotiate for respect and resources is caught in the processes of governmentalization, in the Foucauldian sense of the management of populations. While this governmentalization continues to operate on the basis of biopower (technologies that secure the welfare of the population at the same time as, to this very end, they earmark others for exclusion or elimination; Foucault 1991: 100, 137),[4] it is increasingly the case that *cultural power* is at work. Perhaps the prime instance of this is the permeation of society by a conventional anthropological understanding of groups as defined by cultures, with the political corollary that democracy is to be understood as recognition of these cultures.

Consequently, whether one subscribes to identity politics or presumes that one occupies an unmarked space in which identities are recognizably provincial or interested, subjects are enjoined not only to perform but to imagine their action within a fantasy structure. This structure, which is underpinned by all kinds of institutional contexts, may enjoin us to occupy the normative yet criticizable position of the white middle class or the institutionally sanctioned "alternative" (African American or Latino), or even the (media- and market-conditioned) oppositional stances (lesbians), which is not to say that there aren't "unthought" options. Haraway's proposal to wrest the cyborg from the naturalizing mechanisms of technoscience and its representational machines in "contestations for possible, maybe even livable, worlds in globalized technoscience" (1997: 270) is a version of this unthought or "queering."

But more often than not, the fantasy structure is operative (yet no less real), for example, in the so-called culture wars, when it is imagined that all conservatives take the same position and that all minorities have fundamental grounds for solidarity with each other. With regard to the latter, Michael Warner (1993) argues that liberal pluralism has fostered a cultural climate in which we are enjoined to accept the notion that disparate nonnormative groups are equivalent, a notion captured in the slogan "Racism, Sexism, Homophobia: Grasp the Connections." Rather than an effective political alliance, this "Rainbow" pluralism has projected a "fantasized space where all embodied identities could be visibly represented as parallel forms of identity" (xix). Warner objects that such a model of cultural politics is not conducive to interaction with "movements that do not thematize identity in the same way" (xx).

This same point has been made with respect to audiences for transgressive performance pieces. There is (1) the implicit/complicit audience who shares the same perspective as, say, the NEA Four, who flaunt "return of the repressed" genders and sexualities; (2) the target audience, "polite" society, whether hypocritical (e.g., Jesse Helms et al.) or not, that becomes or acts scandalized by the in-your-face style of the display of obscene "otherness"; and (3) the jaded or "primed" audience of TV talk shows and gossip papers and journals who relish the tension between (1) and (2). Curiously, most performance artists are not aware of or disingenuously deny the differences in audience. In the video installation *Cornered* (1988), Adrian Piper, "cornered" behind a desk, addresses an audience whom the artist accuses of presuming, racistly, that she is white, when "in fact" she is black. Ironically, it is Piper who "corners" her audience, presuming that it is white and racist. Piper thus conflates a range of possible audiences. Guillermo Gómez-Peña and Coco Fusco do something similar in *The Couple in the Cage* (Fusco 1992), a performance in which they present themselves as two undiscovered Amerindians from the Gulf of Mexico. The performance is set inside a cage and the performers wear and use the most outlandish props: presumably they are primitive, but one of them watches TV and the other works on a laptop. The artists claim, nonetheless, that unsuspecting publics mistook them for real Indians, to be mistreated and demeaned. This is clearly disingenuous, for it was the artists who placed themselves in a cage and invited the public to act out the primitivist, absurd fantasy in a pomo register, including feeding them as if they were caged animals. The onlookers were thus invited to "act out" what a target audience would do, and when they accepted the pact—when they were "cornered"—they were taken for that target and labeled racist (Fusco 1995: 47). As Carol Becker (1995: 13) explains, contemporary artists learn to "[push] viewers away" as the result of a moral didacticism born of the presumption that theirs is a "conservative audience that should be radicalized, or a puritanical one that needs to be shocked." But such projections are not limited to the art world.

The overarching social fantasy that compels us to perform conformity with and rejection of a series of roles and identities that give U.S. cultural politics its particular flavor is the product of a conjuncture of conditionings by the media, the market, the welfare state, and the political and juridical systems.

Synergistically, this conjuncture enjoins our performance of what it is to be man, woman, white, black, of color, straight, gay, and so on. For this reason, it is unproductive, in my opinion, to take to task today's performance artists or identity groups for working through and against these injunctions. They, like the rest of us, of whatever ideological stripe or phenotype, are condemned, so to speak, to perform. This imperative extends to all statuses and identities, including what we have become accustomed to imagine as the "dominant." The premise that there is a dominant culture that can go unmarked, unpreoccupied about who they are and how they are represented, is no longer viable. The spate of books on whiteness, identifying it as an ethnicity that cannot go unmarked, suggests that we live in a culture in which everyone is enjoined to confront himself or herself—often recognizing the construction and performance of that identity—in the process of working through the challenges to cultural status from one's "others."[5]

The Historical Roots of "American" Performativity

What I have been calling a national fantasy has a long history, dating back to abolitionism and subsequent strategies of empowerment by and for blacks and other minorities. The spectacularity of Jim Crow laws, and the lynchings that accompanied them, were brutal materializations of whites' fantasies of pollution. The civil rights struggles of the 1950s and 1960s provide the most recent Ur-text that prepares the ground for the performative character of the remaining years of the century. Stanley Aronowitz explains that the novelty of the new politics emerging therefrom is the performative effect that ensues from the staging of contestation (as in civil rights sit-ins): the new politics "[pass] up the traditional wisdom of electoral politics—build a broad based coalition, elect your candidates, work with them to introduce procedural legislation, and so forth—and opts instead for direct microintervention that 'tacitly challenges the *ethical* legitimacy of the majority' " (1995: 362).

These microinterventions were enabled in part by the civil rights struggles.

Indeed, the greater penetration in the Johnson 1960s of the welfare state to channel conduct, what Foucault means by governmentality, was met by struggles around welfare, definitions of the family, and subsequently abortion rights and the cultural ethos of minority groups. The Young Lords Party, for example, organized a "Garbage Offensive" to bring attention to the paucity of Sanitation Department pickups in El Barrio. They planned their action with a "sense of drama and flair" that "everybody could relate to" and that would legitimize the gang-turned-civic-organization in the eyes of the community (Abramson 1971: 75). Denied brooms for their cleanup by the "dogs" (the "Department of Garbage"), they stacked the garbage in the middle of the street "until the pigs came." Such events had enormous performative power, equal to or greater than most performance art, as Agustín Laó (1994–95) suggests in a history of the Young Lords Party. He points to the multiple symbolism of this performative action: it was used in a ritual act of cleansing and as a refutation of the image that the mainstream society had of their community as an abject social pollutant (37). The Young Lords demonstrated a media sophistication comparable to that of ACT UP in the 1980s and 1990s with such actions as take-overs of the Hispanic Methodist Church (December 28, 1969), renamed the People's Church, and Lincoln Hospital (July 14, 1970). These events were not simply vehicles for publicity, they were also means of community organization around such issues as education, nutrition, and health.

That the very rebels who had participated in the 1965 riots in El Barrio "found themselves directors of anti-poverty programs . . . or workers in Mayor Lindsay's Urban Action Core" (37) speaks both to the effectiveness of their actions and to the channeling power of the government programs of the period. This channeling was achieved not only in relation to poverty but, as I have been arguing, in relation to the funding of culture in the newly established state arts councils and the National Endowment for the Arts. The Nixon administration not only continued to fund the arts, but even increased the NEA budget by 500 percent in its first year. Government officials also made sure that subsidies went to the inner cities. In December 1969, Nixon sought congressional approval of his arts budget, citing culture as a "tool for democracy." The idea applied equally to the need to appeal to discontented minorities—Nixon "took an aggressive pro–Black Power posture" in his 1968 bid for the presidency (Marable 1991: 98)—as well as to the opposition to the Vietnam War. Nixon sought to fight on the same grounds as the countercultural elite (Jane Fonda, Susan Sontag, Robert Rauschenberg, the Art Workers Coalition, etc.) who were using culture against the militarist policies of the administration.

Other performative actions born of social and political struggle were the grape boycotts organized by the United Farm Workers (UFW) under the leadership of César Chávez. The Teatro Campesino, which promoted the struggle of the farmworkers as the cultural arm of the movement, contributed to the creation of a new cultural consciousness among Mexican Americans. Muralism, the best-known Chicano art form, was born in the context of this activism. In 1968 Antonio Bernal painted the first Chicano mural on the walls of the offices of the UFW, which housed the Teatro Campesino. The activist feel of the period is captured in the figures portrayed in the mural, beginning on the left with the legendary protagonists of the Mexican Revolution, la Adelita, Emiliano Zapata, and Pancho Villa, continuing with the Mexican American heroes Joaquín Murieta, César Chávez, and Reies López Tijerina, and concluding with a Black Panther and Martin Luther King Jr., in expression of solidarity with the black movement. Esteban Villa, an artist who worked with Mala Efe (an acronym that stands for the Mexican American Liberation Front but also puns on the expression of sedition conveyed by the phrase *mala fe*, "bad faith"), spoke of the direct connection between Chicano activism and performance in an interview with Chicano scholar Tomás Ybarra-Frausto:

> *Esto fue por eso del año '68 . . . Era la época del* [It was around 1968 . . . the time of the] grape boycott *y del* Third World Strike *en* Berkeley. We would meet regularly to discuss the role and function of the artist in El Movimiento. At first our group was composed mainly of painters and we would bring our work and criticize it. Discussions were heated, especially the polemics on the form and content of revolutionary art and the relevance of murals and graphic art. Posters and other forms of graphics were especially discussed since many of us were creating *cartelones* as organizing tools for the various Chicano *mitotes* [spontaneous "happenings"] in the Bay Area. (Esteban Villa, qtd in Ybarra-Frausto 1991: 130)

As Ybarra-Frausto explains, the murals as well as other Chicano art genres, particularly the installation-type altars, had their inspiration in vernacular sources: the images of saints in votive calendars, religious icons (such as the Virgin of Guadalupe), theatrical posters, graffiti, tattoos, even customized low-rider cars (131–132). Despite the defiant character of Chicano performance and murals, or perhaps because of it, funding from antipoverty programs made its way to community centers that sought to empower local residents, in part through community mural painting, funding targeted for crisis management by the federal and local governments. According to Rodolfo Acuña, "The thrust of the War on Poverty to obtain 'maximum citizen participation' drove agency workers who competed with other government agencies to service all sectors of the community. Chicano youths became special targets" (1980: 355). One of these targets, the Young Citizens for Community Action, became the Brown Berets, a group similar to the Black Panthers and the Young Lords. All three groups developed nationalist political and cultural policies, endorsed third world liberation struggles, and engaged in confrontations with the government and the police. All the more reason for the government to try to neutralize them with the carrot of programs for cultural affirmation and the stick of police repression.

The Black, Chicano, and Puerto Rican projects of nationalist affirmation were double-edged. On the one hand, they were necessary for mobilizing their communities to take control of their schools, their social service centers, and other local institutions. One Chicano activist, Rodolfo "Corky" Gonzales, was exemplary regarding this double agenda. He was both a community organizer —he founded Los Voluntarios (the Volunteers)—and became the director of one of the War on Poverty's youth programs. He was also the author of the epic poem "I am Joaquín" about the adversities of barrio life, which was made into a movie by Luis Valdez. By the early 1970s, the activism of Chicano and other ethnic militants had been drawn overwhelmingly into institutionalized cultural and social welfare spheres. Police repression, the end of antiwar activism, and "large doses of federal funds . . . further compromised many former civil rights leaders" (Acuña 1980: 385). Political action gave way to political brokering in increasingly institutionalized settings: university programs in African American, Chicano, Puerto Rican, and women's studies; community cultural programs; bilingual education programs; and more.

This increase in governmentalization is an important conditioning factor in the emergence of the politics of identity, especially the way the late capitalist welfare state translates the interpretations of people's needs into legal, administrative, and therapeutic terms, thus reformulating the political reality of those interpretations. According to Nancy Fraser (1989), the conflicts among rival needs interpretations in contemporary society reveal that we inhabit a "new social space" unlike the ideal public sphere posited by Habermas, in which the better argument prevails. For example, in relation to "gay life," the arts funding controversies of the late 1980s and early 1990s involved a contestation over the "intrusion of a gay 'attitude toward life' " (Helms's objection) or simply a nonnormative attitude into the domain of state bureaucracies (including arts councils and public cultural institutions) established to adjudicate entitlements based on merit, needs, and other criteria. The controversies involved the viability of the "experts" who oversee these institutions, the legitimacy of claims made by groups on the basis of an ethos, and the " 'reprivatization' discourses of constituencies seeking to repatriate newly problematized needs to their former domestic or official economic enclaves" (N. Fraser 1989). The conservative backlash and the "progressive" defense were both premised on the intrusion of or claims on the basis of (private) cultural matters into public life.

In this new social context, and given the conservative move to impede the access to rights, the grounds for entitlement shifted to a paradigm of interpretability. This marks a departure from classic liberal discourse, which accords rights to individuals and not groups. Group entitlement must take place in a *surrogate terrain*, such as language (for Latinos and other ethnic minorities), the family, or sexuality (for gays and lesbians and women's groups), that is, the particular experience around which groups, especially subordinated and stigmatized groups, constitute their identity. But this structuring of the new politics enjoins everyone to take their place within the ensemble of recognized groups or to mobilize to be recognized as such on the basis of "their culture."

Such a politics of identity has to be understood in the specificity of U.S. society, which is not to say that a politics of identity does not operate, in different ways, in other national formations.

"Racial" movements can be understood to be the first of the "new social movements" or "new antagonisms," following Laclau and Mouffe's (1985) theory of radical democracy, that call into question forms of subordination (bureaucratization and consumer commodification of "private" life) in the post–World War II United States (Omi and Winant 1986). Perhaps the greatest change that the civil rights movement brought was a transformation in the means of access to goods and services provided by the welfare state. These programs were an important factor in the redefinition of the terms of group identification, for they helped shift the understanding of the client role from strictly individual cases to those of designated groups, thus reinforcing a consciousness of subaltern group identity. Other minorities — particularly some of the historical Latino (Chicano, Puerto Rican) and Asian American (Chinese, Japanese, and Filipino) groups — were to make claims on the state in these terms, and in time there developed a panethnic approach to this politics of access. We might say, then, that U.S. society changed from one in which racial and ethnic politics were negotiated along the lines of a *war of maneuver*, according to which everyone knew his or her place, to one in which identities were dehierarchized and reconstructed along the lines of a *war of position*, to use Gramscian terms (Gramsci 1971: 238; Winant 1994: 43–45). This transformation also led the way for these groups to think and enact the political in cultural terms as well, the point being that the normativities that held the older order in place had to be struck down in de facto (the terrain of prejudice, habit, and other cultural inertias) as well as the formal de jure terms initially deployed in the civil rights movement. By the end of the 1960s, black, Latino, Asian, feminist, and gay groups were affirming their right to press their group culture into the public and institutional spheres. Black, Chicano, Puerto Rican, Asian, and women's studies departments formed in many universities at this time. And it was in these spaces, as well as in the communities, that the more "properly" cultural expressions of these groups were nurtured and wielded as means to decolonization.

Among their challenges is the push to legitimize the adjudication and legislation of rights on the basis of group need rather than the possessive-individualist terms that traditionally define rights discourse. Martha Minow gives the following explanation of the shift to a politics of identity: "One predictable kind of struggle in the United States arises among religious and ethnic groups. Here, the dominant legal framework of rights rhetoric is problematic, for it does not easily accommodate groups. Religious freedom, for example, typically protects individual freedom from state authority or from oppression by private groups. Ethnic groups lack even that entry point into constitutional protection, except insofar as individuals may make choices to speak or assemble in relation to a chosen group identity" (1988: 319).

Interpretability thus constitutes a "new social space" in which groups claim autonomy and legitimacy on the basis of their particular culture. Such a claim does not take place in a vacuum; it is made possible by the conjuncture of a welfare state that defines clients by group, by a media and market system that targets consumers, by the juridical means available to challenge discrimination. Cultural belonging is not characterized only by the set of practices that a particular community engages in; relations with others and with institutions also demarcate a sense of community. Herein are the grounds on which the impulse toward nonnormativity or abjection serves as a means to rally group solidarity. Culture, understood not only affirmatively but, even more important, as a group's difference from overarching norms, has become the foundation for claims to recognition and resources. In this view, so long as you can assert that you have a culture (a distinctive set of beliefs and practices), you have legitimate grounds for enfranchisement (see the discussion of cultural citizenship in chapter 1).

This premise of cultural legitimacy is usually taken for granted. The first challenge to such a notion would come from the assertion that an identity is *not* a culture. Do Euro-Americans, African Americans, U.S. Latinos, Asian Americans, U.S. gays and lesbians constitute *different* cultures? According to Appiah (1994), none of these groups, by themselves, constitute a *common culture*; rather, they are all positioned vis-à-vis each other in a field of force that could be characterized as U.S. culture. The framing that black activism provided for other group politics in the 1960s is an example of how the most important scale for speaking of culture is the nation, even in this time of rapid change. Whites, for example, adopted many of the forms that blacks themselves generated in relation to white "normativity," a point that has been made by many critics — Manning Marable (1991: 189), Isaac Julien (1992), Paul Gilroy (1992: 15, 307), and Kobena Mercer (1994: 276–277) among them — who argue that blackness is not a monolith enclosed within itself. Isaac Julien goes so far as to argue that there is a cultural kinship between Spike Lee and white supremacist David Duke insofar as both oppose miscegenation on the grounds of racial purity (263). The very fact that the groups referred to are designated as discrete cultures is an "American" phenomenon, one that is inscribed in U.S. national institutions (e.g., the Census Bureau). Furthermore, that such a claim is even possible in the United States is the result of a historical process that culminated in the past three and a half decades. Identity politics is the form that traditional U.S. interest politics takes in the post–civil rights period, one marked by the emergence of other social movements, the reconversion of the U.S. economy along post-Fordist lines and in relation to the new global economic order, and an unprecedented influx of non-European immigrants.

It is precisely as a means to break this frame that Judith Butler's theory of performativity was devised, to account for a politics of "disidentity" that is not premised on visibility but on the failure to reproduce identity. Disidentification can be understood as a form of play with and *within* representations, which is why it has gained currency in relation (or as a challenge) to identity politics. The latter relies on the belief that identities are already given, a belief that presumably forecloses the possibility of recognizing that all identity is constituted in relation to others, in turn a notion that deconstruction captures in the phrase "constitutive exclusions." A "politics of disidentification" enables one to maneuver within identity only by reframing it. Some, for example Butler, have attributed a "subversive" character to this tactical mode of behavior, yet it is anything but limited to a specific group of gender- or sex-benders and it is not necessarily "subversive" in a progressive direction. Disidentity, despite its apparent challenge, is an attempt to resignify a normalizing category or to valorize a "failure of identification." As such, it is a "misreading" that keys from within rather than opposes the normal (Muñoz 1999). Butler's claim that such "rearticulations" lead to a more "democratizing . . . internal difference" in the experience of identity stretches this interpretation beyond its usefulness because disidentification is not limited to those who repudiate the norms of a straight, white, male-valorizing society. Not only do white racists and militia adherents disidentify with what they perceive to be the liberal mainstream, but disidentification is practiced by everyone every day and not only by those who would "[fail] to repeat loyally"(Butler 1993: 219–220).

Ethnomethodologists have accounted for this "failure" by means of the concept of "indexicality." It refers to the context in which utterances and behavior acquire meaning for listeners and viewers (Garfinkel 1967: 36). Context, however, is never fixed but an open and ongoing process that enables all participants to speak, behave, and deny that they have done so in the ways ascribed to them. This doing and claiming to not have done is anchored in the appeal to underlying contextual conditions that are multiple and open to various interpretations. "For the purposes of *conducting their everyday affairs* persons refuse to permit each other to understand 'what they are really talking about' . . . The anticipation that persons *will* understand, the occasionality of expressions, the specific vagueness of references, the retrospective-prospective sense of a present occurrence, waiting for something later in order to see what was meant before, are sanctioned properties of common discourse" (41). We have all at one time or another sidestepped the fixing in meaning (intended or not) of our utterances by using the retort "That's not what I said."

To the degree that any group makes a claim for identity, without recognizing its imbrication in others' discourses, it is, according to Butler (1993), a form of disavowal, a fetishization of identity. Because performativity is the "power of discourse to produce effects through reiteration" of norms (20), identity is a regulated effect rather than the base from which one acts. "If there is *agency*, it is to be found, paradoxically, in the possibilities opened up in and by that constrained appropriation of the regulatory law, by the materialization of that law, the compulsory appropriation and identification with those normative demands" (12). This does not mean, however, that a viable contestatory politics follows from "failure to repeat loyally" in the very process of enacting the "law." This is a disclaimer of interpretations of her earlier book *Gender Trouble* (1990), in which Butler seems to posit drag and parody as viable politics.

However, the disclaimer does not do away with a fundamental problem of deconstructive analyses: they work quite well for texts but seem powerless before the operations of the institutions that exert regulatory force over texts. Butler's contention that the "turning of power against itself to produce alternative modalities of power, to establish a kind of political contestation that is not a 'pure' opposition" (1993: 241), has yet to be elucidated at the level of institutions and their effects (legislative and juridical systems, welfare reform, affirmative action programs, military and foreign policy). To the degree that Butler imagines "democracy"—following the work of Ernesto Laclau and Chantal Mouffe (1985; see also Laclau 1990; Mouffe 1992a, 1992b)—to inhere in such forms of gender trouble, and more generally, cultural trouble, she is caught up in the very fantasy that she aims to elucidate.

Of course, few or none of us in the United States are really outside of this fantasy. Yet it is discernible, quite often by foreigners who experience defamiliarization due to the assumptions that are made about them. Paul Gilroy speaks of the "Americocentrism" of black Americans' "understanding of ethnicity and cultural difference" (1992: 307). My own experience with Latin American activists and intellectuals provides me with a different understanding of the United States, one in which there coexists a deep-seated conservatism and a proliferating politics of identity and disidentity. Most Latin Americans' mistake, in my view, is to liken this state of affairs to the balkanization in Eastern Europe; even careful observers like García Canclini (2001) take this position, largely because, from a Latin American experience, identity is still largely rooted in the nation. To them, U.S. identity politics seems divisive.[6] Instead, the contestations take place *within* a force field that is largely uncontested. To use the Heideggerian terms briefly referred to in chapter 1, it might be said that the "enframing" elicits a summons to a particular kind of ordering "that drives out every other possibility of revealing" (Heidegger 1977: 27). This national fantasy locks "us" into a politics of interpretation and reinterpretation in relation to the many groups that claim recognition of their "culture" and their needs. The conflictive imbrication of the welfare system, the judiciary, the media, and consumer and labor markets holds this fantasy *together*. Thus, the very impulse to "act out" that Butler rightly takes as a sign of contestation is already conditioned by this conjuncture of factors, including "alternative" institutions. Because the criteria of, say, antipoverty programs and arts funding agencies have been devised within a legal order that certifies paragovernmental and nonprofit institutions, U.S. "alternativity" is part of the system (Wallis forthcoming). Two or three generations of artists, activists, and academics have endeavored to stake out a space for alternatives that necessarily exist as such within fantasy as much as within legality.

The impulse to act out has a particular flavor in the United States. This is what I mean by fantasy. It is not limited to progressive activists and performance artists; I have already argued that politicians do it, even archconservatives do it. How else can we understand the backlash of the new "oppressed" group characterized by the media in the wake of the Oklahoma City bombing as the "angry white men"? White men, who have been thought to be beyond representation, that is, unmarked, are now subject to the stereotyping characteristic of other groups. Their abject feature is their supposed murderous racism. A *Village Voice* report on the militia movement would have us think that most white men are ready to act out the racial cleansing (including the revenge on the "race-traitors") that William L. Pierce fantasizes in *The Turner Diaries* (Ridgeway and Zeskind 1995; Woodward 1995; E. Davis 1995: Savan 1995). Various accounts of the motives of the accused bombers, Timothy McVeigh and Terry Nichols, suggest that they were seeking recognition in a culture that conceded it only to the wealthy and those who had a "difference," implying blacks and other minorities. McVeigh "shared feelings of alienation" with the men who compose the militia movement and identified with those "oppressed by the government," like the Branch Davidians who died in Waco, Texas (Kifner 1995). Nichols, in a spirit of dissidence, assumed the mantle of abjection, "declar[ing] himself a 'nonresident alien, non-foreigner, stranger to the current state of the forum' " (Rimer 1995b). Whether or not such protrayals are correct is not as important as the injunction to frame them in this manner. By performative force, I am referring to this framing of interpretation that channels the meaningfulness of speech and acts.

What Regulatory Law Is There in a Society Characterized by Favor?

It is no accident that Butler defines performativity in relation to the law, as a "set of actions mobilized by the law, the citational accumulation and dissimulation of the law that produces material effects, the lived necessity of those effects as well as the lived contestation of that necessity. Performativity is thus . . . a reiteration of a norm or set of norms" (1993: 12). To be sure, she is not speaking of the legal code per se but of disciplinary (in the Foucauldian sense) social or psychosocial norms that produce "sexed," and by a similar logic, "raced" bodies. Nevertheless, her interchangeable usage of the two, law and norm, suggests that in her interpretation of U.S. culture, normalization and law are in close proximity. Foucault claimed that at the turn of the eighteenth century, as "autonomous" subjects were to learn to control themselves, discipline was dispersed throughout the new terrain of the social, wielding greater power than the law, which was still tied to the notion of sovereignty. However, it could be argued that despite the most visible location of observation and discipline in those institutions whose purpose it was to separate out the dangerous elements (e.g., prisons), these activities extended to that normalization generated in knowledge-producing institutions outside the juridical framework. As Boaventura de Sousa Santos argues, disciplinary power and juridical power are not incompatible, as Foucault thought, but shade into and support each other (1995: 3).

Such imbrication is certainly the case in the management of populations in the U.S. welfare state, as is made evident by the connection of "culture of poverty" theses and notions of criminality and rehabilitation. It is precisely by making this connection visible that civil rights and feminist activists sought to extend their struggles against racial and gender discrimination from de jure contexts to the more rooted and cultural de facto spheres (N. Fraser 1989; Quadagno 1994). In this way, they revealed the many ways in which the personal (product of normalization) is political (subject to legislation). Of course, when Butler invokes the law she is parodying/deconstructing a Lacanian style that conceals the constitution of the subject within the social contract, flawed by an "original lack" in those who lack or have relatively less power. Her point is that "cultural intelligibility" is produced via a fantasy/drama whereby some have power (the Phallus, in Lacanian parlance) and others lack it (1990: 44). In other words, the Lacanian "law" is complicit with disciplinary practices in relation to which some subjects are constituted by learning that they lack something.

This is a fantasy that is perhaps more easily discerned from the periphery. It has been suggested that the West's peripheries more easily enable disclosure of the artificiality and power-based criteria for cultural intelligibility. Western constructions of civilization and progress show themselves to be ideological. Analogously, from the "peripheral" perspective of queerness, Butler shows that the acceptance of one's "limitation before the Law" is "ideologically suspect" (1990: 56). Elsewhere, Toby Miller and I argue that cultural policy was formulated largely on the basis of "ethical incompleteness," a lack not unlike the one theorized by Lacan. "The desire was to produce well-tempered, manageable cultural subjects who could be formed and governed through institutions and discourses, inscribing ethical incompleteness in two-way shifts between the subject as a singular, private person and the subject as a collective, public citizen that could govern itself in the interests of the polity" (Miller and Yúdice 2002). Moreover, as Edward Said (1993) has argued, one can discern and unmask, especially from marginal positions, how cultural production (he refers to the nineteenth-century British novel) makes thinkable and normal asymmetrical geopolitical orders such as colonialism.

According to Roberto Schwarz (1992), idealizing discourses based on lack, which would require subjects to repeat norms to approximate an ideal, are necessarily misplaced in colonial and postcolonial societies like Brazil and, by extension, Latin America. He does not mean that such discourses are *inauthentic*, for European ideas of civilization and citizenship are a necessary feature of the colonies' constitutive disjuncture. In Europe, the "autonomy of the individual, [the] universality of law, culture for its own sake, a day's pay for a day's work, the dignity of labor, etc." were liberal ideas that sought universal status versus the irrationalities of feudal privilege (22). In Brazil, however, these liberal ideas were not mobilized against despots but were "adopted with pride, in an ornamental vein, as a proof of modernity and distinction" (28). In other words, rather than serve as part of disciplinary, normalizing practices, they simply adorned the sovereign classes.

The prestige that liberal ideas brought actually functioned in an illiberal social system based on dependency, emblematized in the practice of *favor* from the wealthy, on whom the free man (unlike the large landowner and the slave) depended for survival (Schwarz 1992: 20). "Under a thousand forms and names, favor formed and flavored the whole of the national life, excepting always the basic productive relationship which was secured by force. Favor was present everywhere, combining itself with more or less ease to administration, politics, industry, commerce, the life of the city, the court, and so on" (22). Indeed, favor even permeated liberal ideas, entering into a syncretic relationship with them. Schwarz lays out a kind of form/content disjuncture that operated in syncretic fashion. Institutions were liberal on the outside and dependent on the inside. "*Once the European ideas and motives took hold, they could serve, and very often did, as a justification, nominally 'objective,' for what was unavoidably arbitrary in the practice of favor.*" So wedded were liberalism and dependency that aesthetic practice aligned the disjuncture. Schwarz argues that this syncretic use of liberal ideas generated gratitude, a contradictory symbolic compensation, which was nevertheless "in tune with favor" (23).

It is worth repeating that this syncretism is neither mimicry (à la Bhabha) nor inauthenticity, but rather a different register of the expansion of capitalism in colonial societies.[7] "Difference, comparison and distance are part of its very definition" (Schwarz 1992: 30). Because of this, revealing the complicity of autonomy and dependency, completeness and lack, reason and arbitrariness, which "in Europe was a great feat, could among us be ordinary incredulity . . . the most prestigious ideology of the West was bound to cut the ludicrous figure of a mania among manias." "Embedded in a system they did not describe, even in appearance, the ideas of the bourgeoisie saw everyday life invalidate their pretension to universality from the very beginning" (28). These ideas performed the double-bound debunking of themselves. To the degree that they were accepted, that acceptance, insofar as it was premised on arbitrariness and favor, was unacceptable on liberal terms. This paradox, grounded in the very capitalism that generated liberal ideas, was captured by the ironic, even cynical consciousness of Machado de Assis's narrators (Schwarz 1992: 30), proving that reasoned critique was not the only means to expose the violence at the heart of the system of domination.

Returning to the question of law, we see in Brazil and other Latin American societies the failure of law and discipline to collude in normalization; instead, favor and other pacts between the haves and have-nots provided the background assumptions of a lifeworld permeated by dependency. The lifeworld, according to Habermas, provides the atmosphere in which community members' actions are coordinated toward understanding (1984: 70). Because background assumptions rooted in private relations are quite visible in Brazilian public life, it is readily evident that the public sphere is not as it seems. This disjuncture is even a feature of the legal system, which contrasts "modern, liberal, egalitarian, and individualistic rights" with "conservative legal principles." Roberto Kant de Lima enumerates a number of judicial procedures that demonstrate this contradiction: freedom from self-incrimination is guaranteed by the Constitution, but failure to answer questions can be used against defendants; secretly produced evidence is permitted; defendants may lie on their own behalf; judges may lead witnesses and ask questions not directly related to the facts; inquisitorial-like police practices are written into the records and may influence judges' decisions (Lima 1995: 242–243). Moreover, many of the contradictions in the legal system ensue from a hierarchically defined culture: there are special prisons for people of high status, such as college graduates and members of the military; public officeholders are accorded court privileges when accused of crimes. Rather than universally applicable laws, "different laws rule relationships among distinct layers of citizens, and they are not enforced between the distinct classes but only internally, among peers" (245–246).

Lima couches his analysis of the disjuncture at the heart of the Brazilian legal system in the more general relationship between public and private realms, a relationship that contrasts markedly with that of the United States. If in the United States the slogan "The personal is political" became the feminist-inspired common sense in combating oppression and subordination that went beyond de jure assurances, in Brazil the Portuguese-based judicial tradition fostered making the political a personal issue. The difference, according to Lima, is based on the definite border between the two realms in the United States, in contrast to the porosity of the public to the personal in Brazil. Because conflicts are decided in the public realm by authorities who defer to preexisting hierarchy, the vast majority of Brazilians, subordinated in this social order, make recourse to personal relationships characteristic of the domestic sphere to protect themselves from inevitable arbitrariness. "The extension of this private realm is intended to provide predictable outcomes to public conflicts" (Lima 1995: 259).

The fantasy that the United States enjoys rule of law was explained, against the grain of American exceptionalism, in Gunnar Myrdal's epochal *An American Dilemma* (1996). Despite his ultimate faith that the United States might make good on its ideals, Myrdal is one of the few observers of U.S. culture who argued that national self-understanding is a myth — the egalitarian "American Creed" — that preserves liberal principles while upholding a hierarchical order. He attributed this to a faith in a higher, natural law that justifies disobeying existing laws at the same time that there is a "desire to regulate human behavior tyrannically by means of formal laws" (16). Pointing to the disparity between ideals and actual behavior, particularly in relation to the subordination of blacks, Myrdal describes a structural foundation for a performativity that is unable to understand its inherent contradiction. Americans are not hyprocrites, he argues, but they conform to a strategic attempt to "suppress symptoms of ills while leaving the causes untouched" (20).[8] The strict line in the United States between public and private, especially after civil rights legislation, is what presumably overcame the obstacles in the way of resolving conflicts by a universal application of the law. Indeed, the recourse to publicity is the basic strategy in ferreting out whatever unwanted personal relations might color public life in the school, workplace, and even social and cultural institutions (e.g., disallowing homosexuals to parade as such on public streets in the St. Patrick's Day parade).

Of course, this supposed belief in the effectiveness of public debate and the universal applicability of the law was dealt major blows during the 1960s by the violent repression of the Black Panthers and other anticolonial groups that sought to opt out of the American Creed (Singh 1998: 77). The spectacularity of the U.S. failure of due process has continued in a spate of highly publi-cized cases of state terrorism (against MOVE) and police brutality (e.g., against Rodney King, Abner Louima, Amadou Diallo) and political favors (the Clinton pardons) in which justice did not always seem to be meted out as warranted. Confidence in the police, especially among African Americans, is understand-ably low, although the attacks on September 11 generated significant patrio-tism to temporarily suspend disbelief in rule of law. Nor do U.S. citizens believe that there is no clientelism in their country when George W. Bush's cabinet and policies are oriented to making his oil industry associates even wealthier than they already are. Moreover, the Supreme Court's December 12, 2000 decision that gave the presidency to Bush put another nail in the coffin of confidence in public officials. As Justice Stevens wrote in his dissenting opinion, "It is con-fidence in the men and women who administer the judicial system that is the true backbone of the rule of law. Time will one day heal the wound to that confi-dence that will be inflicted by today's decision. One thing, however, is certain. Although we may never know with complete certainty the identity of the win-ner of this year's Presidential election, the identity of the loser is perfectly clear. It is the Nation's confidence in the judge as an impartial guardian of the rule of law" (U.S. Supreme Court 2000).

The fumbling institution of a new homeland security system in the wake of the September 11 attacks points up the structural duplicity of U.S. attitudes toward law. On the one hand, President Bush, along with myriad Republi-can and Democratic politicians, made an early defense of Arabic and Muslim people, who were targeted by right-wing jingoists. On the other hand, Attorney General John Ashcroft has gotten Congress to legalize the United States' vio-lation of immigrant and citizen rights. Among other reductions of liberty, he has abridged by decree the Freedom of Information Act, which is "an essential check on government malfeasance in peace and war alike," and he has given a new directive "allowing eavesdropping on conversations between some law-yers and clients into the Federal Register" (Rich 2001a). Robert B. Reich, secre-tary of labor under President Clinton, expressed surprise that there hasn't been greater opposition to this slide into a police state (qtd. in Belluck 2001), but, as critical legal scholars have long argued, the rule of law is the rule of expediency. This is the explanation provided by Michael C. Dorf, a professor of constitu-tional law at Columbia University: "Constitutional principles are always, to a certain degree, overridden by certain circumstances" (qtd. in Belluck 2001).

As argued above, civil rights struggles established the paradigm by which identity was constituted as the platform on which access to rights would be legislated. That paradigm is coming apart, not only because mainstream liberal society and institutions have gradually reneged on it, but also because those who seek redress are not content to accept a slow-moving liberal incremental-ism. Indeed, critical race theorists sound a skepticism with respect to the law that echoes Brazilians' suspicions. They argue that the asymmetries wrought by the hierarchy of racism are a *normal* and *normalizing* part of U.S. society; consequently, only color-conscious policies can address racism (R. Delgado and Stefancic 1997). There is a certain irony in that, instead of seeking to end racial categorizations established within liberal legal and institutional dis-course (civil rights legislation, designated groups in affirmative action, census categorizations), they posit that struggle must take place around those very identities. Be that as it may, the means by which both liberal reformists and critical race theorists seek to advance their agendas are quite different from the Brazilian case. And that difference, despite skepticism, hinges on the practice of publicizing/politicizing nonnormative identities, considered to have been sloughed off from the "American" nation. For this reason, critical race theorists are not receptive to such interpellations as "my fellow Americans."

In contrast, Brazilians, including most black Brazilians, are first Brazilian and then something else, as Marcelo Penha explains, drawing on a history of governmentalization that "homogeniz[ed] cultural referents . . . linking them to a national referent" (2001: 373). According to Roberto DaMatta, in contrast to the United States' "separate but equal" commonplace (which, as critical race theorists argue, is a falsehood), Brazilians say " 'different but united,' which is the golden rule of the hierarchical and relational universe such as ours" ([1979] 1991: 4). Indeed, national belonging is something that even the most contesta-tory groups do not deny. This is characteristic of other Latin American societies as well. Perhaps the best example is that of the Zapatistas, who insist on inte-grating into the Mexican nation *for real*, at the same time that they struggle in-tensely for the autonomy of indigenous communities. "We want this nation to legally assume our recognition, not just a moral sentiment that can be silenced according to the manipulation of the media. One which says: 'I legally recog-nize that these who are different have these rights and are part of me.' That is the very role of the Constitution" (Monsiváis and Bellinghausen 2001). This does not mean that they accept clientelism, favor, and other features that have marked Mexican society. On the contrary, integration into the nation means ridding society of those forms of hierarchization.

According to Antonio García de Léon (1998), occupying the pivotal space that the Zapatistas gained was made possible by the Mexican state's failure to resolve a series of crises that began in the early 1980s with the debt crisis. De la Madrid and Salinas attempted a reform centered in the economy, and to bring about this reform they had to resort to corporatism characteristic of the Institutional Revolutionary Party (PRI), but which they tried to keep under control. This process left many empty spaces that undermined previous bases and were filled by myriad local responses: all kinds of civil organizations, economic projects, self-managed groups, civil disobedience, and even armed resistance. The point is that the crisis of the national state enabled the expression of these local responses. While they were indeed heterogeneous and rooted in the local, they were also magnetized by a field of force. In this context, rather than reject the myth of the nation, falsified by exclusion and precarious public spheres, these groups want to supplement and make the myth more encompassing and more effective. I return to the Zapatistas in chapter 3.

DaMatta ([1979] 1991) provides clues for understanding the very different performative force in a Latin American society. The judiciary, the schools, the media, the market, and so on do not produce the same kind of identity politics witnessed in the United States, nor an acting out on that basis. For DaMatta, carnival captures performatively the relation between public (street) and private (home) briefly reviewed here. During carnival, the usually impersonal space of the street is inverted, shedding its impersonality and authority (law) as it is permeated by familial norms characteristic of the home, where people learn "to be someone." Indeed, one of the speech acts most performed by Brazilians who seek a measure of control over public interactions mirrors the ritual inversion of carnival. This attempt to temper the contingency of the public sphere is drawn from their network of personal connections. When a Brazilian asks another, especially an authority, "Do you know who you're talking to?" (this act can be conveyed by other linguistic and performative means as well), he or she is seeking to neutralize the advantage that the other might have by appealing to whatever status migrates to him or her in the network of connections.[9] It is hoped that the appeal to hierarchy will mitigate invocations of the law.

DaMatta discerns "diversity" as the dominant logic of U.S. society, whereas "mixture" characterizes Brazil. This commonplace certainly captures something of the historical apartheid since the days of Jim Crow that put different peoples in their place, a practice that continues in identity politics, which operates through claims to difference. It is as if in the United States the law required people to establish hard and fast demarcations on the basis of which to engage in political contestation. People are pegged into this or that category in the United States, and those categories are believed to be meaningful, even by social constructionists. In Brazil, on the other hand, everyone already "knows his place" (([1979] 1991: 119), but social interaction operates more like a strategic assessment of what advantages or disadvantages that place will provide. For example, Ilka Boaventura Leite's (1991) ethnographic study of racial identification in the southern city of Florianópolis revealed that those people with whom she and her assistants interacted tended to identify relationally, shading lighter or darker in relation to whether they perceived the interviewer as white or black. This study is corroborated by the disjuncture between *Folha de São Paulo/Datafolha's* (1995) research on "cordial racism," which estimated the white and black/mixed population respectively at 39 percent and 59 percent, and the 1996 census that found an inverse proportion of whites, 55.2 percent, to blacks/mixed race at 44.2 percent (A. Nascimento and Nascimento 2000). To be sure, the difference is due to discrepant research methods, but also to the reluctance of the government to deal adequately with race as well as to a continuing strategic approach to identification that ensues in large part from pejorative attitudes toward blackness.

DaMatta's ([1979] 1991) study of carnival demonstrates that public performance, interacting in the street, is largely a ritual personalization of the impersonal. This of course fosters favor, patronage, and clientelism, which undermine the law. These effects are captured by the Brazilian practice of *jeitinho*, which has been translated as "bending rules," "pulling strings," or "cutting red tape." According to Livia Barbosa, it is "a fast, efficient, and last-minute way of accomplishing a goal by breaking a universalistic rule and using instead one's informal social or personal resources" (1995: 36). Moreover, it is another expression of the "in-betweenness" that characterizes Latin American societies in which hierarchies, including those that would relegate them to backwardness and unoriginality, are subverted (S. Santiago 1978). This in-betweenness, moreover, is the situation of those cultures whose originality is neither/nor (i.e., neither European nor equally Eurocentric projections of aboriginality) but both/and.

Taking his cue from Derrida, Silviano Santiago (1978) sees these cultures as supplementary, creating something new by adding to already existing repertoires. Supplementation is a form of disidentification, but the emphasis is neither on the "dis(s)" nor the identification. Santiago refers to a logic of the "both and" rather than "not that." Boaventura de Sousa Santos (1995) attempts to explain the origins of this paradoxical inclusiveness by reference to the alternative, "eccentric modernity" of Mediterranean baroque culture, bequeathed to the Ibero-American colonies. According to Santos, these societies are characterized by the lack of a strong central power, which in turn "endows the baroque with an open-ended and unfinished character that allows for the autonomy and creativity of the margins and peripheries" (499). Appearance, formalism, ambiguity, and mixing (especially race mixing or *mestizaje*) are the salient characteristics of the Latin American baroque. Using Bakhtin's attribution of the paradoxical combination of apotheosis and mockery to carnival, Severo Sarduy (1980) extends this ethos to Latin American societies in general, thus coinciding in part with DaMatta and Santiago.[10] However, the both/and characteristic of the neobaroque and other Latin American styles, such as marvelous realism, have been reified and used to characterize these countries as places of exotic, quasi-supernatural fantasy. These styles have even been invoked to speak of a Latin American postmodernity *avant la lettre* (for a critique, see Yúdice 1992a).

These paradoxical styles share important features with DaMatta's account of Brazilian society: the appeal to personal and religious networks in the negotiation of power, especially by the have-nots, or the *popular* classes, as they are known in Latin America. Indeed, the history of Latin American national identities in the twentieth century is largely that of the representation, courting, incorporation, co-optation, and repression of these popular classes. As in certain European countries (e.g., Italy), "popular" refers to the culture and practices of the peasantry and the working classes. This is why the Gramscian account of the struggle for hegemony, particularly the focus on the failure of an Italian national-popular,[11] is significant in Latin America, where these classes predominate over the small middle class and the tiny *alta burguesía*. In the United States, although "popular" does refer etymologically to "the people," it has become a synonym for mass culture. This may be due to the pervasiveness of mass media and consumer industries that promote progress, in contrast to the maintenance or recreation of rural, indigenous, Afro-Latin, and religious traditions in Latin America, precisely the cultural reservoir from which the above-mentioned styles were mined by intellectuals. More important, the difference is due to the lack of a universal populism that incorporates all subaltern classes in the United States. Though there have been populist moments, especially in the 1890s and 1930s, these did not draw their definition of national identity from an equivalent miscegenated imaginary, as in almost all Latin American countries. The failure to incorporate blacks, especially in working-class struggles, meant that populism could be only partial rather than a national universal. One might say that apartheid has undermined any possibility of a national-popular identity in the United States, and now that neoliberal postmodernity foments the multiplication of differences, this possibility is foreclosed. A democratic national-popular requires generalization across differences in region, politics, and race.

The construction of a national-popular will in Latin American societies faced similar challenges to those outlined by Gramsci. Juan Carlos Portantiero (1981), for example, considered Gramsci's analysis of "Caesarism" and "Bonapartism" applicable to Latin American nationalist populisms, particularly Varguismo in Brazil, Cardenismo in Mexico, Peronismo in Argentina, and Aprismo in Peru. This situation results when a potentially catastrophic contention between social forces is intervened in by a third actor, for example, the military, which brings into play an array of "auxiliary [often popular] forces directed by, or subjected to, their hegemonic influence," and "succeeds in permeating the State with its interests, up to a certain point, and in replacing a part of the leading personnel" (Gramsci 1971: 219–220). In this case, the popular forces do not, obviously, take power, but some of their agendas, particularly those that have been articulated into the third actor's ideological offensive against dominant forces, are incorporated into state policies.

Neobaroque and magical realist narratives may evoke the compromise solutions between the power of those in charge of the state and those who could create disorder on the streets and fields, but contra the culturalist reifiers, they are not the determining factors for the kinds of populism that emerged from the 1920s to the 1940s. This had to do with political compromises, co-optations, and repression in the context of an emerging reaccommodation to the world economy. The name for these compromises is corporatism, whereby individuals participate in the political and social process through state-approved and regulated organizations, which themselves have varying degrees of autonomy from the central government. There is a dissemination of the *personalist* relations characteristic of the patron-client relation based on favor to all state and civil society institutions. Public and private are inextricably bound, thus setting the stage, so to speak, for the cultural-political performativity of the popular sectors. If there is a performative tradition in Latin American countries, it is largely constituted on the basis of the popular, at least since the 1920s.

The most vibrant Latin American economies and societies of the 1920s and 1930s—Argentina, Brazil, and Mexico—were characterized by corporatist pacts between state-aligned élites, who promoted import-substitution industrialization and developmentalism, and an equally state-aligned popular nationalism that sought state welfare. The origins of the huge bureaucracies that provided support for a "national-popular culture" can be traced to this paradoxical situation, which recreated the Western European entities that had been most responsible for supporting culture: education, radio, film, ethnographic museums, and anthropological institutions. "People's culture" was disseminated from these venues, not outside the market, but within the culture industries, which were controlled and sometimes subsidized by the state. The most salient examples are samba and carnival in Brazil, the tango in Argentina, and radio and film *rancheras* in Mexico. It is said that Perón reproduced the smile of the then recently deceased tango superstar Carlos Gardel, in this way seeking to close the distance between the state and the masses that idolized the singer/movie star. The nationalization of samba, for example, involved the intervention of the Vargas regime in the 1930s in the music industries, in various social institutions like carnival and "popular" networks (Raphael 1980; Vianna 1999). This produced the very culture in whose name such arts were supposedly undertaken. In the process, the state became an arbiter of taste.

The salience of state support for certain popular forms and practices since the early twentieth century—Mexican muralism, Brazilian samba, Cuban son, magical realism, and testimonial narratives—bears witness to unique transculturated (F. Ortiz [1940] 1995) or hybrid (García Canclini 1995b) cultures whose significance cannot be adequately captured by the double bind of Eurocentrism and postcolonial nativism. Hybridity was at first an affliction to be contained, impossibly, by the theocratic Iberian colonial state, whose ideal subjects were constituted through repression. But by the early twentieth century, hybridity was becoming the very sign of Latin American modernity, against the citizen-defining Enlightenment and positivist narratives that had taken root there in the nineteenth century. Various populist regimes recognized that the vernacular culture of the working masses would provide the symbolic cement of the nation, necessary to push forward in a new stage of economic development. The populist 1930s to 1960s continue to provide the imagery for what has been accepted at home and abroad as emblematic, even stereotypical of Latin American national identities. The popular classes were idealized on the airwaves and the screen, in part to co-opt their increasing demands, sometimes effectively and often violently, against the state and bourgeois society. Aside from cultural co-optation, they were also met with brutal repression by military governments, with the neoimperialist aid of the United States.

However, the historical circumstances that enabled the rise of this classic Latin American populism changed in the 1960s, emblematized by the crystallization of a common cultural consciousness among so-called popular sectors and leftist intellectuals with the potential to create an alternative hegemony that threatened to change the clientelist arrangements between political elites and increasingly vocal masses. The development projects of the 1950s and 1960s were a catalyst for popular mobilization. The mid-1950s, for example, saw the reformism of the Instituto Superior de Estudos Brasileiros, the Marxist Centros Populares de Cultura, the left-wing Catholic consciousness-raising movement, and the Northeastern Popular Culture Movement (R. Ortiz 1988: 162). Like liberation theology, these movements made an "option for the poor," that is, the popular. They were targeted by the military coup in 1964 and its harder-line coup-within-the-coup of 1968 to 1973. The military formulated clear policies to modernize Brazilian society, that is, to resignify and transform the very notion and reality of the popular away from a perspective rooted in class and cultural struggles, toward a notion of popularity defined by consumer markets.

The Cuban Revolution of 1959 was a powerful stimulus to leftist and antide-pendista thinking throughout the region that also tapped into deep-rooted national-popular movements in most Latin American countries. As these movements played a role in the hegemonic process, their perspectives were relatively mainstreamed, to the point where social science institutes, state agencies, and independent productions all espoused popular culture. However, the radicalization of some "popular sectors" challenged the legacy of corporatism, clientelism, jeitinho, and favor. Consequently, the forces of "order" manifested themselves quite brutally, as per General Jorge Videla's promise/threat that "as many people will die in Argentina as necessary to restore order" (qtd. in Pion-Berlin 1989: 97). Hierarchical negotiations, increasingly repudiated by politicized masses, gave way to the demise of the pact with the popular and the rise of revolutionary initiatives. Hard-line military dictatorships took power in Brazil (1964), Chile (1973), Uruguay (1973), and Argentina (1976).

Import-substitution industrialization was no longer viable in the world economy and power blocs were reunited under the control of transnational capitalism. Leftist articulations of populism, transmuted into guerrilla movements in many contexts, were energetically countered by new military dictatorships (Southern Cone) or authoritarian governments (Mexico). U.S. anti-insurgency policies were an important intervention in these circumstances, offering the carrot of aid for development (e.g., the Alliance for Progress) and the stick of military intervention (e.g., the Chilean coup) and training (e.g., the School of the Americas). Analytically, as the dominant classes could no longer transform and neutralize these radicalized populisms, outright coercion (torture, massacres, disappearances) became the prescribed instruments to rein in the threats. At the same time, new media industries, especially television, whose reorganization under conglomerates like Mexico's Televisa and Brazil's Globo were facilitated by these repressive governments, began to transform the *popular* into *consumers*.

These dictatorships established ironclad political, social, and cultural control of the population, which was met by either armed guerrilla activity or performative styles that elicited political resistance through allegory. Performative force was quite literal, and any gesture of nonnormativity, any telltale sign of subversion could result in disappearance and death (Partnoy 1986). The military generated a "culture of fear," whereby uncertainty, insecurity, and terror paralyzed forms of collective action (Corradi, Fagen, and Garreton 1992); hence the recourse to allegory. But the performative force invoked by allegory goes much deeper than fear of revealing one's opposition. In addition to military repression of the popular, allegorical resistance put another nail in its coffin. This is evident in the allegorical literature of the dictatorship years (e.g., José Donoso's *Casa de campo*), which marked an epochal departure from the popular imaginary as conveyed in magical realism. That is, the aesthetic register (magical realism) of the clientelist compromise (state + popular) is extinguished, but no other evident (or representable) relation takes its place. The result is a mourning for this lost relation. Idelber Avelar characterizes it as follows: "The turn toward allegory spelled an epochal transmutation, parallel to and coextensive with a fundamental impossibility to represent the ultimate ground [of relations], a constitutive failure that installed the object of representation as a lost object" (1999). Moreover, by eliminating the participation of the people, the military dictatorships sloughed off the emancipatory feature of modernity, leaving only "integration into global capital as minor partners" (1999).

The voiding of emancipation did not entail the abandonment of culture. On the contrary, these fascistoid dictatorships installed a strong cultural state largely premised on the modernization of the media, which task was entrusted to technocratic elites (Waisbord 2000: 55; E. Fox 1997: 193). It is precisely in this modernizing context, which promoted forgetting the past and the dictatorships' victims, that the most important performative politics emerged. The Mothers and the Grandmothers of the Plaza de Mayo, diametrically counterposed to the performativity of transgression in the United States, donned all the trappings of family values, motherhood, and personalistic solicitude, *not* to mock or deconstruct them but to shame the military into living up to them. They wore the traditional black dresses of women in mourning and kerchiefs with the names of their disappeared children and marched holding placards with family photographs. Paradoxically, these women extended the domestic sphere into the occupied public sphere to demand not only justice for thirty thousand disappeared Argentines, but a restoration of that which had been eclipsed: their personhood. In other words, the military did not honor their own role as matriarchs in the collapsed public-private sphere of their authority. If justice was to be done, there needed to be a process of mourning that required the restoration of faces and bodies via photo-placards held up in public. As Diana Taylor writes, "The military and the Madres reenacted a collective fantasy" (1997: 205).

Much has been written about the Mothers and the Grandmothers of the Plaza de Mayo, and Taylor has been criticized for suggesting that they engaged in a national fantasy. Although she does criticize the lack of questioning of the domestic sphere within the Grandmothers'/Mothers' movement,[12] the basic premise of her study has to do with how the military represented itself—in the paternal role—as part of its strategy of legitimization, casting others in filial or feminized positions. As in the U.S. cases reviewed above, those who contested the performative force of the power-holders did so by making recourse to the roles projected by that power. This is what Taylor calls "bad scripts." From my point of view, however, the "transgressions" enacted by U.S. "progressives" in the culture wars are equally "bad" scripts, meaning scripts caught in a dynamics—performative force—from which neither protagonists nor antagonists could easily extricate themselves. The problem is not so much the scripts but the stage (force field) on which they are enacted. If what one is seeking is unadulterated agency, the complexity of the stage will not yield that kind of dénouement.

Grandmothers/Mothers and other groups, however, helped transform the stage on which performative force suffused Argentine society. They did not interrogate family roles and their impact in public spheres so much as demand that a traditional performative pact be honored. As we will see, this strategy, which contrasts markedly with U.S. cultural leftists' crusade to break with the past, is also characteristic of many Brazilians' resolve to make good on "racial democracy" rather than follow the path of U.S. civil rights institutionalization or of the Zapatistas, who do not wish to do away with the nation but rearticulate it more inclusively (see chapter 3). We might say that the dictatorships and the processes of democratization operated a sea change as significant in Latin American polities as civil rights struggles in the United States. They set in motion a new performative politics that veered significantly from the enactments of the popular in the earlier period. By turning the personal inside out and back outside in they were able to dramatize a new juridical drama: human rights.[13]

In Brazil, the mobilization of myriad human rights organizations "projected their demands onto the public stage and left their imprint in important victories in the Brazilian Constitution of 1988" (Paoli and Telles 1998: 64), although violence also escalated in the 1990s, tempering if not belying the citizenship gains made in the optimistic and heady years of the previous decade. As in other countries of the region, democratization in the 1980s, in the wake of the dictatorships, was ushered in by social movements whose demands went well beyond the demand for respect for human rights and punishment of violators. Nevertheless, human rights discourse penetrated most social movements (Jelin 1998: 410), including those of women, squatters, indigenous and racial minorities, shantytown dwellers, the landless, and the poor. Human rights provided a language for building a culture of rights and institutionalizing those rights (Jelin and Hershberg 1996: 3). This legacy of the "right to have rights" remained staunchly ingrained and laid the ground for a range of struggles in subsequent years, not only for women's, squatters', and racial group rights, but also for combating violence and labor rights.

But perhaps the most important gain was the *public performativity* of this right to have rights. The citizen actions and the cultural mobilizations analyzed in chapters 3 and 5 reveal that perhaps DaMatta's explanation of the public-private double-bind has been modified somewhat. To be sure, clientelism has not disappeared, as evidenced by the scandals in the alliance that put Brazilian president Cardoso in power. Nevertheless, the mobilizations of the 1980s and 1990s demonstrate that social justice agendas can be promoted even through the networks that characterized personalism, particularly because the very practice of networking has been rearticulated, with the help of NGOs (Fernandes 1994). The networks established by the Grupo Cultural Afro Reggae, on which I comment in chapter 5, have stronger ties to civil society mobilization than to favor and "Do you know who you're talking to?," although those features are also operative.

The publicization of social conflicts and agendas gives a different sense to performativity. "Social movements are important because they constitute, in the conflictive terrain of social life, public arenas in which conflicts gain visibility and collective actors become valid spokespersons. In these arenas, rights structure a public language that delimits the criteria through which collective demands are problematized and evaluated in their exigency of equity and justice" (Paoli and Telles 1998: 66). The impeachment of the first democratically elected president, Fernando Collor de Mello, in 1993 revealed both the outrage over this breach of the new public politics and the intense enthusiasm for the rule of law. This is not to say that everyday life did not continue to see riots (*quebra-quebras*) expressive of the outrage of the weak, as described by DaMatta ([1979] 1991: 31), but these, as I argue in chapter 5, were complemented or supplemented by the new discourse of citizenship.

Jelin argues that the concept of citizenship in a democratic culture must take into consideration symbolic aspects such as collective identity and not just a rationalized rights discourse. In this regard, she comes quite close to Nancy Fraser's (1989) concept of the correlation between identity and the struggle over needs interpretations, which creates a new social space. But this space also becomes permeable to new experts who will extend the reach of demands by channeling them through institutions. According to Fraser, the conflicts among rival needs claims in contemporary society reveal that we inhabit a "new social space" unlike the ideal public sphere in which the better argument prevails. Instead, there are contestations of the interpretations generated by different groups.

Jelin (1998) posits three domains in which citizenship is produced: (1) the intrapsychic, which is the basis for intersubjective relations; (2) public spheres; and (3) state relations with society, from authoritarian to participatory ones, taking into consideration as well forms of clientelism, demagoguery, and corruption. The main question is how to foment a democratic ethos. Jelin's answer is by expanding public spheres, that is, those spaces not controlled by the state in which practices conducive or oppositional to democratic behavior are constrained or promoted. The proliferation of public spheres will ensure that not only one conception of citizenship (rights and responsibilities) prevails. As such, the task of the researcher is to work in collaboration with groups to create spaces in which the identity and cultural ethos of those groups can take shape. Such a project is itself a part of the struggle to democratize society just as the state is brokering free market policies, such as the privatization of all public and cultural space.

However, we may point out two problems with the above discussion. Democratization under neoliberalism has transformed the public spheres in which citizenship can be effectively participatory. Institutional channeling tempers activism, and in the absence of viable state institutions, especially in neoliberalized developing societies, activism must dovetail with the agendas set by NGOs and funders. The social movements that ushered in (or were ushered in with) democratization have undergone NGOization, an institutionalization that has dampened the fire to put an end to clientelism. Let's examine these problems at least briefly, for they condition the kinds of performativity manifest in these countries.

Perhaps the social centerpiece of the neoliberalization of Latin American economies has been privatization. The premise is that greater efficiency will be gained by selling state enterprises (banks, airlines, utilities, etc.) to the private sector, which will also generate revenues with which to pay off the foreign debt and maintain social services. In the majority of cases, things have not turned out as declared, for a range of reasons. Of the largest economies, Argentina exemplifies the worst-case scenario. In addition to the privatization of just about everything, President Menem also put into place a policy of currency convertibility, pegging the peso to a strong dollar, rendering Argentine products uncompetitive due to high wages. Even as the current four-year-long economic crisis deepens, the IMF insists that Argentina avoid a deficit, eliminate government debt (which, respectively, means laying off hundreds of thousands of employees and dealing a blow to local pension funds that are big holders of debt, in a country with strong labor organization), and end the one-to-one convertibility with the dollar (Zlotkin 2001). But just as important, or even more so, is the deep-rooted corruption that has transferred billions into private, even criminal hands (Viau 2000). Moreover, Menem was arrested for illegal arms sales, and his ministers have been implicated in money laundering and thefts in privatized banks that have contributed to the economic crisis. Under these circumstances, the public sphere is paralyzed but also shows signs of being reactivated by outraged citizens who are engaging in a range of demonstrations and civil disobedience. Through such outrage, the constitutionally elected president, Fernando de la Rúa, was forced to resign, like his economic minister, Domingo Cavallo. Subsequent presidents were also forced out until Duhalde, a populist inspired by Perón, was selected by Congress to try to bring Argentina back from default in the remaining two years of de la Rúa's term.

NGOization is not scandalous, but nevertheless contributes to a weakening of the public sphere, precisely the opposite of the intent of the social movements. In the 1990s, the social movements that emerged in the 1980s institutionalized—NGOized—to the point that activism has given way to bureaucratic administration. With NGOization, these movements have been permeated by international discourses on cultural citizenship, where identity is the lynchpin of rights claims. To be sure, how identity is deployed depends on the performative possibilities holding in different societies. In such contexts, there is little to be gained by deploying identity or disidentity if there is no juridical or other institutional uptake to transform rights claims into material changes. This question of uptake is crucial and it has confounded many a study that has presumed the receptivity to identity rights claims on the basis of experiences in other contexts. This is one of the problems, in my view, with some of the positions taken in Sonia E. Alvarez, Evelina Dagnino, and Arturo Escobar's edited volume *Cultures of Politics, Politics of Cultures: Re-visioning Latin American Social Movements* (1998). Although inclusive of Latin American contributors, this book was largely conceived from the vantage point of an unquestioned belief in the power of cultural politics, reflecting to a large degree the U.S. location of two of the editors. Moreover, the book was designed with the express intent of persuading U.S. political scientists that culture matters.

Nevertheless, several of the contributors demonstrate the limitations of a politics of identity in Latin American countries. Olivia Maria Gomes da Cunha (1998) traces the displacement within the Brazilian black movement of a Marxist emphasis on political consciousness to a more culturalist one in identity, which in turn has been displaced by the turn to "citizenship." This turn, moreover, affords this and other movements greater flexibility, particularly as they seek a range of partners for support as well as to extend their reach beyond race and cultural identity. Indeed, Cunha's case study, the Grupo Cultural Afro Reggae, on which I too have written (chapter 5), practices *sampling* in terms of identity (they identify as black, as Brazilian, and as inclusive), political expedience (partnerships), and cultural practice (musical fusions). In other words, jeitinho, mixing, personal relations, and evasion are significant practices that belie the above-board assumptions about democratic mobilization as it is rhetorically portrayed in politically correct spheres in Western Europe. As Paulo Krischke observes, social movement activism and clientelism are crucially intricate and conflictual in ways that are unfathomable to Eurocentric discourses of Weberian and Habermasian public service normativity (2000: 111), which is also not to argue that they are invalidated by failing to meet such criteria.

Verónica Schild's (1998) contribution to *Cultures of Politics* also problematizes the editors' premises by demonstrating how the activism of Chilean women's groups, once absorbed into the machinations of the neoliberal state, became a way of controlling rather than opening up participation. Schild focuses on the ways cultural and material resources are mobilized for the construction of new state forms. From this perspective, "although social movements may, in one conjuncture, challenge domination as a particular 'congealed' structure of power relations (Slater 1994: 27) and of oppressive and exclusionary identities, in another they may themselves contribute to the emergence and development of new forms of domination" (Schild 1998: 95). NGOization, the option in neo-liberal (re)democratization in the postdictatorship years by which activist sub-altern groups have been able, with the help of international organizations and foundations, to have their demands recognized, contributes to repositioning these groups "as new types of *clients* of administrable 'needs' " (110). Culture is at the heart of the politics of interpretation of these needs, and to the degree that they are administrable, the synergy of the market and the state charac-teristic of neoliberalism coproduce identity (as García Canclini [1995a] might say), thus complicating the notion of oppositionality and agency.

The heavy involvement of international NGOs and foundations in pro-moting social agendas in Latin American countries adds another layer of inter-action to the networks in which social movements operate. Aside from the community in whose name social movement leaders speak and act, there are government officials, foundation and NGO personnel, academics, corporate funders in some cases, solidarity groups, the media, and others. What the inter-national NGO or foundation adds is a motivation from outside the receiving society. Sometimes an outside organization provides legitimacy for a particu-lar project. In the case of the Ford Foundation, as Penha (2000) points out, the grants given to the Centro de Estudos Afro-Asiáticos for the study of the Afri-can experience provided funding that, once given, enabled that organization to study local Afro-Brazilian relations as well as African American activism in civil rights struggles in the United States, thus sidestepping the censorious views of the Brazilian government toward affirmative action at home. Penha stresses the brokering actions of granters and grantees of the Ford Foundation's pro-gram on Afro-Brazilians. But the influence of NGOs and foundations is not limited to content. Less visible are certain commonsensical approaches to the study of social groups. Cultural identity, in particular, has been disseminated by U.S. and European organizations, including UNESCO, and it is widely re-garded as the lynchpin of a new kind of citizenship, one based on recognition of difference.

Whether or not grantees start out with these kinds of premises, they adopt them at least for the purposes of writing grant applications. Indeed, I have been told confidentially by some foundation officers that they help grantees write applications according to the parameters of the foundation so that they will be successful. Once they get the grant, these officers will be happy if the grantees do what they want with the funds. This means that there is quite a bit of jeitinho (rule-bending) taking place at several points in the networks that make so-cial action possible. Consequently, not even the stated agenda of the NGO or foundation will ultimately be fully respected. We see at work something akin to the syncretism discussed above, whereby liberal ideas and favor coexist. But it is equally the case that social movement leaders and the communities they represent also do not get their way unilaterally (chapter 5).

To conclude this section, it is worth broaching the brouhaha provoked by Pierre Bourdieu and Loïc Wacquant's (1999) critique of Michael Hanchard's (1993) study of the Brazilian black movement. Despite the many claims that we inhabit a postnational time and space, what the various actors involved in this debate demonstrated is that they were performing in accordance with background assumptions rooted in national culture. Bourdieu and Wacquant accused progressive U.S.-based academics of exporting racial categories to Brazil and focused their critique on Hanchard, whose study of the Brazilian black movement generated critiques from Brazilian and/or Brazilian-based social scientists, largely for the identitarian premise that darker-skinned Brazilians should identify as black as a means to provide the oppositional critical mass necessary to successfully demand a Brazilian version of civil rights and affirmative action. To be fair, Hanchard himself reported that his informants considered it unlikely and perhaps undesirable that in Brazil there would emerge a "racially specific political party, church or other institution on a national level" (82). This premise was read into his work by Bourdieu and Wacquant, but it would have been more accurate if attributed to Howard Winant's extension to Brazil (1992, 1994) of his framework for analyzing race relations, developed in connection to U.S. history.

Bourdieu and Wacquant's critique of U.S. academics' "imposition of racial categories" is very problematic because they base themselves on the myth of Brazilian "racial democracy," which began to be criticized in the late 1940s, especially by Brazilians themselves. This notion, according to which injustice was socioeconomic rather than racial, had been developed by Brazilian anthropologist Gilberto Freyre as a way of distinguishing the Brazilian experience from that of the United States. It provided Brazil a higher moral ground with respect to U.S. apartheid. Some commentators (J. French 1999; Stam and Shohat 2001) have suggested that, like other Frenchmen's alarm at the diminishing international influence of French culture and intellectual tradition, Bourdieu and Wacquant sought to delegitimize the spread of U.S. academic discourse. We see here, then, the makings of an interesting post–cold war international cultural rivalry, echoed in the divergent positions taken by French and U.S. trade negotiators over the definition of culture: heritage (France) versus commodity (United States).

What this brouhaha makes evident is the imbrication of contrasting national background assumptions about the categories we use in understanding different societies. Bourdieu and Wacquant are correct in pointing out that U.S. scholars are permeated by views that emanate from the specific force field of U.S. social relations, yet this does not mean that these views cannot be rearticulated in consonance with social justice. But the important point to be made, following Micol Seigel (2001), is that the comparisons involved in many of the studies of Brazilian race relations by U.S. scholars, and vice versa, are used for purposes that make sense within the scholars' own community: "U.S.-Brazil comparisons are implicated in the differences they chart . . . they are part of the processes of shaping social categories and lived experience. In broadest terms, [I] argue that race and other social categories are shaped in transnational as well as local contexts, and that comparisons are part of that process" (3). Olivia Maria Gomes da Cunha (forthcoming) also demonstrates that U.S. anthropologists of the 1920s and 1930s took an interest in Brazilian race relations to get a better understanding of the U.S. South. The point, then, is that there is a performative force at work in scholarship, as I suggested in opening this chapter with a reflection on Haraway and her audience. I myself, of course, cannot pretend to be free of that force. In what follows, however, I hope to put the competing (U.S. and Latin American) injunctions to perform to work against each other, using each to discern the background assumptions in the other. The objective is not only to criticize those assumptions but to draw lessons from them on the effectiveness of movements for social justice.

The Globalization of Culture and the New Civil Society

In this chapter, I examine how the turn to civil society from the 1980s on was a particularly expedient orientation to culture and identity.[1] Additionally, I explore how the notion of civil society does not take root in the same way in all societies; this is explained in part by the performative force exerted by the web of institutions in which all action is meaningful. Globalization processes certainly have an impact on this field of force, but they are ultimately incorporated as other elements that constitute that field. I am particularly interested in how these processes have generated discussions on the role of civil society as the medium through which the conventional compromise between the state and the diverse sectors of the nation—the E pluribus unum—is renegotiated. This revision is often brought to the fore by localities that have the most to gain or the most to lose from the vicissitudes wrought by globalization. Civil society has become the concept of choice as many movements for reform and revolution have been chastened by the eviction of socialism as a political alternative, at least for the near future. The current dominance of neoliberalism— the set of policies that include trade liberalization, privatization, the reduction (and, in some cases, near elimination) of state-subsidized social services like health care and education, the lowering of wages and the evisceration of labor rights—has contributed to the left's shift in political attention from the take-over of state power (which in many cases has not resolved the question of sovereignty) to issues of civil and human rights and quality of life. Conventional and even progressive political parties have succeeded in doing very little to counter these policies, both because the institutionalized political process is largely dysfunctional in responding to social needs and because enormous pressures from international financial interests not only have discouraged reform but have actually worsened conditions, such as the ever increasing gap in income distribution. Consequently, the most innovative actors in setting agendas for political and social policies are grassroots movements and the national and international NGOs that support them. These actors have put a premium on culture, defined in myriad ways, a resource already targeted for exploitation by capital (e.g., in the media, consumerism, and tourism), and a foundation for resistance against the ravages of that very same economic system.

Globalization has as many explanations as the number of theorists and critics who work with this concept. Many explanations, however, resort to the potent metaphor of the virus to give a graphic sense of the reach and the rapidity of global processes, spurred by technological innovation and deregulation. Throughout 1998 the mass media, with fascinated terror, likened the collapsing global economy to a viral infection. Punning on the Asian flu, commentators observed that Asian countries were gripped by a severe case of monetary inflation and depleted reserves that contaminated Russia and subsequently spread to Latin American countries with alarming speed. Within two months, Brazil was in the death throes of acute economic pneumonia, its immunological reserves having migrated to stronger organisms like the United States, which were likely to resist the assault, albeit menaced by this global influenza. The collapse of several economies produced panic. Within one month, Brazil's reserves had fallen from $75 billion to $40 billion, portending an imminent default on payment of its $350 billion foreign debt.

The IMF and the United States injected $117 billion into Asia (Crutsinger 1998), $22.8 billion into Russia (Cohen et al. 1998), and $41.5 billion into Brazil to safeguard investors (Krause 1998). The vast majority of the population, however, was bled even further by stiff austerity and structural adjustment therapies, applied especially to social services and education. Indeed, higher education budgets were slashed and policies have been instituted for the privatization of the university system (ANDES-SN 2001). As if this weren't enough, the vast majority of Brazilians were bled even more as the bailout did not lead to a recovery and Fernando Henrique Cardoso was forced to devalue the real, which fell precipitously to half its value. This crisis got worse in 2001 and 2002 as the economic crisis that gripped Argentina dampened hopes of improvement in the MERCOSUR countries.

The September 11, 2001 attacks and their aftermath have geometrically multiplied the implications of the viral rundown of capitalism. Not only are terrorist networks conceived of as dormant autonomous cells that can activate spontaneously and attack the system, but the very means of countering them requires that "law enforcement and the military will have to reshape themselves into entities resembling autonomous terrorist cells" (Sloan 2001). Simulation theory proposed such viral self-replication (Baudrillard et al. 1989: 39), which would seem to be verified by the CIA's training of bin Laden's networks and their attempt to topple corrupt monarchies and take their place at the helm of theocratic and neoliberal states (Negri 2001). Such self-replication has become real in the global dissemination and upgrade of surveillance, netwar, and the "new" hot-and-cold war that have translated into the new unstable world order on the verge of careening uncontrollably (Escudé, López, and Fraga 2001).

This viral metaphor has dampened the enthusiasm with which neoliberals celebrated the triumph of capitalism after 1989. For them, globalization is the complete actualization of another fantastic metaphor: the "free" market, which apparently has triumphed over other options. Euphorically, the organic intellectuals of the market (e.g., Francis Fukuyama) declared that the climax of human history had been reached, and that henceforth there would no longer be any ideologies. Nevertheless, the terrain of struggle passed from ideology to culture, if we attend to Samuel Huntington (1996), who prophesied that non-Western cultures, especially Islamic fundamentalism, would oppose the culture of the market epitomized by the United States. Those who criticize neoliberal enthusiasm also emphasize the cultural aspects of globalization, but in order to impugn them. Hence, for example, the critique of the *Global Dreams* of transnational capitalism, the metaphor used in their eponymous book by Richard Barnet and John Cavanagh (1994). For them, McDonalds, Sony, and other transnational conglomerates are responsible for the destruction of local cultures and the erosion of national identities and sovereignties. Leslie Sklair (1991), among others, identifies the culture-ideology of consumer capitalism for keeping in place the hegemony of the transnational bourgeoisie, as much at home in Bangkok as in London, Mexico, New York, or Buenos Aires.

Globalization and Cultural Studies

Until the 1980s, most cultural studies traditions in Europe and the Americas had a national frame. Greater emphasis on the global context of cultural practices in the 1980s and 1990s is the result of the effects of trade liberalization, the increased global reach of communications and consumerism, new kinds of labor and migration flows, and other transnational phenomena. Also significant in this regard was the implosion of the communist bloc, brought about in part by propaganda, economic, and even military warfare on the part of the United States and its allies. This world-historical event not only focused the world's gaze on global economic restructuring and its ideological underpinnings, but it also brought to light a series of conflicts that appeared to be new: the rise of presumably dormant nationalisms, the emergence of religious and ethnic fundamentalisms, and the determination to redraw geopolitical boundaries as a response to globalization. Some of these observations have been factored into assessments of political and cultural conflicts in the United States and Europe, particularly in reference to the rightward turn in politics and the recrudescence of racial and ethnic strife. They have been less important in analyses of the ongoing transformation in the rest of the Americas. However, other aspects of globalization have been particularly significant. Most important, long-standing institutional arrangements, from government proprietorship of industry to public subvention of culture and education, have been undergoing considerable change. This alteration is most often attributed to economic restructuring, particularly policies such as reduction of the public sector, the privatization of national enterprises and social services, and the evisceration of labor laws that create new opportunities for profit and reduce the operating expenses of capital. These have been seen as the means to integration in a streamlined U.S. economic bloc that can compete with the renewed economic muscle of Europe and East Asia. Other global trends considered significant in the transformation of Latin America are the new global division of labor ensuing from global economic restructuring, deregulation, the development of capital markets, the denationalizing impact of new technologies on telecommunications and mass media, the rise of global marketing, the exponential growth of international travel and the tourism industries, and the political and social effects of an expanded narcotraffic industry that has permeated the centers of power not just in Colombia, Peru, and Bolivia, but also in Brazil, Mexico, and, some have argued, even Cuba.

Such a focus on the global was certainly not part of the frame when we think of cultural studies as the field emerged in the late 1950s and was institutionalized in the early 1960s in the Birmingham Centre for Contemporary Cultural Studies. Its frame was English, to the exclusion of other subnations or colonies of the United Kingdom. Richard Hoggart ([1957] 1992), Raymond Williams (1958, [1961] 1965, 1977), E. P. Thompson (1963), and others were interested primarily in helping to shift the focus of national culture away from the tradition of "the best that has been thought and said," characteristic of the legacy of Matthew Arnold, toward a valorization and study of the practices of working-class Britons. In later, Gramscian-inflected characterizations of the enterprise, this shift was described as a complex struggle for hegemony, that is, the shaping of meaning into an articulated whole that makes sense to diverse sectors of the nation, although within that whole the interests of the dominant classes, though contested, are ultimately served (Gramsci 1971). Unlike the more conventional notion of ideology (the worldview of the dominant classes, in its simplest formulation), culture, in this view, was defined as the struggle over meaning. That is, culture is no one's or no one group's property (as would be the case in ideology), but rather a stratified process of encounter. The founders of cultural studies no longer saw culture as a civilizational achievement but as strategies and means by which the language and values of different social classes reflected a particular sense of community while nevertheless accommodating to the place made available to that community within the contest of cultures that makes up the nation.

Transdisciplinary fields of study such as communications and American studies in the United States and the anthropological and sociological study of culture in Latin America were also conceived within a national framework right up to the 1970s. The major exceptions were the dependency theory of the 1950s and 1960s and the critique of cultural imperialism, prevalent among left academics, particularly in the 1960s and 1970s in Latin America as well as in other "peripheral" or third world regions and among the minority academics and intellectuals who struggled to establish ethnic studies departments in the United States. Dependency theorists focused on the unequal exchange imposed by central economies on those of the periphery (Baran 1958; Dos Santos 1970) as well as on the influence that this asymmetry has on structuring internal class relations within dependent countries (Cardoso and Faletto 1973). Cultural dependency is derived from this model insofar as not only class interests but also class tastes and values are thought to be determined by the cultural models of the center (Franco 1975). This perspective was echoed and taken further in books like *Para leer al Pato Donald* (*How to Read Donald Duck*; 1972, 1975). The authors, Ariel Dorfman and Armand Mattelart, like many others at the time, saw the U.S. media as a weapon in the service of U.S. imperialism. Similarly, the Black Power, Chicano, and (Nuyorican) Young Lords movements of the late 1960s attacked the collusion of the media with the military-industrial complex as well as the racist imperialism at the heart of U.S. society and foreign policy. With their focus on the power of institutions of production and distribution to spread capitalist and colonialist values, most of these critics gave little attention to the processes of reception, how readers and viewers might resist, appropriate, or otherwise modify mass-mediated messages. In the British context, even Hoggart, who sought to demonstrate (and advocate) the resilience of British working-class culture, worried that the "newer," U.S.-style "mass art" would lead to a "subjection [that] promises to be stronger than the old because the chains of cultural subordination are both easier to wear and harder to strike away than those of economic subordination." He saw this as a cultural colonization that promised "progress . . . as a seeking of material possessions, equality as a moral levelling, and freedom as the ground for endless irresponsible pleasure" ([1957] 1992: 187, 263).

In tune with the radical tenor of the period, but drawing quite different conclusions from it, Marshall McLuhan, as if dismissing the kind of backward-looking resiliency advocated by Hoggart, urged educators to accept the cultural implications of the new electronic technologies of mass culture. To do so, he argued, would better prepare youth for participation in a media-saturated public culture. Also anticipating the anti-imperialist charges made by Dorfman, Mattelart, and others, he counterargued that "Hollywood is often a fomenter of anticolonialist revolutions" and quoted Sukarno to back up his point: by showing that a "people have been deprived of even the necessities of life . . . [Hollywood] helped to build up the sense of deprivation of man's birthright, and that sense of deprivation has played a large part in the national revolutions of postwar Asia." McLuhan's new world order did not portend greater inequality; instead, it was envisioned to be conducive to a "recreat[ion of] the world in the image of a global village" (McLuhan and Fiore 1967: 100, 131, 67).[2]

McLuhan's global dreams, which were unabashedly utopian, resurface now and then, particularly in the participatory visions that the Internet produces in its most enthusiastic surfers. But even as these dreams are blown to galactic proportions, there are critics like Richard J. Barnet and John Cavanagh, Leslie Sklair, Saskia Sassen, and others who examine the mayhem that hovers at the frontiers of utopia. The protagonists of globalization, according to these critics, are not the new technologies per se but the global corporations that have brought about a simultaneous integration of economies, the disintegration of politics, and a decrease and downgrading of employment or its displacement to the third world, thus leading to the proletarianization of middle sectors and greater immiseration of the poor as corporations thrive. As Barnet and Cavanagh note, the technologies (informatics, telecommunications, biotechnology) on which social transformation is premised are "anything but labor-intensive," thus adding to the scarcity of jobs already effected by economic restructuring (1994: 426). For Sklair, it may not be accurate to consider consumers "cultural dupes," nor to characterize capitalist consumerism as U.S. cultural imperialism; however, national corporations like Mexico's Televisa and Brazil's Globo do just as well or better in promoting the "culture-ideology of consumerism" in those countries (1993: 32). Sassen (1991) shows how finance and media conglomerates have changed the material and social space of global cities, including those in the periphery like São Paulo and Mexico City, forming or deepening new spatial arrangements whereby pockets of wealth are surrounded by stretches of inner cities and shantytowns whose residents provide the cheap labor that underwrites the lifestyle of the professional-managerial classes.

Though most leftist views of globalization are pessimistic, the turn to civil society in the context of neoliberal policies and the uses of the new technologies on which globalization relies have opened up new forms of progressive struggle in which the cultural is a crucial arena. The multiclass Viva Rio movement in Rio de Janeiro, for example, has turned most of the areas of social life abandoned by the neoliberal state—health care, labor, poor neighborhood development, street children and the homeless—into an agenda for organizing civil society. Their most innovative and risky premise is the bridging of concerns of the middle class and the poor. For example, middle-class apprehensions about security (greater and more effective policing) are linked to the poor's demands for civil and human rights (protests against police brutality). Viva Rio also brought together poor youth groups who were feared by the middle classes (particularly enthusiasts of funk music and dance) together with other sectors of society in a project to disseminate funk music as the most important cultural feature of the city. There are risks that such a linking of concerns might yield preference to the demands of elites (as occurred when the military occupied favelas in late 1994), but Viva Rio's emphasis on neighborhood development for the poor serves as an effective counterweight (see chapter 5; Yúdice 1999a, 2000c). The Zapatistas, whom I treat in detail below, have made use of the Internet and other media in new ways to create wide-ranging networks of solidarity, not only to foster the rights of indigenous groups and democratization in Mexico but also to organize a worldwide movement against neoliberalism.

Globalization and Culture in Latin America

In the past two decades, new approaches to the study of culture in Latin America have begun to consider globalization, and the two unconventional examples mentioned above (Viva Rio, the Zapatistas) are only now being incorporated into this new scholarship. As I mentioned at the beginning of this chapter, most interpretations of Latin American cultures were carried out from a national perspective. The major exceptions, dependency theory and anti-imperialism, ultimately hark back to appeals to the purity and health of the authentic nation in the face of foreign cultural contamination. By the late 1970s and early 1980s, as several Latin American countries were making the transition from authoritarian dictatorships to democracy (or, more exactly, to electoral politics without the oversight of the police state), anti-imperialism was left behind as an ineffective analytical framework that did not adequately engage a series of new realities, such as the action of international NGOs with agendas that included human rights, gender and racial equality, and mobilization to help the landless, street children, and the environment. This international linkage to certain social movements, as well as the transnational flows of communications, information, gendered identity images and lifestyles, and their relation to the breakdown of formal politics, created a new imaginary that could not be faithfully captured by the anti-imperialist framework. This is not to say, of course, that enormous inequalities ceased to exist between North and South.

This shift was registered in the very conception and practice in the cultural sphere. As the hold of the national imaginary ebbed due not only to the pull of the transnational but also to the tug of grassroots initiatives, the cultural sphere became increasingly important. The imbrication of the transnational and the grassroots (most evident in the action of NGOs) produced situations in which culture could no longer be seen predominantly as the reproduction of the "way of life" of the nation as a discrete entity separate from global trends. Taking these into account, Chilean sociologist José Joaquín Brunner (1987, 1990), for example, rejected the idea that modernization is inherently foreign to a supposedly novohispanic, baroque, Christian, and mestizo cultural ethos. For traditional elite intellectuals (including major exponents of the literary world), this ethos becomes inauthentic as it is "colonized" by other ethical values. In Brunner's assessment, certain folkloric stereotypes had been folded into a *representation* of the popular as an inherent magical realism, which ultimately smacked of essentialism. The literati put forward this imaginary of the transcultural and hybrid as a means to valorize, and thus legitimize, the contradictory mixtures typical of Latin American cultural formations. This is not to say that the literati were wrong about Latin American national cultural formations; they are in fact hybridized. The critique focuses, rather, on the representations and ideological uses made of that mixture, ones that, moreover, are historically contingent.[3] Brunner argued that these mixtures were generated by the differentiation in modes of production, the segmentation of markets of cultural consumption, and the expansion and internationalization of the culture industry. Latin America's peculiar forms of hybridity were therefore not cause for an essentialist celebration of their marvelous qualities nor for a denunciation of their inauthenticity. Brunner preferred to focus on those features that, from a more historical and sociological perspective, register the emergence of a modern, transnationalized cultural sphere in heterogeneous societies (1987: 4).

Echoing Laclau and Mouffe, Brunner argues that the intellectual of today must necessarily abandon the traditional role of articulating a national common sense, especially if that sense is based on some representation of a generalized popular that *assimilates* myriad differences: "The national-popular preserves the old desire to give culture a unifying ground, be it a class, racial, historical or ideological one. When culture begins to deterritorialize, when it becomes more complex and varied, assumes all the heterogeneities of society, is industrialized and massified, loses its center and is filled with 'lite' and transitory expressions, is structured on the basis of a plurality of the modern; when all this takes place, the unifying desire becomes reductionist and dangerously totalitarian or simply rhetorical" (1990: 21).

Brunner redefines the terrain of cultural activity, such that it necessarily encompasses areas that have been outside the domain of traditional intellectuals (including the literati) and that, in the current conjuncture, run the risk of being left to the experts of technobureaucratic engineering of not only economic but also social and cultural "development." In other words, appeals to the national-popular may actually make it more difficult to address and take some measure of control over the transnational phenomena that increasingly define the culture. It is incumbent on intellectuals and critics, then, to understand how these phenomena are produced and not disdain them because they do not conform to an idealized critical discourse thought to be necessary for the conduct of society.

This is the task that Jesús Martín-Barbero takes on in the sphere of the media, particularly in relation to urban youth cultures, whose symbols depart quite markedly from those of the national-popular. Many activists and scholars of grassroots social movements seem to have a measure of disdain for these youth cultures because they fly in the face of the kind of sovereign culture that affords the nation a foundation for resistance to cultural imperialism.[4] Martín-Barbero's *De los medios a las mediaciones* (1987) put forth an important critique of the idea that transnationalization was just a new and more sophisticated form of imperialism. Transnationalization, despite its homogenizing tendencies, has also been an important factor in helping to see through the "blackmail of the state" and in breaking through the older "totalizing political strategies" of the left, thus enabling a critique of the fetishizations of the "popular" and its reconstitution as the democratic action of "political subjects" (225–226). To register the possibilities of democratic action in these media-saturated civil societies, it is necessary to criticize and move beyond the limiting ideological and theoretical positions that present "the relations and conflicts between culture industries and popular cultures as external to each other or simply as a question of resistance." If we can get beyond this Manichaean dichotomy, it becomes possible to "rethink the relations between culture and politics . . . to connect cultural politics to the transformations in political culture, particularly in relation to the latter's communicational implications, that is, to the weave of interrelations that social actors constitute," and thus to think of mass communications not as a "mere problem of markets and consumption" but as the "decisive space in which it is possible to redefine the *public* and to construct democracy." It is precisely in this endeavor that "Cultural Studies and media studies speak to each other" (1993). The possibility of a progressive politics of mass communications is not only evident in the recontextualized reception characteristic of youth cultures; it is perhaps the most salient aspect of Zapatista activity, as is proposed below.

Situating his media analysis in the context of postmodernity and transnationalization, Martín-Barbero emphasizes two results, one "positive" and the other "negative," of the fragmentations, decenterings, heterogenizations, and hybridizations brought about by these phenomena. On the one hand, insofar as the "traditional spaces of collective gathering are disarticulated, [a process that] de-urbanizes everyday life and makes the city less likely to be used, the audiovisual media, especially television, become the means to return the city to us, to relocate us in it," in its "imaginary territories" (1993). The funk youth cultures about which Vianna (1988) and I (chapter 4) have written make use of pop music and dance as a means to "take back" the city, which, according to elites, does not belong to them. Furthermore, the mass media can recover "the traces which can enable the recognition of 'pueblos' [both people and country/nation—Translator] and the dialogue between generations and traditions." Martín-Barbero also advocates the study of the "changes in images and metaphors of the national, the devaluation, secularization and reinvention of myths and rituals through which this contradictory but still powerful identity is unmade and remade both from a local and transnational perspective" (1992: 50).

Néstor García Canclini's *Culturas híbridas* (*Hybrid Cultures*; 1990, [1990] 1995b) is probably the best-known study of Latin American hybridization in a transnational era. His *Consumidores y ciudadanos* (1995a) and many other books and articles tackle problems presented by processes of globalization and regional integration. Already in the late 1970s, García Canclini had framed his study of Mexican popular cultures, especially the artisanal production of indigenous peoples, within the framework of globalization. It should be noted that in Latin America the term "popular culture" refers to the cultural practices of sundry "subordinate cultures," rather than to "mass culture," as in the United States. This does not mean that popular culture is necessarily considered authentic and untouched by the mass culture industries, a claim that García Canclini, like Brunner and Martín-Barbero, rejects out of hand. On the contrary, García Canclini argues that these "subordinate" cultures "are not allowed any autonomous or alternative development, and their production and consumption as well as social structure and language are reorganzied in order to make them receptive to capitalist modernization" (1982: 29; 1993: 8). In Mexico, this process has been brokered by the state, coextensive with the PRI, which ruled uninterruptedly for seventy-one years. The institutionalization of the ideology of *indigenismo* was carried out as a compromise solution to popular struggles in the aftermath of the Mexican Revolution. Under Lázaro Cárdenas's centralization of a populist state in the 1930s, real gains were made in the redistribution of land to indigenous groups and in labor laws for the emergent industrial proletariat. However, as the state apparatus grew to mammoth proportions, it increasingly put the interests of modernization and development over those of the popular sectors. This ultimately resulted in a sorry situation whereby the peasantry, in particular, indigenous peoples, remained in the position of symbolic base of the nation but were excluded from effective participation and left out of the distribution of resources by the very same state that "represented" them.

The ability of the Mexican state to negotiate its contradictory existence began to founder in the 1960s, as a series of worker and student strikes challenged state repression and corruption. In October 1968, at least four hundred but possibly over a thousand students were massacred at the Plaza of Three Cultures in Tlatelolco. By the late 1970s a cohort of anthropologists and sociologists, including Guillermo Bonfil Batalla, García Canclini, and Rodolfo Stavenhagen, challenged institutionalized indigenism as well as the role of intellectuals and academics. Bonfil, for example, called for a redefinition of the researcher as a collaborator in the projects of subaltern communities. He proposed this collaboration as a needed retooling for social scientists, who were seeing their traditional functions disappear due not only to the paradigm crisis in the social sciences but also to recent political and economic transformations (e.g., neoliberalism and privatization). These changes displaced the anthropologist from his or her function as a facilitator of national integration in the pact that had been struck between the state and civil society in the postrevolutionary period under Cárdenas. García Canclini, in turn, called not only for refashioning the institutions of the organization, production, marketing, and consumption of popular culture, but also the creation of a new public sphere and even a new tourism industry from which to rethink and reexperience culture (1982: 161; 1993: 114).

Culture under Neoliberalism

Such calls for rethinking the relation of state and civil society have become even more relevant since the early 1980s, when the Mexican government adopted neoliberalism. They have also had an enormous impact on cultural identity, particularly because the terms by which the state addressed its national constituency have changed significantly. Under Miguel de la Madrid (1982–88), Carlos Salinas de Gortari (1988–94), and Ernesto Zedillo (1994–2000), nationalist, anti-imperialist discourse was dropped along with trade barriers, long thought to be the bulwark of sovereignty. Now free trade with the United States was courted and decentralization put into operation. In this context, emerging private institutions and public institutions in search of new legitimacy altered their approach to the national identity of culture, which was now put to work in the global arena, as in the *Splendors of Thirty Centuries* blockbuster exhibition. The cultural difference expressed by means of art was no longer used to take a nationalist, defensive position vis-à-vis the dominant models of Western modernity (as in the case of the muralists), particularly the United States, but for staging showcases demonstrating that Mexico was the civilizational par of its trading partner to the north. This seems to have been the purpose of the *Myth and Magic* exhibition in MARCO, Monterrey's museum and exemplar of would-be first world art institutions (Yúdice 1996b).

Anthropological institutions and the discipline itself, like the art world, also found it necessary to "reconvert" in the context of globalization and shifts in the self-perceptions of the Mexican nation. The role of the anthropologist changed vis-à-vis state institutions like the Instituto Nacional Indigenista, which added to the crisis of social scientists and intellectuals mentioned above. The transnationalization of the media, evident in Televisa's offerings, and the prevailing consumerist ethos contributed to changes in cultural identity, evident in the preference for Hollywood and other U.S. audiovisual imports (García Canclini 1995a). Privatization initiatives, downsizing, and decentralization of the public sector, particularly in relation to culture, have begun to shift the center of attention away from a centralized, national context toward regional cultures, a process that is given impetus by the geographically differential impact of the North American Free Trade Agreement (NAFTA). Although it may not be advisable to speak of a culture of neoliberalism, these changes have taken place under neoliberal policies. Before going on to examine new cultural manifestations in this context, a brief account of neoliberalism is in order.

Neoliberal economic policies found fertile terrain in Latin America under the draconian conditions of the early 1980s. An enormous foreign debt had accrued as a result of state-led development and the failure of import substitution in the face of fierce competitiveness unleashed by the global imposition of market values and free trade. The reduction of a state that guaranteed employment and regulated capital, the privatization of state-owned enterprises and services, the targeting of scarce resources, and decentralization were instituted as part of the structural adjustment programs prescribed by such international finance institutions as the World Bank and the IMF, institutions that had the power to sanction investment. Economic integration into the world economy meant reduced state power to shield citizens from the ups and downs of the world market, the disciplining of labor by the criterion of competitiveness, and the unprecedented dissemination of the ideology of the free market. The irony is that trade liberalization, which, it was argued, would increase employment, not only has not done so in the three countries of NAFTA, but it has led to a decrease in real wages and jobs since the early 1980s (Shorrock 1996).

According to Alejandro Foxley (1996), neoliberal policies like stabilization, trade liberalization, and privatization, if implemented successfully, should lead to a final stage of increased investment and productivity. Crucial to the ability to move from one phase to another is political legitimacy, which is countered by increasing poverty and unemployment. Stabilization of the economy in the face of the debt crisis, for example, was carried out by a set of policies that decelerated growth, which in turn led to unemployment, lowered wages, and reduced government expenditures in the social sector. The other phases have also had a negative impact on quality of life issues for the general populace, particularly the lower-class sectors. Privatization, for example, is deployed as a means to greater productivity because state-owned enterprises that are favorable to labor are taken over by private concerns that initiate downsizing and technological modernization, both of which lead to unemployment and a competitive labor market (i.e., lower wages) that enhances participation in the world economy. These social hardships, Foxley argues, must be offset by "a strong social component that will neutralize the negative equity effects" of the first two phases (3).

The question that remains is whether the transition to the third phase of increased investment and productivity can be achieved with a more egalitarian income distribution. For Foxley, this depends on the handling of exchange rate and fiscal policies. Reducing inflation by adjusting the exchange rate can produce a trade deficit and, as in the case of Mexico, not enough reserves to back up foreign investment. Devaluation, which is the usual remedy for this problem, is instituted by increased interest rates and reduced government expenditures, both of which lead to further unemployment and the fraying of the safety net. But even without devaluation, privatization itself leads to a reduction in the safety net and greater hardship for low-income sectors because the state has virtually relinquished its capacity to regulate once state-owned enterprises.[5]

The question then might be why social capital has not been increased. Foxley (1996) suggests that a vigorous civil society may be able to develop the needed social capital to democratize economic and political life. This might beg the question of what will foster that civil society. In many Latin American countries, it is less the state than grassroots initiatives and considerable aid from NGOs, many of which are foreign, that have nourished civil society. We might say that just as the state must manage the contradictions of neoliberalism, so also must civil society, for it has been assigned the role of ensuring "stability along with transformation" (Ronfeldt 1995). Civil society has a double origin in Latin America since the 1980s: in neoliberalism's need for stability and political legitimation, and in grassroots organization for the sake of survival in the face of structural adjustment. There are thus two kinds of civil society activity, or at least two directions in which civil society might move: toward stability or toward ungovernability, both terms used by those analysts, usually on the economic and political right, who favor the transition to neoliberalism.

David Ronfeldt (1995) has formulated a model of national evolution through four "mentalities": (1) tribal, which constitutes the basis of identity; (2) in-

stitutional, which provides efficient decision making and control; (3) *market*, which generates greater productivity and social diversification; and (4) *network*, which fosters "mutual collaboration among members of a distributed, multi-organizational network" resulting in a strengthened civil society through the actions of social movements as well as "environmental, peace, human-rights, and other networks of nongovernmental organizations." This form of civil society offers the stability that the state can no longer provide in periods of great (and painful) restructuring. But this last mentality may also result in the strengthening of "uncivil society," which Ronfeldt exemplifies by reference to criminal networks (e.g., narcotraffickers, terrorists, rightist militias) and other "subversive groups," among them, leftist organizations and insurgents like the Zapatistas.

What is instructive in Ronfeldt's analysis is the notion that civil society must be *managed* in the interest of maximizing political stability and economic transformation. For Ronfeldt and other advocates of neoliberalism, civil society should be linked to the market to nudge it in the direction of maintaining the capitalist system, which he considers to be the only soil fertile enough for democracy to take root. Consequently, even a civil society that works against neoliberalism — for example, the Canadian, U.S., and transnational NGOs that provide support for the Zapatistas — is ultimately a benefit to market society because it "corrects" the excesses of the market and thus stabilizes and legitimizes the system. Civil society will in the long run — if not the medium term — help Mexico evolve into a "true" market society. Such activity will in turn further the destabilization of the corrupt, inefficient, and institutionalized interests of the PRI that ruled for seven decades. It also promotes the diversity that, according to Ronfeldt, is necessary for the market system. The function of the state, then, is to *manage*, not eliminate these forces of civil society, so as to keep "ungovernability" (or, rather, the demands of democratization) at bay. We see here a rightist version of Laclau and Mouffe's (1985) vision of radical democracy, but with the significant difference that the "multiplication of antagonisms" that would presumably further the process of democratization ends up working in the interests of capital.

The contradictory conditions under which civil society is fostered — (1) the state manages and controls third-sector organizations by means of official certification,[6] and (2) these flourish in opposition to or in spite of the state — hold simultaneously as NGOs that have state sanction nevertheless attempt to undermine the very means by which the state attempts to co-opt them. This is the case in organizations such as the *museos comunitarios* that are funded by the state yet in some cases have covert relations with contestatory groups, including the Zapatista National Liberation Army (EZLN). This is also typical of journals and university and cultural organizations that work to disseminate the information that flies in the face of the government's and the international finance institutions' spin on social conditions. Many such organizations receive funding from federal arts and cultural funding agencies.

The Zapatistas and the Struggle for Civil Society

It is true that a renewed civil society, composed of new social movements, emerged in the 1970s as a force mobilized against authoritarian states in Latin America and Eastern Europe, and it is under neoliberalism that it has flourished and integrated with the state and the market. Hence the significance of a movement that would challenge the new status quo precisely on its own terms. However, the possibility of rethinking politics and culture in Mexico received an unanticipated shot in the arm with the insurgency of the EZLN on January 1, 1994. Their action consolidated the frustrations with one-party authoritarian rule, and to this date the calls for reform and relinquishment of that rule have not disappeared from public discussion. The state, together with the media conglomerates, particularly Televisa, blanketed public space with neoliberal hype (a reversal of former nationalist stances) in support of NAFTA.[7] For example, the Zapatistas took the opportunity opened up by NAFTA and capitalized on the public's attention by timing the onset of their insurgency for the day on which the agreement went into effect. The Zapatistas engaged in battle in the first month and in sporadic skirmishes over the next two years; they are not a guerrilla army in the conventional Latin American style, like Castro's rebels, the Sandinistas, the FMLN, or the Shining Path. More than armed combat, they have engaged in a struggle over the definition of the public good, both national and transnational, and have demonstrated an expert use of global resources, particularly network organization, facilitated by the new media and the Internet. As such, they have initiated the kind of intervention into civil society that Bonfil Batalla, García Canclini, and many others had called for but that was impossible to achieve from a purely intellectual or political standpoint.

The call for the new civil society initiative was made on January 1, 1996 in the "Fourth Declaration of the Lacandon Jungle" as a response to a "national plebiscite for peace and democracy," which they conducted in the fall of 1995. The EZLN formed the Zapatista Front of National Liberation (FZLN), "a civil and nonviolent organization, independent and democratic, Mexican and national, which struggles for democracy, liberty, and justice in Mexico." The aim of the Front is to organize the demands and proposals of all sectors of the opposition (although not the conservative National Action Party or PAN) against the "state-Party System [which] is the main obstacle to a transition to democracy in Mexico." Furthermore, the Front will draft a new constitution that includes the demands of the Mexican people, in particular Article 39 of the current Constitution, which states that "national sovereignty resides essentially and originally in the people. All public power derives from the people and is instituted for their benefit. The people have, at all times, the inalienable right to alter or modify their form of government" (EZLN 1994: 34). The Zapatistas' call for a "nation of many worlds" contrasts with the bankrupt national project of the PRI: "In the world of the powerful there is no space for anyone but themselves and their servants. In the world we want everyone fits. In the world we want many worlds fit. The Nation which we construct is one where all communities and languages fit, where all steps may walk, where all may have laughter, where all may live the dawn" (34). More recently, however, the government has adopted much of this multicultural discourse. This is evident in the *Programa de Cultura* 1995–2000 announced in January 1996 by Rafael Tovar y de Teresa, president of the Consejo Nacional de la Cultura y las Artes, which states that "culture contributes to the manifestation of the ethnic and social diversity of the country" (Poder Ejecutivo Federal 1996a, 2; see also Poder Ejecutivo Federal 1996b).

The Zapatista program is unabashedly utopian, particularly in its decision to stay out of electoral politics and yet wield influence over Mexican society, that is, to help create a national forum in which diversity is recognized. This is a new way of conceiving of power, a social power rather than a coercive power. FZLN representative Priscilla Pacheco Castillo characterizes the question of power thus: "When we say we don't want to take power, we don't mean we will remain neutral about power. When we talk of organizing society, we are talking of power, but a different kind of power. We have a different conception of power; it is more a social kind of power. It does not have to be represented in a government" (qtd. in Spencer 1996). The major result of Zapatista actions has been to establish dialogue among the many sectors of civil society, as well as to compel the government to join those discussions (Henríquez and Pérez 1995). Their only safeguard has been the watchful eye of the world, whose attention they have been able to secure, in the first place, by threatening to expose the lack of commitment to democracy on the part of the state. By launching their offensive when they did, they "blackmailed" the state, which otherwise probably would have wiped them out, unfettered by the rhetoric of democratization that accompanied NAFTA. Just as important, the Zapatistas planned an artful guerrilla media war. In a country in which the media are oriented to the state and its policies, the Zapatistas have been able to carve a space for themselves and their civil society project by remaining newsworthy—virtually rewriting the manual for marketing—and pushing the normally unidirectional means of communication into a back-and-forth dialogue (J. López 1996: 30–31).

The emphasis on direct speech, as if a "real" public sphere in a mass-mediated society were possible, has been criticized for its romanticization of indigenous cultural forms (e.g., the priority of face-to-face, collective decision making over electoral representation). When the Zapatistas publish a communiqué in which they state that "the flower of the word will not die . . . because it comes from the depths of history and the land and can no longer be usurped by the arrogance of power" (Hernández and Rojas 1996), they are couching a sophisticated bid for public reception in a language that resonates with the cultural legitimation of premodern discursive forms. The "Zapatista Manifesto in Nahuatl" not only lays claim to a prioritary place in the Mexican nation, but also affirms that democracy will come when the culture of the nation is refashioned from the perspective of indigenous peoples. This entails dredging up the claims to recognition and dignity made thoughout history in the many tongues silenced by the reigning culture, the official indigenismo of the mestizo state. "But the rebellion that rises with a brown face and a true tongue, was not born today. In the past it spoke with other tongues and in other lands . . . in nahuatl, paipai, kiliwa, cúcapa, cochimi, kumiai, yuma . . . By speaking in its Indian heart, the nation maintains its dignity and its memory" (Hernández and Rojas 1996).

The Mexican state's adoption of neoliberalism is expressed not only by a new set of rhetorics, but also by policies that depart from the consensus of the past. The constitutional reform of Article 27 in 1992, for example, reorganized land tenure and permitted titleholders of *ejidos* (land vested in the community) to enter into commercial contracts, thus introducing corporate capital into collective farming. Although this measure pushed some, particularly the larger landholding farmers, into export production, most small farmers were "isolated from the institutional and financial supports that allowed them to continue to farm in the face of unfavorable market conditions" (David Barkin, "The Spectre of Rural Development" 1995, online posting). The result was a further erosion of the material base of rural society, which ultimately contributed to the Zapatista rebellion. Neoliberalism, in fact, has been seen by the Zapatistas and other opposition groups as a threat to their continued existence.

The "national dialogue" convened by the EZLN on the rights and culture of the indigenous peoples called for the dismantling of the "culture of neoliberalism" if indigenous peoples were to gain autonomy under a "new federalism" (M. Pérez and Morquecho 1995).

The Zapatistas have been able to make common cause with many sectors of the Mexican population on this united front against neoliberalism, especially because the government's policies have had a disastrous effect on the vast majority of the population. The Zapatistas have also extended their opposition to neoliberalism to the international arena, calling for an "Intercontinental Forum against Neoliberalism" in their January 1996 "First Declaration of La Realidad" ("Contra el Neoliberalismo" 1996). Besides the meeting held from July 27 to August 3, other meetings were planned in Berlin, Tokyo, an African city, Sidney, and Mexico City. An important feature of the agenda is to organize a broad-based internationalist culture ("a new international of hope") to counter the culture of neoliberalism. It includes "all individuals, groups, collectives, movements, social, citizen, and political organizations, neighborhood associations, cooperatives, all leftist groups, non governmental organizations, groups in solidarity with the struggles of the peoples of the world, bands, tribes, intellectuals, musicians, workers, artists, teachers, peasants, cultural groups, youth movements, alternative media, ecologists, squatters, lesbians, homosexuals, feminists, pacifists."

The discontent with neoliberalism even drove many members of the ruling PRI to fall over themselves in the rush to criticize, opportunistically, their own party's economic policies and to call for a "recomposition of the political system," concurring with the opposition that Mexico's sovereignty is at stake ("La política debe ser instrumento" 1996). The PRI's crisis was brought on by itself, but the new consensus that there must be reform has to be credited to the Zapatistas more than any other sector of the opposition. What exactly, however, does a "recomposition of the political system" mean in Mexico? From a U.S. perspective, one might imagine a system of representation whereby all kinds of interest groups, including the so-called identity groups of multiculturalism, gain proportional representation in the myriad institutions of the state, the corporate sector, and civil society. However, it seems that this U.S.-style representational mode of "distributional equity" has not been incorporated into the newly born Movement of National Liberation or Broad Oppositional Front, which was formed independently, albeit with EZLN guidance, from over five hundred organizations (Correa and López 1996).

Even the agreement with the government on Indian rights, particularly political and cultural autonomy, "the right to adopt their own forms of government in their communities or towns according to their customs" (Preston 1996), was not conceived within such a system of representation. The agreement included the right to multicultural education (whatever that means in the Chiapanecan or Mexican context), including teaching in their own languages. However, the Zapatistas stressed over and over again that they are not an identity group and that their efforts are aimed at transforming the entirety of the nation, at reinvigorating civil society for all. The autonomy they seek is *neither integrationist nor separatist*, as even the government negotiators have come to accept (R. Rojas 1996). This marks a significant departure from the terms of indigenismo, which had presumably integrated indigenous communities since the establishment of the Instituto Nacional Indigenista. As Rodolfo Stavenhagen ("Buenas noticias de Chiapas" 1995, online posting) explains, "The real identity and unity of the indigenous peoples of Mexico is provided at the community level." The administration of municipalities that include indigenous communities will require the negotiation of satisfactory juridicoconstitutional formulas. Autonomy, like integration in the United States, however, "does not produce miracles: it is but a juridical framework within which the national State and indigenous peoples can freely and constructively confront the large-scale problems of poverty and well-being, identity and equality."

Unlike African Americans before the civil rights era, indigenous peoples in Mexico had been represented by indigenista ideology as an *integral* part of the nation. Integration via the Instituto Nacional Indigenista often operated more like an asylum than a home, however. Community was the Indians' own criterion for identity, but the state rearticulated that identity in keeping with its own nationalist project, reifying customs as objects, beliefs as myths, and institutionalizing them in such neutered spaces as the National Museum of Anthropology. The very notion of "heritage" — Whose? For what purposes? For whose observation? — has, indeed, become a contested category, as diverse groups seek to wrest control of the means of symbolization from state institutions that claim proprietary rights over customs, habits, ritual objects, and so on. Mexican critics have spoken of their state's pyramidal cultural apparatuses, and none could be more emblematic than the National Museum of Anthropology. It will be instructive, therefore, to briefly examine the terms according to which a new museological movement was generated among indigenous communities.

The museo comunitario (community museum) movement that began in 1986, although facilitated by national and international professional museological institutions, has sought its raison d'être in local practices and, thus, a relative independence from the proprietary-conservationist ethos of the ideology of national patrimony. As a recent report by organizers from these museums explains, the indigenous people who established them valorize the objects displayed and the practices enacted in relation to the needs of their community, to the reproduction of the community. To the degree that this is the case, "that valorization may contain features that go beyond scientific and aesthetic principles, and [may be legitimized] by the sacred" (Barrera Bassols et al. 1995: 28, 33).

The first museo comunitario was established in Tlalocula, Oaxaca by the decision of the community. After an archaeological find was made in their community, the Shan Dany residents decided to set off a space where they could record and concentrate their activities, including the exhibition of the work of craftspersons and the systematization of their healing practices. Until they established this museum, this community had not revealed in public the activities that are now displayed and performed as part of the museum. The museum itself is not identified by a building, a collection, or a particular audience. Its display is the interaction of the community with itself and other such communities. The exhibits are not planned in writing but are the result of much organization and cultural activity that doesn't depart from their sociopolitical, mythic, and religious rhythms. In many cases, the museological practice is so intertwined with the reproduction of the community that the "exhibition" may consist of practices that further the local economy, such as the systematization of the knowledge involved in coffee growing or the opening up of the community to tourism. The exhibition *La vida en un sorbo: El café en México* (A sip of life: Coffee in Mexico), for example, was initiated by the National Coordinating Committee of Coffee Growing Organizations, which is composed mainly of indigenous producers. The museum not only fulfilled the ritual reproduction of the coffee growing practices but also was a place where they could sell their coffee and thus dispense with the intervention of intermediaries, such as distributors and importers-exporters.

The community museums are interesting in and of themselves. But I raise this example because the community I am referring to was a participant in an international discussion that demonstrates the degree to which even the smallest of indigenous groups can be inserted into transnational networks that have an impact on questions of identity and representation. This community was invited by the Smithsonian Institution's National Museum of the American Indian to participate in a discussion on "Ethnic Identity, Community Museums and Development Programs" in September 1995. Twenty-five other Latin

American Indian groups were invited. The invitation was meant to be the first event in the expansion of the concept of the "American Indian" beyond the borders of the United States. What makes this meeting interesting is that it raised many problems about the conceptualization of identity, ethnicity, and nomenclature, problems that may not become evident until two or more systems of thinking about these issues come into contact.

The director, Richard West, explained that these groups were invited to educate the Smithsonian about the real meaning of the objects that were housed there. The Smithsonian took as its guiding premise that a museum should consult the people who provide the objects on exhibit and not just collect them (Barrera Bassols and Vera Herrera 1996: 23–24). The participants were told that the Smithsonian would use this knowledge to represent native peoples exactly as they themselves wanted to be represented. This raised many concerns and elicited doubts from some that their culture could really be represented. A Mam from Guatemala raised objections about the representativity of the collection and said, "We did not come to exhibit ourselves, we are not objects." Another participant opined that preserving the bones of his forebears was counterproductive. Yet another, a Shuar from Ecuador, objected to the idea that the museum needed to document indigenous cultures because they are disappearing. What is needed, he said, is to document the cultural self-development of the community. The notion of a culture in disappearance is erroneous, he said, "surely put forward by an anthropologist" (24–25). The most heated discussion, however, was about nomenclature and the criteria for assuming the identity of Indian. The museum officials variously used the terms Indian, indigenous, Native American, tribal, people, and community. This made some of the participants feel uncomfortable, as if it did not matter what they called themselves. One participant from Peru said that they only used the term peasant. Instead of el día de la raza (day of the race, a Mexican and Chicano term adopted and "Americanized" in the United States), they should celebrate el día del campesinado (day of the peasant; 26). An observer of a similar event, the Festival of American Folklife, organized by the Smithsonian's Center for Folklife Programs and Cultural Studies in June and July 1994, reported that "the system of racial representations, conflicts, and transactions of U.S. society . . . tends to racialize the lives of other peoples . . . a very complex matter that must be examined in relation to workings of international and transnational agencies" (Mato 1995a, 23).

The differences in systems of identity categorization were commented on with great concern when presented with the fact that in the United States you can be an Indian on the basis of blood, even if you don't "belong" to an indigenous community. For the National Museum of the American Indian, the problem of representativity is solved because 50 percent of its board of directors have at least one-sixteenth Indian blood. The participants expressed their view that such an institution should be administered by Indian communities. It's not enough, they argued, for the director to be a Cheyenne, which raised the question of what is important in the constitution of identity. Some groups considered participation as the way to determine belonging. The Latin American Indian participants were not impressed by the racial component of the so-called ethnic minorities at the Smithsonian. They argued that this was not a blood or race issue. Instead, it is a "wide-ranging set of assumptions, presuppositions, beliefs, myths, values, experiences and ties that researchers themselves have defined as the 'horizon of intelligibility' or 'territory of meaning'" (Barrera Bassols and Vera Herrera 1996: 37). Structures of feeling are what produce group belonging. Not even the use of the "same" language is enough for this sense of belonging.

This discussion brings to the surface the complex negotiations of cultural reproduction and identity, particularly for marginalized or subordinate groups, that are now negotiated in a transnational sphere. I have referred to this process as "transnational cultural brokering" in a study on the exhibition of the work of Latin American artists in U.S. museums and galleries (Yúdice 1996b). The process, however, is endemic wherever "metropolitan" institutions (whether national or international) seek, most often with the best intentions, to help out local communities.[8] This is evident in the "mixed" agenda of the cosponsors of the Festival of American Folklife. The Inter-American Foundation, for example, seems to have a different agenda from that of the Smithsonian. According to reports, it took a somewhat technocratic approach to questions of community development. One participant, "a development specialist at a multilateral banking institution . . . said [he] was very pleased with the program, and added: 'This is not a program on culture and development, but on how the Inter-American Foundation understands culture and development'" (Mato 1995a: 28). While not necessarily accepting the framing terms of the discussions, the participants did not conflict in any significant ways with the hosts. Mato hypothesizes that the lack of conflict reflects a degree of satisfaction with the kinds of projects included in the program, but also a desire not to offend one's hosts and, most important, the "develop[ment of] attitudes of trying to satisfy expectations that [funding recipients] attribute to the donor agencies" (40).

We witness here an interesting negotiation of performative expectations. In their own societies, these Latin American indigenous groups act on the basis of different expectations. This difference explains in part their displeasure with the identitarian protocols and requirements implicit in the behavior and conceptual presuppositions of the Smithsonian's and Inter-American Foundation's officials and also implicit in that of U.S. Native American groups. Nevertheless, they do attempt to "satisfy expectations," both because they are no doubt appreciative of their hosts' hospitality and also because they would prefer not to alienate the "donor agencies." This cautious performative negotiation points up the conflictive imperatives that emerge in any asymmetric and unequal exchange.

An interesting contrast is provided in some of the EZLN's communiqués. Subcomandante Marcos, who has sought out the aid of "international civil society" (i.e., NGOs and solidarity groups from the North), is keenly attuned to the predicaments that arise in the kinds of situations reviewed above. He refers in one communiqué, for example, to two photographers who showed up in the Lacandon forest to "take some shots of Zapatista life in order to present it in a global event on the Internet" (Subcomandante Marcos 1996). They justified their visit by presenting themselves as journalists with "testimonial and artistic intentions." Marcos, somewhat tongue-in-cheek—yet seriously, as becomes evident as the narrative progresses—finds them guilty of perpetrating the "crime" of "image theft." To undo their crime, Marcos takes the camera into his own hands and turns it on the photographers, whom he considers apocryphal agents of public history. By focusing the instrument of representation on them, he aims to "reach the world that looks at their photographs." This reversal, the communiqué continues, is an attempt to bridge the distance between spectator or photographer and the Zapatistas, object of their prurience. Marcos proposes to establish a different kind of relation by turning the gaze onto the spectators and photographers. On this bridge, they are themselves transformed into actors who, by definition, must assume a role. Like one of Julio Cortázar's narrators, Marcos propels the viewers and readers into the story as actors who must take a side: to engage in the always institutionalized quagmire of representation or to act out the relation to civil society in a different way.

Marcos's little allegory does not assume that images tell the truth. Rather, it is in taking hold of the instruments of image making and framing that one can challenge the truth of representations. This is, of course, a tale familiar to anthropologists and media critics who have challenged the conditions under which subjects are turned into represented objects and are thus bereft of the power to tell their own story. In fact, the report on community museums makes explicit reference to the new forms of negotiation of Indian rights that the Zapatista initiated, careful not to be taken in by the intermediary's role (Barrera Bassols et al. 1995: 29). In this particular case, Marcos is referring to the indigenous peoples who make up the mass of the EZLN and who heretofore have "only appeared as images in museums, tourist guides, crafts advertising." "The eye of the camera seeks them out," the text goes on, "as an anthropological curiosity or a colorful detail of a remote past." What is it that has altered the terms of representation? "The eyes [sights] of the rifles that they have taken up have forced the eyes of the cameras to look in a different manner" (Subcomandante Marcos 1996). The Zapatistas may not own the means of representation, but they have found creative ways of exercising a measure of control over representations of their activities. In good part, this measure of control is, as García Canclini would say, a "coproduction": it depends on the solidarity of other agents, particularly sympathetic newspapers like La Jornada, but also local radio stations and transnational media, especially the Internet.

We have come full circle from the anti-imperialist denunciations and fears of Dorfman and Mattelart with this example. The Zapatistas' expert handling of the electronic media shows that there is no necessary contradiction between technological modernization and grassroots mobilization (Halleck 1994; Cleaver 1998). In fact, the Internet has allowed the Zapatistas to question spectators and readers, to "travel through cyberspace and invade, like a modern virus, the memories of machines, and of men and women" (Halleck 1994).

A word of caution is in order. Subcomandante Marcos and other members of the Zapatista directorate are also intermediaries, and as such are themselves susceptible to the critiques discussed here. They are, of course, aware of this; for this reason they have said, "We the Zapatistas want everything for everyone, and nothing for ourselves" (EZLN 1995). It is also for this reason, perhaps, that although they identify as indigenous people and demand political and cultural autonomy, they have not set the terms of the representation of Indian identity. Their slogan is the "organization of civil society."

Conclusion

The organization of civil society is not, as I argued above, an uncontradictory feature of progressive action. It is to a degree imposed by neoliberalism, and as such its success can only be limited, especially if we gauge it against the power-taking dreams of traditional leftist movements. Many of the arguments reviewed and put forth here concerning new kinds of social movements, particularly those that concentrate on organizing civil society, must stand the test of history.

Currently, there is much enthusiasm and hope that civil society will be the ground for renewing the state-nation compact. The problem is that the results can be quite contradictory. Will the state reform called for by the Zapatistas, which the PRI signed in July 1996, give greater political leverage to the conservative PAN? Will decentralization of the state's hold on cultural representation create openings for the media and private enterprise to extend their reach? And does not the effervescence of NGOs cut two ways: helping to buttress a public sector evacuated by the state, and at the same time making it possible for the state to steer clear of what was once seen as its responsibility? There is also the uncertainty that ensues from a movement that to date has waged its most effective battles in the realm of publicity. To what degree does such activity depart from the already overdetermined character of publicity in a capitalist society? Of course, there is no reason why consumer capitalism cannot be wielded against itself. The production of a multimedia CD-ROM in 2001, available from the FZLN's virtual store, may permit interested parties to walk through the Lacandon jungle, get to know the Indians, their plight. But will such a medium take on the character of interactive electronic entertainment?

Such questions form part of a larger context in which any action must be evaluated. Michel Foucault (1983) coined the term "governmentality" to refer to the way action is already channeled by the institutional arrangements of a society.[9] This concept points up the limits to action. Now that the PRI has been defeated and Vicente Fox is attempting to reconfigure the state, will the arrangements that have held for seventy-one years be altered enough for true democratization to take place in Mexico? Can action in the terrain of civil society bring about such an alteration of institutional arrangements?

The notion of governmentality is more or less neutral with respect to social change. That is, it does not evaluate it negatively, as does the concept of governability. What it does emphasize, however, is that all action moves along the tracks of structures of possibility provided by institutional arrangements. This structuring accounts for why the movements may not have the same significance in countries where the institutional arrangements are different. One might ask why a movement like the Zapatistas has not emerged in a country like Brazil, where there are significant numbers of landless groups. There is a movement of landless rural workers (Movimento dos Sem Terra) that has gotten the attention of the government, which has promised action on its behalf. However, the differences and the potential for action are considerable. The Zapatistas achieved the attention of the entirety of the Mexican nation and indeed of the world precisely because Mexico had entered a free trade agreement with the United States. That agreement gave it a certain leverage, that is, the chance to "blackmail" the state (rather than forcing it militarily) into meeting some of its demands. Another feature of the Mexican nation-state is, as I explained above, a seven-decades practice of situating national culture in centralized, pyramidal institutions. Transnational processes, in conjunction with the demands of grassroots organizations, have resulted in numerous protests against that centrality. Brazilian cultural institutions are not similarly centralized, nor does the Brazilian state invest as much as the Mexican state in subsidizing the intellectual, artist class, which ultimately keeps it buffered in a sphere of perhaps ineffective critique. The Zapatista movement, therefore, marks a significant departure from the protagonism of intellectuals.

There are some similarities, of course. The electronic media are monopolized by one meganetwork in each country, Televisa in Mexico and Globo in Brazil. But the control of publicity by such networks has been cannily sidestepped by the Zapatistas. Their use of the Internet, facilitated to a good degree by solidarity groups in the United States and Europe as well as sympathetic intellectuals in Mexico, can serve as an example to movements in other countries. The question is whether the movements will be perceived to have the same extent of legitimacy currently enjoyed by the Zapatistas.

4

The Funkification of Rio

For Hermano Vianna Jr.

This chapter provides a more detailed context for the rise of several social movements, studied in chapter 5, to combat poverty, violence, and racism in Brazil.[1] The allegedly apolitical experience of the mostly black and mixed-race *funkeiros* (funk dance enthusiasts) studied here stands in contrast to the activism of Afro Reggae in Rio. What characterizes these cultural activist movements, as well as the citizen action initiatives examined in chapter 5, is their structure as open-ended networks. Together, these two chapters exemplify how culture is used by social movements and also how such global notions as cultural difference and cultural citizenship are deployed within very specific force fields.

This chapter was written almost eight years ago as a challenge to received ideas about the place of youth in social movements. Given that many years have passed, I was tempted to do a substantial rewriting. I did in fact make some changes, but I left the chapter largely as it was originally, because it serves as a prelude for the work of Afro Reggae especially, and that of the other movements more generally. Funk music and dance have been a way of dealing with racism and social exclusion, and at the same time a way of taking pleasure, something that is often missing in the social movements and the accounts thereof by most social scientists who write about them. As we will see, pleasure is a key element not only of Afro Reggae's cultural activism, but also of the citizen action initiatives.

Claustrofobia	*Claustrophobia*
Ah! meu samba	Ah! My samba
Se tu es nosso, o nosso é samba	If you are ours, then ours is the samba

Se o nosso é o samba, o samba é nosso	If ours is the samba, then the samba is ours
Pra que prisões vais tu	Why prisons within yourself?
Sai, meu samba	Go out, my samba
Porque sei que tu tens claustrofobia	Because I know you have claustrophobia
É tua a noite, a noite e o dia	The night is yours, the night and day
Vai te espalhar pelo pais	Go spread yourself throughout the nation
Vai, meu samba	Go out, my samba
Sem fatiga, estafa o stress	Without fatigue, weariness or stress
não precisa te rezar, kermis	There's no need for prayer, ceremony
ou passaporte do juiz	or a judge's passport
Já se abriu a janela do mundo	The window to the world is already open
E agora não podes parar	And now you can't stop
Tu tens que conquistar	You have to conquer
Tu tens que encantar	You have to enchant
e te fazer cantar	And make yourself sing
com teu la-la, la, la	with your la-la, la, la
com teu la-la, la, la	with your la-la, la, la
com tue la-la, la, la	with your la-la, la, la[2]

Rio 40 Graus	*Rio 104 Degrees*
Rio 40 graus	Rio 104 degrees
cidade maravilha	marvelous city[3]
purgatório da beleza e do caos	purgatory of beauty and of chaos
capital do sangue quente do brasil	hot blooded capital of Brazil
capital do sangue quente	hot blooded capital
do melhor e do pior do Brasil	of the best and worst of Brazil
cidade sangue quente	hot blooded city
maravilha mutante	mutating marvel
. . . .	. . . . . .
quem é dono desse beco?	who does that corner belong to?
quem é dono dessa rua?	who does that street belong to?
de quem é esse edifício?	who does that building belong to?
de quem é esse lugar?	who does that place belong to?
é meu esse lugar	that place is mine
sou carioca, pô	I'm carioca, damn
eu quero meu crachá	I want my I.D.
sou carioca	I'm carioca

. . . .

a novidade cultural da garotada	the cultural novelty of the homies
favelada, suburbana, classe média marginal	slumdwellers, suburban, marginal middle class
é informática metralha	is the informational machine gun
sub-uzi equipadinha com cartucho musical	sub-uzi equipped with a music cartridge
de batucada digital	with a digital drum beat

. . . .

de marcação invocação	a demarcation [beat] invocation
pra gritaria de torcida da galera funk	for the cheering dancers at a funk club
de marcação invocação	a demarcation [beat] invocation
pra gritaria de torcida da galera samba	for the cheering dancers at a samba club
de marcação invocação	a demarcation [beat] invocation
pra gritaria de torcida da galera tiroteio	for the cheering dancers at a shooting spree
de gatilho digital	with digital triggers
de sub-uzi equipadinha	on a sub-uzi equipped
com cartucho musica;	with music cartridges
de contrabando militar	smuggled in by the military[4]

Youth Culture and the Waning of Brazilian National Identity

"Claustrofobia" and "Rio 40 Graus," juxtaposed, give contrasting character-izations of Rio de Janeiro's urban landscape, although they traverse the same terrain. The difference is in the manner of moving through space. The first, a samba, is a mellow, metapoetic composition whose sound is thematized as per-meating the world through its open-ended structure and ethos. Its composer, Martinho da Vila, a highly popular sambista associated since the mid-1980s with a festival of black heritage in Rio, has interpreted the lyrics in an interview with Gary Robinson, the host of the television show Sounds Brazilian: "Claustro-phobia: everyone knows what that is. Here it's a conversation I'm having with samba. It shouldn't stay in the backyards, interiors and shantytowns; it needs to go out and 'spread throughout the world.' And that's happening. 'The win-dow has been opened,' that is, the world is now open to receive samba. And now it's everywhere."[5]

For Martinho, as for many other enthusiasts, samba is a cultural form emanating from "the people" that permeates everything and everyone, blending all into one national identity ("Go spread yourself throughout the nation"). On the same show, Beth Carvalho and Paulinho da Viola emphasize the togetherness that samba inspires and the resistance of the people and the culture to the hardships of everyday life. This resistance is born of samba's propensity to appropriate and mix everything in its way, thus undermining, it is argued, hierarchies of all kinds. National Geographic's documentary *Samba: Rhythm of Life*, about the efforts of the favela Mangueira's *escola de samba* to win the annual carnival competition, gathers every commonplace imaginable about samba: it is what makes life worth living, even in the worst of circumstances; the people may be poor in material goods, but they are rich in spirit; through it they express their social and political aspirations; and, the clincher, in it the people speak with one voice. Samba, of course, has meant these things to many people. As Brazilian music historians Chris McGowan and Ricardo Pessanha write, "In Brazil, millions of people make, sing, dance or just enjoy samba. Its importance in the maintenance of a relative social peace in Brazil is hard to measure, but it is clear. One doesn't need to wait for Carnaval to see how samba brings people from all social classes and races together and keeps them in harmony . . . After all, in Brazil everything sooner or later ends up in samba" (1991: 51).

I would like to suggest, however, that the circumstances have changed and that not everything will "sooner or later end up in samba" or other celebrations of Brazilian identity that "keep all social classes and races together in harmony." The transition to an ever distant democracy in the 1980s and 1990s has brought to the surface the unworkability of social and political enfranchisement through cultural practices that formed part of a "consensus" that dealt material wealth to elites and ever greater hardship to subalterns. Today, the cultural scene is rapidly changing, reflecting the growing dissatisfaction with the nation, as the events that I narrate here confirm. The critiques of Brazilian national identity, particularly by black youth in rap movements, has taken place politically as well as racially and culturally. In the early 1990s, Howard Winant argued, perhaps over-wishfully, "Today, blacks are beginning to challenge the racial 'common sense,' both mainstream and radical, that race and racism are of limited political significance in the Brazilian context" (1992: 87). Given the importance of representations of blacks and mulattos and their cultural practices in the struggles to define Brazilianness, the challenge to racial common sense must focus on the social and economic status of nonwhites and on how the "consensus culture" has symbolized such practices as samba, *pagode* (a neighborhood gathering where samba is played), *capoeira* (an Afro-Brazilian martial arts dance form brought by slaves from Angola), *candomblé* and *umbanda* (Afro-Brazilian religions), and so on. It should be stressed that the critique implicit in "opting out" of the consensus culture does not mean that the above-mentioned practices are somehow alienating or always co-optable as binding elements of a social homeostasis that benefits elites. The point, rather, is that *since the 1930s* they have been mobilized by the media, business (particularly tourism), politics (including the manipulation of carnival), and other mediating instances for the symbolic reproduction of a "cordial" Brazil, with the result that elites reap the lion's share of material benefits. How to disengage these practices at this point from these mediations is a question that is not being asked because the cultural-political negotiations have already yielded something for each party.

Perhaps more than any other sector, including the black and other social movements, which continue to invest their cultural-political capital in Brazil *as a nation*, youth, especially subaltern youth, are leading the way to new experiences, often criss-crossed by transnational cultural forms that confound the consensus culture and often seem to instill fear in the elite and middle classes and suspicion among the leadership of the social movements. The new reality of street gangs, riots, narcotrafficking "commandos," *meninos de rua* (homeless street kids), vigilantism, and so on, has replaced the old myth of conviviality with a premonition of "social explosion," the term used by Brazil's president, Itamar Franco (1992–1995), in setting aside over US$2 billion for food for 9 million poor families ("El gobierno brasileño" 1992; "Governo atenderá" 1992; "Risco de 'explosão social' " 1992).

This new urban landscape is what Fernanda Abreu's funk-rap "Rio 40 Graus" is about. Whereas "Claustrofobia" projects a sense of free access to space, of no constraints on samba's "permeation" of space, the youths sung about in "Rio 40 Graus" must take possession of it through violence, through the display of force that inheres in the machine-gun-like assault of the black U.S. urban rhythms. Brazilian funk occupies the *same physical space* as that of the more traditional samba, but it questions, as does the song, the fantasy of access to social space. Its adherents constitute a new cultural sector, *a novidade cultural*, that does not identify with their sambista elders, although they are equally *garotada favelada, suburbana, classe média marginal* (homies, slumdwellers, marginal middle class). The youths challenge the ownership by the "nonmarginal" middle classes of the city's space, claiming it as their own. Through the new, nontraditional musics such as funk and rap, they seek to establish new forms of identity, but not those premised on Brazil's much heralded self-understanding as a nation of nonconflictual diversity. On the contrary, the song is about the *disarticulation of national identity and the affirmation of local citizenship*.

The cultural glue of this country of 170 million people has been quickly eroding in the wake of the demise of an authoritarian military dictatorship in the late 1970s and the never-ending "transition to democracy" in the 1980s and 1990s, made even more difficult by a substantial decrease in productivity and per capita income.[6] The most telling indicator of this shift is the diversification of youth cultures, almost none of which are holding to the cultural practices that supposedly bound their parents and grandparents in a community imagined through the mise-en-scène of popular culture forms such as carnival, samba, and soccer. Not only have the middle classes veered in a more "modern" direction, away from the celebratory consensus provided by plaza public culture (of the kind celebrated by Bakhtin and numerous Brazilian mythifiers of carnival), but the working classes and the poor have also sought out new cultural forms or transformed more traditional ones like popular music in keeping with the pervasive mass mediation of Brazilian society. If Brazil was once imagined by its national bourgeoisie (and many complicit popular sectors, such as those associated with carnival) as a convivial meeting ground for the diverse groups that inhabit it, most notably the descendants of European immigrants and African slaves, today its cultural critics are increasingly speaking of "difference."

"Cordiality," "racial democracy," and other similar terms have been used since the first decades of the twentieth century as the keywords in the mythic projection of Brazil as a nonconflictual society. Brazilian intellectuals and artists cultivated this myth as a means to recognize the miscegenation that characterized Brazil, at the same time warding off the anxiety that it produced in elites and middle sectors.[7] *Mestiçagem* (miscegenation) was purged of its threatening connotations and dressed up in an aesthetic camouflage that transformed the anxiety into national pride. Gilberto Freyre, who in the 1930s coined the term "racial democracy," an apt catchphrase that evokes a society without "violent racial prejudice," saw in this "tropical *mestiçagem*" a "softening effect" that "tended to dissolve prejudice" (1946: xii–xiii). He went so far as to attribute to the *mestiço*, actually, to the *mestiça*, a new political function that derives from the aesthetic plasticity that she represents: "One may even suggest that mestizos are, perhaps, becoming the decisive force, political and cultural, in a considerable part of the world; and that human aesthetic tastes in regard to human form and particularly to feminine beauty are being greatly affected by the increasing racial mixture" ([1966] 1974: 110). (It should be said, at least parenthetically, that in Brazil, Cuba, and other Ibero-American countries characterized by racial miscegenation between whites and blacks, that the "positive" racist valuation is gendered feminine: the *mulata* is eroticized to mythic proportions, the reverse of Anglo-American mythification of black male eroticism.)[8] In projecting mestiços as the "plastic mediators between extremes," Freyre was in effect making more palatable the black element that Brazilian elite culture found "repulsive." "Racial democracy," based as it is in mestiçagem, thus is consonant with the related myth of *embranquecimento*, that is, the belief that the new national culture can be purged, through a process of "whitening," of its "cacogenic, mongrel, repulsive aspect" (111).[9]

So long as Brazilian subaltern groups accommodate to this image, whereby even social injustice is thought to be better endured and even negotiated through the cultural forms of mestiçagem (e.g., carnival) or the political practices typical of a patriarchal society (patronage and clientelism), they will be tolerated and even imagined as partaking in the rights of citizenship. This is what today's cultural activists of the favela reject.

The Contradictions of Democracy, à Brasileira

In less than three weeks, between September 30 and October 18, 1992, three events took place that catapulted Brazil into a politics of representations unprecedented in its history. In using the word "unprecedented," I am referring to the peculiar mix of representations, not to the persistent social and political asymmetries to which these representations point.

The first event: on September 30, Parliament voted 441 to 38 to impeach President Fernando Collor. The vote capped a five-month process of political jockeying after evidence of corruption was presented, in a fitting telenovelesque melodrama, by the president's brother, who was, among other things, taking revenge for the attempt to seduce his wife. Brazil thus became the first country ever to impeach its president, and the frenzied rush to the streets by more than a million demonstrators outdid Nixon's relatively spineless teledisplay of crocodile tears and the U.S. public's comparatively tepid sigh of relief. The *Jornal do Brasil* described the event as follows:

> The Brazilian people exploded. Throughout the entire country multitudes released the tension of the last two months . . . In an unprecedented demonstration, the crowds, ever attentive to the news of the impeachment, frenziedly commemo-

rated the vote against Collor by the greatest "traitor" of the government and the most celebrated hero of the opposition, deputy Onaireves Moura . . . host of the *feast of curses* [*jantar dos palavrões*] . . .

In Brasilia the people stopped mourning, cast down the black and held aloft the yellow-green [colors of the Brazilian flag]. One hundred thousand demonstrators gave an indescribable spectacle. [An official] set his immense black flag on fire. "Enough of mourning. The yellow-green belongs to the people," he cried. And hundreds of people repeated his gesture, burning their black flags and transforming the lawn outside of Congress into a stage illuminated by fire. Thousands of yellow-green flags became visible among the people who danced, laughed and wept. Fireworks and rockets lit up the sky. Everyone sang, in unison, the National Anthem. Then the Hymn of Independence. ("Jantar dos palavrões" 1992)[10]

This and other articles describe the festivities in good national tradition as a carnival. Not only were there fireworks and chanting, there were music, dancing, and masquerade, the celebrated *caras pintadas* or painted faces of the students, most of them of high school age. Brazil had not seen demonstrations like these since the political heyday of the 1960s. The country seemed to be a nation united again.

I would like to ask readers to hold this image of national celebration in mind—fireworks, national anthem, samba, carnival, restoration of democracy, and so on—as I now turn, for the sake of contrast, to the other two epochal events.

The second event: just two days after the impeachment celebrations, on October 2, the military police invaded the House of Detention in Carandiru, São Paulo, and massacred at least 111 prisoners (some estimates run as high as 280). The police turned machine guns on the prisoners, lining them up against the walls St. Valentine's Day–style or shot them with their hands tied behind their backs. Those who weren't killed by bullets were attacked by dogs specially trained to go for the genitals ("Rebelião em presídio" 1992; " 'Mortos estavam amarrados' " 1992; "Mortos na Detenção" 1992; "Número de mortos" 1992). Prisoners reported being forced to drag the cadavers through puddles of blood because the military police were afraid of contracting AIDS. In fact, it was suggested that the military police took licence to massacre the protesting prisoners as a means to decrease the risk of contamination by continued contact with them.

The tenor of the reports was subdued in comparison to those of Collor's impeachment. Most were descriptive, resorting to sensationalist photographs of mutilated, naked corpses piled on top of each other, Holocaust style, an image that was explicitly evoked by several witnesses. The *Folha de São Paulo* reported:

> "It was worse than World War II. Hitler doesn't compare with this massacre!" cried a woman on Saturday night at the door of the IML (Legal-Medical Institute) in São Paulo . . .
>
> Quite noticeable were the number of perforations in each cadaver: five or six. In at least two the wounds in the back were visible. Many showed large blood stains—even 24 hours after their death. The majority seemed to be under 30 years of age. The long and coarse stitchwork that traversed the corpses, made by the undertakers, put the final touch on the indigence in which they had died. ("Equipe do IML" 1992)

Although the newspapers carried denunciations by intellectuals, politicians, and clergy accusing the state of terrorism, there were many in the population at large who endorsed the massacre, if polls are to be believed. The celebrations of just two days before were succeeded by a substantial show of support for the military police. The *Folha de São Paulo* reported that in a telephone survey it conducted, one third of the population of São Paulo supported the action ("Um terço apóia" 1992). Another newspaper, *O Estado de São Paulo*, found that support to be even higher: 44 percent (D. Caldeira 1992: 2). The interviewees repudiated the denunciation by the Organization of American States and Americas Watch ("OEA 'julga' invasão" 1992), defending the military police as the "moral reserve of São Paulo" ("Assembléia aprova CEI" 1992), and condemned human rights activists as abettors of murderers and rapists. Joanna Wechsler of Americas Watch received insults from many quarters: "I reject the presence of that *gringa*. She's an observer of nothing. Let her deal with the results of the racial conflict between whites and blacks in L.A."; "Demons, tricksters and clumsy fools. Those communists want the corpses for their political proselytizing"; "Useless, vulgar bitch. Go teach your son not to be a thief" ("Assembléia aprova CEI" 1992). The irony, as political philosopher José Arthur Giannotti and urban anthropologist Gilberto Velho explained, is that the mistrust of the justice system leads people to seek violence as a means to ensure security ("Descrédito na Justiça" 1992). Some have even argued that vigilantism and the belief that it is better to kill off criminals represent an internalization of a state of terror, in both senses of the phrase.

This display of violence, reproduced in many other spheres throughout Brazilian society (e.g., the killing of meninos de rua, the widespread narcotraffic, vigilantism) is not proof, of course, that the pro-democracy movement, which has been a complex consensus-building phenomenon cutting across racial, class, and ideological lines, is in any way bankrupt. It is a reminder, however, that talk of democracy in purely political terms is otiose when social and cultural rights are weak and not even enforced.[11]

The third event, which I examine more closely, occurred on October 18. I first found out about it when the mother of the friend at whose house I was staying came running in off the street, alarmed about a riot on the beach (my friend lives where Copacabana turns into Ipanema). It was an *arrastão* or looting "rampage"[12] conducted by "*uma negrada dos subúrbios da Zona Norte*" (hordes of dark kids from the slums in the northern suburbs). The event was registered hysterically by television news shows and newspapers throughout Brazil, as if it were a replay of the L.A. riots. In fact, the television shots of kids running wild on the beach and crowding into overstuffed buses through the windows were clearly meant to provoke such fear. The *Jornal do Brasil* reported:

> Yesterday the *Zona Sul* [south end] of Rio became a battle zone, with *arrastões* carried out by gangs of adolescents from the slums of the suburbs of Baixada Fluminense, armed with sticks. The Military Police, with 110 guards armed with revolvers, machine guns and rifles, had difficulty in putting down the violence of the various groups involved in the attack. Even a parallel police force, constituted by the *Guardian Angels*—a voluntary group aiming to defend the population— entered the fray.
>
> Panicked beachgoers and inhabitants of the area had to take refuge in bars, bakeries and street stands. The attack began about midday, on Arpoador Beach [between Copacabana and Ipanema], where several bus lines from the periphery make their final stop. As the gangs got off, they began to form *arrastões*, spilling over into Copacabana, Ipanema and Leblon. Angry inhabitants demanded the death sentence and Army patrols on the streets. (1992: 1, 14)

Fear of Funk

It didn't take long before the main offenders were identified as funkeiros or the youths from the slums of the north and west ends of Rio who on weekends frequent the dance clubs that play funk music, mostly from the United States. The *Jornal do Brasil*'s Sunday edition carried an article titled "Movimento Funk leva desesperança" (Funk movement breeds despair; 1992) and emphasized the contrast with the student caras pintadas who had engaged in a very different public spectacle on behalf of democracy:

They do not have their faces painted with the colors of the Brazilian flag and, much less, are they any cause for pride, as were the youths who resurrected the student movement in the struggle to impeach president Collor. With no paint on their faces, last Sunday these *caras-pintadas* of the periphery took to the Zona Sul the battle of one of the wars that they have faced since birth—the war between communities. They thus became a cause for shame, directly linked to the terror on the beach: the *arrastões* that sowed panic.

From Leme to Barra da Tijuca, the beaches were partitioned according to gang membership. This army was drawn from the two million frequenters of funk— [which could be described as] a rhythm, a movement, or a force.

This report plays ironically with the two kinds of "painted faces": the middle-class youths who went out into the streets to support "democracy" and the "naturally" painted faces (i.e., with no need for paint) of the black and mulatto youths who took to the beach to cause panic. Their dark skin, in fact, was emphasized in many other reports, such as that by *Veja*, a news magazine comparable to a combination of *Time* and *Der Spiegel*. It carried statements made by middle-class beachgoers who remarked on the dark skin, poverty, and dirty clothing of the kids, some of whom it also interviewed, if for no other reason than to sensationalize them and add to the panic. In a special section of the report, entitled "Baile só é bom se tiver briga" (A dance is only good if it ends in a brawl; 1992), it states:

> The tribes that terrorized the beaches of Rio de Janeiro can be compared to English hooligans or the perverse Mancha Verde gang of the Palmeiras suburb in São Paulo. They are youths who band together to go on rioting sprees wherever and whenever the occasion arises. The name "galera" [dance club] [13] was coined in the funk dance clubs of the Rio suburbs, where gangs from the slums and favelas gather in multitudes of up to 4,000 . . . The aficionados of rioting call themselves *funkeiros* and they cultivate frequent showdowns as a leisure activity.

Not all of the reports pinned the blame exclusively on the funkeiros; in the ensuing days, interviews with them and with youths from the favelas in the Zona Sul itself presented a more ambiguous picture. Yes, the gangs from the funk clubs did engage in commotions on the beach; yes, the beachgoers were scared shitless; yes, there were youths who stole some things from the blankets, although it could not have amounted to much since no *Carioca* (resident of Rio de Janeiro) or tourist in his or her right mind would take anything of value to the beach. As it turns out, what the cameras captured were rival gangs skirmishing on the beach and kids jumping through windows into the few and overstuffed buses that would take them back to their neighborhoods in the north and west ends. Reports from the Guardian Angels and the surfers also suggested that what robberies were committed were probably carried out by the *favelados* of the Zona Sul. But never mind, the funkeiros seem to have been permanently stigmatized by the media and the hysteria of the middle classes of South Rio. A hysteria that was quite productive.

The hoopla around the arrastão took place less than a month before the most important election in Rio's history. The favela-bred and self-taught daughter of a cleaning woman, the black candidate on the Workers Party ticket, Benedita Souza da Silva, who is representative of the above-mentioned cross-class, -race, and -ideology coalition of the pro-democracy movement, was up against a white, middle-class economist from the Zona Sul. Benê, as she is called in Brazil, won a plurality of the votes in the general election but, failing to get a majority, she faced the runner-up, César Maia, in the runoff election on November 15. Samba and the other cultural practices that are supposed to create social solidarity were not sufficient to brake the racial polarization that overtook the city. The upshot is that Benê lost the runoff by three percentage points as many ambivalent middle-class voters, fearing an increase in violence, voted for the "law and order" man.

This event took place while I was conducting interviews with people knowledgeable about music in Rio. I was interested in the reception of rap. Just the day before the arrastão I had interviewed Hermano Vianna, an anthropologist who had written a book on the funk dance clubs. He explained that rap, at least as far as Rio was concerned, was of minor interest. Brazilian youth were basically interested in rock, especially heavy metal and most of it from the United States and England. These were the middle classes. The youths from the suburban slums and favelas of Rio, on the other hand, most of whom are black or mulatto and poor, preferred funk, although rap is on the rise, especially in São Paulo. Reggae, too, is already a permanent fixture in São Luis de Maranhão and Bahia. (It should be said, parenthetically at least, that Brazil is a country of many musics and that one cannot generalize about music loyalty from one city or region to another. If Brazil as a nation could ever have been characterized by samba, that is no longer the case. What is popular in Bahia or Porto Alegre is not necessarily popular elsewhere and may not even get national radio and TV projection. I shall return to the question of distribution.)

Before the arrastão took place even the anthropologist was at pains to explain why these youths would be interested in a music that they couldn't understand and that was not available in stores and until recently didn't even get airplay. The arrastão, however, made it patently clear that the allegiance to funk implied opting out of other musics, particularly those most identified with Brazilian nationalism or, more locally, cultural citizenship in Rio de Janeiro. A *Jornal do Brasil* article that carried interviews with an influential funkeiro DJ and Vianna brought this point home: "According to DJ Marlboro (Fernando Luiz), who since the end of the seventies has promoted these dances, the *funkeiros* are not the source but the victims of everyday violence. They go to the dance clubs—*galeras* named after the hillside slums (*morros*) and *favelas*—seeking the homeland that they do not otherwise know" ("Movimento Funk leva desesperança" 1992).

This DJ had earlier cowritten with other founders of the funk movement, Ademir Lemos and Nirto, a song titled "Rap do arrastão" (Riot rap), which deals with this everyday violence:

Eu gosto de música americana	I like American music
e vou pro baile curtir todo	and I go dancing every weekend
fim-de-semana	to have a good time
Só que na hora de voltar pra	But on the way home
casa é o maior sufoco pegar condução	it's impossible to catch a bus
E de repente pinta até um arrastão	And all of a sudden an *arrastão* . . .
Esconde a grana, o relógio e o cordão	Hide your money, watch or chain
Cuidado, vai passar o arrastão	Careful, the *arrastão*'s coming your way
Batalho todo dia dando um	I work my ass off all day
duro danado mas no fim-de-semana	and on the weekend
sempre fico na mão, esconden-	I always run into problems
do minha grana para entrar	I have to hide my money
na condução	for when I catch the bus.

(cited in Só 1992)

This song emphasizes the problems of everyday violence encountered by the youths who attend funk dances. In Rio, as in other major Latin American urban centers, poor black and mulatto youth have no citizenship rights to speak of. They are not protected by the police; on the contrary, the police, often in cahoots with *justiçeiros* or vigilantes, harass them in the best of cases, and in the worst, murder them and leave their corpses on the street to serve as a warning to others. Human rights organizations' records show that in 1991 in São Paulo alone, the military police killed 876 "street youth." That number was expected to increase to 1,350 in 1992.[14] In comparison, 23 youth were killed in similar circumstances in New York, a city about the same size as São Paulo (Quadros 1992: 16). The point is not so much that in São Paulo the police kill thirty-eight times as many youth as in New York (although that in itself is a telling statistic), but that the method of dealing with unemployment, lack of educational opportunity, hunger, and racism is "social cleansing" of the poor. During the mammoth environmental summit Eco 92 in June 1992, the military police combed the Zona Sul and downtown areas, removing poor youth (most of them black and mulatto) to make the streets safe for the visiting dignitaries. They were taken to and held in outlying areas, such as the nearby bedroom community of Niteroi.

Youths from the slums are detested by the righteous middle classes as polluting elements. Not only geographical but, even more important, social space is clearly demarcated in Rio and other Brazilian cities. The beaches and the leisure that they represent are considered the patrimony of the Zona Sul middle classes and of tourists. Youths from the slums have no patrimony, except that which they stake out for themselves, as evidenced in the arrastão, which became a struggle over space, as the Afro-Brazilian geographer Milton Santos explains. When asked by an interviewer how he assessed the demand by some middle-class Cariocas to cut off bus service to the beaches of the Zona Sul from the northern suburbs, he answered that the multiple spaces of the new megacities of the world are not traversable by everyone and that the poor tend to be prisoners in their own neighborhoods. Multiplicity and heterogeneity do not translate into access (Ulanovsky Sack 1992). Those without the "right" to cross over into a space "not their own" will be stopped by the state on behalf of those who enjoy "citizenship." It should be added that traversability also depends on the purpose for which one moves from one area to another. In the wake of the arrastão, for example, many middle-class people called for the elimination of bus service from the Zona Norte to the Zona Sul. However, they found themselves having to back out of this position when they realized that many of their *empregadas* (maids) lived in the Zona Norte and would not be able to come to cook and clean their houses under such a restriction.

The funkeiros, then, are seen by the "citizenry" as a menace. There were reports that guards hired by the tourist agency Riotur were stopping youths, frisking them, and holding them for the police (1992: 1). And to add insult to injury, even the narcotraffickers declared that they were going to rid the Zona Sul of these youths, for they brought more police to the area and that, as in the tourist trade, was bad for business. In contrast to the image of chaos associated with the funkeiros, the narcotrafficking *comandos* came off as the mirror image of the forces of order, that is, the military and security forces.

Funkeiro culture is both reactive and proactive. On the one hand, funkeiros reject the spectacle of democracy in which the caras pintadas participate. Funkeiros have no cause for celebration. The upper and middle classes have at their disposal the new simulation of democracy, staged by the impeachment of President Collor, and the projection of the poor and the slum dwellers as criminals and lazy parasites. There was a time when the cultural politics of Rio made it possible for these marginal classes to imagine themselves as part of the nation but, as São Paulo sociologist Alba Zaluar explained in an article in the *Jornal do Brasil*: "Rio can no longer be reduced to *blocos de carnaval* or *escolas de samba*, soccer teams and street corner society, the bar hangout or the bohemian boite, all of them creating the cultural politics that always characterized this city that communicated and differentiated itself through music" (1992: 1). She goes on to explain that this construction of a national image is no longer viable. What characterizes Rio and other urban centers in Brazil is a process of differentiation that renders commonality difficult if not impossible to achieve.

> Since the funk clubs do not show any signs of withering away, this still musical city, more consumerist than productive today, will have to learn to deal with the *roqueiros, funkeiros, carecas* [skinheads], *motoqueiros* [motorcycle gangs] that make of small differences signs of an identity to be defended at any cost, even death. Patently narcissistic and without any clear political project or social conscience that might allow us to speak of them as revolutionary in any sense, these groups should gain the attention of the social movements, particularly those of blacks, women and neighborhood societies.

I agree with Zaluar and shall return to these problems. At this point, however, I would like to describe the activities of the funkeiros.

The World of Carioca Funk

Funk culture in Rio de Janeiro implies a total reconfiguration of social space. On the one hand, the million-plus youth who attend the *galeras funk* or funk dance clubs on weekends live in the ghetto suburbs of the Zona Norte and Zona Oeste of Rio de Janeiro. On the other hand, the DJs who play funk, which in Rio includes several black U.S. genres such as soul, rhythm and blues, Motown, and hip-hop, engage in a dizzying transnational traffic in records, tapes, and CDs.

Things have changed significantly since Vianna studied the funk clubs in the late 1980s. Then almost none of the music played was available in record stores and until about 1990 it was not played on the radio. Consequently, the DJs relied on a network of couriers who flew periodically to New York and Miami to buy the music. These couriers were employees of travel agencies and airlines or even DJs themselves from the Zona Norte who arrived in New York in the morning, made their contacts, and returned to Rio on the evening flight. In Rio they sold their merchandise to resellers from whom other DJs got their music. There was stiff competition over the tapes and records because the quality of the music—gauged in terms of danceability, what makes the funkeiros feel most like dancing—is what gives the DJs their place in the world of funk culture. By the time of the arrastões in the early 1990s, however, a thriving local funk music scene had emerged, with producers like DJ Marlboro generating their own recordings.

A bit of history.[15] Funk culture got its start in the early 1970s in the Zona Sul, specifically at the Canecão, which is the principal stage in Rio for pop music. Today it is devoted predominantly to rock and national and international pop. But back in the 1970s several DJs, among them Ademir Lemos and Big Boy, began to give preference to soul artists like James Brown, Wilson Pickett, and Kool and the Gang in the Sunday "Bailes da Pesada" (literally, "heavy" or rowdy, that is, "hip" dances) attended by five thousand youth. But then the Canecão's administration shifted attention to MPB (Brazilian popular music, a rough equivalent of folk rock "incorporating elements of bossa nova, jazz, bolero, sertaneja music, rock, northeastern music, reggae, and other genres"; McGowan and Pessanha 1991: 78). When that happened, the Bailes da Pesada were taken to the Zona Norte, where the dancers most interested in this kind of music resided. To put on the large dances, which sometimes counted over ten thousand youth at a given club, some enterprising individuals put together huge sound systems, *equipes*, in some cases made up of over a hundred speakers piled on top of each other like a wall. These equipes had names like "Revolução da Mente," after James Brown's "Revolution of the Mind," "Soul Grand Prix," and "Black Power."

It was "Soul Grand Prix" that initiated a new phase in Rio funk culture in 1975, a phase the press labeled "Black Rio." Their dances took on a didactic format, introducing black culture through figures already familiar to the dancers (i.e., music and sports celebrities). "Soul Grand Prix" 's dances actually used mixed media—slides, films, photos, posters—to inculcate the "Black is Beautiful" style of the period. The fact that the youth from the Zona Norte were engaging black culture mediated by a U.S. culture industry met with many arguments against their susceptibility to cultural colonization. However, as some of Bahia's most important intellectuals on issues of "Africanization" have argued, soul and funk were important sites for the revitalization of traditional Afro-Brazilian forms such as the Bahian *afoxé* (a rhythm derived from the ritual music of the Afro-Brazilian religion candomblé) and the birth of the first *bloco afro* (an Afro-Brazilian carnival group), Ilê Aiyê. One of the founders, Jorge Watusi, did impugn the commercial character of soul in Rio but also argued that the engagement with black U.S. music could be put to good use in the recuperation of Brazil's own black roots (Vianna 1988: 29).

The passage from the 1970s to the 1980s, which saw the reinvention of Brazilian rock and the transition to democracy, also spelled the waning of the black consciousness of the galeras funk in Rio's Zona Norte. Although it is true that they have maintained their exclusive preference for black U.S. music as a marker of difference from rock, Brazil's most popular music among middle-class youth (who assume "whiteness" in its Brazilian version), the galeras funk no longer make any reference to black pride (Vianna 1988: 32). According to Vianna, "The militants of the various tendencies of the Brazilian black movement seem to have forgotten these dances, no longer considered as proper spaces for '*conscientização*' " (32). Some analysts of the black movement, such as Emília Viotti da Costa, concur with this view, holding that the movement "has remained mostly a middle-class phenomenon and has found little echo among poor blacks" (qtd. in Vianna 1988: 32). It is understandable, then, that some groups of poor youth may turn to cultural forms that are not inscribed within the black movement's counterhegemonic project.

However, these observations, which were made in the mid-1980s, may need revising after the middle-class panic caused by the arrastão and the increasing harassment experienced by the funkeiros and other poor youth. Subaltern youth are responding, particularly those involved with rap, the majority of whom are in São Paulo, although there is significant activity in Rio. The rap movement is becoming more visible and it carries a clear ideological message against racism and the state's complicity with it.[16] Rap and hip-hop organizations have formed in São Paulo and Rio, with the sanction of Workers Party government officials, particularly the Department of Culture in São Bernardo do Campo, one of several industrial centers on the periphery of São Paulo, which subvened the Projeto de Ação Cultural "Movimento de Rua" (Cultural Action Project "Street movement") and its book of rap lyrics and poetry, *ABC RAP: Coletânea de poesia rap*. The editors and contributors defined their demands around issues of "negritude (the majority of the youths are black) and racism, urban violence, poverty (the majority of the youths live at or below the poverty line), the rap movement and ecology" (Oliveira, Borges, and Vieira 1992: 5). The group Esquadrão urbano (Urban Squadron, suggesting an inversion of the violent connotation that death squads have in Brazil) protests the hypocrisy of the notion of security, which is one thing for the elites and another for the poor:

a segurança que a cidade nos ofrece	the security that the city offers us
já não se vê no dia, então quando	you can't even see in the day, so when
escurece	it gets dark
parece que a corajosa polícia some	it seems the brave police disappear
policiáis otários nosso dinheiro	stupid cops spend our money
consomem	cruising in comfortable cars
circulando em confortáveis viaturas	while we poor trudge along barefoot
enquanto nós pobres descalços	(Oliveira et al. 1992: 111)
circulamos nas ruas	

Several groups, such as Panthers of the Night, advocate nonviolence (Oliveira et al. 1992: 115–116); others, such as MC Blacks, claim their rights as black citizens (35–38); and some, like N E P S, even defend feminism:

homens machistas	machista men
nos humilham, não querem saber	humiliate us, they don't want to know
insistem em incitar	they insist upon inciting
dizem donos do poder	they call themselves owners of power
. . . .	. . . .
só pensam em clamar	they only think about making claims
para a violência	for violence
inconformados	disturbed
por estarmos progredindo	by our progress (17)

These uses of rap tend to have a political-intellectual backing from progressive elements in the state, such as São Paulo's Municipal Secretariat of Education, which sponsored the project *Rap nas Escolas: Rap . . . pensando a Educação* (Rap in the Schools: Rap . . . thinking Education; Silveira 1992), and Rio's Ceap (Centro de articulação das populações marginais [Center for the Articulation of Marginal Populations]), which sponsored the Associação hip-hop Atitude Consciente (Hip-hop Association for a Conscious Attitude; A. Curry 1993). The aim of these projects is to "construct a citizenship of the subaltern." Funkeiro culture, on the other hand, from the late 1970s to the present, has rejected the promise of citizenship by politicians and intellectuals, whether populists of the left or right or even from the black movement. It has resisted the terms of participation—cultural representation without access to social and material goods and services—typical of the clientelist relationship accepted by carnival and samba culture. The political significance of funkeiro culture, if any, must be construed otherwise.

In Rio, cultural critics have generally seen funkeiros as nonpolitical and alienated. Rappers endorse that view and have even launched a project to "convert the *funkeiro* tribe" (A. Curry 1993). For Vianna, however, this opting out of politics does not mean that they are alienated. Taking the lead from critics of the idea that, in contrast to elites who live with one eye on the international scene, popular sectors maintain the "authentic roots of national culture," Vianna, somewhat in the spirit of Dick Hebdige's claims about subcultural groups, sees funkeiro culture as resisting "official or dominant culture," but not through group or ethnic identity or any other worthwhile cause (Vianna 1988: 109). (As we shall see in the following chapter, Afro Reggae aims to channel the pleasure of pop music and dance, including funk, into an alternative and more inclusive notion of citizenship.) His ethnographic work and participant observation in the galeras funk of the Zona Norte lead him to characterize them as "orgiastic feast-like" dances in the spirit of a Batailleian *dépense* (expenditure) (54). Resistance is at best a kind of "poaching," in the sense that Certeau gives the word: a nomadic despoiling of the existing cultural capital (1984: 174). Funkeiros dress like the middle-class *surfistas* of the Zona Sul; appropriate U.S. black music; piggyback on existing networks that serve other purposes (tourism) to get their music, which is then pirated, thus offering no commercial value to the recording industry; and make use of the spaces designated for samba and sports. These appropriations produce little value for the dominant order: the clothes do not distinguish them from other youth (although Nikes and Reeboks do produce profit for shoe manufacturers); U.S. black culture as disseminated through funk does not translate into Afro-Brazilian consciousness; in fact, the lyrics of U.S. black music, which might make reference to racial and cultural politics, are not even understood; funkeiros relexicalize the English on the basis of homophony: "you talk too much" and "I'll be all you ever need" become the nonsense Portuguese *taca tomate* (tomato beat) and *ravioli eu comi* (I ate ravioli; Vianna 1988: 82).[17] With the exception of rap and the music of pop stars like Michael Jackson, U.S. black music is not sold in Brazil, therefore producing no profit for record companies, although the sound system *equipes* make their living from the dances; the use of the spaces of samba and sports does not suture them into the national culture. (The *Rio Funk* program of the municipal government, discussed in the next chapter, is a counterexample that signals greater consciousness raising after 1994.)

Poaching, *dépense*, and Dionysian orgiastic dancing, though necessary correctives to the stereotypes of media consumers as the dupes of the culture industry and cultural imperialism, are not the only ways of interpreting the practices of these youths. The poaching model takes to an extreme a gesture of contemporary critical theory that projects all kinds of everyday people and particularly subaltern groups in charge of the representations that constitute their world as "active producers and manipulators of meanings" (H. Jenkins 1992: 23). The depiction of funkeiro culture that I have provided certainly recognizes the active role of these youths in staking out their own territory, constructing their own means of pleasure, often against the grain of national or regional cultural identity. I characterize the poaching model as an extreme, however, because in attempting to overturn one stereotype it fails to give sufficient attention to the *negotiated character of reception*, which is never squarely in the hands of any one person or group.

Funkeiros, whether they wanted to or not, have found themselves in the center of public sphere debates about culture. The arrastão, if nothing else, put them in the middle of an ongoing conflict about the place of the poor, their access to the goods and services of citizenship, and their vulnerability to vigilantism and state violence, so pointed in the case of the meninos de rua. Funkeiros have now become part of a new urban lore, projected as a polluting menace. Television and the press show them as have-nots seeking to take what belongs to the elite and middle classes in exchange for a fear that "justifies" their repression. In fact, images of violence in the arrastão served to fix the spatial fluidity of funkeiros' nomadic poaching, thus demarcating in a Manichaean way the differences between Zona Sul and Zona Norte. Images of violence have demonized and thus, to a degree, controlled them, making funk productive of the culture at large, a productivity that it sought to opt out of.

Funkeiros are only one sector of Brazilian youth whose representations are transforming the traditional mediascape. Youth culture is highly differentiated, as we have seen. It consists of politicized rappers; the caras pintadas who celebrated the "democratic" triumph over President Collor, most of whom listen almost exclusively to rock and international pop; the meninos de rua, thousands of whom are brutally murdered throughout Brazil and who have recently organized a new social movement with their first international convention in Brasilia (G. Nascimento 1992; Dantas 1992; Mendes 1993; "Encontro reúne" 1992), surfistas ("Surfista do morro" 1992), guardian angels ("Anjos da Guarda" 1992; "Anjos' usam" 1992), and funkeiros. But also *metaleiros* (heavy metal aficionados), punks, skateboarders, *motoqueiros, neobeats, neohippies, carecas* (skinheads),[18] neonazis and "nationalist" *whitepowers* ("Fanzines pregam" 1992; "São Paulo organiza" 1992), black Muslims ("Ódio ao branco" 1992; "Grupo negro declara" 1992), and the rastas, reggae, and calypso enthusiasts and other youth who cultivate the musics and cultural practices of the African diaspora, especially in Bahia and other cities of the Northeast. Brazil, which has a land mass larger than that of the continental United States, has never been a homogeneous country, although samba, carnival, bossa nova, and MPB did represent it as more or less coherent. From the mid-1990s on, however, a *new politics of representation* has emerged that places the emphasis on difference. The media, the new social movements, and the asymmetrical but pervasive consumer culture all engage in this politics of representation, making it impossible for any one group to maintain control of how it is imaged.

The newspaper accounts that I have cited throughout this chapter are filled with accusations, contestations, and recriminations about funkeiros. But the images that have been generated around them are not all negative; in the past two years, just like hip-hop culture in the United States, they have made their way from the periphery to prime-time TV and chic boutiques in the Zona Sul: *O funk caminha das festas da periferia para novelas de TV e lojas da Zona Sul* (Funk migrates from the parties of the periphery to telenovelas and [upscale] shops of the Zona Sul) (D. Caldeira 1992). New pop stars are beginning to gain recognition in Rio and other Brazilian cities as funk singers or by appropriating elements of funk. There is a tendency in U.S. cultural criticism to impugn white middle-class musicians and artists who appropriate elements from subaltern cultural practices: Elvis and rhythm and blues, Madonna and vogueing, for example. Similar charges could be made about Fernanda Abreu, whose "Rio 40 Graus" opens this chapter, or some of the DJs who have begun to "mainstream" the Brazilian-composed funk, particularly DJ Marlboro, who has produced three *Funk Brasil* albums (DJ Marlboro 1989, 1990, 1991). What is important to keep in mind, however, is that such artists and producers are helping to open up public spheres to which funkeiros had no access. If the funkeiros themselves have not politicized their dances and emergent music, they are now, in the wake of the arrastão, inevitably involved in a conflict of valuations that takes place in public spheres. And their contribution to Carioca cultural politics has been to open up a space of taste, style, and pleasure that is not permeated by national or regional identity, even though they may be using the same physical space of samba, soccer, and carnival.

The Cultural Politics of Carioca Funk

How to evaluate the cultural politics of funkeiro culture? This, of course, cannot be an innocent enterprise. Contemporary cultural criticism, particularly in studies of reception and youth culture, tends to endow viewers and listeners with substantial political(?) power as a corrective to the elitist attitude that mass culture only alienates its consumers. I would like to opt out of this kind of discussion, for it does not tell us very much about the larger institutional and transnational context of popular practices. I prefer to situate the question of Carioca funk's cultural politics in the terrain of conflicting public spheres. In this regard, I think funkeiro practices offer a new cognitive mapping in which transnational culture and technology are used for their own purposes, which are clearly not political. This is a cultural mapping quite different, however, from the kind that Marxist theorists from Lukács, Adorno, and Benjamin to Eagleton and Jameson differentially advocate: namely, that artworks are heuristic devices through which the critic gains a knowledge of social reality otherwise unavailable.

Funkeiros do not need the culture critic to tell them how their social reality is structured; they know it quite well and make use of that knowledge to further their own ends. We might call this a "cultural reconversion" after Néstor García Canclini's ([1990] 1995b) study of the strategies for "entering and exiting modernity" in a transnational world. This kind of cognitive mapping is more a *practical* matter than an epistemological one.

On the other hand, the claims made for identity politics typical in U.S. cultural criticism make no sense whatsoever in Brazil. Many of the groups mentioned above have an ephemeral existence. Identity does not go very deep, especially in this age of denationalizing culture. Nor does the poaching model help to explain the political dimensions of practices that seem to be quite apolitical but that have significant repercussions in the conflict of public spheres. Ultimately, I think a public sphere approach to the conflict of styles and forms of pleasure goes further in accounting for why space is so hotly contested in Rio and other Brazilian cities. Certainly, something of the poaching model is operative in this contestation of space, but it is the permeation of space by style and ethos that carries the political impact the new funk artists are tapping in their songs. In an uncanny anticipation of the arrastão and the "law and order" re-action of the white candidate for mayor, César Maia, the title song on Fernanda Abreu's album *Be Sample* starts with a demagogic representative of the middle and upper classes who calls in the military police to remove *o povo* (the people, i.e., the popular classes) so that the "marvelous folklore" of the nation can be presented with *melhor brilhantismo* (better brilliance).[19]

This call for national pride is immediately undercut by the emphasis on the sampled character of culture in the voice that sings "Play it again Sam / Sam-pleia isso ai" (Play it again Sam, Sample this here), an interlingual pun, by in-version, on the anglicism *sampleia* (sample), which in Portuguese sounds like "Sam play." What follows is a kind of funk manifesto about sampling as op-posed to any fixed national identity. The entire album, in fact, is a virtuoso performance of sampling, establishing interesting relations with the musics of U.S. blacks and Latinos, a kind of "transbarrio" sampling from one sub-altern group to another. "Sigla Latina do Amor (SLA 2)" (Latin initial of love [SLA 2]) samples the voices of Puerto Rican youths in El Barrio, among them a rap in Spanish by a woman who says "Hacerlos bailar es mi misión y Latin ACT UP es mi canción" (To make them dance is my mission and Latin ACT UP is my song). The Puerto Rican rap group Latin Empire is also sampled making the kind of claim that funkeiros no doubt fully agree with: "Yo tengo derecho de ser una estrella/porque mis rimas son más bellas/somos muchachos latinos y mi lenguaje es más fino/porque yo soy latino activo" (I have the right to be a star/because my rhymes are more beautiful/we are Latino boys and my lan-guage is finer/because I am an active Latino). This is a claim to value, a claim that funkeiros make through their style, their pleasure, and above all their dancing. The popular funk hit "Dance" by Skowa and Tadeu Eliezer places identity and value in dance itself:

As minhas raízes são passos de dança	My roots are dance steps
Quando ouço um funk, nunca perco a esperança	When I hear funk I never lose hope
Dentro do salão não penso duas vezes	In the dance hall I never think twice
Eu danço com emoção e durante vários meses	I dance with emotion and for several months
Eu danço com raiva.	I dance with rage. (Skowa e a Máfia 1989)

Unlike Martinho da Vila's samba, there is no extension here of the emotion from the individual to a larger social formation, such as a social movement or the nation. This funk song expresses, rather, the desire to let go, to have the freedom to let go, which is continually denied whenever the favelado or *sub-urbano* steps off the dance floor. The emotion, which is experienced as rage in the act of dancing, is untapped for a "greater" social or political purpose. It is the manner in which poor youth construct their world, against the restrictions of space and against the correctly deduced conviction that to channel the rage toward some social or political goal may lead only to being duped. And yet, fun-keiro culture is being heard, it is opening spheres of discussion on television and in the press, entering the market, creating new fashions, generating new music stars. This may not gain these youth greater material resources, it may not save them from violence; but then again, such expectations are not their specific hope, which is, rather, to clear a space of their own.

5

Parlaying Culture into Social Justice

In chapter 4, I examined how the largely black and mixed-race youth who frequent the bailes funk (funk dances) in Rio de Janeiro dealt with marginalization, devaluation, and harassment.[1] In this chapter, I examine the activism of citizen action initiatives and youth cultural organizations themselves to, respectively, heal the wounds of the divided city described in the previous chapter and to empower poor, racialized youth. Chapter 4 dwelled on both the violence and the pleasure of funk; here I examine the channeling of that violence and pleasure into what these groups call cultural citizenship. In effect, popular music and dance became opportunities to perform practices of public participation (or citizenship) otherwise left unverbalized.

Violence in the Divided City

It wasn't long after his election that César Maia, the white economist who won the election against Benedita da Silva, had to confront the escalating violence in Rio, particularly the narcotraffickers entrenched in the favelas and the military sent in to root them out when it became evident that local police were either poorly prepared or on the take. Operação Rio, as the campaign was called, barely managed to contain criminal activity. It had no effect on the (often political and elite) forces external to the favelas that coordinated this activity, but it did leave an enormous toll of victims, especially among poor youth, a major reason it was opposed by those who saw real democratization as a more viable counterforce. Many, like Luiz Eduardo Soares—organizer of a working group on violence for the Institute for the Study of Religion (ISER) at the time of the arrastões, subsequently coordinator of Security, Justice, Civil Defense and Citizenship for the governor of Rio de Janeiro in 1999, and now National Security for Public Safety in President Luiz Inácio "Lula" da Silva's new government— were critical of the abuse of favela residents' citizenship rights (Luiz Soares 1996). A double-pronged solution emerged in the midst of the violence: the use of the new favela culture to enfranchise poor youth and a "citizen action initiative against violence" called Viva Rio.

In 1994, César Maia's secretary of Social Development, Wanda Engel, together with other municipal secretariats (e.g., Leisure and Sports) and NGO activists, launched Rio Funk, a project to use funk music and dance as a means to develop creativity and notions of citizenship among favela youth. Besides bringing professionals to the favelas to teach music, percussion, dance, theater, and DJ—putatively to increase employment opportunities—the goal of the project was to identify *cultural difference* with belonging. By disseminating this notion of belonging, thus reprising the generalization of samba as the city's music seventy years before, it was hoped that the fragmented constituencies might come together. The secretariat's video *Rio Funk* (1995) brought home the message that funk culture was not a criminal culture, but a "way of being and doing" that might serve as a social glue and thus lead to the healing of the city. I shall return to this argument when I discuss the cultural group Afro Reggae.

In the video, Rubem César Fernandes, organizer of the citizen action initiative against violence Viva Rio, makes this argument: although the arrastões of 1992 and 1993 sent the middle classes into panic, it was the brutal violence against the poor that immediately prompted the formation of Viva Rio and that brought Afro Reggae to the favela that most symbolized conflict. On July 23, 1993, eight street children were murdered by a "social cleansing" death squad made up of off-duty police in front of the Candelária church, at the major intersection of Rio's downtown avenues. At the end of August, twenty-one innocent residents of the favela Vigário Geral were massacred. Apparently, on the previous day, the local chapter of the narcotraffic gang Comando Vermelho (Red Command) had killed four cops who tried to extort a drug shipment from them. The police stormed the favela the next day and shot people indiscriminately. In one house they murdered all eight family members, who were parishioners of the evangelist church the Assembly of God. The parents died Bible in hand. All three of these events disrupted the sense of place that Cariocas (Rio's residents) associated with the spaces in which they occurred (Luiz Soares 1996). The arrastões on the beaches introduced an element of fear into the space of leisure.

The murders in front of the Candelária church undid the assumed sociability among classes that is taken for granted at this inevitable space of encounter. The massacre in the favela reversed the role of the police, much like the Rodney King beating in Los Angeles. The police became the criminals who defiled a now sacred space otherwise identified with abjection. Whereas the arrastões saw quick action from the authorities, as described in the previous chapter, the response to the other two events came from "civil society." Viva Rio emerged not only to demand effective action from the authorities but to communicate a new sense of citizenship, of belonging and participation, that included all classes, especially the poor.

Caio Ferraz, a young sociologist and the first resident of Vigário Geral ever to attend college, created the Community Movement of Vigário Geral to analyze what had happened, to demand justice, and to develop ways of enhancing citizenship values and access to social services. The movement also took on the task of demonstrating to the rest of the city that "the people who live in shanty towns are honest; that we exist, that we can also be intellectual, that we can also produce culture" (Colombo 1996). The movement decided to transform the "house of war," in which the family of eight had been murdered, into the Casa da Paz, or House of Peace. To get support for this project, Caio turned to ISER, an NGO with wide-ranging networks throughout society, government, and international foundations and organizations. Rubem César Fernandes, director of ISER, who had been invited to form part of a group to initiate actions to stop the violence, in turn invited Caio to the first meeting. That group included the heads of the major newspapers and television networks of the city (and of Brazil) and, most important, Betinho (Herbert de Souza), leader of Citizenship Action against Hunger and director of the Instituto Brasileiro de Análises Sociais e Econômicas (IBASE), Brazil's most important NGO for social research and activism on behalf of a wide range of social issues.

It was at this meeting that the "two halves" of the city came together, as journalist Zuenir Ventura (1994) narrates in his account of the emergence of Viva Rio. Ventura also came to form part of the initiative, along with other writers and academics, business executives, religious leaders, union representatives, and interested citizens from middle-class neighborhoods as well as favelas and subúrbios. The significance of Viva Rio's press and television coverage from the very beginning make it, along with Betinho's contemporaneous Campaign against Hunger, the best-publicized citizen action initiative ever in the history of the city. Indeed, Ventura's book, Cidade Partida (1994; Divided city), like his earlier chronicle on the cultural politics of the dictatorship years,

1968, *O ano que nunca terminou* (1968, The year that never ended) (1988), became a best-seller, only this time concentrating on the energies for renewal within "civil society." This was and continues to be a rather idealistic concept, one that gained currency when it became evident that the "transition to democracy" would not usher in governments with the capacity (or will) to bring about more equitable distribution of wealth and services. In other words, it fell to the grassroots to resolve their own problems.[2] To get the citizenry to feel a part of this movement, it had to be dramatized. Rio, the marvelous city of carnival and spectacle, had contracted the taint of violence, as reported in the print and electronic media.[3] To exorcize it and heal the rifts required performing a series of actions, ritualized by the media, so that the city could see itself going through the curative process. This meant acting out rituals of respect and concern for each other, which Ventura chronicled.

That the haves and the have-nots should meet was, of course, a sign that the violence had become intolerable, that it could no longer be confined to the spaces of the poor. With the decrease in programs that benefit the poor, many young men, and even preadolescent boys,[4] from the favelas and subúrbios turned either to petty criminality or to the drug traffic for survival. In both cases, the increasing violence in the favelas and subúrbios made its way to the chic middle-class areas that constitute the showpiece of the city, particularly the beachfront areas of the Zona Sul (South Side) that attract the majority of tourists. All this was threatened.

Ventura discovered, however, that the real source of the problem did not emanate from the favelas but from the very guardians of the citadel. The drug traffic, which was and continues to be seen as the major source of the violence, has its source elsewhere, as suggested by Flávio Negão, then head of the local chapter of the Comando Vermelho,[5] whom Ventura interviewed: corrupt businessmen, government officials, and, most important, the police. Even the secretary of the Civil Police, Nilo Batista, admitted that there were vigilante groups among the police. A secret informer reported that the "entire police system — from the very top to the lowest orders, from the precinct head to the detective, from the commander to the officers — is infected by the virus of extortion," siphoning off a share of cache for resale (Ventura 1994: 67).

The demonization of the favelas thus functions in part as a smoke screen, a way to throw most observers off the scent. Benedita da Silva, the shantytown leader who ran unsuccessfully for mayor at the time of the arrastões — and the first black woman to be elected to the federal Senate in 1994, subsequently vice governor, governor of Rio de Janeiro, and since 2003 Secretary of Public

Welfare and Promotion in President Luiz Inácio "Lula" da Silva's new government—warned that the negative hype would lead to an invasion of the slums
by the military, "only to satisfy a frightened elite" (Brooke 1994a: 4). The print
and electronic media contributed to this situation, stoking the public's fears
and transforming the marvelous city into the very image of hell on their front
pages and lead stories. The tourist industry, the city's economic mainstay, took
a nosedive.[6]

The panic caused by the two arrastões in 1993 was to a large degree a media
construction, as I explained in the previous chapter. An important study of
representations of violence and citizenship among various social strata of Rio
youth confirms that the media distort the roots of violence, attributing it to
youth in the favelas and outlying shantytowns, particularly those who frequent
funk dances (Minayo et al. 1999).[7] The association with funk was then generalized to the favelas as a source of pathology. It is true, of course, that youth
who have no other source of income or sociality have had to turn to the drug
traffic, as in so many other cities of Latin America and the United States.[8]
But it is the very division of Rio into two (or several) parts—the "divided city"
of which Ventura writes—that enables middle- and upper-class residents and
most observers to overlook the class and racial factors that have transformed
the favelas into bastions of abjection. Fear, although not totally unjustified,
draws attention to violence among and by the underclasses and away from the
responsibility of political and economic leaders. The fears generated by this
quasi-hysterical reaction were used in the election against Benedita da Silva. As
a candidate for the Workers Party, she was committed to bettering the conditions of the have-nots, although elites perceived her to condone the supposed
lassitude and criminality of the favelados.

As in every other megalopolis, it is becoming increasingly difficult for Rio
to provide services to the citizenry. Not only has Rio's economy fared badly in
the past decade, with deleterious effects on the tax base, but the image of violence further eroded the tourist industry for much of the 1990s. Reductions in
health care and education as well as the federal government's increasing commitment to neoliberal policies have contributed to a shortage of resources. The
effects are felt most acutely by the poor, of course. The gap between elites and
underclasses has widened, straining the bonds that have given the city its quasi-
mythical aura of conviviality. One example of these strained relations is the
initial hysterical repudiation of funk music, quite the opposite of the conviviality experienced in samba. As explained in the previous chapter, 1980s funk
exploited aggressive sounds and lyrics, analogous to those of rap. Through

funk, lower-class youth expressed the desire to claim the social space denied to them. As Ventura suggests, beneath the myth of conviviality, there has been an abysmal divide historically between *asfalto* (the paved streets of the middle-class neighborhoods) and *morro* (the hillside shantytowns).

The premise of Ventura's book is that the violence in Rio is the result of a long-held policy of social apartheid: "In truth, during this century, from the reforms initiated by Pereira Passos up to the [urban beautification and modernization] plans of Agache and Doxiadis, the option [for the elites of the city] was always one of separation, if not a more outright segregation. The city was civilized and modernized by expelling its second-class citizens to the local hillsides and the outlying areas" (1994: 13).

An even stronger indictment of the violence and poverty in Rio was expressed by filmmaker Arnoldo Jabor in the aftermath of the arrastões and massacres. He begins by stating that "all the plans against violence and poverty in the city are vitiated by an ideology of exclusion" (1995: V10). His point is that it is too late to repair that exclusion, or, in any case, it is not up to the elites to carry out that work of reparation. The reason for this is that the "whitish" middle classes ("população branquinha") have not shown a real ability to live side by side with the darker denizens of the favelas and subúrbios. (This is actually the opposite of what most Carioca elites think because of the inescapable proximity of favelas and luxury highrises, a proximity that contrasts with the urban geography of the bunkered elite enclaves of São Paulo; T. Caldeira 1996b.) According to Jabor, what disturbs the elite of the Zona Sul is not the mugger: "It is the walker [*passeante*], the poor flâneur. Dark strollers in sandals and shorts fill the streets of the Zona Sul. They intuit the fear of the 'middle classes' and promenade with pride. White *cariocas* become indignant, as if only they were the true native city dwellers" (V10). Being seen and being heard—and just occupying space—is thus a way of asserting belonging, as was evident during the funkeiros' arrastões.

For Ventura, the separation of classes, which presumably enabled the good life of the Zona Sul in the Golden Years of the 1950s, turned out to be the nightmare of the middle and upper classes in the 1980s and 1990s. His point is that this policy of apartheid was not only disastrous from a humanitarian and moral point of view. It turned out to be a disaster from the standpoint of efficacy in administering the city. The policy, that is, boomeranged on the elites.

> The *barbarians* are the great source of malaise at this century's end. The [policy of] exclusion turned out to be the greatest social problem. There seemed to be

no problems so long as all we heard were the sounds of samba coming from the favelas. But now we also hear gunshots. This is not a civil war, as some mistakenly think, but a postmodern, economic war, which depends on the laws of the market as much as on the arts of war. We are dealing here with a kind of commerce. That is why there is no magic solution within sight. It's obvious that the "vanguards" — the drug traffickers who practice the barbarities — have to be destroyed in an implacable show of force. But to exterminate them is easier than to dismantle the economic circuit that sustains them and whose center of gravity — production and consumption — is not in the favelas themselves. (1994: 14)

The point of Ventura's book, however, is that the two parts of the city can be reconnected. It is for this purpose that he undertakes to become the flâneur of the barbarians' territory, to discover, or better yet to confirm, that they are no more barbarian than his own neighbors. But Ventura is not under any illusion that his book will in itself bring about a change; he expects it, rather, to be a contribution to the necessary mourning that the city must undertake, as well as publicity for the various related movements working to bring about a positive change in Rio.

Bridging the Two Halves

Rubem César Fernandes, coordinator of Viva Rio, has often used the metaphor of the bridge, "a bridge on which diverse sectors of the citizenry can meet with the private sector and the state" (personal interview, August 6, 1996). Hence the fundamental role of the media, for the bridge metaphor is simply an approximation to the idea, and practice, of communication.

> Viva Rio is working on the simple, elementary things that unite us all, despite our many differences of opinion, ideology, religion, and politics. What is fundamental is that we are all from Rio. This feeling of belonging to the same city is what characterizes Viva Rio's field of action. We are making a great effort to bring together the State government, the mayor's office, the federal forces, and the citizenry. Communication across classes is a long-standing tradition in Rio. The beach, carnival, religion, football. The links between the morro and the asfalto are quite strong. But these have been strained enormously in the past few years, giving way to a vast fear of each other. Hence, we are doing our utmost to reverse this tendency, to reestablish the lines of communication between the middle and poor classes in Rio. (qtd. in Barros 1994: 4)[9]

Who is this "we" to whom Fernandes refers? Officially, it is an NGO with a co-ordinating council of thirty-six, among them union officials, religious leaders, business executives, community organizers, newspaper and television directors, journalists, and other NGO leaders like Betinho and Fernandes.[10] In practice, this council facilitates — seeks contacts, helps raise funds, and so on — the many actions that Viva Rio sponsors, usually in partnership with other organizations from the communities as well as the business, government, and civil sectors. "It operates like a 'network of networks,' whereby a small permanent team makes possible activities throughout the Greater Metropolitan Area of Rio de Janeiro," reads an outreach flyer detailing the actions sponsored from October 1995 to June 1996 (*Ações do Viva Rio* 1996). It is active in over 350 favelas (Viva Rio 2001).

Fernandes is candid in pointing out that Viva Rio is a citizen action initiative and as such does not pretend to "represent society." It "represents only those people who support the movement and its ideas," which, he adds, "has the right to take action like any other group" ("Maia proíbe Viva Rio na prefeitura" 1995). In more theoretical writings on the character of the "third sector" in Latin America, Fernandes distinguishes such citizen action initiatives as Viva Rio from representative movements, whether trade unions, neighborhood associations, or even social movements. Citizen action initiatives "do not rely on the complex political game that is obligatory in representative systems in order to legitimize their decisions" (Fernandes 1994: 71). The point is maneuverability, to move others to action without the drag of inertia or the hindrance of red tape. This is the kind of action that the antiglobalization movement made notorious in Seattle and that Arquilla and Ronfeldt (2001) have characterized as networking. Such action can be of a symbolic or ritual nature. It is often sudden, to catch its targets off guard. It can be aimed to prod government to be more responsible. It may encourage people to value themselves as citizens and hence to demand service and access to decision making on issues that affect them. Or it can tackle more pragmatic problems, such as delivering clean water to a neighborhood, by means of partnerships between resident groups and local NGOs, private enterprise, and international NGO funding.

Among the more symbolic or ritual actions, the most notable are the transformation of the house in Vigário Geral whose eight occupants were murdered into a House of Peace, the observance of two minutes of silence throughout all of Rio as a commemoration of all victims of violence, and the demonstration to protest a spate of kidnappings (Reage Rio home page). As a result of the continual news coverage of the project to renovate the House of Peace, from

September to December 1993 the plight of the residents of Vigário Geral was brought into the homes of the middle and upper classes. Caio Ferraz, the young sociologist mentioned above, mobilized local residents, negotiated ownership of the house with the help of a donation from an evangelical church included in Viva Rio's coordinating council, had it renovated by architect Manoel Ribeiro, who also sat on the council, and planned a series of cultural and educational activities for the youths. The House of Peace, in partnership with Viva Rio and several pop stars, celebrities, and entertainment entrepreneurs, was pivotal in spreading funk, rap, and other forms of youth music and culture throughout the city, thus seeking to undo the demonization to which it had been subject on account of the arrastões. By such means, in Ribeiro's words, "the entirety of carioca society will come to know the true face of the favela, not the face of jailed or dead thugs, but that of the citizens" (qtd. in "Uma Casa da Paz em plena guerra" 1994).

Betinho also used the image of reversal to speak of the cultural action of the House of Peace and analogous initiatives that his own movement, Ação da Cidadania, sponsored. Fearful of the effects of a military occupation of the favelas, Betinho stated that "it will not be with tanks in the favelas or reinforced doors that cariocas will succeed in transforming the city. The invasion that the favela is asking for is an invasion of citizenship," a "cultural revolution" (qtd. in Gonçalves 1994: 78). This includes the public performance of the cultural resources of the favela, according to Fernandes, as another bridge toward a more inclusive Carioca culture (Rio Funk 1995). Cultural production and distribution are also conceived as a livelihood for favela youths. Although funk was initially seen by the middle classes and the authorities as a weapon used by poor youths to intrude into the social space of the elites, in the context of the initiative to renew the city with the participation of all this music movement has become a resource, much like the samba of yesteryear, for the integration of those sectors of society segregated from each other.

Clarice Pechman, an economist on the coordinating council of Viva Rio, advocated a social investment in funk as an alternative to the allure of narco-traffic. "In order to get the attention of these youths for other activities, we have to use already existing forms of organization. One option is provided by the funk dance clubs in Rio, that gather around 1.5 million youths. Today, this movement is known for its violence, but we have to support its positive side, which is greater. These dance clubs are an alternative form of livelihood and leisure for these youths . . . who can receive professional training in music, dance, video production, and the promotion of events. They may even become a tourist attraction to be included in the calendar of cultural activities" (qtd. in Faria 1994). This view is consensual, shared by the above-mentioned leaders as well as organizers from the favelas and subúrbios. Caio Ferraz created the Casa da Paz precisely to disseminate the solidarity values of community culture. Itamar Silva, a black intellectual and leader in the favela Santa Marta, concurs that cultural action is just as important as political activism and economic aid (Ventura 1994: 141). What or whose culture and how to lay bridges by means of its dissemination are examined below. At this point, I would like to turn to the second symbolic action mentioned above.

Imagine New York City, from the upper Bronx to Jamaica Bay, Brooklyn, and Staten Island, or Los Angeles from the San Fernando Valley to Long Beach, totally silent at midday, with people from every walk of life gathering in major intersections, dressed in white, holding hands, commemorating the victims of violence, and praying for peace. Neither the return of the Iran hostages to bowers of yellow ribbons, nor Martin Luther King Jr.'s funeral procession years before, nor even the quasi-analogous "Clean Up the Streets" efforts after the L.A. riots achieved a citywide stoppage of these proportions. From the beginning of September, right after the massacre in Vigário Geral, to December 17, Viva Rio's council members did not rest until they had contacted every newspaper, radio and television station, police precinct, school, university, political party, labor union, neighborhood association (including the famous samba schools), religious group, business organization, and tourist agency. Even outside the city, figures of symbolic importance such as then-president Itamar Franco observed the two minutes of silence. The observance of silence was a ritual, a demonstration by Cariocas to themselves that they had to confront violence, not militarily (although this subsequently became one controversial method), but by expressing community and solidarity.

There was considerable risk in compromising the future of such a citizen initiative on a chancy public ritual that could go awry if even one car tooted its horn, if a taxi driver refused to stop, or if the skeptics whistled or booed in mockery. Rio is, after all, the city of carnival, whose public ethos is ironic and iconoclastic, as Luiz Eduardo Soares, one of the organizers, observed: "Observing silence, dressed in white, under the rain, we were a hair's breadth, or a honk, from a fiasco, a ridiculous display" (Soares 1996: 261). Such moments can be awe-inspiring, which is what the newspapers and other commentators reported: harmony, solidarity, unanimity, and a belief in the future.[11] An astute political philosopher not often given to naïveté, even Soares exulted with wonderment: "I have never seen, as clearly, the intensity and scope of the coercive and affective power of the social, as Durkheim and Mauss might have said. Or the tremendous spectacularity of the spectacle of the masses, in Gabriel Tarde's words. The non-action of the others inhibited each and every individual. The contagious current of violence and the impression of violence had been operated in reverse. This proved that powerful social processes are reversible and travel rapidly, in opposite directions, along the same tracks" (1996: 261). At the same time, he paused before the temptation to give reality a "cosmetic makeover." The ritual would not, in itself, provide the cure for intractable problems like "white collar" corruption and narcotraffic. The enormity of the event did, however, instill feelings of solidarity that established a context in which Cariocas would remain open to social justice initiatives. As such, it stretched the span of time within which Viva Rio could find willing collaborators. In other words, it gave them a long running start, before indifference might settle back in place.

The Predicaments of Publicity

Like political campaigns, citizen initiatives like Viva Rio have their ups and downs. Much depends on their visibility, their newsworthiness, and the endurance of the coalitions they put together. By the time of Reage Rio (Rio Reacts), approximately one year after the other two actions, several important elements of the coalition were defecting. Chief among these were the governor and mayor and Caio Ferraz, the director of the Casa da Paz. Before delving into these defections, a brief account of this third symbolic action is in order.

Reage Rio was conceived as a citywide, multisector mobilization of the population of Rio to demonstrate against a spate of kidnappings. The most significant kidnapping for Viva Rio was that of the son of one of the coordinating council members, Eduardo Eugênio Gouvêa Vieira. Vieira had just taken over the leadership of the Federation of Rio de Janeiro Industries (FIRJAN); as a major spokesperson for the social responsibility of business, he sought to upgrade business's role in helping solve the city's problems. In Fernandes's opinion, Vieira's son was kidnapped in retaliation for his social protagonism and participation in Viva Rio.[12] Given that the son was kidnapped a couple of days after Vieira held a ceremony to launch FIRJAN's new role, Fernandes considered it a "coup against Viva Rio." This act placed renewed attention on violence, which had lost some of the newsworthiness that accompanied the arrastões in 1992 and the massacres in 1993. One of the reasons for its diminished prominence had to do with the recovery of business and the economy after Operação

Rio, the occupation of Rio by the armed forces at the end of 1994. Business-men and tourists felt that the city was safer, and even the majority of favela residents, despite several acts of arbitrary military action against poor youth,[13] expressed their support for this state of siege on narcotraffickers. The kidnap-ping was, therefore, a symbolic action, and not just for the ransom money. Taking this act as its cue, Reage Rio was planned as a series of peaceful street protests against kidnapping, but focused on schoolchildren. Organizational discussions opened the initiative to a protest to all kinds of violence.

The renewed newsworthiness, however, had its price. Both the governor, Marcello Alencar, and the mayor, César Maia, opted out. Political interest was clearly at stake. Neither of the two thought they could benefit from participa-tion. By some press accounts, the governor feared that Reage Rio would place demands on him that he would not be able to make good on.[14] He did not allow his staff to have dealings with anyone from the movement (Rubem César Fer-nandes, personal interview, August 6, 1996). The governor, according to these accounts, went so far as to accuse Caio Fábio (the evangelical minister who obtained the funds to purchase the Casa da Paz) of collaborating with narco-traffickers at the renovated Fábrica da Esperança (Factory of Hope) that he founded in the subúrbio of Acari to sponsor cultural and educational activi-ties, job training, and salaried employment for poor youth. Caio Fábio ended up fleeing to Miami.

Mayor César Maia's reversal regarding Viva Rio is explained by his advo-cacy of a military solution to the problem of violence in Rio, particularly in the favelas. He was especially critical of the defense of peace put forth by Reage Rio, labeling it a jazzed-up version of populist politician Brizola's politically inter-ested tolerance of *malandragem* (roguery).[15] This is the characteristic "tough on crime" discourse that overlooks questions of human rights but nevertheless wins votes. Two options were made available to the populace at this time: either the "bridge between the favelados and the middle class" laid down by Viva Rio, or a reversion to the social cleansing discourse that often threatens to prevail in Brazil. A workman who said he "would not bother with the protest" was re-ported to endorse "only one solution" to violence: more violence. "We have to get guns to defend ourselves" (Brooke 1994c: A3). Sensing a receptivity to his programs on the part of the middle *and* working classes, the mayor also forbade all municipal government officials from talking with representatives from Viva Rio ("Maia proíbe Viva Rio na prefeitura" 1995).

The cracks in the coalition were also evident in the divergent press coverage. The newspaper directors within the Viva Rio coalition more or less guaranteed

Reage Rio favorable coverage. However, other papers, reflecting the biases of the governor and the mayor or widely read papers like the Folha de São Paulo from out of town, rained on the initiative's optimistic expectations. Betinho, Caio Fábio, and Rubem César Fernandes had projected 1 million participants. The estimates varied from 60,000 (according to the military police) to 100,000 (media reports) and 150,000 (a Workers Party count), which Betinho attempted to downplay by arguing that due to the rain, each demonstrator actually counted as ten ("Passeata do Reage Rio" 1995). Not only were the numbers far from the goal, but the crowd was reported to be composed mostly of middle-class people. Consequently, reports seemed to bear out the criticisms leveled at the initiative. From the beginning, critics took to calling it "Reage Rico" (The Rich React), pointing up a fracture in the coalition between rich and poor that Viva Rio avowed (Molica 1995: section 3: 1). One reporter went so far as to suggest that NGOs come in all varieties to serve the poor, but are staffed by the middle class, who therefore make their living parasitically. "There are NGOs for all tastes, even one working in behalf of plumbers. They give the impression of a top heavy structure without a base. That is our tradition" (Filho 1995: 1–2).

This was precisely Caio Ferraz's argument. What had started as a reaction against the social cleansing of the poor ended up, he thought, as a public display of the elite's concern for security. He coined the term "Reage Rico" and accused Viva Rio of abandoning its advocacy on behalf of the poor. He accused Fernandes of allying with him and the residents of Vigário Geral out of interest and even suggested that Fernandes, as treasurer of the Casa da Paz, had extorted the funds for its activities ("Caio Ferraz diz que Reage Rico é elitista" 1995). Rather than boycott the event, Ferraz and his associates decided to wear blue instead of white and to walk sideways to convey the point that the poor are "always pushed to the side." Fernandes responded sympathetically to Caio's accusations and pointed out that he was under great stress, having received death threats (from the military police; "Rubem César prefere evitar discussão" 1995). Caio Ferraz, like Caio Fábio, ended up fleeing to the United States.[16]

The Work of Citizen Action Initiatives

Viva Rio, like the Ação da Cidadania, bet on media coverage to get leverage in its campaigns. This strategy worked on many occasions. But it also backfired at times, as in Reage Rio, belying the marketing approach that the founders of IBASE brought with them from the United States (Guedes 1996). For Betinho, "the media had a fundamental role in the Ação da Cidadania; it was a strategic policy from the beginning and it is still the instrument for the revitalization of the movement" ("Tres linhas estratégicas" 1995). As Viva Rio's newsworthiness waned, many people began to think that the initiative was dying out. When asked about this, Fernandes explained that Viva Rio was actually carrying out more programs than ever before, all of them in partnership with business, neighborhood organizations, churches, other NGOs, and hybrid welfare organizations like Comunidade Solidária, which has government members on its board. Consequently, newsworthiness is not an accurate gauge of activity, an observation that runs counter to new kinds of action initiatives like ACT UP in the United States and elsewhere (Aronowitz 1996). Nor does Viva Rio entice the media by means of in-your-face, confrontational actions characteristic of ACT UP and other radical groups. In any case, even these radical strategies do not always find receptivity in the media.

Viva Rio has over five hundred projects in over 350 favelas. These projects are focused on five areas: public security and human rights, education, community development, sports, and the environment. All projects produce actions or other results in accordance with simple and clear methods that enable them to be reproduced; they are formulated in relation to public demands and are thus amenable to the generation of public policies; they come into being through partnerships that straddle public agencies, private enterprise, and third-sector organizations; they strengthen civil society by working from a base in neighborhood and favela associations. Given that most schools in favelas and subúrbios do not provide a viable education that leads to employment or entry into college, Viva Rio has coordinated special courses for over fifty thousand students at the primary and secondary levels. Moreover, it has augmented education with computer and Internet training for over twenty-five thousand low-income students in its Informatics Clubs (Vargas 2001). Viva Rio even has its own portal, with news and feature articles on such issues as rights, antiracism, social movements, and youth music and culture of interest primarily to low-income communities (Vivafavela.com). In matters of security, Viva Rio, in partnership with the state government of Rio de Janeiro, negotiated and oversaw the destruction of over one hundred thousand weapons, the largest such act in world history.[17] As for citizenship rights, it attended, at its Balcão de Direitos (Rights Service Center), over fifteen thousand cases of rights violations in eight favelas. As part of community development, Viva Rio has provided R$12 million in credit to seven thousand small businesses and has set up credit and loan establishments in favelas throughout the city (Viva Rio

2001). Viva Rio is involved in hundreds of other activities (see Viva Rio home page and previous reports).[18]

Fernandes has emphasized that Viva Rio is dedicated exclusively to public service, especially of three kinds at present: creating a bridge between slum dwellers and the middle classes at the neighborhood level, connecting human rights and public security issues, and strengthening community development. Its greatest commitments are in the favelas and outlying suburbs. Most of the projects listed above and in note 18 are situated there. Over the years, Viva Rio has also upgraded the professional character of these projects, particularly those in the medium to long range. But rather than bring in corps of professionals from outside poor neighborhoods, Viva Rio has striven to help local residents themselves professionalize. This is the reason for raising credit for small businesses and for spearheading partnerships to develop new and better housing.

All of this has had to be done largely without the collaboration of the government. Originally, the coordinators wanted government involvement, despite their desire to stay out of politics. However, due to the coalitional fractures mentioned above, Viva Rio has changed course. This decision represents a step backward from the position taken at the inception of both Viva Rio and the Ação da Cidadania. Indeed, Betinho resigned in May 1996 from Comunidade Solidária because he objected to government officials—the director, Ruth Cardoso, is the wife of former President Fernando Henrique Cardoso—sitting on its board (Campos 1996). He also criticized what he considered to be meager results—six hundred thousand jobs—of the US$20 billion invested.

Mediating Citizenship and Values

Asked whether he conceived Viva Rio and Ação da Cidadania as charity organizations, Fernandes wavered. Though not exactly charitable organizations, these initiatives do not reject the notion of charity. Instead, they try to bridge it—along with other similar notions like solidarity, gift giving, pity, and compassion—with the value of citizen responsibility and the development of expertise. In this way, they achieve two results: they mediate among diverse sectors of civil society so they can meet and work together, and they encourage the development of professionalism. Betinho's and Fernandes's efforts are aimed at creating multiplier effects in third-sector initiatives. This means working with the "fluid language of values," developing the "art of translation" of those values "beyond cosmopolitan circuits" where rights and other conceptual categories can be too abstract. More than publicity, which is what boomeranged on Viva Rio on some occasions, what Fernandes and Betinho mean by communication is developing the ability to bring the "individualistic language of rights" into contact with "other principles that regulate social life." To this end, they advocate becoming "polyglots of sociability" (Fernandes 1994: 171).

Citizenship initiatives imply a different role from the ones traditionally ascribed to intellectuals, on the one hand, and social movements (grassroots or otherwise), reformers, and revolutionaries, on the other. The former seek to generate views of the world, the latter to change social structures. Viva Rio and Ação da Cidadania include these in their agendas, but they do not attempt to achieve these worldviews and changes directly. Rather, their strategy is to bring people together so that they can negotiate their differences and find common ground, that is, set the parameters for coordinating social change.

> Such coordination, to have effective receptivity in plural societies, must have the ability to engage with a multiplicity of languages, symbolic codes, and social and cultural forms. How to relate [citizenship, i.e., participation] to the hierarchies based on kinship, to different upbringing and ethnic backgrounds, to respect for one's elders, to the protection one expects from one's superiors, to informal networks of mutual aid, to motherhood, to the cult of saints, to witchcraft, to mediumship, to charismatic gifts? These are the questions Third Sector activists must face if they really mean to move beyond Westernized social circuits. And there are no immediate answers to such questions. They are typically contextual, varying according to the specific partners involved in a communication, the issues in question, the dynamics in operation. (Fernandes 1994: 171)

Afro Reggae

Fernandes could have been referring to José Júnior, director of the Grupo Cultural Afro Reggae (GCAR), when he coined the expression *polyglots of sociability*. He was a former petty participant in the narcotraffic economy and himself a favela resident who became a funk DJ and saw the potential to draw youth away from the drug trade, virtually the only source of employment for poor youth. Júnior organized a series of dance parties, which eventually became the spawning ground of Afro Reggae. Because the police backlash after the arrastões led to the closing of many funk clubs, DJs and black movement activists began to promote reggae parties to get around the restrictions. Júnior's first "Rasta

Reggae Dancing" party in October 1992 "brought together large sectors not only of the black movement, but also political parties, the women's movement, ecologists, human rights activists, and union leaders . . . [including] many non-initiates in the so-called organized civil society" (R. Santos 1996: 6). Júnior realized that these parties "could finance GCAR and also serve as an apt site for disseminating a 'pedagogy of pleasure' " (Roque 2000: 7).

The massacre in Vigário Geral provided Júnior with a mission not to change youth culture but to use music and dance to attract youth to a "new ethical and moral field"; rather than claim the moral high ground he sought to instill recognition and affirmation of these youths' "beauty and positivity" (Roque 2000: 11). In the spirit of Viva Rio and Caio Ferraz's House of Peace, Júnior sought to institutionalize GCAR as an NGO to expand activities from cultural self-esteem to the provision of social services. To do this he needed support, which he got from Fernandes and by forming a dense network of connections with local and international NGOs, human rights organizations, politicians, newspaper reporters, writers, academics, and entertainment celebrities. At the heart of Júnior's initiative was the idea that music, as the practice that best characterizes fusion or sampling, could serve as the platform on which favela youth would be able to dialogue with their own community and the rest of society. Although he may not have thought of it at first, the musical practice of Afro Reggae was to become the polyglossia of sociability that he imparted to these youths.

The basic principle of their work is embodied in the practice of *batidania*, a portmanteau neologism that suggests that *cidadania* or citizenship dwells in the *batida* (beat) and *batucada* (music and rhythm of Afro-Brazilian dance) of favela youth who were blamed for the wave of arrastões. A community's resistance and survival don't always come "spontaneously," according to Júnior; "specific initiatives have to be devised for that purpose" (Zanetti 2000: 15). Afro Reggae has extended this consciousness-raising activity to concrete civic action in health, AIDS awareness, human rights, and education, particularly training for a range of jobs in the service and entertainment sectors (percussion, dance, capoeira).

Afro Reggae's expansion to other poor communities (Parada de Lucas, Cantagalo, Cidade de Deus), its national and international fundraising campaigns, and its plans to increase the number of international performances of its various bands—Afro Reggae, Banda Afro Reggae II, Afro Lata (10–15 years old), Afro Samba (7–12 years old)—which produce income for its civic projects, has led them to prioritize their Communications Program, which links them to "an almost infinite network of people" who receive their newspapers and see their TV appearances and with whom they interact by email, the radio program *Baticum* (a partnership with the Centro de Tecnologia Educacional da Universidade do Estado do Rio de Janeiro and transmitted by the Community Radio Bicuda in Vila da Penha), the AFRONET listserv, and the Internet. As in the antiglobalization movement, the Internet is increasing Afro Reggae's ability to establish networks of articulations that extend from the *barrio* to the largest NGOs and foundations from the United States (e.g., Ford Foundation) and Europe (e.g., Médécins sans frontières). GCAR is also linked to municipal, state, national, and transnational agencies (from the local tourist board to UNESCO). In Rio itself, Afro Reggae is linked to IBASE, the bank Caixa Econômica Federal, the citizen action initiative Viva Rio, Ceap (Center for the Articulation of Marginalized Populations), and many other NGOs, corporations, and grassroots groups. The same is observable at the national level, in partnerships, for example, with Comunidade Solidária, a semigovernmental agency serving the needs of the poor. And now, like the Zapatistas, Afro Reggae has representatives in Brussels, New York, Stanford, France, and fifteen other cities in Brazil.

Afro Reggae's partnerships extend, of course, to other musical groups and cultural initiatives on television and in video. They had the support of television music host Regina Casé and the singer Caetano Veloso early on (1994)[19] and subsequently have networked and collaborated with groups, singers, and rappers like Olodum, Fernanda Abreu, Gabriel O Pensador, João Bosco, Milton Nascimento, MV Bill, and Cidade Negra. The band opened shows for some of the most popular artists: Marcelo D2, Thaide & DJ Hum, and Câmbio Negro in Hip Hop Pelo Rio; Ilê Ayê, Olodum, and Daniela Mercury in the Show das ONGs or Show of the NGOs; and Rock in Rio. GCAR's relationship with the group O Rappa is quite special; the latter invited GCAR performer Paulo to apprentice and eventually form part of the band. When he returned to Afro Reggae, he was able to help the group professionalize, a necessity for raising funds not only for their own maintenance but also for their civic activities.

Revenues come mostly from spectacles in which they combine music, dance, capoeira, circus acts, and theater; they have taken these shows all over Brazil and various cities throughout the world, most recently in France, Germany, Holland, and England. They are also planning shows in Washington, D.C., and New York. Last year, under the musical direction of Caetano Veloso, Afro Reggae recorded the CD *Nova Cara* with a major label, Universal Records. To hold onto their nonprofit status as an NGO and also to manage their income-producing activities, GCAR created a parallel for-profit corporation, Afro Reggae Produções Artísticas, which is now their own production company.

Nova Cara (New face [of the favela]) can be seen as the autobiography of the favela Vigário Geral and a healing act of mourning. The band Afro Reggae sonorously reenacts the war between narcotraffickers and police, the demise of so many youth, the death of the twenty-one residents, and the clamoring for peace and justice. In "Poesia Orgânica" (Organic poetry), the singers blame the police and apartheid for the massacre of the twenty-one innocents and denounce the suspicion with which black youth are held by the middle classes of Rio's Zona Sul. In this cut, the singer claims a more active role beyond denunciation, that of a reporter who narrates his own protagonism in leading other youth to a better life, yet bringing it all back to the neighborhood. In "Conflitos Urbanos" (Urban conflicts) the singer stakes out a new "struggle for dignity" against the subordination and stereotypes to which he and other favelados are subjected. "Capa de Revista" (Magazine cover) identifies that new face (that new cover) with the new style of urban black youth:

É uma nova era	It's the new era
esse é o novo estilo	it's the new style
de uma galera	of a new gang
que ninguém segura	that no one controls
dança, capoeira	dance, capoeira
tambores em fúria	drums in frenzy
funk, hip-hop,	funk, hip-hop
samba e percussão	samba and percussion
Dread e adrenalina	Dread[s] and adrenaline
pagode na esquina	pagode on the corner
www ponto emoção	*www dot* emotion
tudo aqui é brother	everything here is brother
tudo é sangue bom	everything my man
. . . .	. . . .
Tudo vai mudar, vai mudar	everything is going to change, to change
vai mudar	to change

The lyrics reproduce the fusion of sounds and styles that characterizes the articulations that put Afro Reggae at the center of a network of groups and individuals working to change their circumstances. If nothing else, we might say that Afro Reggae produces a culture of change, specifically, in music and

1. Cover for Afro Reggae's CD with Universal (2002).

2. Afro Reggae on roof of a house in Vigário Geral. Photo by Ierê Ferreira.

3 and 4. Afro Reggae, posed on stage.
Photos by Ierê Ferreira.

5. José Júnior, Afro Reggae coordinator, and Altair, Afro Reggae member, walking through Vigário Geral with Caetano Veloso. Photo by Ierê Ferreira.

spectacle oriented both to attract youth and to entertain the local and foreign middle classes who are their accomplices. In "Som de V.G." (Sound of Vigário Geral), that struggle is identified with the new sound/new face of the favela, which brings justice via culture.

É através da música e da cultura	Through music and culture
está aqui mais um movimento	this is one more movement
que luta em prol da paz, pode crê	that struggles for peace, believe it
Pow, pow, pow, pow	bang, bang, bang, bang
taí o meu recado, o recado de Vigário Geral	that's my message, message from Vigário Geral

The NGOization of Culture

According to the video *Batidania: Power in the Beat* (1998) on Afro Reggae, music and performance are acts of citizenship because they present a different portrayal of poor black youth and because it is an intervention into public spheres, or better yet, a way of opening them up. Afro Reggae takes its shows and messages to television with great frequency, appearing on talk shows, variety shows, music specials, and the like. One of their greatest concerns is to counter the stereotypes of criminality and victimhood. Nevertheless, another stereotype is reinforced: black kids from the favela are shown as inherently musical, moving to the batucada, only now not for the ritual purposes of Afro-Brazilian religions like candomblé but to demonstrate their self-esteem. It might be said that they are caught in a double bind of representation. On the one hand, they repudiate the culture of poverty, that is, the social pathology associated with urban poverty; on the other hand, they invoke the commonplace of "poor but dignified" people making community. The latter is the image they disseminate on TV shows and to foundations and other institutions.

Batidania is a promotional tool that seems tailor-made to present to NGOs, foundations, and government agencies that seek to empower grassroots groups. The audiovisual language is the standard third-sector fare. The video begins with black children beating drums, while a voice-over tells us that "their culture" keeps them from the drug trade and contributes to changing stereotypes. The video, like the CD, is a kind of group Bildungsroman, beginning with the massacre in Vigário Geral and concluding with the success of Afro Reggae not only as a music and performance group but also in wooing kids away from criminality. A range of social workers and NGO personnel who collaborate with Afro Reggae appear, giving testimony on the depth of the problem and the success of the group in bettering circumstances. They all reiterate the basic premise that culture is empowerment. We might speculate that these are the images with which foundations that promote cultural citizenship are likely to adorn their annual reports.[20]

Afro Reggae and other initiatives like it might be seen as co-optable and criticized on that basis. This is something on which they have reflected in print. Aware of the dangers of putting all the eggs of their activism in the basket of civil society, they warn of the "dilemma in which all nongovernmental organizations find themselves. On the one hand, they help construct the process of civil society and democratization, which is laudable ... On the other hand, however, they run the risk of facilitating the State's retreat from social programs. Consequently, NGOs should not aim to take over State functions. The ideal is to establish an interface between civil society and the government" ("Afro Reggae vira tese de mestrado" 1997). This is not a language learned spontaneously in popular mobilization, but is part and parcel of the activities of the networks brought together by the likes of the Citizen Action Initiative against Hunger and Poverty and Viva Rio. Of course, ventriloquizing NGOspeak as a means to gaining support is not in and of itself the problem.

The problem, to my mind, is not co-optation, for everyone in the network of articulations briefly described (and certainly we as academics) must negotiate. My concern is that cultural practice runs the risk of responding to performative injunctions that leave little space for experiences that do not fit an NGOized depiction of development, worth, and self-esteem. Cultural production and distribution become a way to keep favela youth from "making trouble"; they provide a livelihood for some, and even, according to some NGO and government planners, enable them to take advantage of the emerging favela tourism, which extends the "family of man" to the ghetto (Favela Tour). I imagine that José Júnior would not object to these characterizations, but instead see them as the means by which urban youth can become a recognizable part of the city and partake in some modest way of its assets in a context in which government social services have dwindled and never really worked well in any case, especially for the racialized poor. They thus become performers of individual or collective selves that are at least partly scripted to provide the life and spice and, indeed, the salve of the city.

Poor populations, often immigrants and minorities, are implicated in the maintenance and reproduction of the urban middle classes. Writing about the new economy, Manuel Castells (2000) has argued that "alongside technological innovation there has mushroomed an extraordinary urban activity . . . fortifying the social fabric of bars, restaurants, chance encounters on the street, etc. that give life to a place." Rio de Janeiro is the site of a very special cultural economy, and Afro Reggae has found a way to give life and partake of it as well in the process. If one is left asking what there is to that life aside from spectacle and performativity, I suggest focusing on the community-building activities undertaken by Afro Reggae. Although they may depend on the media and markets, this is not an exclusive dependence. Moreover, the networks of articulations in which they operate include NGOs and international agencies like UNESCO that, despite promoting the instrumentalization of culture, nevertheless also promote social justice.

In several presentations on Afro Reggae and similar groups, skeptical listeners have remarked that NGOizaton and consumer-media politics, convergent in the lyrics of the *Nova Cara* CD, simply integrate a few such groups at the expense of the vast majority. This is inevitably the case. But it must be said that Afro Reggae also condemns class privilege, racism, sexism, homophobia, and political corruption. That these protests have become part of the genre that is consumed in pop music—most rap in Brazil, for example, is a form of social protest, as in the work of 1998 MTV award winners Racionais MC—should not become the reason for condemnation but a call for reflection on the ways politics takes place in urban, consumer-mediated societies. Asked about the depoliticizing risks of absorption by the entertainment industry, a DJ writing in the journal *Afro Reggae* responded that the wager is to dance with the devil and not be burned. He recognizes that the industry "capitalizes on some aspects of black culture, while relegating others" (DJ T.R. 2000: 4–6). The trick is to intelligently take advantage of the exposure, for example on MTV, all the while making sure to promote those artists who can get their message across (2000: 5). There are even music industry executives who have been won over to the cause of culture in the service of social justice. This is the case of André Midani, until recently president of International Music at Time Warner. He returned to Rio after twelve years in New York to use his executive skills in raising Viva Rio's fundraising capacities. He also decided to promote quality musicians who are bringing something new and vibrant to the cultural scene. He recognizes that Afro Reggae's work helps to bridge the gap between the middle classes and the favelados and also contributes to self-esteem in the favela (Midani 2002). Revolution this is not; but Afro Reggae is building community and advancing a range of causes that will get further exposure among the youth with whom they work.

To the degree that Afro Reggae networks with institutions that include the state and enterprise, one may question their effective opposition to domination, as their participation in these networks may be characterized as absorption into top-down initiatives. Curiously, this interpretation would return to invisibility the kind of agency that, in my view, Afro Reggae skillfully practices. Among cultural leftists, agency—the ability to take up action—is usually interpreted, following the likes of James C. Scott (1985, 1990), as the opposition and resistance of the weak against top-down initiatives. However, it should be clear that there usually is no unilateral action. Agency in this sense is a faulty concept. We might say the same about agency that Bakhtin said about language: it is never wholly one's own. One has to appropriate it by rearticulating others' voices. Agency succeeds to the degree that an individual or a group can make its own the multiplicity of venues through which initiative, action, policy, and so on are negotiated. But orchestration and negotiation require standing one's ground in the face of co-optation. And rather than a frontal action against a single source of oppression, it requires working in a range of groups and organizations, working with and mediating to help provide interfaces among diverse agendas, say those of a neighborhood group vis-à-vis a church, a local government, a national or regional NGO, and international foundations. This, again, is what Fernandes meant to communicate with the phrase "polyglots of sociability."

In one of the cuts on their CD *Iguais sobrepondo iguais* (Like dominating like), Afro Reggae denounces those who hold power, a drug just as devastating as those trafficked by drug dealers who, despite false romanticization as Robin Hoods, lead favela youth to addiction and death. The solution? "You can count/on culture/it's the main instrument/for change." They thus counterpose a civil society grounded in cultural citizenship to the savage society above and below. But civil society increasingly looks like an alibi for neoliberalism and provides the terrain in which it takes root. In its current incarnation, civil society has a double origin: in neoliberalism's need for stability and political legitimation, and in grassroots organization for the sake of survival in the face of structural adjustment. These are the contradictory conditions under which civil society is fostered: the state controls third-sector organizations, the markets manage citizens-as-consumers, and both of these attempt to have their way in Certeauian fashion. Culture has become the slippery terrain on which change is sought. But it is on that very terrain that Afro Reggae has had its successes, claiming the territory of their neighborhoods from both the police and narcotraffickers. This too requires that their activism operate on the level of spectacle, competing with and appearing on the stages in which value circulates.

Afro Reggae is not alone, of course, in making recourse to culture and media worthiness to promote their causes. As Gohn explains, because "new technologies have enabled the globalization of information and communication, the internal practices of social movements have been altered in the 1990s. The result is that the style of communication and the strategy of the leaders of these movements are transformed as they adjust to the requirements of the new technological model" (2000: 23). For example, the marches of the Movimento dos Sem Terra (Movement of the Landless, MST), like those of the Zapatistas, have received wide media coverage. This coverage in turn has had an impact on the way the landless choreograph their marches and the way they present themselves visually (bright red scarves, etc.) as a means to garner visibility and, concomitantly, solidarity in Brazil and abroad. But mediated action also has its limits, which are evident in Viva Rio and in the failure of MST demands that the World Bank abandon its policy of "enforcing payment for lands bought and credits received via subsidy" (Gohn 2000: 157). Moreover, the celebrity that media coverage produced led to "overestimation of the power of the media" (158). Ultimately, Gohn concludes, change requires a strong political culture as well as a cultural politics of visibility. Although Afro Reggae does not generally engage in traditional politicking, the network of articulations they have achieved does enable the linkages between their civil or citizen action and concrete results. These results are far from changing the "real relations of production" and accumulation, but they are greater than what populist politicians, narcotraffickers, or NGOs have brought to the favela. The cultural activists of Afro Reggae have at least positioned themselves pivotally in their networks and in the public spheres. Rather than belittle such achievements by assuming that they simply make it easier for elites to wax enthusiastic about bootstrap efforts while holding onto their purses, more attention should be given to Afro Reggae's insistence, in collaboration with their partners, that governments and NGOs aim to change social relations.

As I was revising the final draft of this book, I received a posting from Afro Reggae's Conexões Urbanas (Urban Connections) listserv. "*Os Pingos nos 'Is'*" (Dotting the i's) is a response to two journalists who criticized the group for jumping on the modish bandwagon of culture "for the sake of the social." Aside from pointing out that this bandwagon was rolled out by Afro Reggae itself, who were by no means *following* a fashion, they stressed that although the artist's responsibility should be to artistic quality, however that is defined, that should not imply that those who, like Afro Reggae themselves, wield that art for bettering social circumstances should be disqualified. Responding to the journalists' suggestion that there is now a "dictatorship of the social," Afro Reggae wrote: "We disagree. Dictatorship is social exclusion, violence in the favelas, hunger, lack of hospitals and schools and so many other issues that never go out of style. This is not a reality that we have chosen; it has been imposed on us for centuries. The social was not. Those of us who believe in the social basically want to change that reality. You do that if you want to; it's your choice. Even if it seems *demodé*" (July 20, 2002).

Consumption and Citizenship?

Consuming Identities

In a 1993 essay that appeared in *Harper's* magazine, David Rieff launched an attack on multiculturalism, arguing that it was a bedfellow of consumer capitalism: "The collapse of borders, far from being the liberating event that the academic multiculturalists have envisaged, has brought about the multiculturalism of the market, not the multiculturalism of justice." Rieff berates multiculturalists for having turned their backs "on what is valuable about Marxist theory" and gives words of comfort to conservatives who worry that multiculturalism is a bid for power when it is nothing short of "a demand for inclusion, for a piece of the capitalist pie" (1993: 70). He also observes that, whereas on the apparent upside, capitalism is "increasingly eager to let in women, blacks, gays, and any other marginalized groups," for they "legitimize whole new areas of consumerism" (64), on the downside, capitalism is selling short everyone but the professional-managerial class as it increases its profits at the expense of the working class through the elimination or at best reduction of wages and health benefits. The social contract is being replaced with a conservative contract on society which the multiculturalists, in all their zeal for bringing down the Western canon, overlook. Capitalism, he argues, is already way ahead of multiculturalists on this count, having at best a "vestigial or sentimental interest in Western civilization, as it is roughly understood by campus radicals and conservatives alike" (69). Instead, it makes profit on the new wares of diversity.

Rieff is disingenuous. His essay no doubt was meant to resonate with 1960s leftists like Todd Gitlin, who bemoan the multicultural turn in activism, and conservatives who fear that multiculturalism actually brings about change. But it is not altogether clear that Rieff invokes Marxism because he believes in any of its premises. This seems to be his cocky way of getting in his digs at the "cultural left." I sense that, in the tradition of his mother (Susan Sontag) and other "public intellectuals" who have not allowed themselves to be "prostituted" by the "easy perks" of academia (Jacoby 1987), "earning" their way (as John Houseman used to advertise) by hard and disinterested critique instead of identity grandstanding, he harbors a resentment at the little attention given those who, like him, have little appeal in an age in which cultural studies and multiculturalism have a better market share.

On the other hand, I think Rieff is mostly correct. During the past two decades, multiculturalism grew exponentially from contestatory, alternative stances to the point today when no program in education would dispense with it and when even the U.S. State Department makes the diversity characteristic of multiculturalism a *requirement* for those who seek grants from the Bureau of Educational and Cultural Affairs. The Bureau's "Proposal Submission Instructions" (2001) states, "Pursuant to the Bureau's authorizing legislation, programs must . . . be . . . representative of the diversity of American political, social, and cultural life. 'Diversity' should be interpreted in the broadest sense and encompass differences including but not limited to ethnicity, race, gender, religion, geographic location, socio-economic status, and physical challenges."

That said, however, the fact that circumstances have not gotten better for minorities in the past twenty years is not a consequence of multiculturalism, nor is it the fault of progressives who just can't see that, as Rieff alleges, they are simply buying into capitalism. To begin with, multiculturalists are not and have never been in power, no matter what Rieff might think about their predominance in the academy. The downward slide, of course, is largely attributable to a well-organized Republican strategy. It is also due to the failed Democratic administration that moved rightward in deeds while it dressed up its windows with a few good intentions. On that count, George W. Bush has done even "better," putting together a much more "diverse" cabinet, if by diversity one thinks in the limited terms of race and gender. The united colors of the Bush administration may be varied, but its politics is homogeneously conservative.

I agree that there is a rapprochement between consumer capitalism and multiculturalism, which I address in this chapter, but the argument needs to be made differently, without responding to the casting call of the culture wars, as explained in chapter 2. It is not so much that multiculturalists are fools who cannot see that they are purchasing revolution in the shopping mall. Rather, I think they believe that it is possible to play the game of citizenship through the medium of consumption, not only of commodities but, more important, of representations. Underlying this politics of consumption is the assumption that there is an adequate rule of law. The drawback is that, for the reasons given in chapter 2, *performative force* (a term I prefer over the "society of the spectacle") is to a good degree overdetermined and capitalized on by the media and the market, or it circumscribes the beneficiaries of inclusion in compensatory networks for the alternative distribution of value (in parts of the academy, the art world, and the corporate sector), as I explain in chapter 8. This latter "marginalized" space is an eminently capitalizable one; like organic farming, it has its alternative forms of niche marketing in museum exhibitions and journals of cultural criticism.

Citizenship is about membership and participation, but it is overdetermined in complex ways that mitigate claims to "empowerment," particularly those carried out in the domain of representation. Drawing on Foucault's notion of governmentality, by which he means the channeling of individuals' conduct through the strategies for "disposing of things" for the welfare of society (1982: 221; 1991: 95–103), we might say that strategies and policies for inclusion are an exercise of power by which institutions construe women, "people of color," and gays and lesbians (the "others"). By invoking the notion of governmentality I do not mean to suggest that there aren't processes of exclusion and subordination. Rather, my argument is that these processes involve the production and channeling of representations that are managed by power brokers.

Barbara Cruikshank gives a similar analysis of the ways progressive organizers, to empower the poor during the War on Poverty, ended up "help[ing] to invent and operationalize new means for acting upon the subjectivities of the poor" (1994: 48). The "politics of representation" is the new means by which multiculturalists are brokering citizenship, and in the process "structuring the field of action" (Foucault 1991), or access. But access to what? To a compensatory network for an alternative distribution of value? And why not act, instead, to end this structuring of the field of action into a mainstream and its alternatives?

Like Cruikshank's critique of empowerment, which mobilized the poor to constitute themselves as such, as a "group with interests and powers" into which the government could then intervene (1994: 52), my critique of multiculturalism focuses on the brokering role that contributes to the consolidation of groups that can be capitalized on by academic, art, media, and market institutions. Of course, there may be no getting around this, especially in the United States. But it is incumbent upon the brokers to confront their own complicity in governmentality. As I argued in chapter 2, this complicity is evident in the way conservatives and cultural leftists are locked into a reciprocal fantasy, with the right presumably seeking to reimpose a common culture and the left brokering the validation and enfranchisement of diversity. Often, this structure is characterized in the crudest stereotypical terms: the white guys versus the "others." Part of the problem is that "both sides" are invested in this confrontation, draw their energies from it, like the NEA Four, whose value within alternative performance circuits increased, Antaeus-like, each time Jesse Helms became outraged. On the other hand, whenever an NEA-funded artist programmatically breached the norms of conviviality, Helms's political capital hit a new high. The NEA Four and their apologists argued that they were simply exercising their artistic freedom; Helms, that public decency should not be violated by the pornographic or otherwise offensive use of public funds. Ultimately, they needed each other. Together they coconstructed the field of action.

For the right, multiculturalism espouses a kind of libertinism, one already reviled by Christopher Lasch (1978) before the term had even gained currency. According to Lasch, the decline of conventional authority brought about by the 1960s and 1970s activism of youth, women, and gays and lesbians, as well as the dependency and erosion of family life, particularly that of blacks, promoted by the "paternalistic" welfare state, converged in the emergence of a "culture of narcissism." Nostalgic for the fading double ethic of freedom and responsibility, Lasch mourned the degeneration of the citizen and the worker. The hegemony of the professional-managerial class (in business as well as in government) and the dominance of market and media, which subsumed knowledge and information into advertising and spectacle, constituted, for him, a "historical development that turned the citizen into a client and the worker from a producer into a consumer" (235). Compared to the conservatives of the 1990s, Lasch at least had the openness of mind to recognize the degree to which the very capitalism that made the United States an economic power was in part accountable (in the cultural field) for its supposed decline. This is a premise that was forgotten by most on the right and left in the 1980s and 1990s. The right, for example, has attempted to attenuate through cultural, especially religious, conservatism the innovations wrought by "technical progress, capitalist growth and rational administration" as if its own policies did not contribute to the unleashing of consumer-based cultural changes (Habermas 1981: 13). The multicultural left, on the other hand, has generally overlooked the overdetermination of "contestatory" identities by the media, the market, and government bureaucracies; it has staked its future on the struggles of groups whose identities correspond at least in part to the imaginary of diversity projected by consumer culture.

The *backlash* against affirmative action, against the extension of the rights of the so-called new immigrants, and against the reforms in public culture advocated by women, racial minorities, and gays and lesbians constituted a necessary condition for the turn to a politics of interpretability and representation in the 1980s and 1990s. This is a politics, moreover, that signals the transformation from what was traditionally deemed properly political to cultural mediation. The politics of representation seeks to transform institutions not only by means of inclusion but also by the images and discourses generated by them. As such, this politics locates citizenship issues within the media of representation, asking not *who* count as citizens but *how* they are construed; not *what* their rights and duties are, but how these are *interpreted*; not *what* the channels of participation in opinion formation and decision making are but *by what tactics* they can be intervened on and turned around to the interests of the subordinated. New interventions that challenge both right and Gitlin-like left positions on multiculturalism and identity suggest that consumer capitalism has much to do with the ongoing redefinition of citizenship, a contradictory process that, though not a cause for celebration, is not to be lamented either.

Citizenship

The starting point for contemporary discussions of citizenship is T. H. Marshall's ([1950] 1973) extension of the notion from one of membership in a community as a political matter to social and civil dimensions. Each of these dimensions of citizenship is supported by an institutional context: the juridical system as regards civil rights, education as regards the social, and the electoral system and political parties as regards the political. Furthermore, the relationship among these three spheres tends to be conflictual, which is most directly expressed in relation to class. Citizenship, Marshall argues, provides a means to attenuate the inequalities generated by the economy, thus intervening in class relations. Understood in this way, the compromise sought in the terrain of citizenship is mirrored in the compromise struck between capital and labor in the Keynesian welfare state. The social rights institutionalized by the welfare state "subordinat[e the] market price to social justice," although that takes place within the market system itself (111). So long as the welfare state provided a stable context for economic growth, particularly in the 1950s and 1960s, the compromise held. However, the transition to a post-Fordist regime under the hegemony of multinational and global corporations exacerbated the underlying tensions, leading to a concomitant trend to reorganize the institutional contexts that supported citizenship rights in all three dimensions. This is most evident in neoliberal policies to reduce and privatize welfare state services. Culture and civil society play a hand in this.

It could be argued that the transition of the welfare to the neoliberal state has generated, in the process, a new dimension of citizenship rights. I am thinking here of cultural citizenship, a by-product, so to speak, of the confluence of civil rights legislation, increases in immigration (both documented and undocumented), the permeation of the social by foundations and third-sector institutions specializing in welfare services, the electronic media, and the post–mass market (i.e., the turn to specialized niche marketing). A social logic emerged in the late 1970s that reconstituted the social dimension of citizenship along the lines of group needs, desires, and imaginaries. These are today the most significant constituents of what I refer to as the *cultural ethos* that serves as the warrant for making claims not only on service and educational institutions but also on the media and the market (Yúdice 1993a). This development, by which cultural claims, according to Young (2000), become political resources, marks a departure from the individual-based tradition of citizenship rights, but one supported by the targeting of consumer publics. Both the state and the market coconstruct the serviceable and capitalizable needs and images of these groups, in relation to their own struggles to extend their social franchise.

The struggles around immigration, affirmative action, welfare, abortion rights, health care, even the arts funding controversies, and the ways they involve the politics of identity, cannot be fully understood without taking into account that the capitalist welfare state, the media, and the market translate the interpretations of people's needs into legal, administrative, therapeutic, and imagistic terms, thus reformulating the political reality of those interpretations. According to Nancy Fraser, the conflicts among rival needs interpretations in contemporary society reveal that we inhabit a "new social space" in which claims are legitimized not by the "best argument" in an idealized public sphere, but by the cultural ethos that accounts for the needs in the first place (1989: 157). Politics thus takes the form of cultural antagonisms in a context of structured inequalities between dominant and marginalized positions (Young 2000: 98).

In this new social context, and given the conservative move to impede the access to rights, the grounds for entitlement have shifted to struggles within the paradigm of interpretability.[1] Because the legal framework in which citizenship rights are distributed refers to individuals and not groups, entitlement must take place in a *surrogate terrain*, such as language (for Latinos and other ethnic minorities), the family, or sexuality (for gays and lesbians and women's groups), that is, the particular experience around which groups, especially subordinated and stigmatized groups, constitute their identity. It is in this sense of group self-formation, in which the media and the consumer market have an important, targeting role, that I would agree with Fredric Jameson's (1991) assessment of the cultural turn in contemporary society. In its convergence with the economy, it has not so much dissolved as "explo[ded] throughout the social realm, to the point at which everything in our social life—from economic value and state power to social and political practices and the very structure of the psyche itself—can be said to have become 'cultural.'" (48).[2]

Perhaps the most important factor in this "cultural turn" is the impact of the informationalization of the economy. Manuel Castells (1989) speaks of a "new technological paradigm" characterized by the primacy of information processing (requiring a workforce different from that which served Fordism) and of the emergence of process-oriented technologies that "[lead] to modification in the material basis of the entire social organization . . . transforming the way we produce, consume, manage, live, and die." These processes are the "mediators of the broader set of factors that determines human behavior and social organization" (14–15). This mediation can be understood most clearly in the shift in the labor force toward services, which increase productive and social diversity (130), and in the permeation of the entirety of social space by consumerism, which serves not only to spur production, but also to "wire" the citizenry into the new technologies.

Jameson's notion of the explosion of culture (or, as Baudrillard would say, the "implosion" of everything into it) so as to exhaust the space of the social has recently been echoed by critics who feel that culture can no longer be construed as false consciousness, as something "foisted on gullible populations by hype and the lust for profit" (Mort 1990: 167). This form of ideology critique encourages a pessimistic view of the possibilities for an effective social intervention, especially among today's youth. In contrast, others have posited the possibility of turning the greater penetration of capital around to one's advantages, particularly through consumption. In *The Consumerist Manifesto*, Martin Davidson puts forth the claim that consumption, not production, "is the basic mode of activity in our society" (1992: 203). David Chaney finesses this claim by construing consumption itself (the recycling of images and representations) as the very mode of production in our epoch (1994: 86).

These changes in the mode of production correspond to an extension of disciplinary institutions (in the Foucauldian sense) beyond the state, which does not mean that the state itself has been weakened but, rather, that it has been reconverted to accommodate to new forms of organization and capital accumulation. Flexible accumulation, consumer culture, and the "new world information order" are produced or distributed (made to flow) globally to occupy the space of the nation, but are no longer "motivated" primarily by any essential connections to a state. The motivations are also infra- and supranational. We might say that, from the purview of the national proscenium, a posthegemonic situation holds. That is, the "compromise solution" that culture provided for Gramsci exceeds the territorial boundaries of the nation-state; the "culture-ideology of consumerism" serves to naturalize global capitalism everywhere (Sklair 1991). Nevertheless, as I explained in chapter 2, both the infra- and supranational forces at work contribute to a performative field of force that is still largely national.

Following these leads, there are at least two ways to think through a (nationally based) politics of culture premised on the convergence of consumption and citizenship: the extension of citizenship can be seen either in relation to diversity as projected in the media and consumer markets, or in the exploitation of the "multiaccented" images of commodities "in the service of resistant demands and dreams" (Mort 1990: 166). Let's examine these options.

Point-of-Purchase Politics

The term consumerism is historically associated with movements to protect consumers. The most recognizable name in this history is that of the "crusader" Ralph Nader, whose book Unsafe at Any Speed (1965) revolutionized the regulatory institutions of the state. The history of consumerism, however, goes back to the late nineteenth-century movements against Big Railroad and Big Business, dramatized in Frank Norris's The Octopus (1901) and Upton Sinclair's The Jungle (1906). Today the notion of consumerism no longer refers predominantly to consumer protection, which is housed squarely within the state, but to the permeation of all aspects of life (home, leisure, psyche, sex, politics, education, religion) by an ethos (or lifestyle) of "all consuming images" (Ewen 1988: 14). From a social movement that contested the undemocratic monopolistic power of Big Business, consumerism was transformed into a corporate movement for the "democratic engineering of consent," as Edward Bernays presciently proposed in 1947. The history of consumer culture in the United States has only borne out Bernays's prediction; democracy itself advances through spectacle, style, and consumption.

This holds not only for the aestheticization of mainstream politics, which became quite self-reflexive in the Reagan-Bush era and which continued with the MTVization of the Clinton administration and of the right in the guise of Newt Gingrich in the mid-1990s and now G. W. Bush. It also pervades what goes on in the name of "oppositional" politics. In the 1980s and 1990s, every issue, from antiracism and antisexism to antihomophobia, but also evangelism, antiabortion, and right-wing antigovernment stances, was politicized in the medium of consumable style (Niebuhr 1995a, 1995b; Rimer 1995a; Berke 1995). As Heather Hendershot argues, white youth can find countercultural expression in fundamentalist culture: "In contrast to the harsh denial of old-fashioned fundamentalism, Focus [production company of fundamentalist youth culture] promotes what is apparently a kinder, gentler activism" (1995: 19). Even academic enterprises, such as cultural studies, have been promoted by some of their practitioners and critics as a matter of fan appreciation or as a "profess[ion] of hip" (Mead 1993).

In part, the permeation of all of life by consumption has been made possible by the shift from mass marketing to an ever more specialized targeting of consumers. In 1994 an executive at Warner Music spoke of the possibility of reaching fifty thousand individuals throughout the world interested in post-punk Cypriot music via an electronic cable "juke box" system (André Midani, personal communication, October 28, 1994). Napster, Nullsoft, Gnutella, Lime-Wire, and others have made that aspiration a reality, albeit hotly contested by corporations that will not easily relinquish the profits brought by control of copyright and intellectual property rights.

Even political activism has been affected by these new technologies. Niche marketing, turbocharged by the Internet, enables corporations to promote their wares for both profit and ethical responsibility, by the appeal of political images and messages, most often progressive ones. Ben & Jerry's, for example, made it possible for consumers to act on their political convictions simply by purchasing and consuming their products, having their cake and eating it, so to speak. When they tried to extend the performative character of their corporate democracy beyond the politics of style and consumption into business administration itself, as in the highly publicized campaign to hire a CEO through an essay-writing contest, the contradictions became overwhelming. Not only did they backtrack and hire a headhunting firm to find the new CEO, but they also went against policy and paid him more than seven times the wage of the lowest-paid employee (Gillespie 1999). Not only did Ben & Jerry's resist unionization of its workforce, but it eventually sold out for $326 million to the mammoth food-processing and household goods company Unilever, whose revenues alone in 2000 were nearly $44 billion (Edmond 2001). Unilever made a pledge to maintain the founders' political commitments, but it is clear that no matter who benefited from the Ben & Jerry's Foundation's donations, these were no larger than a PR budget, and quite successful in attracting customers. Consequently, though the founders' politics may be different in substance from those of, say, the Ronald McDonald Foundation, the promotional style is the same. It would not be an exaggeration to say that style is the substance of such promotions, for it effectively transubstantiates ethical values.

If anything, the spate of companies that engage in point-of-purchase politics (the display of political positions on packaging and signs at cash registers), among them Esprit de Corp, Kenneth Cole Productions, Working Assets, and the more controversial Body Shop and Benetton, makes it evident that civil society is also the society of consumption and spectacle. However, recognition of this does not mean that older Marxist notions such as the commodity fetish and alienation necessarily apply in the same ways in which the concepts were originally formulated. In these cases, consumption functions as a means to counter alienation in at least one sense: the separation of the consumer from the rest of society. Political consumerism can also be quite activist. Working Assets, the socially conscious credit card and long-distance telephone company, not only contributes a small percentage of its profits to clearly progressive causes, among them gay and lesbian organizations, for which they have been targeted for boycotts by the religious right (Elliott 1992: 37), but they also serve as a convenient vehicle for enabling massive protest and lobbying. Every month Working Assets' customers can exercise "automated activism" by scheduling letters and calls, partly at company expense, to lobby politicians. For example, a 1995 invoice invited its customers to make free calls to Senator D'Amato to express opposition to the cuts in school lunches and to Senator Moynihan to urge him to vote no on the Comprehensive Regulatory Reform Act of 1995, which "would handcuff both the OSHA and the EPA by putting industry profits ahead of the public interest" (Working Assets, invoice and annual review, 1995). From 1985 to 2001, Working Assets "generated $25 million in donations to nonprofits working for peace, equality, human rights, education and a cleaner environment" by taking a portion of the monthly charges on long distance, credit card, and online services for the "causes you help select—at no extra cost to you" (Working Assets 2001).

Like a few other companies, Working Assets takes a deeply partisan position in its attacks on the undemocratic policies of the right. The summary of activities in the May 1995 annual report, for example, states:

> Last year's swing to the right stirred us into action as never before. In December alone we protested Newt Gingrich's Contract With America with a record-breaking 65,000 calls and letters. Any contract that cuts off basic assistance to 7 million children, trashes environmental laws and pumps more money into the Pentagon is not our contract with America. Last year, simply by making long distance calls, rounding up your phone bill and using a credit card, you raised an impressive $1.5 million for 36 nonprofit groups working to protect the environment, fight bigotry and feed the hungry. You registered your political discontent with over 450,000 calls and letters.
>
> Newt and company, though, are not going to let up. So neither must we. Your political involvement is more important than ever. TOGETHER WE CAN MAKE A DIFFERENCE.

Working Assets' recipients are among the most progressive NGOs that espouse environmental, geopolitical, and human rights and that practice democracy on a globolocal scale. The Center for Third World Organizing "improves living conditions for people of color in low-income communities through training and leadership programs"; the Center on Social Welfare Policy and Law "fights for a welfare program for the poor"; the Farmworker Network for Economic and Environmental Justice "works with farmworker organizations in Caribbean, U.S. and Mexico to change environmental and economic policy in agriculture"; Rainforest Action Network "fights deforestation, supports tribal people and promotes economic alternatives for sustainable societies"; the Mexican Human Rights Commission "exposes and combats government violations of human rights in Chiapas and other parts of Mexico"; the Society for Women and AIDS in Africa "mobilizes African women to fight the HIV/AIDS epidemic"; the ACLU Lesbian and Gay Rights/AIDS Project "litigates and advocates to protect and enhance the rights of lesbians, gay men and people with HIV disease nationwide"; the Center for Democratic Renewal "confronts the most naked hatred and racism in the country . . . monitor[ing], document[ing] and educat[ing] the public about the detestable activities of the Ku Klux Klan, Aryan Nation, Christian Patriots and other hate groups."

Nevertheless, this activism has also been the target of muckraking critics like Jon Entine (1997a), who points out that, whereas its political ethics are clearly progressive, its actual operations may be less so. Working Assets' attempt to provide "green power" was all smoke and mirrors, according to Entine, because the energy it purchased from mainstream sources and resold to consumers was not "renewable." Working Assets operates as "a shell that buys products at wholesale (long distance access, Internet, paging, electricity), then slaps on a green label and a steep green premium" (Entine 1997b).

Although Working Assets' politics clearly go beyond hype, that is not true of the politics of consumption of companies like The Body Shop, a British cosmetics chain with 1,694 stores in forty-eight countries, which ran afoul of its image as a company with a conscience, particularly on questions of human rights, environmental protection, animal testing, and fair trade with developing nations. Although The Body Shop claims to have made significant contributions to the homeless and animal rights groups (Roddick 1991), doubts were raised about the accuracy of the company's contract terms with workers in developing nations and its franchising practices (Entine 1994).

The most notorious of all politically oriented marketers is Benetton, whose "United Colors of Benetton" advertising campaign generated a veritable growth industry in the field of cultural studies (Deitcher 1990; Back and Quaade 1993; Rosen 1993; Giroux 1994). Benetton's campaign has included the images of a war cemetery, an oil-soaked seabird, a nun kissing a priest, children laboring in Colombia, the bloody uniform of a Croatian soldier, a terrorist's car bombing, and sundry multicultural yokings of blacks, whites, Asians, Arabs, and Israelis, albeit representations that strain the "good intentions" of portraying social harmony, as in the supposedly amusing photograph of two dogs, black and white, kissing. Oliviero Toscani, the company's advertising director, has upped the ante in the postmodern practice of 1980s "appropriation art," reappropriating the style that ACT UP/Gran Fury (composed of a number of advertising artists and directors) had itself poached for some of its "guerrilla" "demographics" (Crimp 1990). Intending to raise awareness about AIDS, Toscani situated the company's "concerns" in a humanistic setting—David Kirby surrounded by family—that ACT UP has eschewed for various reasons, some of which have to do with the problematic repercussions of family in relation to queer identities. Benetton's AIDS, death row, and other catastrophe-themed ads have raised the hackles not only of activist groups like ACT UP and victims' rights groups (Neff 2000), but, perhaps more important, many of its own customers. Benetton franchisers in Germany posted large losses due to a consumer boycott protesting the "us[e of] human tragedy and suffering to sell clothes" (Nash 1995). To add insult to injury, Benetton does not even fund causes as other companies do. The CEO, Luciano Benetton, has "justified its policy of not donating to charity because they 'invest in advertising campaigns which promote social harmony' " (Back and Quaade 1993: 72).

Companies less invested in "radical" or "progressive" causes also engage in socially conscious advertising with an aim to promote "social harmony." It can be found quite explicitly in a Mobil ad (1990) that reproduces a series of past ads that have incorporated such a notion of solidarity into their global propaganda. Mobil makes the claim that their advertising functions as a kind of global public sphere, in which discussion of critical issues such as the environment, democracy, recognition of difference, and so on are taken up. The print version of their voice-over reads:

> Clean streets and remedial skills, architecture that works and great art by Maoris, Soviets, Indonesians, Turks, Australians, Americans . . . all enrich the quality of life. Yes, we've talked about all these topics and more in our recurring op-ed messages on the quality of life—from a Norwegian fjord to our own backyard. Why? Because we're a global company with business interests and social concerns in more than 100 countries. Because we think it's important to recognize achievement—here and abroad. One way is through cultural exchange [and] public debates such as National Town Meetings, summer jobs, sponsorship of sporting events, programs for the disadvantaged, and computer-assisted remedial courses in math and reading for culturally deprived youngsters. Mobil underwrites all of these activities, and more. And by writing about them in this space, we call attention to works and institutions that enhance the quality of life for all of us.

The flip side of the ad reads:

> Over the past 20 years, we've used our op-ed space from time to time to rally corporate and public support for scores of worthy causes. Shown here are just some of the organizations we've supported—and urged others to do as well . . . our messages—and our grants—have helped to get out the vote, fight crime, stock the blood bank and much more. They've encouraged young blacks and Hispanics to become engineers, spurred women to start their own businesses, and advised retired executives on lending their skills to fight social ills.

Mobil's appeal to the classic and idealized public sphere of the eighteenth century is explicit in the final sentence of the ad: "And like the pamphleteers of earlier times, we feel one way [of making an impact to solve social problems] is by proclaiming our support—in our corner of the op-ed page."

Without necessarily politicizing consumption, the gay market is instructive as regards the correlation of participation, consumerism, and cultural reproduction. Michael Warner (1993), for example, sounds a caution to an unproblematized application of Marxist assumptions that serve as obstacles to sexual politics for gay people, which are worked out in "close connection [to] consumer culture and the most visible spaces of gay culture": bars, advertising, fashion, brand-name identification, mass-cultural camp, 'promiscuity.' " "Gay culture in this most visible mode is anything but external to advanced capitalism and to precisely those features of advanced capitalism that many on the left are most eager to disavow. Post-Stonewall urban gay men reek of the commodity. We give off the smell of capitalism in rut, and therefore demand of theory a more dialectical view of capitalism than many people have imagination for" (xxxi n.28).

A 1994 marketing video by Telemundo, *Hispanic USA: Marketing Niche of the 90s*, says virtually the same about U.S. Hispanics, but in a different, more normalizing style. We find out that Hispanics are the "consummate consumers." They can no longer be derided as the serape-wrapped stereotypes astride a burro, the coffee-picking Juan Valdezes or dancing chiquitas of yesteryear; today they are upward-moving professionals, driving expensive cars, walking briskly through airport terminals, yet maintaining their culture, sitting down to elaborate family meals, and using the Spanish language. They have large families growing at a rate more than twice as fast as the rest of the U.S. population, which, together with a disposable income estimated in 1994 at nearly $300 billion, makes them the most coveted market. The video does not, of course, show one single poor Hispanic; they are all solidly middle or professional-managerial class.

Also touting gay consumerism but downplaying Warner's in-your-face style, a special section of the June 1993 *Advertising Age* on "Marketing to Gays and Lesbians" refers to a "newfound acceptance" of gay and lesbian newspapers and magazines (*The Advocate, Deneuve, Genre, On Our Backs, Out, 10 Percent, QW*) by mainstream advertisers who seek to capitalize on a market that is perceived to be somewhere between $394 and $514 billion (Levin 1993: 30). But the "gay market" is not a monolith, and advertisers and marketers are acutely aware of this as they seek out a "subset . . . that, based on anecdotal evidence and market research, is urban and has above-average disposable income" (B. Johnson 1993: 29). An analysis of the "first mainstream television commercial [for Ikea] starring uncloseted gay consumers" also bears out this upscale selectivity, as if the very phrase "gay market" meant affluence (Rich 1994). They live in a designer loft, drink designer water, eat a designer dinner, and are connoisseurs when it comes to tasteful furnishings. Another report on an executive search firm for gay talent also focuses on the middle-class and professional-managerial-class positioning of the market to which they cater. Despite the continued existence of hate groups and the still unresolved discrimination of gays and lesbians in the military, the director of the firm believes that to attract this targeted market, "companies . . . from liquor makers to insurance companies are starting to look for executives who know the territory" (Noble 1993).

It is evident, if marketers for Hispanics and for gays and lesbians are correct, that to a good degree, membership in and access to the institutions of "civil society" via consumerism are limited on a class basis. The promise of franchise for minorities is disseminated throughout the (consumer) culture, but despite its glaring obviousness there is little critical reflection in the public sphere on the fact that targeting is aimed primarily at the middle class. Or, perhaps, as Arlene Dávila explains, what TV and advertising images generate are normative images, meaning "unthreatening" demeanor and behavior that assimilate them to "symbolically white," whereas the "deviant" images that one may see in talk shows like El Show de Cristina are "raced" and "othered" (2001: 169). Indeed, audiences to whom I have shown Telemundo's Hispanic U.S.A. marketing video have remarked that all the Hispanics in it are white, which is not the case, leaving aside for the moment the obvious fact that race and ethnicity are cultural constructs, if one carefully looks at skin color. But the predominance of businessmen and other successful figures assimilates them to symbolic whiteness. Similarly, the gay couple in the Ikea ad are shown acting like a heterosexual couple. As Dávila remarks concerning other Ikea ads, images of buying furniture conveys commitment (256). Nevertheless, the failure to include the poor is widespread. After all, marketing vehicles are meant to sell images of buying power to businesses. I now turn to "corporate diversity," where the absence of the poor is even more glaring.

The Consumption–Corporate Diversity Connection

As in the case of consumption, there is no paucity of critiques of corporate diversity. Most focus on the difference between the multicultural rhetoric of corporations' public personas and the actual composition of their workforce and management personnel (A. Gordon 1995; Moylan 1995; Newfield 1995). As in the case of multiculturalism and socially conscious marketing, some progressive critics yearn for an untainted politics of difference, one not beholden to consumer capitalism. I question whether this is at all possible in the contemporary United States. In fact, it seems to me that despite the relative downgrading of real empowerment through these forms, there is nevertheless support for antiracist, antisexist, antihomophobic, and pro-immigrant policies aimed at countering the right.

It "makes sense" that a global capitalism that seeks to attract new consuming publics as well as manage a diverse workforce (both because that is increasingly the demographic reality of the United States and because this diversity is positioned to extend a bridge to international markets) should dress itself in all the trappings of multiculturalism and the empowerment of diversity. It also "makes sense" that as the welfare state, with its regulatory institutions to ensure equal opportunity, shrinks, the mechanisms introduced in the civil rights era and its wake to compensate minorities and women for past discrimination are now to be left to the promises of the corporate world to be more inclusive, more diverse. These are not, as Avery Gordon points out, totally empty promises: "[Proponents of diversity management think] it will replace crude racial social control, including that primarily driven by 'innocent' ignorance, with a solution designed to work within the class parameters that link an increasingly racially diverse professional managerial class. Diversity management thinks it could lead to the 'internal decomposition' of what Etienne Balibar calls the community of racists" (1995). Diversity management consultants like Robert L. Davis (quoted in *The Diversity Challenge* 1995), the advocacy partner of the American Institute for Managing Diversity at Morehouse College, proposes "negotiat[ing] a psychological contract" between managers and employees, such that providing a bias-free environment (via "bias-reduction seminars"), mentoring, learning, upward mobility, and other features of a democratic workplace can be planned.

This position is taken not only for political reasons; there is also an expedient, economic reason for accommodating cultural difference. As Marlene L. Rossman argues in *Multicultural Marketing: Selling to a Diverse America*, the corporate world must turn to "Hispanics, Asians, African-Americans, and other culturally distinct segments" out of necessity, that is, to capture the hundreds of billions of dollars of minority spending power (1994: 7). Another marketing professional, Sidney I. Lirtzman, acting dean of Baruch College's School of Business, corroborates this view: "Capitalizing on the talents of a diverse workforce can enable companies to tap new sources of customers in the U.S. and abroad" (*The Diversity Challenge* 1995: 2). This means that even new immigrants (most of whom are non-European) will be wooed "because there are so many, and regardless of [marketers'] personal feeling about immigration policy" (Rossman 1994: 10). In fact, following this logic, sociologists and demographers have argued that immigrants lift sagging local economies mostly through their impact as consumers and as workers in the service sector. Significantly, culture is thought to be at the heart of this urban renewal, for it is the "cultural complexity" itself that makes metropolitan areas like New York City so dynamic (Levine 1990; Goode, Schneider, and Blanc 1992; Sontag 1993).

Such rhetoric of diversity is open to different ideological articulations, and it must be noted that while the Buchananesque far right had a privileged position within the Republican consensus, the corporation and its ties to global trade could be seen as the enemy by the right. An article in a special issue of *International Business* devoted to examining the "threats to Latin American business" took a dim view of the nationalist-populist character of the conservative wing that dominated the Republican Party. Focusing on the deep ideological split on the issue of free trade, the author cites a specialist on Japanese trade with the Congressional Research Service: " 'My impression of a lot of these people, especially those on the religious right, is that they tend to be fairly isolationist, wary of something like a world trade organization or anyone telling the U.S. what to do' " (Moskowitz 1994: 78–79). Conservative, born-again, and hawkish, George W. Bush's candidacy nevertheless emerged as an antidote to the anti-immigrant, anti–free trade right that was perceived as a liability by Republican strategists. Bush, moreover, has a reasonably good chance to woo Hispanics to the Republican Party, as I argue in chapter 8.

The foregoing discussion makes it evident that a diversified U.S. corporate world and a global workplace cannot be seen solely in economic terms; they also have social and cultural dimensions. National and transnational corporations have to deal not only with the increasing diversity of the workforce, particularly as populations migrate around the world, but also with new avenues of marketing. A mid-1990s textbook on global marketing highlights the "cultural values that make them useful in formulating strategic plans and programs in the global marketplace" (Sandheusen 1994: 99). Drawing on a range of research into national and local cultures, this approach attempts to approximate a "global cultural studies." Global marketing pays attention to changing, "secondary and subcultural" values, as well as "core or persistent" values. The approach also takes into consideration how the particular values cluster to form what we might call ideologemes. Ultimately, the purpose is to predict the correlations between "value/lifestyle orientations and their buying behavior pattern" (105). We might say, then, that diversity marketing in some ways developed some of the "cultural indicators" that social scientists interested in assuring the well-being of minorities in inner cities would begin to develop later (see chapter 1).

The focus on the diversity of values in the global marketplace so as to capture and retain an expanding range of publics is not limited to marketing research but extends to education and employment (witness the emergence of numerous MBA and other training programs in global business). Diversity has the greatest impact on the redefinition of the U.S. workforce, even if only at the rhetorical level. As the rhetoric goes, a diverse managerial leadership will ensure exploitation of all possible markets, precisely because only through attention to cultural diversity can these markets be discerned. For example, an ad for MCI in *Hispanic Business* states: "Capturing the essence of diversity makes MCI a leader. Leadership comes to those who possess an entrepreneurial spirit. The vision to recognize emerging trends. And the determination to succeed. You'll find all these attributes at MCI, and something more: the rich diversity of resources required to meet new challenges. We're applying diverse services, technologies and people to the realization of a communications revolution." Similarly, an ad for Microsoft, also in *Hispanic Business*, features the photograph of a 10-year-old Hispanic girl standing in front of the classroom and reading a report to her classmates. The caption states: "You've always enjoyed having a stage from which to excel. Ever since you were a kid, you've been driven to add your unique flair to everything you do. That's exactly what we're looking for at Microsoft. We depend on diverse opinions and viewpoints. Which is why we're actively seeking to add diversity to our workforce. If you want to join in on helping to redefine the software industry, talk to us." A Frito-Lay ad featuring a human rainbow of executives boasts of its understanding of the importance of mixing diverse ingredients: "Frito-Lay understands that producing the best snack foods does not happen by chance. You must follow a proven recipe made with only the finest ingredients. The proper mixture of quality minority vendors will always produce the best." Another ad that features a human rainbow, this time of children of all races, begins "This is our view of Corporate America's future" and ends with the slogan "The difference is Merrill Lynch." The copy reads: "At Merrill Lynch we believe that diversity in Corporate America will be as commonplace in the future as it is in the playgrounds today. As one of the premier financial firms in the world, we work toward that goal every day." Another human rainbow ad, for the biotechnology company Amgen, combines its area of research with diversity, rooting that diversity in biology: "All kinds of people have science in their genes. We recognize that diverse perspectives are a key factor in the process of discovery."[3]

A 1994 report on corporate philanthropy to minority education and arts begins by noting, "Corporate America . . . identifies educational efforts in the minority community as a top priority" (Dutko 1994: 60). However, the reality of corporate philanthropy belies the rhetoric: out of an estimated $6 billion given in 1994 to nonprofit organizations, only $26 million was directed toward minority populations. Precisely because the corporate ideology of diversity focuses on middle management (as a means to control lower-echelon workers), it does not coincide with the "radical democratic" project's aim to link questions of class to those of race and gender, the categories according to which minoritiness is measured. In fact, corporate diversity covers over that connection by a positive and trendy appeal to opportunity and success. Furthermore, although its discourse is multicultural, judging by company dossiers, advertising, and PR, studies show that 95 percent of senior management positions are held by white men, who make up only 43 percent of the workforce (Holmes 1995a; Kilborn 1995; Andrews 1995). Black men and women, who, respectively, hold 4 percent and 5 percent of middle-management jobs (as compared with 40 percent held by white women), continue to be underrepresented at this level, despite a 36 percent increase in availability of African Americans with B.A. or postgraduate degrees (Kilborn 1995). No wonder, then, that, as in the title of a critical report, "companies embrace diversity, but are reluctant to discuss it" (Dobrzynski 1995).

There are more skeptical studies that point up some of the root causes of the so-called glass ceiling. According to Sharon Collins (1997), black entry into executive positions in public and private enterprise is part of a governmentalizing strategy of control rather than a result of better education or sincere affirmative action initiatives. This strategy has two tracks. The first is a new employment structure from which blacks benefited, ensuing from "the need felt by the federal government and private employers to abate black upheaval and restore social order, which had been disrupted by civil rights activities" (11). Second, many executive jobs for which blacks were hired were "in personnel departments and labor- and public-relations jobs . . . to administer corporate policies sensitive to blacks and, hence, lessen racial pressures on white corporate environments" (12). We see here a racial version of the progressive corporate citizenship discussed above in relation to politics through consumerism. In both cases, corporations get good publicity and avoid criticism by resorting to "business ethics" (Entine 1995). These strategies are also analogous to the routing of African American and other minority artists into the Expansion Arts and Folk Arts programs at the NEA, as reported in chapter 8.

Companies may not want to discuss these issues openly, but the juridical system will sometimes pry open company practices regarding equal opportunity and discrimination. The juridical system is an important component in the conjuncture of factors that put diversity agendas up for constant evaluation. I have argued elsewhere that the conflictive formation of Latinos as a panethnicity and the gains and losses they won and suffered take place in such a convergence of factors, including the struggle to be recognized as consumers and workers in welfare state agencies and state and nonstate public institutions such as schools and universities, particularly in relation to language rights (Yúdice 1993a). Such processes do not occur in the same way in all societies, precisely because the above-mentioned factors are not structured in the same way. Nevertheless, it should be recognized that the juridical solution to these problems is as ideological as diversity rhetoric. As I argued in chapter 2, the belief in the rule of law makes it possible to lessen social strife. As in the case of consumerism, there is just enough legal redress to keep frustration at social immobility from escalating into unleashed outrage.

In the United States much political negotiation operates through a complex that includes the client role imposed by the welfare state; the legacy of the civil rights era, particularly affirmative action and equal opportunity, which defines the citizen in terms not only of individual rights but, increasingly, of collective interpretations of those rights; the targeting of groups by consumer capitalism; and the struggles over representation that take place in the media and other venues. These factors converge in ways that allow for disjunctures of a qualitatively different character from what is possible in a country like Brazil. Just for the sake of contrast, consider the fact that the $54.4 million settlement won by the African American plaintiffs who claimed that the restaurant chain Denny's discriminated against them (Kohn 1994) is currently impossible in Brazil, which has a population of African descent larger than that of the United States. There have been lawsuits to enforce laws against discrimination, but Brazilian society and culture have not undergone a civil rights revolution, nor does the judiciary operate to the benefit of most Brazilians, nor is there a welfare safety net that does justice to the concept, nor is consumption a viable medium for even rhetorical democratization. To this day, no one has been found guilty for the murders of street children, which number as high as nine hundred per year for São Paulo alone (see chapters 4 and 5). As I noted in chapter 2, there is a disjuncture at the heart of public culture in Brazil, such that the law and other "liberal ideas" are conjoined with favor and other social practices based on a hierarchical, clientelist society. This is brought home in a report on the culture of impunity in Brazil: "On paper, Brazil's legal system is a model of fairness. But in reality, it fails to punish criminals" (Brooke 1993). Of course, there is no impunity for those who are born poor and black. Instead, as Teresa Caldeira, a researcher of violence on the poor, observes, there is a tendency to class cleansing analogous to the ethnic cleansing practiced, say, in Bosnia (1993: 2).

The point is not that redress for discrimination is adequate in the United States, but that the means of struggling for it are imbricated in a complex set of factors that condition the formation of identity as well as the practices of the state, the economy, and the media. This is evident in Denny's settlement with the NAACP, which set the goal that the chain should add fifty-three minority-owned restaurant franchises by 1997. By November 1994, forty-seven of Denny's fifteen hundred restaurants were owned and operated by a black company (Kleinfeld 1994). Consider also that if the "Buying Black" approach in L.A. "pays off," as Calvin Sims (1993) reports, such that a consumer-oriented version of citizenship rights reproduces identity, if Latinos can sue Disney World over "English Only" policies (Lewin 1994), and if deaf people have sought recognition not as a handicapped minority but as an autonomous culture (Padden and Humphries 1988; Dolnick 1993), it is because there is an imbrication of politics and culture that works through the terrain of state, media, and market that has been internally structured, so to speak, in radically different ways than in Brazil and, for that matter, other developed nations such as Britain, as is evident in a comparative study of McDonald's U.S. and McDonald's U.K. John Gabriel (1994) cites not only the existence of affirmative action laws in the United States as a fundamental distinguishing feature, accounting for the greater number of minority franchises than in Britain, but he also notes that the size of minority communities cannot be overlooked when considering the bottom line. "Maintaining links with minority communities, given their significance in numerical terms, is clearly part of a wider marketing strategy that aims to add to McDonald's 60 million customers per year" (120, 118).

Consumer activism can produce many gains when there is the perception that the juridical system works and when the rhetoric of consumption is engineered to be sensitive to a diversity already overdetermined in the society at large. Thus, even advocates of healthier foods have been able to pressure McDonald's successfully to change the fat content of their burgers and fries.

One activist, Peter Sokolof, bought full-page ads stating, "McDonald's, your Hamburgers have too much fat" and "Your french fries still are cooked with beef tallow" (Gabriel 1994: 123). It should be noted, however, that successful activism around consumption does not affect the tendency toward downgrading workers' benefits, salary, the routinization of everyday life in service sector work (Leidner 1993), the negative impact of packaging (a form of marketing) on the environment, or the exploitation of cheap labor and valuable resources in developing countries. Fast food restaurant chains such as McDonald's contribute to the worsening diet of poor people and those of modest income in the developing world, encouraging, when not engaging in, agribusiness that intensifies underdevelopment. The displacement of staples by cattle raising, which also lures farmers away from raising dairy cows, makes it difficult for the poor to maintain a balanced diet, particularly because beef is raised for export (Lappé and Collins 1979: 290). Considerations such as these make it necessary to explore the possibility of bringing to bear the rights of citizenship on a global basis, to offset the asymmetries effected by consumerism and its sponsorship by U.S. foreign policy agencies such as the Agency for International Development, which fostered (or imposed) models of development, such as agribusiness, that have succeeded mostly in making access to nutritional food more difficult for the majority in developing nations.

Consumerism and the Call for Global Citizenship

Under the new mode of global capitalism, with its policies of deregulation and defunding of government, immiseration has increased exponentially. In 1992, 14.5 percent of all Americans — 36.9 million — lived in poverty. The poverty rate was 33 percent for African Americans and 29.3 percent for Latinos. Analysis of the 1990 Census found that the richest 1 percent of Americans (101 billionaires and 1 million millionaires) had a greater net worth than the bottom 90 percent of the population (Katz-Fishman and Scott 1994; Batra 1993). Throughout the 1990s, the income gap widened, according to the Center on Budget and Policy Priorities and the Economic Policy Institute ("Income Gap of Richest and Poorest Widens for U.S. Families" 2000); by 2000, the number of billionaires had nearly tripled to 271 (Minade 2001). Despite this downward slide, consumption patterns in the United States and Europe far outstrip the survival level of 3 billion people worldwide and another 1 billion who live in extreme poverty, mostly in Africa and South Asia (Durning 1992). The global economy relies on the "surprising resilience of consumer spending" even as wages fall and benefits are eliminated; this was the claim made for the relative strength of the U.S. economy in 2001 despite the "stock market drop, rising layoffs, and heavy debt loads" (Koretz 2001). This is facilitated by the ever increasing percentage of world trade (estimated at 33 percent and 40 percent by the World Bank in 1993 and 2000, respectively) that takes place as intracompany transfers within the largest 350 multinational corporations, with the result that less and less income finds its way into workers' pockets ("The Philanthropy" 1993; Padmakshan 2000). Two billion people earn less than $2 per day (B. Scott 2001: 160). The rise of market and consumption values and the increase in immiseration go hand in hand and are integral factors of the redefinition of the cultural field.

Of the five forms of global citizenship that Richard Falk examines — world government and the politics of deterrence; the cosmopolitan or transnational habitus; management of the global order for the sustainability of middle-class lifestyles; regional integration projects such as the European Union; and transnational activism embodied in transnational social movements and NGOs — only the last is centered on respect for human rights, grassroots democracy, environmental reform, and local identities. It is by no means a coherent movement, as evidenced in the myriad conferences and discussions on the Internet, which bring together elite organizations like the Nature Conservancy and transnational development agencies alongside foundations from Europe and the United States, quasi-governmental diplomatic agencies, and grassroots groups dealing with urban, environmental, indigenous and women's issues. They meet at international fora and have begun to play a greater role in the work of the United Nations (Mawlawi 1992).

At the World Summit for Social Development in March 1995, delegates to the NGO Forum established the Alternative Declaration of Principles to ensure participation in decision making. These included access to information; transparency and public participation in the development of laws, regulations, and policies; fair and open election processes; and participation of indigenous peoples. After the 1992 Earth Summit in Rio de Janeiro, the NGO Forum formulated a set of principles on consumption:

> The most serious global environment and development problems facing the world arise from a world economic order characterized by ever expanding consumption and production, which exhausts and contaminates our natural resources and creates and perpetuates gross inequalities between and within nations. We can no longer tolerate a situation which has brought us beyond the limits of the earth's

carrying capacity and where twenty percent of the people consume eighty percent of the world's resources. We must act to balance ecological sustainability with equity between and within countries. It will be necessary to develop new cultural and ethical values, transform economic structures, and reorient our lifestyles. ("Treaty on Consumption and Lifestyle" 1992)

Among the recommendations are the restructuring of the economic system away from the production and consumption of nonbasic goods; ensuring that developed countries assume the primary responsibility for compensating for the disproportionate use of resources; easing of consumption and production commensurate with the regenerative carrying capacity of the earth; curtailing the production of goods with a built-in obsolescence; reusing and recycling; and the creation of partnerships of governments, business, voluntary and community organizations, and academia for further planning and implementation of guidelines.

Evidently, the kinds of proposals set forth by those who would seek a global citizenship run counter to the politics of consumption as I have described them in the preceding sections. It is not clear, however, how the cultural turn in citizenship will gain leverage for its proponents in a global context. What force, aside from that of solidarity, will the claim of, say, an indigenous person from Peru have among delegates from Croatia and Ghana? And how will academics, intellectuals, and activists accustomed to working within the cultural politics of consumerism (e.g., interpreting texts against the grain) participate in a forum in which the realities have less to do with consumption of images than lack of consumption of nutrients? Nothing is said in *The Consumerist Manifesto* about the kinds of issues raised by the NGOs. Indeed, it is difficult to imagine a reconciliation of an "aspirational consumption," which means that we "consume [the world around us] more not less" (Davidson 1992: 203), and the call by the advocates of a global citizenship that we ease back our consumption. The UN Population Fund (1999) published a "U.S. Scorecard" relating to the disproportion of population size and consumption of world resources. With only 4.6 percent of the world population, the United States produces 24 percent of the world's carbon dioxide output, and "directly or indirectly, each U.S. citizen consumes his or her own body weight in primary resources every day: oil, coal, other minerals, and agricultural and forest products." To Davidson and many other first world consumption and cultural studies scholars, this comes off as "moralism." But that response is increasingly illegitimate in the context of antisweatshop and antiglobalization protests.

Regional Federalism

There are, however, other, if not local, more regional positions, that neither celebrate nor simply dismiss the market and the mass media. Jorge Castañeda, for example, argues that these phenomena must be dealt with if there is to be a left alternative to neoliberalism. He takes the Latin American left to task for leaving these out of their agendas for taking power. I touched briefly on leftist traditions in chapter 2, but it is clear that few oppositional leftist forces have been able to stake out new positions with respect to the market and the media. And those center-left coalitions that have ascended to power have succumbed to the neoliberal policies bequeathed to them by previous administrations (Lagos in Chile, de la Rua in Argentina). There are, moreover, weak relations between the rich activism of civil society in Latin America and formal institutionalized political forces.

What I would like to highlight from Castañeda's (1993b) critique in *Utopia Unarmed* is the notion of civil society identified with consumer capitalism on the one hand, and, on the other, one that hitches its hopes to a social movement or "grassroots explosion" independent of the state. If a consumption society is a model of wasteful use of resources, the social movements, even with their important transnational linkages, "risk being rendered marginal" by not participating in electoral politics and thus attempting to redirect state policies (234–235). "Without the electoral connection and the association with parties, the movements were often condemned to fester and vanish, as the reasons that brought their emergence disappeared" (201).

Muniz Sodré (1992) has an even more pessimistic interpretation of the institutionalization of what Castañeda calls the "grassroots explosion." His argument is that, though important, the survival strategies of subordinated groups should not be touted as solutions to the absence of civil society, for that is precisely how elites seek to absolve the state of its responsibilities. In other words, the celebration of the marginal and heterogeneous, so dear to those who overvalorize the agency of, say, mass media audiences or squatters, becomes a way of shifting the burden of responsibility to the subordinated. The rise of technobureaucratic forms of domination and the increase in self-help strategies are, according to Sodré, two sides of the same coin. For example, as the technobureaucratic Brazilian state developed informatics, agrobusiness, and other advanced production, political society was overwhelmed by new forms of illegal (narcotraffic) and informal urban economies and social and religious mobilizations. Instead of seeing these as signs of new, autonomous formations, Sodré finds that the state simply takes the opportunity for relinquishing its traditional responsibilities (1992: 56).

The valorization of heterogeneity and marginality that Sodré refers to is characteristic of a cultural politics approach to social movement mobilization, like that of S. Alvarez et al. (1998). The practitioners of such criticism regard their work as a contribution to the struggles of the oppressed. Sodré's argument provides a sobering caution. It suggests that perhaps intellectuals who work in the field of representations may actually be contributing to a politics that makes it easier for states to engage in control, particularly at levels scaled larger than the conflict of interest groups. It also suggests that critique may be more useful if it focuses on the relations among the state, the consumer market, and civil society, and if it adopts as a given that there is no autonomy of civil society from the state and the market. It may continue to be useful to think of civil society as the institutionalized terrain of the lifeworld but one that is continuous and in tension with the state, with legality, with the market, and with transnational entities.

The problems pertaining to what is usually thought of as civil society seem quite intractable in Latin America, even in (perhaps particularly in) the largest countries, such as Brazil and Mexico, where distributional inequities are the most acute. In the absence of any viable utopias, Castañeda (1993b) makes a controversial proposal for a new "cross-cutting, longitudinal nationalism" or "regional federalism." It includes a strong presence in the emerging "global civil society" dealing with "the environment and human rights [as well as] broader economic policy matters" (311) and, most important, regional economic integration, "an intermediate solution between a largely unsustainable status quo and a highly harmful progression toward the dissolution of sovereignties" that results from being drawn in to "one of the three large economic spheres of influence," particularly the free market–oriented sphere of the United States (313). Instead, Castañeda advocates a confederal union of semiautonomous communities that includes:

> compensatory financing funded by windfall profit taxes and duties, labor mobility, a common external tariff to protect sectors of industry and agriculture that are jointly considered strategic and worthy of support, subsidies and credit facilities in order to make them competitive, in a business-government alliance and industrial policy along East Asian lines, a social charter or its equivalent and an environmental charter that harmonize up, not down, and include financing provisions for the adoption of superior norms in one area or another, common sub-

sidies, and expenditures for research and development, and dispute settlement mechanisms open to all interested parties and relevant issues. (317)

For Castañeda, Latin America can neither opt out of the world economy nor revert to national-protectionist positions if it is to have the resources to advance in the democratization of distribution. This intermediate solution, moreover, would require "ratcheting up the noneconomic domains in which integration takes place . . . grass roots regional integration and the creation of regional political, social, and legal institutions" (320). This still leaves out an important dimension that would contribute to making sense of integration. I am referring to regional cultural integration, which would include the arts, the media, and their relationship (most significantly through consumption) to economic and political factors. In reality, these aspects are simultaneously cultural and economic, as Néstor García Canclini argues in his own proposal for a regional federalism.

In *Consumers and Citizens*, García Canclini (2001) posits consumption as "means of thinking" that creates new ways of being citizens. However, the mediated public sphere, particularly in the context of globalization and regional integration, overflows the classic sphere of political interactions. The public nowadays is the mediation by which social institutions (re)present multiple aspects of social life to their interlocutors. In this regard, traditional and even recent progressive thinking on the expansion of citizenship to the "popular" (or "subaltern") sectors is outdated, according to García Canclini, insofar as traditional imaginaries of these sectors hold to the national frame as the proscenium of action and a "Gutenbergian" conception of how to negotiate the public sphere. García Canclini advocates rethinking politics in relation to consumption, although not in accordance with the U.S. model. Globalization has transformed the traditional sentimental-educational terrain of citizenship formation. National patrimonies, folklore, and the high arts are losing viewers and users, or their functions have shifted. Consumption, then, has to be rethought in relation to the culture industries. But in Latin America, this means confronting the problem of "Americanization."

This is precisely why García Canclini, like Castañeda, considers it important that states have a meaningful role in brokering a regional federalism, particularly in setting regulatory policies so that the affective aspects of cultural interpellation—identity formation—are not so overwhelmingly articulated by U.S. and other transnational entertainment conglomerates. For García Canclini, as for Castañeda, neoliberalism and privatization are not the answers; these just enable transnational corporations to gain greater control in Latin America. He argues that because experience has shown that privatization has not made utilities function any better, the state should get back into the public interest, helping to create better systems of cultural intermediation. In this regard, the activities of the "grassroots explosion," which must form part of any regional federalism, nevertheless cannot substitute for the conventional responsibilities of states: education, health, and social and cultural services. More specifically, García Canclini's own model of a culturally integrated regional federalism includes policies to create a Latin American media space; the creation of book, magazine, film, TV, and video common markets in the region; setting quotas of 50 percent Latin American production and distribution in movie theaters, video outlets, radio broadcasts, television programming, and so on; the creation of a foundation for the production and distribution of Latin American media; the regulation of foreign capital and policies to strengthen Latin American economies; and the development of citizenship by giving greater attention to a politics of recognition in keeping with a democratic multiculturality.

Anglo-American cultural studies approaches to cultural consumption speak of "interpretive communities"; García Canclini extends the notion to local and transnational "interpretive communities of consumers" (2001: 43). As such, he seems to provide the cultural adhesive for Castañeda's more economically conceived regional federalism. The two can be imagined to work in tandem, particularly in promoting the recognition of the diverse cultural formations of the region. If properly worked out, federalism could create an enabling environment for minority and marginal cultures throughout, insofar as they would have greater representation in the wider space of Latin American civil society, which would redraw the boundaries between nation and state.

The challenges are great. Neoliberalism, García Canclini writes, has "accentuated poverty and marginalization among Indians and mestizos," aggravating displacement and power struggles. As intercultural and interethnic conflicts and racism become ever more rampant, policies to encourage democratic coexistence are necessary. If we add to these problems the fact that most goods and messages are produced and circulated transnationally, the great difficulty of regional cultural integration and citizen participation becomes readily evident. Hence, national governments need to rethink conventional modernization programs and eliminate the cultural incomprehension inherent in their national consolidation projects (2001: 126–127).

Given the resistance of most Latin American nation-states to recognize multiculturality, one that is substantially different from what we in the United

States call multiculturalism, regional federalism would, at least at the level of cultural production and distribution, help remove the ideological state apparatuses from the grasp of an oligarchic state, thus potentially promoting a more democratic relationship between state and nation. In effect, cultural representation would no longer be pressed into the service of political representation. As García Canclini sees the problem at hand, it is a matter of rethinking civil society in an age of globalization and regional integration.

Potentially upsetting this rosy picture is the recognition that a regional-federalist solution still has to confront the pressures of the global economy on labor and the exploitation of resources. Furthermore, the rearticulation of culture at the continental level will still be subject to a consumerist model, with the only difference that it is a Latin American rather than an "American" model. To a great degree, such a notion of culture might be (in fact, is already being) underwritten by consumer-corporate enterprises (particularly from media-dominant Mexico, Brazil, Argentina, and Venezuela) that would gain a comparative advantage. This is not necessarily a damning problem, for societies may have reached a historical threshold in which it is no longer possible to think such ideals as citizenship and democracy in the absence of consumption.

The regional federalist model might make sense, for example, in negotiating the ongoing struggles over cultural representation and capital accumulation development plans in Colombia's Pacific rainforest. According to Arturo Escobar (1994), the Colombian government's Plan Pacífico for developing the infrastructure of the rainforest for capital accumulation and another, more modest government plan sponsored by the World Bank's Global Environment Facility for the Conservation of Biological Diversity have converged on an area inhabited by a majority Afro-Colombian population. The objective of the Plan Pacífico is integration into the Pacific Rim economy at the risk of vast ecological deterioration, for the biodiversity conservation plan would exploit gene pools for pharmaceutical companies. The two projects conflict in their modes of accumulation (destructive/conservationist) as well as in their rhetorics (progressive-modernizing/respect for diversity). The third and most important actor in Escobar's account is the Afro-Colombian community. Caught in the midst of these development projects, it has organized, especially under the auspices of the black movement, against development and in a "struggle articulated around the fact and defense of cultural difference" (4). Black identity has become a particularly strong position for the defense of the region, which has been undergoing farming and fishing industrialization that has displaced many and brought about "important cultural, ecological and social transformations." In this context, the nature conservation discourse of the biodiversity project has appealed to the black movement for what it might offer in "ways of strengthening local cultures in coexistence with nature. Notions such as 'culturally sustainable development' and 'ethnodevelopment' are being used to convey the need for culturally-based economic and social projects" (5).

Escobar notes that the common denominator of nature conservation that may prove of mutual benefit to biodiversity and the Afro-Colombian population does not in itself lead to the formulation of concrete projects. This is typical, he adds, of the difficulty third world communities confront in attempting to "articulate 'alternatives' to conventional development schemes" (1994: 5). This difficulty opens up this three-way struggle to a fourth actor: the " 'experts' (planners, anthropologists, ecologists, etc.)" who can be invited to collaborate to mediate with the state (which relies on "expert knowledge").

I have raised the Afro-Colombian example to suggest that the regional-federalist civil society that García Canclini proposes might further the cause of this community. The media and the marketing of consumer products made in this and other rainforest regions could promote natural biodiversity and cultural diversity. In fact, the collaboration between professionals and social movements that Escobar points to necessitates these other instances. From a regional-federalist perspective, the community might have greater leverage because representations relating to it would not necessarily share the same goals as the Colombian state, thus opening the way to other partnerships. In a sense, this is already at work in a smaller-scale and more fragmentary way in the representations disseminated by alternative media, the NGOs, and Internet discussions.

Another example in which a community has been caught in the pincer movements of powerful state and economic forces is that of the poor youth who frequent funk dance clubs (funkeiros) in Rio de Janeiro. In Rio, samba and carnival have been the traditional means by which the poorer classes (who are predominantly black) have participated, albeit in a controlled manner, in cultural life, giving the city one of its most characteristic images. As forms of cultural reproduction of identity, they are clearly part of civil society. However, as forms that inscribe those identities within a national or local setting that disables or compromises oppositional practices, samba and carnival are productive for the state. Through such structures and forms of enabling and disabling, the state can inscribe citizens. Even a form of popular music that has broken with the national connotations of samba, carioca funk, has become functional in several ways. It was attacked as the source of criminality; it legitimized, in part, the rejection of a leftist black woman candidate for mayor (Benedita da Silva); and it was tapped by the candidate who won as a means of recognizing, symbolically, poor youth.

In chapters 4 and 5 I detailed the kinds of networks that community activists have developed to deal with what look like such intractable problems. These networks are very important locally, but they also extend beyond the municipal and the national. Rubem César Fernandes, an important agglutinator and facilitator of such networks, including Afro Reggae, has written on Brazilian NGOs, defining them as promoters of citizenship rights, using practices resembling those of private organizations to deliver services that the state has failed to provide. They draw their funding from "churches, States, private foundations, volunteer associations, trade unions, individuals, businesses, and even the anonymous mass called the public opinion, that donate part of their income in order to contradict the contradiction of the market" (Fernandes and Piquet 1991: 13).

Conclusion

Viva Rio understands that it cannot limit its actions to a politics of recognition for the subordinated sectors of civil society, that citizenship issues involve the state, the military, the police, NGOs, and even the business and tourism sectors, and not only the autonomous activity of social groups. The recognition of diversity cannot substitute, cannot be a surrogate for state responsibility and the involvement of market sectors. The actions of Fernandes and Viva Rio point to other possibilities, particularly involvement in action aimed at articulating the various spheres through which a difference can be made. As explained in chapter 5, Viva Rio has brought together particular social groups, the state, the military, and other sectors, as well as transnational entities (foundations, NGOs, human rights organizations, churches), which provide funding as well as other services. The examples I have examined involve the imbrication of consumption and citizenship just as much as the examples I gave from the United States. However, the articulations are different, as are the theoretical proposals put forth by the likes of Castañeda and García Canclini. The politics of consumption in Latin America does not refer, in the first place, to actions wielded in the activity of purchasing (or boycotting) consumer commodities. There isn't confidence in the rule of law that would back up such initiatives. Rather, Latin American cultural politics point to a collaboration of diverse actors working in different scales of social space: from the local group to transnational businesses, financial institutions, media, and NGOs.

I am not suggesting, however, that Latin American cultural politics is more effective, not even in its own terrain of action. If anything, it is weak, precisely the reason Castañeda, García Canclini, and others are promoting ways to strengthen it. In fact, it may not be easily transferable to the United States. The institutionalization of just about every form of activity here makes it difficult to cut across different spheres of action, for institutions tend to police their borders quite assiduously. On the other hand, the absence or weakness of similar institutions in Latin America, most of all universal access to commodity consumption (e.g., there, McDonald's is for elites), makes the U.S. example virtually untranslatable.

In the following three chapters, I examine how culture and commerce drove the development of Miami in the past decade (chapter 7), how free trade involves culture in a difficult negotiation of citizenship and equity (chapter 8), and how a binational triennial art program, inSITE, originally spurred by NAFTA, creates an innovative, if problematic, model for the integration of the Americas (chapter 9).

7

The Globalization of Latin America: Miami

Globalization and Cities

Miami has been classed as a "minor world city" in the company of Amsterdam, Barcelona, Berlin, Buenos Aires, Caracas, Geneva, Montreal, Shanghai, Taipei, and Washington, D.C.[1] World or global cities are generally defined by the concentration of command and control headquarters for transnational corporations and a concomitant critical mass of complementary *advanced* producer services, particularly accounting, advertising, banking, and law. Although these services are found in all cities, only in advanced "postindustrial production sites" do we find the innovations in services that play "a specific role in the current phase of the world economy" (Sassen 1991: 126). New practices like "just in time" production and outsourcing require capitalization, systems analysis and management, and increased telecommunicational capacities, in addition to accountancy and law. These services are concentrated in cities, as Manuel Castells (1996) argues, where innovation results from the synergy of networks of complementary enterprises and from reservoirs of "human talent," much of it composed of intra- and international migrants. To attract such talent, Castells (2000) adds, cities must offer a high quality of life, which means that such cities are also major generators of cultural capital and value. The role of culture in capital accumulation, however, is not limited to this ancillary function; it is central to the processes of globalization, as we will see below, taking Miami as our case study.

Most cities, and Miami is no exception, have experienced globalization according to two logics that have been operative since the 1970s, when a worldwide inflationary crisis brought the Keynesian compromise between capital and labor to an end: the assault on labor via neoliberal policies and the related development of new technologies that have enabled capital to reorganize commensurate with a new world economy in which operations are articulated planetarily in real time. Globalization did not just happen "naturally" but has been the result of policy and conflict.

Falling wages in the developing world, due to U.S.-biased IMF structural adjustment or austerity programs, enabled corporations to relocate manufacturing "overseas." On behalf of transnational corporate reorganization and the new international division of labor, the U.S. government spearheaded the elimination of barriers to trade in goods and services and to portfolio and direct foreign investment. This entailed devaluation, privatization, deregulation, reduction of public programs, and the elimination of protectionist policies that had been used to support national enterprises and that often maintained wage levels. U.S. government and transnational protagonism in this regard has taken place on the stage of GATT and its successor, the WTO.

While labor has certainly felt the stab of these policies, workers have increasingly struggled to maintain the public weal and have disrupted capital at both national and global levels, evident, respectively, in the so-called IMF riots and more recently in the mass demonstrations against the WTO in Seattle, Davos, and Washington, D.C. Protestors have yet to target the globalization of culture, including music and the new media, maybe because they are some of their more avid consumers. Perhaps for this reason, technological innovations have provided a more successful opportunity for capital's new regime of accumulation. The telecommunications and Internet technologies that enabled roboticized just-in-time production in both first and third world factories, geographic reorganization of corporations, and decreasing production costs (Cleaver 1995: 166–167) have also made possible the decentralized flow of information on which the anti-WTO protestors rely. Indeed, it has been argued that the Internet is not a technology but an organizational form that fosters network relations (Castells 1996), which characterize the new practices of both the transnational corporate sector and civil society (see chapters 3 and 5). The rapid development of these technologies has enabled the so-called new information- and knowledge-based economy to supersede the old industrial economy; 80 percent of the U.S. workforce, for example, does not make things but works in offices generating information and providing services (Progressive Policy Institute 2000). A June 2000 U.S. Commerce Department report indicates that the information technology industry is the major engine of economic growth in the country, accounting for one third of that growth (Claus-ing 2000).

As the price of labor has decreased, largely by relocating it to the develop-ing world, knowledge and information have become the major generators of value. Indeed, "wealth creation" is premised on the production of intellectual property, which requires highly developed and capitalized university systems and the assiduous policing of those who resist capital's regime of appropria-tion, such as local peoples who have devised herbal medicines or rhythms over many generations, or who poach on it, like unlicensed manufacturers of CDs and video tapes sold by street vendors and software engineers and companies (e.g., Napster) that make it possible to freely exchange music and video with anyone else on the Internet. The United States is far ahead of all other countries in the number of patents registered. Just to give a sense of the importance of knowledge production, the U.S. genomics industry alone is about the size of the entire Argentine economy (Enríquez 2000). As capital accumulation increas-ingly depends on scientific and technological innovation and as commodity production is further devalued, Latin America and other developing regions will decline even further. Under the current neoliberal consensus among Latin American elites, university research agendas are increasingly driven by market criteria, particularly in the private universities that have sprouted over the past decade or two in every country and even in the increasingly underfunded public universities (Gentili 2000: 13). The result is brain drain from public to private institutions within Latin America and from Latin America to the United States, where scientifically competent immigrants are needed to fuel the new econ-omy, according to Federal Reserve Chairman Alan Greenspan's depositions be-fore Congress in 2000 and 2001. Indeed, pressed by Internet and high-tech companies, Congress will raise the number of HI-B visas in 2000 ("Ali Asked" 2001). The problem, of course, is not limited to developing countries like those in Latin America or to the United States. Germany, which has "an estimated 75,000 to 100,000 jobs vacant in the booming Internet sector, with few Ger-mans apparently qualified to fill them," is courting high-tech-proficient im-migrants from India, a policy that is met with protest and greater appeals for increases and changes in the German university system. According to one ob-server, "German education with its focus on heavy philosophical concepts does not turn out the people we want" (R. Cohen 2000). An expression of a new inter-national division of knowledge production is the new Indian policy to produce information technology workers to meet demand in Germany, Japan, Singa-pore, Britain, and the United States as well as locally ("India Plans" 2000).

Whether the new economy succeeds to the extent of its potential depends on government spending on education, transportation, communications, and, ultimately, technological research. In the past (and indeed in the origins of the Internet) the U.S. government financed the development of new technologies and industries and then put them in the private sector as sources of wealth creation (Madrick 2000). Current policies militate against a direct government intervention, but there are a range of alternatives, among them local public investment and incentives. The creation of Silicon Alleys, Valleys, Parks, and Beaches throughout the world is not solely the product of entrepreneurial genius in the private sector but also of public-private partnerships. Such partnerships have significant transformative effects on the urban fabric, from the renovation of decaying areas (often at the expense of vestigial industrial activity or of poor communities) to the creation of new educational and cultural venues that are being touted as generators of value in their own right. That value, of course, is not distributed evenly, but accrues to those classes that are positioned to gain access. Yet poor populations, often immigrants and minorities, are implicated in the maintenance and reproduction of the digerati: "Alongside technological innovation there has mushroomed an extraordinary urban activity . . . fortifying the social fabric of bars, restaurants, chance encounters on the street, etc. that give life to a place" (Castells 2000). "Giving life" is a matter of policy in many cities, as culture increasingly becomes a part of business and economic development departments, as was recently the case in the City of Miami Beach with the creation of a liaison for the entertainment industry in the Economic Development Division (Dennis Leyva, interview, March 14, 2000; City of South Miami Beach 2000).

Miami: Cultural Capital of Latin America

But it is culture—not raw technology alone—that will determine whether the United States retains its status as the pre-eminent Internet nation.
—Steve Lohr, "Welcome to the Internet, the First Global Colony"

Internet portals will be the engine of development of the entertainment industry and Miami will prosper to the degree that content can be produced there.
—Sergio Rozenblat, interview, March 10, 2000[2]

It has been argued that in the new economy the manufacture and transfer of goods increasingly will take a secondary place with respect to culture. The cultural economy is already defined as the "selling and buying of human experiences" in "themed cities, common-interest developments, entertainment destination centers, shopping malls, global tourism, fashion, cuisine, professional sports and games, film, television, virtual worlds, and [other] simulated experiences." These "represent the new stage of capitalist development" (Rifkin 2000: 29, 265). Such a depiction is sure to induce allergic reactions in those with Adornian proclivities, but neither simulated experiences nor the "elimination" of work are the end-all and be-all of contemporary cultural life. Castells's argument about "giving life" makes it clear that culture encompasses more than the entertainment and tourism industries; it is also a medium in which new intellectual capital is reproduced and maintained in a range of experiences that cut across different classes and social and ethnic groups. This is not fully evident because we are accustomed to thinking of capital in terms of property and commodities. To be sure, the production of the culture industries fits this conception, but there is more to the success of these industries than selling and buying. We might ask what it is about city life, particularly its immigrant populations and their cultures, that can be transformed into value, and what kind of value. I hope to give a sense of this in my examination of Miami as the "cultural capital of Latin America."

Most studies of Miami, especially from the mid-1980s on, focus on the protagonism of the Cuban exile community and its relations with other ethnic groups, particularly Anglo-Americans, African Americans, and Haitians, in a series of power struggles and compromises (Croucher 1997; Didion 1987; Portes and Stepick 1993; Rieff 1987). This view captures to a great extent the course that the region, south Florida, has taken, but it nevertheless overlooks the most dynamic changes that have been taking place from the early 1990s into the twenty-first century. I am referring to the transformation of Miami and surrounding counties and cities by the fashion, entertainment, communications, and new media industries.[3] They provide the momentum that has already led to characterizations of Miami as a global city based on the numerous multinational articulations that take place in the area (Beaverstock, Smith and Taylor 1999; Beaverstock, Smith, Taylor, Walker, and Lorimer 2000). To be sure, the possibility of making these articulations was facilitated by Cuban exiles with business expertise, hemispheric connections, and cultural talent, as well as two other historical precedents: Miami was chosen as headquarters of the U.S. national security state vis-à-vis Latin America in 1898 and the U.S. government pumped billions of dollars into the Cuban exile community to transform it into a showcase of success vis-à-vis the economically strangled Cubans who remained on their island and vis-à-vis other U.S. minorities at a time when they were attracted to Marxist and anti-imperialist critical frameworks in the 1960s and 1970s. Even in entertainment, which constitutes the backbone of the new industries that are transforming Miami, Cubans have already cleared the way, for example, the Miami Sound Machine, Emilio Estefan Enterprises, El Show de Cristina, and various magazine publishing enterprises. But in the 1990s the impetus of these new industries came from other sources and often chafes against the Cuban exile community. As these new industries give the region a new face, it becomes possible to speak of a post-Cuban and even a post-Caribbean Miami.

Cubans will continue to play an important role in the new Miami, particularly as new generations are weaned from the fervent anti-Castroism of the older generations. But this weaning has to be carefully negotiated, particularly when there are flare-ups like the Elián González affair, which brought many strays back into the fold or at least obliged them to remain silent (Forero 2000). It is important to note that some Miami Cubans, particularly those connected to the arts and entertainment industries, voiced dissident views regarding the Miami-Dade ordinance that prohibited the county from contracting with any entity that does business with Cubans from the island. Their pressure and the increasing power of arts and entertainment made it possible for Cuban musicians to play in Miami, although most recently the Latin Grammy Awards were forced to relocate to Los Angeles because the organizing institution, the National Association of Recording Artists (NARAS), would not go back on its intentions to invite Cuban artists. This turn of events infuriated people in the industry and cost the city millions of dollars (Cobo-Hanlon 1999a, 2000). On the other hand, even opponents of the Miami-Dade ordinance, like *Miami Herald* columnist Liz Balmaseda, took the side of the exile community over custody of Elián. While the Elián flare-up rallied even third-generation Cubans to the exile perspective (Robles 2000), it also backfired, producing great resentment among non-Hispanic whites, African Americans, Haitians, and even other Latin American immigrant groups (Adam Ramírez 2000). There were counterdemonstrations to the exile community's protests against the U.S. government for removing Elián from his Miami relatives ("Protesters Support" 2000). Ethnic tensions flared when banners bearing images of bananas were sported throughout town and bananas were thrown at Miami City Hall, a parodic criticism of the "Banana Republic"–like actions of Mayor Joe Carollo (F. Santiago 2000). Moreover, the (always temporary) "warming" of relations between the U.S. and Cuban governments, particularly as regards trade (Perlez 2000), as well as the repeal of the Miami-Dade ordinance banning business with Cuba (Weaver, Levine, and Finefrock 2000; Kidwell 2000), were also off-shoots of the Elián affair.[4]

Cuban exile leaders made a serious miscalculation as to the likelihood of support for their position and thus lost considerable symbolic capital over the Elián González case. They are now regrouping, but it will be difficult to re-gain the prestige they once enjoyed (C. Marquis 2000). They clearly do not see that Miami is changing and that they no longer occupy the leading role in the next stage of the region's development. This case fits the pattern that Sheila Croucher discerns, whereby the images of different ethnic groups and of the city itself are part of the struggles among non-Hispanic whites, Cubans, and African Americans as they jockey for power (1997: 173–174). But there is more than jockeying for power; politics and ethnicization keep memories alive or revive them when change is on the way. The current prosperity of Miami, led by the entertainment industry, which needs space for its expansion and has spurred new waves of tourism, has led to a run on yet undeveloped areas, such as the initiative to transform deserted Virginia Key into an upscale resort area. Conceded in the immediate postwar period to black Miamians who were banned from most other beaches in South Florida and subsequently abandoned in the wake of civil rights and devastation by a hurricane in the mid-1960s, it is now caught in a struggle between development plans and an initiative to create a civil rights park that would honor black residents who fought against segregation (Bragg 1999).

As Croucher (1997: 179) argues, multiculturalism was largely accepted in the 1990s by the non-Hispanic white elites as their power waned. It was a way of maintaining a place in the new power dynamic, which was largely underwrit-ten by Latin culture, and a way of dealing with ethnic conflict, particularly the claims of African Americans who were left out of the spoils of development. The discourse of multiculturalism, which can be found in the local govern-ment promotional documents and reports as well as those of the initiatives of the new industries, is a means to put a positive spin on the unequally dis-tributed new prosperity. As I argue below, this is not the same multicultural-ism found throughout the United States. The Latin-based entertainment-led boom in Miami has contributed features of Latin American discourses of mes-tizaje and hybridity, which are generally thought to be more inclusive than U.S. identity politics. The result is the simulacrum of a level playing field, in which African Americans and Haitians continue to lose.

I will return to this line of argument in my conclusion. Now I would like to make my case for a post-Cuban Miami as a new economy that cannot be separated from culture—let's call it a cultural economy, on the model of political economy—takes root there.

Miami has many attractions for people who are seeking to work in entertainment, new media, and related enterprises that do business in Latin America and/or that cater to U.S. Latino markets. Compared to Latin America, it offers economic stability; the most convenient location in the entire hemisphere for those who travel tricontinentally in Latin America, Europe, and the United States; the lowest cost of living of the major concentrations of Hispanics in the United States (Los Angeles, New York, Miami); excellent communications and mail services; a critical mass of production companies and advanced producer services (accountancy, advertising, banking, law, etc.) and technological production services (studios, laboratories, postproduction, and distribution facilities); high intellectual and artistic capital (composers, arrangers, producers, musicians, scriptwriters, visual, internal, and fashion designers, multilingual translators, universities and specialized training centers); attractive locations for film, video, and photography; tax breaks and other government incentives for production and commerce; and high quality of cultural life (restaurants, bars, nightclubs, galleries, museums, beaches). Moreover, for many people who have relocated there it has the feel of a Latin American city without the crime, grime, and infrastructural dysfunctionality and all the advantages of a first world city (Bruno del Granado, interview, March 13, 2000; Néstor Casonu, interview, March 14, 2000).

People in the entertainment industry list three mid-1980s phenomena as the sources of the new Miami: the Miami Sound Machine, *Miami Vice*, and the renovation of the Art Deco District. It is no doubt an exaggeration to base the genesis of the new Miami on new sound and visual imagery, but entertainment people explain that these attracted film producers and celebrities like Stallone, Madonna, and Cher as well as gave a shot in the arm to a small modeling industry that burgeoned as designers like Giorgio Armani and Calvin Klein established branch offices there and Gianni Versace bought a mansion in the restored Art Deco District. Gay culture also burgeoned, especially in South Beach, and contributed significantly to these industries and consumer lifestyle (e.g., shops, discos, and other entertainment venues). By the early 1990s, the major music multinational corporations like Sony and Warner reestablished offices there, and throughout the 1990s all majors had their regional headquarters (i.e., headquarters for Latin America) in Miami, specifically in South Miami Beach, spurring the renovation of already existing sound studios (e.g., Criteria, active since the 1960s and where artists like Aretha Franklin, Eric Clapton, and Bob Marley recorded) and the construction of others, like Emilio and Gloria Estefan's Crescent Moon Studios, the Mecca for many Latin American singers like Luis Miguel and Shakira.

Any viewer of Spanish-language television in the United States knows that the dominant network, Univisión, concentrates its production and other operations in Miami, although it maintains its headquarters in L.A. Telemundo recently moved its headquarters there from Los Angeles to take advantage of lower production and service costs as well as a more Latin American as opposed to the predominantly Mexican American population of L.A. Together, these two networks reach over 100 million viewers in the United States and Latin America. Music and television attracted thousands of celebrities, artists, producers, arrangers, executives, and other entertainment service professionals from Latin America. In addition to the Anglo-American celebrities mentioned above, we can list an ever-growing number of Spanish-speaking artists and professionals, including Julio Iglesias, his son Enrique Iglesias, and the pioneer of the romantic ballad, Raphael; important telenovela actors like the Venezuelans José Luis Rodríguez ("El Puma") and Lucía Méndez, who is also a popular singer; and many television personalities, such as the Dominican comedienne Charytin, the Cuban talk show host Cristina Saralegui, and the Chilean Don Francisco, host of the variety show *Sábado Gigante*; important producers like the Cuban American Rudy Pérez, the Colombian Kike Santander, the Argentine Bebu Silvetti, and the New Yorker Desmond Child; major singers like Ricky Martin and Shakira, and, of course, the staple of Cuban singers and musicians, including Israel "Cachao" López, Arsenio "Chocolate" Rodríguez, and Albita.

The music and entertainment infrastructure has grown to the point that any imaginable service can be found in Miami, from producers, arrangers, backup singers, writers, sound engineers, technicians, and film and video personnel to specialized musicians. For the past five or six years, Latin music has enjoyed robust growth unseen in any other segment of the music business, with a 12 percent jump from 1998 to 1999. The U.S. Latin music industry's strong performance is, according to Hilary Rosen, president and CEO of the Recording Industry Association of America, additional to "the Ricky Martin/Jennifer Lopez phenomena, as these artists' recent English language recordings are not classified as Latin" (Cobo-Hanlon 1999b). In Miami Beach alone more than 150 entertainment companies have been established in the past five years (Dennis Leyva, interview, March 14 2000). Almost half of these companies (among them Sony, EMI, Starmedia, MTV Latin America, and WAMI TV) are concentrated in a five-block-long outdoor mall—Lincoln Road—amid stores, restaurants, theaters, and art galleries (Potts 1999). Growth has been so rapid that from September 1990 until March 2000 another twenty-eight companies opened there and it is estimated that another five hundred thousand square feet were to be renovated later that year for office space for the new "dot-coms" and Internet portals that were created in the past couple of years. These new media companies are full-service entertainers providing movies, television, videocassettes, CDs, books, interactive games, theater, and Internet sites (Gabler 2000). Indeed, the building industry has received a potent shot in the arm from all this activity. Even real estate companies have formed partnerships with entertainment concerns. For example, real estate developer Michael Comras has wagered on the continuing prosperity of Miami's entertainment industry by forming a special entertainment division with Miami International Studios that will steer companies from Los Angeles and Latin America to Miami, in particular to Comras's buildings ("Comras" 1998).

The synergy of all of this activity made Miami the most attractive headquarters location for most dot-coms seeking to break into Latin American markets. Although most of these initiatives failed, due to the burst Internet bubble, they did constitute a major site for investment, particularly for portals specializing in entertainment or financial information and counseling. For example, AOL Latin America, Eritmo.com, QuePasa.com, Yupi.com, Elsitio.com, Fiera.com, Aplauso.com, Starmedia.com, Terra.com, and Artistsdirect.com sought to offer music information, download, and services such as Web page creation for musicians; Subasta.com offers an online auction; SportsYa.com and Totalsports.com broadcast sports news and ecommerce; R2.com deals strictly with the futures market; and Consejero.com and Patagon.com offer online stock transactions ("Spanish-language Web Sites Specialize" 1999). These new enterprises had wagered that the development of the Internet market in Latin America would grow exponentially, following market studies like International Data Corp.'s, which foresees 19 million subscribers by 2003 (Graser 1999). Brazil alone is expected to have 30 million users in 2005 (DaCosta 2000). Since it was predicted that the Internet would revolutionize the entertainment industry, vast sums of money were invested as part of a Darwinian gambit for survival. The Cisneros Group invested over $200 million in its 50/50 partnership with America Online, and spent $11 million on a media blitz featuring actor Michael Douglas just to launch its Brazil site (Faber and Ewing 1999).[5] Similarly, StarMedia raised $313 million in public offerings in 1999, much of which will be used for marketing and acquisitions, which are estimated to produce a loss of $150 million in 2000 (García 2000). Perhaps the most spectacular merger and acquisition was the deal between Spain's global telecommunications corporation Telefónica and Germany's global media conglomerate Bertelsmann to give Terra, Telefónica's Internet service provider, a boost by acquiring and merging with Lycos (Carvajal 2000). This is the first purchase of a major U.S. Internet company by a European corporation. Terra is expected to make sizable gains in Latin America; nevertheless, it is a global initiative, with significant activity in Europe and the United States as well. Miami, easily accessible to these three regions, is the most convenient site for its headquarters. Together, these companies have carved out a piece of South Miami Beach that is now called "Silicon Beach."

Miami Beach has been particularly active in wooing industry. The Miami Beach Enterprise Zone offers incentives to businesses expanding or relocating there that include property tax credits, tax credits on wages paid to Enterprise Zone residents, and sales tax refunds. The Façade Renovation Grant program provides matching grants to qualifying businesses for the rehabilitation of storefronts and the correction of interior code violations (City of South Miami Beach). As a consequence of this promotional activity, Miami entertainment industries generated about $2 billion in 1997, more than any entertainment capital in Latin America, and boasts a workforce of ten thousand employees (García 1998; M. Martín 1998). By November 1999 volume had increased to $2.5 billion (Leyva interview 2000). Other Miami counties are also renewing their initiatives to woo the entertainment industries. To counteract the difficulties that producers and film companies encounter in dealing with the complicated bureaucracy of the numerous municipalities in the area that have their own regulations, Jeff Peel, Miami-Dade film commissioner, is leading an initiative that includes his counterparts in other municipalities to change the bureaucracy and draw more film and TV business to South Florida (T. Jackson 2000). The importance of entertainment in Miami is not only that it supplies most programming for the U.S. Latino market but its attraction of an increasing share of the Latin American market. Miami is the third-largest audiovisual production hub in the United States, after Los Angeles and New York (LeClaire 1998). Currently, Miami entertainment and new media are expanding to global markets ("Boogie Woogie" 1997).

Entertainment and new media have an advantage in relocating to Miami, where the financial sector has established a highly developed infrastructure for business and where transport and communications provide the best connections to Latin America, Europe, and the rest of the United States. Since the 1980s, the location of the largest free trade zone in the United States in the vicinity of Miami airport has attracted more than two hundred corporations specializing in international trade. Some, like Dupont, selected Miami as their regional headquarters over Mexico City, San José, Bogotá, Caracas, São Paulo, Rio de Janeiro, Buenos Aires, and San Juan (Grosfoguel 1994: 366–367). Almost all of the people I interviewed for this study remarked on this convenience. For Néstor Casonu, an Argentine who, in his capacity as regional managing director for EMI Music Publishing, moved from Buenos Aires to Miami, the airport is a much more convenient gateway to all Latin American cities (interview, March 14, 2000). Producer Bruno del Granado, who moved to Miami from Los Angeles in 1994 for the same reasons as Julio Iglesias, recalls the singer's advice: "Julio Iglesias told me that when he came from Spain to the United States he wanted a base. He researched the different cities looking for a convenient central location between Europe, the United States, and Latin America. He was already famous everywhere else, aside from the U.S. Miami furnished him with a base for launching into the U.S., while he was only a few hours from Europe and Latin America" (interview, March 13, 2000).

Entertainment and tourism nourish each other. The critical mass of entertainment companies situated in South Beach have transformed it into a major international promenade for the "beautiful people" and those who yearn to walk in their wake. In the early 1990s, following Versace and all the glitz of fashion and entertainment celebrities, "the beautiful people came to town," and, as Neisen Kasdin, mayor of South Miami Beach explains, "people wanted to be around them." Together, these phenomena produced a synergy that increased exponentially the "nonstop creation of new businesses in modeling, new media, broadcasting and electronic commerce" (Kilborn 2000). And of course, this "Hollywood East" or "Hollywood Latin America" has spawned a self-congratulatory hype, embodied in Will Smith's *Miami Mix*, produced by Emilio Estefan at Crescent Moon. Such hype belies the urban conflicts referred to in the beginning of this chapter but also captures the spirit and no doubt part of the reality of what makes Miami so dynamic in the 1990s and early twenty-first century. Let's examine some of this hype.

From the perspective of the financial or entertainment and new media industries, Miami is a gateway or a crossroads. The reason for the location in Miami of the major entertainment conglomerates has more to do with command and control of transnational operations—a major feature of global cities—than with edenic bliss, one that, like every utopia, is ringed by the dystopia of conflict and corruption. As Gabriel Abaroa, executive director of the Latin American Federation of Producers of Phonograms and Videograms, explains, it is much more advantageous to monitor all aspects of the music industry from Miami "since everyone has to go through it" ("Q & A with Gabriel Abaroa 1998). By "everyone," Abaroa is referring not to the new migrations that are swelling the ranks of the Latino community, but to the critical mass of artists from throughout the Hispanic world who have moved to Miami or who continuously shuttle there from regional capitals. The very logic of capitalizing on Latin culture as a resource is internalized in the discourse of many of the entertainment celebrities in Miami. Miami, in fact, becomes a synecdoche and a metonym of that resource. The variety show host Jaime Bayly refurbishes Simón Bolívar's dream of an integrated Latin America with all the trappings of media glamor: "If what you want is a real Latin American program that will reach an international public, you have to be where all the celebrities are, and that means Miami" (qtd. in Rohter 1996).

This hype and the commercial reality that largely corresponds to it provide the major rationale for business and political leaders' strategies to locate the Center of Hemispheric Integration in Miami. As the rhetoric goes, only in Miami are there significant representatives from each country of the region. Furthermore, Florida sends 48 percent of its exports to Latin America, most of which travel through Miami. According to Luis Lauredo, U.S. ambassador to the Organization of American States, Miami "is a blend of the best of the cultures of the Americas, both North and South" (quoted in Rivera-Lyles 2000). As a center of commerce, technology, and communications whose personnel are at the very least bilingual, it has a comparative advantage. This advantage is expected to increase with the "expansion of its intellectual capital," mostly by way of immigration but also by targeted training programs at institutions like the University of Miami and Florida International University. That FIU graduates more Spanish-speaking students than any other university in the country is not an expression of concern for Latinos as an underprivileged minority but a strategy for reinforcing the business and high-tech sectors. This strategy ensues from the observation that, in the words of FIU's president, the most dynamic "technological and economic urban centers are connected with major research universities" (Rivera-Lyles 2000). As the site of business and trade summits, Miami is touted as a New World Brussels. Should the Free Trade Agreement of the Americas (FTAA; ALCA in Spanish) be sited in Miami, where negotiations have been held over the past couple of years and in whose Intercontinental Hotel its headquarters are temporarily situated, it is likely that the OAS and the Inter-American Development Bank (IADB) would move there. This opportunity will enable Miami to redefine itself when the embargo on Cuba is lifted and tourism, still Miami's largest industry, is siphoned off to that island. The location of a critical mass of communications and Internet companies in Miami is already a step in that direction (Katel 2000).

Magazines in south Florida also have capitalized on the Latin resource. They are having a boom, in great part because advertisers can reach several markets via Miami. The concentration of businesspeople in south Florida makes the area a convenient location for Latin Trade, covering the Latin American markets, the U.S. Latino market (with its considerable buying power of $325 billion in 1999, estimated to reach $458 billion in 2000), and readers who enjoy the attractions of South Beach and the rest of South Florida. Ocean Drive took its name from the beachfront street on which Gianni Versace bought his mansion in 1992. Similarly, Channels features the "beautiful people" and fashions of South Beach; initiated as a regional publication, it went national in 1998. Latin Girl and Generation ñ are two new magazines for teens and the twenty-something generation, who also flock to Miami Beach (Martínez 1998). Florida International Magazine was started in 1998 with a print run of 75,000; by the end of 1999, it had reached a circulation of 100,000. Political and economic instability in Latin America have led to the relocation of publishers and other companies to Miami. For example, the most influential Latin American art journal, Art Nexus, relocated there permanently from Bogotá in 2000 (Celia Bibragher, interview, March 15, 2000).

Latin Multiculturalism: Transculturation as Value Added

As suggested earlier, Latin Miami is no longer an exclusively Cuban city. There are hundreds of thousands of immigrants from Nicaragua, the Dominican Republic, Colombia, Venezuela, Argentina, Brazil, and other countries. Some have been in Miami for only a few short years, but they already have national festivals. Argentines' first festival in May 1999 attracted 150,000 people; several hundred thousand Colombians, from Miami, other parts of the United States, and the homeland, swelled Tropical Park on July 17, 1999. Whereas many immigrants have come out of economic necessity or for political reasons, quite a few have come to work in the entertainment and new media industries. Many come for both reasons: telenovela actress Alejandra Borrero and talk show host

Fernando González Pacheco both left out of fear of kidnapping by guerrillas and moved to Miami, where they could continue doing television work (Rosenberg 2000).

The new immigrants to Miami fit neither the assimilationist nor the identity politics paradigms familiar to U.S. scholars of race and ethnicity. They maintain ties to their homelands and travel back and forth with frequency, but they have also developed a new spirit of belonging to the city. Daniel Mato's research on the telenovela industry indicates that many new transplants feel comfortable reflecting the reality of Latin American immigrants in the United States (Mato 2000; Yúdice 1999b). Some, particularly those in the corporate and entertainment and arts sectors, have developed a new sense of cultural citizenship and seek to reinforce local cultural institutions. Unlike most Latin American immigrants and Latino minorities in other U.S. cities, most of the fifty people I interviewed in March 1999 characterized Miami as an "open city" that accepts new migrants. Not all new transplants are from Latin America; many people have relocated to Miami from other parts of the country and from Europe to take advantage of opportunities. There is a recognition that entertainment, the new media, design, fashion, tourism, and the arts are helping to transform Miami, to give it the cultural sophistication it never had before.

This largely multicultural image of the city was sounded time and again by my mostly middle- and upper-class interviewees. They are cosmopolitans for whom Miami is a convenient hub for their travels throughout the world. Nevertheless, their esprit de corps and will to create a cultural infrastructure for all Miami residents does not emanate only from their role as managers and producers in the center of command and control for Ibero-American culture industries. In the past five years, the new cultural producers, while maintaining a strong Latin flavor, have nevertheless opted for an international image. This is evident in the art world, in which Miami is no longer being promoted as the capital of Latin American art. Although much Latin American art will continue to be shown and bought and sold there, art institutions are focusing increasingly on international trends and on developing local talent. Both of these developments are taking precedence over worn tropicalist stereotypes that have sold well. The new spirit in the art world, as in the entertainment industry, is manifesting itself in the major contributions that Miami artists, Latin or not, are making to contemporary art.[6]

This means that Latinness or Latinoness is undergoing a transformation in Miami; it is less rooted to a specific or minority identity. Perhaps this is because of all U.S. cities (indeed, all cities in the Americas), Miami is the only one from which a generalized international Latin identity is possible. This internationalization is even taking place in the music industry, in which two worlds continue to exist side by side, especially in their administrative aspects: the U.S. Latino (and the aspired-to crossover) market, characterized mostly by Latin pop and salsa (Gloria Estefan, Jon Secada, Albita, and a host of other Latino singers from elsewhere produced in Miami), and the Latin American market, which is largely managed out of Miami. But these two worlds do communicate and thus create an important source of hybridization between the North and the South, between Latinos and Latin Americans. And together they are producing a range of international megastars like Ricky Martin, Shakira, and Enrique Iglesias, in addition to mainstays like Julio Iglesias.

Because Miami has long been held to be a cultural backwater, the fact that it is now a major production hub for the culture industries is providing the impetus to legitimize the city as a cultural capital in the more traditional artistic sense. Latin American and Latino producers, artists, entertainers, managers, and executives are participating in the establishment or redefinition of museums, educational institutions, and philanthropic and training initiatives to produce new cohorts who will feed into the burgeoning entertainment industries. One such initiative is One Community, One Goal, which has targeted specific industries for employment growth. The culture industries are in the forefront of this initiative (Peggy McKinley, interview, March 13, 2000). Among its projects is Arts Related Technology for Entertainment Careers, a program designed to prepare students for technical careers in the arts and entertainment industries.

Composer and producer Rudy Pérez, first president of the Latin American Association of Recording Artists, introduced into Miami various philanthropic programs implemented earlier by the parent NARAS. For example, Pérez is a regular lecturer and performer for the Grammys in the Schools program spearheaded by Quincy Jones for NARAS. Additionally, Pérez has been an outspoken advocate for arts (particularly music) education in the schools. He himself is in the process of opening a school of the arts, with a focus on music and recording/engineering and the music business, and also a children's talent agency. The school is conceived as a complement to the New World School, patterned after the High School of Music and Art in New York, which has stringent requirements in all subjects, making it difficult for musically talented minority youth to gain admission. The school that Pérez has proposed will provide special tutoring to talented black and Latino kids. Like many other people in the arts and entertainment, Pérez finds that although Miami has a high profile it lacks a cultural infrastructure, particularly in performing venues. This problem has been overcome to some degree in the visual arts, where new museums have been built or renovated. And the art scene has gone from one dominated by Cuban and Latin American artists to an international scene that puts a premium on diversity. "Miami is no longer just Cuban or even Latin American. Now there are Italians, Russians, and other Europeans in addition to Brazilians, Colombians, Dominicans, Puerto Ricans, and Central Americans" (Rudy Pérez, interview, March 11 2000). Despite this cosmopolitanism, Pérez prefers to focus attention on the local communities: "Latins are coming to Miami, having kids here who speak English, and at 16 or 17 they resonate to their Latin cultural background. This is the case with English-language artists like Cristina Aguilera, Jaci Velázquez, and Oscar de la Hoya, who have decided to be produced in Miami for their Spanish-language versions. Instead of looking for artists in Latin America, we need to scout for talented kids from the barrios." Some artists, like Aguilera, have turned to producers in Miami to get in touch with roots they have never known. This desire to learn Spanish and make records in that language is no doubt motivated by a desire to further capitalize on sales of over 10 million copies of some of her singles, but also, according to Pérez, because she wants to draw on her heritage for her music. For Pérez, anyone who has not been part of a Latino community in the United States can partake of the transnational Latinness that Miami offers.

Markets and identity evidently go together in Miami's Latin-inflected multiculturalism. The effects of all this Latin cultural production in a U.S. city, no matter how Latinized, is of concern to many Latin Americans, who fear that national and local cultures will be homogenized by this "Miami sound machine." But hybridity and transculturation are the name of the game of pop music in all Latin American entertainment capitals (Yúdice 1999b). The results are not a flattening out of music but, on the contrary, its pluralization, observable in the rock of groups like La Ley from Chile and Maná from Mexico, or the "ethnic" musics of Olodum from Salvador and Afro Reggae from Rio de Janeiro. Moreover, there is a constant flow of musics from Latin America into Miami, in the person of the musicians who go there to produce their records, as well as in the influences that arrangers and producers introduce into their work. This emphasis on local taste markets is increasingly reflected in the organizational structure of some entertainment companies, especially the most global ones. Mato points out that some telenovela and serial production companies are selling modular formats that can be tailored to the demographic characteristics of audiences in different localities ("Miami South Florida" 1999: 6). Something similar is taking place in the corporate reorganization of MTV Latin America. Programming and marketing were completely done in the Miami office when MTV Latin America got started with one signal for all of Spanish America in 1993 and another for MTV Brazil. In 1996 it took its first step toward regionalization by doubling the Spanish American signals, centering the northern one in Mexico City and the southern in Buenos Aires. In 1999 it began to produce programming in the regions, following the adage "I want my own MTV." Rather than homogenization, a global corporation like MTV wants local relevance, in every locality. The next step will establish full programming, production, and marketing offices in each of twenty-two countries. Its center of operations will remain in Miami, but direction of content provision will be much more flexible and nomadic as managers and producers move or communicate between Latin American localities and the Miami office (Antoinette Zel, interview, March 14, 2000).

Miami is a major center for the fusion of dance and house musics, especially the Latinization of disco, funk, rap, and jungle. The source of this fusion is the DJs and the groups, which hail from all the various ethnicities to be found in Miami. More than in the production side of the entertainment industry or the art scene, dance is the place for the commingling of bodies. As one observer reports, "The cultural mix brings together races, diverse sexual orientations, languages and incomes" (Kilborn 2000). And it is from this commingling that a good part of the creativity that animates the music industry is drawn. Midem, the largest industry showcase for Latin music, showcased dance at its 1998 convention in Miami Beach. Among the local musics featured were the house music of Tito Puente Jr., the Latin-influenced hip-hop acts of 2 Live Crew and DJ Laz, and Afro-Cuban house music by LatinXpress (Cobo-Hanlon 1998). The influence of this music can be found in Gloria Estefan's gloria!, which overlays salsa onto disco, and Ricky Martin's dance-mix version of "The Cup of Life." According to recording star Alegra, "This music is a breeding ground for experimentation" (qtd. in Cobo-Hanlon 1998).

Experimentation in dance, house, salsa, hip-hop, and other musics is regular fare in the lively nightclub life of Miami. From there it moves up the industrial stream to those stars who make records for the majors: Jaci Velazquez, Shakira, Albita, Ricky Martin, and Gloria Estefan. The Chirino sisters have recorded a Spanish-language record with "Latin/rock/pop/gypsy rhythms, produced by the Colombian Juan Vicente Zambrano of Estefan Enterprises" (E. Pérez 2000). As Latinized music makes its way beyond the clubs and Latin artists, it serves up the promise of the crossover.

This mainstreaming is also being pursued on television, which is not limited to the production of telenovelas. Producers Mo Walker and Robert Fitzgibbon have teamed up with Francisco García in the design of a Latinized *American Bandstand*–like music show for network television. Its pilot show features a block party in South Miami Beach where youth of all ethnicities engage in transculturating Latinness through rhythm, movement, and language (Mo Fitzgibbon, interview, March 10, 2000).

These musical and bodily fusions reflect the dynamism of Miami's dance clubs, where very diverse groups come together, yet there are considerable ethnic conflicts over access to jobs and (un)fairness in immigration policy. The tendency of culture, particularly Latin culture, and economy to merge, embodied in the entertainment industry itself, provides greater opportunities for the bicultural and bilingual professional class in Miami than in any other U.S. city. This transformation is likely to exacerbate the subordination of certain immigrant populations, such as Haitians and other non-Spanish-speaking groups, particularly if they are black. Of the Cubans and Haitians who, if lucky, arrive intact on Miami shores, only the former get to stay. The Elián González affair only heightened this difference, leading Haitians and many other observers to suspect racism at work (Putney 2000; Adam Ramírez 2000; Simmons-Lewis 2000). The multiculturalism that is being showcased is not that of the poor and working classes, but of the professionals and middle classes that have given Miami an economic boost. It has been argued that Miami is adopting a typical Latin American discourse of racial democracy, whereby Latinness is inclusive of all races and classes except for blacks (Grosfoguel 2000). Contrary to Cubans' and Cuban Americans' denials that they harbor any racism or color prejudice, many scholars of race relations readily point to the fact that dark-skinned Cubans have always been on and continue to occupy the lower rungs of the socioeconomic ladder in Cuba and Miami (Casal 1980; Croucher 1997; Helg 1990; Zeitlin 1970). A report on two recent immigrant friends from Cuba, one black and one white, part of a *New York Times* series on race in the United States, detailed how they were each incorporated into separate communities based on their color. The report brings home the point that racial differentiation is greater in Miami than in Cuba, perhaps because of accommodation to the U.S. model of ethnic competition and identity politics (Ojito 2000). The report belies the claims to color-blindness that abound among Latin Americans.

Latin American claims to color-blindness are founded on the myth of the racial melting pot or mestizaje. National identity in many Latin American countries since the late 1930s and early 1940s was premised on a cultural citizenship identified with a racially hybrid subject. Fernando Ortiz ([1940] 1995), Cuba's best-known scholar of Afro-Cuban culture, advocated the abandonment of the concept of race in favor of the notion of *transculturation*. In those countries in which this transculturated, mestizo identity was accepted by whites and most racially mixed people, blacks found it difficult to make claims for equal treatment on the basis of race and were often accused of racism for even raising the issue. A Latin American equivalent of normative whiteness in the United States, mestizaje presumably included everyone as a member of the nation, but not necessarily as a beneficiary of the privileges of citizenship.

It is beyond the scope of this chapter to elaborate on the precedents of this issue in Cuba and Latin America.[7] Suffice it to say that music and dance are two privileged areas of appropriation whereby a national cultural style is fashioned from the practices of subordinated groups. This observation makes it important to take into consideration the racial repercussions of Latin entertainment industries in the United States.[8]

It is this very appropriation of the vernacular cultures, of what happens in the dance clubs, to get back to Miami, that ultimately produces value for the entertainment industry. It is here that another aspect of immigrant cultures — the meeting places of different classes — is productive of value, adds value to a cultural commodity. Latin culture industries in the United States derive a double value. On the one hand, they have a growing *market* value in Latin America, the United States, and elsewhere; on the other hand, they gain an extra *political* value as they are embraced by U.S. discourses of diversity and multiculturalism. Latin culture in Miami can even claim, as we have seen, to provide a solution to the social and racial problems that rack U.S. cities. As such, it has a comparative advantage over the cultures of other groups.

The value added by transnational, transcultural immigrant cultures to the entertainment industries in Miami is an excellent example of a new international division of cultural labor. Toby Miller (1996) proposes using this term to capture the split in production of cultural commodities across continents, taking as his model the imbrication of transnational industrial production across first, second, and third worlds. Mental and physical labor hail from varying locations, disrupting the mercantilist model whereby raw materials from the third world were transferred to the first for the manufacture of commodities. In the post-Fordist era, culture, like the clothes we wear, may be designed in one country, processed in several other countries, marketed in several locations, and consumed globally. Nation of provenance is increasingly an insignificant notion, although the post-Fordist model retains the basic insight that surplus value accrues to power elites, in this case transnational corporations, despite the disseminated structure of leadership, production, and consumption.

Hollywood, maintaining control over all operations despite geographically fragmented territories, exemplifies the new international division of cultural labor for Miller. Latin entertainment industries in Miami, though not exactly counterhegemonic, do present some significant manifestations of production and distribution that are not fully and maybe not even significantly in the hands of U.S. corporations. This last statement requires an analysis of just what the status of corporations like Sony and the Cisneros Group, to mention two global corporations, is when sited in the United States. According to Carlos Cisneros, CEO of Cisneros Television Group, a subsidiary of the Cisneros Group of Corporations (CGC) that moved to Miami from Caracas in 2000, "Miami is becoming a world production city . . . no longer limited by region" (qtd. in Moncrieff Arrarte 1998). That is, relocation to the United States, especially Miami in the case of Latin entertainment, enables corporations from other places to use the United States as a springboard to increase their global reach. That CGC is (or was) a Latin American corporation, that it has divested itself of all commodity production and distribution to concentrate on the media enhances the possibility that it can, at least in its executives' eyes, penetrate the United States. Indeed, it aims to do so *culturally*. Gustavo Cisneros, CEO of CGC, claims that "Latin American culture has truly invaded the United States . . . Our local content is going to make it to the United States. We planned it that way. So I wonder who is invading whom?" (qtd. in Faber and Ewing 1999: 52).

Is this a delusion or the manifestation of something else? It seems to me that as a complement to the new international division of cultural labor proposed by Miller, we need also to focus on a new international networking and partnering of cultural production, which, though headquartered in places like Miami, is also structured like an archipelago of enclaves that cut across the developed and developing world. Does it make any difference, especially to the poor consumers of this cultural production, whether it is Hollywood or Latin CEOs who reap the profits? Yes, for two reasons. In the first place, relocation to the United States means that these companies and the immigrant intellectual and cultural labor they hire pay fewer taxes in their country of origin. Why shouldn't Buenos Aires or Bogotá increase its tax base as Miami does? In the second place, it does seem to make a difference that Latin American executives, producers, and arrangers can and indeed do produce culture that speaks to people throughout the subcontinent, even if that production takes place in Miami. The culture industries, as Mato writes, are not deterritorialized as much as they are transterritorial (2000: 4, 6).

Perhaps the problem is less this transterritorialization than the various means by which these industries produce, or better yet, extract value. To get an idea of how this takes place, we need to follow the network economy of which Castells writes, to all of its connections. Some of those connections, the advanced producer services, are characterized by more or less equitable contractual relations. Others, often involving independent producers and content providers, are less than equitable. But there are still others that are almost invisible. Network relations imply some kind of collaboration. I underscore the root "labor" in the word "collaboration" to emphasize that two or more parties who undertake a task or contribute to it are doing work. As Miller and Leger (forthcoming) note, culture industries are among the most labor intensive. Many tasks are socially constructed in such a way that only some of the parties engaged in the activity are to be remunerated financially. The other collaborators, who contribute value added to the activity, presumably derive a nonmaterial return for their participation. As I explain in greater detail in chapter 9, this differential distribution of value for labor is similar to that of "women's work," especially their collaboration within the family unit, where the satisfaction of motherhood was considered proper remuneration. Cultural work often goes unremunerated financially because it is assumed that those engaged in it derive spiritual or aesthetic value from it. In a cultural economy like that of the Latin entertainment and new media industries in Miami, there are many collaborators, especially those immigrants and other groups that provide the rhythms, fusions, and hybridities that drive "content" or, in Castell's words, "give life" through new musics or situations for a telenovela.

Free Trade and Culture

What is free trade, what is free trade under the present condition of society? . . . Whose freedom? It is not the freedom of one individual in relation to another, but the freedom of capital to crush the worker . . . When you have overthrown the few national barriers which still restrict the progress of capital, you will merely have given it complete freedom of action . . . So long as you let the relation of wage labor to capital exist . . . there will always be a class which will exploit and a class which will be exploited . . . The free trade system is destructive. It breaks up old nationalities and pushes the antagonism of the proletariat and the bourgeoisie to the extreme point. It is in this revolutionary sense alone, that I vote in favor of free trade.
—Karl Marx, "On the Question of Free Trade"

NAFTA has the virtue of making integration visible; it certainly did sharpen the contradictions, as the Old Man might have put it. If capital insists on integrating, those who joust with it have to do the same.
—"The Philanthropy of Financiers"

What Does Culture Have to Do with Free Trade?

Free trade and culture do not, by any means, have transparent meanings.[1] For example, the qualifier "free" suggests that government and international accords envision trade as unrestricted. Nothing could be further from reality now or at any time in the past. Free trade is anything but unrestricted; it must be managed, as is evident in the hundreds of protocols, declarations, and articles that constitute trade agreements. The last set of protocols generated by GATT in 1993 consisted of twenty thousand pages weighing over eighteen hundred pounds. Moreover, participating corporations receive subsidies, bailouts, and tax credits from their home government for their "competitiveness." Similarly, the term culture is not transparent. Depending on the context—national or local cultural policy; artistic and academic traditions; anthropological and sociological theory; feminist, racial, (post)colonial, and cultural studies approaches; law and the litigation of discrimination; and, of course, political discourse—the term may refer to the arts; to the media; to the rituals and other practices by which nations or smaller-scale social groups reproduce themselves symbolically; or to the differences by which some groups, usually defined as subaltern, distinguish themselves from (or resist) other, dominant, groups. As we saw in chapter 1, the very notion of innovation as an engine of capital accumulation is often identified with culture; in this chapter, we see how the strategies of global trade are rearticulating all conceptions of culture, even to the point that some of the most economically profitable products and services, say computer software and Internet sites, are treated, respectively, as cultural forms of intellectual property and cultural "content." Also examined are strategies for cultural integration in Latin America that, even as they counter the inordinate influence of U.S. and transnational entertainment culture, also increasingly rely on partnerships with private capital and neoliberal policies. Although the relationship between trade and culture is woefully understudied in the United States, it nevertheless has brought about many transformations.

I do not pretend to give hard and fast definitions of these two terms. I approach them, rather, by examining what other issues are being negotiated through the linking of free trade and culture. Culture is invoked, Virginia R. Dominguez has argued, to "make strategic social and political interventions." She goes on to recommend displacing studies "*about* culture—what belongs, what doesn't belong, what its characteristics are, whose characteristics are being imposed and whose are being excluded—... [with] asking *what is being accomplished* socially, politically, discursively when the concept of culture is invoked to describe, analyze, argue, justify, and theorize" (1992: 21).

It is in this sense that I explore the shift (or the contribution to the shift) that free trade has produced in the arts and notions of citizenship and public culture, particularly the relationship of the state to civil society. What are the state's responsibilities? What are the means available for citizens to participate in shaping opinions and engaging in decision making? How do changes at these levels involve changes in how we understand cultural issues, not just those of national identity but, more fundamentally, how the constitution of community, identity, solidarity, even artistic practices are transformed by new technologies and market values? Free trade has an important role in the redefinition of all of these dimensions.

Beginning in the 1980s, free trade was repackaged as a means to manage a worldwide economic crisis. Economic restructuring became a necessity as a result of a conjuncture of factors. The foreign debt of countries in the southern hemisphere grew to the point of economic crisis (a result in large part of the structural adjustment policies of the IMF and the World Bank under U.S. tutelage), and the rate of profit in the production of goods and services had fallen due to the glut of commodities produced in the reemergent economic powers of Germany and Japan and to innovations in new information and labor-saving technologies. The new president of the World Bank reoriented its poverty-reduction policies by putting greater emphasis on "rent seeking." This change made it easier for the Bank to follow the criteria of the IMF, whose approval was needed to make loans. Consequently, both institutions became "missionaries" that imposed free trade and structural adjustment programs on poor countries that had no choice but to assent (Stiglitz 2002: 13–14). In this context, free trade means deregulation, that is, the elimination of barriers (tariffs) to trade but also the curtailment of state support of industry (never fully achieved in developed countries), and, most significant, the forsaking of labor protection (more easily achieved), resulting in lower wages and benefits, the reduction of welfare and social services (health care, education), and the rollback of environmental safeguards. These changes not only ensure greater profits for corporations, particularly multinational enterprises, but guarantee that there will be little interference with the conduct of business because the organizations that manage trade (those that negotiate tariffs *and* regulations on production and distribution) are not subject to oversight by any electorate. In effect, GATT, its successor the WTO, NAFTA, the World Bank, the IMF, and others have not been empowered by voters and yet impose their policies virtually unchecked, although there is an emerging antiglobalization movement aimed at the irresponsibility of these institutions.

The repercussions of this restructuring, although presumably generated at the transnational level in trade agreements and structural adjustment policies, are experienced acutely at the local level, as witnessed by the loss of jobs in the United States and the defunding of school systems in Latin America. Immigrants—Mexicans in the United States or Bolivians in Argentina—are often blamed for the problems faced by the working class, as politicians characterize them as a drain on society, making parasitic use of "undeserved" benefits at the expense of taxpaying citizens (as if immigrants didn't pay taxes). Moreover, they are portrayed as a threat to the national culture. The global economic impact is redirected such that different sectors of society as well as different societies are pitted against each other in the competition for ever scarcer jobs, occluding the sources of the competition (displacements of production in search of ever cheaper labor) in the first place. Such ideological projections have a profound effect on how citizens and other residents understand themselves, their identities.

Transnational corporations manage to have it both ways under WTO ordinances: they can operate more freely across borders at the same time that they are considered local firms in host countries (Dobson 1993). Yet, even as transnational corporations have such an impact on labor issues, they produce very different images of their relationship to diverse workers, consumers, and publics. As I argue below, the hegemony of "corporate diversity," as the ideological face of global capitalism, is reproduced by the millions of public relations images in which social harmony is achieved through relations of difference. Or it might be more accurate to say that the successful (consumer) society is projected as one in which difference works as the motor of marketing. Market values come to prevail as the services that the Keynesian state had been providing are now privatized. Even in the realm of social provision, difference is also what drives conceptions and practices of "cultural citizenship," such as making claims for inclusion and participation in specific countries and even transnationally via the "global civil society" projected in the discourse of NGOs, foundations, and intergovernmental organizations like UNESCO. In UNESCO discourse, "economic and political rights cannot be realized separately from social and cultural rights" (Pérez de Cuéllar 1996).

We might ask at this point if such notions of cultural citizenship, though important for eliminating the impediments to inclusion, have not, especially when understood through the medium of consumer-oriented representations, obfuscated increasing class difference, which can be measured more or less objectively in terms of income disparity. Katz-Fishman and Scott (1994) report that poverty has been on the increase throughout the 1980s and 1990s, such that the "polarization of wealth and poverty is greater than at any time since the government has been tracking such data." A more recent analysis of the 2000 Census data shows that poverty is deepening in the United States as the rich get richer (Bernstein 2000). This is the situation in the United States; in other parts of the world the number of people barely surviving on less than $2 per day increased by 100 million from 1990 to 2000 (World Bank 2000: 29).

In Latin America, the widening income gap is more acute due to the inability of those countries to compete in the global economy. The prevalence of market and consumption values and increasing poverty go together as integral factors in the redefinition of the cultural field. This alarming development is not naturally given but has been produced and thus requires a critical reinterpretation of the relation of citizenship and consumption to capital (see chapter 6).

Intellectual Property and the Redefinition of Culture

The rise of market values is an important factor for the redefinition of culture in another sense. As the Europeans have argued, U.S. GATT and WTO negotiators have defined cultural goods such as films, television programs, video and audio recordings, and books as commodities subject to the same kinds of trade conditions as cars and clothing. Consequently, the Europeans contend, such trade arrangements legitimize the colonization of the European imaginary by Hollywood images, not to speak of filling the pockets of the shareholders of transnational entertainment conglomerates with most of the profits generated by films and other audiovisual products. In 1992, for example, Europeans "exported $250 million to the U.S. while the latter had sales of $4.6 billion in Europe" (Balladur 1993). U.S. audiovisual sales in Europe continue to rise: the 1992 figure for exports had been matched in half the time, by midyear in 1994 ("After GATT Pique" 1994: 16). Globally, sales figures surpass US$12 billion per annum in foreign revenues (Motion Picture Association of America 1999). And when one looks at the sum of revenues from the copyright industries (theatrical films, TV programs, home video, DVDs, business software, entertainment software, books, music and sound recordings), that figure rises to US$535.1 billion, or 5.24 percent of the GDP (Motion Picture Association of America 2002).

Culture has become a grab bag into which all kinds of technological innovations are deposited as a means to protect the ownership claims of transnational corporations. The clearest example of this trend is the displacement of the categories to which the concept of "intellectual property" applies. NAFTA, following the example of GATT, redefined the notion of culture as forms of property that include copyrights, patents, trademarks, plant breeder rights, industrial designs, trade secrets, integrated circuits, geographical indications, encrypted satellite signals, and so on. Furthermore, such intellectual property is protected insofar as it belongs to individuals (including corporations), obviating any recognition of collective rights, particularly the notion that communities generate culture and other forms of intellectual invention, such as seed varieties devised by peasant communities. Instead, according to NAFTA, "computer programs [are protected] as literary works and databases as compilations" (North American Free Trade Agreement 1993: 36). The agreement states that "intellectual property rights [will be provided adequate and effective protection] on the basis of national treatment," but computer programs are hardly an example of a cultural product that merits evaluation on the basis of national identity.

The Clinton administration's Working Group on Intellectual Property Rights recommended decisions that further redefined culture and enhanced benefits for commercial interests (McKenna 1995: 8). The impact of these decisions contributed to changes in the character of authorship, production, publication, and retransmission; rights were increasingly put in the domain of corporations, with privacy intervened by state and business enterprises. Even human life is increasingly subject to patenting and copyrighting (Dillon 1993: 11), and the rights to the digital reproduction of art and music have largely been acquired by entertainment conglomerates and telecommunications companies rather than the museums or original recording companies that own or owned the works (Powell 1995: 31). The extensive catalogues of national musics are now owned by the five major entertainment conglomerates, thus delinking value from national origin (Yúdice 1999b). Noncompliance with intellectual property laws advanced particularly by the United States has already brought threats of punitive trade sanctions. International "piracy" of U.S. "culture" (software, books, music, video) reached $8 billion in 1993, rising by more than 50 percent to $12.38 billion in 1998, according to the International Intellectual Property Alliance (Wellman 1999), leading U.S. enterprises to seek greater adherence to copyright and trademark protections.[2] Mexico was virtually forced to change its intellectual property laws and to enforce them as of 1994, and China was threatened with a $30 billion sanction to discourage the piracy of trademarked products (Sciolino 1995; Faison 1995a, 1995b; Sanger 1995c).

Although there are controversies revolving around the difference between authors' rights and copyright, the global knowledge-based economy nevertheless operates on the basis of the latter, in great part due to U.S. dominance in the organizations that oversee intellectual property rights. The United States and other postindustrial countries have recourse to international law and to the sanctions they can bring to bear on transgressor countries. Developing countries and fourth world indigenous peoples do not have the same clout, despite the drafting of international covenants by their own representatives (International Covenant on the Rights of Indigenous Nations 1994) and UNESCO (Recommendation on Safeguarding Traditional Cultures and Folklore 1989; Chartrand 1999). Western intellectual property law ascribes rights only to those who operate an alteration on a substance from the natural state such that the resulting product is "non-obvious" (Roht-Arriaza 1996: 18). Consequently, intellectual property law does not recognize the forms of labor, especially immaterial or ritualistic forms such as shamanism, at the heart of indigenous knowledge and cultural forms like rhythms. This difference ensures that the asymmetry in capital accumulation between developed and developing countries and native peoples will become greater. The hegemonic redefinition of culture raises problems for the legal protection of community and other collective practices that generate marketable knowledge (folk remedies, seed varieties) and products (music, crafts) that are not recognized as such by states and transnational corporations, the major brokers in the arena of international law. Particularly in regard to popular music, such as the Afro-Brazilian rhythms of Bahia, controversies have arisen because these cultural forms do not receive the kind of protection from usage (appropriation by pop and rock musicians from the North such as David Byrne and Paul Simon) that is accorded to computer programs. On the other hand, the very notion of what appropriation means has also undergone major redefinition in the recent past, as appropriative practices such as sampling (assimilable to influential postmodern theories of pastiche and parody) have gained currency.

The transnational character of much cultural production and distribution, particularly in music and entertainment, makes it unlikely that the protection of culture can be effectively legislated on the basis of national states (which are already marked by the lack of recognition [protection] of many collective cultural practices, as noted above). As Garnham states, "An analysis of culture structured around the concept of the cultural industries . . . directs our attention precisely at the dominant private market sector. It sees culture, defined as the production and circulation of symbolic meaning, as a material process of production and exchange, part of, and in significant ways determined by, the wider economic processes of society with which it shares many common forms" (1987: 25). The repercussions for how we understand and relate to the public realm are enormous. Public space, in which cultural forms circulate, is increasingly conditioned by commodified and transnational discourses and ideologies that combine and conflict with local forms in ways that disrupt the coherence of traditional national discourses, particularly those founded on conventional notions of the popular (see chapter 2). As García Canclini argues, "It is not that national culture is extinguished but, rather, that it is converted into a formula for designating the continuity of an unstable historical memory that is now being reconstituted in interaction with transnational cultural referents" (2001: 8). It has become an "international popular" (R. Ortiz 1988: 182–206),[3] or better yet, a "transnational popular."

In the two sections that follow, on the cultural impact of free trade on Canada and Mexico and on the United States, I examine the reconstitution of national "historical memory" in the three partners in NAFTA.

Free Trade and Culture in Canada and Mexico

There has been very little discussion in the United States of the cultural implications of NAFTA, the very reverse of the situation in Canada and Mexico. The free trade debates in the United States have revolved around job flight to cheap labor markets in Mexico and the negative effects on labor conditions at home; on the deregulation of government policies, resulting in a downward harmonization with legislation in other countries in such areas as environmental protection, socialized health care (an evident risk for Canadians), and workers' rights and benefits; and on the deregulation of the economy, particularly in relation to privatization, not only of national resources but also of social and public institutions now redefined as "service commodities open to competitive pressures and the dictates of the marketplace" (Bernard 1994: 20). But who in the United States has engaged in debates on free trade in relation to culture?

The "Battle of Seattle" at the end of November 1999, which launched a continuing series of antiglobalization demonstrations throughout the world (Davos, Prague, Washington, D.C., Bangkok, Porto Alegre, Buenos Aires, Quebec), provides an important but only partial answer to this question. Demonstrators addressed deregulation, privatization, liberalization under the hegemony of corporate capitalism, global consumerism, the attack on labor protections, the rise of sweatshop labor, the imposition of austerity and restructuring programs imposed by the IMF and World Bank, the introduction of user fees, cuts in agricultural subsidies and the rise in incentives for export-oriented industrial agriculture, the abandonment of redistribution programs, the environmental devastation caused by oil and mining industries, and the lack of citizen input in any trade decisions. But the cultural issues themselves have not been raised. To be sure, McDonaldization, the emblem of the culture of consumerism, has been ever-present in the protests, but the main issue is that intellectual property rights and other provisions that favor entertainment conglomerates and the new economy are structured in such a way that the consumption of "immaterial" culture (information, digital services, entertainment, mediated experiences, etc.), which nonetheless requires *physical* labor, has become a potent engine of economic development, perhaps greater than any other kind of economic activity.

A look at the antiglobalization demonstrations reveals little protest over the subsumption of culture by new capital accumulation strategies. A good many of the critiques aimed at consumption are self-righteous, raising the curious contradiction that most of the protesters were weaned on television and have learned to wield a "politics of consumption" (see chapter 6). But it is the way consumerism and "immaterial" capital accumulation are structured that harbors the greatest threat to social well-being. I shall return to the antiglobalization movement in the conclusion. Here I would like to focus on the responses to NAFTA's effects on culture.

In the Canadian debates, it was argued that Canada's entry into the U.S.-Canada Free Trade Agreement (FTA), NAFTA's precursor, was a symptom of a weakening national culture. Anthony Westell (1991), director of Carleton University's School of Journalism, contended that Canada's "kinder and gentler" social policies emerged from a social formation essentially different from that of the United States, one that put greater stock in the state, as witnessed by socialized health care and state sponsorship of cultural production. The signing of the FTA was a symptom of the weakening of this difference, produced by "the trend toward a global economy and a homogenized popular culture which is rapidly eroding the sovereignty of national states . . . So what we see in Canada today is a struggle between those who believe that the world has shrunk and become more competitive and that we must change with it, even to the extent of abandoning our distinctive culture, and those who believe that we can and must preserve what remains of our culture, our dream of a distinct society" (266).

Not all commentators endorsed Westell's view that "nationalism has been concerned with preserving the notion of a society different from, and better than, the U.S. society" (1991: 265). Dorland characterized Canadian culture as a repressed form of "nationalist ressentiment" (1988: 130), and Brimelow (1991), from a conservative, free trade position, argued that there is no difference between Anglo-Canadian and U.S. culture. In his view, what is claimed to be a distinctive culture is composed of the policies of a "new class" of "civil servants, educators, and assorted political media hangers-on . . . inventing policies that benefit itself and its clients," such as federal bilingualism or the National Energy Program (273–274). This is also the "class" that pressed for a "cultural exemption" in the FTA, that is, an exemption from regulations on state subsidy (or "protectionism" from the U.S. business vantage point) of the arts and the culture industries.

Jingoist Anglophile Brimelow no doubt had an ax to grind against any definition of North America that moves away from its "base" in Anglo-American cultural formations. Indeed, in a later book, *Alien Nation* (1995), he takes the peculiarly re-revisionist position that the United States is not a country of immigrants. His views on Canada, however, focus attention on the confluence of nationalist capitalists and progressive activists who seek to preserve what they claim is their "distinct culture." This insight is corroborated by Claire F. Fox, who notes, from a different political position, that Harold Greenberg, president of the production company Astral and chair of the Canadian Cultural/Communications Industries Committee, makes an anti-imperialist argument against U.S. penetration of Canadian media that "closely resemble[s] that of Canadian activists, intellectuals, and labor leaders" (1994a: 11; 1999: 22).

Alison Beale (2002) goes even farther in her demystification of both the call for a cultural exemption and the more recent demand for assurances of cultural diversity in French and Canadian negotiations in free trade forums. She demonstrates that under the cloak of protecting national culture, capital interests in both of these countries (and in the European Union under French leadership) are actually promoting their own cultural industries and *not* what we in the United States call nonprofit arts and heritage, which would presumably be the bulwark of national identity. Moreover, these countries do not propose a serious defense of their internal minority cultures. To the degree that this is the case, the neoliberal-compatible premise of *cultural diversity* that has displaced *exemption* in trade fora winds up operating as a rhetorical stand-in for international markets (14).

The inclusion of a cultural exemption in the FTA was never really effective, for it was already preempted, according to Colleen Fuller (1991). Mosco explains that the exemption was largely rhetorical, for it was rendered ineffective by a loophole that enabled the United States to retaliate to "equivalent commercial effect" for what it considered protectionist subsidies of cultural products (1990: 63; qtd. in C. Fox 1999: 146, n.9). As Fox reports, Westinghouse Electric Corporation's complaint before NAFTA arbitrators in 1995 against the Canadian government for blocking its subsidiary Country Music Television (CMT) from two million Canadian homes ended in a new, partly U.S.-owned, Canadian country music network (1999: 146, n.9). Not only was the cultural exemption clause ineffective, but it brought about a result even more characteristic of corporate transnationalization; the merger of CMT and the Canadian broadcaster on whose behalf local viewership was blocked. The new company, New Country Network, controlled by Canadian media/telecommunications conglomerates Rogers Broadcasting and Shaw Cable, the latter of which was subsequently spun off into Corus Entertainment, was renamed Country Music Television Canada after viewers complained about changes in programming, and a minority stake was sold to Viacom, the new parent company of CMT ("Country Music Television Canada" 1999). In this new guise, a company can have legal local status at the same time it is part of a global enterprise.

Free trade agreements have thus had the ironic effect that even as they incorporate measures to protect national cultures, international commercial law ends up prevailing. The timing for this impact on national culture could not have been more fitting because the debate on free trade in Canada was articulated to ongoing changes in national culture on which all parties in the political spectrum took a position. In part, the transformation of national culture has some of its roots in the particular circumstances of Anglo-Franco bilingualism-binationalism and its multiculturalist complement aimed at integrating, without necessarily assimilating, immigrant groups. Indeed, as Allor and Gagnon (1997) argue, the cultural field itself emerges as the set of policies, practices, and discourses, including debates on free trade and cultural exemption, that displace the action on population as the means to govern. This field is structured by the encounter of discourses and actions emanating from cultural and civil society institutions, corporations, the media, and artists, producers, and critics that juxtapose questions of national sovereignty and identity with economic development and internationalization. Even as these discourses "steer away from endorsing free market mechanisms" they wield "culture [as] . . . a resource to be developed and exploited for the sake of Quebec's economic development and that of enhancing its international profile" (43). In other words, free trade is not in itself the issue; it is the occasion for discussion of the increasing protagonism of culture in the articulated management of the economy, mediated representation, and citizenship.

To put it more simply, following Carlos Fuentes's discussion of alternatives to NAFTA, free trade agreements are an attempt to deal with the global paradox, which he describes as follows: "If economic rationality tells us that the next century will be the age of global integration of the world's national economies, cultural 'irrationality' steps in to inform us that it will also be the century of ethnic demands and revived nationalisms" (1991: 15). In Mexico, however, the opening to trade—imposed, among other measures, by the IMF as

a remedy to the failure of import-substitution industrialization in the 1970s
and acute debt crisis in the early 1980s—was accompanied by tempering of a
nationalism identified with protectionism. Culture had an important role in
ushering in the so-called Salinastroika. For Salinas, many centuries of cultural
mettle would maintain Mexico's autonomy as it upgraded into the first world
NAFTA bloc. Fuentes himself argues that the heterogeneity of Mexican—and
by extension, Latin American—culture "does not propose religious fundamentalisms or ethnic intolerance," such that the internationalization that comes
with trade liberalization does not lead to fragmentation (16). Fuentes neglects
to say, however, that culture is not a natural given but that it is produced, an
obvious point with respect to Mexico. Those centuries of Mexican culture that
Salinas refers to can be understood as the construction of a governmentalizing
(in the Foucauldian sense) heritage, whose history goes back to the 1920s. Although that heritage and the institutions that ground it are quite strong, many
cracks in the foundation are now appearing, not the least of which is the challenge to the dominant construction of the nation by the Zapatistas on the very
day—January 1, 1994—that NAFTA went into effect.

Mexico's entry into NAFTA was celebrated as a positive development by
many in the business and financial sectors, but there were also arguments
against it. Many intellectuals repudiated free trade in the name of economic and
cultural sovereignty. Some commentators, while rejecting the reach of transnational corporations, nevertheless greeted deregulation with approval, relying
on it to shake up the mammoth bureaucratic infrastructure of the one-party
political system. According to Peruvian novelist Mario Vargas Llosa (1991), who
had been invited by Octavio Paz to a round table discussion (no doubt to support Paz's views as a fellow conservative), that system had achieved the most
effective totalitarian rule in Latin America. Mexico's PRI, which faced a series of
serious challenges since President Salinas signed the NAFTA legislation, controlled for seventy years every sphere of life, from industry and the economy to
indigenous crafts and the institutionalization of the arts. It is worth remem-
bering that in Mexico the postrevolutionary state pressed intellectuals, artists,
and academics into the service of creating an integrated cultural identity—
founded on the three principles of normative melting pot mestizaje, bureau-
cratized indigenismo, and modernizing anti-imperialism—that would appeal
to peasants and workers on the one hand, and to the middle classes and the
national bourgeoisie on the other. According to Guillermo Bonfil Batalla, who
wrote on the role of social scientists, particularly anthropologists, in the construction of this national identity: "The State . . . took on the task of construct-

ing a nation that it desired homogeneous; furthermore, to this end it forged a national culture which, from the top down, would finally become the patrimony of all Mexicans. This was to be a *mestizo* culture, a noble amalgam of the best that the matrix cultures offered. The State, the force behind this project, imposed itself in diverse ways and with different faces throughout the entirety of the land" (1993: 20).

However, due to various forces predating the move toward neoliberalism and free trade in the 1980s, Mexican society was already splintering, despite the vast reach and corrupt operations of the PRI-ista state. A very brief historical sketch of the past three decades will help explain this process of splintering.

By the time of the 1968 student revolt at Tlatelolco, in which hundreds were massacred by police and soldiers, modernization had created a sizable middle class that sought to increase its purchase on education and upward mobility. The transnationalization of the mass media since the 1960s further contributed to the reluctance of youth to adopt national symbols that had ceased to be convincing. The increasing impact of migrants to the United States and of Chicano and (Mexican) border cultures also contributed to the questioning of a pristine Mexicanness. The challenges to the PRI from within and without explain, in part, the increasing power and the electoral success in 2000 of the conservative party PAN and, to a lesser extent, the Partido Revolucionario Democrático, as well as the tragicomic downfall of ex-president Salinas. He had been groomed by the United States for the presidency of WTO but was shunned after the economic debacle of December 20, 1994, as well as the political scandals involving his family.

Indeed, although the recovery of the Mexican economy has been characterized as "vibrant" through 2000 (Organization of Economic Cooperation and Development 2000), despite the ups and downs due to sensitivity to international finance markets and dependence on the U.S. economy, the crisis unleashed in 1994 has not been overcome for the vast majority of Mexicans. Right after the crash, Bloomberg Business News statistics showed that whereas the "palace economy" (the stock market, the macroeconomy) seemed to have regained its level prior to the devaluation that led to the crisis, the "plaza economy" (survival conditions for the majority) plunged to its lowest level in history. In 1995, official unemployment figures stood at 2 million or 6.3 percent, but they were misleading because even chewing gum street vendors were included among the employed. The real percentage of unemployed was at least three times greater, about 19 percent, according to one report (DePalma 1995: 11). More recently, the International Labor Organization reported that despite decreasing unemployment, the "buying power of salaries . . . is much lower [in 2000] than twenty years ago" (Jaura 2000). And, as in the past, a leader of the workers' union pointed out that real unemployment far outpaces the euphemistic figures put out by the government ("Proponen" 2001). The impact has been even greater in the countryside. The demands by peasants in poor areas for a more equitable distribution of land and resources escalated into revolts throughout the years, the most recent of which, the rebellion of the EZLN, coincided with the inauguration of NAFTA (see chapter 3). The point is that *although free trade may not have caused, it certainly sharpened the contradictions that were already auguring a reconfiguration of national culture.* This is true of the Canadian case as well.

This scenario does not suggest, however, that Mexican intellectuals like Bonfil Batalla and Carlos Monsiváis jumped on the free trade bandwagon; they took the different tack of pointing up the hypocrisy of those who sounded the anti-imperialist call of yore yet continued to maintain the repressive status quo. Anticipating NAFTA, Bonfil Batalla, Monsiváis, García Canclini, José Manuel Valenzuela, and others published an analysis of the likely impact of free trade on education and culture the likes of which did not even appear as articles in specialized journals in the United States (Guevara Niebla and García Canclini 1992). In it they question the entry into a trade agreement whose only effect, at least on the level of culture, is to intensify a consumerist ethos among those who have the means while excluding 17 million of 85 million Mexicans living below and another 30 million living at the official poverty line (Monsiváis 1992: 194). They greet with cautious reception the decentralization of Mexican culture, and they also question the neoliberal conditions under which private and transnational media are laying the foundations of a new cultural formation.

In an assessment of film distribution and viewing in Mexico in the late 1980s and early 1990s, García Canclini observes that 80 percent of the supply came from the United States. Driven by the profit motive, even Televisa, the major network and fourth largest in the world, shows mostly U.S. films. A team of ethnographers led by García Canclini found that the narrative imaginary of most Mexicans is populated by the stars of U.S. films (2001: 114–116). Most alarming is the classification of U.S. film as film tout court by video rental outlets. Blockbuster of Mexico, for example, carries all U.S. films under the category "film"; Mexican film is kept in a small "national" section, and Latin American film in the "foreign" section. Such a classification naturalizes U.S. movies as the most intrinsically filmic; yet that characterization depends on the "foreign policies" of this global industry, which bears out, perhaps, its essentially nonfilmic character.[4] And because viewing has increasingly relocated from the movie house to home video (García Canclini 2001: 99),[5] such a classification system has an even greater impact.

Before turning to the almost nonexistent debate on the impact of free trade on U.S. culture, it will be useful to consider briefly the divergent possibilities in the Canadian and Mexican cases for charting cultural policies that neither nostalgically return to a once-hegemonic national culture that was also repressive nor simply embrace the kind of transnationalization promoted by the U.S. culture industries. It is instructive to remember in this regard that the European Union, pressured by France and Spain as well as numerous filmmakers from other countries, prevailed in exempting audiovisual distribution from the concluding agreement of GATT's Uruguay Round. From the U.S. vantage point, film and television were regarded as commodities; the Europeans, however, insisted that they be understood as cultural constituents of civil society, and insofar as they would safeguard European culture from foreign monopoly or total commercialization, they argued that these constituents should be exempted from trade agreements (R. Cohen 1993a; T. Friedman 1994). U.S. advocates of free trade retorted that they would accept the idea of exempting high culture but noted that it is hypocritical to "put a quota on an American cop show so that French studios can crank out their own car chases" (Passell 1994; T. Friedman 1994).

Both positions might be seen, ultimately, as "the outcome of contingent moralisms," for they both offer problematic justifications for the putative subject they are protecting: the "fabled sovereign consumer" on the one hand, and the "fabled sovereign citizen" on the other (Miller 1993: 79). This vexing double fiction is at the heart of both the U.S. arguments against a cultural exemption for entertainment on the basis of a culture/industry dichotomy (they are willing to allow it for the arts and connoisseur's delights like fine cheeses and wines) and European contentions that their movies and TV shows transcend that dichotomy because what is at stake is the expression of a way of life that nurtures citizenship. What are the repercussions of this debate for rethinking free trade in the Americas?

According to García Canclini, the model of a negotiated continental culture, analogous to the cultural space being constructed by the European Union, can be viable for Latin America, even more so because of the commonality of language and other cultural features. Creating a market for the culture industries and a system of incentives and subsidies for high and artisanal cultures at the continental level would serve to counter the monopoly from the North and also to counter the hegemony of national cultures that have outlasted their historical potential and that in most cases have repressed groups that do not fit the normative profile of the nation. Furthermore, a continental, confederational approach, if properly worked out, could create an enabling environment for minority and marginal cultures throughout, insofar as they would have greater representation in the wider space of Latin American civil society, which would redraw the boundaries between nation and state. This process is already taking place, to an extent, in the "strong drive toward regional economic integration" in Latin America (Brooke 1995: 1) and more recently with the push toward Ibero-American confederation that Fuentes referred to as an alternative (1991: 17), but which is now looking like a Spanish version of U.S. economic neoimperialism as Spanish foreign direct investment reaches new heights and Spanish banks and telecommunications corporations buy up privatized state enterprises throughout Latin America. I address cultural integration in more detail below and in chapter 6.

Turning attention to the Canadian case, it is not evident that a confederational solution is possible, for the very source of the problem, as far as many Canadians are concerned, is the United States. Consequently, merging into a confederate civil society with the neighbor to the south would only deepen the problems. The distance that separates Canada from the other British Commonwealth nations militates against the possibility of a viable cultural formation at that remove. It therefore makes sense to maintain some kind of protection for culture, although it is crucial that it be delinked from status quo nationalist frameworks. Gathering evidence for this position, Berland (1991) comments on the ironic international success of Canadian musicians, facilitated by changes in the production and distribution of cultural goods, particularly recording and broadcasting, in the 1980s and 1990s. The economic liberalization promoted in this period made it increasingly difficult for Canadian artists to gain access to their own national market, for distribution is completely under foreign control. This situation has forced many musicians to seek their primary distribution abroad: "The rising costs of recording and video-making mean that few albums can recoup costs of production . . . from domestic sales alone . . . As a consequence more Canadian musicians now bypass Canadian companies, whose ability to function in the American market is not increased by these measures, and seek record deals with the home office of the major companies" (323).

From a citizenship perspective, the unlikely confederation of Canada and the United States is the reverse of the confederational model that García Canclini and others envision for Latin America. "Canadian agents, producers, musicians and owners of independent labels have been angry and disturbed at the difficulty of working within their own national market. This doesn't mean that they don't share the aspiration of making it in the U.S., but rather that they want to retain their own country — still a different country with different experiences, tastes, sounds, not to mention economic institutions and ideologies — as somewhere to start and somewhere to come back to, and for some, as somewhere to stay" (Berland 1991: 324). Retaining their own country also seems to be the reason more Canadians oppose NAFTA (48 percent) than support it (28 percent), according to the Environics survey in January 1999. Canadians are generally distrustful of the effects of NAFTA, "not only across Canada's regions but also across political and economic lines" (Scoffield 1999).

Free Trade and Culture in the United States

What has been argued with respect to Canada and Mexico — that free trade has intensified ongoing changes in national culture over the past two decades — could be said about the United States. This would include the debate between, to simplify, multiculturalism and a conservative backlash to reinstall traditional American values. I myself do not believe that the situation is as simple as this, as I argued in chapter 1. It is quite obvious that the celebration of "American" diversity is consistent with the "We are the world" attitude of the U.S. corporate and other sectors as they stand poised to capitalize on their global pretensions. That this corporate ethos crosscuts and inflects the discourse of multiculturalism does not bode well for a truly democratic recognition of all constituencies, if by that is meant equitable redistribution of resources and not only the tutti frutti representations of U.S. marketing that are now evident throughout other continents. Even the right has Benettonized its face and President G. W. Bush's cabinet in ways that both confirm and belie criticism of the right's visions of "a more monocultural society that puts tight limits on people's participation" (Pharr 1994). In this section, I attempt to contextualize the forms that liberal-corporate and conservative positions take in the national debate, as a starting point for the analysis of free trade's impact on U.S. culture.

THE RIGHT To the degree that the debate on national culture, the so-called culture wars, involved various groups that were characterized in the media and academia as the right and the left, it seems fitting to examine, within this framework, the reception of arguments for and against free trade and the related controversy over immigrants' rights. The first point that might be made in this regard is that even after the Seattle antiglobalization protests, there seems to be no hard and fast correlation between a given political position and a pro or con position on free trade. Free trade did not generate clearly defined polarization as did the debates on welfare entitlements and affirmative action. What might be said is that there was a struggle among diverse groups in both camps to define such notions as conservatism, progressivism, American values and national culture, the role of the state, and so on. In this contest over ideological positions, there was little coherence on an issue like free trade. Phil Gramm, Pat Buchanan, and Ralph Nader, from opposing camps, were against it. Indeed, at the anti-IMF protest in Washington in April 2000, Buchanan was cheered by Teamsters when he said that as president he would appoint James Hoffa as U.S. trade negotiator and would have the Chinese sell the "last pair of chopsticks in any mall in the United States" if they didn't "shape up" (T. Friedman 2000). Conversely, Newt Gingrich and Robert Reich, also polar opposites, were for free trade. Of all Clinton's programs, free trade was the only one ushered through Congress successfully, this despite his putative alliance with labor, which opposed NAFTA.

NAFTA seems to have become an albatross for its supporters. Despite the appearance of a recovery in 1997 and 1998, the Mexican economy weakened considerably (a condition that was covered over by the Zedillo administration), many Mexican businesses went bankrupt, and hundreds of thousands of jobs were lost since the fateful December 20, 1994. As of this writing (April 2001), the stock markets are rising and holding steady, while the new president has sent Congress a tax reform bill that would increase the price of food and medicine (Tricks 2001). Free trade enthusiasts, moreover, reveal themselves to be *cheap labor* advocates, for that is what enables corporations to maneuver as markets strengthen and weaken, closing and reopening factories at will, largely on the backs of Mexican workers, who have seen poverty rise and real wages fall five years after NAFTA went into effect (Brandon 1998). The trend has continued into 2001 (N. Klein 2001).

Despite Mexico's being a "privileged" partner in NAFTA, a downward spiral in regional trade and retail sales in all of Latin America, low commodity prices, and the fear of rising interest rates in the United States augured slower economic growth into the late 1990s. Exports to the United States are expected to fall by 5 percent from already weak performance in 1998 (C. Krauss 1999). In the United States, Clinton had at best tenuous support for the $20 billion (the U.S. contribution to the total international $50 billion) bailout package for Mexico. In fact, Senator Alphonse D'Amato, epitome of conservatism, attempted to mobilize Congress to prevent the administration from "dispensing anything beyond the $5.2 billion that Washington has already sent" (Sanger 1995b: 16). Curiously, D'Amato's argument against the bailout was that it would help only "rich investors," the very purpose of much of the legislation that he and his fellow Republicans traditionally sponsor. In any case, now that G. W. Bush is in the White House and Vicente Fox in Los Pinos, even such staunch opponents of NAFTA as Jesse Helms are coming around (G. Thompson 2001).

Among the reasons for the ambiguous correlation between ideological positions and support for or opposition to free trade are the perplexing reports on NAFTA's track record. On the one hand, at the same time that large increases in trade among the three partners in the agreement are reported (e.g., a 40 percent increase between Canada and Mexico [NAFTA and Inter-American Trade Monitor 1994d] and a greater than 20 percent increase between the United States and Mexico in 1994 [Myerson 1995: D7]), figures show that the U.S. trade deficit grew at a record annual rate of $152.5 billion (Gilpin 1995: 1) and was estimated to break all records at $200 billion by the end of 1999 (J. Peterson 1999). Regarding unemployment and quality of jobs, there have been losses and downgrading of jobs that are making workers, especially those who are unionized, wary of the effects of free trade. The early trade victories of the Clinton administration have been reversed as unions and skeptics who fear that the expansion of free trade, as stipulated in the defeated Multilateral Agreement on Investment, will erode national sovereignty through extension of national treatment to foreign investors. The WTO, which was promoted by the Clinton administration, permitted other countries to bring lawsuits to change U.S. industrial and environmental standards, thus offending constituents of all ideological persuasions, including conservatives like Jesse Helms (J. Peterson 1999). Moreover, while U.S. jobs were lost in the manufacturing sector, increases were registered in low-paying industries that offer little or no benefits to workers, such as poultry processing, municipal recycling facilities, financial services, prisons, nursing homes, and urban renewal. The Wall Street Journal found that "many of today's toughest occupations offer little compensation [from a (then) minimum wage of $4.25 to $7 an hour], either in pay or in skills that might allow workers to move on to more rewarding jobs" (Gundrey 1994). Furthermore, the confusing picture created by conflicting reports on whether NAFTA would stem the tide of undocumented workers only added to the uncertainty felt in the United States about keeping the standard of living from falling any further by the loss and downgrading of jobs.

Why raise such issues in an examination of the impact of free trade on culture? Because the economic insecurity that many people in the United States felt in the early to mid-1990s was channeled into an obsessive dread of immigrants, particularly their supposed drain on services and their transformative effects on national culture. Given that a good part of that dread is operationalized by the racialization of immigrants, especially from Mexico and Latin America, it makes sense to consider how the right is constituted around the issue of race, which conditions to a great degree how the "new," nonwhite immigrants are seen. I take as my starting point Howard Winant's (1990) model of the various forms of the new "racial politics." He identifies several sectors that have formed coalitions in certain conjunctural moments, such as the coming together of the Christian right and neoliberal wings of the Republican Party. Winant discerns three right projects and one he calls the "radical democratic project." Of the three rightist discourses, the first, the "far right," which for him includes the Christian right, establishes organizations that resemble those of minority groups in order to counter them. The second, the "new right" project, aims to reverse gains by women and minorities through state activity. The third, the "neoconservative" project, counters the claims of minorities and women by denying racial and gender differences. One can discern still another racial project somewhere between the three identified by Winant as being on the right and the progressive "radical democratic" project. This sector of the right would be composed of those "moderates" who differ from the three on social issues, although on financial issues they are united with the Republican majority (Wines 1994). This sector not only recognizes racial and gender differences but seeks to link them to class difference as part of a political program to overturn economic and social inequalities.

But it is important to note that the coalitions Winant refers to can also come apart, for example, around women's right of choice, the defunding of the NEA and NEH, the elimination of children's school lunches, the denial of full citizenship for gays and lesbians, and the withdrawal of rights to health care and education from undocumented and in some cases even documented immigrant workers. Consider as examples of this the defeat of an amendment to triple the cut in the 1995 NEA budget in which 75 Republicans sided with 185

Democrats (Rich 1995). A New York Times article of March 16, 1995 reported that "rifts [are] emerg[ing] inside the GOP" around abortion and the "$200 billion in tax cuts to systematic welfare restructuring" (Toner 1995). On March 21, "nearly half of the 230 Republicans in the House urged their leaders . . . to scale back a proposed $500-a-child tax cut to families" (Wines 1995). Moreover, the Christian Coalition, which led the right's offensive in national politics, came apart due to debt, the departure of its leaders, and the admission that it never really commanded large numbers of adherents (Goodstein 1999).

Nevertheless, what we are currently witnessing may be more of a reconversion of the far or hard right, not the extreme right represented by Buchanan, but a conjunction of conservatives, cold warriors, antilabor corporate interests, and the religious right, all of whom are embodied in G. W. Bush's administration. Indeed, Bush's appointment of John Ashcroft as attorney general bears out this radical turn to the right. But it is counterbalanced, at least in appearance, by the appointment of the most "multicultural" cabinet to date. This does not transform the Republicans into radical leftists, but it does demonstrate that the right is not monolithic, eternal, or invulnerable, as some critics have suggested. Moreover, the Bush administration has already shown signs that it is aware that Republicans need to maintain the semblance of multicultural participation, both for the sake of increasing their share of the Latino vote as well as to seem culturally receptive to the new free trade partners to the south. Indeed, U.S. congressmen's visit to Mexico in April 2001 to discuss a migrant worker pact with Vicente Fox and Foreign Minister Jorge Castañeda "turned into an unlikely love fest between Mr. Helms and Mexican officials — especially Mr. Castañeda, a leftist intellectual and former Communist Party activist recently branded as unfriendly to the United States in a report written by Mr. Helms' aides" (Sandoval 2001). With both Bush and Fox closely linked to the Christian right, the likelihood of growing "diversity" among conservatives is not to be ruled out.

What Winant may not have noticed in his 1990 analysis is the convergence of Democratic liberals and moderate Republicans in a project that eschews some of the programs legislated in the civil rights period and its aftermath, particularly affirmative action. This sector seeks to refashion rather than totally eliminate affirmative action. It is split around support for social programs (for health care, against welfare), and pretty much lined up to support a corporate ethos. It is in this latter regard that this sector becomes relevant for my discussion of free trade.

Corporate Diversity

Free trade is ideologically pitched predominantly as a means for the United States to regain its economic dominance in the world in the face of advances from Japan and East Asia on the one hand, and the European Union on the other. It is a strategy for constructing "competitiveness" in a global age characterized by three economic hegemons, although the Asian is currently debilitated. Free trade is touted as a means not only to renewed dominance but to the national rebirth of the United States, particularly in the creation of new jobs and a reversal of the downward slide in the standard of living. In tandem with this pitch is the claim that to compete in the global economy, U.S. corporations must be more diverse. This secondary premise appeals to cultural diversity, contrary to the agenda of the three sectors of the right briefly reviewed above. But the right, which has managed to come together to take electoral power in recent elections, is like any other ideological bloc sundered by contradictory forces.

We might say that at the heart of rightist ideology the impulse to stem social and cultural modernization contradicts the very effects of economic modernization. The culture wars were in part the result of the receding compromise between sociocultural and economic modernization struck in the U.S. version of Keynsianism. The compromise is now largely situated in the market, with a concomitant reduction of the (welfare) state and modifications in regulations to favor trade. Consequently, the mechanisms introduced in the civil rights era and its wake to compensate minorities and women for past discrimination are now to be left to the promises of the corporate world to be more inclusive, more diverse. Avery Gordon (1995) notes that the corporation offers a new contract for America, one rooted in the managerial powers of the middle class. But insofar as its project for a consensual culture is based on difference and diversity, corporate culture runs counter to the rightist projects reviewed above, although, as already mentioned, G. W. Bush staged a greater display of "diversity" than the Democrats ever did. The number of blacks and Hispanics in Bush's administration points to the absorption of "diversity" into a conservative sphere, a necessity if the Republicans are to survive in an increasingly nonwhite world.

The rhetoric of diversity may be open to different ideological articulations, and although one can assume that Republican inclusion of minorities in visible positions is due to political expediency, this in itself is a sign that the party is finding a way to reconcile the Christian right with corporate capitalism. That would explain the disaffection of the extreme right from the Republican Party that repudiated Buchanan. An expression of this disaffection may well be the right-wing participation in the antiglobalization protests in Seattle and elsewhere. Louis Beam, a white supremacist leader, characterized the protests in Seattle as a "new politics of America [that] is liberty from the NWO ['New World Order'] Police State" (Southern Poverty Law Center 2000).

The rhetoric of diversity operates like a smoke screen that enables Republicans to make the claim that they are inclusive while at the same time opposing affirmative action and other entitlement programs for minorities and moving the entire juridical system to the right, as in the penetration of the government by appointees who belong to the conservative Federalist Society (N. Lewis 2001). In the past, the highly publicized campaigns that foster diversity in the management of transnational corporations, on the basis that diversity facilitates business with other cultures, have not been well received by several sectors of the right, particularly those that would like the United States to take a more isolationist course, in keeping with a strong nationalist mood that transcends the right.

But the Republicans seem to have reconciled their nationalism with the global entrepreneurialism of the new world capitalist order by a new form of isolationism: unilateralism (Schlesinger 1995: 5). With the Soviet threat gone—a major reason for financing the capitalist world order—conservatives, and many liberals, see no justification for continued participation in internationalist causes such as the crusade for human rights and democratization abroad or the multiculturalist-oriented work of UNESCO, none of which in their view directly advances the interests of the United States. A different kind of multiculturalism has emerged, in which, for example, the image of Mexico has been "cleaned up," even in the eyes of former denigrators like Jesse Helms, who said on a recent goodwill trip to Mexico that he is seeking to "establish a new spirit of cooperation between our two countries" ("Helms Trumpets" 2001).

The salience of the far right in the Republican Party, particularly in Clinton's first term, led him to move many of his policies to the center, abandoning some progressive social issues and in some cases seeking common ground with Republicans, particularly in the endorsement of free trade. This common ground "almost surely means the president will have to jettison hopes for a new fast-track authority that would permit the inclusion of environmental, civil rights and labor standards in future trade agreements. It's no accident that Clinton argued that moves toward free trade by themselves fulfilled his commitment to fostering human rights improvements abroad because such trade creates an entrepreneurial class that pressures for democracy" (Moskowitz 1994). In typical Clinton style, the administration attempted to have it both ways: defuse the appeal of Republicans by watering down its own advocacy of civil rights and affirmative action, and shift such concerns to a market approach to the public sector. In effect, both Gingrich's "contract" and the administration's "reinvention of government" became mirror images of each other: "In their search for a successor to government as usual, Mr. Gore and Mr. Gingrich symbolize approaches that exactly reciprocate each other: a market-oriented public sector versus a non-market-oriented private sector" (Stark 1995). In either case, the result was a bid to revise the dividing line between public and private by shifting the ways government addresses values.

Commerce is not solely an economic phenomenon. National and transnational corporations disseminate all kinds of values, from notions of citizenship to consumer ethos. And as they incorporate an increasingly diverse workforce, they develop new marketing strategies such as those reviewed in Sandheusen's (1994) *Global Marketing* textbook (see chapter 6). That text highlights the diversity of "cultural values that make them useful in formulating strategic plans and programs in the global marketplace" (99). Diversity, however, is not unleashed but managed; indeed, "diversity management" has become a major area of business administration (A. Gordon 1995; R. Thomas 1991; chapter 6).

Of course, access to the global workplace is uneven depending on the group examined. An assessment of immigrant access to the global economy published in *World Trade* celebrates immigrants' contribution to the rebirth of America, despite the passage of Proposition 187. The article begins by noting the high number of minorities and immigrants among the list of *World Trade* 100 CEOs and the fact that their companies are housed in California. Not only are immigrants responsible for 39 percent of the U.S. population growth in the 1980s, but they are also among the biggest contributors to the U.S. export boom. As global trade rhetoric would have it: "From Poles to Mexicans, 'the utility of the immigrant groups is that they bring with them their fearless spirit of competing globally'" (Delaney 1994). It is important to recognize that this celebration of global capitalism is accompanied by an apparent antiracist counter to the extreme right, presumably belied by Bush's 2000 campaign pageantry: "Anti-immigrant groups claim that new arrivals consume a disproportionate share of social services and frequently end up on the dole. Although they frequently deny it, an invidious nativist—even racist—tone colors their arguments" (Delaney 1994). The global corporate diversity pitch is not so much that immigrants are good for America, although that statement is surely made, but that free trade brings greater prosperity and democracy. Hence Bush's campaign promise to "look south . . . as a fundamental commitment of my presidency . . . overcome the North-South divide [just as we ended the great divide between East and West]," with diversity considered "differences among family" (Bush 2000).

Free Trade and Transnational Cultural Brokering

THE "PROGRESSIVE" BROKERING OF DIVERSITY AND THE "WE ARE THE WORLD" SYNDROME Consider these two passages:

> Given the global realities of the 1990s, NAFTA represents a vital strategic national interest for the U.S. Mexico stands waiting for an infusion of U.S. know-how, technology, and investment capital . . . This policy has the potential to extend to even more Latin American countries a critical platform for modernization of economic infrastructure . . . Most economists predict that U.S. Hispanic business owners and professionals may be among those who benefit the most. (Chavarría 1994: 3)

> The U.S. stands on the edge of a new frontier—a world both home and abroad, that is in flux and out of balance . . . The new frontier is a complex global society that will demand the power of the imagination and the forces of regeneration to meet its challenges.
>
> For America's artists and cultural institutions this is a time of great opportunity. We can offer more than a colorful banner and a theme song in support of this quest. We bring our untapped capacities as bridge builders, translators and problem solvers. We bring the language and technology of transformation . . .
>
> America, the lone remaining "superpower," must now learn to operate in an environment of shifting, toppling, and even flattening hierarchies—a world where information technology, multinational finance, world famine, ethnic conflict and ozone depletion are but a few of the interconnecting threads in the emerging global fabric . . .
>
> While we were watching the transformation of the world on CNN, the U.S. has undergone a metamorphosis as well. The dramatic shift in population from north/east to south/west, the move from an industrial to a service- and information-based economy, the ongoing deterioration of our human services, edu-

cation and public works infrastructures, our wide-spread political disaffection, and our emergence as the globe's first truly multicultural society, are but a few indications of the monumental changes taking place. (Cleveland 1992: 84–85)

These two excerpts, taken from what most readers would consider diametrically opposed venues—the first is an editorial from *Hispanic Business* and the second an advocacy piece in a progressive art journal, *High Performance*—nevertheless coincide in one respect: the great gains they expect for themselves as relatively subordinated groups (Hispanics, progressive artists) from interaction with their peers in other countries in this age of globalization and regional integration processes. While progressives have predicted mostly negative effects from such processes, these two writers (one an ardent capitalist, the other an activist artist) see opportunity calling, particularly as "bridge builders, translators and problem solvers." I have obviously juxtaposed the two passages to highlight the fact that in the context of globalization both see the possibilities of capitalizing on talents that others will consume. How different are these statements from the more or less crass or more or less subtle public relations advertisements for corporate diversity? I would like to delve further into the intermediary role these statements propose, for which I have coined the term "transnational cultural brokering."

AN OVERVIEW OF CULTURAL BROKERING   The negotiation of culture in relation to national expression in an international arena is not new. Balfe analyzes the transformation of this function of "artworks as symbolic carriers, as mediators of politics" in the current conjuncture in which the "orchestration has become more complicated and more necessary in recent years as the world's great artworks have been increasingly used in the competition between various 'imperialistic' powers and assigned various roles in international propaganda" (1987: 195).

Among the new roles for artworks from third world and peripheral countries, we might mention the transformation in the modes of reception. Increasingly, exhibitions are partnerships among sponsors from the South as well as the North. The curator has become the major symbolic actor in the art world, eclipsing artists themselves. Curatorship, more than ever before, now involves complex collaborations such that the flows of influence no longer travel from center to periphery but circulate multidirectionally among global cities throughout the world, much like the transactions of transnational corporations. Like the CEOs of those corporations, curators are the "institutionally recognized experts" of their markets, steering the meaning and status of their products and their image through the system of distribution (acquisition, exhibition, and interpretation as regards art). Mari Carmen Ramírez (1996), in one of the few studies of the phenomenon as it relates to Latin American and U.S. Latino art, has noted that the curatorial function is framed by an infrastructure of institutional, financial, and professional networks that necessarily inscribes art exhibition within a complex "web of market or institutionally dominated interests" such that any "preten[se of alternativity] is at most a fallacy." In what follows, I examine the transnational brokering of art in its high corporate mode as well as in the U.S.-based compensatory "alternative" market for the distribution of value to those (particularly minorities) whose work does not circulate in the dominant art circuits.

We might point to the symbolic power of blockbuster exhibitions like *Mexico: The Splendors of Thirty Centuries* (1990), which served to usher in NAFTA, at least at the level of "high" culture. The artworks included in the exhibition were meant to operate as a medium of negotiation, a form of cultural brokering. This is evident in Octavio Paz's inaugural lecture for the exhibition, in which he reconciles the "otherness" of Mexico's past, with the future (present) of its modernity: "The radical 'otherness' of Mesoamerican civilization is thus transformed into its opposite: thanks to modern aesthetics, these works that seem so distant are also contemporaneous" (1990: 19). Not unlike advertising for tourism, such exhibitions appeal to the metropolitan desire to indulge in a "comfortable exoticism," with all the luxuries of air conditioning, multilane highways to move from place to place, and supermodern hotels. In one of those ironic flips that history can subject us to, Paz, who has produced some of the keenist insights into the rhetorical workings of power, had now become the spokesperson of free trade, the flip side of his assimilation of Mexico's otherness to a grand historical design. In an op-ed piece published in the *New York Times*, Paz (1993) identifies "NAFTA [as] the first step in [this] grand design." If he had once written in *The Labyrinth of Solitude* and other works about revolution, love, and poetry as the forces that transcend all antinomies in the "self-realization of history," that role is now bestowed on NAFTA: "Nafta looks like the first step in a grand design. Its goal, therefore, is historical, transcending economics and politics. It is a reply to the terrible challenge of our historical moment, which is being torn asunder by the rebirth of the most ferocious nationalisms." Purged of its communist specter, the new internationalism can now resolve questions of national identity at a higher level. Thus, thirty centuries of Mexican culture can circulate as a testament to the new historical mission. Indeed, this is an excellent expression of the new international division of cultural labor: the appeal to local difference within global circuits.

As Goldman (1991a, 1994) notes, the new transnational world order has made one-way cultural imperialism obsolete, together with its contestatory counterdiscourse of anti-imperialism. According to Goldman, culture is brokered at this "high" (finance) level by "power elites from nations of the First and Third Worlds . . . whose objective is the control of resources and cultural configurations across national boundaries" (1991a: 17). It comes as no surprise that Mexican media conglomerate Televisa was a major actor in the brokering of the *Splendors of Mexico* exhibition, for it had a significant stake in NAFTA. Just as the agreement was about to go into effect, Emilio Azcárraga, then principal owner of Grupo Televisa, sold a stock issue worth $1 billion to position his company to reap the windfalls of the privatization of state-owned Mexican stations and to strengthen its investments in U.S. Spanish-language television. Although only a minority shareholder, he seemed to "call the shots" at the U.S. Spanish-language network Univision, as suggested by a *Hispanic Business* report (Mendosa 1994: 58). Thus, while U.S. enterprises are moving into Mexican media and telecommunications (in 1994 NBC signed an agreement to purchase a 10–20 percent share in Grupo Azteca, Televisa's far-off second-place competition [NAFTA and Inter-American Trade Monitor 1994a]), Televisa took control of four new Spanish-language channels in the United States through the intermediation of its subsidiary Galavision (Mendosa 1994: 60).

Another exhibition that seems to have had the goal of ushering Mexico symbolically into the first world was *Mito y Magia en América: Los Ochenta (Myth and Magic in America: The 1980s)* at the Museo de Arte Contemporáneo de Monterrey in 1991. According to one of the consultants I interviewed, the directors' underlying agenda was to present a history of the art boom of the 1980s with Mexican artists as the protagonists. Although nineteen countries were represented, the emphasis was on Mexico and the United States. This was a way of suggesting cultural parity between both countries, with the Monterrey Group, Mexico's most dynamic national bourgeoisie, at the center of the equation. Regardless of what one may think of the "autonomous" artistic value of the works exhibited (the criteria of evaluation, in any case, are being renegotiated worldwide in relation to shifting institutional bases not totally independent of the pressures of civil society and corporate capital), the curatorial intent seemed to be the equating of artists like Julio Galán, Dulce María Núñez, Rocío Maldonado, and Nahum B. Zenil with the superstars of the U.S. art scene of the 1980s: Eric Fischl, Cindy Sherman, David Salle, Kenny Scharf, Julian Schnabel,

Sherry Levine, Jean-Michel Basquiat, Keith Haring, and others. In his catalogue essay, Alberto Ruy Sánchez argues that the 1980s saw the constitution of a "new imaginary geography," whereby "the United States and Canada are seen as belonging more and more to the same continent as Mexico" (1991: 156). The common denominator in this shared imaginary is "exuberant" ritual, which in Sánchez's essay is characterized as a kind of reconditioned, even postmodern, magical realism. Jean-Michel Basquiat's "exuberance" consists of the "transporting [of 'savage,' albeit] everyday primitive figures into the world of everyday contemporary figures," and Dulce María Núñez's exuberance "becomes a strictly personal mythological code derived from Mexican creation myths" (160–161). As Mari Carmen Ramírez (1995) argues concerning the marketing of Latin American art in the 1980s and 1990s, "Cultural identities" become the medium through which value circulates for this newly exoticized art. What the *Myth and Magic* exhibition did was extend the bridge of consumable identity across the Rio Grande.

In the context of then ongoing negotiations for drafting a free trade agreement, the purported equivalence with the United States underscored the desire to enter the first world both economically (the show was sponsored by Televisa) and culturally. This entailed the elimination of whatever was deemed not to contribute to this display of first-worldness, including what Edward Sullivan, in his contribution to the catalogue, characterizes as the "rhetorical[ly political] gestures that made the last gasps of the muralist movement so redundant" (1991: 170). But, as Ramírez argues, the framing of Latin American artists does not take place in a vacuum, at a remove from economic and institutional inducements and constraints. Instead, such a framing "reveal[s] the conflation of competing interests and objectives in the marketing of . . . identities" (1996: 6). The above-mentioned consultant reported that he had to pressure the museum to include U.S. minority artists as well as artists from the Anglo- and Francophone Caribbean who were relatively unknown.

Understandably, those Latin American artists selected who reside in the United States were labeled "American," for they developed their reputation in U.S. institutions (e.g., Carlos Almaraz, Luis Cruz Azaceta, and Juan Sánchez). Once located within the force field that is U.S. cultural politics, one's "difference" operates differently: one becomes a Latino. Furthermore, the preference for painting over other media, particularly the more politicized installation format, suggested an accommodation to the art world status quo at the time.

Underneath, then, the show supported the gallery system in which the valuation of art is more an economic than a socioaesthetic matter. These criticisms are actually brought home in the catalogue in an essay by Charles Merewether (1991), who gives a quite different portrayal of the art scenes in the United States and Latin America. The inclusion of this essay seems to have been an attempt to ward off the criticism.

This phenomenon of cultural brokering does not originate and end at the office doors of such corporate sponsors as Televisa or the national oil company PEMEX. The packaging of Mexican identity attempted by these corporations opens up spaces of negotiation for other actors, both in Mexico and the United States. The emphasis on Mexico's indigenous past enabled marginalized indigenous minorities to launch a critique of the *Splendors* show and of the institutions that sponsored it. In fact, the Zapatista liberation struggle in Chiapas was in part enabled by the disjuncture between the packaging of Mexico for NAFTA and the hardships of indigenous peoples in Chiapas and other states. Similarly, in the United States, Chicanos and other minorities (particularly Native Americans) organized alternative exhibitions to make visible that which *Splendors* did not recognize, particularly popular arts and the cultural production of Chicanos in the United States. It is precisely in the struggle between minority communities and the mainstream art world, a struggle that corporations cautiously negotiate in their strategies to legitimize their own discourse of crossing borders, that the place of a parallel market can be analyzed most fruitfully.

A PARALLEL MARKET Merewether's (1991) essay points to the ongoing struggle between mainstream art world institutions and what I call an *alternative* or *parallel* art market, one that attracts (and *manages*) artists like those excluded from the *Splendors* and Monterrey exhibitions. To a great extent, this parallel market is supported by public institutions that have adopted new approaches to art, especially the turn toward an anthropological construal of everyday and vernacular cultures (Clifford 1988, 1991), the aesthetic evaluation of works traditionally kept in ethnological museums, and the "new curatorship" in the United States, with its emphasis on difference and diversity. All of these new tendencies, which are presented in two anthologies edited by Ivan Karp and Steven Lavine (1991) and Karp, Kreamer, and Lavine (1992), aim to displace the self-legitimizing strategies of art institutions that were established in the heyday of modernism. These approaches also move the practice of art further from its self-understanding as an autonomous realm of culture. Instead, its meaningfulness is understood to derive from the needs, demands, and desires of the constituents of civil society. Art moves ever closer to a practical reason as opposed to a cognitive or aesthetic rationality.

It is important to understand that this turn in cultural production toward a parallel or alternative market is motivated in great part by minority artists' difficulty of access to or the repudiation of the gallery-cum–auction house infrastructure of the art market oriented toward profit, which most art museums have supported. This infrastructure has, of course, integrated certain "alternative" practices, such as the graffiti art of Basquiat and Haring, but always as a means to profit. The mainstream art world has tried to respond to the alternative market, as in the much criticized 1993 Whitney Biennial. Such a rapprochement is also motivated in part by pressure from foundations like Rockefeller, Ford, MacArthur, Lila Wallace–Reader's Digest Fund, even Coors and Phillip Morris (both of which have had run-ins in the past with minority cultural institutions).[6]

It may be instructive to contrast the ethos of alternative work in Mexico with that in the United States. The *Myth and Magic* exhibition largely excluded the "really alternative" from both countries. Olivier Debroise (1990) characterized the excluded Mexican art as that of a "different Mexico." Starting with the massacre of hundreds of students in the Plaza de las Tres Culturas in Tlatelolco in 1968, there emerged an "irreversible 'Chicanization' of everday life" that contributed to the redefinition of Mexican identity, which from 1975 to 1985 in turn "substantially revitalized forms that artists of the mid-century had sought to dissolve in their haste to integrate their work into the universalism of modern art" (28). This process became even more intense after the mid-1980s, particularly with the emergence of a self-organization movement to deal with the ravages of the 1985 earthquake, which the state seemed incapable of tending to adequately. Such self-organization left an impact on young artists, who opposed the official art market that gained prominence as an investment vehicle in the wake of the 1987 stock market crash.

We might emphasize one feature in Debroise's description of this youth art movement that contrasts markedly with the practice of young U.S. artists in the 1980s and that will help explain the function of the cultural brokers of alternativity. It can be said that in Mexico there was a veritable explosion of noninstitutional exhibitions and festivals organized by the young artists themselves in their apartments, in "microgalleries," in invaded public spaces, and through the media of cheaply produced journals and fanzines, some of which were linked with parallel art trends across the border. In the United States, however, many of these parallel art trends, particularly multicultural and, more specifically, identity-oriented and "border" art, found some means of public and third-sector or "nonprofit" support. According to Whittaker (1993), *arts organizations*, particularly those that promote "social action art," drew most of their funding from municipal and state arts councils and the NEA before it was transformed by the culture wars of the late 1980s and 1990s.

Throughout the 1970s and 1980s, the NEA's commitment to "diversity" increased (one of the reasons for conservative opposition to it during the culture wars). This was also the case in most local agencies, many of which serve as conduits for NEA dollars (DiMaggio 1991: 227). According to Langley, "The funding of ethnic artists and multicultural companies has become a stated priority at most federal, state, and city arts agencies, as well as at many private and corporate funders" (1993: 189). Even with the cuts to the NEA, some of the slack is picked up by foundations such as Rockefeller, which promotes minority artists. And as Zolberg (1994) notes, some of these foundations, like the Carnegie and the Ford, have "oriented their support toward bringing in groups relatively excluded from access." Moreover, the Lila Wallace–Reader's Digest Fund made "grants of $50 million in the largest national effort to help art museums shed their image as elitist institutions . . . [and] to target very specific new audiences: young people, residents in rural communities, the disabled, ethnic minorities" (286).

Alternativity, whether we define it in terms of race, ethnicity, gender, sexual orientation, or a multicultural combination, was reined in by what Brian Wallis characterizes as the managerial procedures whereby arts agencies—the NEA, state and municipal arts councils—created special niches, or "ghetto[s] for artists of color" (forthcoming a). Moreover, alternative arts spaces, the R&D of what galleries and contemporary art museums will capitalize on, began to set the trends, and in the process were drawn into the mechanisms of professionalization. "What can be read from one angle as a successful takeover of the governmental cultural apparatus by artists, might from another view be seen as a textbook case of [Foucauldian] governmentality in action" (Wallis forthcoming b).

The rallying concept for many of these support efforts is the category of the community. Art is supposed to serve the interests of communities, rather than appeal to universal autonomous values, which critics argue end up buttressing the status quo. This ethos helps explain why NEA minority arts funding responds to more "general" or "multidisciplinary" than specifically aesthetic criteria. Concentrated in just two of the NEA's twelve programs (Expansion Arts and Folk Arts), grants to "minority arts organizations [are made to seem] less compatible with the specifically focused disciplines that concentrate on contemporary work and more compatible with 'general' programs that are eclectic enough to handle a range of aesthetic criteria" (Gilmore 1993: 147–148). This policy, which made good sense to progressively minded arts groups, was challenged from both the right and the left in the 1990s. For example, a recent study criticizes foundations' community-oriented funding criteria because they encourage the formation of a welfare service mind-set among artists. Some funders have decided, ironically, to make the awards directly to communities rather than to the artists-"middlemen" (Rabinowitz 1994):

> The function of the community artist can, in at least some respects, be productively compared with that of the reformer or social worker. Both the community artist and the social worker possess a set of skills (bureaucratic, diagnostic, aesthetic/expressive, and so forth) and have access to public and private funding (through grants writing, official status, and institutional sponsorship) with the goal of bringing about some transformation in the condition of individuals who are presumed to be in need . . . For the community artist the community's guardianship of "art," "creativity," or the "aesthetic" plays the same role that "science" does for the reformer. It is a universally applicable language that allows them to transcend the specificity of their own social and cultural positions.
>
> Obviously the institutional apparatus that administers and supports welfare is much larger than that which supports community art, but the growing interest among foundations in "community" issues is precisely such that the distinction between community art and welfare or social policy is in some cases quite fine. (Kester 1995: 8)

The infrastructure that supports the parallel market, managed largely by liberals and progressives, including many women and minorities, is intended to facilitate the construction of bridges to all those "others" who have been excluded or marginalized in mainstream culture, particularly in the aesthetic public spheres. Private and public foundations (the NEA and state arts councils) require that exhibitions be legitimized on the basis of wider and more diverse audiences. They also frequently make their grants contingent on matching funds, which arts organizations can provide or serve as conduits to obtain. Arts organizations in turn cannot obtain their own funds "without proving their relevance to the communities that they serve" (Whittaker 1993: 32). Gilmore adds that the NEA, like any other federal agency, must answer to Congress, "who in turn represents diverse and different communities . . . so that the matter of distributional equity of public funds is becoming ever more problematic" in the context of the culture wars between conservatives and progressives (1993: 138).

How does all of this impact the relation between the arts and free trade? Free trade, I have argued, has adopted a discourse of diversity. And corporations eager to legitimize their contribution to diversity and to expand into new markets are sponsoring exhibitions that deal with such topics, the result being that a multicultural ethos has a (contested) place in the mainstream art world. This is consistent with the corporate ethos that is permeating all aspects of life, even more so as neoliberalism promotes privatization. The parallel art market (increasingly seeking entry into the dominant one) shares at least this aspect of the corporate ethos: "making consumers [or audiences] feel valuable" (Langley 1993: 185). I am not speaking only of U.S. corporations. As Mari Carmen Ramírez (1996) explains, Latin American art markets in Mexico, Colombia, Venezuela, and Miami (i.e., "Cuban America") have promoted their own artists, leading to what some have seen as a Latin American art boom in the 1980s and 1990s. These are the artists who are carried by mainstream galleries in the major art centers and whose work is auctioned at Sotheby's and Christies. The problem is that the promotion of these artists has been done by means of the same discourse of diversity that has emerged in the parallel market for minority artists.[7] Often, exhibitions lump together Latin Americans and Latinos, thus masking the compensatory reasons for the existence of a parallel market. On the one hand, this practice incenses Latinos, who have worked hard to get a parallel market to respond to their own work, expressive as it is of minority communities. On the other hand, Latin American artists, who are usually solidly middle class, feel diminished by getting into the art market through the back door, so to speak.[8]

Transnational culture is also local culture. This was evident in the response of Chicanos to the *Splendors* exhibition. The alternative exhibitions and lecture series aimed at introducing into the public sphere the everyday cultural practices of people of Mexican origin. Where did the funds for these alternative exhibitions come from? In part, they came from community cultural and social institutions. But these in turn received their resources to a large degree from state and municipal arts agencies whose mandate is the proportional distribution of resources earmarked for cultural activities. Several analysts of arts management have pointed to the recent reduction in funding for arts organizations and to the need to attract new publics to increase revenues, both from ticket sales and from government agencies that foster inclusion of all sectors of society. Foundations like the Rockefeller also sponsored many of the alternative activities that supplemented the *Splendors* exhibition.

As we are all aware, most conservative Republicans have sought to cut off public funding for the arts precisely because of such community concerns and to discourage the private funding of diversity. All the more reason for the new transnational partnerships that have emerged, in which Mexican government foundations such as the Consejo Nacional para las Artes y la Cultura and the U.S.-Mexico Fund for Culture and corporations like Televisa can compensate when U.S. government support is cut. The Mexican consular system has also invested heavily in the sponsorship of art and other cultural events, particularly those organized by Chicanos and other Latinos, thus providing important support.[9] Raúl Hinojosa, a former policy analyst and advisor with the NAFTA Bank in the U.S. Treasury Department, compared such sponsorship of cultural and other social and political activities to Israel's efforts to infuence U.S. society through the philanthropy of Jewish organizations (personal communication, September 1993). Transnationalization extends to all possible spaces, transcending national boundaries for commercial as well as minority political interests. García Canclini's proposal for considering citizenship in tandem with consumerism should thus be extended to these more intricate transnational processes. What has yet to be done, however, is to bring them to open discussion in a transnational forum that includes representation of all affected parties, and which we see emerging in the Southern Cone with the MERCOSUL da cultura, examined in a subsequent section of this chapter.

Given the transnational and translocal character of several ethnic groups in the United States, it is not surprising that the concerns of their countries of origin should get bound up into the mechanisms devised in the United States for "distributional equity." Such issues are addressed, for example, in museum exhibitions like *Beyond the Borders: Art by Recent Immigrants* (1994) at the Bronx Museum of the Arts. According to the catalogue essay, "For most immigrants now arriving in the U.S., 'American' culture is not a newly encountered concept. The innovations of global telecommunications and travel have reshaped crosscultural knowledge and fixed notions of cultural proximity and distance." Consequently, these new immigrants have already worked out some accommodation to "American" culture and seek to make an input that creates a space for their own ideas. "The work by immigrant artists thus becomes a basis for questioning established ideas and cultural positions within American culture" (13–14).

Another example of how the funding situation of cultural institutions opens up spaces of negotiation among minorities, big business, and foreign governments and institutions is offered by Jane Stevenson Day (1994), who found herself embroiled in unexpected negotiations among such parties when she curated an exhibition of Aztec art at the Denver Museum of Natural History. Her first concern was to attract new audiences for financing purposes: "Successful museums today are playing new roles in their communities. Not only are they meeting new educational challenges but they are attempting to draw new visitors into the museum and to address the concerns and interests of non-traditional audiences. Reasons for this vary. Partially, it is based on institutional financial requirements; obviously new audiences bring in additional memberships and admission fees. In addition, diverse audiences often open up new opportunities for funding from foundations and government agencies" (309). Introduction of new constituencies into the museum generated a whole new set of demands. Latino groups wanted a say in the presentation of the history of the Aztecs. They also lobbied for a more accessible, as opposed to a scholarly, catalogue. The popular character of the catalogue also turned out to be an expedient means to raise funds: an unprecedented twenty-five thousand copies were sold. To satisfy the educational requirements of such an enterprise, the museum offered seminars, involving volunteers from the larger Denver community, half of whom were Latinos. Native Americans also sought to have some say in the presentation of the exhibition, particularly in the matter of the treatment of skeletal remains, which are sacred in their culture.

The pressures brought by the local minority communities involved the museum in an unusual negotiation with lending institutions in Mexico, "institutions whose political and cultural concerns we needed to consider" and which did not initially understand the inclusion of Hispanics and Indians in the planning of the exhibition (Day 1994: 313). Finally, because the exhibition was a costly event, but an event that highlighted relations between Mexico and the United States, corporations "were particularly anxious to add the cultural excitement of the Aztec exhibition to their economic concerns. Both cash contributions and 'in kind' donations from these international businesses were a significant funding factor in the larger exhibit budget." The upshot was both cultural and economic, confirming García Canclini's arguments about "cultural reconversion" in his book *Hybrid Cultures* ([1990] 1995b). He puts forth the view that "culture" is reconstituted in relation to a combination of political negotiations and marketing concerns. "We know that about 725,000 people saw the exhibit; that the impact on the Denver economy was between 60 and 70 million dollars; that about 60 percent of our visitors came from outside the Denver area (100,000 of these from foreign countries); and that almost 125,000 school children visited Aztec" (Day 1994: 315).

The transnationalization of museological and social concerns, as in this case, can have quite positive outcomes. Involving the different constituencies (perhaps a more accurate expression would be "producing" different constituencies) in the process of designing an exhibition and presenting knowledge about it can be seen in part as de-emphasizing the professional's role in such a cultural intervention. On the other hand, bringing in or producing these constituencies, following Foucault (1982), Bennett (1995), and Wallis (forthcoming a, forthcoming b), is a way of managing social interaction as museum professionals mediate the potential conflicts arising from encounter. Moreover, these groups are partly constituted in the relationship that social and museological issues bear to funding and accountancy, a classic medium through which, in Foucauldian language, populations are managed.

These and other examples make it evident that in the current context the relationship among art, community, and the negotiation of diversity cannot be divorced from the economic factor. We have already seen that more "diverse" audiences will generate greater revenues, either directly in admissions or by means of government agency grants that require such diversity. In fact, the very discourse of diversity reconciles the prevalence of multiculturalism in educational, artistic, corporate, and "progressive" spheres with the belief in the new exceptionalism of "America" as a leader in world culture and economy: "the globe's first truly multicultural society" (Cleveland 1992).

Progressives and capitalists alike have seen a kind of salvation in the hybridity generated by the so-called new immigrants who, to paraphrase performance artist Guillermo Gómez-Peña, are redrawing the map of America. "Mexican and Caribbean cultures," he states, romanticizing them, in my view, "can offer the North their spiritual strength, political intelligence and sense of humor in dealing with crises; as well as experience in fostering personal and community relations" (1993: 60). On the other hand, advocates for large urban metropolitan centers see the cultural resources of diversity as one of the most important forms of economic revival. A "comprehensive, yearlong research project" carried out by the Port Authority of New York and New Jersey reports that "the arts and other cultural activities have grown substantially in importance over the last decade. They now pump at least $9.8 billion a year into the New York metropolitan area and, directly and indirectly, support more than 107,000 jobs. The arts directly employ some 41,000, appreciably more than the 36,000 employed in advertising" (Redburn 1993: B6). The authors of the study conclude that the very cultural complexity of the New York area, which has intensified in the past decade and helped "lift the New York economy" (Levine

1990; Sontag 1993), is the major factor in the growth of the arts and other cultural activities.

Ultimately, the rhetoric of diversity is supposed to generate enthusiasm among people who are losing jobs to "developing" countries and to workers earning survival wages in those countries whose *value* is measured in terms of cultural identity. It is no accident that free trade and diversity can get along so well together. Add to this the currency of diversity in the third sector, both national and international, the latter led by UNESCO, and even the U.S. Information Agency/Department of State, whose grants for partnerships with foreign institutions *require* incorporating diversity into all aspects of proposals (U.S. State Department, Bureau of Educational and Cultural Affairs 2001). Although the valuation of cultural identity is no doubt an important part of current thinking on citizenship (see chapters 1 and 6), this diversity *value* nonetheless operates as a resource for accumulation in some contexts and as a compensation for the lack of economic value in others.

Capitalizing (on) the Border

It is a commonplace to recognize that the setting of boundaries is achieved through violence, a "violent spacing" that produces value and culture (Derrida 1976: 107). "The realm of culture," Bakhtin has said, "has no internal territory: it is entirely distributed along the boundaries, boundaries pass everywhere . . . Every cultural act lives essentially on the boundaries" (1984: 301). Indeed, this seems to be the logic of Frederick Jackson Turner's (1920) "moving frontier" trope for the process by which the page of "American" civilization is written.[10] Economy and culture go together in the process of "writing the frontier," or the "border," as Chicano historians and critics prefer to call it, pointing out that value is produced by the "incessant expansion" to which Turner (37), and Marx and Engels ([1848] 1967) before him, refer.[11] The Chicano borderlands, then, may be understood as a trope for the persistence of and resistance to this process of transnationalization, which, according to Marx, rendered "the old local and national seclusion and self-sufficiency" outdated, replacing them with "intercourse in every direction, [with] universal inter-dependence of nations." This process of material expropriation is also one of intellectual and cultural appropriation. Indeed, in addition to the swallowing of borders that occurred when the United States took over the lands that constitute the Southwest, such cultural intermediaries as Charles F. Lummis, Aurelio M. Espinosa, and J. Frank Espinosa appropriated the "border" by projecting a romanticized Spanish or Mexican past that edited out the cultural attributes of the majority of inhabitants of the region.

This quaint and exoticized portrayal of Mexican Americans was redrawn by the Chicano scholars of the 1960s, who struggled in an inhospitable academic milieu (albeit one opened up by political pressure and the liberal espousal of representativity in the wake of the civil rights movement) to highlight the bicultural and working-class characteristics of Mexican Americans. The new interdisciplinary work on Chicano border culture has gone through several phases — from a nationalist to a hybridist recognition of gender, racial, and sexual orientation factors — nevertheless constituting a "local" canon ranging from the border balladry that Americo Paredes identifies as a major leavening of cultural identity in his *"With His Pistol in His Hand": A Border Ballad and Its Hero* (1958), to the poetry, novels, popular theater, and murals of the 1960s and 1970s, to the "mestiza border writing" of Gloria Anzaldúa (1987) and other contemporary writers and critics in the 1980s and 1990s.[12]

I would argue that despite the emphasis on hybridity that has come to dominate thinking on Chicano and other Latino and U.S. minority groups, the "border culture" referred to in such works is a particularly local one and, as such, one that has become susceptible to poaching by the ubiquity or "border crossing" of capital and transnational artists. This practice is made evident in the epigraphs from *Hispanic Business* and *High Performance* in the previous section. Guillermo Gómez-Peña, to give another example, flaunts his ubiquity as if the very ability to travel and mutate has greater value than the rootedness of the local:

> Today, eight years after my departure [from Mexico], when they ask me for my nationality or ethnic identity, I can't respond with one word, since my "identity" now possesses multiple repertoires: I am Mexican but I am also Chicano and Latin American. At the border they call me *chilango* or *mexiquillo*; in Mexico City it's *pocho* or *norteño*; and in Europe it's *sudaca*. The Anglos call me "Hispanic" or "Latino," and the Germans have, on more than one occasion, confused me with Turks or Italians. My wife Emilia is Anglo, but speaks Spanish with an Argentine accent, and together we walk amid the rubble of the Tower of Babel of our American postmodernity. (1988: 127–128)

Gómez-Peña sees himself poised on the cusp of a new era, characterizing himself as the Zelig-like pioneer who will bring us visions of a hybrid utopia that he no doubt presumes has value for the reader. But such ubiquity and hybridity have a localized value that circulates in a particular way in the academic, art, and cultural circuits in the United States. In other words, it sells well in the United States. Néstor García Canclini interviewed many residents of Tijuana, just on the other side of the border, one of the sites of operation of Gómez-Peña's "Taller de Arte Fronterizo/Border Arts Workshop." The "locals" expressed serious reservations about this "border-crosser" 's ubiquity:

> Other Tijuana artists and writers challenge the euphemistic treatment of the contradictions and uprooting that they discern in the work of *La Línea Quebrada/The Broken Line* [the journal of Taller/Border Arts Workshop]. They reject the celebration of migrations caused by poverty in the homeland and in the United States. Native Tijuanos or those who have resided there for fifteen years or longer are outraged by the insolence of these artists' unconcerned parodies: "These are people who have just arrived and immediately they tell us who we are, they dictate how we should discover ourselves." (García Canclini 1992a: 42)

Careful ethnographic research by Pablo Vila (2000) provides a thorough critique of the hype in border theory. The notions of hybridity and border crossing do not do enough justice to the specificity of place and how people in given situations deal with the challenges posed by migration, "flexible" labor conditions (maquiladora work with low compensation), transnational TV and communications, and so on. While writers like Gómez-Peña, Anzaldúa, and even García Canclini tend to generalize one notion of border culture, Vila's work demonstrates the complexity and multidimensionality of identification in the El Paso–Juárez region that cannot be reduced to homogenizing spatial metaphors and where several competing and often coincident narrativizations of identity are deployed to negotiate the status, value, or devaluation to which people are subject. He argues convincingly that there is no *one* border identity, something that is assumed by so many other writers on the topic. To a good degree, his method, the use of narratives, or what he calls emplotments, of encounters with others (i.e., not belonging to the same set of categorizations as the informant) provides dependable empirical evidence (to the extent possible) of how the classifications invoked by the informants are contradictory, reflecting the changing frameworks of self- and other-conception as they move from one location to another or refer to different "others." Particularly revealing is his explanation of El Pasoans' (even Mexican American El Pasoans') preference for measures to limit immigration from Mexico.

The appropriation of border culture was also evident in the media hoopla that ushered in NAFTA. There were celebrations of economic reform, similar to those reported in the New York study referred to above. A *New York Times* report, "San Antonio's Wild about Free Trade," cited corporate executives who waxed enthusiastic about the cultural as well as economic aspects of the accord: " 'People here have really made an effort to understand the Mexican culture,' said Blair Labatt, the president of the Labatt company" (Verhovek 1993). Reports on the opening day of the agreement noted that "the warming of trade relations is welcomed on both sides of the border," observing, however, that such an economic welcome was accompanied by redoubled "crackdown[s] on illegal immigration" (Reinhold 1994). Such crackdowns, in fact, also contribute to the capitalization of the border, pumping in large amounts of money, like Operation Gatekeeper's $25 million, for the construction of barriers, the purchase of equipment, and the hiring of guards (Ayres 1994). Such measures only increased with the debacle of the peso in December 1994 and the bailout package offered by the Clinton administration. In fact, the bailout was implicitly made contingent on the Mexican government's "commit[ment] to crackdowns on emigration and narcotics without making that a strict condition of the loan" (Sanger 1995a).

Some of the crackdowns can rival conceptual art performance pieces like *Arte-Reembolso/Art Rebate* (discussed below) or environmental art like that of Christo, who wraps buildings and mountains and has cut through landscapes with miles-long fences. The consequences of this erection of barriers against illegal immigration are both symbolic and material, as in the *Arte-Reembolso/Art Rebate* event, but unlike this event they reach the hysterical dimensions of an obsession. Conservative politicians participated in "Light Up the Border" events, which included the erection of a "10-foot-high border fence north of Tijuana [stretching] 14 miles inland from Imperial Beach, south of San Diego. Steel pilings 340 feet into the Pacific Ocean [have also been installed] to thwart illegal immigrants arriving by boat" (Reinhold 1994). Residents on the Mexican side, mobilized by artists from the Border Arts Workshop, engaged in their own performance of "lighting up the border" by holding up large mirrors that reflected the car lights back onto the U.S. side. Indeed, the border has been the major inspiration for site-specific art events, such as those included in the triennial art festival known as inSITE (see chapter 9), although one might argue that what takes place on and around the border cannot be matched by any artwork.

Despite this heated anti-immigrant sentiment, especially in California, corporate capitalism has supported public relations mega-art events at the border, including "Chicanos and U.S. artists of color," who, contrary to Gómez-Peña's predictions, were not "bypassed." In fact, it might be said that corporate capi-

6. "Playas de Tijuana: Border Fence." Photo by George Yúdice.

7. "Tijuana: Border Fence." Photo by George Yúdice.

talism has been able to keep pace with "decentering" at least as well as, if not better than, progressive performance artists. According to Gómez-Peña, free trade art impresarios "would rather bypass the border zone, with its mine fields of race and gender and its political geysers, and deal directly with what they perceive as 'the center' (New York, Los Angeles, Paris or Mexico City). Unfortunately they ignore that today in 1993 culture has been completely decentralized, and the old centers are being reconquered by the margins" (1993: 61). If the border hype that has been reported in the media brings home any message, it is quite the opposite of Gómez-Peña's claims. In the spirit of his own rhetoric, one *New York Times* report forecasts that San Antonio is "a city poised to be a kind of Hong Kong to Mexico's China" (Verhovek 1993). Furthermore, in such mega-art events as insITE, held in the border cities of San Diego and Tijuana, one gets the feeling that art and trade shows have found a common ground in flexing recently acquired economic muscles.

It could be said that, in keeping with free trade rhetoric, the San Diego–Tijuana region is epitomized both by the border and the 63 million crossings that belie it. Gómez-Peña, frustrated by the easy appropriation of the once "alternative" border trope, insists that it is time for border artists to "look for another paradigm to explain the new complexities of the times," because "the hybrid model . . . precisely because of its elasticity and open nature . . . can be appropriated by anyone to mean practically anything . . . Eventually, even the official transculture will use the hybrid to baptize transnational festivals, boring academic conferences and glossy publications" (1993: 62). If nothing else, Gómez-Peña is right on the mark about the border and hybridity metaphors constituting the basis of academic conferences, which may, in fact, be no more and no less boring than some performance art pieces structured around the same metaphors. Indeed, there has been a spate of conferences on the economic and social consequences of NAFTA, sponsored by the likes of the Center for U.S.-Mexican Studies at the University of California at San Diego and other specialized programs at the Colegio de la Frontera Norte in Tijuana, the University of Texas in Austin, the University of Arizona in Tucson, Tulane University in New Orleans, and the University of Maryland. Gwen Kirkpatrick examines several conferences — "Scientific and Technological Education" (Ciudad Juárez, October 1991); Wingspread Conference on Trilateral Education Issues (Racine, WI, September 1992); the "International Symposium on Higher Education and Strategic Partnerships" (Vancouver, September 1993); "Latino Educators Conference on Free Trade and Education" (Tucson, April 1993) — in which were discussed the possibilities and risks of " 'harmonizing' educational standards and certification, [with an] emphasis . . . on the scientific and technological aspects of education" (1993: 6).

In the area of culture, there has been much less activity.[13] The Universidad Nacional Autónoma de México and the Universidad Autónoma de Ciudad Juárez sponsored a groundbreaking conference in November 1991, which was published as a book titled *Education and Culture under the Free Trade Agreement* (Guevara Niebla and García Canclini 1992). In 1993 and 1994, the Inter-American Cultural Studies Network held conferences in Mexico City, Bellagio, Italy, and Rio de Janeiro on various aspects of the general topic of globalization and culture (Yúdice 1996a). Other important discussions have been held at Modern Language Association conventions in 1993 and 1994, where the impact of free trade was examined in relation to three main issues: national identity, globalization and supranational integration, and the media. The conference "Borders and Cultures," held at McGill University in Montreal in February 1995, focused on the formation of disparate and hybrid cultural interactions resulting from the "crumbl[ing of geographic boundaries] under the assault of economic requisites or pressure of transnational ethnic loyalties." As comprehensive as the McGill conference was, ranging from "a history of the ideologies of mapmaking to local issues with significant implications along the U.S./Canada border, from legal questions facing the European Union to projected impacts of Proposition 187 in California, from the breakdown of borders due to the electronic flow of information to the status of refugees in Chiapas to issues relating to the legacy of colonial borders" (George Szanto, personal communication, March 1995), very little here or elsewhere, except for the two MLA panels mentioned above (especially Claire F. Fox's contribution, which was incorporated into her 1999 book), engaged specifically the relation of the arts to free trade.

However, discussion is finally coming around to the impact of free trade on the arts. The Rockefeller Humanities Fellowship Program of the Latin American and Latino(a) Art Research Center at the University of Texas at Austin was established in the late 1990s to train "professionals to lead and advise" in "museums and universities in the United States that are now contending with issues of cultural representation and program development centering on Latino-American art." Funded for three years by the Rockefeller Foundation, it focused on South American art, Mexican and Mexican American art, and Latino(a) art and its cultures of origin. The latter two themes emphasize, among other things, transnational relations, the increasing visibility of Mexican and Latino(a) art in the United States, and the "changing role of curators and collections . . . in a culturally diverse society." This program was crucial not only for understanding the tensions between Latin American and Latino artists, as well as the contradictions that rack the institutions that seek to exhibit their work, but also for intervening in that process. Mari Carmen Ramírez, who has written eloquently on this problem, was the moving force behind this residency program (Rockefeller Curatorial Residence Program in Latin American and Latino AA 1994–1997). Moreover, panel discussions complementing inSITE1997 and inSITE2000, as reported in chapter 9, like many of the artworks, have addressed the relationship between free trade and culture head on.

Artists too, chief among them Guillermo Gómez-Peña, despite having sworn off "boring academic conferences," have organized discussions to examine the impact of free trade on their practices. A group called Life on the Water, for example, "a non-profit arts organization in San Francisco, held a conference and residency workshop programs for artists and critics on the "Reality/Realidad/Realité [of the] Free Idea Zone" brought about by NAFTA. Funding was provided by the Rockefeller Foundation, the California Council on the Humanities, the Ministry of External Affairs of Canada, FONCA-Mexico, and USIA. The last funding source may raise eyebrows, as it was once considered an arm of intelligence operations in Latin America. The fact that artists, particularly "radical" progressive artists, such as the ones who organized this workshop, are willing to seek funding from sources like these results in the contradictory situation of working within the conditions provided by the very governments and institutions that have promoted free trade at such a high cost to workers, the environment, and citizenship rights. One wonders to what degree the critique of free trade becomes blunted or absorbed by its institutionalization. The topics slated for discussion at the "Free Idea Zone" conference were directly linked to global trade: "the impact of globalization on culture, new information technologies and cultural distribution, issues of historic and current cultural and political inequities within and between the different countries. The goal of the residency and the conference was to build a foundation for a new network for promoting an uninterrupted exchange of ideas, cultural practice, and political information between artists and cultural activists from each country" (*Free Idea Zone Residency* 1994).

Such cultural activism approximates government policy, in a manner similar to that which Kester (1995) observed about community arts. In Gómez-Peña's sassy essay "The Free Art Agreement/El Tratado de Libre Cultura," one reads, "The job of the artist is to force open the matrix of reality to admit unsuspected possibilities," including the "redefinition of our continental topography" (1993: 59). To a great extent this redefinition is based on the experiences of undocumented immigrant workers, whose migrations are deemed analogous to the flows of a parallel "Free Art Agreement" among "nonaligned artists" (60). Sympathetic critics, for example, have commented approvingly on Gómez-Peña's projection of a free space of multicultural encounters. James A. Linker (1997) writes, "A border vocabulary is constructed from the multiple jargons which converge on the deterritorialized frontier. No longer geographically fixed, simultaneously everywhere and nowhere, the border is now recognized as a cultural formation, common but no longer restricted to those regions astride international boundaries. No longer containable by a site-specific definition, every major city of the Americas now constitutes a borderland, populated by multiplicity." Their *zona franca*, or free idea zone, is held up as a solution to the asymmetries exacerbated by free trade. This faith in art and culture may seem quixotic, yet it was very much in the spirit of the times, at least within the circle of progressives who advocate recognition of ("crossracial, polylinguistic and multicontextual") diversity.

Nevertheless, after years of advocating multiculturalism, Gómez-Peña subsequently eschewed it for its susceptibility to a "homogenized global culture" and turned to more interactive forms resulting from "diaspora, hybridization and 'borderization' " (Free Idea Zone Residency 1994). This utopian space, despite claims to recognition of the local, tends toward the universal and the abstract, a feature that may have to do with the peculiarly static ubiquity of these border artists. The "Free Idea Zone" residency workshop was actually a summit of "cross-cultural diplomats," who claimed to traverse borders with an ease not given to those "others" for whom they serve as "cultural brokers." For them, the border is thus a space of otherness disengaged from the experienced otherness of migrants. Again, critics like Linker (1997) celebrate this postmodern global wanderlust: "Gómez-Peña reminds us that to embrace a global pluralism is to reconnect to the collective social assemblage that has been so neatly fragmented for so long, a reconnection that will also require recognition of the inadequacies of conventionally constituted political structures." He even attributes a political valence to this deracinated globalism: "Thus it follows that these works are political insofar as they engage the relational functions of the social, the virtual community of global pluralism becoming actual in the borderlands that constitute the Americas." Claire Fox provides a lucid critique of this posturing, pointing out these artists' lack of awareness that their abstract mobility is not unlike that of other privileged actors: "The U.S.-Mexico border has rarely presented itself as a hindrance to artists, intellectuals, and tourists, for example, but then again, these crossings are not demographically representative of other large-scale flows of border traffic which currently characterize the region, such as that of undocumented workers northward and that of U.S. capital southward" (1999: 130).

Evidently, the implied surrogacy for the outcast, the dominated, the marginal, and particularly the undocumented worker—"poster child" of border art—is rendered problematic by the global ubiquity of the postmodern bordercrosser, which, according to Fox, Gómez-Peña casts as shamanistic figures who "[have] 'primacy' in processes of social transformation, because their jobs give them a unique position from which to 'dialogue' with 'Others' " (1999: 129). Displacing the "experience of dealing with a dominant culture from the outside," from the undocumented worker to the "free idea" artist, the latter is enabled in his or her ability "to tresspass, bridge, interconnect, translate, re-map, and redefine" (Gómez Peña 1993: 59). Ultimately, the emphasis on "borderization" in relation to culture further complicates any understanding of the specificity of art and the aesthetic. Perhaps the complication has to do with the hold the avant-garde ethos has over postcolonial, border-crossing, diasporic artists. Gómez-Peña, for example, writes in the egocentric manifesto style of the historical avant-gardes: "I am a migrant performance artist . . . I connect groups who think like us"; "I oppose the out-dated fragmentation of the map of America with that of Arte-America, continent made out of people, art and ideas, not countries"; "I oppose the sinister cartography of the New World Order"; "In my conceptual world, there is no place for static identities, fixed nationalities or sacred cultural traditions. Everything is in constant flux, including this text" (1993: 59). Not surprisingly, the ever desperate search for the new makes itself felt in this kind of work, so conscious of its place on a cutting edge that becomes dull as it gets "appropriated by anyone to mean practically anything" (62).

My own survey of the interrelationship of activist art and new "communities of difference" shows that there is a great deal of confusion in dealing with aesthetic issues and questions of representation. A questionnaire addressing such issues was sent to one hundred arts professionals and artists, of which about half were returned, and in some cases there were follow-up interviews. The introductory paragraph stated:

> The following survey is being conducted for the purpose of collecting the opinions of museum and gallery directors, curators, art critics and historians, artists, and foundation personnel on several related issues: the importance given (or not

given) to writing about, exhibiting or subsidizing artists variously characterized as "minority," "Third World," "of color," "subaltern," "marginalized," and so on. A related concern is the impact of transnational trade agreements on art exhibition (and subvention). To what degree is (will) art and other cultural production (be) affected by the restrictions on immigrants in supranational entities like the European Union or the countries participating in the North American Free Trade Agreement (NAFTA)? Or do (will) these entities have a favorable effect on the exhibition or subvention of the work of artists such as those referred to above?

Those surveyed were asked to provide information on such matters as whether their institution subsidized or exhibited Latin American and/or other third world artists and for how long; what criteria they used in writing about, subsidizing, and/or exhibiting these artists (e.g., a particular liking for the artist's work; the application of traditional criteria of excellence and connoisseurship; the innovative character of the work; the desire to include artists belonging to historically underrepresented groups; or the allure of a good art world reputation); whether the institution subscribes to some notion of multiculturalism; whether the respondent thinks there should be norms or laws to ensure inclusion and representativity; whether immigrant and foreign artists should be included in exhibitions of "American" art; and whether and for what reasons art should be included in trade agreements.

The following information was collected. All respondents subscribed to some form of multiculturalism, of which various definitions were given, including those based on race, gender, sexual orientation, ethnic, class, and geopolitical (i.e., third world) factors. Little consensus was observed in the means deemed appropriate to democratize the arts in keeping with a multicultural perspective. A majority (60 percent) rejected legal decrees as a means to include artists from underrepresented groups. Of the remaining 40 percent, only one respondent advocated the legislation of inclusion; most considered that institutional "norms" or "guidelines" should suffice. In other words, a form of affirmative action was thought to be desirable, but not a "quota" policy. Nevertheless, only 10 percent of the respondents thought that their institutions met a "distributional equity" commensurate with the proportion of "designated" groups in the general population.

Of great interest for an assessment of the place of aesthetic judgment today were the choices of criteria for exhibition, subsidy, and review. The vast majority (90 percent) of respondents opted for a mix of "traditional criteria of excellence for evaluating art works," "the desirability of including artists belonging to underrepresented groups," and the application of "social factors" in this regard. That is, they appealed to questions of "quality" as well as to those of "parity," pointing up a degree of uncertainty about what exactly makes an artwork a good one. Evidently, "content" (what is evoked discursively and politically) was deemed to be as important as, if not more important than the formal and material features of the work.

Perhaps the most interesting response concerning the exhibition of art in the transnational context of free trade was the desirability to open up the definition of "American" art to artists from the entire Western hemisphere. About 90 percent endorsed this option, although a majority of respondents (60 percent) also thought that foreign artists (no matter how [Latin] "American") should not be given preference over U.S. minority artists. These results confirmed the declarations of a Chicano art critic who, in a letter concerning the criteria for selection for the 1993 Whitney Biennial, objected to the museum's plans to broaden the definition of American art to include Latin American artists, fearing that the latter, most of whom come from a middle- and upper-middle-class background, would preempt U.S. minority artists: "There is a . . . danger in using non-American artists to challenge the notion of a homogeneous national culture. One does not have to cross borders to find artistic practices that— whether through their outright difference, or through their critical engagement of dominant aesthetics—upset, expand, subvert, and undo the category of 'American' art . . . At the very moment when the Whitney Museum should identify and proclaim racial and sexual minorities as part of a new American patrimony, the curatorial agenda is redirected to the international sphere, instead" (Chon Noriega, personal communication, 1993). This critic puts his finger on the use of multiculturalism against the very groups that the rhetoric says it seeks to empower. The other side of the coin is, of course, the stereotyping of the culture of Latin Americans and other third world subjects, who are sought out by curators to demonstrate that "American" culture can be "inclusive." By appealing to the "difference" of these widely varying groups, multiculturalism ironically ends up homogeniz~~~ ~~~~ ~~~~~~~~~~~~ ~~ ~~~~~culturalism has been looked on with muc~~ ~~~~~~~~~~~~~~~~~~~~~~~~ectuals, artists, and activists, to the point ~~~~~~~~~~~~~~~~~~~~~~~~~~ance to cultural imperialism. This is also ~~~~~~~~~~~~~~~~~~~~~~~~~nterprise of American studies to a hemisp~~~~~~~~~~~~~~~~~~~~~~~~

Though not necessarily rel~~~~~~~~~~~~~~~~~~~~~~~~onventional sense, the so-called new Ame~~~~~~~~~~~~~~~~~~~~~~~ the American Studies Association (Rad~~~~~~~~~~~~~~~~~~~~~~~~ in the trade in intellectual trends as they have moved to incorporate the "differences" that ensue from the other countries of the hemisphere via migrant cultures. The impetus to recognize the relational coconstitution of "America" (the United States) and other American countries certainly merits tracking the cultures that form within the United States and in transnational migratory transit to other American nations. However, there also has to be recognition of the specific force field that organizes how one conceives of these moving cultural formations in relation to the inertia/momentum of U.S. institutions, political movements, the media, and the academy. As Jane Desmond and Virginia Domínguez (1996) caution, the focus on difference by the new American studies is not sufficient to achieve self-understanding and knowledge of other societies because there isn't sufficient participation of foreign-residing scholars in establishing research agendas that are viable because they are fundable.

Worse still is the export of U.S.-designed agendas, especially cultural studies trends that deal with the Americas while corroborating U.S. experiences (Desmond and Domínguez 1996: 477). For example, the introduction to *Postnationalist American Studies* makes the claim that black studies, Chicano studies, women's studies, ethnic studies, and gay and lesbian studies decentered the nationalist framework (Curiel et al. 2000: 6). They did in fact burst the myth that there was a national consensus on values, but it is hard to see how these particularist nationalisms and other group formations were not overdetermined by the force field of U.S. society. Moreover, the dynamic manifests itself as a kind of momentum to include the rest of the world according to a vision that was generated in the United States. This observation is not meant to impugn the new American studies but only to point out its practitioners' own blindness in imagining that adoption of multiculturalism is somehow beyond the national frame. Indeed, how can the new American studies be postnational when so inordinately much of its epistemological framework does not easily incorporate or at least enter into dialogue, tension, and debate with other views from other societies, without at the same time imagining that they confirm American diversity or that they are somehow related to the way ethnoracial minorities are situated in the United States? Internationalizing American studies, as Desmond and Dominguez as well as "other American" scholars like the Brazilian Sônia Torres (2001) advocate, is, in my view, not enough.[14] There must also be a direct engagement with the way the U.S. university systems collude in the underdevelopment of university systems elsewhere (Yúdice, 2003b).

Returning to the expansion of "American" art by including Latin Americans, the problem is that the criteria of evaluation, even if they "favor" inclusion of

Latin Americans in their status as "subalterns" or "excluded," are generated in the United States, in a context that is different from their own. For all the talk of globalization and translocality, there still are different contexts that have not simply become suburbs of the United States. Well-meaning foundations favor the inclusion of Latin American artists in exhibitions on the basis of notions of identity that reflect the U.S. situation more than that of the foreign or immigrant artists. The globalization of border pluralism is thus a version of a "We are the world" complex. This global pretension was quite pervasive in "alternative" art venues in the 1980s and early 1990s. For example, the information brochure for *The Decade Show: Frameworks of Identity in the 8os* (1990), explains that the show was a "proclamation that 'history' is not objective and that the American experience is much more heterogeneous than generally asserted." Significantly, the heterogeneity of the "American experience" extended to the whole world and to a multiple historicity: "The work included in this exhibition may be seen as material evidence of alternate viewpoints. Many artists of color, for example, in their philosophical, aesthetic, and spiritual linkages to the precolonial societies of Africa, Asia, and America, legitimize diversity, resist Eurocentric domination, and create a foundation from which to analyze and explain contemporary social phenomena. Feminist, gay and lesbian artists similarly affirm that there are other ways of seeing, ways equal to existing cultural dictates."

Latin American and other "foreign" artists have been defined in similar ways, that is, against the mainstream of "existing cultural dictates." There is a double bind here that makes the "peripheral" artist feel damned whether he or she is included (because the organizers "second-guess" how his or her art articulates "cultural identity") or excluded (because the organizers feel that an art that departs from the expected "difference" is merely derivative). This dilemma is evident in the catalogue essay to *Het Klimaat* (The Climate), an exhibition held in Maastricht in 1991 with the express attempt to exhibit art dealing with cultural identity without, however, falling into the exoticizing pitfalls of the much criticized *Magiciens de la terre* (Paris, 1989). *Het Klimaat* was organized with multiculturalism (a "term which is now commonplace throughout all the political corridors of Europe") as its guiding concept, one seen as a "corrective mechanism" to the imbalances unleashed in the new Europe (*Cultural Identity* 1992: 4–5). According to curator Ine Gevers:

> It may be an intellectual challenge to see notions such as identity and cultural identity as relative, but this comes from the privileged position of Western thinking.

Such a line of argument may reduce identity to a fiction, but for a non-Western individual, standing outside this narrative, it is an absolute necessity. His or her identity, seen in relation to Western culture, its monopoly position and its conventional, linear historiography, has never had any significant right to exist. For the non-Western artist or intellectual it is essential not only to be able to distinguish oneself but above all to create or recreate the historical and ideological conditions which at least provide the possibility to do so. (*Cultural Identity*: 12)

Ironically, some of the "foreign," presumably "non-Western" artists magnanimously included in *Het Klimaat* repudiated the very terms and conditions of their inclusion. Sebastián López, for example, brought attention to the use of terms, such as *Gastarbeiders* (guest workers), *etnische Minderheden* (ethnic minorities), *Migranten* (migrants), and *Allochtonen* (nonnative or nonautochthonous) as a means to segregate those who do not originate from within Western Europe. This is particularly the case with the last term, which arose in the 1980s when there was a "project to repatriate foreigners — mostly Moroccans and Turks who together made up a large minority community in the Netherlands" (S. López 1992: 21). Allochtonen "has become a synonym for the non-European geographically, for the non-white racially, and for those outside the mainstream culturally" (22). Like the term "people of color" prevalent in the United States, Allochtonen is applied even to Dutch citizens who happen to be the children, born in the Netherlands, of foreign parents. It is a term used officially but also in matters relating to art and culture, including the designation of the "foreign" artists in *Het Klimaat*, much to their chagrin. Noting that the work of Dutch artists has never been labeled *Autochtonen kunst*, López points to the asymmetries that the Allochtonen are forced to accept if they wish to exhibit their art. They are asymmetries not unlike those that characterize the "parallel market" or "alternative" system of distribution of value for minority artists that I described above:

Many artists often refused to ask ministries and municipalities for special subsidies, because that would put them in a complicated political position regarding the conditions for showing work. They found themselves trapped in a patronising system which, while giving them a chance to work with subsidies, at the same time closed the door that would enable them fully to enter and play a role within the Dutch cultural climate. Those who accepted their ethnicity and official definition could only show in alternative art circuits and marginal exhibition spaces. (23–24)

Refunding Art in an Age of Free Trade Agreements

In July 1993, three artists staged an art event that brought together all the contradictions mentioned by López plus the most important issue of the period, free trade. In fact, the very materials of the art event were the forms and media through which it questioned the categories that separate the Allochtonen from the Autochtonen in the United States. In that very month, Pete Wilson, governor of California, announced a program that eventually evolved into Proposition 187. Among its points were the denial of citizenship to U.S.-born children of unlawful residents as well as termination of their health and education benefits (Curtis 1993: F11). Politicians and a broad range of interest groups had become embroiled in a national debate on NAFTA, which highlighted, among other issues, the supposed drain on jobs and services by "illegal immigrants." Perhaps the most ingenious way of upping the ante of the debate and forcing the rights of immigrants onto the agenda was the art event conceived and carried out by the three Southern California artists: David Avalos, Louis Hock, and Elizabeth Sisco. On July 23, 1993, and for several months afterward, they distributed $10 bills along the San Diego–Tijuana border to "undocumented workers." The event, titled *Arte-Reembolso/Art Rebate*, was commissioned for $5,000 by the Centro Cultural de la Raza and the Museum of Contemporary Art in San Diego as part of *La Frontera/The Border*, the first major binational art exhibition/installation. The three artists aimed to address simultaneously several issues of civic importance: the treatment of undocumented Mexican immigrants in the United States; the use of civic space itself—and the circulation of citizenship benefits such as sharing of public art funding—as an artistic material; and a challenge to the funding criteria of the NEA, $1,250 of whose monies the museum had apparently included in the project's budget and which were replaced in an effort to attenuate the storm that brewed among infuriated sectors of the public and Congress. The event was announced by a press release with passages extracted from think tank studies, national magazine articles, and studies by monitor organizations.

The passages on undocumented workers brought home the point that they are also "undocumented taxpayers." For example, "immigrants contribute more to public revenues than they consume in public services" (Vernez 1993); "Approximately 11 million immigrants are working, earning $240 billion a year, and paying more than $90 billion in taxes . . . outweighing by far the $5 billion that immigrants receive in welfare" (*Business Week* July 13, 1992); and "Most of the [existing] studies suggest that immigration has not had a significant impact on the employment of native workers" ("Impact of Undocumented Persons" 1992; all cited in *Arte-Reembolso/Art Rebate* 1993).

The press release also brought attention to the event as a work of conceptual art, one that made quite visible the normally abstract meanderings of the circulation of money. What the artists bring into view by handing out "rebates" is that undocumented workers do not as a rule get back anything for the taxes they have paid. The art event completes the cycle because the recipients reintroduce the bills into the economy, thus producing a ripple effect throughout the space of the region, the nation, and, indeed, the world. The press release states: " 'Arte-Reembolso/Art Rebate' is public art and not art in public. This art operates at the intersection of public space (the streets and the sidewalks), informational space (radio, television and print media) and the civic space between the public and government officials. It activates a discourse that reveals the shape of contemporary social thinking about immigrant labor. Conceptually, this art traces the network describing our economic community as it follows the circulation of the rebated $10 bills from the hands of the undocumented to the documented."

Arte-Reembolso/Art Rebate was so successful that its concept circulated widely through the media, infuriating politicans in California and Washington over the idea that arts funding would be used to "give away" what belongs to citizens. Of course, what such lawmakers overlooked was the degree to which the very definition of citizenship, and its relation to work and workers' rights, was what the artists intended to thematize and put up for discussion. Also intended was the witting or unwitting mise-en-scène of these officials as actors in the very midst of the art event. In effect, they became performers. As Avalos remarks, "The politicians are acting like performance artists while we're trying to be political" (qtd. in Pincus 1993a: E8).

As actors, these officials reacted to the "buttons" the artists pushed. The controversy over NEA funding was used to bring a new issue into public circulation. In that sense, *Arte-Reembolso/Art Rebate* entered the ongoing "culture wars." Immigration, as conservative columnist George F. Will wrote at the time of this art event, is not only economic but also cultural:

> The cultural argument about immigration begins with this fact: immigration at the end of this century occurs in a social context different in two crucial ways from the context at the beginning of the century. Today immigrants are received into a welfare culture that encourages an entitlement mentality. That mentality

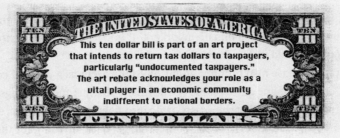

THE UNITED STATES OF AMERICA

This ten dollar bill is part of an art project that intends to return tax dollars to taxpayers, particularly "undocumented taxpayers." The art rebate acknowledges your role as a vital player in an economic community indifferent to national borders.

TEN DOLLARS

- The economic growth of California and the Southwestern U. S. could never have happened without the labor of undocumented workers.

- Historically, the U.S. government, business and society have been willing to look the other way as long as they are enjoying the profits afforded by undocumented labor.

REEMBOLSO ART Rebate

- Today, in a wrecked economy, the so-called "illegal alien" is once again blamed for the social problems of the region and portrayed as a drain on the economy. In fact, there is no credible statistical evidence that undocumented workers take more in social services than they give in combined local, state and federal taxes.

- Not only are the crucial economic contributions of the undocumented overlooked or denied, these workers pay federal income tax, social security, state income tax, DMV fees, sales tax and more.

- Undocumented workers are undocumented taxpayers.

- You pay taxes when you eat a taco at 'berto's, shop for socks at K-Mart, buy toilet paper, hand soap or razor blades at Lucky or fill up your tank at Thrifty Gas.

- Regardless of your immigration status, if you shop you pay taxes. Period.

"Art Rebate" is a project by Elizabeth Sisco, Louis Hock and David Avalos. It is part of the "La Frontera/The Border" exhibition co-sponsored by the Centro Cultural de la Raza and the Museum of Contemporary Art, San Diego, and made possible, in part, through the generous support of the National Endowment for the Arts, a federal agency, The Rockefeller Foundation, the City of San Diego Commission for Arts and Culture, and the California Arts Council.

Undocumented Workers Taxpayers

8. "Art Rebate" English flyer. Provided by Louis Hock.

Este billete de diez dólares forma parte de un proyecto de arte que pretende devolver dólares de los impuestos a los contribuyentes, particularmente a los "contribuyentes indocumentados". Este arte-reembolso reconoce que estás integrado a una comunidad económica a la que le son indiferentes las fronteras nacionales.

- El crecimiento económico de California y el suroeste de Estados Unidos jamás podría haberse dado sin la mano de obra de los trabajadores indocumentados.

- Históricamente, el gobierno, los empresarios, y la sociedad de Estados Unidos han estado dispuestos a hacerse de la vista gorda mientras disfrutan de las ganancias que les proporciona la mano de obra indocumentada.

- Las importantísimas contribuciones económicas de los indocumentados no sólo pasan desapercibidas, o se dice que no existen, sino que además estos trabajadores también pagan impuestos federales, seguro social, impuestos estatales, cuotas del DMV, impuestos sobre ventas, y más.

- Los trabajadores indocumentados son contribuyentes indocumentados.

- Tú pagas impuestos cuando comes en la taquería de 'berto, cuando compras calcetines en K-Mart, cuando compras papel del baño, jabón o navajas de rasurar en Lucky, o cuando llenas el tanque en Thrifty Gas.

- No importa tu estado migratorio: si haces compras, pagas impuestos y eres contribuyente. Punto.

REEMBOLSO ART Rebate

"Arte–Reembolso" es un proyecto por Elizabeth Sisco, Louis Hock y David Avalos. Forma parte de la exhibición "La Frontera/The Border", partrocinada por el Centro Cultural de la Raza y el Museo de Arte Contemporáneo de San Diego, y apoyada en parte por el Partrimonio Nacional para las Artes (National Endowment for the Arts), una agencia federal, y una donación de la Fundación Rockefeller.

Trabajadores
Contribuyentes Indocumentados

9. "Art Rebate" Spanish flyer. Provided by Louis Hock.

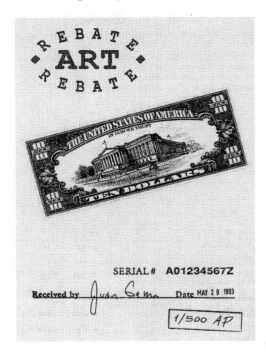

SERIAL # A01234567Z

Received by *Juan Sima* Date MAY 2 0 1993

1/500 *AP*

10. "Art Rebate" receipt.
Provided by Louis Hock.

weakens the mainspring of individual striving for upward mobility. A generous welfare state such as the United States, and California especially, can be a "magnet" for migrants [such that] the argument for immigration as a source of social invigoration fails.

The second difference . . . that makes problematic the tradition of liberality regarding immigration, is the weakening of the ideal of assimilation [into American culture]. (1993: A15)

Will's position is echoed in Peter Brimelow's (1995) *Alien Nation*, evoking the specter of a fragmented land in which the Allochtonen will transform cities like Atlanta, Miami, and San Antonio into "communities as different from one another as any in the civilized world." Brimelow does not only not consider the children of the "new" immigrants to be "real" Americans, but he tends to misidentify immigrants as the major drain on welfare services. Contrary to his claims, an Urban Institute study shows that immigrants create more jobs than they fill. In 1989 total immigration income was $285 billion, about 8 percent of all reported income (immigrants made up 7.9 percent of the population). Much of this money was spent on U.S. goods and services. Undocumented workers also relied less on public assistance than documented ones — 6.2 percent compared to 6.6 percent—and much less than natives, whose share is 87.2 percent (Fix and Passel 1994). By sounding the "entitlement mentality" of immigrants, Brimelow doubly alienated them.

But such a characterization of "others" is precisely what needs to be re-considered, from all political and cultural perspectives. The multicultural approaches that I have reviewed here, whether those emanating from "progressive" sectors or those legitimizing the corporate world, ultimately reproduce a sense of the world that is *alienating*. Art events have capitalized on this alienation, both in Gómez-Peña's shamanistic claims to heal the wounds and in insITE94's celebration of border trade. To my mind, *Arte-Reembolso/Art Rebate* is the rare art event that has made the connections among free trade, immigration policy, and national culture with a different relation to capital: its attempts to de-alienate, to return what is theirs to the workers. To the extent that *Arte-Reembolso/Art Rebate* permeated public space, it served to counter the billions of dollars spent on the promotion of free trade and to subject to full public scrutiny its misleading implications for U.S. citizens, immigrants, and cultural life. If anything, this event made it evident that any trade agreement, if it is to be democratic, must address the question of citizenship rights for immigrants in an era of massive migrations.

Cultural Binationalism and Integration

"We require bi-national, bi-cultural programs to influence how we think about each other." This statement, made by Mexican Consul General Luis Herrera-Lasso (qtd. in Sinkin 1999), seems to occupy the same discursive ambience as Gómez-Peña's cross-border, bridge-building pronouncements. It also refers to the context in which insITE, one of the most ambitious and compelling public art events, was initiated and developed over the past nine years. All of these attempts to imagine culture in the same terms as free trade necessarily turn on the contradiction between the local and the cosmopolitan, as we shall see in chapter 9.

Aside from exhibitions and other binational and multinational events like insITE, there are specific regional integration projects directly related to free trade. Among them, I consider several competing projects to construct a Latin American cultural space. Such a plurality is consistent with the various interests at work there, including the different levels of development in the nineteen countries of the region and the kinds of cultural programs deemed appropriate for these different realities. That there are different and differently positioned contexts does not mean that they have nothing in common or that they cannot construct a supranational cultural space. To this end, it is crucial that integration projects do not simply respond to the will of the larger countries because they have more representatives on a supranational council or because they contribute more resources. Negotiating equity is difficult, as exemplified by Mexican representatives to the binational U.S.-Mexico Fund for Culture, who objected to expanding the program to other countries because that would mean fewer resources for Mexicans. To date, that Fund has symbolized for Mexicans a very special relationship with the United States. In matters of culture, this puts Mexico on a par with the major trendsetter on the international scene. A hemispheric or Latin American emphasis might seem like a step backward from this vantage point. Nevertheless, there are exigencies (such as the search for new partners in the wake of political and economic changes) that may lead a country with major resources for cultural support like Mexico to advocate a supranational fund (Yúdice 1999d).

What, then, are the motivations for the construction of such a space? First, the most obvious reason for constructing a continental cultural space is to moderate or even invert the inordinate power of U.S. audiovisual products to monopolize programming on Latin American networks, cable, and satellite systems. If Latin American countries want to hold on to the culture industries that they developed since the 1930s, they need to develop policies that can respond to the integration of the Americas that is already taking place on terms set by the United States and transnational corporations. The irony, as Octavio Getino (2001) points out, is that integration is already being carried out *on* Latin American countries.

For small countries, it may not make too much of a difference if Brazilian or Mexican telenovelas instead of U.S. sit-coms and soaps dominate their screens. As cultural producer and administrator Sylvie Durán explains, in Central America "our TV is basically a subsidiary of Mexican and U.S. industries, especially the cheapest canned entertainment available in discounted markets" (2001: 5). Against the backdrop of U.S. or Mexican or Brazilian domination, local writers and TV producers and directors do not get much of a chance to showcase work that relates more closely to the local culture. Something similar might be said about the power of U.S. art institutions to showcase "American" artists throughout Latin America, or to pull from their contexts Latin American artists to represent a packaged-in-the-U.S. multicultural internationalism. A second, likely project, which would ameliorate the problems just raised by a large-country-dominant cultural space, would attempt to create spaces for local cultures, either through programming on public access venues subsidized by a supranational fund or through incentives provided by a network of countries for development of such programming in collaboration with local producers and directors, with input from viewing communities. Such a project would provide greater room for local cultures outside the purview of national frameworks and even enable partnerships among localities in different countries, following the model of networks of first peoples and in collaboration with NGOs and foundations, which have contributed to the maintenance and endurance of these networks. Such networks, often created "informally," are more likely to generate creative responses and more fluid organizational arrangements, "from the family, to the friends who offer collateral for loans and the in-kind exchanges among the cultural workers of the professional and particularly the grassroots sectors, where they are quite common" (4). A third project might support the production and dissemination of materials and practices in languages other than Spanish and Portuguese. To this end, it would also have to support supranational ethnic networks, like those of Maya or Quechua or Guaraní speakers.

The point I am obviously making is that there are many Latin Americas and various projects for integration that might be developed separately or in combination. There is even a project for Latin American cultural integration being promoted by the entertainment conglomerates headquartered in Miami. One might think that this is exclusively an anti–Latin American project (in the sense of having all control of decision making and profit taking in the United States), which to some degree it is. However, the viability of made-in-Miami entertainment increasingly recognizes the value of producing locally (see chapter 7). MTV Latin America, for example, is in the process of relocating all production of "content" and advertising, which is currently made in Miami and three annexes in Argentina, Brazil, and Mexico, to local producers and directors in all nineteen countries (Antoinette Zel, interview, March 14, 2000). The point is that transnationals recognize that it may enhance profitability to geographically diversify production, decision making, and so on to better serve local markets.

One could refer to other projects such as the expansion of regional cultural spaces or the creation of an Ibero-American space that would include Spain and Portugal (Fuentes 1991). Indeed, increasing Spanish dominance in telecommunications and displacement of the United States as the largest foreign direct investor in many Latin American countries has led to several initiatives to create an Ibero-American cultural space. The invention of the Universal Forum of

Cultures, "a new type of world event, of spirit and scale similar to the Olympic Games and International Expositions, but based on the cultures of the world," by the Catalonians with the backing of UNESCO, to give protagonism both to culture in global politics and economy and also to their own subnation within the European Union, has already led to several organizational initiatives in Latin America (Universal Forum of Cultures 2002).

Cultural integration, absent from NAFTA and relatively weak within the European Union, is poised to become a major engine of activity and capital accumulation. Founded on the principles of human rights and cultural diversity, as overseen by UNESCO, the Common Market of the South (MERCOSUL),[15] Arte Sem Fronteiras (explained below), and the Universal Forum of Cultures stand as effective counterinitiatives to U.S.-led trade in cultural production and services. The headway made in these initiatives means that Latin American countries may not be locked into exclusive arrangements with the United States, which is taking the initiative to create a Free Trade Area of the Americas. As G. W. Bush (2000) observed, "If the United States cannot offer new trade with the nations of Latin America, they will find it elsewhere — as they are doing already in new agreements with the European Union."

Given this heterogeneity and competition of interests, is it possible or even desirable to create a Latin American cultural space? Conversations on this topic over the past five years suggest that it is both possible and desirable, so long as certain pitfalls of national policies are avoided: monopoly by hegemonic centers (i.e, Brazil, Mexico, and Argentina, or Spain in the Ibero-American case), minoritization of certain groups and their subordinated incorporation on that basis, and surrender to market imperatives, which should not be understood as synonymous with exclusion of the culture industries, as Getino (1997, 2000, 2001) never tires of pointing out. It should be said that there is still great hesitancy about inviting the culture industries to the cultural policy table. However, they do have the resources that are lacking in the absence of significant government subsidy, and it is also recognized that they have a better track record attracting "popular audiences," more profitable than the tiny audiences for the arts or folk culture. It should be remembered that in many Latin American societies, where functional and even complete illiteracy can still reach 30 percent or more of the population, the authority of public culture passed almost immediately from the oral to the audiovisual "without crossing the intermediary stage of the written word" (Coelho 1999: 19).

Amazing as it may seem, attention to audience is something new to Latin American cultural policy, which has focused almost exclusively on production, with scant attention given to distribution. Even then, however, the relatively laissez-faire attitude toward the traditional and the new media in Latin America is quite problematic. This means that foreign product, especially from the United States, has the largest market share. Governments have not yet taken an active interest in developing these media. Indeed, governments don't even have the requisite data to assess how the media contribute to the economy, much less, it goes without saying, to understand how the media shape social and political life. According to Getino, who has done the most encompassing research on Latin American cinema and television, their current crisis has less to do with the production of these media than with their traditional modes of circulation and reception, which have largely been neglected by state policy. Without a clear policy framework for the introduction and dissemination of the new audiovisual technologies, they have been left to languish in a state of dependency, relinquishing a sense of public responsibility to market criteria most often designed by transnational enterprises that have succeeded over national television networks in producing a fit between the increasing fragmentation of Latin American urban societies and the proliferation of channels on cable and satellite. Once accused of homogenizing their publics, transnational media conglomerates exacerbate fragmentation by producing multiple and partial subjectivities in each viewer, that is, producing the niches within the subject, thus promoting the appearance of "consumer 'tribes' " whose demands, far from leading to democratization, reproduce demands for the "same types of audiovisual products across territorial borders" (Getino 1998: 225).

Regional and local broadcasting, on the other hand, have succeeded in producing programs (e.g., "live" shows and serials made from a local point of view) that cannot be replaced by those of the transnational conglomerates. But these unsubstitutable programs grounded in local realities (yet with the potential of continental and sometimes even transcontinental export) are at best complementary. To enhance their chances of survival, Getino advocates investment in and development of knowledge of the most advanced technologies and of local creativity, reinforced by a humanistic and democratic ethos (1998: 226–228, 257–263). These possibilities can be furthered by transnational Latin American training centers, as well as Latin American networks for the production and dissemination of national, regional, and local cultures. If Europe has failed in this regard, perhaps a Latin American audiovisual space largely constructed on the basis of two related languages, as well as democratically incorporated minority languages, has a better chance.

In the past decade. the two major reasons for interest in creating a supranational cultural space have to do with the simultaneous reduction in national cultural budgets and the greater demands for decentralization of national cultural policies. The first ensued from the subjection of Latin American countries to the structural adjustment programs of the IMF and World Bank, applied during the so-called lost decade of the 1980s, when budget deficits skyrocketed. By the 1990s, most countries had accepted neoliberal policies that required reconceptualizing and finding nongovernment sources for financing the public sector. In contrast to the privatization of public enterprises, such as utilities, which were sold off to private companies, usually based in Europe or North America, governments sought to relocate cultural support in public-private partnerships. This is the case especially in Mexico and Brazil, where a conjuncture of economic and political circumstances required change in the state's approach to national identity.

In the wake of Mexico's economic crisis during Miguel de la Madrid's *sexenio* or six-year presidential term, which saw a decrease in funding for education (and less so for culture, a fact that is revealing about the importance of cultural subvention as a form of legitimation for the state), President Salinas sought to bolster cultural support on new terms. Rafael Tovar y de Teresa was named president of the National Council for the Arts and Culture (CONACULTA), established in 1989 as part of Salinas's new cultural program to reconcile Mexicans with a new modernization project. In his account of the project, Tovar y de Teresa (1994) suggests that modernization entails trade deregulation, political liberalization, and institutional decentralization, which have social and cultural effects that must be offset. Tovar tells the story of "the close connection that a modernization project recognizes in and maintains with culture" (20).

Culture here is the terrain of negotiation around the social and political changes wrought by the acceleration of capitalist development. Faced with the threat of homogenization and the erosion of sovereignty, Tovar advocates a "return to roots," for culture is a "point of reference, unique and unsubstitutable, for the assumption of changes in such a way that our national identity is not put at risk" (1994: 12–13). To this end, he invokes the concept of *patrimonio* (heritage), whose preservation and dissemination is the first of the six functions of CONACULTA. At the same time, however, the point of the new cultural program is that the state must open the notion of heritage to the ethnic and social diversity that was overlooked by the centralized corporatist programs of the past.

Democratic participation was to be enhanced in two ways: first, by the decentralization of cultural institutions; second, by encouraging the private sector to invest in culture through tax incentives (Tovar 1994: 103). The National Fund for Culture and the Arts (FONCA) was established in 1989 to serve as the pivotal institution among government, the private sector, and the cultural community (59–60). The ratio of state to private investment in culture through FONCA went from US\$125,000 to \$0 in 1989 to US\$7.2 million to US\$16.5 million in 1993.

In Brazil, two days after taking office in 1990, President Collor de Mello announced a number of decrees that effectively extinguished all government-generated support for the arts. The changes included the abolishment of the Lei Sarney, a law initiated in 1985 that offered tax incentives for industries that supported cultural production, the reorganization of the Ministry of Culture into a secretariat of the Ministry of Education, and the termination of the National Arts Foundation (Funarte), the Scenic Arts Foundation (Fundacen), the Brazilian Film Foundation, and the National Film Distributing Company, which were reincarnated on a smaller scale in the minimally funded National Institute of Cultural Activities (Catani 1994: 98). Under Collor, the Lei Sarney was redefined in the Lei Rouanet, written by a renowned intellectual, Sergio Paulo Rouanet, author of, among other things, books that offer a Foucauldian-inspired critique of a Habermasian public sphere.

After Collor's impeachment and the interim presidency of Itamar Franco, Fernando Henrique Cardozo, elected in 1995, sought to attenuate strong challenges from the left and, like Salinas in Mexico, used cultural policy, in particular the Lei Rouanet, both for shifting cultural initiatives to a more entrepreneurial private-oriented program and for decentralizing support. "Culture is good business" was the Brazilian Ministry of Culture's slogan when it reintroduced in 1998 a refurbished Lei Rouanet under Minister of Culture Francisco Weffort. As part of its efforts to shift support in a more private direction, the Ministry of Culture generated numerous statistics to prove that cultural investment spurred export earnings, created jobs, and fostered national integration. At the same time, however, the new incentive laws put into place a system whereby support for cultural projects is largely up to corporate sponsors, who decide, usually on the basis of the projects' marketing value, which ones they will underwrite. The Ministry of Culture is left the limited task of deciding on projects' eligibility for support under the incentive laws. The result has been the emergence of a new kind of cultural entrepreneur and new kinds of not-for-profit corporations that broker cultural projects (Ottmann forthcoming). Most of the projects that have been funded have had to do with *cultural mar-*

keting, which is the title, in English, of a special trade journal that was born simultaneously with the Lei Rouanet.

According to Ministry of Culture documents, the objective of this shift has less to do with fiscal thrift than with a philosophy of giving greater responsibility to civil society, largely under the guardianship of the private sector. Indeed, the United States' well-developed public-private system of cultural support has served as a model for the restructuring of the Brazilian (and the Mexican) system. John Wineland refers to various meetings at which semiprivate, parastate corporations like Arte-Empresa: Parceria Multiplicadora, sponsored by the Serviço Social do Comércio and the Serviço de Apoio ás Micro e Pequenas Empresas, which have become powerful middlemen in São Paulo's cultural funding processes, have sponsored meetings with U.S. executives to discuss corporate philanthropy. At one such meeting "were representatives from the automotive, tobacco, information, electronics, cosmetics, audiovisual, petroleum, chemicals and food and beverage industries, as well as a number of marketing executives. Also present was AT&T vice-president and director of the Business Committee of the Arts, Timothy McClimon, who represented the 'American example' of how to properly include the arts in a corporate marketing philosophy" (Pompeu 1994, qtd. in Wineland 1999).

This public good heralded by the new corporate philanthropy is most often rhetorical, for these societies, which have never fostered a thriving public culture, are interested either in the cultural capital generated by sponsorship of the traditional arts or, increasingly, in the emergence of culture as a resource for the generation of profit. This is the case with most cultural heritage and tourism projects, many of which are financed by the Inter-American Development Bank and the World Bank. The impact on art, dance, film, and popular culture programs, not to mention critical cultural practices, has been quite marked; on the other hand, banks and some large corporations have been able to finance their own cultural foundations, which produce cultural marketing exclusively for the parent corporation, and deduct most if not all of the amounts invested from their taxes. Despite claims to decentralization, the successful projects tend to be concentrated in the wealthiest states, especially São Paulo, Rio de Janeiro, Minas Gerais, and Rio Grande do Sul, to which, with the exception of certain tourist-attracting states in the Northeast like Bahia, much of the Ministry of Culture's resources went traditionally.

The Mexican reformers, on the other hand, had to contend with a more stubbornly rooted symbolic system of populism and social reform, leading to a centrally coordinated aesthetic strategy aimed at weakening revolutionary symbolism. Cardozo's regime, on the other hand, couched the Ministry of Culture's program in a pragmatic free market approach that was embedded in the larger claims of Brazil's "transition to democracy." In neither case is there room for critical art and culture. The above-mentioned partnership schemes are wedded to new cultural programs whereby the state is enjoined to pry open the notion of patrimony to the ethnic and social diversity that was overlooked by the centralized corporatist programs of the past. This legitimizes the changes in forms of cultural support, largely preempting critiques from the more elitist arts, including tendencies that espouse social critique. There is sometimes a political standoff over the role of culture on the left political spectrum between leftist intellectuals and artists on the one hand, and popular or populist politicians and local leaders on the other. It is beyond the scope of this chapter to elaborate on this further, but it is worth noting that intellectuals and artists since the 1960s have customarily relied on the assumption of a critical power in cultural work as a kind of legitimizer of their interventions, whereas populists have tended to disqualify even critical culture by taking popular tastes as their compass. The creation of a Latin American cultural space might contribute to taking attention away from this defeatist dichotomy. Criticality and an interest in the needs and struggles of popular classes need not operate according to such a national(ist) framework (see chapter 2, n.11).

We see here the opening up of cultural policy not only to national corporations but also to international multilateral financial institutions, transnational corporations, and tourism concerns, which almost by definition are international, and relatedly to some NGOs who lobby on behalf of culture and development projects. The challenge is to internationalize rearticulated notions of culture and cultural policy practices that do not reduce culture to economic or political resources while recognizing that corporations and NGOs can help in furthering the interests of those who have been heralded (and exploited) as the epitome of the popular. One of the major difficulties in creating a continental cultural space has to do with the enthusiastic turn to or the resigned acceptance of the notion of culture as a resource, the only surviving definition in contemporary practice. I argued in chapter 1 that when culture is touted as a resource, it departs from the Gramscian premise that culture is a terrain of struggle and shifts strategy to processes of management. Compatible with neoliberal reconversions of civil society, culture as resource is seen as a way of providing social welfare and quality of life in the context of diminishing public resources and the withdrawal of the state from the guarantees of the good life. What we have commonly thought of as the often contentious new social movements have made common cause with international foundations and many government agencies in creating a "collaborative" civil society (S. Alvarez, forthcoming; chapter 3). This tendency is global and local at the same time and indeed marks a new development in conceptualizing the scope of culture, politics, and agency.

There are also challenges to and opportunities for the creation of a Latin American cultural space in the cultural initiatives that complement regional trade agreements: NAFTA as it relates to the United States, Canada, and Mexico, and MERCOSUL as it relates to Brazil, Argentina, Uruguay, Paraguay, Chile, and Bolivia. These trading blocs are regional responses to global economic competition and they entail the subordination of satellite economies to those of the core country: the United States in NAFTA and Brazil in MERCOSUL. The danger to regional or supranational cultural networks is that the interests of the core country will prevail. As we will see, this does not have to be the case. Moreover, the cultural complements to these trading blocs bring into greater relief both the desire to decentralize cultural support and to project greater symbolic inclusion of some groups that historically have been excluded. We're dealing here again with a sword that cuts both ways, which is evident in the important differences between the cultural expressions accompanying NAFTA and MERCOSUL. Some binational projects, like the U.S.-Mexico Fund for Culture and inSITE, have a great capacity for inclusion of marginalized sectors of the population, in large part because these venues are not directly connected to NAFTA, although they were instigated by the premise that if there could be collaboration in business, why not also in culture.

The U.S.-Mexico Fund for Culture, a partnership of FONCA (a public-private national cultural fund), Bancomer (Mexico's second-largest bank), and the Rockefeller Foundation, has followed the model of the NEA in establishing expert panels for the distribution of resources for artistic, scholarly, and community cultural projects in Mexico and the United States (Fideicomiso 1997). Although not fully autonomous of government and business (some trustees are government or corporate officials), the selection panels and overall process have been remarkably independent. It is in this forum that some of the initiative for a continental culture has been discussed (Yúdice 1999d). Similarly, inSITE has commissioned curators and artists from throughout the Americas, not only to design site-specific exhibitions and public interactions, but also to hold workshops and discussions on the role of art and culture in dealing with contemporary problems, including symbolic rearticulations of the Americas. An important feature of both these initiatives is that, though they do promote a binational and even a hemispheric cultural space, they are open to interventions from other regions, particularly Western Europe.

MERCOSUL, in contrast to NAFTA, has an official cultural complement, evident in the many organizations, especially professional ones, that have been meeting over the past ten years to discuss social, educational, business, and cultural issues on a regional basis. At the first meeting of the ministers and secretaries of culture of the member nations, a MERCOSUL da Cultura, or integrated cultural zone of the countries of MERCOSUL, was announced, emphasizing the promotion of Spanish/Portuguese bilingualism in education and other spheres of life, the free circulation of cultural goods and services, and a "cultural cable system for MERCOSUL" largely dedicated to educational and other public programs to make the different countries known to each other ("El mercosur de la cultura" 1995, online posting). There are, nevertheless, troubling aspects to the cultural integration envisioned at this meeting. In the first place, the basic reason for the creation of a cultural MERCOSUL was the melding of economics and culture, as then Argentine Minister of Culture Pacho O'Donnell said. Moreover, trade agreements not only redraw national geographies in ways that exclude certain parts of the member countries (the Brazilian Amazon and Northeast and the Argentine South share little of the dynamism introduced by the agreement), they also foster the creation of a new imagined community that has new constitutive exclusions. Taking the perspective of the new labor migrations in the region, some critics have convincingly argued that the creation of new borders is a retrograde step, sloughing off a southern region from the rest of the South American continent (Grimson 1998).

As in the United States, economic integration has not bettered the conditions for migrant workers, who are minoritized much like Mexican workers in the United States or extracommunitarians in the new Europe. This is the case of Bolivian migrants who seek work in Argentina and whose presence, coincident with the waning of class-based politics, has led Argentines to speak publicly of ethnic and racial difference for the first time since the consolidation of an immigrant national identity in the early twentieth century (Grimson 1999: 177–189). As in other Latin American countries, nineteenth-century Argentina was under the spell of social Darwinist theories of race and for that very reason sought European immigration as a means to progress. While class politics was the salient mode of incorporation of European immigrant workers and their children, there was also prejudice toward the *cabecitas negras* or dark-haired, largely indigenous and mestizo migrants from the northern provinces. The attitudes toward the cabecitas negras can now be seen as racialized, yet neither race nor ethnicity emerged in Argentina as a category for social analysis at the time. Now the cabecitas negras from Bolivia and other adjoining countries have an emerging ethnic or racial relationship to the normative whiteness of Argentineness. Cultural integration, if taken in a wider sense than the usual showcasing of the arts, as in the MERCOSUL Biennial examined below, would provide a forum for discussion of transborder minoritization and discrimination. As laid out by García Canclini and the architects of Arte Sem Fronteira's integration project, a Latin American cultural space has specific policies for the democratic inclusion of all constituencies.

But most of MERCOSUL's cultural efforts have thus far been concentrated on the arts and communications from a business perspective, leaving aside other forms of cultural expression. Indeed, despite the salience of the MERCOSUL Biennial's focus on education, the project is conceived as "taking culture to the people." As we will see in the chapter on inSITE, the attention paid to "community culture" in the United States does not necessarily solve the problem of outreach but may instead institutionalize cultural difference and transform it into an even more instrumentalized resource. In any case, the reason the business elites from the city of Porto Alegre, capital of the southernmost Brazilian state, sponsored this mega art event including over nine hundred works by three hundred artists and costing $6 million, is that the arts are an excellent form of PR and, in this case, largely at public expense, as the Fundação Bienal de Artes Visuais do Mercosul was able to take advantage of enormous fiscal incentives amounting to over $3.5 million plus an extra $1.25 million in federal funds (Luiz Carlos Barbosa 1998). Justo Werlang, local businessman, art collector, and president of the foundation that organized the Biennial, acknowledged that the MERCOSUL trade agreement was a strategy for the Southern Cone's competitiveness in global processes that are otherwise led by the United States. But economic competition, according to Werlang, is not enough; the economic has to be facilitated by the intermediation of culture. There has to be cultural integration, meaning mutual knowledge and respect (Welang 1997). In other words, the very idea that MERCOSUL is oppositional within (not to) the struggle for hegemony in the global economy—for example, in opposition to the Free Trade Area of the Americas, disseminated hemispherically by the United States and centered in Miami, an analogously emerging art and culture center (see chapter 7)—has to take root in consciousness, and culture is, in this view, the best means to raise consciousness.

Herein lies the gist of Luis Camnitzer's (1998) excellent critique, the unusual rapprochement of anti-imperialist discourse and neoliberal economic strategies. Indeed, the three themes of the Biennial—politics, constructivism, and cartography—not only provide a platform for an oppositional cultural politics to U.S. and European hegemony but demonstrate that culturally, the Southern Cone, and by extension Latin America, does not have any reason to envy the North. Curator-general Federico Morais cites Henry Kissinger at the very beginning of his catalgoue essay to disprove the stupid remark that "nothing important ever came from the South; history is never made in the South" (1997: 12). Of course, the very denial of subordinate status inevitably performs that status. Nevertheless, the political dimension points up the struggle against capital accumulation strategies devised in the North that underdevelop the South as well as the disparities and injustices that arise due to local dynamics. Morais writes, "Daily life in Latin America is contaminated by politics, by social and economic problems. We are always conversing about inflation, recession, corruption, death squads, the extermination of Indians and children; child prostitution, the landless and homeless, kidnappings, political violence, etc. Beyond regional and historical differences, what we have in common is that emerging character of problems. Thus it is often impossible for Latin American artists to abandon their context in the name of a presumably universal, atemporal and ahistorical language" (17).

The second theme, the constructivist dimension, points up a different role for Latin American culture vis-à-vis Europe and the United States. The constructivist legacy, exhibited quite lavishly in the exhibition, demonstrates that Latin American artists, especially from the Southern Cone and Venezuela, not only contributed to but also took that legacy in directions relatively unexplored elsewhere. In this view, the South has its own expression of modernity. Finally, the focus on alternative cartography, rooted in Joaquín Torres-García's *Upside-down-map* (1943), a visual expression of the motto "Nuestro norte es nuestro sur" (Our North is our South), conveys the will to displace the hegemonic North.

Camnitzer (1998) points out that under Morais's curatorship, the artworks were not grouped by "national divisions" but instead were "organiz[ed according to] an expressive fabric in terms of aspects," thus approximating an imagined community thought to be necessary for economic integration. The Biennial would contribute to this imagined community by providing a space for the "exchange of people, ideas and values that only culture knows how to provide" (Britto 1997). This idea is given clearer expression by the secretary of culture of the state of Estado do Rio Grande do Sul: "This endeavor, by paying tribute to Latin American creativity, places the State of Rio Grande do Sul squarely in the center of the movement to cultural integration that should guide the consolidation of MERCOSUL" (Boeira 1997). The Web site for the second edition of the MERCOSUL Biennial in 1999 stresses the "diversity and plurality, the significant differences in the artistic and cultural production of the countries" to be integrated in the trade agreement. The curator of the second edition, Fábio Magalhães, stresses the idea that globalization forces regions to consolidate in order to survive: "Some have seen globalization as contributing to the loss of identity, but I believe that even if globalization weakens national political and economic action, it also strengthens regional and local cultures" (qtd. in Moraes 1998). Magalhães thus maintained the focus on resistance, but he deepened the sense of a specific regional identity.

Conclusion

As I argued in chapter 1, culture has indeed become expedient insofar as it is instrumentalized for both economic and social reasons. The coincidence of technological development and the virtualization of the resources for capital accumulation (subtended by intellectual property regimes disseminated globally by trade legislation) make this almost inevitable. The imbrication of culture with economics and the solution of social problems is a conjunctural phenomenon analogous to the Keynesian compromise between capital and labor brokered by nation-states. The problem today, however, is that the site and the scale for resolving the conundrum of this imbrication are not obvious. Hence the perplexity registered by Camnitzer (1998) at the "disconcerting commercial-ideological" regional strategy that combines anti-imperialism and neoliberalism. As I also argue in chapter 1, UNESCO and civil society initiatives have entered into similarly hitherto difficult to understand imbrications of projects for social justice with a neoliberalized focus on diversity. Even the antiglobalization movement has not given this less visible conundrum its due.

Precisely because it attempts to engage this conundrum head-on, I conclude with the Associação Internacional Arte Sem Fronteiras' project for a Latin American cultural integration. A Brazilian nonprofit organization, Arte Sem Fronteiras was created in 1996 for the purpose of integrating Latin American peoples by articulating disparate activities in the arts and civil society. Two fora were held in November 1998 and November 2000 that brought together representatives from all Latin American countries working in state and local cultural ministries, artists and artist networks, civil society groups, cultural institutions, arts administration professionals, businessmen and politicians interested in promoting the arts, and international organizations like UNESCO, the Inter-American Development Bank, the Organization of Ibero-American States, and the Andrés Bello Convention to discuss the challenges to and the possibilities for increasing cultural exchange.

At first, it was thought that facilitating the circulation of cultural goods and artists—a more practical version of Gómez-Peña's "Free Art Agreement"—was the most important goal. But such a heterogeneity of people and interests soon made it evident that Arte Sem Fronteiras had to serve as a forum in which these different actors could talk to each other and debate the relative merits and drawbacks of their understandings of culture and its uses. At the conclusion of the first forum it was decided that Arte Sem Fronteiras would compile all data available on laws controlling the circulation of arts and artists across borders as well as all cultural policy laws with the aim of beginning the process of integration.

At the second forum, it also became obvious that, as Teixiera Coelho (1999), one of the architects of the initiative, wrote, cultural policy had to address questions of and establish a political culture. To this end, the General Estates of Culture were formed with the aim of taking to all national legislatures the articulated concerns of the representatives at the two fora. Because Arte Sem Fronteiras had gained the legitimacy to convoke representatives from the MERCOSUL parliament and the Latin American parliament (Parlatino), these became two bodies in which it could begin to act immediately. The most direct action could be taken with regard to MERCOSUL, because Arte Sem Fronteiras has its headquarters in Brazil and its steering committee includes representatives from all the member countries. Moreover, because some of the members of the steering committee are involved with the 2004 Barcelona Universal Forum of Cultures, Arte Sem Fronteiras will present the ministers of culture who will gather there with a charter to be adopted in the countries of the region.

Of course, Arte Sem Fronteiras cannot resolve the contradictions ensuing from the many different interests involved. For example, just as there is a concern for the artistic and cognitive viability of cultural institutions like museums, there are also advocates for privatizing them and using them in the "culturally sustainable" renovation of postindustrial cities. At the same time, representatives who work with marginalized populations demand that these other initiatives open up and make a place for the cultural practices of the poor and those not integrated into Western-oriented culture. There are also efforts to get the major television and audiovisual corporations to the bargaining table to have them take on their responsibility as corporate citizens.

The importance of Arte Sem Fronteiras in the Latin American context should not be underestimated. This is probably the first time in history that a local NGO with ample representation from all sectors interested in culture has achieved both a necessary exchange of views and effective action. Arte Sem Fronteiras also bears some resemblance to the citizen action initiatives that I discussed in chapter 5. Both are broad-based articulations of actors from all sectors of society who seek to take a multidimensional approach to problems. Arte Sem Fronteiras has the added feature that it is international, bringing together actors not only from given societies but also across societies. It is also important that it is not a foundation with a huge endowment that can establish agendas through its power to fund initiatives. On the contrary, the participants are the ones who push Arte Sem Fronteiras to take on this or that issue, to the extent of its capabilities. Although it would overstate the case to liken Arte Sem Fronteiras to the rhizomatic movements that engage the WTO and other forces of globalization where they meet to make decisions, it can be seen as an initiative that harnesses the forces that it can interpellate through its ethical discourse to serve the interests of those who usually get only the stick but never the carrot of globalization.

Getino (2001) points out that the demands of regional and local cultures are increasing, and Gohn (2000) adds that movements like the Zapatistas in Chiapas and the *sem terra* or landless in Brazil are using the media to make those demands more visible. In other words, myriad actions are taking place, but there hasn't been sufficient articulation across regions and countries. Because it is unlikely that the most successful border crossers—the transnational corporations—will collaborate in projects that have local significance in cultural, economic, and labor terms, Getino, a member of Arte Sem Fronteiras' steering committee, calls for both government regulations on capitalist enterprises and incentives for local and regional production and distribution of work that would otherwise not be competitive in the market. MERCOSUL is a starting point, just as NAFTA is, for hemispheric integration. But the dynamism within the MERCOSUL da cultura is for public culture.

This chapter on free trade and culture has made it evident that there is no way out of the expedient uses of culture. Rather than out, Arte Sem Fronteiras points the way into dealing with the problems, ultimately ones of cultural policy, which should not be understood as the exclusive province of governments. On the contrary, issues of trade and nongovernmental initiatives demonstrate that cultural policy is also made by corporations, the media, foundations, politicians, and sometimes even citizens.

9

Producing the Cultural Economy:
The Collaborative Art
of inSite

The [apartheid] machine [at the intersection of the United States and Mexico] is increasingly indifferent to democracy on either side of the line, but not indifferent to culture, to the pouring of oil on troubled waters.
—Allan Sekula, "Dead Letter Office"

The Emergence of Binational Cultural Collaboration

This epigraph is the caption to a photo in an installation by Allan Sekula, *Dead Letter Office*, whose various components capture images of the power differentials at the intersection of the United States and Mexico.[1] We see photos of the border patrol and wealthy Republican politicians on the San Diego side, and on the Tijuana side, images of poverty and industrial blight. Sekula also follows the trail of poverty into San Diego in the person of a "scavenger at work during the Republican Convention" and, reciprocally, registers the encroachment into Mexico of the culture industry in the guise of a Twentieth-Century Fox set constructed for the making of *Titanic* in Popotla, a village in the border region. The metaphor of oil poured on troubled waters is meant to be ironic, an indictment of the toxic social spill produced by the "apartheid machine" at the border: the disenfranchisement of cheap labor in asymmetrical exchange for commercial culture. A further, self-reflexive irony in Sekula's statement may be that the very venue in which he articulates it is an expression of the problem he identifies. inSITE97, the venue in which this installation is included, can, like the movie set, be conceived of as an artistic maquiladora whose executives (the directors of the art event) contract with managers (the curators) to map out the agenda for flexible workers-for-hire (artists) who in turn produce or extract (cultural) capital by processing a range of materials: the region (especially the border and the neighboring urban ecologies), the publics and communities who invest their collaboration in the success of a "project,"[2] social issues transformed into "art," and local cultures and international artistic trends that constitute the two poles of the new international division of cultural labor (Miller 1996). insITE is composed of a network of assembly sites where the artists and their collaborators put together cultural events of increasing national and international recognition. By equating culture with oil, Sekula captures the contradiction inherent in a program that would use culture to salve wounds and heal the binational rift on the one hand, and exacerbate the asymmetries of the region on the other, perhaps by showcasing it for international audiences. Indeed, when "culture" is made to happen at the border, the effects exacerbate the inequalities there, especially if the cultural capital derived therefrom accrues to those who already have plenty of it: the sponsors, directors, curators, artists, and art-going publics. Because culture capital is translatable into aesthetic, social, political, and even commercial value, there is a "return" on the investment of capital and labor. But what is the return for the local population?

Sekula's *Dead Letter Office* and many other compelling insITE97 projects among the fifty-eight installations, site-specific works, and community-based processual collaborations speak to the power of this binational art "festival" or "series of installations throughout the San Diego/Tijuana region" (insITE92). The first version in 1992 was organized by Installation Gallery to "celebrate our binational arts community" over a two-month period and involved the participation of other institutions: community colleges, public and private spaces, the Centro Cultural de la Raza, and the Museum of Contemporary Art in San Diego. This first version was a small operation, largely carried out among friends of the organizers at Installation Gallery and with the participation of local museums and galleries, which established close interinstitutional ties for this purpose. The exhibitions were repeated on a much larger scale in 1994, 1997, and 2000–2001, evolving into a triennial with increasing national and international recognition. Most press and review coverage has been local, but the 1997 version had greater exposure in the mainstream art world, with over twenty reviews and feature articles in journals like *Art in America, Art Nexus, Artfocus, Artforum, ART-news, Contemporary Art, Flash Art, International Contemporary Art, New Art Examiner, Public Art Review, Sculpture,* and *World Sculpture News,* as well as the most important newspapers in Los Angeles, Mexico City, São Paulo, and Toronto. Although inSITE may not have attained the status of biennials in Venice, Sidney, Johannes-burg, and São Paulo and art "festivals" like Documenta, some of the reviews and articles compared it favorably to these larger venues as well as to "younger art bashes such as the Korean Kwangju Biennial, the Münster Sculpture Projects, or the American SITE Santa Fe festivals, [because] inSITE distinguished itself from these by being both a residency and exhibition program," commission-ing new work rather than recycling work exhibited elsewhere (Chattopadhyay 1997: 23).[3]

Indeed, many of the artists who have done projects for these international venues have been invited to inSITE. The exhibitions expanded widely after 1992 to include anywhere from twenty-seven to thirty-eight nonprofit institutions located in San Diego and Tijuana as well as sponsorship from the private, nonprofit, and foundation sectors, including several government agencies in Mexico. The roster of artists also increased exponentially to over one hundred in 1994. Although originally meant to showcase local talent, from 1994 on inSITE has counterbalanced localism with such internationally recognized art-ists as Vito Acconci, José Bedia, Chris Burden, Mark Dion, Andrea Fraser, Allen Kaprow, Vitaly Komar and Alex Melamid, Alfredo Jaar, Allan McCollum, Allen Sekula, Lorna Simpson, and Krzysztof Wodiczko.

inSITE also belongs to a new genre of exhibitions, or more accurately, public art programs for which artists are commissioned to create new works, usually installations involving performance, film, and video, developed over weeks and months in specific sites and in interaction with local publics, communities, institutions, and corporations. In this regard, inSITE differs from the typical biennial that displays already existing works. Moreover, the city or region in which this new genre of public art is held, in this case the San Diego–Tijuana corridor, is crucial to the elaboration of the projects. There is a two-decades-long history of community-based and activist art projects that deal with the border region, the best known of which are those organized by the Border Arts Workshop/Taller de Arte Fronterizo (BAW/TAF), which was formed in 1984. The very idea of a binational project, eventually brought to fruition as La Fron-tera/The Frontier, had already been proposed in 1989 to the NEA and the Califor-nia Arts Council by the La Jolla Museum of Contemporary Art. This proposal, however, generated a struggle over who "owned" border art; its formulators, mostly white and institutionally accredited, had borrowed freely from texts on border art published in the BAW/TAF's journal Broken Line and were therefore accused by the largely Chicano workshop membership of extracting cultural capital from this margin of the art world, of "appropriating our ideas, our lan-

Photos on pp. 290–295 by Allan Sekula, from the "Dead Letter Office" exhibition at Centro Cultural Tijuana in 1997. Originals in color.

11A and B (above and opposite). *Hyundai container factory and trucker's graffito, Tijuana.* Diptych.

12A and B (above and opposite). *Twentieth Century Fox set for Titanic and mussel gatherers, Popotla.* Diptych.

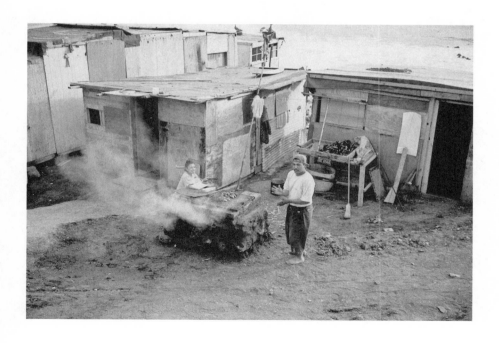

13A. Shipyard welder cutting steel for Hyundai truck chassis, Ensenada.

14A and B (above and opposite). *ABC News crew covering the Republican convention, San Diego.* Diptych.

13B. Metalworkers employed by a Hyundai subcontractor signing authorization papers for an independent union, Tijuana.

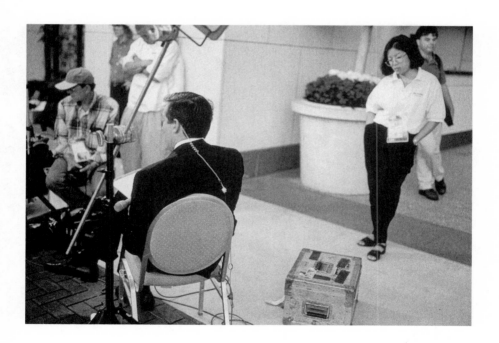

15A. *Scavenger at work during the Republican convention, San Diego.*

16A and B (above and opposite). *Tuna cannery, Ensenada.* Diptych.

15B. *Lobbyist's son at the Republican convention, San Diego.*

guage, our culture . . . now . . . that it is a fashionable and grantable thing to do."[4]

The struggle over the ownership of the border and binationalism left many unhealed wounds, but the directors of insITE, who would inherit this hot potato, have managed to negotiate quite skillfully and wisely to avoid (although not completely) the impression that they are accumulating the region's cultural capital and on this basis broker its distribution. The binational partnership with Mexican institutions established for insITE94 a major step in spreading the responsibilities and the benefits of the program.[5] The incorporation of community engagement projects in 1997 was an important step toward inclusivity and a means to temper suspicions. Unfortunately, the fifteen "unabashedly participatory and process-oriented projects" were separated from the "exhibition" projects, suggesting a hierarchy according to which the latter belong to a more "artistic" class and the former to a more "communitarian" one (Yard 1998b: 170). The very attempt to balance the local and the international, a necessity for art world recognition, sponsor satisfaction, and the civic demands of foundations and state arts councils, offset the good intentions, lubricating the slide back into a hierarchical arrangement. To show that its programs are relevant to nontraditional publics, insITE accommodated an already existing bureaucratic rhetoric whereby "community" functions as a code word for poor and racialized people.

Of course, insITE is not alone in having to manage the distribution of cultural capital, an issue that is particularly sticky when it migrates from communities to institutions, whether this involves the "development" of tribal uses of rainforest plants for producing pharmaceuticals, the fusion of indigenous rhythms into world music, or the "processing" of community practices by relatively well-off directors, curators, and artists for the biennial and art festival circuit. When it comes to artist-community relations, it really doesn't matter whether we are dealing with "minority" artists such as those involved in BAW/TAF or the directors and curators of museums and new institutional venues like insITE; they both exploit communities on the basis of culture-as-resource for solving social problems. The pursuit of legitimacy for claims to represent a community adequately, that is, to exercise cultural property rights with respect to community experiences and resources, is certain to produce tensions. Native Tijuanos, for example, have taken exception to BAW/TAF's representations of their experience, protesting that "these . . . people . . . have just arrived and immediately they tell us who we are, they dictate how we should discover ourselves" (García Canclini 1992a: 42). It is thus clear that neither the artists in BAW/TAF nor the directors, curators, and artists participating in inSITE are "organic" to these communities. Legitimacy can be established only by discursive strategies, and when these lack verisimilitude, it may be best to take another tack.

Perhaps for this reason, it made sense for the directors and curators of inSITE to de-emphasize "border art." Cocurator Sally Yard explained that to impose the border theme would "pose questions that predict their own answers," thus reproducing what local artists had already done (Ollman 1997). Instead, the curators encouraged the mobilization of cultural practices that transform public space and modes of transit in the "transnational metropolis" (Mesquita et al. 2000). Downplaying border art, however, is a veritable impossibility because many of the artists invited from outside the area become enthralled by the border.[6]

Indeed, the border can be said to be inSITE's prime "natural" resource. This has been noted by cynical critics as well as by activist artists. In the former category, Thomas McEvilley wrote that inSITE94 artists "cashed in on the fence that runs across the Northern edge of Tijuana and divides it from the U.S. as if it were the new p.c. hot spot—California's own Berlin Wall" (1995: 113). In Michael Duncan's review of inSITE94, the graffiti on the fence—"Welcome to the Berlin Wall"—is not seen as "p.c." but as portentous and "daunting" (1995: 51). The comparison with the Berlin Wall is not fortuitous. Long a site of "daunting" conflicts between two geopolitical and cultural worldviews and more recently carved up, cynically and profitably, into bric-a-brac, the transformation of the Berlin Wall emblematizes what is taking place at the U.S.-Mexico border. However, inSITE does not deserve comparison with these two characterizations. Although the border is "in reality" daunting and although it is subject to much commercialization, inSITE attempts, in the best tradition of "sustainable cultural development," to transform it and the local social ecology into an opportunity for reflection that goes beyond cultural and economic capital, which of course are also generated in the process. inSITE shares many of the concerns voiced at the "Summit Meeting of Museums of the Americas on Sustainable Museums and Communities," where it was declared that "sustainable development is a process of bettering the quality of life in the present and for the future, of promoting a balance between environment, economic growth and cultural equity and diversity, requiring the participation and recognition of everyone" ("Cumbre" 1998). The border, like the Berlin Wall, is one of those sites where the intangible value predominates, like concentration camps and other places where disaster has struck or where people have been enslaved and oppressed, and that cultural administrators institutionalize as heritage sites for commemoration, ritual, and testimony, as well as for cultural tourism and economic development. Such initiatives also "help to develop in the population a 'pride of place,' a knowledge of the history of their region and its value" (Clarke 2000). So long as these sites yield value by their conversion into art, social healing, and tourist attractions, they will remain potent catalysts for cultural projects.

The border, its steel fence in particular, exerts such a potent magnetic force that it is almost impossible for many of the artworks sited there to project energetically enough to break away from its pull. Indeed, extending along the border for miles and leading right into the ocean, the fence is a de facto installation that might make Christo envious. Made from corrugated steel landing strip panels left over from the Gulf War, the fence calls attention to the border for some twenty-five miles. And as if that weren't significant enough, it overshoots its limits and plunges into the ocean for another hundred yards.

Among the projects that worked directly with the border, most of which assayed a conceptual punchline or an ironic reversal of its function, are Terry Allen's Cross the Razor/Cruzar la navaja (1994), which consisted of a van equipped with a loudspeaker on each side of the border suggesting that now, finally, Mexicans and Americans could speak to each other, and Helen Escobedo's By the Night Tide/Junto a la marea nocturna (1994), an installation on the Mexican side of three wire-mesh sculptures resembling ships armed with coconut-loaded catapults, suggesting a defiant but quixotic counteroffensive against the power of the Goliath next door. Similarly, Vito Acconci's unrealized Island on the Fence/Isla en la muralla (1997), each of whose halves was to be placed on either side of the piece of fence that extends into the ocean, would have risen and fallen with the tide, thus constantly separating and joining the persons standing on it. More subtle, perhaps, were Silvia Gruner's The Middle of the Road/La mitad del camino (1994), a series of plaster figurines of Tlazoltéotl, a filth-eating goddess in the act of giving birth, perched on the fence as if guarding over the symbolic death and rebirth of the would-be border-crossers, and Ulf Rollof's 23 September 1994/23 de septiembre de 1994, (1994) five spruces mounted on a circular railroad track pivoted to a seat at the center of the circle, forcing the viewer to keep his or her "background assumptions" in focus (thus reversing the usual train ride in which the background is blurred) while confronting the alien reality of the border.[7]

At a further remove, there were more allegorical projects like Francis Alÿs's The Loop (1997), which avoided the border altogether. It consisted of a twenty-day trip around the world, starting in Tijuana and following a "perpendicular

route away from the fence . . . heading 67° SE, NE, and SE again until meeting [the] departure point," but on the San Diego side. What the audience got
to see was documentation from his brief stopovers in airports and hotels in
tourist must-visit cities. According to 1997 curator Olivier Debroise, there was
a "very political stake" in Alÿs's effort to not cross the border the way Mexican
migrants do, going to the extent of circumnavigating the globe. For Debroise,
Alÿs's politics reside in his self-reflective cynicism. Rather than sympathize
with the "wretched of the earth" by assuming their plight, Alÿs turned his gaze
on himself as a relatively privileged artist who, rather than parachute into a
site, took a round-the-world tour. In this way, he endowed the site with spatial insinuations, particularly cosmopolitan ones, not usually associated with
this border. In doing so, however, he brings us back to one of the aspects of
the material conditions of insITE that is usually lost in the various projects that
commiserate and collaborate with the downtrodden or attempt to unveil the
ideological underpinnings of power differentials between the two countries.
Alÿs's allusive project reminds us of the cosmopolitan character of art festivals
and biennials. Cosmopolitan artists who are "in the loop," many of whom have
participated in insITE, are commodities " 'packaged' . . . for this new, apparently
marginal, diplomatic industry called a biennial" (Debroise 1998: 58).

There are precedents for insITE's elaboration of its regional and site-specific
resource. The murals and other public works commissioned by the Secretaría
de Educación Pública in the 1920s and 1930s in Mexico and the U.S. Federal
Arts Program during the New Deal were expressive of a national-popular ethos,
but remained monumental in ways that current community art eschews. The
Art in Public Places and Art in Architecture programs of the 1960s, which involved modernist works, generally had little connection with the communities
in whose surroundings they were sited.[8] Arts institutions, especially museums, have of course debated their relationship to education, audiences, and
local community involvement since at least the 1930s (Rea 1932; Riviere 1949),
but the emphasis on drawing relevance from the experiences of audiences and
communities is characteristic of debates since the 1960s (Hoving 1968; Larrabee 1968; Martin 1967; Oliver 1971).[9] The mandate to decentralize and democratize culture, to be carried out by the institutions established in that decade (NEA, state arts councils), led to increasing demands for inclusion and
community relevance, still operative today, which some see as a means to empowerment and others to co-optation.[10] In the early 1980s, increasing critique
of public art led to the inclusion of the artist in the choice and planning of
the site and to the involvement of the community, according to NEA direc-

tives (Lacy 1995: 22–24). The "community engagement" projects introduced by inSITE in 1997 have as their direct predecessors the alternative (feminist, ethnic, Marxist, and other activist) practices that by the 1980s began to be incorporated into the bureaucracy of government and foundation arts departments.[11] Diversity and multiculturalism became rallying cries for the new public art, "emphasiz[ing] Otherness, marginalization, and oppression" and questioning prevailing (andro- and Eurocentric) values and privilege (Lacy 1995: 31). By the mid- to late 1980s, the role of the artist as educator, activist, and collaborator was firmly established, although the effects of this "aesthetic evangelist" role have been questioned, both for the bureaucratization that resulted from it as well as for the governmental or pastoral function that artists took on with respect to poor communities (Kester 1995). Indeed, as neoliberalism took root and the responsibility for the welfare of the population was increasingly shifted onto "civil society" (as in Bush Sr.'s Thousand Points of Light), the developed arts administration sector saw an opportunity to tap resources for the arts, claiming that they could solve America's problems: enhance education, salve racial strife, help reverse urban blight through cultural tourism, create jobs, reduce crime, and so on.

Within this framework, public art programs have drawn much of their significance from the history and social problems of a given place. Racism, class differences, and other social fissures are some of the historical legacies available to the "healing" and "problem-solving" power of community-based art practices, as described by Michael Brenson (1995) and Mary Jane Jacob (1995) in the catalogue for *Culture in Action*. In addition to *Culture in Action*, curated by Jacob for Sculpture Chicago over a period of two years (1991–93), some of her other projects, like *Places with a Past* for the 1991 Spoleto Festival in Charleston, *Points of Entry* (1996) for the Three Rivers Art Festival in Pittsburgh, and *Conversations at the Castle* for the Arts Festival of Atlanta (1996), have established Jacob as the leading curator for a collaborative art "appli[ed] to all walks of life," particularly communities outside the loop of mainstream institutions, to "demarginalize contemporary art and artists, [build] new bonds with the public, and [establish] a valued place for art in our society" (Jacob 1995: 60). Outside the United States there are also large-scale urban art programs, such as Nelson Brissac Peixoto's series of City Art (Arte Cidade) projects, which, although different in scope and intention from those of Jacob, also mobilize the features of their locale (in this case, the urban blight of a deindustrialized São Paulo) as a resource that elicits the intervention of artists and architects, in collaboration with researchers, communities, and public authorities, to provide new mappings for a more accessible habitation in and transit through the increasingly fragmented landscape of the postindustrial megacity (Peixoto 2002). It is no coincidence that many of the artists invited to *insITE* in the past two versions (e.g., Krzysztof Wodiczko, Andrea Fraser, Iñigo Manglano Ovalle, Mauricio Dias, and Walter Riedweg) have also participated in Jacob's or Peixoto's events.

Like these kindred projects, *insITE* departs from the attachment to site as that set of physical (rather than social or historical) attributes prioritized for placing a sculpture or carrying out an "intervention," as was characteristic of the quite different work of Robert Smithson, Carl André, Richard Serra, and appropriation artists like Jenny Holzer.[12] Instead, the city or region is supposed to provide the opportunity to explore the tendencies to publicization and privatization, especially as its residents and itinerants experience them. Rather than simply "parachute" into a site, artists are invited to spend time there, often more than a year, get to know its history and the community, and on this basis arrive at the concepts and materials that will constitute a project. In the case of *insITE*, thematizing the region or some aspect of it is not mandated, but the issues associated with it are expected to serve as a point of departure for the artists' projects. It could be said that the artists are enjoined to produce surprise, although that is not always the outcome, especially in those projects that attempt to best the border. And because a good number of the artists come from afar and have international reputations, many works involve an imbrication of the local and the transnational or global, as well as outreach to institutions and venues not usually associated with art. Indeed, as *insITE* evolved, its focus shifted from showcasing finished works to process-oriented projects that, according to the prepublication copy of the catalog for the 2000 version, "enlist the active participation of the public in their development" and "interweav[e] artists and works into the fabric of communities . . . sustained over an eighteen-month period."[13]

According to the curatorial statement, *insITE2000–2001* abandons treating the region as a "large-scale gallery [or] stage for the display of aesthetic objects and/or artistic interventions," encouraging instead a *collaboratory* model in which publics are coinvestigators and institutions "become colaboratories" (22). Nevertheless, the stage-like features characteristic of *insITE* in previous versions do not disappear. The laboratory and the stage are not counterposed spaces. The stage is still there even in the most successful *collaboratory* projects. One can imagine *insITE* as a "living theater" in which the region is the stage and a range of intermediary participants (who cannot be identified with traditional audiences) steer the production as much as the directors or actors/artists do. The "script" or curatorial theme to be enacted on this stage is not a template to be followed but an open-ended invitation to engage the locations, communities, and institutions. Consequently, the program of events is much less coherent than one might be led to assume from the catalogue.

Curatorially, inSITE expanded greatly in 1994 to encompass thirty-eight institutions and over a hundred artists, but in 1997 and 2000–2001 curatorship was streamlined to enable a more coherent aim. If in 1994 the artists were "left to their own devices" (Forsha 1995: 6) and the "exhibition took no central theme beyond the general parameters of installation and/or site-specificity" (Yard 1995: 34), the four-curator teams of the 1997 and 2000–2001 versions attempted to give conceptual guidance to the proliferation of perspectives that the many artists brought to inSITE. According to Executive Directors Michael Krichman and Carmen Cuenca, "It was decided early on in the conceptualization of insITE97 that the terms 'installation' and 'site-specific,' which had figured in the programs of insITE92 and insITE94, would be set aside in favor of an investigation of public space—as a *subject* to be explored, not merely as a *site* for locating works" (1998: 8). Accordingly, insITE97 was given a title, "Private Time in Public Space," which was to serve as a "suggestion" (rather than a mandate) for the "guises in which artists would deploy their projects" (Yard 1998a: 12). Analogously, insITE2000–2001 sought to "challenge the concepts that have oriented previous versions of inSITE and similar international exhibitions: site specificity, community engagement, artistic practice, and public space." To this end, the curators devised a set of conceptual axes—"landscape-traffic-syntax"—along which artists might work in collaboration (insITE2000–2001). The resulting "reconfiguration of space" and new knowledge of the two cities are seen by the curators as political acts that generate "new cultural articulations." It should be noted that the artists do not necessarily abide by such curatorial themes, which are perhaps more a reflection of the curators' intellectual interests and the art world's demands for exhibitions to come up with something new.[14]

The Laboratory and the Maquiladora

This collaboratory model animated most aspects of insITE2000–2001, including its planning. A series of residencies were held at which the organizers, curators, artists, and invited speakers discussed the issues involved in providing cognitive and visual and other sensory registers of the region and its locales, institutions, and people. The purpose of debate and discussion at these residencies was to hone the conceptual tools and practical strategies for seeing through the alienating structures in place and for "enabling unpredictable exchange" (insITE2000–2001). The invocation of the laboratory metaphor, presumably aimed at shifting the focus of insITE from exhibition to exploratory and collaborative process, raises as many problems as it seeks to avoid. At the July 1999 residency, geographer Aníbal Yáñez Chávez (1999) pointed out that space is not a void waiting to be filled and that when seen as a laboratory, the San Diego–Tijuana region is a palimpsest of experiments that have been carried out there. One can immediately think of the experiments that served the interests of the military-industrial complex located in San Diego, the experiments with surveillance devices and methods to stem the flow of undocumented workers across the border, and those experiments, beholden to the military foundations of San Diego, that have transformed the city into a leader in the telecommunications, computer, and biotechnology industries. These experiments also extend to the other side of the border, where the knowledge generated is put to use in the assembly of new products for global markets. If analyzed in all its dimensions, then, the laboratory metaphor brings into view insITE's articulations with the maquiladora metaphor introduced above.[15]

These connections were not lost on some of the artists and reviewers of insITE97. Judith Barry created a video installation, *Consigned to Border: The terror and possibility in things not seen* (1998) in which she focuses on the contradictions of labor exploitation and land use in the maquiladora zone in Tijuana. The collage sequences of these videos reproduce, insofar as it is possible, an otherwise invisible geography materialized here in the images of flows of capital and technology. Writing on *The Popotla Wall*, an insITE97 project by the binational art collective Revolución Arte (RevArte), Melinda Stone offers a convincing account of a community-based art project that successfully reworks and reappropriates the five-hundred-foot-long cement wall in order to counteract the "calculated capitalist interests of Hollywood, thus intervening 'between the movie *maquiladora*' — i.e., the Twentieth Century Fox movie set built for the making of *Titanic* — and the 'communal character of the fishing village' " (1998: 14).[16] Much labor was expended on reworking this wall, but the result was "mak[ing] it fit better with [the villagers'] surroundings," a compensation that cannot be evaluated in strictly economic terms.

But what are the terms of compensation?

Maquiladoras are the locations of flexible production, which in the post-Fordist era rely on three key principles: a premium on knowledge, labor flexibility, and mobility. insITE's brainstorming residencies thus bear a family resemblance to the knowledge production necessary to generate innovation or "unpredictable exchange," as the directors characterized it. Where inSITE departs—but only in part—from the maquiladora model is in dedichotomizing the intellectual/manual labor divide that characterizes the operations of transnational corporations, producing knowledge on the "developed" side of the divide and disseminating labor throughout the "developing" world. inSITE draws its intellectual/artistic capital more or less equally from North and Latin America. But inSITE's departure is qualified because intellectual production, even if disseminated across the border, is nevertheless in the hands of people (curators, artists, critics) with high institutional capital, whose work takes them through an archipelago of centers enclaved throughout the developing world, even as they presumably seek to engage and empower nontraditional (i.e., disadvantaged) publics. In other words, once we abandon the outdated model of center and periphery, we see clearly that power circulates from enclave to enclave regardless of whether it is located in New York, San Diego, Mexico City, São Paulo, or San José. This arrangement is evidence of a new international division of cultural labor whereby executives and knowledge producers can hail from anywhere so long as accumulation (in this case, cultural capital) flows along transnational networks of power. In the new economy, whether financial or cultural, the network provides the structure for the flexibility required in production, promotion, circulation, distribution, and consumption (see Castells 1996).

A similar qualification holds for the manual labor side of the equation; those who fuel transnational corporate or cultural institutions with their labor, including collaboration with artists, can also be found on either side of the border: poor Mexicans who work in maquiladoras and poor immigrant Mexicans and their U.S. kin who work in the service industries. The ruse, of course, is that inSITE and its kindred art venues may collapse the two kinds of services that now drive the "alternative" art world: those services rendered by the artist, with his or her highly developed intellectual capital, and those rendered by "communities," whose cultural capital, gauged in measures of marginality, provides relatively uncompensated value added to art.[17]

There are a few moments in the spate of reviews that shed some light on this problem. Commenting on native Canadian artist Rebecca Belmore's project *Awasinake (On the Other Side)*, photos of an unnamed Mexican woman with marked indigenous features projected onto the marquee of the Casino Theater in downtown Tijuana, Sarah Milroy (1997) points out the irony of one indigenous person attempting to make a point about invisibility by nearly exploiting her own indigenous sitter. Milroy seems to suggest that even though the sitter was paid $400 for two days of posing (less than 10 percent of the artist's fee for the work), there was little in the way of a nonpecuniary compensation that art should presumably provide. How is this any different from the exploitation of marginality by a Tolouse-Lautrec or a Sebastião Salgado?

The laboratory metaphor is expressive not only of the curators' desire to realize the most ambitious goal of the avant-garde, which is to sublate art into the *process* of life; it also sheds light on the very organization and administration of inSITE. Aside from the partnerships established with corporate and civic institutions that I explore below, labor is probably the most pervasive yet invisible aspect of the program. It takes an enormous amount of work to realize the projects, a good part instigated by the artists, and much of it done by the directors and their staff, as well as by collaborative publics and communities. The curators write that in the laboratory model, "the role of the public shifts from audience to co-investigator" (inSITE2000–2001). Directors, curators, and artists are all remunerated and derive cultural capital from their labor, albeit differentially distributed. The question needs to be asked, however, in what ways the labor—the coinvestigation—done by "publics" and "communities" is compensated.

Compensation, of course, should not be measured exclusively in economic or other utilitarian terms. Whether or not material or utilitarian forms of compensation are distributed equitably is relatively easy to ascertain; it is not at all clear, however, in what ways communities derive a noninstrumental benefit. How can we know, for example, that "communities" are indeed partaking, as cocurator Sally Yard claims, of "art's capacity to operate as a field of memory and a space of critical reflection, as a zone of attending and an arena of expression" (1998b: 170)? One might ask the same questions of Michael Brenson's claims for *Culture in Action*. According to Brenson, the paint chart developed by artists Kate Ericson and Mel Ziegler for the residents of a Chicago housing project, which included naming colors after local events and individuals, is a "political [act] exposing the role of institutional indifference in the widespread stigmatization of public housing and in the stereotyping of its residents as unknowing, uncommitted people . . . In so many ways, the paint chart expands outward, unfolding in many directions, flowing into personal, social, and political worlds" (1995: 21–22).

My query does not imply that what Yard and Brenson claim does not take place; I question, rather, curators', artists', and critics' *assumptions* about the art experience. In any other sphere of activity, such claims need to be backed up by some form of verification. How do we know that the "participants" brought in by invitation or attracted by some contingent aspect of an event (e.g., featuring a celebrity at the opening) necessarily walk away with—and retain as memory—the significance given to the event by the curators, artists, and those who write on their behalf?

One way to ascertain this is to involve the participants in a discussion of their involvement, a discussion that does not simply elicit the one-minute testimonials captured in documentaries about how much fun it was to paint a mural on a building or to create a community garden. The discussion I envision involves understanding one's role not only in applying paint or transplanting saplings but also in giving shape to the project at all levels, from making recommendations to the community artist to engaging the leadership and staff of the sponsoring institution and its funders, including municipal, state, and federal agencies, foundations, and corporations. Only by establishing the participants' protagonism and even authorship at all of these levels can one begin to understand what it means for a community to benefit from a project in ways that go beyond limited inflections of "enrichment" (i.e., established notions of cultural, economic, and social capital). Paulo Freire, in the context of liberation theology in the 1960s, devised a method for establishing the community's authority in educational programs and discussions in the public interest. These were taken into the artistic realm by Augusto Boal and others, such that publics were as much the authors of theatrical work as traditional script writers. There are also precedents in the United States for the encounters of publics with artists, curators, critics, and organizers, such as several of the community-based works in *Culture in Action* and *Conversations at the Castle*, both curated by Mary Jane Jacob, or Suzanne Lacy's youth projects in Oakland. As Jacob writes in her introduction to the *Conversations* catalogue, the point is for all the participants to discuss "who is authorized to communicate their experience of art to others" (Jacob and Brenson 1998: 24). As I argue below, however, there is more to the public's protagonism than the involvement in discussion. The role of publics and, more generally, culture (which is the currency now at play in access to such events) can only be made fully evident if the circumstances of organization, including sponsorship and its raison d'être, are part of the encounter (which may and perhaps should be more conflictive than a "conversation").

Mobility, of course, is the principal characteristic of the flow of labor and culture across borders. And "regional cooperation" is the manner in which that mobility can be made to yield a "comparative advantage" in an "increasingly competitive global economy." This is the view expressed by Richard N. Sinkin

(1999), managing director of the InterAmerican Holdings Company, an international management and consulting company specializing in "adding value to companies in Latin America" by means of "market intelligence, project implementation, start-up in Mexico, and investment." In his article, "Mexico's Maquiladora Industry," Sinkin argues that the trade arrangements that underpin the maquiladora industry must be bolstered by regional cooperation that is not limited to the economic sector but must also strengthen "our cultures." He thus establishes an analogy regarding knowledge/labor relations in both the economic and cultural spheres. Tellingly, the Mexican consul-general in San Diego, Luis Herrera-Lasso, gathered senators and "business executives from companies that have established maquiladora assembly plants, like Honeywell, financial corporations like CASAS, tourism agencies, and Tijuana chamber of commerce members" to discuss binational, bicultural programs that will provide the "mutual understanding" necessary for cooperation. It is no coincidence that the consul-general, honorary cochairman and board member of inSITE, should see and promote the congruence of economic and cultural cooperation.

Cultural Capital

Many of these issues have been dealt with by participating artists, some directly and others more covertly. And the curators have attempted to infuse their projects with a political significance that derives from the remapping of space and networks of interaction that the collaboratory model entails: "The collaborative impact of the insITE2000 projects will be to challenge the syntax of the city that orders and organizes the multiple economies of daily life, determining circulation, power lines and institutional access" (inSITE2000–2001). Notwithstanding these attempts to inform the works conceptually and politically, the scope of the enterprise remains too vast and the sensibility of the artists is so varied (and often recalcitrant to "guidance") that it is difficult to see the directors' and curators' mission borne out in each and every work. This is inevitable not only because artists may eschew programmatic themes, but also because different kinds of artists are invited according to different criteria, often beyond the control of the curators. For example, the substantial support provided by the Mexican government (through the Instituto Nacional de Bellas Artes and CONACULTA) means that a significant number of Mexican artists, and not necessarily those from the border region, must be included, regardless of whether they share the commitment to process and community-based work. One of the curators interviewed for this chapter observed that inSITE "was funded to make sure that we found Mexican artists since funds were not available to make studio visits in any other country,"[18] despite the Americas-wide scope of the event. For inSITE2000–2001, the only significant individual Mexican sponsor, Eugenio López, CEO of the transnational juice company Jumex, is from the capital. Curiously, Mexico City officials and curators seem to have at least as much and maybe even more of a stake in inSITE than anyone from Tijuana. Aside from the specific mission of inSITE in terms of putting Mexican artists on the map and providing important institutional capital for officials, the program has endowed the figure of the curator, particularly the "independent" curator, with a salience that has only recently emerged in Mexico. Historically, government-appointed directors called the shots in keeping with state agendas like brokering national identity. inSITE is one of several initiatives that emerged in the late 1980s and early 1990s that has created a new practice for the "independent" curator (Cuenca 2000).

According to Olivier Debroise (forthcoming), the conditions for the emergence of the new curatorial practice in Mexico are found in the restructurng of the state under President Salinas de Gortari in the late 1980s in response to the economic crisis and to the spirit of privatization that accompanied NAFTA. In the cultural sphere, this has meant greater institutional autonomy from direct government mandate at the same time that curatorial agendas were devised according to the public relations ethos of corporate executives. This change was evident in new private museums and cultural centers like the Centro Cultural/Arte Contemporáneo, financed by Televisa, and the new museums established by corporate elites in Monterrey (Museo de Monterrey and Museo de Arte Contemporáneo de Monterrey).[19] Privatization brought new demands from museum-going publics and from sponsors who wanted greater competency and professionalization according to international norms. In less than a decade, however, these "independent" curators who had fostered alternative practices and who were part of a new international scene, evident in the workshops at CURARE (directed by Debroise until 1998), were transformed into "producers" at the service of the new institutional agendas of private spaces like X-Teresa and the Carrillo Gil Museum or binational public-private partnerships like inSITE. Debroise's account thus bears out my argument about the place of cultural workers as the model of the new flexible service workers who produce knowledge and process, whether for business enterprises or cultural institutions. In either case, the services straddle the local (e.g., "communities") and the global (the new international division of cultural labor).

On the San Diego side, local sponsors desire to see their city profile lifted on the international scene, a major reason for the creation of new biennials. By 1997, inSITE was recognized as an established triennial. ARTnews's focus on San Diego that year gave inSITE as much or more space than other local art institutions, noting that it played an important role in "rais[ing] the city's profile in a constructive way." Another reviewer crowed that "thanks to art, San Diego is on the national map to an extent seldom attained by Chamber and ConVis propaganda" (D.S. 1994). Indeed, inSITE gained recognition just when city officials and elites were seeking to "help the world community turn its attention to San Diego" (" 'Insights' " 1994). The ARTnews piece goes on to point out that since 1994 inSITE had "garnered a prodigious amount of ink and a sizable audience on both sides of the border" (Pincus 1997). inSITE's press books list 265 articles for the 1994 version and 268 for the 1997. Reflecting on her experience with inSITE, 1997 cocurator Jessica Bradley (2000) remarked that elites want their city to have ownership of events like these. Moreover, the survival of cities is increasingly tied to tourist dollars, and the arts are a major resource in this regard. Indeed, inSITE has been seen as the catalyst, along with the biomedical and computer industries, for putting San Diego on national and international cultural maps and helping it get through the "economic dependency adjustment" that ensued with the "loss of the defense and military support [on which it] has relied for so long" (S. Johnson 1994).

Conceived when negotiations were about to culminate in the signing of NAFTA, inSITE directors contributed to crafting a new binational model of cooperation and resource sharing that was as much cultural as economic ("inSITE97 Takes Shape"). They participated in some of the activities of the Binational Committee of Education and Culture and the Committee on Binational Regional Opportunities, whose mandate was to "creat[e] a space that will facilitate the implementation of binational projects in the areas of education and culture" (Binational Committee of Education and Culture). The public-private partnerships (particularly public institutions on the Mexican side) brokered by inSITE are unique, and together with the U.S.-Mexico Fund for Culture, inaugurated in 1991, are the only initiatives that have created long-lasting binational institutional unions in the cultural sphere.[20]

Codirector Carmen Cuenca (2000) observed that the binational and the public-private-nonprofit partnership established by inSITE makes it unlikely that any single contributor can bring about a shutdown. If, for example, one of the Mexican government funders were to withdraw support, then private Mexican support as well as funders from the United States would enable the program to continue. Because CONACULTA, FONCA, and the Instituto Nacional de Bellas Artes are government agencies, it is not unlikely that the new ruling party, the PAN, might want to redirect their agendas and thus channel funds elsewhere. On the other hand, Tijuana is a city ruled by the PAN and inSITE can become an even more salient player in the symbolic work that culture does for politics. Though it cannot be said that there aren't interests at play and some minimum level of monitoring to ensure that no scandals take place, this leveraged form of support gives inSITE directors a good measure of independence. And of course, endless work and meetings to patch together this impressive assortment of supporters.

The binational, public-private arrangements of both inSITE and the U.S.-Mexico Fund for Culture were facilitated by the new direction that the Salinas government gave to many government agencies. With the advent of NAFTA, there was an increasing interest in partnering with U.S. institutions as well as with the move to new corporate and semicorporate structures, such as the nonprofit corporation, which did not exist in Mexico. For the cultural sphere, the first step in this direction was the creation of FONCA in March 1989, with a mandate to increase support by means of hybrid public-private capital for the preservation of the country's heritage and to foment new cultural production and dissemination. Octavio Paz emphasized this mission at the inauguration of FONCA, noting that culture's social responsibilities and its freedom had to be supported by both the state and the economic community (Tovar y de Teresa 1994: 59). FONCA, in turn, became a natural partner in the creation of the U.S.-Mexico Fund for Culture, whose other partners are Bancomer (Mexico's second-largest bank) and the Rockefeller Foundation. As Alberta Arthurs (2000), then director of the Arts and Humanities Division at the Rockefeller Foundation, remembers it, a Wingspread report had given a bleak picture of distrust and little understanding between the two countries just as the talks leading to NAFTA were gearing up. By the time the Rockefeller Foundation stepped up the initiative for the partnership, relations between the countries had improved. There was a lot of action and optimism in the early days of the Salinas presidency and much of the enthusiasm stemmed from Mexico. Arthurs, Ercilia Gómez Maqueo Rojas, head of Bancomer's philanthropic department, and José Luis Martínez, director of FONCA, were able to tap this enthusiasm when they proposed shared funding and binational collaboration on behalf of the arts and culture. The initiative would also be a way of encouraging philanthropy in Mexico.[21] In turn, FONCA, the U.S.-Mexico Fund for Culture, and the Rockefeller Foundation have supported inSITE.

The partnership mentality that was in the air around the time of the negotiations for NAFTA, rather than any particular cultural program complementing trade (of which there were none), also extended to FONCA, the U.S.-Mexico Fund for Culture and inSITE.

These cultural programs are every bit as impressive as the flexible production, labor, and trade arrangements of the binational Maquiladora Program. An important feature of these resource-sharing programs is the value added by Mexican labor, whether in the guise of assembly work in the industrial parks of the border region,[22] or in that of communities that infuse inSITE projects with the "reality" that art demands today. Consequently, even those programs that feature what Mary Jane Jacob once referred to as "unfashionable audiences" (i.e., poor, racialized, or otherwise marginalized communities distant from the museum-going public) have a role in this endeavor, especially as the idealism of community-based art is incorporated into the rhetoric of "rebuilding cities." Redevelopment projects in blighted areas, which can bring new jobs, "increase property values . . . and increase receipts from the tax on hotel rooms," and are enhanced by art, which provides "visual reinforcement . . . helps accelerate th[e] revitalization process" (Klein 1997). It also doesn't hurt that foundations and municipal and state arts councils, particularly on the U.S. side, encourage art institutions to provide proportional representation of the local and national demographics (i.e., artists of color) and the involvement of nontraditional (i.e., non-museum-going) publics. Nevertheless, to maintain a high profile in the art world, a number of internationally renowned artists must be invited. The directors and curators thus have a difficult and often precarious balancing act to perform, yet inSITE seems to have been quite successful at bringing it off.

This balancing act is a major achievement, requiring ingenuity, tact, and influence. Such an achievement, particularly the *organizational work* done by inSITE directors and staff, deserves at least as much attention as the most successful art projects in the program, for it can tell us much about the human and institutional potential of the region as well as the creativity in interaction and setting up networks that has enormous reality effects. Shouldn't the balancing act be part of what inSITE has to reveal about the region? We can learn a lot about dealing with inequalities, incongruities, and contradictions, understand how all the parties—from the directors and curators to the artists, corporate executives and workers, elite sponsors, government and foundation funders, cultural institution personnel, local community leaders, and the Mexican fishermen of Popotla who counterbalance the disruption of a movie set by painting a mural around it—relate to each other and how measures might be devised and

taken, concretely, to mobilize the considerable forces of the program to produce effects that are not limited to the idealistic statements of the catalogue.
Indeed, the organization of insITE points in the direction of action over hype,
although the latter is necessary for promotional and fundraising purposes.

Cultural Politics

I shall return to the organizational dimension of public art programs as catalysts for action. First, however, I would like to explore further the rhetoric found
in the promotional materials and catalogues and the analyses of previous insITE
versions.

insITE's own materials abound in pious discourse about the rich diversity and
the vast inequalities of the region (ranging from squatters to developers), which
legitimize the need for art that offers "encounter[s] with history, memory,
identity and personality" and "activate[s] self-awareness—articulating individual and collective experience" (Yard 1998a: 13). The curatorial statement for
insITE2000–2001 takes the discourse even further, advocating a cultural salve
for social lesions: "We want to trace the activities that cause the transnational
metropolis to expand and contract—the daily trafficking in goods and people,
frustrations, desire and dreams. When cultural practices are injected into these
flows, or when they redirect them by detours, they open up new possibilities
of linking people and places. Here artists' laboratories become experiments
in the removal of institutionalized blockages, providing remedies against the
inertia of everyday life." But why not include an examination of insITE's own
institutional effects, not necessarily in the mode of institutional critique, but
at the very least as an exemplification of what exactly takes place when new
forms of art experience and "cultural practices are injected into [the] flows" of
daily life?

Despite a commitment to the "real world," most often accessed by reference
to "communities," no window is provided onto the process itself of bringing
art to the public. Curators' and critics' understanding of the reality of an art
event is most often expressed thematically, that is, couching the interpretation
of the significance (or failure) of artworks and practices in the context of social,
cultural, political, and economic realities, such as immigration or the fragmentation of the city. I suggest that we focus on the structure and organization
generated by insITE directors and staff. Promotion and criticism, in contrast,
tend to be interpretive. For example, commenting on insITE94, Cuauhtémoc
Medina argues that "each work in the exhibition had to be judged in terms of

how it momentarily converted this dividing line [of the border] into a common element in dissimilarity, how it suspended the reality of this strip of borderland, if only to wipe away its cosmetic mask" (1995: 55). Faced with an art object or process, the proper response seems to be a thematics of unveiling, of probing an underlying reality that is not the work itself but to which the work refers and that it perhaps affects. Reviewers tend to cast their gaze over the wildly varying projects and attempt to discern a set of themes that underpin the heterogeneity. This is done by exercising an allegorical and/or metaphorical discernment that yields insight into the otherwise ungraspable whole. In this sense, most of the writing about inSITE is quite traditional, even art historical.

Writing in the 1994 catalogue, Olivier Debroise frames the series of works within the thematics of mediation. He finds that the nonarticulated dissemination of disparate installations over an eighty-mile stretch requires the intervention of commentary—the mediation of the press, video, and photography—to get a sense of the exhibition as a whole (1995: 23). The virtuality implicit in this mediation encapsulates the entire experience for him, particularly of those works that cross or straddle the border by putting into play the "comings and goings of people . . . the ebbs and flows of information" (29). Sally Yard (1995), in turn, organizes the exhibition along four axes: the excavation of remembrance, representation shaped by singular narratives and complacent models, the wresting of publicness from privat(ized) space, and the attenuation of the estrangement imposed by the border fence. Medina (1995) finds several coincidences that distinguish the exhibition from an "undifferentiated amalgam": the representation of crossing as a "funereal passage" and/or a mythic death and rebirth; the "illusion of free movement," particularly repetitive or circular movement; the contradiction of communication and other structures of mediation, including curatorship, which "mak[es] them esthetic, decorat[es] them, and extend[s] them to the point of irony"; the ephemerality of archaeologies and monuments vis-à-vis the unearthed histories of the San Diego–Tijuana area; and the use of toys as emblems of the military-industrial-informational complex.

Despite the tendency to transmit information, David Hickey (1995) found that most of the artists in inSITE94 tended to "parachute" into locales, thus failing to translate cultural differences, a failure based on presuppositions ensuing from fixed ideological and culturalist views. He illustrates this problem by reference to Jean Lowe's recreation of a classroom in Tijuana's Casa de la Cultura Municipal, where the critique of the exploitation of animals based on Protestant assumptions overlooks its ideological foundation in Catholicism

(66–68). Other critics have pointed out that Patricia Patterson's attempt to get a Tijuana family to paint their house in more "Mexican colors" (pinks, greens, blues) and put family photos on the walls as part of her project La Casita en la Colonia Altamira ran against her intention to capture the indigenous and avoid spectacle (García Canclini 2000: 12). Apparently, she brought her preconceptions ("the touristic exoticism of imported criteria"; Arriola 1998: 88) of what a popular Mexican home should look like and sought to recreate it in Tijuana. Pieces like this can be very productive, for they bring to the surface the underlying assumptions of artists and curators from one country working in another. In this regard, Ivo Mesquita retorted insightfully in a dialogue with the other curators that the "question of public space is a U.S. issue, more than an issue pertaining to the rest of the Americas. The distinctions between private and public space are much less clear in Colonia Libertad in Tijuana, for example, than in La Jolla" (Bradley et al. 1998: 55). Many of the other guiding concepts of inSITE — community, diversity, identity, politics — offer similar pitfalls when deployed interculturally.

The catalogue for inSITE97 shied away from the interpretive essays characteristic of the 1994 catalogue, embracing instead more theoretical interventions on public art, political art, urbanism, and transnationalism, as well as more ethnographic explorations of community experiences. The catalogue thus provided a context in which readers might grasp the works on a more abstract level, particularly as a response to global forces, as well as more directly at the experiential level, presumably partaking of the reactions of community participants. Nevertheless, this attempt to merely insinuate these macro- and microframes of interpretation or experience does not avert more direct interpretation, as in Néstor García Canclini's essay and the discussion among the four curators. García Canclini interprets the works in inSITE97 as reactions to the degradation of public space, community, and civility brought about by development, privatization of gathering places, and the decentering of traditional Latin American cities (1998: 41). The works evoke for him a sense of the intimate, especially where the monumental has lost its power to enthrall the users of the city; they deinstall or change the meaning of the urban and its trappings; trouble or accommodate to the stereotypes on either side of the border; capture the "fleeting connections that are made between objects, people, and spaces" (47).

Similarly, the four curators' reflections on the works selected for inSITE97 framed and circumscribed the chaotic heterogeneity sprawled throughout the region. The emphasis on the reworking of public space and the border setting exerted an overarching unity, in their view (Bradley et al. 1998). The curators gave considerable priority to those works that disrupted the temporality or timing implicit in the most basic feature—communication—of the Mexican-U.S. relationship; focused on the diverging significance of public space in Mexico and the United States; took the guise of an everyday thing or event (a house, a water fountain, a business, an inaugural speech); centered on tourism as part of the transience of being a public artist or performer; invoked the thematics of surveillance; took the border as a goal rather than a barrier; generated images of doubles and reversals that troubled the notions of cooperation and dominance at the border; and exceeded their artistic presentation in their factual presence and survival beyond the exhibition. This last aspect, evident in David Avalos's *Paradise Creek Educational Park Project*, constituted the utopian aspiration of the exhibition.

Avalos's piece raised the question of an effective politics of art, of what an artistic intervention into the real beyond "mere" consciousness raising and critique might entail. The latter were considered by some artists, curators, and critics to not be enough to make an effective difference on inSITE's publics. Co-curator Ivo Mesquita wrote, "David did something here that was real, rather than operating in a more ethereal critical space" (Bradley et al. 1998: 52). This "public works collaboration-in-process" involved the creation of an educational, environmental park for a half-mile stretch of Paradise Creek, just behind a school in National City. As such, it would have an ongoing impact on the students' understanding of the local ecology. For Mesquita, this wasn't an abstract or "merely" poetic crossing between the borders of art and life. The politics that Avalos seeks to elicit are not based on resistance, at least not as it is understood in most avant-gardist versions, including that of Susan Buck-Morss, in her contribution to the inSITE97 catalogue. Avalos pretty much dispenses with "art" and instead adopts the role of catalyst in creating a collaborative, learning experience. Buck-Morss, on the other hand, draws her inspiration for a political art from the resistance of the phenomenological body, whose aesthetics or sensory perception dispenses with or resists socially and culturally construed meaning. The body has the capacity to "[blow] up the significance of our seemingly insignificant everyday practices of compliance . . . As a form of cognition through the bodily senses, aesthetic experience has the power to undermine official cultural meanings, and inform our critical, corporeal side, the side that takes the side of human suffering and bodily pain wherever it occurs, and supports the possibilities for social transformation that present structures disavow" (1998: 24–26). For Buck-Morss, all other political art practices are easily absorbed by the institution of art.

It is true that resistance can be conceived as rooted in bodily departures from norms, as Judith Butler has argued,[23] or in "anarchic" expressions that disrupt the social, as embodied in Julia Kristeva's notion of the semiotic *chora*.[24] It is also the case that those departures can themselves be incorporated into more flexible forms of socialization. It is often argued that ethnoracial or sexual "minorities" are "subversive" of the mainstream, but the very means by which they have access to making claims (usually for redress of exclusion) facilitates their acceptance of ethnoracial or sexual categorizations, and thus of "alternative" forms of normalization and representation within the larger process of socialization in liberal and neoliberal democracies. Butler's account suggests a way of getting at the politics of these processes of normalization, but only up to a point. Because a normalizing injunction (e.g., "to be a given gender") "produces necessary failures," for Butler its subversion ensues only from within that process where a "variety of incoherent configurations . . . exceed and defy the injunction by which they are generated" (1990: 145). This account suggests that focusing on the performance or performativity of normalization and socialization yields a politics. This may indeed be a productive strategy for discerning the politics of cultural events, particularly if we focus on how the organization of an event produces its effects. However, Butler's formulation would have to be revised to take into account that the normalizing identities that we may want to focus on are not just the white, middle-class, museum-going publics, but the nonmainstream publics themselves, because they too are usually understood only through repetitive representation and categorization: principally as African Americans, Latinos, Native Americans, or gays and lesbians. In other words, the politics of an alternative cultural event may be most productively approached not by assuming that the political effect ensues from the exclusion or nonrepresentativity of the nonmainstream publics. Instead, politics might best be discerned in the performative force by which institutions produce cultural events that assume and in the process normalize nonmainstream categorizations.

To the extent that this is the case, an avant-gardist approach, no matter how defiant of institutionality,[25] is less likely to yield a viable politics. For example, when community-based art first became a major presence on the art scene in the 1980s it was thought to be "unfashionable," particularly because much of it engaged poor and racialized non-museum-going audiences. However, by the mid-1990s, promoters of these alternative events were lamenting that the "attention afforded community-based art of late [had] become a stylistic term," had been "broken down into a formula" (Tormollan 1995: 58). Focusing on the machinery of production of a cultural event's effects can make visible the transformation from unfashionableness to accommodation in this example. More generally, this machinery or archaeology, to use Foucault's term for showing how a system of statements works, will help us understand how inSITE patches together a heterogeneity of discourses and practices that produce subject positions and in so doing is itself a social intervention. It is for this reason that I advocate examining the organization of inSITE, and indeed suggest that inSITE reveal its own operations as part of its display, not simply as a form of institutional critique but for the purposes of devising plans for action.

Avant-garding Publics and Process

These dynamics of the avant-garde are rehearsed time and again in criticisms of inSITE art projects' inability to "really" achieve the empowerment they set out to mobilize because they are hampered by the art institution. It is beyond the scope of this chapter to elaborate on the premise that there is no outside of institutionality and that it will not do to expect an external force — the real — to solve the problems of an institutionally bound practice. Suffice it to suggest, however, that institutions can be reconverted, particularly within broad historical changes like those of the past two decades that have transformed their significance and function. Accordingly, I find it more useful to ask not how the real intervenes into practice but to turn this preoccupation on its head and ask what the reality effects of inSITE itself are as a project.

To the degree that the artists addressed a range of issues, from immigration to poverty, policing, and crossing borders, they succeeded in producing experiences of politics. For example, Marcos Ramírez Erre's shack, titled *Century 21* (1994), was intended to restore, synecdochically, the shantytown Cartolandia that had been leveled to build the modern Centro de la Cultura Municipal in Tijuana, thus raising issues about land ownership and zoning policy. BAW/TAF's *ESL: tonguetied/ lenguatrabada* (1994) was an indictment of the suppression of Spanish in U.S. schools. Pepón Osorio's *Public Hearing* (1994) was meant to raise concern about police brutality, particularly toward Latinos. The Chicano Park Artists Task Force's *Four Our Environment* (1997) raised questions about cultural ecology; Rebecca Belmore's *Awasinake (On the Other Side;* 1997) dealt with the neglect of indigenous women's problems; feminist ecology and the racial ecology of sound were referenced, respectively, by Deborah Small's *Rowing in Eden* (1997) and George E. Lewis's *The Old People Speak of Sound: Personality, Empathy, Community* (1997). Other political interventions took the form

of explicit critique or more implicitly attempted to make visible the contradictions and inequalities on the divides of class, race, and nationality in the border
region. Some artists alluded to the military and technological forces that dominate the region. Chris Burden's *A Tale of Two Cities*, a scale model of the region,
emphasized the "war toys" of San Diego's military-industrial complex, as well
as Japanese techno-apocalyptic creations, which, when viewed through bin-
oculars, suggested complicity, as Medina observed in the inSITE94 catalogue
(1995: 63).

The demand for reality over critique seems to be a never-ending quest of the
avant-garde. After reviewing several pieces whose politics consisted in raising
consciousness of pressing issues like racism and complicity with military agendas, Medina asked "whether this exhibition can have some impact beyond instigating a more full awareness" (1995: 63). This question was echoed by the
critics and by some of the artists participating in inSITE. At the July 1999 residency in preparation for inSITE2000–2001, artist Armando Rascón suggested
that an art project should have lasting effects in the community in which it is
sited, that is, should leave something that goes beyond instigating awareness
of the contradictions attaching to a particular place or situation. Both Medina
and Rascón asked for effectiveness, but with different effects in mind. Medina's
response to his own question turns on the transformation of Helen Escobedo's
installation of three ships with coconut-loaded catapults at the border into
more than a symbolic challenge to the offensive border fence. Local residents
had substituted the coconuts with stones, suggesting, in Medina's view, that
they had empowered themselves as latter-day Davids to defeat the neighboring
Goliath. Although the residents surely upped the political ante of Escobedo's
piece, the so-called transformation seems to be no more than another turn in
the dialectic of the avant-garde. The piece may have inspired residents to replace the symbolic bombs with more material ones, but what makes Medina
think that the stones are any less symbolic than coconuts?

Rascón's question also suggests that public or social art should be held to
criteria of effectiveness. He is not alone; these criteria have become an integral
part of arts administration, as evidenced by a 1997 report, *American Canvas*, for
the NEA. The premise of the report is that to survive, the arts must embrace
a new pragmatism involving the " 'translat[ion of]' the value of the arts into
more general civic, social, and educational terms"; in this way, they will be more
convincing to the public and elected officials (Larson 1997: 81).[26] The result is
a troubling bureaucratization of the avant-gardist blurring of art and life:

No longer restricted solely to the sanctioned arenas of culture, the arts would be literally suffused throughout the civic structure, finding a home in a variety of community service and economic development activities — from youth programs and crime prevention to job training and race relations — far afield from the traditional aesthetic functions of the arts. This extended role for culture can also be seen in the many new partners that arts organizations have taken on in recent years, with school districts, parks and recreation departments, convention and visitor bureaus, chambers of commerce, and a host of social welfare agencies all serving to highlight the utilitarian aspects of the arts in contemporary society. (127–128)

What characterizes our period is that prior premises of resistance and community have been articulated to a notion of service that makes of the arts and culture techniques of government, which, following Foucault, means establishing techniques for managing people that are situated in civil society. In this context, the historical avant-garde project of drawing art from its institutional enclave to the "intoxicating" contingencies of life no longer makes sense. Instead, as Andrea Fraser (1994; "Services" 1997) has pointed out, the evolution of arts administration since the 1960s has increasingly encouraged artists to become service providers. This refunctionalization is not limited to the United States but is characteristic of the role of artists as catalysts for cultural citizenship in the new cultural policies throughout Latin America and many other regions.

Mary Jane Jacob, champion of community-based collaborations, has sounded a caution with regard to criteria of "functional effectiveness" applied to such work because, as she observes, the fact that art affects people does not mean that it is the same as "day-to-day social programs." "Artists are not miracle workers — they are just another alternative" (1996: 45). If we ask the question, Alternative to what? the answer will most likely be the mainstream art institution. And if this is the answer, then "communities" become a way for artists to achieve the avant-gardist dream of opting out of institutionality. Pushing the envelope of art-beyond-the-institution is what delivers the artists from the charge of practicing social work. "For us [Michael Clegg and Martin Guttmann], the idea of working with a community relates to the question of how to expand the frame of twentieth-century art to other areas and not, primarily, to the question of addressing communities. We are artists. We are not social workers" ("Services" 1997: 144). To address one's work *against* the institution of art is, however, another way of allowing that institution to frame the understanding of the practice and to seek to incorporate it. Artists who accept the avant-gardist goal of reconciling art and life (especially social issues and community-based work) thus run the risk of carrying out the injunction to deliver the real at the expense of their art. This, no doubt, is what provoked Iñigo Manglano-Ovalle (1999), renowned as a community-based artist after his critically acclaimed participation in Jacob's *Culture in Action*, to respond to Rascón's question at the residency by noting that art exhibitions and events may be no more than opportunities for artists to show their work. Like Guttmann, he objected to the call in contemporary public art circles for artists to negate their art, to subordinate it to more visible social agendas that seem to carry greater legitimacy: "Artists can't abandon their own histories as artists or our own critical site of artmaking." Manglano-Ovalle's (2000) critique of the institutionalization of community-based art is worth citing in full:

> Since the landmark program "Culture in Action" (1993), and the recent inducements to create a new genre of collaborative work, we have in many ways burdened art with a curatorial theme that historically was already a theme of art: how it connects to a public, how it is social, how it extends the parameters of being art, how it extends audiences. A problem with the new genre public art (as evidenced in Suzanne Lacy's *Mapping the Terrain*) is positing it as a new avant garde. But historically this was always its logic. And this history, from which we seem to be separated, is important to us. Curatorially, there is an attempt to mine this new field. But artists are interested in the continuity of history, in recognizing that their work has connections to site and community but also to a larger practice into which it also fits. The problem is that for a program to be successful in its overall context, it pigeon-holes the artist into a completely local site, dislodging him or her from larger historical issues. It does the same for questions of work and community. In achieving success as a local, community-based project brought to international attention, it localizes that community even more, disconnects it, disallows it to participate in the larger discourse that surrounds the project.

The claim to be doing art, however, does not do away with the interrogations about what, exactly, the artist is doing by engaging communities. Hal Foster has criticized the artist as ethnographer who engages the "real," particularly in the guise of cultural other, without taking into account the critique of ethnography. The artist as ethnographer emerges as "art pass[es] into the expanded field of culture," thus reconfiguring the very materiality and location of art to the space of the museum, to discursive networks, and even social conditions "like desire or disease, AIDS or homelessness" (1996: 184). Add to this culturalization of art the instrumentalization of arts funding, which promotes it, and the "rise of the migrant ethnographic artist" can be seen as a logical outcome (282 n.44), indeed, one that provides service and value for reconfigured arts institutions as well as social service institutions like foundations. It is ironic that the cultural turn or the anthropologization of the arts and other disciplines like criticism and politics, which makes this instrumentalization a means by which the "excluded" make claims to cultural worth, ends up producing authority and legitimacy, particularly in educational and philanthropic settings.

This said, it is also the case that some critics are too fast to dismiss the materials and methods with which these artists work. Such critics are also holding these artists to avant-gardist criteria of effectivity: if the art does not transform the world, if it lapses into a partial nourishment of institutions, then it is a failure. Artists respond in several ways. Manglano-Ovalle points out that the artist may simply be taking advantage of the opportunity for commissions that the current patrons provide. After all, exhibitions are venues for achieving recognition, and they also increase the value of works that circulate in the market. Judith Barry (1998b), another insITE participating artist, argues that critics do not make enough effort to get beyond their own ideological axes. She turns Foster's questions back on him: "Are art writers trained to value our extra-artistic research?" Mauricio Dias and Walter Riedweg, who prepared a project involving the border patrol for insITE2000–2001, also prioritize the intervention of art over a romanticized acquiescence to an overinstrumentalized rhetoric of community and otherness. They prefer to interact with "groups that don't usually work with culture" by provoking questions that enable a vulnerability that in turn yields "more complex and fragile perceptions of them and of ourselves . . . We understand art as a tool to raise questions. Not to solve them but to point to them, making them present and important as the resulting end-products. Art can create space for doubts and fragilities that have more to do with real life than specific results do." [27]

Creating these experiences on one's own, which would be an alternative to inclusion in a project-work program, can be quite arduous, as Dias and Riedweg explain. Their first project, *Devotionalia*, which involved making daily wax castings of the hands and feet of six hundred youth living on the streets of Rio de Janeiro during six months in eighteen poor communities, was self-financed through other kinds of work and the accumulation of substantial debt. Subsequently, they were able to get grants and commissions to exhibit the project in several countries over the next two and a half years (1994–97). Dias and Riedweg tell of the difficulties in carrying out this project on their own in order to make their case for the importance of institutional support, particularly venues like inSITE and other project-work programs, including some biennials. "We simply see that depending on the physical size and the complexity of intentions that an event of contemporary art has, it is absolutely necessary, even desirable, to have a very complex structure of group organization to achieve the original intentions." They speak for many artists in their appreciation to "Carmen [Cuenca], Michael [Krichman] and their staff [for] conduct[ing] communication and making possible the interventions of the artists within this event [which] seem to us not only natural, but logical, since our experience with Devotionalia has taught us that sponsors (private and public) trust institutions, directors, boards and curators more than artists."

Another piece that raises these issues is Krzysztof Wodiczko's video projection of the talking heads of six female maquiladora workers onto the dome of the Centro Cultural Tijuana. They denounced the bosses and men in their lives who abused them. According to the project description, Wodiczko (2000) sought to "give visibility and voice, through the use of advanced media technologies, to women who work in Tijuana's maquiladora industry." At the discussion of his work after the projection (García Canclini, Wodiczko, and Yúdice 2001), Wodizcko explained that he sought to bring into public space controlled by class and gender hierarchies, especially in the Mexican context, the privatized suffering of women. An interesting question is Who worked with those women to achieve those effects? Was it only Wodiczko? What about staff and interns? And if the latter were involved, how do they fit into the artistic process?

Discussions with inSITE staffers Cecilia Garza and Tobias Ostrander revealed that the women had been meeting for about one year from the time Wodiczko first enlisted support in identifying appropriate participants for his project. Garza explained that the process was akin to that of group therapy, and indeed it took a lot of working through — what Wodiczko called "psychological development" at the panel discussion after viewing his project — for the women to get to the point at which they felt they could reveal their lives, above all, the abuse they suffered at the hands of their bosses, husbands, lovers, and authorities. Wodiczko's intentions were to politicize what remains suppressed due to the strong public/private divide in Mexico. The projection of these women's testimonials on the dome of the Centro Cultural Tijuana, the major public building in the city, thus performed the opening up of public space to those who, in an undemocratic society, do not have access to it.

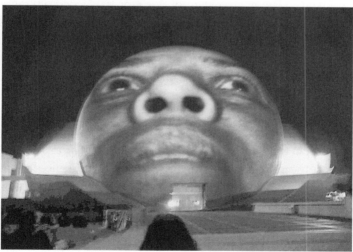

17 and 18. Projections by Krzysztof Wodiczko onto dome of the Centro cultural Tijuana (2000). Photos by George Yúdice.

But it is for this very reason that some critics likened this project to talk shows like *Oprah* and *Sally Jessie Raphael*, where people who are "pathologized" or who suffer their abuse in secret are able, according to pop therapeutic models, to "take charge" of their lives. Some of the show hosts even arrange professional therapy for their guests.[28] Wodiczko countered that his work is not entertainment, where people seeking their fifteen minutes of fame will do anything to display themselves. But a more important difference is that talk shows tend to confine the discussion of pathology to the family setting, whereas Wodiczko sees it as a failure of democracy, understood in psychological terms as the limitation of access to and the staging of conflicts over values in the public sphere or agora, to use the term that he borrowed from Hannah Arendt. Indeed, the space in which private and psychic life are shielded from the public space of the stage was known to the Greeks as *obscene* or offstage. And that is surely how one can characterize a social space in which it is not acceptable for the subordinated (or the "vanquished," to use Wodiczko's term) to enact a public memory of what happened to them.

But, as mentioned above, it took the work of many individuals, in addition to Wodiczko and inSITE staff, to achieve the testimonials we all saw. NGOs like Factor X (grassroots advocates of women's labor and reproduction rights) and a group of women lawyers were part of this process. Aside from the year of preparation, these women must face the prospect of reprisals in response to their testimonials. In one case, a woman revealed to the public that her husband had not sympathized with her suffering from a rape fifteen years before; instead, he asked her if she didn't bring it on herself or even enjoy it. What might that woman's return to her home that night have been like after making such a revelation? What is the artist's responsibility? And what about the staff who worked with these women over the previous year? What will be their continuing investment in this quasi-therapeutic relationship? Is the relationship over for them once the piece is shown? And what are the consequences of bringing the piece (and the relationship) to an end? Indeed, this very question might be asked of inSITE as a whole, for as in the case of Wodiczko's piece, it is the ongoing process rather than the exhibited product that provides the life of the art.

Organization and Insight

I have suggested that the avant-gardist model is no longer in place when art becomes service. Attempts to smash or extend the frame of art's institutionality have been the typical modalities for reconciling art and life. From futurism, dadaism, and surrealism to community-based art, the transubstantiation of art into "reality," bypassing or questioning the frame of museums and galleries, has always seemed to be reined back into some form of institutional explanation. Other strategies, such as accentuating that frame in various quasi-philosophical experiments with the boundaries of the museum (e.g., Daniel Buren's work), have situated the critique of the avant-garde in purely institutional terms. Institutional critique does something similar, with the additional twist that the frame of the institution is further defined in terms of the legitimacy it provides to funders and others who derive cultural, social, political, and economic capital therefrom. It seems, then, that all attempts to get beyond or to highlight the frame accommodate to an avant-gardist upping of the ante such that art and critique gain value at the same time that they are ultimately incorporated into the institution that defines the terms of valuation in the first place.

Instead of accepting the avant-gardist impulse or accommodating art practices into its dialectic, we might inquire into the organization of initiatives like inSITE to understand both what an art event can do and to transform that understanding into a plan of action. If one focuses on inSITE not as an exhibition of authored projects to be interpreted and/or critiqued but as a work in its own right, produced by the actions of the directors, staff, curators, and artists and often redirected by the coinvestigators and collaborators, its reality effects will be more readily discernible. This does not mean, however, that one has to consider inSITE's "complex organization [as] perhaps more impressive than its esthetic results" (M. Duncan 1995: 51). A consideration of the terms on which the legitimacy of conceptual art and community-based art, both of which work with nontraditional materials, is established will lead us to the role of venues like inSITE in producing a range of reality effects.

One work that begins to explore the imbrication of art, organizational arrangements, and sponsorship interests in such an event is Andrea Fraser's *Inaugural Speech* for inSITE97. The speech is prefaced by an explanation that points to the very circumstances of the exhibition as the inspiration for the speech: "The fact that the federal government of Mexico contributed half of the exhibition's budget was largely responsible for the unusual (in the United States) scheduling of official public opening ceremonies, complete with speeches by public officials." Fraser's speech is both an ironic pastiche of these ceremonial discourses as well as an invitation to reflect on the interests that have brought everyone to the exhibition, herself included. The speech opens a window onto the political significance of inSITE through her irony and sarcasm, aimed at the organizers, local institutional brokers and trustees, showcase-seeking politicians, corporate executives, and philanthropists. By highlighting the roles that these actors play, she gets at the contradictions of the region and the exhibition: for example, the recourse to a rhetoric of diversity at the same time that migrant workers are exploited; the desire for activation of public space at the same time that (in another speech, by a "public official") public space is restricted and government's (and therefore corporations') contributions to the tax base for social welfare programs are reduced; the growth of the economy (for business and tourism) in contrast to low wages in the service sector (culture included). The contradictions are to be found not only in the region as territory (i.e., the sites); they are at work in the very venue—insITE—through which the artists' work is made available.

Of the 650 reviews and critical essays written about insITE94, insITE97, and the preparations for insITE2000, not one deals with the year-long preparations, negotiations with public, private, and community organizations, the acquisition of permissions, and so on that make a work possible. In the reviews and critical pieces, collaboration and interaction seem to mean the encounter or working together of two sets of actors, poor (often racialized) people and artists, as if "engagement" were important only in the coming together of these two groups. For the reasons reviewed above, this is a somewhat fetishized understanding of collaboration and public, particularly insofar as the labor of publics goes largely unrecognized. Moreover, there are many other actors, many intermediaries who collaborate in the authorship of these works. For a year or more, artists work with the curators, directors, the directors' staff, and corporate, public, and community representatives (contact with whom is almost always facilitated by directors and staff). Writers often hark back to the avant-gardist notion of bringing art and life together, yet do not appreciate that life (including the everyday arrangements for the projects developed for insITE) flows through a capillary profusion of macro- and micro-institutions and networks of individuals. An understanding of collaboration that takes into account all aspects of the development of projects, and of the larger event (insITE) in which they are included, may imply, without detracting anything from the artists' activity, that they are coauthored in this complex process.

We can begin to inquire about authorship at the most macro level, that is, the sprawlingly vast and open-ended text that insITE provides for all interpreters, including participants of all walks. A feature of this complex process is that it puts the artist in a very particular actantial role. He or she is a content, or better yet, process provider for the directors and curators. I have invoked two metaphors to understand the process. According to the first, the theatrical production, the producers hire directors/scriptwriters, which in the case of insITE97 and insITE2000–2001 are the four curators. They provide an open-ended "script" or agenda for the event, which is not to imply that artists simply carry out any preconceived plan. On the contrary, the curators "already know" that artists are "unpredictable," and it is for this very reason that certain artists are selected to produce "process." Indeed, artists like Iñigo Manglano-Ovalle and Roman de Salvo point out that regardless of the curatorial mission, many artists gladly accept the opportunity to participate in these high-profile programs and then do whatever it is they are most inclined to.[29] That is, recognizing that institutions *use* artists, the artists must try to stake out a space of possibility or an opportunity for a "line of flight" within those constraints.[30] The script or set of program themes is only a point of departure, and the artists do depart (Manglano-Ovalle 2000; de Salvo 2000). For codirector Krichman (2000), what drives insITE conceptually and what he finds "fascinating and amazing is to see how artists can construct and deconstruct space; cause us to look at things in a different way, such as what results from, say, a video montage of flows across the border or from the dialogue between an artist and an engineer at Qualcomm." Although insITE is not a traditional art institution like a museum, it has, like museums, particular needs, which artists' projects, following Andrea Fraser's service model, can provide (1997: 115).

When viewed from the "services" perspective, it becomes obvious that the serendipity of artists getting us to see things in a different way is an institutional need—regarding their publics, their educative mission, their fundraising responsibilities for outreach to nontraditional "communities," their cutting-edge or international status—specific to the context of an institution, which does not "just happen" but which must be produced (A. Fraser 1997). Krichman and Cuenca have a staff that assists artists at almost every step in the process. As one staff member reported, "We are frustrated about the extent to which artists are asking that we help produce their work. Artists get frustrated by bureaucracy, but they are asking staff to help in the production."[31] Often, this involves solving difficult problems, such as finding the right service provider for, say, drilling holes in monumental granite cubes to transform them into large die, or even doing the impossible, such as getting permission from the Immigration and Naturalization Service and/or the border patrol to open holes in the border fence. When such endeavors do not, predictably, pan out, staff helps to conceive alternatives. Staff members also make an enormous personal investment in the projects and the artists, including ferrying them to sites and suppliers, having long discussions with them into the wee hours, and investing the unmeasurable labor of love (of art) and the labor of producing process. This investment includes critical work that does not always surface in the exhibition materials like the catalogue and guide. Many of the staff, in fact, have studied art or are interns from curatorial programs. Indeed, some of the information on the day-to-day mediations by staff briefly described here as well as a wealth of artistic/bureaucratic troubleshooting episodes are eloquently captured in Sofia Hernández's *Transitio*, a semifictional chronicle of her stint as an insITE intern. The staff's function as a sounding board for an artist's project is a kind of labor that extends beyond wage work and approximates the emotional and nonpublic labor usually associated with unrecognized and uncompensated "women's work."

For insITE2000–2001, the script was structured by a thematic complex of landscape-traffic-syntax. The artists were to flesh out this script with their process-oriented works and installations. The entire region — historical, territorial, cultural, political, and virtual — was their stage. The audience was differentially constructed, according to the various needs and demands of the event. High-profile works brought in the international art community (even if they resided in the region). Educational and community engagement projects brought in the "nontraditional audiences" (i.e., poor Chicanos, Native Americans, and African Americans). Residencies, workshops, and symposia brought in the academics, critics, and other intellectuals who produce and distribute the meaningfulness of insITE at various levels and scales. The injunction to involve the community resonated, for example, with the agendas of the Rockefeller Foundation[32] or the mandates of municipal, state, and federal arts agencies. There was also an urban-institutional audience, which dovetailed with corporate (especially high-tech), real estate, and tourism interests. The binational audience is of great interest to political actors and intellectuals. The international scale glazes the parties and receptions given by public and private sponsors with the cultural capital exuded by high-profile biennials. This multipurpose, multiaudience, multilabored event must be produced. And it is in the production process that the theater and the maquiladora work well, superimposed on each other.

I hasten to add that I use these metaphors not to suggest that there is anything sinister about this process-oriented art or that the artists' labor is alienated, but to focus on production (of artworks, of interactions, of audiences, of sundry forms of cultural capital). Moreover, whether artists are independent enough to do what they want is not the point of my reflection. They are, in fact, supposed to do what they want. As Mary Jane Jacob has said with regard to *Culture in Action*, "I did not invent or tell these artists to make this kind of work. This type of activity was already happening; I just drew a frame around it" (1996: 43). It is precisely that frame that raises the virtual walls of the artistic theater or maquiladora within which authority is instantiated. Indeed, to frame is to author (Derrida 1979), to marshal into one's own intentionality a range of varying phenomena.[33] The directors and curators, wittingly or not, hire the artists to be flexible, to rearrange institutions and sites, to set off chemical reactions among publics. That nontraditional audiences are both embraced and contribute to a less institutionally sanctioned experience is important, particularly to the institution of art, regardless of whether these audiences are "unfashionable." In any case, as Jacob herself recognizes, community-based art can have a downside. For Jacob, the danger is its transformation into a style that can be embraced by the institution, thus subordinating the empowerment of people to the advancement of art as institution. This incorporation should come as no surprise; it is the experience of the historical avant-garde, which has always sought to break the frame of the institution, only to have that very rupture installed within it. As such, the incorporation is expected and familiar, and curators and artists are compelled to push the envelope—the institutional frame—once again, this time establishing a "dialogue" with the community from which they would want the art to "spring organically."

However, the critique of collaborative, process-oriented, and community-based art goes deeper than the deconstruction of this avant-gardist condition, raising problems that will not be solved by pushing the envelope further. In fact, it is likely that in working through cultural and political rifts, the turn to culture implicit in collaboration, process, and community is reaching hitherto unmined recesses that are socially and economically productive for new structures of power under the aegis of new global-local logics of accumulation. This is not to echo Timothy Luke's (1996) cynical critique of *Culture in Action*: that artists and curators build their careers because corporations and foundations are the main sponsors of activist art and that they in fact do not eliminate the social problems they presumably set out to address. To be sure, these are very real problems inherent in the contradictory space that community-based, activist art practices inhabit. But this is a critique that Jacob has already anticipated and dealt with by eschewing the formulaicization of activism, which will only lead to status within institutionality. Miwon Kwon comes closer to the problem in her critique of site-specificity: "Inasmuch as the current socioeconomic order thrives on the (artificial) production and (mass) consumption of difference (for difference's sake), the siting of art in 'real' places can also be a means to *extract* the social and historical dimensions *out* of places to variously serve the thematic drive of an artist, satisfy institutional demographic profiles, or fulfill the fiscal needs of a city" (1997: 105).

This is not a contradiction or problem that can be eliminated by more of the same: pushing the envelope further or latching onto an "externality" (displacing mainstream with excluded constituencies), both of which only exacerbate the avant-gardist compulsion to absorb the margins. Kwon argues convincingly that the embrace of a nomadic deterritorialization as a response to the enlistment of culturally and historically specific sites for new forms of capital accumulation is not a panacea because "the ability to deploy multiple, fluid identities in and of itself is a privilege of mobilization that has a specific relationship to power" (1997: 109). But her solution—"finding a terrain between mobilization and specificity"—a kind of Bhabhaian "third space" of relationality that addresses "differences of adjacencies," though it does make for an aesthetics, does not escape the dilemma of making that space available to power, thus accommodating to the dialectic of the avant-garde's compulsive discovery of new spaces and practices to be absorbed by institutionality. Indeed, many third spaces are enjoying curatorial attention as well as the attention of publishers, marketers, and even social theorists with new governmental agendas.[34] The search for an art or a cultural practice to reconnect us against the alienating force of the museum is akin to Habermas's postulation of an ideal face-to-face communication that stands outside of or preexists modern institutionality. It may be, however, that the advent of presumably alienating modern communications has brought that ideal into existence as the counterfactual to which it aspires. That ideal subjectivity identified with culture, which Brenson identifies with healing, can be characterized as the fuel on which modern institutions feed. The unfolding of art into culture, which promises to heal the rift between everyday life and institutions, ends up providing more fuel. It is then to culture, as the set of processes whereby community and social life are produced and reproduced, that we might venture to understand the creation of the new public art.

The Expediency of Culture

As processes of production and reproduction, labor stands at the heart of culture. Such a formulation should constitute a rule of cultural analysis. It is a useful rule in examining, for example, the production of value in the media.

Labor is the attention extracted from audiences, which is in turn sold to advertisers. Perhaps at the heart of this process is the mediation provided by curators, who can commission artists to mobilize the labor of publics. Their function goes beyond that of auteur to that of producers who carry out the curatorial, administrative, educational, marketing, and public information tasks as well as serve as intermediaries of global politics.[35] In inSITE all of these tasks are carried out by the codirectors, who work closely with the curators, artists, and contacts (coinvestigators) necessary to carry out the projects. Part of this has to do with the salience of issue-oriented exhibitions or project-work programs. These exhibitions and programs require high managerial expertise, the kind necessary for devising marketing plans, and the curators (like the artists) are brought in to realize these plans. The new structure of cultural institutions requires such knowledge/cultural management. Relatedly, a new form of labor is emerging in our so-called postmodern age, a form of labor patterned on the creative, innovative practices of the artist. We might say that artists are the "mental workers" who bring the notion of "assemblage" into the postmodern era of flexible production (A. Ross 2000). The very term "cultural workers," so dear to those who advocate the shift from art to culture, conveys the specialization in the production and reproduction of publics.

Nonalienated activity is, of course, the major utopian aspiration in capitalist modernity, and the artist's creativity is the emblem par excellence of nonalienation. Marx located workers' loss of humanity, their alienation from themselves, in wage labor, which alienates the products of their activity from their "inner world" (1959: 70). Because labor does not belong to the worker's "essential being," by which Marx means social being, "in his work therefore, he does not affirm himself but denies himself, does not feel content but unhappy, does not develop freely his mental and physical energy but mortifies his body and ruins his mind" (72). Subjection to the machines of capitalist production, which transforms workers into a veritable "industrial army" (Marx and Engels [1848] 1967: 17), actualizes what should otherwise be a process of self-activity into wage labor. In contrast, culture expands self-activity.

Some recent discussions of the new economy, however, argue that as culture, largely defined as "self-activity" within a collectivity, becomes an increasingly functional part of the economy (in communications, the media, and the Internet), it is itself transformed into a commodity. Marx, and the Frankfurt School after him, remarked on the illusory character of commodification, whereby "definite social relations between men [are transformed into] the fantastic form of a relation between things" (1977: 105). That is, the quantification of labor congealed in exchangeable products conceals the collective character of labor. But in our postmodern period, capitalism does not so much conceal as continually transform into commodities whatever quality or use-value is left. As Jameson (1984) characterized it, late capitalism has penetrated the last two recesses of modernity: the third world and the unconscious. Curiously, both of these spaces are implicated in the importance for cultural institutions and foundations of community-based and processual works. Marx had written that in the mystified understanding of economists, " 'riches' are the attribute of men . . . or a community [whereas] value is the attribute of commodities" (1977: 120).

The mystification persists, with communities "enriched" or "empowered" by art while directors, curators, and artists derive value.[36] Artists can be conceived as the service providers who extend the reach of capital to those poor communities who represent the third world, or the third world within the first, enabling them to yield value for cultural institutions that play an important if not always direct role in urban redevelopment, cultural tourism, and, most important, a social return on investment for cultural development that can be transformed into market value. Social theory has taken up community as a new ethical space in which people are supposed to find their well-being.

This is not the same community of nostalgic thinkers who, in the nineteenth and twentieth centuries, lamented the loss of organic connection in the face of bureaucratization and the market. Community is a governmental concept, a strategic notion for the shaping of behavior because it enables the production of value where previously it was not thought to inhere. For this reason, as Nikolas Rose has observed, "communities became zones to be investigated, mapped, classified, documented, interpreted, their vectors explained to enlightened professionals-to-be in countless college courses and to be taken into account in numberless encounters between professionals and their clients, whose individual conduct is now made to be intelligible in terms of the beliefs and values of 'their community' " (1999: 175). And the labor of this making intelligible is what culture has become, an insight that enables us to rethink political economy as cultural economy.

Following Bourdieu and Foucault, we can discern a dual role in the deployment of culture in capitalist modernity. On the one hand, culture (including knowledge of the arts and education) is a noneconomic mode of establishing distinction, which in turn reinforces class position. This account is a variant of Marx's account of ideology—inscribed in law, morality, religion, and culture—that supports the bourgeoisie's ethics of individuality and freedom, which in turn enables the bourgeoisie to "[recognise] this self-alienation as *its own power* and thus ha[ve] the *semblance* of a human existence" (Marx and Engels 1975: chap. 4). Within this framework, the bourgeois museum became the elite temple of the arts. Complementarily, culture also reins in the proletariat, as a form of discipline or set of behavioral techniques that "ma[k]e it possible to increase the useful size of multiplicities by decreasing the inconveniences of the power which, in order to make them useful, must control them" (Foucault 1977: 3).

Tony Bennett has described the very same nineteenth-century museum that produced the cultural capital of the bourgeoisie as a disciplinary apparatus for rendering the working class docile: "Through the institution of a division be-tween the producers and consumers of knowledge—a division which assumed an architectural form in the relations between the hidden spaces of the mu-seum, where knowledge was produced and organised in camera, and its public spaces, where knowledge was offered for passive consumption—the museum became a site where bodies, constantly under surveillance, were to be rendered docile" (1990). This shaping activity is not necessarily a punishing one; combin-ing some of the features of the fair, the museum's spatial arrangement and set of rules trained visitors in ways of dressing, walking, speaking, and behaving in public (Bennett 1995: 102–103).

The historical avant-garde challenged both the cultural capital and disci-pline of the arts but was ultimately incorporated into the institution of art by way of the market, new fetishizations of otherness, or bureaucratization. By the 1960s, anticommercial "alternative art spaces" were founded by grassroots artist groups, and otherness could no longer be conceived of abstractly but as marginalized groups in the United States. Then decolonizing intellectuals de-manded recognition for non-Western cultural formations. By the 1970s, how-ever, the arts organization bureaucracy of the NEA and state arts councils had begun to incorporate and in the process rein in these groups. The result has not been primarily the marketization of alternativity, although this has hap-pened, but the extension of the alternative into projects that furthered state and capital interests such as "boosting local economies (through the gentrify-ing influence of artists' organizations in certain neighborhoods, particularly in small cities), reviving old buildings (particularly abandoned or disused govern-ment or industrial facilities), promoting research and development (by offering 'laboratories' or 'institutes' for creative experimentation in the knowledge in-dustry), and providing reskilling for underemployed citizens (highly educated artists)" (Wallis forthcoming b).

Such alternative groups also extended into the community, "empowering" non-art-going groups, largely based on notions of cultural citizenship, whereby democratic participation was thought to be fostered by activating non-mainstream cultures in public space. This is a global phenomenon with specific applications in different societies. In chapter 5 I examined the effects of this discourse of community in connection with the cultural economy of youth culture in Rio de Janeiro. Mary K. Coffey (forthcoming) has written a ground-breaking study of community museums in Mexico, taking the new governmental discourse as her point of departure. The Mexican state has not weakened, at least not with respect to its service to a new regime of capital accumulation, which requires a different notion of self-actualization. Mexicans are no longer to find this ethical foundation in the national state, which promoted mestizaje under the leadership of the PRI. As the national model was eroded by post-Fordism and neoliberalism, a new communitarian discourse emerged such that in the new decentralized institutions (especially the community museums), "the community gains agency as a producer of knowledge about itself. The rationalizing and professionalizing process involved in becoming competent historians and curators helps to construct autonomous groups equipped to self-govern." This emphasis on community across North America provides a common ground for the relevance of the artist or curator as service provider in venues like inSITE. Indeed, even if this still goes unrecognized in Mexico as supporters of inSITE seek to position Mexican artists among the international cultural elite, this coincidence is advantageous for arguing for the continued support of inSITE on the part of the new government. This recognition, moveover, will put the last nail in the coffin of the avant-garde.

Culture, in this view and following Gramscian theory, was understood as a "terrain of struggle." But the content of culture receded in importance when the instrumental usefulness of the claim to difference as a warrant gained legitimacy. It might be said that previous understandings of culture—canons of artistic excellence, symbolic patterns that give coherence to and thus endow a group of people or society with human worth, or culture as discipline—give way to the expediency of culture. In our era, *claims* to difference and culture are expedient insofar as they presumably lead to the empowerment of a community.

There are several senses in which the idea of the expediency of culture as resource might be understood here, but I should like to make clear that it is not my purpose to dismiss this strategy as a perversion of culture or as a cynical reduction of patterns of symbols or ways of life to "mere" politics. Such dismissals are often premised on a nostalgic or reactionary desire for the restoration of the high place of culture, presumably discredited by philistines who really don't believe in it anyway. My argument is that the cultural economy to which I have briefly referred is not alone in making recourse to culture as an expedient, as a resource for other ends. We can find this strategy in many different sectors of contemporary life: the use of high culture (e.g., museums, cultural development areas, cities transformed into theme parks) for the purposes of urban development; the promotion of native cultures and national patrimonies to be consumed in tourism; the creation of transnational culture industries as complements of supranational integration, whether in the European Union or Latin America; and the redefinition of intellectual property as forms of culture for the purposes of spurring capital accumulation in informatics, communications, pharmaceuticals, and entertainment.

In chapter 1 I reviewed several expedient projects of this instrumentalist character of cultural policy. *American Canvas*, a report commissioned by the NEA, synthesized six town hall–like discussions with people from all sectors of society interested in salvaging the support system for the arts. It made recommendations to tap into venues that command public funds, even those earmarked for roads, sewers, and prisons (Larson 1997: 83).

Larry Grossberg (1999) makes the interesting argument that in the postmodern period, ideology is increasingly beside the point. His end-of-ideology proposition is premised not on the demise of communism but on the rearticulation of political economy. Unlike Fukuyama's formulation, however, the new global conjuncture of today does not portend the end of history. Modernity required ideology to camouflage the instrumentality of cultural management. But today, as Grossberg argues, the globalization of culture has led to an "increasingly cynical inflection to the logic of ideology," such that it no longer operates unconsciously. Paraphrasing Slavoj Žižek, he argues that if ideology implies that "people don't know what they are doing but they are doing it anyway," then the expediency of culture as instrumental performativity implies that "they know what they are doing but they are doing it anyway" (43–44 n.52). Engaging in the struggle for hegemony, then, means that we know what we do and we do it to further our interests. Once we recognize that only interests are at play, then there is no role for the avant-garde, which endeavored to uncover the intoxication of life buried under ideology. We do not have to understand this postmodern condition only in the cynical mode proposed by Grossberg. What we have, quite simply, is the untenability of any ultimate ground of authority and legitimacy. The avant-garde's recourse, for example, to the value of intoxication or the phenomenological body's resistance is now readily dismissed as based on the intoxication or resistance of specifically gendered or raced or sexed or aged bodies.

Bill Readings (1996) elaborates further on the transformation in the experience of culture. In the post-Fordist era, culture no longer mediates between the ethnic nation and the rational state to produce a distinct national identity. This does not mean that culture disappears, but only that it is reconverted; it becomes useful but no longer legitimized as the medium through which subjects are civilized or, to use the language of early twentieth-century cultural policy, become "ethically incomplete" (Miller 1998). Ethical incompleteness, indeed, is a variant of that performative force that requires subjects to come into being by reiterating norms. According to Readings, the emerging global system of capitalism no longer needs "a cultural content in terms of which to interpellate and manage subjects," which is not to say that subjects do not consume culture more voraciously than ever before. In other words, as culture expands and becomes ever more central to the economy, its importance in establishing a Bourdieuian distinction wanes. Capitalism now is committed only to "monetary subjects without money" who are merely "the shadow of money's substance." Consequently, "if the sphere of the ideological [and, I would add, the cultural] has become visible (not only in critical theory and the academy but literally everywhere), this is because it is not where the real game is being played anymore" (Grossberg 1999: 5). This displacement of the real renders ineffectual avant-gardist drives to sublate art and life.

It is not so much that power dispenses with culture, but that it no longer needs it to shape ethical subjects of the nation. Culture is "freed," so to speak, to become a generator of value in its own right. And it is increasingly traveling speedily along the same media as finance capital and especially the new economy. If, in capitalist modernity, all other spheres of life were subordinated to capitalist production, in so-called postmodern society, culture plays the major role. According to Marx, "The Communist revolution is the most radical rupture with traditional property relations" (Marx and Engels [1848] 1967: 36), but it must be recognized that capitalism itself has transmutated for its survival by shifting from a regime of ownership to a network-based global economy founded on ideologies of "systems thinking and consensus building" underpinned by telecommunications and "access networks" rather than direct ownership (Rifkin 2000: 13–21). Within this framework one can envisage artists like Jordan Crandall working with high-tech corporations on the development of new uses for their technologies as "free labor" that may yield new, hitherto unimagined uses of a Qualcomm or Packet product. Similarly, one can think of community-based artists working in poor neighborhoods that are poorly served by city services or that are racked by violence and racial conflict as "outsourcers" and suppliers of process that enhances the value of cities.

As Barbrook argues, the "free labor" that is touted as part of the high-tech "gift economy" where people "work, play, love, learn and discuss with other people . . . collaborate with other people" (1999: 135, qtd. in Terranova 2000: 36), is an "important force within the reproduction of the labor force in late capitalism as a whole" (Terranova 2000: 36). Like the collaboration of communities and other constituencies in the production of insITE projects, we do not always recognize forms of labor such as "chat, real-life stories, mailing lists, newsletters, and so on" (38). The important point made by Terranova is that although these forms of cultural activity have not been brought into existence to meet the economic needs of capital, they are nevertheless "part of a process of economic experimentation with the creation of monetary value out of knowledge/culture/affect" (38). This does not mean that cultural labor is only co-opted or exploited labor; we must remember that it is willingly given and not on the basis of financial remuneration.

To the degree that this is the case, we cannot simply dismiss collaboration of the type fostered by insITE. Instead, insITE itself becomes the site for examining the relations between cultural labor and value as well as in the value-producing circumstances of binationality and transnationality. insITE should not conceive of itself only as a venue for artists' projects. More than any other biennial or art festival, it has brought together all the different forms of cultural labor and in doing so has established a hemispheric processing zone whose organization makes visible and palpable how the cultural economy functions. But what do we do once we see how it functions? Critique of this venue will not produce the disalienating effects believed to ensue from the uncovering of ideological structures and processes characteristic of ideology critique. Nor will we get in touch with our phenomenological body or have a limit experience. What insITE calls for, in my view, is to become a user, a collaborator who intervenes in order to have the labor expended recognized and compensated. Venues like insITE become important sites for the reformulation of cultural policy in a post-Fordist, globalizing world, not from the vantage point of a government agency, foundation, or university office, but by engaging as an archaeologist-practitioner in the process.

CONCLUSION

Culture in a Time of Crisis

Most of the uses of culture that I have reviewed in this book have been prem-ised on a reasonably stable world. Under those circumstances, museums and renovated waterfronts can contribute to the economic development of cities and attract innovators for local industry; community artists can help trouble-shoot acute social problems like racism, segregation, and residential displace-ment; supranational cultural integration can provide the means for practi-tioners from peripheral countries to compete with those in the first world; consumption can be a means for practicing citizenship; and so on. But what happens when there is economic crisis, terrorism, or war? Can we always rely on a stable world? And if not, what is the role of culture in times of ongoing crisis, as has been the case in Bosnia and Colombia?

I broach these questions in relation to the September 11 attacks. Indeed, I was working on this conclusion when the attacks took place and put it on hold for several months as I endeavored to understand the political and cul-tural underpinnings of the tragic events, both the attacks themselves and the U.S. government's responses within the country and abroad. In the face of all this, my arguments about the expediency of culture seemed incredibly petty. What did it matter, I thought, if culture was invoked to bolster civil society, solve social problems, or aid in urban development, some of the uses of culture that I examine in this book? The world seemed to be on the verge of catas-trophe and there was no cultural practice that would change that dreadful eventuality.

Culture, of course, was not absent. It is constitutive of the very spectacu-larity—pastiched from Hollywood, that most American of exports—that the terrorists sought and achieved. They struck at the symbols of global power that subtend the reach of Hollywood; indeed, representatives of the U.S. audio-visual industry have been leaders in the global trade accords of GATT and its

successor, the WTO. But even if we understand culture more anthropologi-
cally—as the encounter and reproduction of values, identities, and rhetorics—
the reaction at home of both the conservative government and the multicultural
left, was to perform also, with great spectacularity, the new "American Creed"
of cultural diversity, so pervasively shaped by identity politics, the media, and
consumerism, as the touchstone of our "freedom," confirming what is, in my
view, a deep-rooted collective delusion of exceptionalism.

September 11, Diversity, and Racial Profiling: Americocentric Views

The Bush administration astutely sought to parlay its tutti frutti (albeit homogeneously conservative) multicultural composition into political capital, reconciling diversity and national unity, and simultaneously blanket-bombing
Afghanistan (champing at the bit to strike at Iraq as well) while making
diplomatic efforts to elude an all-out "clash of civilizations." In his influential
Clash of Civilizations and the Remaking of World Order, Samuel Huntington (1996)
argues that the post–cold war rivalry among seven distinctive world cultures
or civilizations could set off new wars, particularly against the West: "Such a
war . . . could come about from the escalation of a fault line war between groups
from different civilizations, most likely involving Muslims on one side and non-
Muslims on the other." In Huntington's view, the United States, the leader of
the West, nationally and morally weakened by tolerance for diverse cultures, can
implode and take down with it all of Western civilization. Under the current circumstances, however, the Bush administration, contra Huntington, tempered
the affirmation of European-derived Western heritage as a means to facilitate
an alliance of Muslim and other nations needed in the counterattack on terrorism. Donning the mantle of diversity, it sought to create a bridge between the
national agenda of unity and the international political agenda of gaining support for military strikes against countries that not only harbor terrorists but
also suppress diversity. Indeed, such tolerance for diversity is touted as a unique
feature of U.S. society. Rarely invoked as "hyphenated cultures," we now hear
references to Arab-Americans, Pakistani-Americans, and the like, in part because the hyphen is seen as a cultural resource for explaining the compatibility
of the American Creed with Islam. "We're going to tell Pakistanis how good a
life, we as Muslims, live here in the U.S. Freedom of speech, freedom of religion, human rights, justice for all—this is exactly what Islam is," said one of
eight Pakistani American goodwill ambassadors who traveled to their country
of origin to explain U.S. society (Domowitz 2001).

On September 13, Assistant Attorney General Ralph F. Boyd Jr. of the Civil Rights Division released the following statement:

> The Attorney General has made clear that any act of violence or discrimination against a person based on the perceived race, religion or national origin of that person is contrary to our fundamental principles and the laws of the United States. His statement is a reminder to all Americans that Americans of Arab or South Asian descent and people of the Muslim faith were also injured and killed in Tuesday's attacks. In addition, they also are — along with other Americans — involved in relief operations, and other efforts to alleviate suffering. Any threats of violence or discrimination against Arab or Muslim Americans or Americans of South Asian descent are not just wrong and un-American, but also are unlawful and will be treated as such. (U.S. State Department 2001d)

At the National Day of Prayer and Remembrance Service, President Bush invoked the maxim "Adversity introduces us to ourselves," recognizing therein "a national unity . . . of every faith, and every background" (U.S. State Department 2001a). Meeting with Muslim community leaders, Bush affirmed that "Arab Americans, Americans who are Muslim by faith" are just as patriotic as other Americans (U.S. State Department 2001c). And in mid-December, he welcomed twenty Muslim children to the White House to celebrate Eid al-fitr, the Muslim holiday marking the end of Ramadan (U.S. State Department 2001b). The most spectacular multicultural expression, however, was the interfaith prayer service organized by the Giuliani administration at Yankee Stadium. It was like a Benetton ad brought to life, with rabbis and imams holding hands in prayer alongside priests, politicians, and myriad media celebrities, African Americans and Latinos well represented among them. The United States needed to demonstrate via spectacle that it is indeed a community of diverse cultures united behind the American Creed of freedom and justice.

President Bush himself essayed various genres of spectacle, resorting at times to a John Waynesque "we want him dead or alive" in reference to bin Laden, or mimicking Indiana Jones in the latter-day crusade billed as Operation Infinite Justice. At the same time as his administration celebrated Arab and Muslim Americans and repudiated attacks on them, it also launched a racially profiled covert witch hunt of these very residents. Even one of Bush's own bodyguards, an Arab American, was detained at an airport ("Guard for Bush Isn't Allowed Aboard Flight" 2001). The Bush administration issued executive orders for trials by military commissions of suspected terrorists, the indefinite detention of some noncitizens, and the "voluntary" interviewing of more than five thousand mostly Middle Eastern men living in the United States. And to deflect criticism, it stopped tallying the number of people hauled in by the antiterror dragnet, which at last count in November was almost twelve hundred (Randall 2001). According to an ACLU report dated December 14, the administration held over five hundred detainees in federal prisons and refused to provide any information on them (Nojeim 2001). Another ACLU report points out that the USA Patriot Act, in accordance with which these actions have been taken, was at odds with the Constitution by holding "detainees . . . for weeks, sometimes months, before charg[ing them] with a crime or immigration offense" (ACLU 2002). Almost a year later, the Defense Department refused to state how many detainees it held or to release their names (Shenon 2002).

This blatant lapse in the rule of law (a lapse in the American Creed or a constitutive feature of it, as Gunnar Myrdal suggested nearly sixty years ago?) was deemed beyond criticism by Attorney General Ashcroft. He lambasted critics of the covert detentions and military tribunals with the following words: "To those who scare peace-loving people with phantoms of lost liberty, my message is this: Your tactics only aid terrorists . . . They give ammunition to America's enemies" (qtd. in Balmaseda 2001). The media, especially Fox, MSNBC, and CNN, which virtually became propaganda organs of the administration, and tabloids like the Daily News and New York Post that echoed its recriminations in their jingoistic and hypocritical defense of "freedom and democracy," failed to provide a serious exploration of root causes. One can, to be sure, read critical op-eds in the New York Times and the Washington Post, not to mention more progressive fora like The Nation or Z Magazine, or access the Web sites of the ACLU, Counterpunch, the World Socialist Web Site, Global Solidarity Dialogue, or the International Network on Disarmament and Globalization. But a critical media pedagogy is not a fundamental aspect of the American Creed. Without it, the vast majority of people seek their information from network news, CNN, and the tabloids, precisely those venues that foment jingoism.

Civil society joined the fray, with right-wingers like Jerry Falwell and Pat Robertson reviling not only terrorists and critics of the administration, but extending their bile to those with whom they disagree and reprising the culture wars: "the pagans, and the abortionists, and the feminists, and the gays and the lesbians who are actively trying to make that an alternative lifestyle, the ACLU, People for the American Way—all of them who have tried to secularize America" (Falwell 2001). Many commentators have argued convincingly that these right-wingers and the Taliban share the same impulse to banish those with whom they disagree. This attitude extends to academia, which these zealots fantasize as a hotbed of traitors and degenerates. Right-wing organizations like the American Council of Trustees and Alumni, a conservative non-profit watchdog group against liberal tendencies in academia, listed the names of scholars and students whose criticisms of the Bush administration have earned them the infamy of being anti-American (Eakin 2001). Beginning with a quote from board member Lynne Cheney encouraging the study of American history, the Council's statement was aimed at those, mostly U.S. professors, who put that history at risk by "morally equivocating" or denouncing the United States as it wages war against terrorism. Liberals who invoke "tolerance and diversity as antidotes to evil" are thus painted as the "the weak link in America's response to the attack" (J. Martin and Neal 2001).

U.S. civil society also rose to the occasion by helping the victims, collecting funds, and organizing commemorations like the ones at Union Square and Washington Square in New York City; nevertheless, the media provided little coverage of the antiracist and antiwar events throughout the country. I will return to these protests below. Here I would like to continue with an examination of the American Creed of diversity.

Despite the Bush administration's staging of diversity, many progressives were worried about attacks on Arabs and South Asians and other "people of color" who might bear the brunt of nationalist lust for vengeance. Notwithstanding progressives' fears of racial profiling, many blacks and Latinos declared their allegiance to the Bush administration's war on terrorism, if we are to believe the press and pollsters.[1]

Another curious "fact" that was reported is that "the public has a better opinion of Muslim-Americans than it did before the attacks." Polls show that favorable views increased from 45 percent in March to 59 percent in December 2001 (Pew Research Center 2001b). In view of the above-mentioned detentions and covert investigations, antiracist activism is crucial, for it is clear that race — in this case, the racialization of as yet "uncategorized" Arabs — continues to draw a line in the sand of U.S. society. The very image of the "terrorist" can be racialized. But the worldwide complexity of the terrorist attacks and the ensuing U.S. "war on terrorism" cannot be explained away by recourse to this interpretive schema. U.S. government and corporate elites' interests in the oil and weapons industries may be inflected by race, but these interests and the myriad machinations on their behalf are much larger and more complex than questions of "color."

In this book, particularly in chapter 2, I have questioned the applicability of U.S. interpretive categories to Latin America, and the same can be done for the

Middle East and South Asia. It is not surprising that racial profiling should have emerged as such an important issue, both for the government agencies that practiced it as well as for the college and university critics who saw that practice as yet another expression of racism. Fortunately, experts in Middle Eastern and South Asian studies were sought out to provide analyses based on in-depth knowledge of these regions that did not simply reproduce U.S. presuppositions or social imperatives to perform. Contrary to some press reports, these explanations did not involve justifications of the attacks, but the U.S. role in stoking terrorism was clearly laid out. At my university, these experts explained Islamic law, the social, cultural, and political differences in Islam, the contradictory expressions of modernity in the countries of the region, the colonial and postcolonial struggles both during and after the cold war, and the legacy of wrongheaded U.S. support for profoundly undemocratic groups, such as the fundamentalists who eventually made up the Al Qaeda terrorist network to battle the Soviet Union, which had backed the socialist modernizing government of Noor Mohammed Taraki, president of Afghanistan's Revolutionary Council (1978–79).[2]

Much has been written about the conditions that generated terrorist networks against the United States and other Western/Northern countries. The progressive left, which is by no means homogeneous, has more or less arrived at a consensus on "why they hate us." It is not on account of culture or the freedoms embodied in the American Creed. Many Arabs and Muslims were radicalized or came to sympathize with radicals because of the United States' steadfast support for Israel; the bombings of Iraq during the 1991 Gulf War and so many other U.S. military interventions have nurtured that "hate." British foreign correspondent Robert Fisk (2001a) writes, "This is not the war of democracy versus terror that the world will be asked to believe in the coming days. It is also about American missiles smashing into Palestinian homes and U.S. helicopters firing missiles into a Lebanese ambulance in 1996 and American shells crashing into a village called Qana and about a Lebanese militia — paid and uniformed by America's Israeli ally — hacking and raping and murdering their way through refugee camps." Fisk (2001b) even suggests that bin Laden might have lured the United States into bombing Afghanistan to turn the Islamic world against it. The more the United States bombs these countries, the more will some of their citizens be driven to the desperation of suicide bombing, as in the Israeli-Palestinian conflict.

In an attempt to get beyond thinking as usual, some of the teach-in organizers formulated topics of discussion that would "look more toward the future than the past: What should be our national response to the calamitous events of last week? How does a civil society function in light of terrorist threats? How does the Left articulate its vision(s) of peace and democracy in the face of knee-jerk nationalism? Is it possible for us on the Left to be patriotic, and, if so, how can we articulate our patriotism in ways that won't be co-opted by warmongers? How do we empower ourselves to have an impact on policy?" (email memo, September 19, 2001). These are crucial questions and signal a need to consider premises, such as patriotism—and I would add religion and international tribunals for trying terrorists—that are not characteristic of the cultural left. But they have to become part of its agenda. Does September 11 mark a new direction for progressive activism? How did it affect the antiglobalization movement that emerged in Seattle in 1999?

The Cultural Consequences of September 11

To get a sense of the cultural impact of September 11 in its most immediate form, consider the devastation of the infrastructure that supports cultural activities. The destruction of the Twin Towers resulted in a loss of "office-space equivalent to entire downtown areas of major American cities": 13.5 million square feet destroyed and another 17 million square feet rendered useless in damaged buildings in the area. This affected 10 percent of the total available office space in the city (Staley 2001), as well as diminished the economic activity that fifty thousand workers and seventy thousand daily visitors generated. The attacks also tripped an already failing economy into a tailspin, with a budget deficit of $5 billion for 2002. It is estimated that the damage from the World Trade Center attack will reach $83 billion and cost the city over 114,000 jobs in 2002 in addition to the 125,000 lost in the fourth quarter of 2001 (Joyce 2001; Lipton and Cooper 2002). Aside from the sadness and shock produced by the destruction of a crucial part of the cityscape (even if, in this writer's estimation, the towers were an architectural eyesore) and grief over the loss of three thousand lives, an enormous blow was dealt to museums, theaters, galleries, concert halls, and other cultural institutions. The tourism industry, which contributed nearly $30 billion and 282,000 jobs to the New York economy in 2000 (NYC & Company 2001) and which is a mainstay of the arts, will "be severely curtailed from almost all [travel] markets," according to a report of the International Labour Office (2001). Hotel occupancy went from 84.6 percent in 2000 to 72.5 percent in 2001 and is expected to fall even further to 68.5 percent (McDowell 2001). In less than two weeks after the attack, five Broadway plays had closed, one hundred actors were laid off, and the theater sector had lost $5 million (McKinley 2001). These figures escalated in the ensuing weeks and months, and will lead to a cut of 20 percent in the city's arts and culture budget, which was $137 million in 2001 ("Survival of the Arts" 2001). Another victim was the Guggenheim Museum, which had already suffered from overexpansion before the attack and now had to deal with 60 percent fewer visitors,[3] a reduction that seriously impacted revenues because a significant portion of the operating budget is from earned income. Moreover, it was forced to lay off 40 percent of its employees, close its Lower Manhattan annex, and defer the ambitious new museum that Frank Gehry was to build on the East River (M. Lewis 2001). Additionally, it put on hold the construction of new museums in other parts of the world.

We're dealing with the cultural-economic consequences here. But the very conception of art and the aesthetic was also left in turmoil. The seven artists who were asked to reflect on the state of the arts in the aftermath of the attack for a feature article in the *New York Times* all registered a "common feeling . . . of helplessness" (Rockwell 2001). Culture—in this case, the artist—was not necessarily up to the task of helping residents mourn and heal; rather, artists themselves needed "help[in] recover[ing] from the effects of the attacks and find[ing] ways to renew their lives and careers" (Kinzer 2002a). The magnitude of the trauma produced misgivings that perhaps prior to September 11 the arts, along with other activities, were part of an oblivious and glitzy courtship with superfluous entertainment. Such suspicions are, of course, part of the moralizing that arises from the need to blame. Perhaps, as another report suggested, the arts would contribute to healing, but most of the recommendations for this healing process look as expedient as the strategies for legitimizing the arts in *American Canvas*, the 1997 NEA report (Larson 1997) discussed in chapter 1.

From the Americans for the Arts Web site on September 11, 2001 came suggestions for "Ten Ways to Promote Healing, Civic Dialogue and Community Building":

> The arts and humanities can play a pivotal role in helping Americans begin the healing process following the aftermath of the September 11 tragedies. It is particularly important to engage Americans of all ages to participate in cultural group activities during this period. Americans for the Arts recommends the following ten ways for cultural groups to reach-out to their community.

> 1. Immediately preceding or following performances at cultural events, performers could lead audience members to join them in singing a song of unity.

Community-based cultural groups will know their audience to determine whether a patriotic or spiritual song or something else will be the most effective.

2. The arts and humanities can be used as a vehicle to engage the public in meaningful civic dialogue about values we cherish as a democracy, fears we have as individuals, and hopes we have for the future. For specific ideas of how to create cultural forums for civic dialogue, visit our website at www.AmericansForTheArts. org/AnimatingDemocracy.

3. Cultural forums could be created to have animated readings with follow-up audience discussion of important historical documents and speeches, including the Constitution, and speeches articulating the importance of freedom, tolerance and unity.

4. Cultural groups and artists could work further with children both in-school and after-school to lead students in group projects through drawing, music, dance, drama, writing and photography. These groups could also work with PTAs to educate parents how they can use the arts at home to engage their children about their thoughts and emotions.

5. Cultural groups could assist schools in organizing trips to local historical war monuments and memorials in order to better educate children about our past and reassure them of our future.

6. Cultural groups could do further outreach to local military bases, veteran groups, elected officials, police and fire workers and their families to specifically include them in local arts and healing activities.

7. Cultural groups could produce cultural events with specific messages of tolerance and understanding of different religious and ethnic groups. Art forums could be created involving community members from a variety of backgrounds, and specifically Muslim-Americans, to discuss cultural traditions, rituals and religious beliefs.

8. Cultural groups could help raise funds and supplies for charities assisting in disaster relief by donating a percentage of their proceeds from cultural events, providing donated advertising space in Playbills, benefit auctions, and requesting donations from audience members. Americans for the Arts has created a national fund on its website www.AmericansForTheArts.org for disaster relief of New York–based cultural organizations specifically impacted by the tragedies of September 11, 2001.

9. Cultural groups could invite members of the community to take photographs around themes of love, compassion, fear, or freedom for public exhibitions. Cultural groups could also engage professional storytellers to work with various groups within the community to use this wonderful art form to help people talk about their thoughts and emotions.

10. Cultural groups could engage artists and the community in the development of public art ideas around issues of healing, remembrance, freedom and other topics. Projects such as temporary installations or murals could also include community participation.

The language of these recommendations smacks of foundationspeak, art therapy, and arts organization initiatives to succor "community," a concept that is left unexamined and is quite problematic in its presupposition of a "unified" civil society.[4] This is a major drawback in Robert Putnam's (2001) appeal to the reconstitution of cooperation among government, civil society, and the entertainment industries in the aftermath of the Pearl Harbor attack in 1941. There is a danger that in accepting the government's rallying of national spirit, the citizenry will leave aside those critical faculties that point to the government's own collusion in the "blowback" of its many interventions abroad, not least the Al Qaeda network that is responsible for the September 11 attacks. It is not enough to turn to interfaith services or to expand national service programs like AmeriCorps as a means to reinstill the civic lessons that Putnam tells us the Boy Scouts learned at filling stations during World War II; critique is also an essential citizen activity. Nowhere do Putnam's recommendations say anything about exploring fear, horror, mortality, crisis, puzzlement, or about the exercise of critical reflection on, say, the mendacity of our politicians and marketers. The assumption is that in times of fear we need to regroup via experiences that provide the same kinds of assurance as religion. But should culture be limited to the constitution of such community? If other institutions of the public sphere will not take us there, then perhaps only art can mine the muck of our fears and confront the clandestinity of corrupt military, oil, pharmaceutical, and surveillance-security enterprises aided and abetted by those who rule.

Culture is indeed expedient when the media collaborate with government in keeping the populace in ignorance about the motives and the extent of the damage wrought by U.S. military interventions abroad. This collaboration and the unquestioning civic-mindedness broached above are more in keeping with a society of control than the more traditional notion of civil society. The problem is not, as Putnam suggests, that people no longer associate; just look at all the identity groups that have formed throughout the United States. The problem, rather, has to do with the emergence of a society of spectacle, of the decline of labor unions, the privatization of welfare state services (e.g., education and health), and, ironically, the rise of a radical right that has appropriated the tactics of the social movements (including a civil disobedience often escalating into terrorism), all of which bear witness to the unworkability of the notion of civil society. The debacle of Enron, Halliburton, Harken, WorldCom, and other U.S. corporations and the arms scandals of the Menem government in Argentina demonstrate that political society has lost all legitimacy. Can culture take up the slack?

As several observers of netwar have remarked, those who control information and its framing will win a war that is neither of maneuver nor position (Arquilla and Ronfeldt 2001; Garreau 2001). The U.S. government thus turned to advertising to get its message across. To this end, the government enlisted the entertainment industries. Muhammad Ali and other celebrities were sought out for propaganda films shown in Islamic countries ("Ali Asked" 2001). According to a *New York Times* report, the State Department planned "a television and advertising campaign to try to influence Islamic opinion; one segment could feature American celebrities, including sports stars, and a more emotional message" (M. Gordon 2001). The military also invited filmmakers like Steven E. De Souza and Joseph Zito, who directed *Delta Force One*, to generate new terrorist scenarios so that the United States wouldn't be caught unawares (Roberts 2001). The collaboration with Hollywood goes even further, to the exchange of simulation techniques used for special effects in film and for training in warfare (Bart 2001; Hart 2001; Sieberg 2001; "U.S. Army Goes Hollywood" 1999). The Institute for Creative Technologies at the University of Southern California, for example, is a $45 million partnership of L.A. high-tech companies, the academy, and the entertainment industry for "joint modeling and simulation research [with] high-value applications for the army as well as for the entertainment, media, video game, film, destination theme park, and information technology industries" (Der Derian 2001: 163). This is a very different use of the media from what is usually studied in media and communications research. The more viewers partake of these scenarios and parameters to interpret the world, the greater the control wielded by what Der Derian has called the military-industrial-media-entertainment complex.

Censorship is another tool used for controlling interpretive frameworks. Much has been made of the way the military imposed strict control over access to images of war and introduced new views of war (e.g., video cameras on the putative "smart bombs") during the Gulf War in 1991 (Denton 1993; Gerbner 1992; Livingston 1997). For Virilio, it introduced "new logics of perception" via satellite imaging that enabled remote control (qtd. in Der Derian 2001: 64–65). This sense of control, and of the equally deceiving images of "surgical" strikes against the enemy, gave viewers a false sense of security. The U.S. government would never again let the news and the media present information that gave citizens grist for their protests. The government would now lead journalists to the places and settings that it wants them to see, or it would simply use manipulable satellite images. The war in Afghanistan has been even more shameful. On October 10, Condoleezza Rice, Bush's national security advisor, requested that television networks refrain from broadcasting unedited messages sent by Osama bin Laden. Almost all networks acquiesced (Roberts 2001). U.S. government pressure on the media has extended beyond national borders; much of this influence is driven by the "CNN effect," deriving from its synergistic global corporate ownership, around-the-clock coverage, and its ability to interconnect video sources, newsrooms, and foreign ministries to television sets around the world. Throughout Latin America, viewers were subjected to edited sound and video images, "violating CNN's own style manuals . . . and the norm of providing equal access to alternative opinions. In all of these respects, CNN broke its own codes, compelled by jingoism and blood-thirsty vengeance" (Piscitelli 2001). But more than these subjective motives, CNN set the standard for global television as a conflict-driven medium (Semati 2001).

Coverage of opposition to the war has not been part of network news agenda-setting policies, perhaps a significant reason for such widespread support for the war. Yet opposition to war was quite palpable on the streets of New York almost immediately after the attack on the Twin Towers (e.g., warisnottheanswer.org). It was interspersed with spontaneous commemorations to the victims and unprecedented street debates. The night of September 11 and on the following days, one could see people holding photos of their loved ones, captioned with descriptions and requests for information. Those photos were taped to lampposts, mailboxes, and the fences around equestrian statues in parks and plazas, transformed by an accumulation of statements, flowers, flags, and candles into makeshift shrines. The entrances to firehouses and police stations were similarly decorated with the names of those who died trying to save lives.

What struck me the most about these activities, aside from the expression of solidarity so unusual in New York, were the debates in which people of sometimes quite incongruous backgrounds and beliefs engaged. One juxtaposed a twenty-something black woman who opined that the country should retaliate with an older black man who had served in Vietnam and was opposed to military attacks. Curiously, the woman argued that this was an opportunity for blacks to show common cause with whites in a defense of the nation, while the black man observed that despite his service in Vietnam, opportunities available to his white cocombatants were not made available to him. In another corner of the square, a Jewish man who advocated an attack on Afghanistan to root out Osama bin Laden argued with a Palestinian man who felt that the United States had looked after Israel's interests for too long, and another white man opined that oil interests were behind Bush's plan to secure the Middle East and South Asia. Voices were clearly strained, but there were no expressions of outright hostility. Total strangers felt the need to engage each other in the midst of this array of commemorative activities, which included a group of flag-bedecked Sikhs singing "We Shall Overcome" and making statements about their allegiance to the United States. As far as I can tell, it took the newspapers and networks weeks to report on these vernacular commemorations (Kimmelman 2001). They have yet to chronicle the emergence of public debates on city streets.

This was an extraordinary moment and the activities that engaged it were equally uncommon. Yet there were aspects that reminded a few commentators of previous events in U.S. history: Vietnam memorials, be-ins in Central Park, participatory public art murals and graffiti in East Los Angeles and the South Bronx (Kimmelman 2001). The musicians who gathered in the parks and plazas also provided continuity between this extraordinary moment and the usual entertainment available on weekends ("Performances and Shrines" 2001). There were artists who sought to engage the trauma and provide some kind of alternative ritual to the flag-waving that would "unite" the country. Among artist-initiated events, *Our Grief Is Not a Cry for War* was one of the most interesting and meaningful.

Organized by the Artists Network of Refuse and Resist, over one hundred artists wearing black clothing and white dust masks joined hands in a semicircle along part of the perimeter of Union Square on Saturday, September 22. They each held a poster with the motto: "Our Grief Is Not a Cry for War." This performance was repeated in Times Square on September 25 and on October 5 (Artists Network 2001). On October 7, several thousand protestors met in Union Square and marched to Times Square. The march was organized by a coalition of groups from diverse communities and constituencies who reject war and racism and refuse to be silenced in the face of government, institutional, and media portrayals of a nation united behind war (New York: Not In Our Name Web site, 2001).

The performances and the march, while claiming to be acts of mourning, felt more like the antiglobalization protests that began in Seattle in December 1999. Or perhaps like the marches of the Mothers and Grandmothers of the Plaza de Mayo. The performances went beyond the documentation of the missing on placards and posters. The following editorial appeared in the *New York Times* on October 19:

> Most of us have been forced, in the past few weeks, to reconsider the assumptions we have quietly, unconsciously made about death and dying. One of the most basic is the assumption that whatever else death takes away, it leaves behind a body. This is a truth profoundly ingrained in us by religion, by experience, by simple biological order. The body that remains after death becomes a locus for grieving, a comfort, strangely, because its very presence helps define what has been lost. In the rituals that attend burial and cremation, there is a gravity, a certainty, that in time helps replenish those who live on . . . New York City is doing what it can to bring definition to this mourning by consecrating powdered debris from the trade center site and depositing it in small mahogany urns that will be given to the victims' families at a memorial service later this month. ("In the Body's Place" 2001)

A little more than a month later, however, the shrines were largely gone and as I write today, four months later, the memory of those shrines is itself disappearing.[5] Some might say that the war in Afghanistan, and the nationalist sentiments through which politicians have sought to legitimize it, are a way of coming to terms with the trauma. But it is more like an *acting out* of violent impulses toward a reified and profiled enemy than a *working through* that keeps memory in place, that does not let all responsible parties off the hook. There is very little popular participation in the construction of memory in such a process. The erection of monuments will also fall short of a reckoning with what took place. Despite protestations to the contrary (Dunlap 2002), memory is not activated by monuments. The vast majority of people walk by them without even seeing them. Moreover, our public space is saturated by the news-entertainment industry to help us forget or misconstrue the facts of our geopolitical strategies. These media have operated as a wing of the Defense Department since the Gulf War and they have hijacked the rituals of spectacle and meaning creation that are the province of mourning.

A Culture of Memory

Throughout this book I have examined cultural activism, civil society organizing, and cultural development initiatives in both the United States and Latin America. Mourning, a process that is deeply cultural, also offers an insightful staging that helps us discern and thus have a better understanding of what I call the social imperative to perform. In a 1994 article in *Punto de Vista*, Leonor Arfuch uses the phrase "the disappeared" to refer to those who died in the terrorist bombing of the Israel-Argentine Mutual Association, thus situating that event within the legacy of disappearances during the "dirty war" waged against its own citizenry by the military dictatorship. Whereas the notion of "disappearance" predominates in Argentina and other Latin American countries, the word "missing" belongs to U.S. tradition. This word was applied to those victims of the World Trade Center attack whose bodies had not been found. The notion of missing keeps in place the hope that they will be found; disappearance requires a different operation, a symbolic one that makes the disappeared become visible and present in some way. One does not erect monuments to the disappeared; instead, one interrogates the process of their disappearance. Finding and bringing to justice those who are guilty of disappearing others is part of the process of political healing. Insofar as September 11 is concerned, Osama bin Laden and Al Qaeda are not the only ones responsible. Those who facilitated their position in Afghanistan also share that responsibility.

The tradition of seizing public space to reclaim the bodies and persons of the disappeared, epitomized in the ritualistic performances of the Mothers and Grandmothers of the Plaza de Mayo, contrasts markedly with the relative oblivion regarding September 11, even in New York. Arfuch (1994) inscribes "los 'desaparecidos' de la calle Pasteur" within the "cuentas pendientes" (unpaid debts) and remarks that "those hastily tacked photos, captioned with childlike scrawl, were doubly wounding. And perhaps for that reason we also have to treasure those names and their histories, not let them be erased from an 'us,' no matter how inclusive we have to make that 'us.' " In contrast, the makeshift shrines in New York were removed and there is little memory of them, perhaps because the terror in New York was more circumscribed and without further attacks things were bound to return to business as usual. The viewing platform over Ground Zero at the World Trade Center, which should bear some relationship to memory, has become more of a tourist draw for those who might not otherwise risk coming to New York. As such, Ground Zero has become another site of trauma (like the Berlin Wall and the border fence between Mexico and the

United States, discussed in chapter 9), transformed into a touristic resource for generating economic activity. Mayor Giuliani himself suggested that a memorial built at Ground Zero would compensate for some of the loss of business by becoming a tourist must-see.[6] Or a place for gawking, which is not the same as a place for commemoration or revelation.

In Argentina, as in other countries of the region, decades-long dictatorships created cultures of fear (Corradi et al. 1992), but when the dictatorships gave way to democratically elected governments, the insistence on recovering the disappeared was powerful and has remained a constant inspiration for mobilization to demand justice and the expansion of rights. For example, Elizabeth Jelin (1991) and other members of Centro de Estudios de Estado y Sociedad worked in the 1980s and early 1990s with victims of human rights violations in Argentina, seeking to understand new forms of citizenship and democratic culture originating in the symbolic aspects of collective identity and not just a rationalized rights discourse. Hence the importance of memory, aesthetic imagination, and new ways of framing narratives (Antonelli 2001).

The dictatorships had not permitted certain discussions and images to circulate, a reason there was a turn to allegorical modes of communication that gave them political relevance. But in the wake of the withdrawal of the dictatorships, human rights activism proliferated, and with it the right to memory, to that which had been disappeared, including through corruption and abuse of power. Indeed, throughout the dictatorship years the state was the terrorist, as well as all those who collaborated with it. But even in the period of so-called redemocratization justice was prematurely abridged by President Menem, who sought amnesties (or social amnesia) for the victimizers. Menem, that darling of Washington in the late 1980s and early 1990s, is also responsible for the most radical application of neoliberal policies—slashing tariffs, privatizing state enterprises, giving carte blanche to transnational corporations, and pegging the peso to the dollar—that resulted in the largest foreign debt default in history. Menem belongs to that generation of Latin American political leaders who abandoned traditional anti-imperialist rhetoric to adopt new U.S.-led recipes for economic growth after the "economic miracles" of the 1970s failed. By the mid- to late 1980s, Mexico, which was always within the economic orbit of the United States yet maintained a critical-rhetorical distance, sought to become a junior partner in NAFTA. After the Brazilian crisis of 1998 and the Argentine default in 2001, Latin Americans are again pressing the charge of imperialism.

Even before September 11, the Bush administration was poised to take a hard line on economic bailouts. After September 11, Latin America was no longer a priority, permitting the United States to dispense with legitimation measures—such as poverty reduction and aid to bolster civil society—as part of aid packages. The only legitimation in the wake of September 11 is aid for the expansion of the military and security and surveillance technologies, two of the industries that, along with petroleum and pharmaceuticals, are protected by the Bush administration.

Consider that just three weeks after the attacks, the U.S. Congress approved a $15 billion aid package to bail out the airline industry (with nothing earmarked for the more than 100,000 workers laid off in that industry) and another $40 billion for other salvage operations for those sectors affected by the crisis, half of which would go to New York. More recently there have been discussions about a $60 billion aid package. The airlines alone are asking for an additional $10 billion, and travel agencies another $4 billion. The Department of Defense has sought a budget increase of $17 billion. Homeland Security will see its budget rise from $8.6 billion in 2002 to $10.7 billion in 2003 (Stout 2002). Another $1.3 billion will go to combat terrorism and biowarfare. Moreover, the Fed reduced interest rates to the lowest level ever in the history of the country: 1.5 percent by mid-December 2001. These cuts are part of an integrated strategy worked out with the other central banks of the G-7, including $100 billion earmarked to increase liquidity. Other measures include $71 billion for fiscal incentives, subsidies for high-speed railroads, increase in unemployment insurance to the tune of $8 billion, and $20 billion for health insurance for those who lost their jobs (Folha de São Paulo, qtd. in Bolaño 2002).

The fact that the administration approved the $30 billion bailout of Brazil in early August does not entail great concern for Latin America but, as a New York Times reporter suggests, safeguards the huge interests of American banks like Citigroup, FleetBoston, and J. P. Morgan Chase and the billions of dollars of American industrial investment (Andrews 2002). As of August 2002, the United States still stands adamant against a bailout for Argentina, where there are fewer U.S. interests. Elsewhere in Latin America, the events of September 11 and their aftermath saw the immediate closing of the U.S.-Mexico border and a concomitant shelving of amnesty for undocumented immigrants that the Mexican government was hoping to broker. Moreover, the United States cast its antiterrorist net ever wider by assimilating drug traffic and guerrilla movements into an integrated antiterrorism policy that provides for more military buildup than aid to help find solutions to the economic crisis of farmers and the citizenry. Even the piracy of media and software products has been included as part of the terrorist networks to be combated, on behalf of corporate interests, as is evident in the targeting of Ciudad del Este in Paraguay and Manaus in Brazil as places requiring greater surveillance. Latin American militaries, having lost their legitimacy in the dictatorship years, have eagerly jumped on the security bandwagon (e.g., in Operación Centauro) as a way to increase their budgets (Bonasso 2001).[7] But even worse is the inclusion of progressive Latin American groups, especially antiauthoritarian insurgencies, among the terrorists identified by the Bush administration. The stated purpose of the actions of the U.S. Southern Command in Latin America is to curtail arms and drug trafficking (Pace 2001), but the spillover effect and most likely real objective is the control of popular opposition to neoliberalism, such as the protests that brought down the Argentine government several times in December 2001 and January 2002.

The connections between Latin American insurgent groups and Middle East and South Asian terrorists are often quite tenuous, as in this statement by Anne Patterson, U.S. ambassador in Colombia. She alleged that the Colombian guerrillas, "FARC and bin Laden share the same moral hypocrisy and lack of ideas. The Afghani Taliban do not represent Islam just as the Colombian guerrillas do not seek social justice" (qtd. in Kollmann 2001). Military aid to Colombia is justified only as a war on the drug and arms traffic, but as analysts of this situation point out, U.S. policies in Colombia are for the protection of U.S. corporations, whose profits are compromised by civil war. Despite the great loss of civilian lives and the violation of human rights by the guerrillas, the drug traffickers, the military, and the paramilitary forces, corporations have been the beneficiaries of $1.6 billion of U.S. military aid to defend their property and interests (Staples 2001). And if this weren't enough, U.S. propaganda is busy establishing links among bin Laden, the FARC, heroin and cocaine traffickers, and the Triple Border of Argentina, Brazil, and Paraguay.

Why these connections? According to Kollman (2001), the war in Afghanistan resulted in the move of heroin operations—with seventeen times the value of cocaine production—from there to Colombia. Moreover, the United States fears that the Colombian conflict will spill over into Venezuela, whose president, Hugo Chávez, has declared on more than one occasion his solidarity with Colombian guerrillas. These connections are part of a U.S. strategy to reinforce military and surveillance networks in the region, at the same time bringing in Argentina and Brazil to negotiate an "arms elimination pact," or more likely to intervene in an "armed conflict against the Colombian revolutionaries, whom the U.S. calls, as in Afghanistan, the narcoguerrilla" (Kollmann 2001). However, as Petras (2001) argues, the vast majority of profits from drug trafficking are in the processing and export market, which flow through U.S. client states in the Caribbean and Central America. It is, rather, the "narcoparamilitaries" in these client states, as also in South Asia and the Middle East, that present the major problems. These clients, who "combine drugs, white slavery and gun-running" along with proxy warfare have "blown back" on the United States, as was evident in the Al Qaeda bombing of the World Trade Center in 1993 and its destruction in 2001.

But such critiques of U.S. policies do not make their way into mainstream news sources. U.S. military policy and the attendant cooperation of news organizations like CNN, Fox, and MSNBC have virtually closed Latin American media and news systems to objective and multiperspectival reporting, as in the United States, thus rivaling the Big Brotherism of Huxley's or Orwell's fiction. Moreover, as Paul Krugman (2002) notes, the IMF and the Bush administration are now busily rewriting history, "blaming the victims" of their policies. Currently, the greatest ire of the Argentines is aimed at their corrupt and inept politicians for bringing about the worst debacle in their history as a nation. But they also recognize that the international financial institutions that the United States controls had a significant role. Argentines are not radical fundamentalists seeking to strike out at U.S. symbols of power, but they recognize the abuses of that power in ways that the majority of Americans do not. Krugman adds that "we are notoriously bad at seeing ourselves as others see us. A recent Pew survey of 'opinion leaders' found that 52 percent of the Americans think that our country is liked because it 'does a lot of good'; only 21 percent of foreigners, and 12 percent of Latin Americans agreed."

It is no wonder, then, that some groups who historically have voiced the most acerbic critiques of U.S. interventions should express satisfaction at the trauma dealt the United States. In Argentina, a wing of the Mothers of the Plaza de Mayo, that most exemplary of human rights groups, expressed joy at the toppling of the World Trade Center and the damage to the Pentagon. This unfortunate reaction is significantly different from the majority of opinions in Latin America that expressed sympathy for the victims. The Cuban government, for example, denounced the terrorists and took a reasoned position in calling for an international, UN-based solution to terrorism (Castro 2001). But even these sympathetic expressions did not pull punches in condemning U.S. military and economic interventions, noting that it was high time that the United States get a taste of what was the daily experience of people in Israel, Palestine, Iraq, and other parts of the world. It is instructive to review the Mothers' reaction and some of the critiques they generated.

Hebe Pastor de Bonafini, a founder of the Mothers of the Plaza de Mayo, declared her admiration for the men who piloted the planes that struck the World Trade Center and the Pentagon. She opined that they "declared war with their bodies, driving a plane that smashed and knocked the shit out of the greatest power on earth. It made me happy. Some may think that is wrong. Each will have to evaluate it and think about it. I will not be false. I will make a toast to my children, for so many who have died, for the end to the [Cuban] blockade." She also saw the deaths in the World Trade Center as payback for the thousands of disappeared Argentines. "Now [North Americans live] the same fear that they produced in us, with persecution, disappearances and torture . . . The [North American] people remained silent and even applauded the wars." Bonafini said these words during a class session on "imperialist war" (Sobre la guerra imperialista) at the Universidad Popular de las Madres de la Plaza de Mayo. There were conflicting opinions expressed in this forum (Natalichio, Freyre, and Fuchs 2001; Iramain 2001), yet intellectuals ranging from the most important, such as David Viñas, to other significant figures, such as Sergio Schoklender and Vicente Zito Lema, expressed similar opinions in the same forum.

Viñas characterized the attacks as an expression of class struggle, a retaliation from below against the "institutional violence of empire," against the "violence encysted above," and compared these actions of the "subjected and humiliated of the world" to those of Robespierre and Castelli.[8] Zito Lema agreed with this "class analysis" and characterized Osama bin Laden as a revolutionary comparable to San Martín, Belgrano, Artigas, Che Guevara, and his "comrades fallen in battle" during the cold war. Schoklender did not see these as terrorist acts but, using the rhetoric of the U.S. government, as "surgical operations against specific power centers" of the "enemy that is destroying us." He added that he was happy to see that the United States was not invulnerable and that "we have the possibility to resist it and confront it."

Latin Americans certainly are entitled to begrudge and to resist U.S. interventions in their countries, yet the idea that the death of three thousand people from eighty countries, many of them workers and an inestimable number of them undocumented, can be regarded as retribution shows an egregious lack of judgment and a lapse in the human rights activism for which people like Bonafini are known. As Verbitsky and Rolando Astarita (who resigned from the

Universidad Popular de las Madres de la Plaza de Mayo after the session on imperialist war) argue, bin Laden does not represent the cause of the wretched of the earth, nor are the attacks on the World Trade Center and the Pentagon part of the class struggle or a socialist vision. Much the contrary, according to Astarita (2001), for whom socialism is a social and political vision to "put an end to private property in the means of production." These attacks are instead part of a complex geopolitical struggle in which Pakistani and Saudi Arabian interests, allied with those of the United States, used Islamist extremism to fight a number of proxy wars for the sake of territory, emerging markets in Central Asia, oil, arms, and power, the details and dimensions of which are not the subject of this conclusion or this book. Suffice it to say that the blowback from the CIA's machinations has been devastating for the entire world (Cooley 2000).

If, as Staples suggests, the September 11 attacks have given a shot in the arm to the political and economic forces that have generated globalization such that we are entering a new historical period, it is worth considering how all this affects Latin America. First, however, we should review the global context into which the Latin American case is inserted.

The new regime of surveillance and security threatens not only the possible successes of social movements and civil society organizations, but also how we understand them. They are either neutralized through repression or absorbed into the machinery of security. And both of these outcomes have profound social and cultural repercussions. Hence the importance of cultural policies for this new era. The globalization generated by the transnationalization of corporate-based accumulation and the flows of financial speculation have produced greater inequality than in the years immediately following World War II. Instead of designing policies to halt the immiseration generated by globalization under the sign of neoliberalism, international financial and trade institutions (IMF, World Bank, WTO) limit themselves to timid debt-reduction programs for the poorest of countries, at the same time that they resort to culture as a panacea (Wolfensohn 1998; World Bank 1999a, 1999b). But debt reduction does not alter the structure that generates inequality, which is the juridification of the international division of labor and the transformation of everything, including experience, into property.

The Corporate Highjacking of Latin American Culture

The privatizations enacted in Latin America are only one example of the transformation of the collective good or patrimony into private property, as the modern nation-state gives way to the neoliberal state. Herscovici explains that the valuation of patrimony or private property in market terms is not something that takes place naturally: it ensues from political decisions, shaped in turn by their contextualization in a global economy (1999: 55). The control that central economies wield over those of other countries is nowhere more evident than in the intellectual property and copyright regime that regulates the international production of pharmaceuticals. Brazil, India, and South Africa struggled for years to attain a modicum of autonomy with respect to intellectual property laws that prevented them from producing generic versions of AIDS drugs at a price that would enable distribution to all citizens (Consumer Project on Technology 2001). At the same time the WTO declared at its November 2001 meeting that the safeguard of patents and copyrights "does not and should not prevent [countries] from taking measures to protect public health" (Bluestein 2001), activists and critics from developing countries observed that "the conference declaration . . . does little beyond codifying existing practices, and concedes that the world's poorest countries and those with no pharmaceutical manufacturing capacity will not benefit" (International Union 2001). Indeed, pharmaceutical industry spokespersons made statements to the effect that the declaration does "not change the way [they] sell [their] medicines," that their "intellectual property rights are [not] in any way diminished," and that they are "satisfied with the language" (UNwire 2001). As for the United States and European countries that sought to protect the pharmaceutical corporations from exemptions to intellectual property laws, it should be noted that they themselves favored the production of generics or cheaper prices on brand names when it came to first world security against bioterror. As Bob Goldberg, senior fellow with the Manhattan Institute for Policy Research, put it, "The question became, how can the U.S. pull rank on patents in the case of Cipro but not when it comes to needs of the Third World?" (qtd. in K. French 2001). This is one more instance of "American hypocrisy: free-trade rhetoric combined with increased trade barriers" (Stiglitz 2002).

The political economy of intellectual property regimes deepens inequality in other ways. The very fact that all major corporations are headquartered in G-7 countries militates against not only developing countries but also peripheral metropolitan countries (Southern and Eastern Europe) developing significant and autonomous intellectual property production systems. Not even an economy the size of Brazil, the ninth largest in the world (U.S. Commercial Service 2001), has been able to capitalize on intellectual property generation. U.S., European, and Japanese universities, in partnership with those corporations that are the engines of innovation for the sake of accumulation, do not have any counterparts in Latin America. In fact, the independent research university, associated with the failed import-substitution industrialization model, is now being destroyed. Even such flagship institutions as the Universidad Autónoma de México, the Universidade de São Paulo, and the Universidad de Buenos Aires have seen their budgets severely reduced and have been encouraged to develop R&D programs in partnership with transnational corporations. The corporations, of course, get to keep the patents and hold the intellectual property rights. This restructuring of the university also has the drawback of closing off access to disadvantaged groups and even the middle classes, thus increasing the already huge income gap.

According to Brazilian Minister of Education Paulo Renato de Souza (1996), "The emphasis on university education was a feature of a model of self-sustaining development that required one's own research and technology . . . today this model is in its death throes." He adds that the international imbrication characteristic of globalization makes such autonomy impossible; consequently, the Ministry supports "access to knowledge production through partnerships and joint ventures that provide the companies in countries like Brazil with all the needed know-how." He also advocates the tertiarization of the university, as in Korea, which "makes more sense from an economic point of view." A critique of these educational policies, "Em defesa da Universidade Pública" (In defense of the public university) points out that because 99 percent of patents belong to the multinational corporations of the G-7, the high cost of intellectual property rights makes it difficult for the majority of the population in developing countries to have access to medicines, agricultural products, and so on (ANDES-SN 2001).

The weakening of the Brazilian university system and its capacity to function as a generator of intellectual property has already taken place via budget cuts for the thirty-nine federal universities, which have not seen an increase since 1995. Worse yet is the 80 percent cut to university libraries. The situation is even worse in Argentina, which defaulted in early January 2002, devalued its currency, and withheld salaries for several months, not to speak of research funding. This on top of various measures that the Ministry of Education presented to the National Congress, auguring the transition of the university system to the private sector and abolishing employment stability. Under these circumstances, it is impossible for professors to plan their programs independently of the interests of the private sector (ANDES-SN 2001).

As Verbitsky (2001) points out, the attacks on the United States have in no way "destroyed the greatest power on earth," as Bonafini had thought. On the contrary, the very "software that measures country risk was already installed in other buildings." That is to say, the technologies of control operate in the background, without anyone taking notice. There isn't sufficient historical perspective to determine the future of this system of accumulation nor how the "war against terrorism" will pan out. What does seem evident is that a new mode of controlling contingencies is claimed to be possible via such new technologies. This new control regime is also cultural, although not necessarily in the cultural-imperialism terms that Dorfman and Mattelart (1975) criticized three decades ago, even if, as Benjamin Barber (1995) tells us, Jihad has risen up against McWorld. Barber's, like Huntington's, is a civilizational analysis according to which fundamentalist haters of modernity repudiate the fast fooding and infotainment of the world (Barber 2001: xxi). But, as I have already argued in this book, the new system of control is premised less on commodification—the Adornian critique—than on the property and accumulation regime that underpins it.

Global conglomerates rely on security forces to ensure their profits. This is evident in the entertainment industries (film, TV, music, books, videogames) and other digital products, whose profits are threatened by piracy, or what a Time-Warner executive calls "traffic in entertainment" (André Midani, interview, July 17, 1998). To get an idea of the enormity of that "expoliation," consider that piracy in some subsectors takes at least 50 percent of the legitimate market, and that in 1998 the arts, entertainment, communications, and copyright sector reached $360 million in the United States alone (Arthurs and Hodsoll, 1998: 104). As neoliberal *New York Times* columnist Thomas Friedman himself admits, "The hidden hand of the market will never work without a hidden fist. McDonalds cannot flourish without McDonnell Douglas, the builder of the F15 warplane. And the hidden fist that keeps the world safe for Silicon Valley's technologies is called the United States Army, Air Force, Navy and Marine Corps" (qtd. in Staples 2001).

Brazil's public policies for the production of inexpensive AIDS medicines and their free distribution to all HIV+ residents, which prevailed over the intellectual property regime that the pharmaceutical industry imposed on national and international markets, is evidence that it is still possible to protect the public good. And the so-called antiglobalization movement shows that it is still possible to appropriate technological advances and cultivate an interactive and oppositional community. Nevertheless, as César Bolaño warns, for these possibilities to be effective and to go beyond "symbolic war," concrete political strategies "will have to be activated in their proper spaces" (1999: 39). Foundations and NGOs have a role to play in the financing of critical literacy in activism against the transformation of public goods into private property. Until now, most of their cultural policies have been concentrated in the recognition of cultural differences, on the premise that such recognition will provide access to citizen participation. In other words, the work of these organizations has been limited to opening access to fora of interlocution (Antonelli 2002), without noticing that these fora have already been structured according to corporate arrangements and protocols, often with their collaboration, as in the UNESCO-Disney partnership (Fawcett forthcoming). The antiglobalization movement will thus have to turn its attention to its own collaboration with the globalized civil society of NGOs and weed out the appropriation of the public good by the new regime of accumulation based on intellectual and cultural work.

NOTES

Introduction

1 The Convention defines biodiversity as "the variability among living organisms from all sources including, *inter alia*, terrestrial, marine and other aquatic ecosystems and the ecological complexes of which they are part . . . within species, between species and of ecosystems" (1992: 5).

Chapter 1. The Expediency of Culture

1 One definition for expediency given by the *Oxford English Dictionary* is "suitability to the circumstances or conditions of the case."

Chapter 2. The Social Imperative to Perform

1 This image and the discussion referring to it do not appear in any of the three books by Haraway mentioned here. See, however, Haraway 1989a.

2 I use the term "cultural leftist" for those who espouse social justice for a range of minoritized groups. This less than adequate definition extends to those who believe that social justice can be achieved largely by cultural means, especially the critique of biased representations, founded on status quo normative assumptions. Much of what Haraway writes could be characterized by this statement. Like other current political terms today, there is not great coherence among those to whom the label is applied. There is no satisfactory term to refer to positions on the political spectrum, in great part because politics are not only defined by ideological stances regarding economic and class-based issues but are permeated by more slippery questions of identity and culture. A "leftist" in the 1960s could be expected to be welfare-statist, if not anticapitalist, anti-imperialist, supportive of working-class struggles, and antiracist in the terms generated by the civil rights movement. Women's liberation, nationalist positions among ethnoracial minority groups, lesbian and gay liberation activism, however, crosscut that conception of leftist, such that it is not necessarily predictable that a gay activist would also be antiracist or anticapitalist, despite the presumed generalization of minority struggles. Todd Gitlin (1995), for

example, argues that these "particularisms" have sundered the left: "The left . . . has come to be identified with special needs of distinct culture and select identities." He does not attribute this political fragmentation only to the cultural left (conservatives and white supremacists are also "identity" groups), but he does attribute ineffectiveness on the progressive front to the range of positions characteristic of multiculturalism. Although critical of Gitlin's position, I agree that there isn't yet a well-formulated leftist position for social justice in the post–cold war era. The so-called antiglobalization movement, launched in Seattle in 1999, for example, is a collection of quite disparate positions, ranging from environmentalism to third world debt reduction, anticapitalism, labor unionism, and even nationalist jingoism (e.g., Pat Buchanan, who addressed an antiglobalization rally in Washington in April 2000).

3 I object to characterizing U.S. citizens as "Americans" (because the appellation is an expropriation by the United States of the name of an entire hemisphere, in which other countries also make claims on that name). However, I believe that it is analytically important to convey the sense in which people, including social interpreters, use categories to refer to their discursive objects and themselves. For U.S. citizens to refer to themselves as American shows either obliviousness regarding the hemispheric contestation over this arrogation or, more tellingly, a conscious belief that the contestation has been won and that they are the only ones who can, through the legitimacy that power bestows, use the appellation, usually to convey the belief that "we" are the bastion of freedom and justice and the world's future. On this issue, see Fernández Retamar 1976, Hanchard 1990, and Saldívar 1995. The critiques of the Bush administration's recourse to the traditional American Creed during the war on Afghanistan, albeit giving it a multicultural updating, is another expression of this arrogation.

4 Biopower "brought life and its mechanisms into the realm of explicit calculations and made knowledge-power an agent of transformation of human life." Bodies were identified with politics, because managing them was part of running the country. This has continued into contemporary life. For Foucault, "a society's 'threshold of modernity' has been reached when the life of the species is wagered on its own political strategies" (1991: 97, 92–95; 1984: 143).

5 Whiteness studies became a growth industry in the 1990s. It can no longer be said that white is unmarked. To be sure, when the popular press picks up the topic ("Whiny White Men" 1995; Kinsley 1995), it has percolated quite deeply. I cite only the most salient studies; there are many more: Appiah and Gutmann 1996; Babb 1998; Bay 2000; Bonilla-Silva 2001; Bonnett 2000; Clark and O'Donnell 1999; Conley 2000; Cuomo and Hall 1999; R. Curry 2000; Daniel 2002; R. Delgado and Stefancic 1997; Dobratz and Shanks-Meile 1997; Dyer 1997; Ferber 1998; Fine et al. 1997; Frankenberg 1997; Hale 1998; Hartigan 1999; Helms 1992; Hill 1997; Howard 1999; Ignatiev 1995; Ignatiev and Garvey 1996; Jacobson 1998; Jurca 2001; Kincheloe et al. 1998; Kivel 1995; Lamont 1999; Levine-Rasky 2002; Lipsitz 1998; I. López

1996; McKee 1999; McKoy 2001; Nakayama and Martin 1999; Rasmussen et al. 2001; Rodriguez and Villaverde 2000; Roediger 1991, 1994, 1998, 2002; Rothenberg 2001; Sartwell 1998; Takaki 2000; Thandeka 1999; Walle 2000; Ware and Back 2001; Wetherell and Potter 1992; Wray and Newitz 1997. As of September 15, 2002, Michael Moore's *Stupid White Men and Other Sorry Excuses for the State of the Nation* was on the *New York Times*' best-seller list for twenty-eight weeks and was still in eighth place, with over five hundred thousand copies sold.

6 This is a point that I emphasize in my introduction to García Canclini's *Consumers and Citizens*. See Yúdice 2001a.

7 If we accept Boaventura de Sousa Santos's Weberian- and Habermasian-derived account of the development of modernity, we see in Latin America, inversely, the development of those aspects of modernity that are marginalized in the North. Santos, like Habermas, posits two poles of modern development: the regulatory and the emancipatory. Each of these has three constituent logics. Regulation is provided by the state, the market, and the community; emancipation is sought in the aesthetic-expressive, cognitive-instrumental, and moral-practical spheres. According to Santos, hegemonic modernity is characterized, on the one hand, by the predominance of the market and, on the other, by an instrumentally oriented science (1995: 2). Angel Rama (1967, 1970, 1985) is, perhaps, the critic who most advocated the view that the high accomplishments of the aesthetic sphere, particularly in literature, from the late nineteenth century on, are both a reflection of Latin America's insertion into the world economy and a symbolic compensation for the underdevelopment of the economic, political, and scientific spheres, largely due to European colonialism and subsequently U.S. neocolonialism. Santos himself, taking political theorists-activists such as Orlando Fals Borda and Paulo Freire as his point of departure, puts forth the premise that the rich development of novel forms of community (from participatory research-action, popular, grassroots, revolutionary, human rights, and liberation theology movements) is Latin America's contribution to egalitarian forms of regulation, despite the authoritarian and clientelist character of the state and the law (1995: 38). Aesthetics and community, the two underdeveloped logics of modernity, work in tandem to produce some of the most potent critical and emancipatory movements, as witnessed by the emergence of a form of expression from within contestatory communitarian struggles that came to wield great influence in other parts of the South and in the North. *Testimonio* is the example most commented on (see the essays in Gugelberger 1996).

8 This statement provides a valid analysis of the current U.S. war on terrorism, for it would have to question its own policies that enabled that terrorism in the first place, as explained in the conclusion.

9 According to DaMatta ([1979] 1991), in the United States people don't perform "Do you know who you're talking to?" to a cop or an authority. However, the problem in the United States is likely to be the inverse: it is the cop who says it to the discriminated person: "Who the fuck do you think you are?" for example, to someone

"driving while black." Such behavior on the part of the police is characteristic of racial profiling. Alvin Pouissant, a psychology professor at Harvard, has described his fear and anger when addressed in this way by a cop (Kochman 1973). A black rap impresario, co-owner of *The Source*, who attempted to use "Do you know who you're talking to?" to a cop in Miami had the unpleasant but predictable response of being arrested (and, allegedly, beaten; Odierna 2001). What goes through the reader's mind in reading about this is the cop's probable retort, similar to the one reported by Poussaint. Another example is a train conductor's response to Congressman Arthur Mitchell (D-IL) when he attempted to travel first class: "He said it didn't make a damn bit of difference who I was, that as long as I was a nigger I couldn't ride in that car" (*Mitchell v. United States* 1941).

10 A lot has been written on the Latin American baroque and neobaroque, especially concerning literature. Severo Sarduy (1980, 1982, 1987) is perhaps the most original theorist of this trend.

11 The notion of the popular was used by Gramsci in his diagnosis of the rise of fascism in 1920s Italy and as part of his program for moving Italian politics in a more revolutionary direction. In his estimation, progressive Italian intellectuals were out of touch with the social forces, particularly the "popular masses," necessary for the construction of a "national-popular" consciousness or "collective will" that in turn was necessary for revolution. According to Gramsci, every social group that plays a role in economic production "creates together with itself, organically, one or more strata of intellectuals which give it homogeneity and an awareness of its own function not only in the economic but also in the social and political fields." Such unified awareness requires "cultural battle," not only to create a class consciousness but also to generalize that consciousness to other classes to achieve hegemony, which is a historical act (1971: 3, 348–349). In France, the Jacobins ushered in a national-popular bloc by creating an alliance with the "popular masses," in particular the peasantry, which enabled the creation of a modern state (131–132). But the legacy of quasi-feudal "economic-corporate" domination in Italy, characterized by autonomous city-states, dependent regions, and a mechanical bloc of social groups, was not conducive to national unification until the Risorgimento in the mid-nineteenth century, and then only "inorganically" under the leadership of Cavour and the Moderate Party, without significant involvement of popular classes. Indeed, the absence of popular elements enabled the Moderate Party to absorb the more liberal-democratic intellectuals of the Action Party of Mazzini and Garibaldi, thus serving the interests of northern (Piedmontese) capitalists (204). Gramsci calls this northern dominance a "dictatorship without hegemony," in which Piedmont stood in for but did not properly function as a "leading" social group (106). The northern bourgeoisie did not show the "inflexible will to become the "leading" party," as did the Jacobins (80). Instead, the Piedmontese state " 'led' the group which should have been 'leading.' " This state loosely held together ruling class "nuclei" throughout Italy, but these nuclei "did not seek to 'lead' anybody, i.e. they

did not wish to concord their interests and aspirations with the interests and aspirations of other groups" (104–105). The result was the failure to achieve a "national-popular collective will," particularly without a "[*simultaneous*] burst into political life" of the "great mass of peasant farmers" (132).

12 So too does Elizabeth Jelin, perhaps the scholar who has had the greatest influence on the discourse and politics of human rights in Argentina: "I also find it regrettable that the imagery of the family and the defense and reproduction of family ties have been so present in this part of the human rights movement" (Jelin and Kaufman 1998: 17 n.10).

13 In the conclusion I review the sad turn to acceptance of violence and, by extension, the abandonment of human rights discourse, by Hebe Pastor de Bonafini and other pivotal figures connected to the Mothers of the Plaza de Mayo. Bonafini reported feeling joy when she learned that terrorists had destroyed the Twin Towers and part of the Pentagon. She took these acts as retribution for the disappeared in her own country.

Chapter 3. The Globalization of Culture and the New Civil Society

1 A previous version of this chapter appeared under the same title in *Cultures of Politics, Politics of Cultures: RE-Visioning Latin American Social Movements*, edited by Sonia E. Alvarez, Evelina Dagnino, and Arturo Escobar (Boulder, CO: Westview Press, 1998), 353–379.

2 It is significant that McLuhan conceived this global village within the tradition set forth by one of the major formulators of the cultural legacy against which the Birmingham Centre worked: T. S. Eliot, in particular, his "Tradition and the Individual Talent." The reworking of tradition, which is how Eliot conceives the act of poetry, is invoked by McLuhan to characterize the means by which the new electronic media will organize the global village as a work of art (McLuhan and Powers 1989: 180 n.3).

3 In contrast to more affirmative assessments of "marvelous realism," such as that of Michael Taussig (1987: 165–167), I, along with other critics of literary and intellectual production in Latin America, find that much of the discourse on the Latin American marvelous was produced in a contentious relation to a supposedly stultifying and inauthentic European surrealism. Such a contention is at the very heart of, for example, Alejo Carpentier's novel *Los pasos perdidos* (*The Lost Steps*; 1953) and his programmatic preface to *El reino de este mundo* (*The Kingdom of This World*; 1949). Carpentier resorts to essentialism of the most crass type when he embodies Latin American origins in his protagonist's newfound lover in the heart of the jungle (stand-in for the "real" Latin America), the indigenous mother-earth Rosario. She stands for everything that negates the culture of the protagonist's upper-class European father. Consequently, the binary representations that Carpentier wields in this novel are ultimately beholden to the European model that they would undo. Such

a narrative strategy is typical, in my view, of Latin American elites in search of a national cultural identity that supports the independence from Europe that these elites sought. But such an autonomy, which reflects by means of narrative allegory the will to economic sovereignty evident in the work of dependency theorists and advocates of import substitution, is a far cry from any effective advocacy of or collaboration with the popular or subaltern classes in Latin American nations. It is this kind of imaginary, projected by the intelligentsia, that the indigenous movements have repudiated. Such a surrogate manifestation of culture is ultimately a drawback for the uses of culture by grassroots groups. This is an argument, as I explain below, that the *museos comunitarios* movement in Mexico has made.

4 This point needs greater analysis, which I cannot provide here. Suffice it to say that youth cultures, whose very existence runs counter to the rejection of capitalism typical of many grassroots movements, flourish *within* consumerist capitalism, despite the fact that the majority of these youth do not have much buying power to speak of. Their culture, like that of grassroots movements, is one of survival, but much more identified with using to their own advantage the structures that capital opens up for others, the elites. Studies of youth cultures tend to work within the "practices of everyday life" framework laid out by Michel de Certeau (1984). See, for example, Vianna 1988, Franco 1993, and Yúdice 1994c. Other, more Marxist approaches that deal with youth cultures sympathetically are Valenzuela Arce 1988, 1993.

5 Victor Thomas-Bulmer summarizes these contradictions of the New Economic Model thus: "Privatisation leads to rising unemployment, but labour market reform may not be sufficient to absorb surplus labour. Export promotion requires a depreciation of the real effective exchange rate, but inflation stabilisation may require the opposite. Technological modernisation requires access to capital, but the reform of domestic capital markets may make the needed investments more expensive. Fiscal reform requires increases in revenue, but tariff reductions and the elimination of employment taxes lead to a fall" (1996a: 12).

6 The recently instituted process of certification of NGOs under the Ley de Fomento a las Actividades de Bienestar y Desarrollo Social in Oaxaca is an example of government control. The junta established by this law has the authority to create, modify, or eliminate NGOs. The NGOs must even pay fees for the maintenance of this junta ("Mexican government controls non-government organizations" 1996, online posting). It is obvious, then, that civil society does not function in practice as a "third sector" independent of government and productive enterprises, as the recently formed Mexican Center for Philanthropy would have it (*Directorio de Instituciones Filantrópicas* 1995: ix), but rather as the handmaiden of both.

7 During visits to Mexico in 1992 and 1993, I saw many television and print commercials that advised citizens to meet the challenge of economic adulthood (NAFTA) with social maturity. The commercials urged viewers to keep streets clean, get to work on time, and so on.

8 Transnational brokering is even more complicated, as Daniel Mato (1995b) points

out in his study on the phenomenon. Not only are there foreign and national metropolitan agents (banks, the UN, government institutions, etc.) on the one hand, and local and social movement agents as well as the target community on the other. There is also an entire spectrum of intermediary organizations, particularly NGOs. All of these constitute "complexes of brokering" that must negotiate a plethora of competing agendas (8). Even among NGOs there is great diversity, starting with the difference between international nongovernmental organizations (INGOs) and NGOs. For example, "unlike the INGOs, many of the Latin American human rights organizations have close ties to political parties," including commissions created by governments, which adds another dimension: the degree to which they are independent of the governments that created them (B. Torres and Toro 1992: 20–21).

9 "Governmentality" should not be confused with "governability." The latter is of utmost concern to conservatives and all those who see social change in the direction of democratization as a form of chaos. This is exactly the way Ronfeldt (1995) assessed the action of civil society organizations, or what he called the network society.

Chapter 4. The Funkification of Rio

1 This essay has benefited from the generous commentary of Rob Anderson, Idelber Avelar, and Ana Lúcia Gazolla of Duke University, my comrade-in-criticism Juan Flores of the City University of New York, and Heloísa Buarque de Holanda, Patrícia Farias, and Carlos Alberto Messeder Pereira of the Escola de Comunicação at the Universidade Federal do Rio de Janeiro. I am indebted, above all, to Hermano Vianna's pioneering work on *funkeiro* culture.

2 "Claustrofobia," written by Martinho da Vila, in Byrne 1989.

3 "Marvelous city" is Rio's motto.

4 "Rio 40 Graus," written by Fernanda Abreu, Fausto Fawcett, and Celso Laufer, in Abreu 1992.

5 Martinho da Vila performed on the weekly television series *Sounds Brazilian* in 1989.

6 According to a *Los Angeles Times* report, "Industrial production is now 7 percent less than in 1980 and still dropping, while per-capita income is 5 percent less and also dropping." The rate of decrease has accelerated in the 1990s: 4 percent in the first three years of the decade ("Inflation, Despair Reign as Brazilian Confidence in New President Wanes" 1993).

7 For a critique of the "limits of a racially based liberal nationalism," see Hanchard 1993.

8 The difference between Ibero- and Anglo-American sexual objectification of blacks may be explained, in part, by the fact that few Portuguese (and Spanish) women came to the "new world," whereas many U.S. colonies consisted of entire communities, including women and children. Brazil did not acquire a high percentage of whites until the end of the nineteenth and beginning of the twentieth century. Consequently, black and mulatto women were usually the sexual object of white men's

desire. In the United States, where white women were more numerous (and Puritan culture supposedly more repressive), white men's desires might have been inflected by the anxiety of "their" women being taken by the evidently more physical black men.

9 This brief discussion of the heritage of the cultural politics of race in Brazil is necessarily inadequate. To do justice to it, were it the central topic of this chapter, I would have to lay out how the ideologemes of mestiçagem and "racial democracy" were important factors in the construction of a "modernized" Brazilian identity from the 1920s on, according to which the largely "colored" working classes, especially those who were migrating from the economically declining Northeast, were imagined as citizens with the responsibility of being productive. (This ideology made few claims about their rights.) One of the reasons "people of color," a term that means something very different in Brazil than in the United States, have had such a difficult time pushing forward an agenda of social justice is that the consensus culture included them as the basis of the nation, thus leading many "white" (again a term with different meanings in Brazil) elite and middle sectors to claim that there is no racial prejudice in Brazil and thus no need to make changes for this purpose. See Hasenbalg 1992 and Hasenbalg and Silva 1988.

10 The "feast of curses" refers to a dinner that Collor's ally Onaireves Moura gave for him. The press reported on Collor's use of foul language at that dinner. Everyone expected Moura to vote against the impeachment, but, public pressure being so strong, he voted to oust Collor. Hence the celebration. (I owe this explanation to Ana Lúcia Gazolla.)

11 I owe this qualification to Rob Anderson. On the unworkability of democratization without the enforcement of social rights, see D. Caldeira 1992.

12 Arrastão is derived from arrastar, the verb for net fishing. In a looting "rampage," youths from the favela line up shoulder to shoulder for distances as long as a quarter of a mile and run across the sand toward the water, taking whatever they can from the panic-stricken beachgoers. It can also be translated as "dragnet."

13 The word galera is used metaphorically, by the youths themselves, to refer to the dense crowd that gathers in the dance clubs. Galera is the word for the hold of a ship, where the slaves were kept on the voyage from Africa to Brazil.

14 As the first version of this chapter was being revised for publication, a massacre of street children in Rio by a death squad composed of military police in plain clothes was reported widely. See Human Rights Coordinator 1993.

15 A good part of the following account is based on Vianna 1988.

16 Several reports and newspaper articles have drawn attention to the political focus of rap in the wake of the arrastão. See, for example, Orsini 1992.

17 See also D. Caldeira (1992) and the special "Galeras Funk" on Programa Legal, aired on Brazil's Manchete Network in 1991.

18 The lead article in a special section of O Globo de São Paulo (October 4, 1992: 34–

36) was titled "As tribus do Rio em pé de guerra" (Rio's tribes are up in arms). The first line reads: "A cidade está dividida em territórios—muitos deles minados—de gangues rivais" (The city is divided into territories—many of them mined—held by rival gangs). The section included articles on several of these groups: "Metaleiros invadem os cemitérios e violam túmulos" (Heavy metal aficionados invade cemetery and violate graves); " 'Neohippies': Viagem no túnel do tempo" ("Neohippies": A trip in a time tunnel); " 'Funk' reproduz guerra de bandidos" ("Funk" reproduces the battles among narcotraffickers); " 'Carecas': Contra 'gays' e drogados" ("Skinheads": Against "gays" and drug addicts).

19 The text of the speech is "Atenção, senhor, tenente comandante da patrulha da polícia militar do estado, pedimos o seu comparecimento para ver se retira o povo que invadiram, para que possamos e tenhamos qualidade de apresentar com melhor brilhantismo, com mais gesto, esta coisa maravilhosa que é o nosso folclore." (Attention, sir, lieutenant commander of the military police of the state, we request your presence to see if you can remove the people who have invaded, so that we can, and have the quality to, demonstrate with greater brilliance and more grace this marvelous thing that is our folklore.)

Chapter 5. Parlaying Culture into Social Justice

1 This chapter builds on previous research presented in Yúdice 1999a.

2 The promotion of self-help among grassroots mobilization has been criticized for letting the state off the hook, so to speak. The appeal to government to act responsibly is, however, a central effort of Ação da Cidadania and Viva Rio.

3 Like Los Angeles, another city of spectacle, Rio was portrayed as pathological, a "sick organism," in the words of a newspaper editor cited by Ventura (1994: 69). Even in the United States, the metaphor of illness was picked up, as in James Brooke's reports: "Rio de Janeiro, long romanticized as a beguiling cocktail of sea, sun, sex and mountains, is now Brazil's sickest city" (1994b: A4).

4 According to a member of Viva Rio's coordinating council, urban violence mostly affects young men. "By the age of 20, they have either made it to the top or they are dead" (Faria 1994). For this reason, Viva Rio aimed one of its principal actions at young favelados and encouraged them to give up their weapons (provided by the narcotraffickers) for food and toys. The weapons were transformed into a "sculpture for peace" by the artist Vilmar Madruga (Escóssia 1994; "Crianças trocam suas 'armas' por brinquedos" 1994).

5 Flávio Negão was killed by the police in 1994. He was 24 years old.

6 The role of the media was a topic of heated discussion at a 1994 conference on "The Media, Drugs, and Criminality," held in the wake of several high-profile killings, apparent social upheavals, and the formation of Viva Rio. Rondelli, for example, argues that the image of Rio and its residents (Cariocas) is "constructed by conta-

gion, more the creation of a discursive foundation laid by the press than necessarily a real referent" (1994–95: 106). She goes on to argue that the violence is portrayed as pervasive, as if the whole city were involved in criminality, instead of quite specific actors in particular places. Neto, Castro, and Lucas focus at one point on the synecdochal treatment of the episode in Vigário Geral, laid out serially like a telenovela and extending to the entirety of the city (1995: 125). Such images have been exploited especially by São Paulo newspapers, ever interested in downgrading their rival city.

7   The study also confirmed that youth of all strata take issue with the representations of Rio as the most violent city in Brazil and are quite aware, as I argued in chapter 4, of the forces—and the related interests—that account for both the violence and the representations. Favela residents interviewed in focus groups, for example, adamantly challenged the representation that poor youth are criminals and instead quite accurately blamed the violence on unequal social conditions, narcotraffic and corruption, and lack of respect for rights among the police. See especially chapters 6 to 8 of Minayo et al. 1999.

8   According to Paulo Sérgio Pinheiro, director of the Núcleo de Estudos da Violência (Center for the Study of Violence) at the University of São Paulo, the high rate of deaths among shantytown (or "inner-city") youths "is a phenomenon which also has been taking place in Europe and the USA. The social differences are the causes of the problem. These youths do not have access to social benefits, which bespeaks the failure of the public authorities" (Servico Brasileiro de Justiça e Paz, "Brazil: Growing Urban Violence," July 14, 1994, online posting).

9   Communication is also one of the main forms of action taken up by the Ação da Cidadania (Citizen Action Initiative) and its parent organization, IBASE. According to the organization's newsletter, "IBASE operates fundamentally in the field of communication. It promotes public debate with the goal of strengthening movements to shape opinion, capable of addressing civil society, political parties and the State, as well as corporations and the business world. The focus of the citizen's message is participation, the surpassing of individualism and indifference, public action to orient the State and the economic system to questions of citizenship" (Jornal da Cidadania 37, online posting).

10   For a list of the members of the council, see Viva Rio 2001 home page.

11   See "Rio dá uma chance à Paz" 1993; "Vereadores dançam na chuva" 1993; "Carioca enfrenta até chuva e pára por uma cidade melhor" 1993; "Viva Rio é para sempre" 1993.

12   Much of this account is based on an interview with Rubem César Fernandes at ISER's offices (August 6, 1996). Contrasting opinions are drawn from other interviews, some with parties that preferred to remain anonymous, and from press reports.

13   Luiz Soares reports that General Câmara Senna, chief of Operação Rio, did not deny

press accounts that he said "the military were not social workers and were sure to leave a few scars on the Constitution" (1996: 271).

14 This account of press coverage was received by the Reage Rio home page on November 24, 2001.

15 *Malandragem* is the poor man's way of "getting over" in Brazilian society. The *malandro*, celebrated in samba lyrics, much like the roguish protagonists of the blues, lives off of women, does not work, engages in petty thievery, in sum, embodies a "culture of poverty." It is believed that populist politicians tolerate malandragem because they are supported politically by organized crime and the poor generally through networks of clientelism and patronage. Flávio Negão, the local chief of the narcotraffic gang Comando Vermelho, when asked about his political leanings, responded "with almost rote pride of his neighborhood, 'Vigário Geral is Brizolista' [Brizola being one of the best-known populist politicians in Brazil]" (Brooke 1994c: A3). The classic studies of malandragem are Antônio Cândido's "Dialética da malandragem" (1970) and Roberto DaMatta's *Carnavias, malandros e heróis: Para uma sociologia do dilema brasileiro* (1979).

16 Amnesty International issued an "Urgent Action Bulletin" on Caio Ferraz's behalf on November 1, 1995: "Death Threats/Fear for Safety" (Anistia Internacional 1996). A "Real Brazil" online posting reports that "Ferraz will study international relations at the Massachusetts Institute of Technology" and "direct his N G O by e-mail" ("Fleeing the 'House of Peace' " 1995).

17 Antônio Rangel Bandeira and Viva Rio director Rubem César Fernandes, both appointed to the Brazilian delegation to the U N Conference on Illegal Traffic in Small and Light Weapons, reported in August 2001 that the United States, in a telling alliance with China, Russia, and Arab countries, refused to sign two of the more than eighty-five articles approved by all other nations. In light of the September 11 attacks, it is ironic that the two articles rejected by the United States had to do with the prohibition of arms sales to nongovernmental actors such as terrorists and guerrillas and greater control of arms sales to civilians (Bandeira and Fernandes 2001).

18 Viva Rio's home page gives detailed information on all its projects and campaigns (Viva Rio 2001). To get a sense of its activities throughout the years, see the following summary:

Viva Rio Projects 1995–1996

HEALTH CARE PROJECTS

Walk-in clinics in Canal do Anil, Jacarepaguá: center for training of community health care agents, with basic medical attention, in partnership with I S E R. The clinic is a result of intense activity of this group giving attention to victims of floods in February 1996.

Center for Liver Transplants in the Hospital do Fundão: mobilization of resources and lobby for credentialing, starting from the case of the child Gabriel. *Partnership with the Hospital do Fundão.*

HOUSING PROJECTS

"Residential Condominium Rio das Flores": construction of homes for those left homeless by the floods in February 1996 in Rio das Pedras, for 93 families. A collective, self-help initiative carried out in collaboration with SMH of the Mayor's Office, C&A department stores, and Centro Bento Rubião.

Street Paving Collective Action in Chapéu Mangueira, Leme: partnership with the Neighborhood Association.

PUBLIC SECURITY AND CITIZENSHIP PROJECTS

Monitoring of emergency report number: analysis of performance of emergency report number, with production of monthly reports for the Secretariat of Security and for public opinion. Partnership with Rio against Crime and ISER.

Rights Service Center: citizenship service centers in favelas, offering conflict mediation, defense of rights, and facilitation of access to justice. Agreement with the Ministry of Justice: to be initiated in August 1996. Partnership with Public Defender's Office, Public Ministry, and Tribunal of Justice.

"Public Security . . . Everyone's Responsibility": coordination of seven regional seminars examining new initiatives of cooperation among public security, state organs, and civil society initiatives. Agreement with the Ministry of Justice.

"Law and Liberty": biweekly interdisciplinary seminar on alternative policies in confronting urban violence. Partnership with ISER.

The Numbers of Violence: collection, organization, and analysis of data on violence in Rio de Janeiro. Partnership with ISER.

CAMPAIGNS

Reage Rio: campaign against the violence that culminated in the "Walk for Peace," on November 28, 1995. It had two main themes: reform of the police, integration of favelas with the city.

Solidarity with the Victims of February 1996 Floods: more than 400 tons of gifts were collected throughout the city and distributed in critical places in the Rocinha, Barra da Tijuca, Jacarepaguá, Cidade De Deus, and Itaguaí. R$425,000 of gifts in construction materials to build homes for those left homeless.

Environment Week: June 4–10, 1996: march on Copacabana beach with 40 municipal schools to publicize urban garbage, environmental education, and sport marathon "Mareé de Patins" at the MAÉ Complex. In partnership with ISER, Maré Limpa, and the local neighborhood associations. Also included bicycle tours, with 5,000 participants, in Nova Iguaçu. In partnership with Onda Verde (Green Wave).

Generation: primary and secondary school campaigns, conducted by students, to promote the idea of "Good Neighborhood" with the schools and communities of the poor in the neighborhood. Students from the schools tutor favela children and youth. Partnership with Ação da Cidadania, Grupo ECO, Afro Reggae, and others.

PROJECTS FOR THE GENERATION OF INCOME AND WORK

Credit for Micro-Businesses in Favelas: in development, with support of the Inter-American Development Bank. To be initiated in the second semester of 1996.

Training for Micro-Businesses in Favelas: in development, with support of the Inter-American Development Bank. To be initiated in the second semester of 1996.

Sebrae Service Center/Viva Rio in Rocinha: services for microbusinesses, adapting Sebrae methodology for the environment of the favela. Initiated in July 1996. Once implemented, to be extended on a large scale.

Training and Agency of Baby-Sitting Services: in Borel, for the public of Tijuca. In partnership with the Catholic Church of Borel and the Psychoanalytic Association. To be initiated in July 1996. A second center is being programmed for Pavão-Pavãozinho-Cantagalo, serving Copacabana, Ipanema, and Leblon.

Training of poor youth in restaurant services in historic buildings: in partnership with the Roberto Marinho Foundation, SANAE, and Central de Oportunidades. Initiated in July 1996.

Tourist Guides- Mirins: in Cerro Corá, serving tourists who go up to Corcovado. In partnership with the Neighborhood Association and the Church of São Judas Tadeu. Initiated in April 1996.

Graxa no Pé: reintegrated street children work as bootblacks in downtown businesses. Initiated in March 1996, at O Dia and Bozano Simonsen. Partnership with Se Essa Rua Fosse Minha (If That Street Were Mine).

EDUCATIONAL PROJECTS

TeleCourse 2000/Community: primary school for youth and adults, with methodology adapted to the environment of the favela. Experimental teleclassrooms in the favelas of Santa Marta, Borel, Cantagalo-Pavão-Pavãozinho. Partnership with Roberto Marinho Foundation and FUNENSEG. Initiated in July 1996. Once initiated, to be reproduced widely.

Youth Link: BBS connecting favela computer schools, open to the link with public and private schools in the city. Partnership with the Committee for the Democratization of Informatics, supported by Solidarity Community.

Peace Games: grand championship for children and youth (10–17 years of age), extending from the poor neighborhoods to the city, in the spirit of Olympic culture. Partnership with Rio 2004, Ministry of Sports, Solidarity Community. To be initiated in second semester of 1996.

Day Nursery in the Factory of Hope: in Acari. Support for day care center serving 50 children, with foreseen expansion to 400 children in 1996. Support in partnership with Solidarity Community.

Day Care Center "Heart of Geneva": in Vigário Geral. Support for the initiative of the

Comité Pour La Vie, with fundraising events in Geneva that resulted from the construction of a community day care center to be administered by the Secretariat of Social Development of the Mayor's Office in Rio de Janeiro. Initiated in March 1996.

Day Care Center in Chapéu Mangueira: support for Center of Coexistence, Batista Church of Leme. Partnership with Solidarity Community.

Urban Social Center of Antares, Parada de Lucas: support for sporting services and culture for youth. Partnership with local community organization. Supported by Solidarity Community.

Center for Culture and Citizenship: in Borel. Renovation of Neighborhood Association. A self-help, collective initiative.

Acari Day Care Center: renovation and equipment for Community Center in Acari. Day care for 100 children.

Sports Park in Maré: consultantship in planning project of Gestão do Parque. Partnership with Mayor's Office and neighborhood associations in the Complex of Maré.

19 Júnior and the members of the first Afro Reggae band met Regina Casé and Caetano Veloso at a conference that I coorganized with Heloísa Buarque de Hollanda at the Federal University of Rio de Janeiro in 1994. "Sinais de Turblência" (Signs of Turbulence) brought together academics, DJs, musicians, and community activists.

20 See chapter 9, note 32.

Chapter 6. Consumption and Citizenship?

1 See the commentary in chapter 2 on Paul DiMaggio's research findings on beliefs of political and cultural polarization in the United States.

2 Although I agree with Young (2000) that cultural claims are a political resource for claims for or against inequality, I do not understand culture as simply a pretext for politics. That particular understanding is fostered in the new epistemic conjuncture. In other words, politics is not constitutive of culture; instead, the two, along with economic rationales, are coconstitutive.

3 The ads cited are from 1994 and 1995 issues of the monthly magazine *Hispanic Business* (Santa Barbara, CA).

Chapter 7. The Globalization of Latin America: Miami

1 In "A Roster of World Cities," J. V. Beaverstock, R. G. Smith, and P. J. Taylor (1999) discern three types of world cities—alpha or full-service world cities; beta or major world cities; gamma or minor world cities—on the basis of the number of advanced producer services in accountancy, advertising, banking/finance, and law. In their first tier of full-service cities we find New York, London, Tokyo, and Paris; in their

second tier, Chicago, Frankfurt, Hong Kong, Los Angeles, Milan, and Singapore. Beta or major world cities include Brussels, Madrid, Mexico City, Moscow, San Francisco, São Paulo, Seoul, Sydney, Toronto, and Zurich.

2   Sergio Rozenblat was president of WEA Latina from 1992 to 1997 and president of the Latin American Recording Artists Society from 1999 to 2000. He is currently CRO of a new Internet portal, Aplauso.com, and a partner with the singer Julio Iglesias, the talk show host of *Sábado Gigante*, Don Francisco, and Larry Rosen, ex-manager of a record company, founder of the Internet company N2K, and a pioneer of music online.

3   It should be noted that the entertainment industry is spread out beyond Miami–Dade County and the City of Miami Beach; it includes a range of municipalities along the corridor from West Palm Beach, about fifty miles to the north, including Fort Lauderdale and Broward, and to the south, Coral Gables and Miami Beach. This fragmentation of the area into different political zones makes coordination of entertainment and new media policy difficult.

4   The Elián affair, capitalized on by Castro, also cost Cuban exiles some of the prestige they enjoy among many Cubans on the island. As one interviewee for a *Miami Herald* report said: "Trying to fight Fidel Castro by politicizing the plight of a 6-year-old boy was absurd" ("Exiles' Elián Protests" 2000).

5   To date, AOL's venture into Brazil has proven to be a fiasco, largely because of lack of local experience (Ferreira 2000).

6   This view was borne out by my interviews in March 2000 with Celia Bibragher, editor of *Art Nexus*; Bill Begert, director of the Rubell Family Collection; Amy Capellazzo, independent curator and former director of the Wolfson Galleries at Miami-Dade Community College; Carlos Cisneros, CEO of Cisneros Television Group; Bonnie Clearwater, director of the Museum of Contemporary Art, Miami; Rosa de la Cruz, collector of contemporary art; Peggy McKinley, chair of the One Community, One Goal initiative; Dahlia Morgan, director of the Florida International University Art Museum; Vivian Pfeiffer, Christies Miami; and Fred Snitzer, gallery owner. It is also confirmed by Roni Feinstein's 1999 comprehensive report on the Miami art scene.

7   A close reading of Ortiz's work and that of other writers and social science essayists like the Mexican José Vasconcelos and the Brazilian Gilberto Freyre reveals that the negative implications and degenerative diagnoses of nonwhite races in nineteenth-century social Darwinism are never fully exorcized from the celebratory constructions of hybrid national identities in the 1930s and 1940s. Until recently, transculturation was characterized by social commentators as an apt recognition of the contributions made by indigenous, African, and European peoples as they mixed, physically and/or culturally, in the national formations of Latin America. When Ortiz introduced the term in 1940 it was received positively by critics concerned with the democratization of culture. It signaled for them the importance of the popular (working-class and peasant) "stock" in which the ingredients of the national *ajiaco* ("stew") were blended (Ortiz 1939: 6). More recently, however, the

emphasis on synthesis inherent in this model has come under critique, for it subordinates the constituents that went into the cauldron. Indeed, a less nationally based conception of democracy has put the emphasis on the ingredients themselves rather than their absorption for the sake of union. In accordance with this contemporary critique of transculturation, it is possible to see the legacy of social Darwinism as a critical factor in the suppression of individual constituents in the process of narrating a hybrid nation (Yúdice 2003a).

8 Music and language are the two privileged grounds of transculturation. Materially, they most embody the processes of hybridization evident in the degenerations decried by social Darwinists as well as in the positive mestizajes celebrated by those who sought to lay bridges between the different constituencies of the nation. This process is best seen in Fernando Ortiz's and Alejo Carpentier's books on Cuban music and dance, which serve "to orchestrate the social, the perennial symphony of a culture" (Ortiz [1951] 1981: 41). African-derived musics are the quintessential meeting place of the inside and outside of a community that changes and yet remains the same. Rather than mimicry or outright plagiarism of European musics, of which Afro–New World musics are usually accused, they should be considered a "remodelación de lo ajeno" (remodeling of what is not one's own) (112), echoing Mikhail Bakhtin's insight that expression or language is never wholly "one's own" but is "populated" with others' value-laden voices. It is, rather, in the creative appropriation of others' words, accents, nuances, and styles that one acquires "one's own" voice (Bakhtin 1981: 294).

Chapter 8. Free Trade and Culture

1 I would like to thank Donna Lazarus for research assistance and much initiative in conducting the survey of arts professionals.

2 In Latin countries the rights of authors or *droits d'auteur* (based in the Civil Code) imply a moral tie between authors and their works. In the Anglo-American tradition (based in Common Law), the *copyright* literally means that whoever has the right of ownership can set the terms of a work's reproduction, independently of the will of its author. In the increasingly transnational world of cultural markets, Latin countries consider it crucial to maintain the rights of authors over works, especially in view of the premise that creativity is the major engine of accumulation in the new economy.

3 In *A moderna tradição brasileira*, Renato Ortiz (1988) uses the international reworking of Gramsci's "national popular" to refer to the integration of Brazil into an international order of mass media that requires certain standards of production. The fact that Brazil is one of the largest producers of television programs for export has been internalized into the styles of popular consumption and in ways that do not correspond to the cultural imperialism hypothesis ("Do popular-nacional ao internacional-popular?" 182–206). Of course, this sleight of phrase does not carry

with it the Gramscian assumptions about the ability of popular groups to influence the "leading" groups, which in any case have been internationalized.

4 For several decades the movie industry has been a thoroughly transnational operation, with substantial corporate ownership by Japanese, French, and Australian companies, transnational production arrangements with European studios, overseas location shooting, and the integration of European and Latin American actors, directors, and producers. Los Angeles continues to be the site of central decision making and postproduction facilities, thus maintaining efficiency while maximizing innovation in global audience attraction (Miller 1993: 9). In Miami, new studios have opened for the production of made-for-TV movies and telenovelas for Spanish-language television in the United States and Latin America. Mexican and Venezuelan networks like Televisa and Venevisión have major shares in these initiatives (Yúdice 1999b and chapter 7). These initiatives will further integrate Latin American audiovisual styles with U.S. production values.

5 Although movie theaters made a comeback in the late 1990s, largely due to the acquisitions and mergers of theaters by cineplex conglomerates (García Canclini 1999: 41–42), the increase in cable and satellite delivery, with the exponential increase in program offerings (mostly of U.S. movies and TV programs), means that the notion that U.S. film is film tout court is still prevalent. That more people go to well-built, comfortable cineplexes in malls and shopping centers to see mostly U.S. films contributes to this "naturalization."

6 Chapter 3 elaborates on governments' and foundations' interests in culture as a resource for healing social rifts, "empowering" communities, and even providing teaching.

7 In chapter 7, however, I find evidence that the art scene in Miami is leaving multiculturalism behind or realigning it with the international, hoping to set some of the trends.

8 The marriage of the local and the international in the case of the art triennial insITE partly gets around this double bind of lumping together Latinos and Latin Americans, but it also raises other problems that I analyze in chapter 6.

9 A recent report shows that under Fox's presidency, Mexico continues to use its embassies and consulates to sponsor artistic and cultural events to influence foreign relations, above all in the United States (Kinzer 2002b).

10 "Line by line as we read this continental page from West to East we find the record of social evolution. It begins with the Indian and the hunter; it goes on to tell of the disintegration of savagery by the entrance of the trader, the pathfinder of civilization; we read the annals of the pastoral stage in ranch life; the exploitation of the soil by the raising of unrotated crops of corn and wheat in sparsely settled farming communities; the intensive culture of the denser farm settlement; and finally the manufacturing organization with city and factory system" (F. Turner 1920: 11).

11 "The need of a constantly expanding market for its products chases the bourgeoisie over the whole surface of the globe. It must nestle everywhere, settle everywhere,

establish connections everywhere. The bourgeoisie has through its exploitation of the world market given a cosmopolitan character to production and consumption in every country" (Marx and Engels, [1848] 1967: 83).

12 For accounts of border culture, see Calderón and Saldívar 1991, Ybarra-Frausto 1992, and McCracken and García 1995.

13 Claire F. Fox (1999: 7) conducts a brief review of the proportional weighting of social science and humanities or cultural issues taken up by educational institutions and think tanks that deal with the U.S.-Mexico border.

14 The introduction to *Post-nationalist American Studies* criticizes Desmond and Domínguez for the "optimism" of their supposedly "cosmopolitan" perspective, taking issue with the idea that a more global framework will produce a more equitable production of knowledge. The authors of that introduction back up their critique with the wholly unsupported allegation that the race, gender, and sexuality biases of forces in the world economy will prevail under such a cosmopolitanism (Curiel et al. 2000: 8). But Desmond and Domínguez never say that race, gender, and sexuality are not important; they say that U.S. perspectives on these are not sufficient to produce a decentering of paradigms necessary to have a better view of oneself. The introduction argues that cosmopolitanism buys into capitalism but presumably has no similar critique of multiculturalism. In any case, the status of international networks depends on *who* gets together in those networks. And that is likely to follow from the proclivities of *those who invite* the international partners, or who have U.S. minority scholars stand in for people from third world countries. For a critique of this "We are the World-view," see Yúdice 1992b.

15 The acronym for the Common Market of the South is MERCOSUL in Portuguese and MERCOSUR in Spanish. I use the Portuguese version because Brazil is leading this initiative.

Chapter 9. Producing the Cultural Economy: The Collaborative Art of inSite

1 Many people have collaborated in thinking through the issues in this chapter. I would like to thank David Avalos, Judith Barry, Norton Batkin, Jo Anne Berelowitz, Jessica Bradley, Nelson Brissac, Susan Buck-Morss, Jordan Crandall, Carmen Cuenca, Olivier Debroise, Roman De Salvo, Mauricio Dias and Walter Riedweg, Andrea Fraser, Néstor García Canclini, Silvia Gruner, Sofia Hernández, Mary Jane Jacob, Michael Krichman, Miwon Kwon, Dermis León, Iñigo Manglano-Ovalle, Linda Merritt, Ivo Mesquita, Tobias Ostrander, Mari Carmen Ramírez, Armando Rascón, Melania Santana, Osvaldo Sánchez, Sohnya Sayres, Lorelei Stewart, José Manuel Valenzuela Arce, and Teresa Williams. I would also like to acknowledge the support of the U.S.-Mexico Fund for Culture.

2 I underscore the root "labor" in the word "collaboration" to emphasize that two or more parties who undertake a task or contribute to it are doing work. Many tasks are

socially constructed in such a way that only some of the parties engaged in the activity are to be remunerated financially. The other collaborators, who contribute value added to the activity, presumably derive a nonmaterial return for their participation. The classic example of this differential distribution of value for labor is "women's work," especially their collaboration within the family unit, where the satisfaction of motherhood was considered proper remuneration. Artists' work often goes unremunerated financially because it is assumed that they derive spiritual or aesthetic value from it. But artists' collaborators derive even less financial remuneration, for they are not perceived as the authors or coauthors of the activity. Financial remuneration is not, of course, the end-all and be-all of cultural activity; in our society, however, it is the form of recognition par excellence. The problem is that recognition flows in multiple and contradictory tracks. I take up this line of argument below, when I examine the organization of insITE and other similar art programs that rely on the collaboration of the "community," a word that is open to many interpretations but in most instances refers to people of low economic status, usually racialized and confined (by class and race and sometimes gender) to poorly served neighborhoods. It may be ironic, yet nonetheless a fact, that poor communities' share of compensation for collaboration in cultural programs is usually conceived of as some "higher" form of enrichment rather than financial remuneration; this fact is consistent with the social construction of inequality, evident even in do-good programs that seek to "empower" the disadvantaged. Stephan Dillemuth, a participant in "Services: Working-Group Discussions," remarks that when artists reflect on "serving audiences, serving communities: actually, they serve you. Don't forget it" ("Services" 1997: 141).

3 The reviewer for the Los Angeles Times also finds that "there's more interesting new art in insITE97 than in all of Documenta X" and that it "gives the Sculpture Project in Münster a good run for its money" (Knight 1997).

4 The words cited are those of Hugh Davies, the museum director, paraphrasing the accusations made by members of the BAW/TAF (Berelowitz 1997: 74).

5 According to Sofia Hernández (1997), the inclusion of Mexican institutions was suggested by the insITE partners at the Centro Cultural de la Raza in San Diego.

6 Vito Acconci's reaction when he first saw the border fence, as related in Hernández's Transitio (1997:77), is characteristic: "I had never seen anything so striking. When I saw that site, it couldn't be refused or denied. It was a sign of the most malicious . . . it functioned as a gesture of malice . . . I returned to my studio in New York and could not get that image out of my mind."

7 Other examples of the conceptual punchline or ironic reversal are Louis Hock's International Waters/Aguas internacionales (1997), twin water fountains on either side of the fence from which a window has been cut that enables the drinkers to see each other and thus become aware of their reliance on a common resource; and Marcos Ramírez Erre's Toy an Horse, a huge bifrontal Trojan horse placed at the border check-

point and meant to generate reflections on the border experience. Many more artists elected to situate their projects on the border for insITE2000–2001, among them Gustavo Artigas's staging of soccer and basketball matches to highlight the cultural commonalities and differences among the populations of both countries; Judith Barry's projection of a video above the border crossing booth, directly engaging the images of globalization as they are produced by television and the media; Arturo Cuenca's satellite images of the two cities projected onto billboards on either side of the border; Mauricio Dias and Walter Riedweg's video documentary of their interviews with border patrol officers regarding their trusting and affective relations with their dogs and mothers; Silvia Gruner's video documentary of her sessions with psychoanalysts from both countries as they analyze and drive her across the border; Alfredo Jaar's one thousand cloud-like elastic white globes floated over the border to commemorate the thousands who died crossing it; Iñigo Manglano-Ovalle's installation of weather stations on both sides of the border, highlighting the shared environment and information that shapes daily life; and Valeska Soares's border-straddling garden, meant to create a communal space across the line of difference.

8 Programs like Art in Public Places and Art in Architecture were ancestors of the current U.S. system of arts administration put into place with the creation of the NEA and the state arts councils in the mid-1960s. Most of the artworks commissioned under the auspices of these programs and in most community development block grants did not take the ecology of the local communities into consideration. In many cases, these mostly modernist public artworks were adjuncts to the gentrification process. Even pieces that pretended to question their surroundings, like Richard Serra's *Tilted Arc*, were not sensitive to community.

9 In 1972 the Regents of the University of the State of New York issued a report, "Culture and Education: A Statement of Policy and Proposed Action," that indicted cultural institutions for their lack of credibility, which fed into their financial difficulties, and their "lack of understanding as to their educational role in what is increasingly becoming a 'knowledge society' " (179). Formulated in the wake of a decade of tumultuous urban "disorder" and the claims for inclusion by ethnic, racial, and sexual minorities as well as by women, the report advocated the involvement of cultural institutions in rebuilding the fabric of society. These issues have been chronicled in many places. For a discussion of the shift toward social relevance in the 1960s and 1970s, see chapter 2 and Yúdice 1999c. See also Hancocks 1987.

10 One particularly relevant precedent is the "maintenance art" of artists like Mierle Laderman Ukeles, which by fiat endowed maintenance (particularly women's) work with artistic value. By the mid-1970s it was exhibited at the Whitney and funded by the NEA. See Phillips 1995.

11 For a comprehensive analysis of the arts as governmental procedure, see Yúdice 1999c.

12 Miwon Kwon (personal communication, August 10, 2000) points out that the apprehension of history through geological time in Robert Smithson's work makes

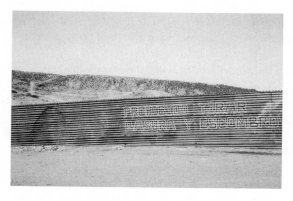

19, 20, 21. "Las Reglas del Juego/The Rules of the Game" by Gustavo Artigas, at inSITE2000. Photos by George Yúdice. "The Rules of the Game" consists of (19) Game = a simultaneous basketball/soccer game in a stadium in Playas de Tijuana; (20) Fronton = a handball court or Fronton built by the artists at the border in a poor outlying area of Tijuana; (21) FenceProhibitionSign = a sign written on the border fence near the handball court, which prohibits throwing garbage onto the U.S. side.

it much more complex than a simple siting in physical space. The same goes for Serra, for whom, as in Smithson's case, a site is not a tabula rasa. While this is never the case—we can add Jenny Holzer to this list of site-specific interventionists who choose their sites for particular effects—my point has to do with the new governmental injunction (emanating from funders like the Rockefeller Foundation and local arts councils) that requires artists to be "sensitive" to and involve the inhabitants and users of the space in which they situate their work. That injunction elicits certain rhetorics and procedures on the part of the artist, which are often concealed or displayed as part of a political (dare I say politically correct?) agenda. Serra, of course, operates in a different circuit that depends less on public and nonprofit agencies; but that circuit also has its own rhetorics and procedures concerning the value of art. Some might want to see these two circuits—the mainstream in which Serra operates and what elsewhere I have called a parallel and compensatory market for minority, feminist, and "progressive" artists—as pitched in a cultural struggle for hegemony in the field of art. I think that together they structure that field of art, incising the grooves of what can be thought and envisioned. Together they provide the legitimacy and authority of that thinking and envisioning. The point of my critique, then, is not to opt for one or the other but to produce an archaeology, that is, to map out the networks according to which both discourses on art construe the thinkable in this subfield of culture.

13 The published version of the catalog abbreviated the statement to "what the curators had in mind was the installation of a cultural practice in the region . . . It freed insITE to look beyond traditional notions of site specificity . . . and to think about the ways in which artistic practice might engage various sectors of our two communities" (Krichman and Cuenca 2002: 14).

14 I am indebted to Mary Jane Jacob for this observation (personal communication, July 22, 2000).

15 I would like to thank Sofia Hernández for discussing the maquiladora metaphor with me.

16 David Kushner (1998) points out that critics of the Twentieth-Century Fox studio took to calling it a Hollywood maquiladora, thus underscoring its placement in Mexico as a way of reducing the operating costs of making films. This Hollywood maquiladora and the struggle of Popotlans over its transformation of the community is a good example of the problems that arise in the new international division of cultural labor.

17 For a pioneering account of the artist as service provider, see Fraser 1997. Grant Kester extends the critique of artists as service providers for communities, noting that their representational practice on behalf of communities is premised on the "convenient alibi" that they "always seem to move from a position of greater to lesser privilege" (1995: 5). But an analysis has yet to be written of the community as service provider. A point of departure would be the recognition that neoliberal forms of management have displaced the responsibility to provide welfare onto the

communities that make up civil society. In other words, communities, particularly disadvantaged ones, are enjoined to provide the means of their own survival as well as the legitimacy for neoliberalism. I discuss this type of government in chapter 3.

18 Some interviewees have requested confidentiality. In keeping with that request, there are places in this chapter where statements remain unidentified.

19 The Centro Cultural/Arte Contemporáneo and the Museo de Monterrey were recently closed by their backers for financial reasons.

20 inSITE has gotten funding from many sources, but mainstay contributors have been the California Arts Council, the City of San Diego Commission for Arts and Culture, the NEA, CONACULTA, FONCA, the Instituto Nacional de Bellas Artes, and the Mexican Government Tourism Office, on the public side of the partnership. On the foundation/not-for-profit side: the James Irvine Foundation, the Lucille and Ronald Neeley Foundation, the Peter Norton Family Foundation, the Rockefeller Foundation, the Schoepflin Trust, the Warhol Foundation, the Jumex Foundation, and the binational and public-private hybrid U.S.-Mexico Fund for Culture/Fideicomiso para la Cultura México-Estados Unidos. The Catellus Development Corporation, Qualcomm, Aeroméxico, the Fondo Mixto de Promoción Turística de Tijuana, Grupo Calimax, Barbara Metz Public Relations, and Telecomunicaciones de México are some of the corporate contributors, which are recruited on a per-version basis. inSITE has also received important sponsorship from many San Diegans, including family members of the U.S. codirector.

21 For a fuller account of the emergence of the U.S.-Mexico Fund for Culture, see Yúdice 1997.

22 See "Parque Industrial Pacífico"; Tijuana Economic Development Corporation 2000; "Border Corridors: When Borders Become Bridges" (2000).

23 "When the disorganization and disaggregation of the field of bodies disrupt the regulatory fiction of heterosexual coherence, it seems that the expressive model [of gender identity] loses its descriptive force. That regulatory ideal is then exposed as a norm and a fiction that disguises itself as a developmental law regulating the sexual field that it purports to describe" (Butler 1990: 136).

24 The "semiotic" is the term that Kristeva uses to refer to Plato's *chora*, the place or receptacle where representation occurs but which cannot be represented. As a "process . . . [of] rhythmic space" preceding the making of meaning, the chora precedes the symbolic. Kristeva goes on to conflate the chora and the mother's body, thus providing a (disputable) foundation for the pre-Oedipal, that is, for processes of significance (in contrast to signification) that are unintelligible from the purview of the social. Another (nonfeminist) version of this would be pre-Oedipal polymorphous perversity (1984: 26–27).

25 Taking his cue from Marx's dialectical insight in the *Grundrisse* that the critique of any phenomenon is only possible when it has become cognizable by unfolding to its completion, Peter Bürger proposes that the institutionalization of art as a realm separate from the rest of life only unfolded to its perfection in European aes-

theticism at the close of the nineteenth century, thus constituting the precondition for the "historical" avant-gardes to recognize art's full accommodation to bourgeois ideology. This recognition opened the way to a will to reconnect art and life (1984: 17).

Bürger's account may be amended by acknowledging that the avant-gardes are not just an immanentist expression of the "unfolding" of bourgeois art. The rejection of institutionalization also stems from the embrace of other life experiences, such as those of subordinated classes and regions as well as colonized peoples. The institutionalization of art, in fact, negated these experiences, opening itself to challenges from these "nonmainstream" constituencies in a postcolonial or post-Eurocentric era. Furthermore, from a dialogical perspective, it is quite illusory to think that there is any one moment when a form or a practice unfolds to completion. Instead, the avant-gardes can be located in different contexts, in which they may fulfill a diversity of particular symbolic responses to a historical conjuncture of social, political, economic, and cultural circumstances. Indeed, an avant-garde may be a contradictory response, furthering a cultural or political demand at the same time that it corroborates a social or economic status quo. For a critique of avant-gardist aesthetics in the context of postmodernity, see "Postmodernism in the Periphery" (Yúdice 1993b) and "Rethinking the Theory of the Avant-Garde from the Periphery" (Yúdice 1999e).

26 For a critique of this report, see Yúdice 1999c.

27 Personal communication, June 26, 2000.

28 The suspicion that the therapeutic ethos of talk shows had crept into this kind of collaborative work with victims was voiced by many people in the audience at "ConversationIV."

29 Anyone who has applied for a grant is familiar with the experience of tailoring a proposal to meet the funder's criteria, figuring that the process has enough play to allow one to do what one wants in the first place. Tailoring, however, can vary markedly. As someone who has many years of experience evaluating applications for grants and fellowships, it is often quite evident when an applicant puts aside his or her trajectory to accommodate the parameters of the grant description. This means that the funding agency exerts a conditioning force on the field, often producing the behavior that it is seeking. This "conduct of conduct," or channeling of behavior, is what Foucault meant by governmentality. See Foucault 1991 and Yúdice 1999c for an application to the cultural sphere, especially cultural policy.

30 Stephan Dillemuth advocates "us[ing] the institutions [that use you] to the extent possible" ("Services" 1997: 141). Gilles Deleuze and Félix Guattari's expression "line of flight" is a more mobile, "deterritorializing" strategy, implying that one can somehow outrun the incorporative force of institutionality. See Deleuze and Guattari 1987.

31 Interviewee requested confidentiality.

32 Indeed, the Rockefeller Foundation recently changed the name of its Arts and Humanities Division to the Creativity and Culture Program to highlight its increasing interest in the underrepresented. See Rockefeller Foundation 1999: 9. Though this is a laudable emphasis, it should be pointed out that its discourse of "enrichment" (not to be confused with "material well-being") for poor communities falls into the trap of dichotomizing "riches" and "value," on which, following Marx, I comment below. This despite the attempt to not treat issues of health, work, food, and creativity in isolation. One curious result of a perspective founded on "enrichment" is the Rockefeller Foundation's 1999 *Annual Report*, which is largely a photoessay that explores the daily life of two poor families, one in San Diego and the other in Epworth, Zimbabwe. The photos and text are in the tradition of *The Family of Man*, the Foundation playing the role of anthropologist bent on showing the humanity of these families while at the same time arguing that globalization is the culprit that threatens their traditions. Notwithstanding, in the second part of the report, "1999 Financial Reports," we find out that the Foundation invests in international securities, that is, that it itself is a part of the globalization that is impugned in the first part of the report.

33 Jacob has a different interpretation of the act of framing: "A frame also calls attention to something, gives us an opportunity to recognize and reflect, brings it from the margins (albeit perhaps to be consumed!), and doesn't necessarily author it" (personal communication, July 22, 2000).

34 Jeremy Rifkin (1995) has argued that the "third sector" of the civil society community, situated between the state and the market, takes up the slack of the retreating neoliberal state at the same time that it provides an ethical alternative to consumerist culture as the conduit for identity. Incentivized by the state, it can become an even greater engine of job creation as most social welfare needs are carried out in this not-for-profit sector. Rifkin speaks of the decline of work, but if we posit a cultural economy, as I do later in this chapter, we see that new forms of value production or labor have emerged.

35 For the various functions of the contemporary curator, see Nathalie Heinich and Michael Pollak 1996; Yúdice 1994d, 1995; M. Ramírez 1996; and Brenson 1998.

36 See note 32 above for a brief commentary on how philanthropy envisions the "enrichment" of the poor.

Conclusion

1   The survey on Bush's performance conducted by the Pew Research Center for the People and the Press (November 28, 2001) showed that 84 percent of the population approve. In the case of African Americans, "who were most critical of Bush in the early months of his presidency, 60% currently approve of his job performance, up nearly two-fold since before the attacks" (Pew Research Center 2001a). The Repub-

lican National Committee issued a report (November 12–16, 2001) on a *Los Angeles Times* survey that shows African American and Latino approval of Bush's handling of the war on Afghanistan to be 59 percent and 86 percent, respectively.

2 President Zia of Pakistan wanted to create an Islamic opposition to the Soviet Union in Central Asia. The CIA collaborated with Pakistan's Inter-Services Intelligence to recruit radical Muslims from around the world to join the Afghan Mujaheddin's attacks on Tajikistan and Uzbekistan (Rashid 2001). After the Taliban took control in the mid-1990s, the United States continued to provide support, even until 2001, when it provided $143 million for humanitarian aid and to curtail production of opium (Kellner 2001). Reflecting on the U.S. role in Afghanistan, Zbigniew Brzezinksi (1998) said, "What was more important in the world view of history? The Taliban or the fall of the Soviet Empire? A few stirred-up Muslims or the liberation of Central Europe and the end of the Cold War?" Asked if he regretted this policy, he responded, "Regret what? That secret operation was an excellent idea. It had the effect of drawing the Russians into the Afghan trap and you want me to regret it? The day that the Soviets officially crossed the border, I wrote to President Carter: We now have the opportunity of giving to the USSR its Vietnam war."

3 To give a sense of the extent of the fall in tourism, the São Paulo consulate processed 1,600 visa applications per day before September 11. After that date and until the end of November, the number of applications had not risen above 40 per day (César Borza, personal communication, November 22, 2001).

4 As Ana María Ochoa Gautier (2002) explains, the use of art and culture for the purposes of peace often covers over deep-rooted conflicts that need to be brought to the surface if there is to be effective negotiation. Cultural pageantry of the type performed by most 9/11 commemorations engaged in practices that shoved onto the "enemy" all that is wrong in the world. This indeed is the strategy of most politicians and official actions, and culture was, with few exceptions such as those of "Not in Our Name" and "Refuse and Resist," harnessed to do their bidding.

5 As I revise the manuscript of this book nearly a year after the attacks, myriad commemorative events have been planned in New York City. However, the institutionalized mourning and the official character of many art projects, particularly those that stage multicultural pageantry, point up what is most missing in our society: working through the issues and giving voice to real public critique. There are a couple of Web sites where a good deal of the ephemera of the commemorations is archived: http://www.nyu.edu/fas/projects/vcb/case_911_FLASHcontent.html. Reports and critical assessments are available at http://september11.archive.org/; http://www.counterpunch.org/archive.html.

6 "If the memorial was done correctly, he said, 'millions of people would come here. And you'll have all the economic development you want, and you can do the office space in a lot of different places'" (Cardwell 2001).

7 Operación Centauro was developed by the CIA and the Argentine Intelligence Secretariat on the triple border of Argentina, Paraguay, and Brazil after the terrorist

attack on the Israel-Argentine Mutual Association. The purpose was to infiltrate presumed Islamic fundamentalist groups, such as the Hezbollah, which, according to Argentine intelligence, was planning to bomb the U.S. embassy in Asunción (Bonasso 2001).

8 All of the quotations from the discourses of Viñas, Bonafini, and Shoklender and Lema can be found in Verbitsky (2001). The complete text of Bonafini's discourse can be found in Bonafini 2001.

WORKS CITED

Abaroa, Gabriel. 1998. "Q & A with Gabriel Abaroa." *Latin Music Quarterly* 24 January 1998.

Abbe, Mary. 1994. "Walker Seems Surprised at Reaction to Mutilation Show." *Star Tribune* (Minneapolis) 29 March: 8E.

Abramson, Michael. 1971. *PALANTE: Young Lords Party.* New York: Pantheon.

Abreu, Fernanda. 1992. SLA_: *Be Sample*. Recording. Emi-Odeon Brasil 368 780404 2.

ACLU. 2002. "Safe and Free in Times of Crisis." Press release. 24 January. http://www.aclu.org/safeandfree/index.html

Ações do Viva Rio. 1996. Brochure. Rio de Janeiro: Viva Rio.

Acuña, Rodolfo. 1980. *Occupied America: A History of Chicanos*. 2d ed. New York: Harper and Row.

Adelman, A., and P. Somers. 1992. "Exploring an Academic Common Market in North America." *Educational Review* 73.4: 33–38.

Adorno, Theodor. [1938] 1978. "On the Fetish-Character in Music and the Regression of Listening." In *The Essential Frankfurt School Reader*, ed. Andrew Arato and Eike Gebhardt. New York: Urizen, 270–299.

———. 1984. *Aesthetic Theory*. London: Verso.

Afro Reggae. 2000. *Nova Cara*. Recording. Universal Music. 73145427972.

"Afro Reggae vira tese de mestrado." 1997. *Afro Reggae* 5.25 (January).

"After GATT Pique, Pix Pax Promoted." 1994. *Daily Variety*, 8 June: 1, 16.

Aletti, Vince. 2000. "Eyewitness Photographers at Ground Zero Start Making Sense." *Village Voice*, 10–16 October.

"Ali Asked to Film Public Announcement." 2001. *New York Times*, 23 December (online edition).

Ali, Tariq. 2001. "Germany's Green Police State Busted in Munich." 30 October. http://www.counterpunch.org/wtcarchive.html

Allor, Martin, and Michelle Gagnon. 1997. *L'État de culture: Généalogie discursive des politiques culturelles québécoises*. 2d ed. Montréal: Groupe de Recherche sur la Citoyenneté Culturelle, Concordia University, Université de Montreal.

Alvarez, Marcelo, Mónica Lacarrieu, and Verónica Pallini, eds. 2001. *La (Indi)Gestión Cultural*. Buenos Aires: CICCUS.

Alvarez, Sonia E. Forthcoming. *Contentious Transformations: Feminist Readings of Civil Society*,

Social Movements, and Transnational Organizing in Latin America. Berkeley: University of California Press.

Alvarez, Sonia E., Evelina Dagnino, and Arturo Escobar, eds. 1998. *Cultures of Politics, Politics of Cultures: Re-Visioning Latin American Social Movements.* Boulder, CO: Westview Press.

American Review of Canadian Studies. 1991. Special issue on Canada–United States Free Trade Agreement. (summer/autumn).

ANDES-SN (Seção Sindical dos Docentes da UFRJ). 2001. "Em defensa da Universidade Pública." *Boletim especial.* 20 August. http://www.adufrj.org.br/2001/jornar200801/debate%20010820.pdf

Andrews, Edmund L. 1995. "Court Stalls F.C.C. Program for Women and Minorities." *New York Times,* 16 March: A22.

Andrews, Edmund L. 2002. "I.M.F. Loan to Brazil Also Shields U.S. Interests." *New York Times,* 9 August.

"Anjos da Guarda negam versão da PM." 1992. *Folha de São Paulo,* 20 October: 3–3.

"Anjos' usam artes marciais." 1992. *Jornal do Brasil,* 22 October: 5.

Ante América, Regarding America. 1993. Catalogue. Gerardo Mosquera, Carolina Ponce de León, and Rachel Weiss, curators. Bogotá: Biblioteca Luis-Angel Arango.

Antonelli, Mirta. 2001. "Memorias: Entre el acontecimiento y la diseminación. (Aportes para una 'periodización' de la experiencia democrática argentina)." Paper presented at the 2001 meeting of the Latin American Studies Association, Washington, DC, 6–8 September.

———. 2002. "Nuevos escenarios/ nuevas interlocuciones: Para re-pensar las exclusiones." Elizabeth Jelin, Néstor García Canclini, Daniel Mato. In *Globalización, Cultura y Transformaciones Sociales,* ed. Daniel Mato. Special issue of *Relea.*

Anzaldúa, Gloria. 1987. *Borderlands/La frontera: The New Mestiza.* San Francisco: Aunt Lute.

Appiah, K. Anthony. 1994. "Culture, Subculture, Multiculturalism." Paper presented at the Bohen Foundation, New York City, 3 March.

Appiah, K. Anthony, and Amy Gutmann, eds. 1996. *Color Conscious: The Political Morality of Race.* Princeton: Princeton University Press.

Apple, Jacki. 1994. "Performance Art Is Dead. Long Live Performance Art!" *High Performance* (summer).

Aranda Márquez, Carlos. 1994. "Alternativas Phoenix-México Alternatives." *Poliester* 3.9 (summer): 62–63.

Arfuch, Leonor. 1994. "Memorias de la Calle Pasteur." *Punto de Vista* 50 (November): 10–13.

Arian, Edward. 1989. *The Unfulfilled Promise: Public Subsidy of the Arts in America.* Philadelphia: Temple University Press.

Armstrong, Elizabeth, and Joan Rothfuss, eds. 1993. *In the Spirit of Fluxus.* Minneapolis: Walker Art Center.

Aronowitz, Stanley. 1994. "The Situation of the Left in the United States." *Socialist Review* 23. 3.

————. 1995. "Against the Liberal State: Act Up and the Emergence of Postmodern Politics." In *Social Postmodernism: Beyond Identity Politics*, ed. Linda Nicholson and Steven Seidman. Cambridge, England: Cambridge University Press.

————. 1996. "Against the Liberal State: Act Up and the Emergence of Postmodern Politics." In *The Death and Rebirth of American Radicalism*. New York: Routledge.

Arquilla, John, and David Ronfeldt, eds. 2001. *Networks and Netwars: The Future of Terror, Crime, and Militancy*. Rand. http://www.rand.org/publications/MR/MR1382/

Arriola, Magali. 1998. "insITE97 San Diego–Tijuana." *Art Nexus* (Jan.–March).

Arte-Reembolso/Art Rebate. 1993. Press release. Elizabeth Sisco, Louis Hock, and David Avalos, artists. Part of *La Frontera/The Border* exhibition, cosponsored by Centro Cultural de la Raza and Museum of Contemporary Art, San Diego.

Arthurs, Alberta, and Frank Hodsoll. 1998. "The Importance of the Arts Sector: How It Relates to the Public Purpose." *Journal of Arts Management, Law, and Society* 28.2 (summer): 102–108.

Artists Network of Refuse and Resist. 2001. "Artists' Performance in New York City: Our Grief Is Not a Cry for War." 10 October. http://www.artistsnetwork.org/news/news14.html

Aspe, Pedro. 1993. *Economic Transformation: The Mexican Way*. Cambridge, MA: MIT Press.

"Assembléia aprova CEI em sessão tumultuada." 1992. *Folha de São Paulo*, 9 October: 1–12.

Astarita, Rolando. 2001. "Crítica al discurso de Hebe Bonafini y renuncia a la UPMPM." 16 October. http://www.antroposmoderno.com/antro-articulo.php?id_articulo=12

Auslander, Philip. 1994. *Presence and Resistance: Postmodernism and Cultural Politics in Contemporary American Performance*. Ann Arbor: University of Michigan Press.

Avelar, Idelber. 1999. *The Untimely Present*. Durham: Duke University Press.

Ayres, B. Drummond, Jr. 1994. "Stepped-Up Border Patrols Halve Unlawful Crossings." *New York Times*, 13 December: A22.

Babb, Valerie. 1998. *Whiteness Visible: The Meaning of Whiteness in American Literature and Culture*. New York: New York University Press.

Baca, Judith. 1985. "Our People Are the Internal Exiles." In *Cultures in Contention*, ed. Doug Kahn and Diane Neumaier. Seattle: Real Comet Press.

————. 1987. "Murals/Public Art." In *Chicano Expressions: A New View in American Art*. New York: INTAR Latin American Gallery.

————. 1995. "Whose Monument Where? Public Art in a Many-Cultured Society." In *Dream Utopias, Nightmare Realities: Imaging Race and Culture within the World of Benetton Advertising*, ed. Lacy Back, Les Back and Vibecke Quaade. Special issue of *Third Text* 22 (spring).

Back, Les, and Vibecke Quaade. 1993. "Dream Utopias, Nightmare Realities: Imaging Race and Culture within the World of Benetton Advertising." *Third Text* 22 (spring).

"Baile só é bom se tiver briga." 1992. *Veja* 28 (October): 22.

Bakhtin, Mikhail. 1981. "Discourse in the Novel." In *The Dialogic Imagination: Four Essays* by M. M. Bakhtin. Ed. Michael Holquist. Trans. Caryl Emerson and Michael Holquist. Austin: University of Texas Press.

———. 1984. *Problems of Dostoevsky's Poetics*. Ed. and trans. Caryl Emerson. Minneapolis: University of Minnesota Press.

Balfe, Judith Huggins. 1987. "Artworks as Symbols in International Politics." *International Journal of Politics, Culture and Society* 1.2 (winter): 195–217.

———. 1989. "The Baby-boom Generation: Lost Patrons, Lost Audience." In *The Cost of Culture: Patterns and Prospects of Private Arts Patronage*, ed. Margaret Wyszomirski and Pat Clubb. New York: American Council for the Arts.

Balladur, Edouard. 1993. "Entrevista a Edouard Balladur, primer ministro francés. ¿Qué es lo que quiere EU . . . la desaparición del cine europeo?" Interview. *El Nacional* (Mexico), 23 October: 27.

Balmaseda, Liz. 2001. "Ashcroft Gives Ammo to Critics." *Miami Herald*, 10 December (online edition).

Bandeira, Antônio Rangel, and Rubem César Fernandes. 2001. "Armas sem controle." *no.com* 1 (August). ttp://www.no.com.br/servlets/newstorm.notitia.apresentacao. ServletDeNoticia? codigoDaNoticia=27943&dataDoJornal=996706814000

Banes, Sally. 1993. *Greenwich Village 1963: Avant-Garde Performance and the Effervescent Body*. Durham, NC: Duke University Press.

Baran, Paul. 1958. "On the Political Economy of Backwardness." In *The Economics of Underdevelopment*, ed. A. N. Agarwala and S. P. Singh. Bombay: Oxford University Press.

Barber, Benjamin R. 1995. *Jihad vs. McWorld: Terrorism's Challenge to Democracy*. New York: Ballantine.

———. 2001. "2001 Introduction: Terrorism's Challenge to Democracy." In *Jihad vs. McWorld: Terrorism's Challenge to Democracy*. New York: Ballantine.

Barbosa, Livia. 1995. "The Brazilian Jeitinho: An Exercise in National Identity." In David Hess and Roberto Da Matta, eds. *The Brazilian Puzzle: Culture on the Borderlands of the Western World*. New York: Columbia University Press.

Barbosa, Luiz Carlos. 1999. "Lastro cultural na Bienal do Mercosul." *Extra Classe* 4.33 (July).

Barbrook, Richard. 1999. "The High-Tech Gift Economy." In *Readme! Filtered by Nettime: ASCII Culture and the Revenge of Knowledge*. Ed. Josephine Bosma et al. New York: Autonomedia.

Barnet, Richard J., and John Cavanagh. 1994. *Global Dreams: Imperial Corporations and the New World Order*. New York: Simon and Schuster.

Barrera Bassols, Marco, Iker Larrauri Prado, Teresa Márquez Martínez, and Graciela Schmilchuk. 1995. *Museos AL REVÉS: Modalidades comunitarias y participativas en la planificación y el funcionamiento de museos*. Report submitted to Fideicomiso para la Cultura México/USA.

Barrera Bassols, Marco, Iker Larrauri Prado, Teresa Márquez Martínez, Graciela Schmilchuk, and Ramón Vera Herrera. 1996. "Todo rincón es un centro: Hacia una expansión de la idea del museo." Project report for a Fideicomiso de la Cultura México–EAU / U.S.-Mexico Fund for Culture award.

Barros, Jorge Antônio. 1994. "O conciliador da cidade." Interview with Rubem César Fernandes. *Domingo*, Sunday supplement of *Jornal do Brasil*, 21 August: 3–5.

Barry, Judith. 1998. "Questioning Context." Lecture presented at Nexus, Philadelphia; in *Context* (fall).

Bart, Peter. 2001. "Bush Crusade Goes Hollywood: Will He Bomb at Box Office?" *Variety*, 7 November.

Bateson, Gregory. [1972] 1985. *Steps to an Ecology of Mind*. New York: Jason Aronson.

Batra, Ravi. 1993. *The Pooring of America: Competition and the Myth of Free Trade*. New York: Collier Macmillan.

Battcock, Gregory, and Robert Nickas, eds. 1984. *The Art of Performance: A Critical Anthology*. New York: Dutton.

Baudrillard, Jean. 1983. *Simulations*. Trans. Paul Foss, Paul Patton, and Philip Beitchman. New York: Semiotext(e).

Baudrillard, Jean, et al. 1989. *Looking Back at the End of the World*. Ed. Dietmar Kamper and Christoph Wolf. Trans. David Antal. New York: Semiotext(e) Foreign Agents Series.

Bauer, M. Delal, and Sidney Weintraub, eds. 1994. *The NAFTA Debate: Grappling with Unconventional Trade Issues*. Boulder, CO: Lynne Rienner.

Baxandall, Michael. 1991. "Exhibiting Invention: Some Preconditions of the Visual Display of Culturally Purposeful Objects." In *The Poetics and Politics of Museum Display*, ed. Ivan Karp and Steven D. Lavine. Washington, DC: Smithsonian Institution Press.

Bay, Mia. 2000. *The White Image in the Black Mind: African-American Ideas about White People, 1830–1925*. New York: Oxford University Press.

Beale, Alison. 2002. "Communication Policy, Media Industries, and Globalization: Identifying a Policy Hierarchy." In *Global Culture: Media, Arts Policy, and Globalization*, ed. Diana Crane, Nobuko Kawashima, Kenichi Kawasaki, and Roseanne Martorella. New York: Routledge.

Beaverstock, J. V., R. G. Smith, and P. J. Taylor. 1999. "A Roster of World Cities." *Cities* 16.6: 445–458. http://info.lboro.ac.uk/departments/gy/research/gawc/rb/rb5.html

Beaverstock, J. V., R. G. Smith, P. J. Taylor, D. R. F. Walker, and H. Lorimer. 2000. "Globalization and World Cities: Some Measurement Methodologies." *Applied Geography* 20.1: 43–63. http://lboro.ac.uk/departments/gy/research/gawc/rb/rb2.html

Becker, Carol, ed. 1994. *The Subversive Imagination: Artists, Society, and Social Responsibility*. New York: Routledge.

———. 1995 "The Education of Young Artists and the Issue of the Audience." *Performance and Pedagogy* 30 (winter).

Bello, Walden, and Anuradha Mittal. 2001. "The Meaning of Doha." Independent Media Center, 15 November. http://www.indymedia.org/front.php3?article_id=90263&group=webcast

Belluck, Pam. 2001. "Hue and Murmur over Curbed Rights." *New York Times*, 17 November.

Benamou, Michel. 1977. "Presence and Play." In *Performance in Postmodern Culture*, ed. Michel Benamou and Charles Caramello. Madison, WI: Coda Press.

Benedict, Stephen, ed. 1991. *Public Money and the Muse: Essays on Government Funding for the Arts*. New York: Norton.

Bennett, Tony. 1990. "The Political Rationality of the Museum." *Continuum: The Australian Journal of Media and Culture*. 3.1.

———. 1995. *The Birth of the Museum: History, Theory, and Politics*. London: Routledge.

Berelowitz, JoAnne. 1997. "Conflict Over 'Border Art.' Whose Subject, Whose Border, Whose Show?" *Third Text* 40 (autumn).

Berke, Richard L. 1995. "Murdoch Finances New Forum for Right." *New York Times*, 30 April: 20.

Berland, Jody. 1991. "Free Trade and Canadian Music: Level Playing Field or Scorched Earth?" *Cultural Studies* 5.3 (October): 317–325.

Bernard, Elaine. 1994. "What's the Matter with NAFTA?" *Radical America* 25.2 (April/June): 19–31.

Bernays, Edward L. 1947. "The Engineering of Consent." *Annals of the American Political and Social Science Association* 250 (March): 113–120.

Bernstein, Nina. 2000. "Widest Income Gap Is Found in New York." *New York Times*, 19 January (online edition).

Berríos, Rodrigo, and Felipe Abarca. 2001. "Ranking de ciudades: De Puerto Madero a Puerto Digital." *América Economía Publishing*. Interlink Headline News 2297.20 supplement (May). http://www.ilhn.com/indice.php3

Bertoncini, Deanna. 1989. "El arte latino en Estados Unidos." *La Jornada Semanal*, 24 December: 35–37.

Beverley, John. 1999. "Our Rigoberta? I, Rigoberta Menchú, Cultural Authority, and the Problem of Subaltern Agency." In *Subalternity and Representation: Arguments in Cultural Theory*. Durham, NC: Duke University Press.

Beyond the Borders: Art by Recent Immigrants. 1994. Catalogue. Bronx Museum of the Arts, February 18–June 12.Binational Committee of Education and Culture.

Bluestein, Paul. 2001. "Getting WTO's Attention: Activists, Developing Nations Make Gains." *Washington Post*, 16 November (online edition).

Blumrosen, Alfred W. 1993. *Modern Law: The Law Transmission System and Equal Law Employment Opportunity*. Madison: University of Wisconsin Press.

Boeira, Nelson. 1997. Preface to *I Bienal de Artes Visuais do Mercosul /I Bienal de Artes Visuales del Mercosur, de 2 de outubro a 30 de novembro de 1997*. Catalogue. Porto Alegre: Fundação Bienal de Artes Visuais do Mercosul.

Bolaño, César. 1999. "La problemática de la convergéncia informática-telecomunicaciones-audiovisual: Un abordaje marxista." In *Globalización y Monopolios en la Comunicación en América Latina*, ed. César Bolaño and Guillermo Mastrini. Buenos Aires: Editorial Biblos.

———. 2002. "Pós-modernismo, Islã e o futuro do capitalismo: Uma contribuição latina ao debate sobre a concepção de Império." *Eptic.* http://www.eptic.com.br/textdi3.pdf

Bonafini, Hebe Pastor de. 2001. "El 11 de septiembre sentí que la sangre de tantos caídos era vengada." *Revista Pretextos.* http://www.nodo50.org/pretextos/bonafini1.htm

Bonasso, Miguel. 2001. "La CIA traslada a su agente local por una revelación de Página/12." *Página 12,* 14 January. http://www.pagina12.com.ar/2001/01-01/01-01-14/pago3.htm

Bonfil Batalla, Guillermo. 1991. "Desafíos a la antropología en la sociedad contemporánea." *Iztapalapa* 11.24.

———. 1992. "Dimensiones culturales del Tratado de Libre Comercio." In *La educacion y cultura ante el Tratado de Libre Comercio,* ed. Gilberto Guevara Niebla and Néstor García Canclini. Mexico City: Nueva Imagen.

———, coordinator. 1993. "Introducción: Nuevos perfiles de nuestra cultura." In *Nuevas identidades culturales en México.* Mexico City: Consejo Nacional para la Cultura y las Artes.

Bonilla-Silva, Eduardo. 2001. *White Supremacy and Racism in the Post–Civil Rights Era.* Boulder, CO: Lynne Rienner.

Bonnett, Alastair. 2000. *White Identities: Historical and International Perspective.* New York: Prentice-Hall.

"Boogie Woogie." 1997. *Latin Trade* (July): http://www.latintrade.com/archives/july97/tradetalk.html

"Border Corridors: When Borders Become Bridges." http://www.conway.com/shighlites/august/border.htm. 25 January.

Bourdieu, Pierre, and Loïc Wacquant. 1999. "On the Cunning of Imperialist Reason." *Theory, Culture and Society* 16: 41–58.

Bradley, Jessica. 2000. Interview. July 6.

Bradley, Jessica, Olivier Debroise, Ivo Mesquita, and Sally Yard. 1998. "Private Time in Public Space: A Dialogue." In inSITE97.

Bradsher, Keith. 1994. "Panel Clears GATT Accord without Fast-Track Proviso." *New York Times,* 3 August: D1, D6.

———. 1995a. "Low Ranking for Poor American Children." *New York Times,* 14 August: A9.

———. 1995b. "Skilled Workers Watch Their Jobs Migrate Overseas: A Blow to Middle Class." *New York Times,* 28 August: A1, D6.

Bragg, Rick. 1999. "Alliance Fights a Plan to Develop a Florida Gateway Born of Racism." *New York Times,* 28 March (online edition).

Brandon, Karen. 1998. "NAFTA at Five." *Chicago Tribune,* 29 November.

Brandt, Daniel. 2001. "The 'Patriot' Act and Internet Surveillance." 9 November. http://cryptome.org/spy-dotnet.htm.

Brenson, Michael. 1995. "Healing in Time." In *Culture in Action: A Public Art Program of Sculpture Chicago,* 16–49.

———. 1998. "The Curator's Moment." *Art Journal* 57.4 (winter):16–27.

Brett, Guy. 1990. *Transcontinental: An Investigation of Reality: Nine Latin American Artists*. London and New York: Verso.

Brimelow, Peter. 1991. "The Free Trade Agreement: Implications for Canadian Identity?" *American Review of Canadian Studies* (summer–autumn): 269–276.

———. 1995. *Alien Nation: Common Sense about America's Immigration Disaster*. New York: Random House.

Britto, Antônio. 1997. Preface to *I Bienal de Artes Visuais do Mercosul /I Bienal de Artes Visuales del Mercosur, de 2 de outubro a 30 de novembro de 1997*. Catalogue. Porto Alegre: Fundação Bienal de Artes Visuais do Mercosul.

Brooke, James. 1993. "Brazilian Justice and the Culture of Impunity." *New York Times*, 23 August: E6.

———. 1994a. "Brazil's Army Joins Battle in Lawless Rio." *New York Times*, 6 November: 4.

———. 1994b. "Crime Reigns in the City Renowned for Romance." *New York Times*, 25 October: A4.

———. 1994c. "Even Rio's Poor Seem Sold on the Inflation Fighter." *New York Times*, 28 September: A3.

———. 1995. "Latin America Now Ignores U.S. Lead in Isolating Cuba." *New York Times*, 8 July: 1, 5.

Brunner, José Joaquín. 1987. "Notas sobre la modernidad y lo postmoderno en la cultura latinoamericana." *David y Goliath* 52: 4–10.

———. 1990. "Seis Preguntas a José Joaquín Brunner." *Revista de Crítica Cultural* 1.1 (May): 19–23.

Brzezinski, Zbigniew. 1998. "Interview with Zbigniew Brzezinski." *Le Nouvel Observateur* 15–21 January. http://www.tao.ca/~solidarity/s11/brzezinski.html

Buchwalter, Andrew, ed. 1992. *Culture and Democracy: Social and Ethical Issues in Public Support for the Arts and Humanities*. Boulder, CO: Westview.

Buck-Morss, Susan. 1998. "What is Political Art?" In *inSITE97*.

Bulmer-Thomas, Victor. 1996a. Introduction to *The New Economic Model in Latin America and Its Impact on Income Distribution and Poverty*, ed. Victor Bulmer-Thomas. New York: St. Martin's.

———. ed. 1996b. *The New Economic Model in Latin America and Its Impact on Income Distribution and Poverty*. New York: St. Martin's.

Bürger, Peter. 1984. *Theory of the Avant-Garde*. Minneapolis: University of Minnesota Press.

Bush, George W. 2000. "George W. Bush Commits to Free Trade with Latin America." Excerpts of a speech given at Florida International University, Miami, 25 August. http://vcepolitics.com/news/2000/00-08-25.shtml

Butler, Judith. 1990. *Gender Trouble: Feminism and the Subversion of Identity*. New York: Routledge.

———. 1993. *Bodies That Matter: On the Discursive Limits of "Sex."* New York: Routledge.

Butler, Judith, John Guillory, and Kendall Thomas, eds. 2000. *What's Left of Theory? New Work on the Politics of Literary Theory*. New York: Routledge.

Byrne, David, compiler. 1989. *O Samba: Brazil Classics 2*. Recording. Luaka Bop/Sire Records 9 26019-2.

"Caio Ferraz diz que Reage Rico é elitista." 1995. *O Globo*, 26 November.

Caldeira, Dulce. 1992. "No embalo do subúrbio." *Jornal do Brasil*. 22 October: 5.

Caldeira, Teresa Pires do Rio. 1993. "Crime and Individual Rights: Reframing the Question of Violence in Latin America." Paper presented at the Seminar on "Derechos Humanos, Justicia y Sociedad," CEDES, Buenos Aires, 22–24 October.

———. 1996a. "Crime and Individual Rights: Reframing the Question of Violence in Latin America." In *Constructing Democracy: Human Rights, Citizenship, and Society in Latin America*, ed. Elizabeth Jelin and Eric Hershberg. Boulder, CO: Westview Press.

———. 1996b. "Fortified Enclaves: The New Urban Segregation." *Public Culture* 8: 303–328.

Calderón, Héctor, and José David Saldívar, eds. 1991. *Criticism in the Borderlands: Studies in Chicano Literature, Culture, and Ideology*. Durham, NC: Duke University Press.

Camnitzer, Luis. 1998. "Letter from Porto Alegre." *Art Nexus* 27. http://www.universes-in-universe.de/artnexus/no27/cam1_en.htm

Campos, Elza Pires de. 1996. "Comunidade Solidária luta contra crise." *Jornal do Brasil*, 6 May: 1–5.

Cândido, Antônio. 1970. "Dialética da malandragem." *Revista do Instituto de Estudos Brasileiros* 8. São Paulo: University of São Paulo.

Cardoso, Fernando Henrique, and Enzo Faletto. 1973. *Dependência e Desenvolvimento na América Latina: Ensaio de Interpretação Sociológica*. Rio de Janeiro: Zahar.

Cardwell, Diane. 2001. "In Final Address, Giuliani Envisions Soaring Memorial." *New York Times*, 28 December (online edition).

"Carioca enfrenta até chuva e pára por uma cidade melhor." 1993. *Jornal do Dia*, 18 December: 1.

Carpentier, Alejo. 1949. *El reino de este mundo*. Mexico City: Edición y Distribución Iberoamericana de Publicaciones.

———. 1953. *Los pasos perdidos*. Mexico City: Edición y Distribución Iberoamericana de Publicaciones.

Carpignano, Paolo, et al. 1993. "Chatter in the Age of Electronic Reproduction: Talk Television and the 'Public Mind.'" In *The Phantom Public Sphere*, ed. Bruce Robbins. Minneapolis: University of Minnesota Press.

Carr, C. 1993. "Telling the Awfulest Truth': An Interview with Karen Finley." In *Acting Out: Feminist Performances*, ed. Lynda Hart and Peggy Phelan. Ann Arbor: University of Michigan Press.

———. 2000. "The Karen Finley Makeover: A Persecuted Performance Artist Gets Past Her Suffering." *Village Voice*, 8–14 November.

Cartographies: 14 Artists from Latin America. 1974. Catalogue. Bronx Museum, 7 October.

Carvajal, Doreen, with Andrew Ross Sorkin. 2000. "Lycos to Combine with Terra Networks in a $12 Billion Deal." *New York Times*, 16 May (online edition).

Casal, Lourdes. 1980. "Revolution and Race: Blacks in Contemporary Cuba." *Working Papers of the Woodrow Wilson International Center for Scholars*. Washington, DC.

Castañeda, Jorge B. 1993a. "Can NAFTA Change Mexico? *Foreign Affairs* 10.3 (September–October): 66–80.

———. 1993b. *Utopia Unarmed: The Latin American Left after the Cold War*. New York: Knopf.

Castañeda, Jorge, and Carlos Heredia. 1993. "Another NAFTA: What a Good Trade Agreement Should Offer." In *The Case against Free Trade*, ed. Ralph Nader et al. San Francisco: Earth Island Press.

Castel, Robert. 1991. "From Dangerousness to Risk." In *The Foucault Effect: Studies in Governmentality*, ed. Graham Burchell et al. Chicago: University of Chicago Press.

Castells, Manuel. 1989. *The Informational City: Information Technology, Economic Restructuring, and the Urban-Regional Process*. Oxford: Blackwell.

———. 1996. *The Rise of the Network Society*. Oxford: Blackwell.

———. 2000. "La ciudad de la nueva economía." *La factoría* 12 (July–August). http://www.lafactoriaweb.com/articulos/castells12.htm

Castells, Manuel, and Roberto Laserna. 1991. *La Nueva Dependencia: Cambio tecnológico y reestructuración socio-económica en América Latina*. Cochabamba: Ed. CERES.

Castro, Fidel. 2001. "Speech by Commander in Chief Fidel Castro, President of the Republic of Cuba." Press release. Ciego de Avila. 29 September.

Catani, Afrânio Mendes. 1994. "Política Cinematográfica nos anos Collor 1990–1992: Um arremedo neoliberal." *Imagens* 3 (December).

Cavanagh, John, and Sarah Anderson. 1993. ". . . And Europe Offers Practical Insight." *New York Times*, 14 November: F11.

Cembalest, Robin. 1992. "The We Decade." *ARTnews* (September): 62–71.

Center on Budget and Policy Priorities. 2001. "Pathbreaking CBO Study Shows Dramatic Increases in Both 1980s and 1990s in Income Gaps between the Very Wealthy and Other Americans." 31 May. http://www.centeronbudget.org/5-31-01tax-pr.htm

Certeau, Michel de. 1984. *The Practice of Everyday Life*. Berkeley: University of California Press.

Chaney, David. 1994. *The Cultural Turn: Scene-Setting Essays on Contemporary Cultural History*. London: Routledge.

Chartrand, Harry Hillman. 1999. "Copyright and the New World Economic Order." MSANEWS 3 July. http://msanews.mynet.net/MSANEWS/199907/19990703.31.html

Chatterjee, Partha. 1993. *The Nation and Its Fragments: Colonial and Postcolonial Histories*. Princeton: Princeton University Press.

Chattopadhyay, Collette. 1997. "The Many Faces of Public Spheres." *World Sculpture News* 3.4 (autumn).

Chavarría, Jesús. 1994. Editorial. *Hispanic Business* (January): 3.

Chicano Art: Resistance and Affirmation. 1993. Catalogue. Bronx Museum of the Arts, April–May.

City of South Miami Beach. 2000. "Economic Development Division." http://www.ci. miami-beach.fl.us/

Clark, Christine, and James O'Donnell, eds. 1999. *Becoming and Unbecoming White: Owning and Disowning a Racial Identity.* Westport. CT: Bergin and Garvey.

Clarke, Bill. 2000. Online posting to the Culture, Heritage, and Development list, 7 July.

Clausing, Jeri. 2000. "Digital Economy Has Arrived, Commerce Department Says." *New York Times,* 6 June (online edition).

Cleaver, Harry. 1995. "The Subversion of Money-as-command in the Current Crisis." In *Global Capital, National State and the Politics of Money,* ed. Werner Bonefeld and John Holloway. London: St. Martin's.

———. 1998. "The Zapatistas and the Electronic Fabric of Struggle." In *Zapatista: Reinventing Revolution in Mexico,* ed. John Peláez and Eloína Peláez. London: Pluto Press.

Cleveland, William. 1992. "Bridges, Translations and Change: The Arts as Infrastructure in 21st Century America." *High Performance* (fall): 84–85.

Clifford, James. 1988. *The Predicament of Culture.* Cambridge, MA: Harvard University Press.

———. 1991. "Four Northwest Coast Museums: Travel Reflections." In *The Poetics and Politics of Museum Display,* ed. Ivan Karp and Steven D. Lavine. Washington, DC: Smithsonian Institution Press.

Cobo-Hanlon, Leila. 1998. "Dance Music Gets Latin Flavor: Mix of Trendy and Traditional Taps Pulse of Nightclub Culture." *Miami Herald,* 23 August (online edition).

———. 1999a. "Latin Music Awards Head West to Los Angeles." *Miami Herald,* 30 December (online edition).

———. 1999b. "Midem Will Be Here in 2000, If Anywhere." *Miami Herald,* 6 October (online edition).

———. 2000. "Latin Grammys Head to L.A.: Organizers Slam Dade Politics." *Miami Herald,* 20 January (online edition).

Coelho, Teixeira. 1999. "From Cultural Policy to Political Culture: Proposals for a Continental Cultural Policy." In *Arte Sem Fronteiras: First Forum for Cultural Integration,* ed. Mônica Allende Serra. São Paulo: Arte Sem Fronteiras/UNESCO.

Coffey, Mary K. Forthcoming. "From Nation to Community: Museums and the Reconfiguration of Mexican Society under Neo-Liberalism." In *Governing the Present: Foucault and Cultural Studies.* Albany: SUNY Press.

Cohen, Ariel, et al. 1998. "The Meaning of the Russian IMF Bailout." Heritage Foundation Lecture, 23 July.

Cohen, Jean L., and Andrew Arato. 1992. *Civil Society and Political Theory.* Cambridge, MA: MIT Press.

Cohen, Marshall A., and Stephen Blank, eds. 1991. *The Challenge of the Canada–United States Free Trade Agreement: An Assessment from Many Perspectives.* Special issue of *American Review of Canadian Studies* 21.2–3 (summer–autumn).

Cohen, Roger. 1993a. "Once Dull, GATT Enters Realm of Pop Culture." *New York Times,* 7 December: D1, D6.

————. 1993b. "Trade Pact Still Eludes Negotiators: U.S. Demands Open Technology Market." *New York Times*, 7 December: D1, D6.

————. 2000. "Germans Seek Foreign Labor for New Era of Computers." *New York Times*, 9 April (online edition).

Collins, Sharon. 1997. *Black Corporate Executives: The Making and Breaking of a Black Middle Class*. Philadelphia: Temple University Press.

Colombo, Paola. 1996. "The Exile of Caio Ferraz in the U.S." *Brazzil* (June). http://www. brazzil.com/p22jun96.htm

"Comras Betting on Entertainment Industry." 1998. *Miami Herald*, 11 August (online edition).

Conley, Dalton. 2000. *Honky*. Berkeley: University of California Press.

"Contra el Neoliberalismo y por la Humanidad." 1996. *La Jornada*, 30 January. http:// serpiente.dgsca.unam.mx/jornada/1995/oct95/951021/cara.html

Cooley, John K. 2000. *Unholy Wars: Afghanistan, America and International Terrorism*. London: Pluto Press.

Consumer Project on Technology. 2001. *New Trade Agreement for the Americas Jeopardizes Brazil's Acclaimed Generic AIDS Drug Program*. 11 April. http://www.cptech.org/ip/health/ trade/FTAArelease 04122001.html

"Convention on Biological Diversity." 1992. U.N. Conference on Environment and Development. Rio de Janeiro, 3–14 June. http://www.biodiv.org/convention/ articles.asp

Cornwell, Terri Lynn. 1990. *Democracy and the Arts: The Role of Participation*. New York: Praeger.

Corradi, Juan E., Patricia Weiss Fagen, and Manuel Antonio Garreton, eds. 1992. *Fear at the Edge: State Terror and Resistance in Latin America*. Berkeley: University of California Press.

Correa, Guillermo, and Julio César López. 1996. "500 organizaciones, en la gestación de una 'gran fuerza social y política.' " *Proceso* 1002 (15 January): 28.

"Corrections." 1998. *New York Times*, 10 July.

"Country Music Television Canada." 1995. *Stickguy: Canada's Media Authority*. http://www. geocities. com/stickguynf/specialities/cmt.htm

Creative Industries Export Promotion Advisory Group. 1999. *Creative Industries Exports: Our Hidden Potential*. London: Department of Culture, Media and Sport.

Creative Industries Task Force. 1998. *Creative Industries Mapping Document*. London: Department of Culture, Media and Sport.

"Crianças trocam suas 'armas' por brinquedos." 1994. *O Globo*, 12 December: 7.

Crimp, Douglas. 1990. *ICaids Demographics*. Seattle: Bay Press.

Croucher, Sheila L. 1997. *Imagining Miami: Ethnic Politics in a Postmodern World*. Charlottesville: University of Virginia Press.

Cruikshank, Barbara. 1994. "The Will to Empower: Technologies of Citizenship and the War on Poverty." *Socialist Review* 23.4: 40–58.

Crutsinger, Martin. 1998. "Asia Crisis To Reduce World Trade, Bankers Say." *Seattle Times*, 8 July.

Cuenca, Carmen. 2000. Interview. 27 May.

Cueva, Héctor de la. 1993. "Side Agreements: Freedom of Trade and Investment without Social Counterweights." *La Jornada Labor Supplement* (September): 3–4. Reprinted in FBIS-LAT-93-07, 28 October: 13–15.

Cultural Identity: Fiction or Necessity? 1992. Special issue of *Third Text* 18 (spring).

Culture in Action: A Public Art Program of Sculpture Chicago. 1995. Seattle: Bay Press.

"Cumbre de los Museis de las Américas sobre Museos y Communidades." 1998. San Jose, Costa Rica. 15–18 April 1998. http://www.ilam.org/forum

Cumings, Bruce. 1992. *War and Television*. London: Verso

Cummings, Milton C., Jr. 1991. "Government and the Arts: An Overview." In *Public Money and the Muse: Essays on Government Funding for the Arts*, ed. Stephen Benedict. New York: Norton.

Cunha, Olivia Maria Gomes da. 1998. "Black Movements and the 'Politics of Identity' in Brazil." In *Cultures of Politics, Politics of Cultures: Re-visioning Latin American Social Movements*, ed. Sonia E. Alvarez, Evelina Dagnino, and Arturo Escobar. Boulder, CO: Westview Press.

———. Forthcoming. "Gaining Intimacy: Brazilian Racial Landscape and National Imagination in the U.S. South, 1937–1945." In *Theories of the Americas*, ed. George Yúdice. Boston: Blackwell.

Cuomo, Chris J., and Kim Q. Hall, eds. 1999. *Whiteness: Feminist Philosophical Reflections*. Lanham, MD: Rowman and Littlefield.

Curiel, Barbara Brinson, et al. 2000. Introduction to *Post-nationalist American Studies*, ed. John Carlos Rowe. Berkeley: University of California Press.

Curry, Andréia. 1993. "O rap briga por dignidade urgente." *Jornal do Brasil*, 9 January: 1B.

Curry, Renée R. 2000. *White Women Writing White: H.D., Elizabeth Bishop, Sylvia Plath, and Whiteness*. Westport, CT: Greenwood Press.

Curtis, Cathy. 1993. "When Legal Tender Hits a Sore Spot." *Los Angeles Times*, 17 August: F1, F10, F11.

DaCosta, Carolina. 2000. "Behind Brazil's Internet Boom." *InfoBrazil.com* 2.55 (28 July–3 August). http://www.InfoBrazil.com

DaMatta, Roberto. 1979. *Carnavais, malandros e heróis: Para uma sociologia do dilema brasileiro*. Rio de Janeiro: Editora Guanabara.

———. [1979] 1991. *Carnivals, Rogues, and Heroes: An Interpretation of the Brazilian Dilemma*. Trans. John Drury. Notre Dame, IN: University of Notre Dame Press.

Daniel, G. Reginald. 2002. *More Than Black? Multiracial Identity and the New Racial Order*. Philadelphia: Temple University Press.

Dantas, Edna. 1992. "Meninos superlotam celas em Brasília." *Folha de São Paulo*, 18 November: section 3, 3.

Davidson, Martin P. 1992. *The Consumerist Manifesto: Advertising in Postmodern Times*. London: Routledge.

Dávila, Arlene. 2001. *Latinos, Inc.: The Marketing and Making of a People.* Berkeley: University of California Press.

Davis, Erik. 1995. "Barbed Wire Net: The Right Wing Hunkers Down Online." *Village*

Day, Jane Stevenson. 1994. "Interpreting Culture: New Voices in Museums." *JAMLS* 23.4 (winter): 307–315.

Debroise, Olivier. 1990. "Desde un México diferente." *La Jornada Semanal,* 28 October: 25– 32.

———. 1995. "By the Night Tide. insITE94: The Archipelago." insITE94.

———. 1998. "Private Time in Public Space: A Dialogue." insITE97.

———. Forthcoming. "The Profile of the Contemporary Art Independent Curator in a Country of the South that Finds Itself in the North (and Vice-Versa)." In *Beyond Identity: Globalization and Latin American Art.* Luis Camnitzer and Mari Carmen Ramírez, eds. Durham: Duke University Press.

The Decade Show: Frameworks of Identity in the 80s. 1990. Catalogue. New York: Museum of Contemporary Hispanic Art (16 May–19 August), New Museum of Contemporary Art (12 May–19 August), Studio Museum in Harlem (18 May–19 August).

Deitcher, David. 1990. "David Deitcher on the United Colors of Benetton." *Artforum* (January): 19–21.

Delaney, Lawrence, Jr. 1994. "Renaissance: The 1994 World Trade 100 Offers Compelling Evidence of California's—and America's—Rebirth." *World Trade* (September): 24–26.

Deleuze, Gilles, and Félix Guattari. 1987. *A Thousand Plateaus.* Trans. Brian Massumi. Minneapolis: University of Minneapolis Press.

Delgado, Eduard. 1998. "Transnational and Regional Support for Culture." Paper presented at the conference "New Trends in Cultural Policy for the Twenty-First Century," New York University, 1 May.

Delgado, Richard, and Jean Stefancic, eds. 1995. *Critical Race Theory: The Cutting Edge.* Philadelphia: Temple University Press.

———, eds. 1997. *Critical White Studies: Looking behind the Mirror.* Philadelphia: Temple University Press.

———, eds. 2000. *Critical Race Theory: The Cutting Edge.* 2d ed. Philadelphia: Temple University Press.

Denny, Charlotte. 2001. "For Richer—and for Poorer." *The Guardian,* 23 November. http://www.guardian.co.uk/Archive/Article/0,4273,4305383,00.html

Dent, Gina, ed. 1992. *Black Popular Culture.* Seattle: Bay Press.

Denton, Robert E., Jr. 1993. "Television as an Instrument of War." In *The Media and the Persian Gulf War,* ed. Robert E. Denton Jr. London: Praeger.

DePalma, Anthony. 1993. "As Free Trade Draws Nations Together, Campus Becomes 'Mexico Think Tank.' " *New York Times,* 22 December: B7.

———. 1995. "After the Fall: Two Faces of Mexico's Economy." *New York Times,* 16 July: section 3, 11.

Der Derian, James. 2001. *Virtuous War: Mapping the Military-Industrial-Media-Entertainment Network*. Boulder, CO: Westview Press.

Derrida, Jacques. 1976. *Of Grammatology*. Baltimore: Johns Hopkins University Press.

————. 1979. "Living On/Borderlines." In *Deconstruction and Criticism*. New York: Seabury.

————. 1980. "The Law of Genre." Trans. Avital Ronell. *Critical Inquiry* 7.1 (autumn): 55–81.

de Salvo, Roman. 2000. Interview with George Yúdice. 18 June.

"Descrédito na Justiça traz apóio à violência." 1992. *Folha de São Paulo*, 8 October: 1–12.

Desmond, Jane C., and Virginia Domínguez. 1996. "Resituating American Studies in a Critical Internationalism." *American Quarterly* 48.3: 475–490.

Didion, Joan. 1987. *Miami*. New York: Vintage.

DiFelice, Attanasio. 1984. "Renaissance Performance." In *The Art of Performance: A Critical Anthology*, ed. Gregory Battcock and Robert Nickas. New York: Dutton.

Dillemuth, Stephen. 1997. "Services: Working-Group Discussions." *October* 80 (spring).

Dillon, John. 1993. "Intellectual Property." *Canadian Forum* (January): 11–12.

DiMaggio, Paul J. 1991. "Decentralization of Arts Funding from the Federal Government to the States." In *Public Money and the Muse: Essays on Government Funding for the Arts*, ed. Stephen Benedict. New York: Norton.

————. 2001. "Social Division in the United States: The Disparity between Private Opinion and Public Politics." Paper presented at the "Privatization of Culture Project Seminar Series on Cultural Policy," New York University and New School University, 26 February.

DiMaggio, Paul J., and Francie Ostrower. 1992. *Race, Ethnicity, and Participation in the Arts: Patterns of Participation by Hispanics, Whites, and African-Americans in Selected Activities from the 1982 and 1985 Surveys of Public Participation in the Arts*. Washington, DC: Seven Locks Press/National Endowment for the Arts, Research Division Report 25.

DiMaggio, Paul J., Michael Unseem, and Paula Brown. 1978. *Audience Studies of the Performing Arts and Museums: A Critical Review*. Washington, DC: National Endowment for the Arts.

Directorio de Instituciones Filantrópicas. 1995. Mexico City: Centro Mexicano para la Filantropía.

The Diversity Challenge: Innovation in the Changing Workplace. 1995. Special advertising supplement to *New York Times*, 7 May.

DJ Marlboro, producer. 1989. *Funk Brasil I*. Recording. Polydor.

————, producer. 1990. *Funk Brasil II*. Recording. Polydor.

————, producer. 1991. *Funk Brasil III*. Recording. Polydor.

DJ T.R. 2000. "A Corda Hip-Hop (Parte 2)." *AfroReggae* 7.36 (March): 5.

Dobratz, Betty A., and Stephanie L. Shanks-Meile. 1997. *White Power, White Pride: The White Separatist Movement in the United States*. New York: Twayne.

Dobrzynski, Judith H. 1995. "Some Action, Little Talk: Companies Embrace Diversity, but Are Reluctant to Discuss It." *New York Times*, 20 April: D1, D4.

Dobson, John. 1993. "TNCs and the Corruption of GATT: Free Trade versus Fair Trade." *Journal of Business Ethics* 12.7: 573–578.

Dolnick, Edward. 1993. "Deafness as Culture." *Atlantic Monthly* (September): 37–53.

Domínguez, Virginia R. 1992. "Invoking Culture: The Messy Side of Cultural Politics." *South Atlantic Quarterly* 91.1 (winter).

Domowitz, Susan. 2001. "Pakistani-Americans Talk to Pakistanis about Muslim Life in the U.S." U.S. State Department. 19 November. http://usinfo.state.gov/topical/pol/terror/01111915.htm

Donoso, José. 1978. *Casa de campo*. Barcelona: Seix Barral.

Dorfman, Ariel, and Armand Mattelart. 1972. *Para leer al Pato Donald: Comunicación y colonialismo*. Mexico City: Siglo XXI.

———. 1975. *How to Read Donald Duck: Imperialist Ideology in the Disney Comic*. Trans. David Kunzle. New York: International General.

Dorland, Michael. 1988. "A Thoroughly Hidden Country: *Ressentiment*, Canadian Nationalism, Canadian Culture." *Canadian Journal of Political and Social Theory/Revue canadienne de théorie politique et sociale* 12.1–2: 130–164.

Dos Santos, Teotônio. 1970. "The Structure of Dependence." *American Economic Review* 60.5: 235–246.

Douglas, Mary. 1969. *Purity and Danger*. London: Routledge and Kegan Paul.

Draper, Lee. 1987. *Museum Audiences Today: Building Constituencies for the Future*. Los Angeles: Museum Educators of Southern California.

D.S. 1994. "Insights to inSite." *San Diego Home/Garden*. December.

Duncan, Carol. 1991. "Art Museums and the Ritual of Citizenship." In *The Poetics and Politics of Museum Display*, ed. Ivan Karp and Steven D. Lavine. Washington, DC: Smithsonian Institution Press.

Duncan, Michael. 1995. "Straddling the Great Divide." *Art in America* 51.

Dunlap, David W. 2002. "In Remembrance of Sorrow from Other Times." *New York Times*, 25 January.

Durán, Sylvie. 2001. "Redes culturales en Centroamérica." Paper presented at the II Euroamerican Campus for Cultural Cooperation, Cartagena de Indias, Colombia, 12 December.

Durning, Alan Thein. 1992. *How Much Is Enough? The Consumer Society and the Future of the Earth*. New York: Norton.

———. 1994. "How Much Is Enough? The Consumer Society and the Future of the Earth." Worldwatch Institute. International Global Communications conference, igc:worldwatch.new, 27 June.

Dutko, Kelly. 1994. "Who Gets the Funds?" *Hispanic Business* (November): 60.

Dyer, Richard. 1997. *White*. London: Routledge.

Eagleton, Terry. 1990. *The Ideology of the Aesthetic*. Oxford: Basil Blackwell.

Eakin, Emily. 2001. "An Organization on the Lookout for Patriotic Incorrectness." *New York Times*, 24 November (online edition).

Edmond, Mark. 2001. "One Thousand Admired Manufacturers." *Start* 5.3 (March). http://www.startmag.com/v5n3/v5n3043.asp

Ehrenberg, Felipe. 1994. "East and West—The Twain Do Meet: A Tale of More Than Two Worlds." In *The Subversive Imagination: Artists, Society, and Social Responsibility*, ed. Carol Becker. New York: Routledge.

Eliot, T. S. 1920. "Tradition and the Individual Talent." In *The Sacred Wood: Essays on Poetry and Criticism*. London: Methuen.

Elliott, Stuart. 1992. "When Products Are Tied to Causes." *New York Times*, 18 April: 33, 37.

"Encontro reúne 1.000 meninos de rua." 1992. *Jornal do Brasil*, 19 November: 8.

Enríquez, Juan. 2000. "Technology and the Future of the Nation State." Paper presented at the symposium "Recentering the Periphery: Latin-American Intellectuals in the New Millennium." New School for Social Research, New York, 7 April.

Entine, Jon. 1994. "Shattered Image: Is the Body Shop Too Good to Be True?" *Business Ethics* (September/October): 23–28.

———. 1995. "The Curse of Good Intentions." *Electronic Journal of Radical Organisation Theory* 1.1 (November). http://www.mngt.waikato.ac.nz/research/ejrot/Vol1_/Dialogue/Entine2.asp

———. 1997a. "Green Shell: Clean Power's Dirty Secret." *Progressive Populist* 3.6 (June). http://www.populist.com/6.97.entine.green.html

———. 1997b. "Jon Entine Replies: 'If You Don't Ask, They Won't Tell.' " *Progressive Populist* 3.8 (August). http://www.populist.com/8.97.letters.html

"Equipe do IML chora entre pilha de corpos." 1992. *Folha de São Paulo*, 5 October: 1–12.

Escobar, Arturo. 1994. "Cultural Politics and Biological Diversity: Nature, Capital, and the State in the Pacific Coast of Colombia." Paper presented for the panel "Cultural Politics and Political Culture(s)." Latin American Studies Association Convention, Atlanta, 10–12 March.

Escóssia, Fernanda da. 1994. "Campanha troca armas por bíblia e comida." *Folha de São Paulo*, 2 December: 1–17.

Escudé, Carlos, Ernesto López, and Rosendo Fraga. 2001. "Tres expertos politico-militares argentinos anticipan lo que viene." *Página 12*, 28 October. http://www.pagina12.com.ar/2001/01-10/01-10-28/pag25.htm

Everitt, Anthony. 1999. *The Governance of Culture: Approaches to Integrated Cultural Planning and Policies. Policy Note No. 5*. Strasbourg: Council of Europe Publishing.

Ewen, Stuart. 1988. *All Consuming Images: The Politics of Style in Contemporary Culture*. New York: Basic Books.

"Exiles' Elián Protests Backfired in Cuba." 2000. *Miami Herald*, 3 July (online edition).

EZLN. 1995. "Tercera declaración de la selva Lacandona." Posted 3 January by Harry M. Cleaver.

Faber, Elio, and Reese Ewing. 1999. "Cisneros Goes Online." *Latin CEO* (December): 46–53.

Faison, Seth. 1995a. "China Closes a Disk Factory as Sanctions Deadline Nears." *New York Times*, 26 February: 6.

————. 1995b. "Razors, Soap, Cornflakes: Pirating Spreads in China." *New York Times*, 17 February: D1, D2.

Falwell, Jerry. 2001. Interview with Pat Robertson. *The 700 Club*, Christian Broadcasting Network, 13 September. Video, http://www.christianity.com/CC_Content_Page/ 1,1182, PTID2546%7CCHID101299%7CCIID,00.html. Transcription available at People for the American Way, http://www.pfaw.org/911/robertson_falwell.html

"Fanzines pregam morte a nordestino e judeu." 1992. *Folha de São Paulo*, 26 September: section 3, 3.

Faria, Antônio Carlos de. 1994. "Rio tenta impedir consolidação do tráfico." Interview with Clarice Pechman. *Folha de São Paulo*, 17 January: 1–6.

Farley-Villalobos, Robbie. 1992. "Museum President Embarrassed." *El Paso Herald-Post*, 25 January.

Fawcett, Michelle. Forthcoming. " 'It's a Small Theme Park After All': Partnerships between UNESCO and the Walt Disney Company." In *The Challenge of Cultural Policy*, ed. George Yúdice. Minneapolis: University of Minnesota Press.

Featherstone, Michael, ed. 1990. *Global Culture: Nationalism, Globalization and Modernity*. London: Sage.

Feinstein, Roni. 1999. "Report from Miami: Part I: Museum Salsa." *Art in America* (May): 63–69.

Felshin, Nina. 1995a. Introduction to *But Is It Art? The Spirit of Art as Activism*, ed. Nina Felshin. Seattle: Bay Press.

————. ed. 1995b. *But Is It Art? The Spirit of Art as Activism*. Seattle: Bay Press.

Ferber, Abby L. 1998. *White Man Falling: Race, Gender, and White Supremacy*. Lanham, MD: Rowman and Littlefield.

Fernandes, Rubem César. 1994. *Private but Public: The Third Sector in Latin America*. Washington, DC: Civicus and Network Cultures-Asia.

Fernandes, Rubem César, and Leandro Piquet. 1991. *ONGs Anos 90: A opinião os Dirigentes Brasileiros*. Rio de Janeiro: ISER.

Fernández Retamar, Roberto. 1976. "Nuestra América y Occidente." *Casa de las Américas* 98: 36–57.

————. [1971] 1989. *Caliban and Other Essays*. Trans. Edward Baker. Minneapolis: University of Minnesota Press.

Ferreira, Alcides. 2000. "Wrong Approach: AOL's Brazilian Fiasco." *InfoBrazil* 2.54 (14–21 July). http://www.InfoBrazil.com

Fideicomiso Para la Cultura México-EUA/U.S.-Mexico Fund for Culture. 1997. http://www.fidemexusa.org.mx/

Fierlbeck, K. 1996. "The Ambivalent Potential of Cultural Identity." *Canadian Journal of Political Science/Revue canadienne de science politique* 29.1: 3–22.

Filho, Otávio Frias. 1995. "Passeata VIP." *Folha de São Paulo*, 30 November: 1–2.

Filibek, G. 1995. "Interventions Concerning Theme 1.1 (The European Convention on Human Rights and Cultural Rights)." Paper presented at Council of Europe, 8th annual international colloquy on the European Convention on Human Rights, Budapest.

Fine, Michelle, et al. 1997. *Off White: Readings on Race, Power, and Society*. New York: Routledge.

Fisk, Robert. 2001a. "The Awesome Cruelty of a Doomed People." *Z Net*. http://www.zmag.org/fiskawecalam.htm. Accessed 5 January 2002.

———. 2001b. "Interview with Robert Fisk," by Matthew Rothschild. *The Progressive* 65.12 (December). http://www.progressive.org/0901/intv1201.html

Fitzpatrick, Sheila. 1992. *The Cultural Front: Power and Culture in Revolutionary Russia*. Ithaca: Cornell University Press.

Fix, Michael, and Jeffrey S. Passel. 1994. *Immigration and Immigrants Setting the Record Straight*. Report for the Urban Institute, May.

"Fleeing the 'House of Peace.'" 1995. Real Brazil. http://lanic:utexas.edu/project/ppb/rb/

Flores, Rafael. 2001. "Carlos Gardel: Desde que se fue, triste vivo yo." El tango. http://www.esto.es/tango/personajes/grangardel.htm

Flores, William V., and Rina Benmayor. 1997. "Introduction: Constructing Cultural Citizenship." In *Latino Cultural Citizenship: Claiming Identity, Space, and Rights*, ed. William V. Flores and Rina Benmayor. Boston: Beacon.

Flynn, Laurie J. 2001. "Online Privacy Expert Shifts Focus to Security." *New York Times*, 12 November (online edition).

Foley, Alejandro. 1993. "Latin America within the World Economy." Interview. *Challenge* (January–February): 18–22.

Folgarait, Leonard. 1998. *Mural Painting and Social Revolution in Mexico, 1920–1940: Art of the New Order*. New York: Cambridge University Press.

Folha de São Paulo/Datafolha. 1995. *Racismo Cordial: A mais completa análise sobre preconcieto de cor no Brasil*. São Paulo: Atica.

Forero, Juan. 2000. "In Miami, Some Cuban-Americans Take Less Popular Views." *New York Times*, 28 April (online edition).

Forsha, Linda. 1995. "Introductory Note." In insITE94: A Binational Exhibition of Installation and Site-Specific Art/Una Exposición binacional de arte-instalación en sitios específicos. Sally Yard, ed. San Diego: Installation Gallery, 6.

Forte, Jeanie. 1988. "Women's Performance Art: Feminism and Postmodernism." *Theatre Journal* 40: 234.

Foster, Hal. 1994. "Cult of Despair." *New York Times*, 30 December: A31.

———. 1996. "The Artist as Ethnographer." In *Return of the Real*. Cambridge: MIT Press.

Foucault, Michel. 1973. *The Order of Things: An Archaeology of the Human Sciences*. New York: Vintage.

———. 1977. *Discipline and Punish: The Birth of the Prison*. Trans. Alan Sheridan. New York: Pantheon Books.

———. 1979. Lecture, Collège de France, 4 April.

———. 1982. "The Subject and Power." In *Michel Foucault: Beyond Structuralism and Hermeneutics*, ed. Hubert L. Dreyfus and Paul Rabinow. Chicago: University of Chicago Press.

———. 1983. "The Subject and Power." In *Michel Foucault: Beyond Structuralism and Hermeneutics*, ed. Hubert L. Dreyfus and Paul Rabinow. Chicago: University of Chicago Press.

———. 1984. *The History of Sexuality: An Introduction*. Trans. Robert Hurley. Harmondsworth, England: Penguin.

———. 1991. "Governmentality." In *The Foucault Effect: Studies in Governmentality*, ed. Graham Burchell, Colin Gordon, and Peter Miller. Chicago: University of Chicago Press.

———. 1997a. "The Ethics of the Concern for Self as a Practice of Freedom." In *Ethics, Subjectivity and Truth*, ed. Paul Rabinow. New York: New Press.

———. 1997b. *"Il faut défendre la société": Cours au College de France (1975–1976)*. Paris: Seuil/Gallimard.

Fox, Claire F. 1994a. "Free Trade and the Cultural Exemption." Revised version of a paper presented at "NAFTA and Culture" panel of the Modern Language Association Convention, 29 December.

———. 1994b. "The Portable Border: Site-Specificity, Art, and the U.S.-Mexico Frontier." *Social Text* 41: 61–82.

———. 1999. *The Fence and the River: Culture and Politics at the U.S.-Mexico Border*. Minneapolis: University of Minnesota Press.

Fox, Elizabeth. 1997. "Media and Culture in Latin America." In *International Media Research: A Critical Survey*, ed. John Corner, Philip Schlesinger, and Roger Silverstone. London: Routledge.

Foxley, Alejandro. 1996. Preface to *The New Economic Model in Latin America and Its Impact on Income Distribution and Poverty*, ed. Victor Bulmer-Thomas. New York: St. Martin's.

Franco, Jean. 1975. "Dependency Theory and Literary History: The Case of Latin America." *Minnesota Review* 5 (fall): 65–79.

———. 1993. Comments made at the first meeting of the Inter-American Cultural Studies Network, Iztapalapa, Mexico, 3–5 May.

Frank, Peter. 1992. "Fluxus Fallout: New York in the Wake of the New Sensibility." In *Fluxus: A Conceptual Country*. Special issue of *Visible Language* 26.1–2 (winter/spring).

Frankenberg, Ruth, ed. 1997. *Displacing Whiteness: Essays in Social and Cultural Criticism*. Durham, NC: Duke University Press.

Fraser, Andrea. 1994. "How to Provide an Artistic Service: An Introduction." Text presented in the exhibition and working group organized by Helmut Draxler and Andrea Fraser, Kunstraum der Universitat Luneburg, 29 January–20 February. http://adaweb.walkerart.org/~dn/a/enfra/afraser1.html

———. 1997. "What's Intangible, Transitory, Mediating, Participatory and Rendered in the Public Sphere?" *October* 80 (spring): 111–118.

Fraser, Nancy. 1989. "Women, Welfare, and the Politics of Need Interpretation." In

Unruly Practices: Power, Discourse and Gender in Contemporary Social Theory. Minneapolis: University of Minnesota Press.

Free Idea Zone Residency. 1994. Brochure. The Ben Lomand Center, Santa Cruz Mountains, CA. 27 June–1 July.

Freire, Paulo. [1967] 1976. *Education, the Practice of Freedom.* London: Writers and Readers Publishing Cooperative.

French, John D. 1999. "The Missteps of Anti-Imperialist Reason: Pierre Bourdieu, Loïc Wacquant, and Michael Hanchard's *Orpheus and Power.*" Working Paper 27, Duke–University of North Carolina Program in Latin American Studies, Working Paper Series, September.

French, Kristen. 2001. "WTO's Drug Deal Will Open Books, Close Markets." http://www.thestreet.com/_cnet/markets/kristenfrench/10004075.html

Freudheim, Susan. 1992. "Centro's Show Loses USIA Help." *Los Angeles Times,* Calendar section, 29 September: F1, F5.

Freyre, Gilberto. 1933. *Casa Grande e Senzala.* Rio de Janeiro: Schmidt.

———. 1946. *The Masters and the Slaves.* Trans. Samuel Putnam. New York: Knopf.

———. [1966] 1974. "Toward a Mestizo Type." In *The Gilberto Freyre Reader.* Trans. Barbara Shelby. New York: Knopf. Originally in *The Racial Factor in Contemporary Politics.* Sussex: Research Unit for the Study of Multi-Racial Societies, University of Sussex.

Friedman, Sheldon. 1992. "NAFTA as Social Dumping." *Challenge* (September–October): 27–32.

Friedman, Thomas L. 1994. "U.S. Sees Hypocrisy on Trade." *New York Times,* 10 March: D1– D5.

———. 2000. "America's Labor Pains: What's Going on with the American Labor Movement?" *New York Times,* 9 May (online edition).

La Frontera/The Border. 1993. Exhibition catalogue. SUNY Purchase, Newberger Museum of Art.

Fuentes, Carlos. 1991. "Latin America's Alternative: An Ibero-American Federation." *New Perspectives Quarterly* 8.1 (winter): 15–17. http://www.npq.org/issues/V81/p15.html

Fuller, Colleen. 1991. "Fade to Black: Culture under Free Trade." *Canadian Forum* (August): 5–10.

Fuller, Hoyt W. 1971. "Towards a Black Aesthetic." In *The Black Aesthetic,* ed. Addison Gayle Jr. Garden City, NY: Doubleday.

Fusco, Coco. 1992. *The Couple in the Cage.* Video documentary of performances by Coco Fusco and Guillermo Gómez-Peña. http://www.artswire.org/cocofusco/FZLN. 2001. La Marcha de los Colores. CD-Rom Multimedia. http://www.fzln.org.mx/

———. 1995. *English is Broken Here.* New York: The New Press.

Gabler, Neal. 2000. "Win Now, or Lose Forever." *New York Times,* 3 May (online edition).

Gabriel, John. 1994. *Racism, Culture, Markets.* London: Routledge.

García, Beatrice E. 1998. "Entertainment Industry Survey Is Off the Mark." *Miami Herald,* 5 December (online edition): 1C.

———. 2000. "StarMedia: The Next Generation: Latin Internet's First Born Fights Growing Competition." *Miami Herald*, 4 June (online edition).

García Canclini, Néstor. 1982. *Las culturas populares en el capitalismo*. Havana: Casa de las Américas.

———. 1990. *Culturas híbridas: Estrategias para entrar y salir de la modernidad*. Mexico City: Grijalbo.

———. 1992a. "Cultural Reconversion." In *On Edge: The Crisis of Contemporary Latin American Culture*, ed. George Yúdice, Jean Franco, and Juan Flores. Minneapolis: University of Minnesota Press.

———. 1992b. "Museos, aeropuertos y ventas de garage: La cultura ante el Tratado de Libre Comercio." *La Jornada Semanal* 157 (14 June): 32–39.

———. 1993. *Transforming Modernity: Popular Culture in Mexico*. Austin: University of Texas Press.

———. 1994a. "¿Macondismo en la época del TLC? Un debate sobre arte y multiculturalidad." *Memoria de Papel* (March): 76–79.

———. 1994b. "Rehacer los pasaportes: El pensamiento visual en el debate sobre multiculturalidad." *Revista de Crítica Cultural* 8 (May): 28–35.

———. 1995a. *Consumidores y ciudadanos: Conflictos multiculturales de la globalización*. Mexico City: Grijalbo.

———. [1990] 1995b. *Hybrid Cultures: Strategies for Entering and Leaving Modernity*. Trans. Christopher L. Chiappari and Silvia L. Lopez. Minneapolis: University of Minnesota Press.

———. 1998. "De-Urbanized Art, Border De-Installations." inSITE97.

———. 1999. "Políticas culturales: De las identidades nacionales al espacio latinoamericano." In *Integración económica e industrias culturales en América Latina*, ed. Néstor García Canclini and Carlos Moneta. Mexico City: Grijalbo, 33–54.

———. 2001. *Consumers and Citizens: Globalization and Multicultural Conflicts*. Trans. and introduction by George Yúdice. Minneapolis: University of Minnesota Press.

García Canclini, Nestor, Krzysztof Wodiczko, and George Yúdice. 2001. "Conversation IV: Image Power: Cultural Interventions as Public Memory in Post-Modern Spaces." Centro Cultural Tijuana, 25 February.

García de León, Antonio. 1998. "Los bordes críticos del sistema." *Fractal* 8 2.3 (January–March). http://www.fractal.com.mx/F8garcia.html

Garfinkel, Harold. 1967. *Studies in Ethnomethodology*. Englewood Cliffs, NJ: Prentice-Hall.

Garnham, Nicholas. 1987. "Concepts of Culture: Public Policy and the Cultural Industries." *Cultural Studies* 1.1: 23–37.

Garreau, Joel. 2001. "Disconnect the Dots." 17 September. http://www.washtech.com/news/regulation/12516-1.html

Gayle, Addison, Jr., ed. 1971. *The Black Aesthetic*. Garden City, NY: Doubleday.

Gentili, Pablo. 2000. "The Permanent Crisis of the Public University." *NACLA Report on the Americas* 23.4 (January–February): 12–18.

Gerbner, George. 1992. "Persian Gulf War, the Movie." In *Triumph of the Image: The Media's*

War in the Persian Gulf: A Global Perspective, ed. Hamid Mowlana, George Gerbner, and Herbert I. Schiller. Boulder, CO: Westview Press.

Getino, Octavio. 1997. Editorial. *Boletín de Industrias Culturales* 4 (December): 1.

———. 1998. *Cine y televisión en América Latina: Producción y mercados*. Santiago de Chile: CICCUS.

———. 2000. "Las industrias culturales y el Mercosur." *Contato: Revista Brasileira de Comunicação, Arte e Educação* 2.6 (January–March): 53–61.

———. 2001. "Aproximación a un estudio de las Industrias Culturales en el Mercosur (Incidencia económica, social y cultural para la integración regional)." Paper presented at the international conference "Importancia y Proyección del Mercosur Cultural con miras a la Integración" Santiago de Chile, 3–5 May. http://www.campus-oei.org/cultura/getino.htm

Gevers, Ine, ed. 1992. *Cultural Identity: Fiction of Necessity*. Special issue of *Third Text* 18 (spring).

Gillespie, Nick. 1999. "Union Crunch."*Reason Online* (June). http://www.reason.com/9906/ci.ng.union.html

Gilmore, Samuel. 1993. "Minorities and Distributional Equity at the National Endowment for the Arts." *JAMLS* 23.2 (summer): 137–173.

Gilpin, Kenneth N. 1995. "Trade Gap Widens in Month: Possible Record for '94 Seen." *New York Times*, 20 January: 1.

Gilroy, Paul. 1992. "It's a Family Affair." In *Black Popular Culture*, ed. Gina Dent. Seattle: Bay Press.

———. 1993. *The Black Atlantic: Modernity and Double Consciousness*. Cambridge, MA: Harvard University Press.

Giroux, Henry A. 1994. "Consuming Social Change: The United Colors of Benetton." In *Disturbing Pleasures: Learning Popular Culture*. New York: Routledge.

Gitlin, Todd. 1995. *The Twilight of Common Dreams: Why America Is Wracked by Culture Wars*. New York: Metropolitan Books.

Glade, William. 1993. "North American Higher Education Cooperation: Overview and Context." Paper presented at Wingspread Conference, Racine, WI.

Glazer, Nathan, and Daniel Patrick Moynihan. 1963. *Beyond the Melting Pot: The Negroes, Puerto Ricans, Jews, Italians, and Irish of New York City*. Cambridge, MA: MIT Press.

"El gobierno brasileño teme un estallido social por el hambre y la desocupación." 1992. *Clarín*, 23 October: 24.

Gohn, Maria da Glória. 2000. *Mídia, Terceiro Setor e MST: Impactos sobre o futuro das cidades e do campo*. Petrópolis: Vozes.

Goldberg, Roselee. 1979. "Seventies' Performance: 'To Be with Art Is All We Ask.'" In *Performance: Live Art 1909 to the Present*. New York: Abrams.

———. 1984. "Performance: The Golden Years." In *The Art of Performance: A Critical Anthology*, ed. Gregory Battcock and Robert Nickas. New York: Dutton.

Goldman, Shifra. 1988. "Latin Visions and Revisions." *Art in America* (May).

———. 1991a. "Metropolitan Splendors: The Buying and Selling of Mexico." *Third Text* 14 (spring).

———. 1991b. "Mirándole la boca a caballo regalado: Arte latinoamericano en Estados Unidos." *La Jornada Semanal* (6 October): 39–44.

———. 1992. "Updating Chicano Art." *New Art Examiner* (October).

———. 1994. *Dimensions of the Americas: Art and Social Change in Latin America and the United States.* Chicago: University of Chicago Press.

Goldring, Marc. 1994. "New Trends in Arts Funding." *High Performance* (summer): 15–16.

Gómez-Peña, Guillermo. 1988. "Documented/Undocumented." In *Multicultural Literacy: Opening the American Mind,* ed. Rick Simonson and Scott Walker. St. Paul: Grayworld Press.

———. 1992. "The New World Border." *High Performance* (fall).

———. 1993. "The Free Art Agreement/El Tratado de Libre Cultura." *High Performance* 63 (fall): 58–63.

Gonçalves, Marcos Augusto. 1994. "Flying Down to Rio." *Revista Folha,* 2 October: 78.

Goode, Judith G., Jo Anne Schneider, and Suzanne Blanc. 1992. "Transcending Boundaries and Closing Ranks: How Schools Shape Interrelations." In *Structuring Diversity: Ethnographic Perspectives on the New Immigration,* ed. Louise Lamphere. Chicago: University of Chicago Press.

Goodstein, Laurie. 1999. "Coalition's Woes May Hinder Goals of Christian Right." *New York Times,* 2 August (online edition).

Gordon, Avery. 1995. "Diversity Management: The Work of Corporate Culture." *Social Text* 44.

Gordon, Michael R. 2001. "U.S. Tries to Rally Public Support Overseas." *New York Times,* 6 November (online edition).

Goswamy, B. N. 1991. "Another Past, Another Context: Exhibiting Indian Art Abroad." In *The Poetics and Politics of Museum Display,* ed. Ivan Karp and Steven D. Lavine. Washington, DC: Smithsonian Institution Press.

"Governo atenderá 9 milhões de famílias com Proalimentos" (Government will assist 9 million families with Proalimentos–Brazilian Program of Nutritional Support). 1992. *Jornal do Brasil,* 22 October: 1.

Gramsci, Antonio. 1971. *Selections from the Prison Notebooks.* Ed. and trans. Quintin Hoare and Geoffrey Nowell Smith. New York: International Publishers.

Graser, Graser. 1999. " 'Silicon Barrio' Getting Latin America Online." *Variety,* 1–7 November: M32-M33.

Grimson, Alejandro. 1998. "Comments on the Cultural Policies of MERCOSUL." Paper presented at the International Seminar on "Economic Integration and the Culture Industries in Latin America and the Caribbean," Buenos Aires, 30–31 July.

———. 1999. *Relatos de la diferencia y de la igualdad: Los bolivianos en Buenos Aires.* Buenos Aires: Eudeba/Felafacs.

Grinspun, Ricardo, and Maxwell A. Cameron, eds. 1993. *The Political Economy of North American Free Trade.* London: Macmillan.

Grosfoguel, Ramón. 1994. "World Cities in the Caribbean: The Rise of Miami and San Juan." *Review* 17.3 (summer): 351–381.

———. 1995. "Global Logics in the Caribbean City System: The Case of Miami." In *World Cities in a World-System*, ed. Paul L. Knox and Peter J. Taylor. New York: Cambridge University Press.

———. 2000. "Multiple Colonialities in a Symbolic World-City: Miami in the World-Economy." Paper presented at the 23d International Congress of the Latin American Studies Association, Miami, 17 March.

Grossberg, Lawrence. 1999. "Speculations and Articulations of Globalization." *Polygraph* 11.

Groupe de Fribourg. 1996. "Project Concerning a Declaration of Cultural Rights." Paris: UNESCO, 4 September. http://www.unifr.ch/iiedh/langues/english/DC/decl_dc.html

Gruben, William C. 1992. "Trade Policy and Intellectual Property Protection: The North-South Dispute." *Economic Review* (Fed. Reserve Bank of Dallas), 4th quarter: 19–29.

Grundberg, Andy. 1990. "Images of Third-World Dislocation (re: Alfredo Jaar)." *New York Times*, 4 May: C30.

———. 2000. "Relátorio Anual do Grupo Cultural AfroReggae 1999." Rio de Janeiro. http://www.afroreggae.org.br/index1.htm

———. "Programas." http://www.afroreggae.org

"Grupo negro declara guerra aos 'carecas.' " 1992. *Folha de São Paulo*, 18 October: section 4, 3.

"Guard for Bush Isn't Allowed Aboard Flight." 2001. *New York Times*, 27 December.

Guedes, Cilene. 1996. "O Brasil numa rua de Botafogo." *Jornal do Brasil Online, Caderno B.*, 28 April. ax.animax in igc:ax.brasil

Guevara Niebla, Gilberto, and Néstor García Canclini, eds. 1992. *La educación y la cultura ante el Tratado de Libre Comercio*. Mexico City: Nueva Imagen.

Gugelberger, Georg, ed. 1996. *The Real Thing: Testimonial Discourse and Latin America*. Durham, NC: Duke University Press.

Guilbaut, Serge. 1983. *How New York Stole the Idea of Modern Art: Abstract Expressionism, Freedom, and the Cold War*. Chicago: University of Chicago Press.

Gundrey, G. 1994. "Where the 'Growth Jobs' Are." *The People* 104.7 (15 December). igc.econ.poverty. Accessed 20 February.

Gussow, Mel. 1998. "The Whitney Cancels a Karen Finley Exhibition." *New York Times*, 4 July.

Habermas, Jürgen. 1981. "Modernity versus Postmodernity." *New German Critique* 22 (winter).

———. 1984. *The Structural Transformation of the Public Sphere*. Cambridge, MA: MIT Press.

Hachten, William A. 1999. *The World News Prism: Changing Media of International Communication*. Ames: Iowa State University Press.

Hale, Grace Elizabeth. 1998. *Making Whiteness: The Culture of Segregation in the South, 1890–1940*. New York: Pantheon.

Halleck, Deedee. 1994. "Zapatistas On-line." In *The Political Uses of Culture*. Special issue of *NACLA Report on the Americas* 28.2 (September/October): 30–32.

Halley, Janet E. 2000. " 'Like Race' Arguments." In *What's Left of Theory? New Work on the Politics of Literary Theory*, ed. Judith Butler, John Guillory, and Kendall Thomas. New York: Routledge.

Hallin, Daniel. C., and Todd Gitlin. 1994. "The Gulf War as Popular Culture and Television Drama." In *Taken by Storm: The Media, Public Opinion, and U.S. Foreign Policy in the Gulf War*, ed. W. Lance Bennett and David L. Paletz. Chicago: University of Chicago Press.

Hanchard, Michael. 1990. "Identity, Meaning, and the African American." *Social Text* 24: 31–42.

———. 1993. *Orpheus and Power: Afro-Brazilian Social Movements in Rio de Janeiro and São Paulo, Brazil 1945–1988*. Princeton: Princeton University Press.

Hancocks, Anthea. 1987. "Museum Exhibition as a Tool for Social Awareness." *American Museum of Natural History* 30, 3: 181–192.

Haraway, Donna. 1988. "Apes, Aliens, Cyborgs and Women: The Intersection of Colonial Discourse and Feminist Theory." Lecture. New School for Social Research, spring.

———. 1989a. "Monkeys, Aliens, and Women: Love, Science, and Politics at the Intersection of Feminist Theory and Colonial Discourse." *Women's Studies International Forum* 12.3: 295–312.

———. 1989b. *Primate Visions: Gender, Race, and Nature in the World of Modern Science*. New York: Routledge.

———. 1991. *Simians, Cyborgs, and Women: The Reinvention of Nature*. New York: Routledge.

———. 1997. *Modest_Witness@Second_Millennium. FemaleMan©_Meets_OncoMouse™*. New York: Routledge.

Hardt, Michael. 1995. "The Withering of Civil Society." *Social Text* 45 (winter).

Hardt, Michael, and Toni Negri. 1994. *Labor of Dionysus: A Critique of the State Form*. Minneapolis: University of Minnesota Press.

———. 2000. *Empire*. Cambridge: Harvard University Press.

Hart, Hugh. 2001. "Bringing Hollywood Pizazz to Military Training." *New York Times*, 15 November (online edition).

Hartigan, John, Jr. 1999. *Racial Situations: Class Predicaments of Whiteness in Detroit*. Princeton: Princeton University Press.

Hasenbalg, Carlos. 1992. "Desigualdades raciais no Brasil e na América Latina: Respostas Tímidas ao Racismo Escamoteado (Notas Preliminares)." Paper presented at the conference "Derechos Humanos, Justicia y Sociedad," Buenos Aires, 22–24 October.

Hasenbalg, Carlos, and Nelson do Valle Silva. 1988. *Estrutura Social, Mobilidade e Raça*. São Paulo: Vértice.

Haynes, Arden R. 1986. "Funding Canadian Culture: A Corporate View." *Canadian Business Review* (summer): 23–25.

"Health GAP Statement on Brazil's Intention to Issue a Compulsory License for Nelfi-navir." 2001. Consumer Project on Technology, Health Care and Intellectual Property, 22 August. http://www.cptech.org/ip/health/c/brazil/hgap-brazil08222001. html

Heidegger, Martin. 1971. "The Origin of the Work of Art." In *Poetry, Language, Thought*. Trans. Albert Hofstadter. New York: Harper and Row.

————. 1977 [1938]. "The Age of the World Picture." In *The Question Concerning Technology and Other Essays*. Trans. William Lovitt. New York: Garland.

————. 1977 [1950]. "The Question Concerning Technology." In *The Question Concerning Technology and Other Essays*. Trans. William Lovitt. New York: Garland.

Heinich, Nathalie, and Michael Pollak. 1996. "From Museum Curator to Exhibition Auteur: Inventing a Singular Position." In *Thinking About Exhibitions*, ed. Reesa Greenberg, Bruce W. Ferguson, and Sandy Nairne. London: Routledge.

Helg, Aline. 1990. "Race in Argentina and Cuba, 1880–1930." In *The Idea of Race in Latin America*, ed. Richard Graham. Austin: University of Texas Press.

Helms, Janet E. 1992. *A Race Is a Nice Thing to Have: A Guide to Being a White Person or Understanding the White Persons in Your Life*. Topeka, KS: Content Communications.

"The Helms Process." 1989. *New York Times*, 28 July: A26.

"Helms Trumpets Mexico's Cooperation." 2001. *New York Times*, 17 April (online edition).

Hendershot, Heather. 1995 "Shake, Rattle and Roll: Production and Consumption of Fundamentalist Youth Culture." *Afterimage* (February–March).

Henríquez, Elio, and Matilde Pérez. 1995. "La transición democrática no la determinará el gobierno, dijo el "sucomandante" en un video." *La Jornada*, 9 August. http://serpiente.dgsca.unam.mx/jornada/1995/oct95/951021/cara.html

Hernández, Helio, and Rosa Rojas. 1995. "Queremos ser parte de la nación mexicana, como iguales," *La Jornada*, 18 November. http://serpiente.dgsca.unam.mx/jornada/1995/oct95/951021/cara.html

————. 1996. "Fourth Declaration of the Lacandon Jungle." http://www.eco.utexas.edu:80/Homepages/Faculty/Cleaver/chiapas952.html

Hernández, Sofia. 1997. "Transitio: Una crónica/ficción de la deslocalización de un sitio específico." Licenciatura thesis, University of Monterrey, Mexico.

Herscovici, Alain. 1999. "Globalización, sistema de redes y estructuración del espacio: Un análisis económico." In *Globalización y monopolios en la comunicación en América Latina: Hacia una economía política de la comunicación*, ed. Guillermo Mastrini and César Bolaño. Buenos Aires: Editorial Biblos.

Hess, David J., and Roberto A. DaMatta, eds. 1995. *The Brazilian Puzzle: Culture on the Borderlands of the Western World*. New York: Columbia University Press.

Hickey, David. 1995. "Sitegeist." In *inSITE94*, 64–71.

Higginbotham, Evelyn Brooks. 1992. "The Metalanguage of Race." *Signs* (winter).

Higgins, Dick. 1964. *Jefferson's Birthday/Postface*. New York: Something Else Press.

Hill, Mike, ed. 1997. *Whiteness: A Critical Reader*. New York: New York University Press.

Hispanic USA: Marketing Niche of the 90s. 1994. Video recording. Telemundo.

Hoggart, Richard. [1957] 1992. *The Uses of Literacy*. New Brunswick, NJ: Transaction.

Holmes, Steven A. 1993. "Pacific Trade Bloc Is Divided over Chile's Membership Bid." *New York Times*, 15 November: A8.

————. 1995a. "Programs Based on Sex and Race Are Challenged." *New York Times*, 16 March: A1.

————. 1995b. "White House Signals an Easing on Affirmative Action." *New York Times*, 25 February: 9.

Houppert, Karen. 1993. "Jamie Does Dallas." *Village Voice*, 10 August.

Hoving, Thomas P. 1968. "Branched Out," *Museum News* 47:4 (1968).

Howard, Gary R. 1999. *We Can't Teach What We Don't Know: White Teachers, Multiracial Schools*. New York: Teachers College Press.

Hufbauer, Gary Clyde, and Jeffrey J. Schott. 1993. *Nafta: An Assessment*. Revised ed. Washington, DC: Institute for International Economics.

Human Rights Coordinator. 1993. "Brazil: Child Murders Shroud Rio." newsdesk@ igc.apc.org, 27 July. igc:ips.english.

Huntington, Samuel. 1996. *The Clash of Civilizations*. New York: Simon and Schuster.

I Bienal de Artes Visuais do Mercosul /I Bienal de Artes Visuales del Mercosur, de 2 de outubro a 30 de novembro de 1997. 1997. Catalogue. Porto Alegre: Fundação Bienal de Artes Visuais do Mercosul.

Ignatiev, Noel. 1995. *How the Irish Became White*. New York: Routledge.

Ignatiev, Noel, and John Garvey, eds. 1996. *Race Traitor*. New York: Routledge.

"Impact of Undocumented Persons and Other Migrants on Costs, Revenues and Services in Los Angeles County." 1992. Report prepared for the Los Angeles County Board of Supervisors, November.

"Income Gap of Richest and Poorest Widens for U.S. Families." 2000. CNN, 18 January. http://www.cnn.com/2000/US/01/18/wage.gap/

"India Plans to Double IT Workers to Meet Global Demand." 2000. *New York Times*, 5 August (online edition).

"Inflation, Despair Reign as Brazilian Confidence in New President Wanes." 1993. *News and Observer*, 18 March: 13A.

Innerst, Carol. 1993. "USIA's Grants Go to Schools in NAFTA Nations." *Washington Times*, 12 September: A5.

"INSIGHTS Fits Naturally into Growth Plan for Greater San Diego Chamber of Commerce and City." 1994. *El Sol de San Diego* 15 September: 20.

inSite92. *A Binational Exhibition of Installation and Site-Specific Art – San Diego/Tijuana: Una Exposición Binacional de Arte-Instalación en Sitios Específicos*. 1992. Brochure. San Diego: Installation Gallery.

inSITE94: *A Binational Exhibition of Installation and Site-Specific Art—San Diego/Tijuana: Una Exposición Binacional de Arte-Instalación en Sitios Específicos*. 1994. Special supplement to *San Diego Daily Transcript*, 20 September.

inSITE97. *Private Time in Public Space/Tiempo privado en espacio público*. 1998. Ed. Sally Yard. San Diego: Installation Gallery.

"insITE97 Takes Shape for Fall of 1997 with an Emphasis on Artists Working in the Americas." 1995. insITE press release, 11 October.

insITE2000–2001. *Parajes fugitivos/Fugitive Sites*. 2002. Ed. Osvaldo Sánchez. San Diego: Installation Gallery.

International Labour Office. 2001. "The Social Impact on the Hotel and Tourism Sector of Events Subsequent to 11 September 2001." Briefing paper for discussion at the informal meeting "Hotel and Tourism Sector: Social Impact of Events Subsequent to 11 September 2001," Geneva, 25–26 October. http://www.ilo.org/public/english/dialogue/sector/techmeet/imhcto1/imhctbp.pdf

International Union of Food, Agricultural, Hotel, Restaurant, Catering, Tobacco and Allied Workers' Associations. 2001. "WTO Doha Conference a Setback for Labour and the Poor." 21 November. http://www.iuf.org/iuf/wp/011121.htm

"In the Body's Place." 2001. Editorial. *New York Times*, 19 October (online edition).

Into the Spotlight: A Survey of Mexico. 1993. Special issue of *The Economist* (13 February).

Iramain, Demetrio. 2001. "Otra campaña contra las Madres de Plaza de Mayo." *Rebelión*, 12 October. http://www.eurosur.org/rebelion/internacional/debate2121001.htm

Iturribarria, F. 1999. "Polémica en Lyon por la idea de construir un museo Guggenheim." *El Diario Vasco*, 27 June (online edition).

Jabor, Arnoldo. 1995. "As favelas do Rio são países estrangeiros." *Folha de São Paulo*, 30 May: V10.

Jackson, Maria-Rosario. 1998. *Arts and Culture Indicators in Community Building Project: January 1996–May 1998. A Report to the Rockefeller Foundation*. Washington, DC: Urban Institute.

Jackson, Terry. 2000. "Lights, Camera. Where Is the Action?" *Miami Herald*, 5 March (online edition): 1M.

Jacob, Mary Jane. 1995. "Outside the Loop." In *Culture in Action: A Public Art Program of Sculpture Chicago*, 16–49.

———. 1996. Interview by Jeffrey Kastner. *Art and Design* 11.

———. 1998. *Conversations at the Castle: Changing Audiences and Contemporary Art*. Cambridge: MIT Press.

Jacob, Mary Jane, and Michael Brenson. 1998. "Reaching the Goal: Curating Conversations." In *Conversations at the Castle: Changing Audiences and Contemporary Art*, ed. Mary Jane Jacob. Cambridge: MIT Press.

Jacobs, Karrie. 1997. "Capital Improvements." *Guggenheim Magazine* (fall): 10–17.

Jacobson, Matthew Frye. 1998. *Whiteness of a Different Color: European Immigrants and the Alchemy of Race*. Cambridge, MA: Harvard University Press.

Jacoby, Russell. 1987. *The Last Intellectuals: American Culture in the Age of Academe*. New York: Basic Books.

Jameson, Fredric. 1984. "Postmodernism, or the Logic of Late Capitalism." *New Left Review* 146 (July–August): 53–92.

———. 1991. *Postmodernism, or, The Cultural Logic of Late Capitalism*. Durham, NC: Duke University Press.

Jamison, Laura. 1993. "Free Idea Zone: A Black Market in Ideas." *High Performance* 61 (spring): 30–33.

"Jantar dos palavrões." 1992. *Jornal do Brasil*, 30 September: 17.

Jaura, Ramesh. 2000. "AMERICA LATINA: Leve mejoría salarial, pero alto desempleo." *Tierramérica*, 17 December. http://www.tierramerica.net/2000/1217/noticias1.html

Jelin, Elizabeth. 1991. "¿Cómo construir ciudadanía? Una visión desde abajo." Paper presented at the CEDES project on "Human Rights and the Consolidation of Democracy: The Trial of the Argentine Military," Buenos Aires, 20–21 September.

———. 1998. "Toward a Culture of Participation and Citizenship: Challenges for a More Equitable World." In *Cultures of Politics/Politics of Cultures: Re-Visioning Latin American Social Movements*, ed. Sonia E. Alvarez, Evelina Dagnino, and Arturo Escobar. Boulder, CO: Westview Press.

Jelin, Elizabeth, and Eric Hershberg. 1996. "Introduction: Human Rights and the Construction of Democracy." In *Constructing Democracy: Human Rights, Citizenship, and Society in Latin America*, ed. Elizabeth Jelin and Eric Hershberg. Boulder, CO: Westview Press.

Jelin, Elizabeth, and Susana G. Kaufman. 1998. "Layers of Memories: Twenty Years after in Argentina." Paper presented at the conference "Legacies of Authoritarianism: Cultural Production, Collective Trauma, and Global Justice." University of Wisconsin–Madison, 3–5 April.

Jenkins, Henry. 1992. *Textual Poachers: Television Fans and Participatory Culture*. New York: Routledge.

Jenkins, Sally. 2001. "Restoring Faith in New York: Religious Leaders Draw 20,000 to Yankee Stadium to Grieve, Pray." *Washington Post*, 24 September.

Jensen, Joli. 1993. "Democratic Culture and the Arts: Constructing a Usable Past." *Journal of Arts Management, Law and Society* 23.2 (summer): 110–120.

Johnson, Bradley. 1993. "The Gay Quandary: Advertising's Most Elusive, Yet Lucrative, Target Market Proves Difficult to Measure." *Advertising Age* (June): 29, 35.

Johnson, Sonia H. 1994. "Thank the Lord for insITE94!" *Arts Monthly* (December).

Joyce, Erin. 2001. "Study: WTC Attacks to Cost NYC $83 Billion." atnewyork.com, 16 November. http://www.atnewyork.com/rebuild/article/0,1471,3041_927631,00.html

Julien, Isaac. 1992. "Black Is, Black Ain't: Notes on De-Essentializing Black Identities." In *Black Popular Culture*, ed. Gina Dent. Seattle: Bay Press.

Juno, Andrea. 1991a. "Carolee Schneemann." Interview. In *Angry Women*. San Francisco: Re/Search Publications.

———. 1991b. "Karen Finley." Interview. In *Angry Women*. San Francisco: Re/Search Publications.

Jurca, Catherine. 2001. *White Diaspora: The Suburb and the Twentieth-Century American Novel*. Princeton: Princeton University Press.

Kafka, Franz. 1976. "A Hunger Artist." In *Kafka: The Complete Stories*. Ed. Nahum N. Glatzer. New York: Schocken.

Kaprow, Allan. 1993. *Essays on the Blurring of Art and Life*. Ed. Jeff Kelley. Berkeley: University of California Press.

Kaptur, Marcy, et al. 1993. "The Human Face of Trade." *Executive Summary, U.S. Congressional Delegation of Women Members to Mexico*, 30 April–3 May.

"Karen Finley: Bill Maher Develops a Taste for Her Performance Art." 1999. *Playboy* (July): 72–77.

Karenga, Ron. 1971. "Black Cultural Nationalism." In *The Black Aesthetic*, ed. Addison Gayle Jr. Garden City, NY: Doubleday.

Karp, Ivan, and Steven D. Lavine, eds. 1991. *The Poetics and Politics of Museum Display*. Washington, DC: Smithsonian Institution Press.

Karp, Ivan, Christine Mullen Kreamer, and Steven D. Lavine, eds. 1992. *Museums and Communities: The Politics of Public Culture*. Washington, DC: Smithsonian Institution Press.

Katel, Peter. 2000. "El futuro de Miami mira hacia el sur." *El Nuevo Herald*, 1 January (online edition): 1A.

Katz-Fishman, Walda, and Jerome Scott. 1994. "The High Tech Revolution and the Permanent Poverty Economy: Educating and Organizing for a New Society." igc.econ. poverty. Accessed 27 July 1994.

Kellner, Douglas. 2001. "September 11, Terror War, and Blowback." http://www. publiceye.org/ frontpage/911/d-kellner-911.htm. Accessed 4 January 2002.

Kester, Grant. 1995. "Aesthetic Evangelists: Conversion and Empowerment in Contemporary Community Art." *Afterimage* (January): 5–11.

Kidwell, David. 2000. "Judge's Edict Formally Ends Cuba Policy." *Miami Herald*, 12 July (online edition).

Kifner, John. 1995. "Bomb Suspect Felt at Home Riding the Gun-Show Circuit." *New York Times*, 5 July: A18, A19.

Kilborn, Peter T. 1995. " 'Glass Ceiling' Still Exists: White Men's Fears Form Barrier, Study Says." *New York Times*, 16 March: A22.

———. 2000. "Miami Beach Clubgoers Creating New, Unwanted Image." *New York Times*, 27 February (online edition).

Kimmelman, Michael. 1995. "Tattoo Moves from Fringes to Fashion. But Is It Art?" *New York Times*, 15 September: C1, C27.

———. 2001. "A Homegrown Memorial Brings Strangers Together." *New York Times*, 19 September.

Kincheloe, Joe L., et al. 1998. *White Reign: Deploying Whiteness in America*. New York: St. Martin's.

Kinsley, Michael. 1995. "The Spoils of Victimhood: The Case against Affirmative Action." *New Yorker* (27 March): 62–69.

Kinzer, Stephen. 2002a. "For Artists, a Sanctuary from Sept. 11." *New York Times*, 23 January (online edition).

———. 2002b. "Mexico's Cultural Diplomacy Aims to Win Hearts in U.S." *New York Times*, 1 August (online edition).

Kirkpatrick, Gwen. 1993. " 'Free as the Wind': The Cultural Politics of Free Trade." Paper presented at the Modern Language Association Convention, 30 December.

Kivel, Paul. 1995. *Uprooting Racism: How White People Can Work for Racial Justice.* Philadelphia: New Society Publishers.

Klein, Naomi. 2001. "FTAA Meeting Buenos Aires, April 6: The Really Tough Question in Buenos Aires." *Globe and Mail*, 28 March.

Klein, Kevin. 1997. "Doorways into the Future." Weekly Wire 10 November. http://weeklywire.com/ww/11-10-97/alibi_feat1.html

Kleinfield, N. R. 1994. "Black Investors Buy Franchises from Denny's." *New York Times*, 9 November: B15.

Knight, Christopher. 1994. "New Border Customs," *Los Angeles Times*, 1 October 1994.

Kochman, Thomas. 1973. *Rapping and Stylin' Out: Communication in Urban Black America.* Chicago: University of Illinois Press.

Kohn, Howard. 1994. "Service with a Sneer." *New York Times Magazine*, 6 November.

Kollmann, Raúl. 2001. "Al-Qaeda en la triple frontera según la CIA: Argentina y el Plan Colombia." *Página 12*, 30 October. http://www.pagina12.com.ar/2001/01-10/01-10-30/ pag04.htm

Koretz, Gene. 2001. "Economic Trends." *Business Week Online*, 2 July. http://www.business week.com/magazine/content/01_27/c3739134.htm

Kowal, Rebekah. 1999. "Modern Dance and American Culture in the Early Cold War Years." Ph.D. diss., New York University.

Kramer, Hilton. 1989. "Is Art above the Laws of Decency?" *New York Times*, 2 July: H1.

Krauss, Clifford. 1999. "New Data Indicate Longer Recession in Latin America." *New York Times*, 30 June (online edition).

Krauss, Rosalind. 1993. *The Optical Unconscious.* Cambridge, MA: MIT Press.

Kreps, Christina. 1994. "The Paradox of Cultural Preservation in Museums." *Journal of Arts Management, Law and Society* 23.4 (winter): 291–315.

Krichman, Michael, and Carmen Cuenca. 2002. "Directors' Statement/Palabras de los directores." InSITE2000–2001 Parajes fugitivos/Fugitive Sites. San Diego: Installation Gallery, 14–19.

Krischke, Paulo J. 2000. "Problems in the Study of Democratization in Latin America: Regime Analysis vs. Cultural Studies." *International Sociology* 15.1: 107–125.

Kristeva, Julia. 1982. *Powers of Horror: An Essay on Abjection.* Trans. Leon S. Roudiez. New York: Columbia University Press.

———. 1984. *Revolution in Poetic Language.* New York: Columbia University Press.

Krugman, Paul. 2002. "Crying with Argentina." *New York Times*, 1 January (online edition).

Kushner, David. 1998. "Titanic vs. Popotla." Wired News 10 August. http://www.wired.com/news/culture/story/14294.html

Kwon, Miwon. 1997. "One Place After Another: Notes on Site Specificity." *October* 80 (spring).

Lacan, Jacques. 1982. *Feminine Sexuality: Jacques Lacan and the école freudienne*. Ed. Juliet Mitchell and Jacqueline Rose. New York: Norton.

Laclau, Ernesto. 1988. "Metaphor and Social Antagonisms." In *Marxism and the Interpretation of Culture*, ed. Cary Nelson and Lawrence Grossberg. Urbana: University of Illinois Press.

———. 1990. *New Reflections on the Revolution of Our Time*. London: Verso.

Laclau, Ernesto, and Chantal Mouffe. 1985. *Hegemony and Socialist Strategy: Towards a Radical Democratic Politics*. London: Verso.

Lacy, Suzanne. 1995. Introduction to *Mapping the Terrain: New Genre Public Art*, ed. Suzanne Lacy. Seattle: Bay Press.

Lamont, Michèle, ed. 1999. *The Cultural Territories of Race: Black and White Boundaries*. Chicago: University of Chicago Press.

Langley, Stephen. 1993. "The Functions of Arts and Media Management in Relation to the Conflicting Forces of Multiculturalism and Mediaculturalism." *Journal of Arts Management, Law, and Society* 23.3 (fall): 181–195.

Laó, Agustín. 1994–95. "Resources of Hope: Imagining the Young Lords and the Politics of Memory." *Centro, Journal of the Centro de Estudios Puertorriqueños* 7.1 (winter– spring).

Laplanche, J., and J.-B. Portalis. 1973. *The Language of Psycho-analysis*. Trans. Donald Nicholson-Smith. New York: Norton.

Lappé, Frances Moore, and Joseph Collins. 1979. *Food First: Beyond the Myth of Scarcity*. New York: Ballantine.

Larrabee, E. 1968. *Museums and Education*. Washington, DC: Smithsonian Institution Press.

Larson, Gary O. 1997. *American Canvas*. Washington, DC: National Endowment for the Arts.

Lasch, Christopher. 1978. *The Culture of Narcissism: American Life in an Age of Diminishing Expectations*. New York: Norton.

Lash, Scott, and John Urry. 1987. *The End of Organized Capitalism*. Madison: University of Wisconsin Press.

Lavine, Steven D. 1991. "Art Museums, National Identity, and the Status of Minority Cultures: The Case of Hispanic Art in the United States." In *The Poetics and Politics of Museum Display*, ed. Ivan Karp and Steven D. Lavine. Washington, DC: Smithsonian Institution Press.

LeClaire, Jennifer. 1998. "Latin America Makes Miami Major Entertainment Player: 'Hollywood East' Is Now Third-largest Production Hub." *Christian Science Monitor*, 17 August (online edition).

Leidner, Robin. 1993. *Fast Food, Fast Talk: Service Work and the Routinization of Everyday Life*. Berkeley: University of California Press.

Leite, Ilka Boaventura. 1991. "Descendentes de Africanos em Santa Catarina: Invisibilidade Histórica e Segregaçao

Lenderking, Bill. 1993. "The U.S. Mexican Border and NAFTA: Problem or Paradigm?" *North-South Focus* 2.3: 1–6 (North-South Center, University of Miami, Coral Gables).

Levin, Gary. 1993. "Mainstream's Domino Effect: Liquor, Fragrance, Clothing Advertisers Ease into Gay Magazines." *Advertising Age* (June): 30–32.

Levine, Richard. 1990. "Young Immigrant Wave Lifts New York Economy." *New York Times*, 30 July: A1, B4.

Levine-Rasky, Cynthia, ed. 2002. *Working through Whiteness: International Perspectives*. Albany: State University of New York Press.

Levins, Hoag. 1998. "The Changing Cultural Status of Tattoo Art, as Documented in Mainstream U.S. Reference Works, Newspapers, Magazines." http://www. tattooartist.com/history.html

Lewin, Tamar. 1994. "Suit Accuses Hotel at Disney World of 'English Only' Policies." *New York Times*, 13 October: A23.

Lewis, Michael J. 2001. "The 'Look at Me' Strut of a Swagger Building." *New York Times*, 6 January (online edition).

Lewis, Neil A. 2001. "A Conservative Legal Group Thrives in Bush's Washington." *New York Times*, 18 April (online edition).

Lima, Roberto Kant de. 1995. "Bureaucratic Rationality in Brazil and in the United States: Criminal Justice Systems in Comparative Perspective." In *The Brazilian Puzzle: Culture on the Borderlands of the Western World*, ed. David J. Hess and Roberto A. DaMatta. New York: Columbia University Press.

Linker, James A. 1997. "The Minor Art of Guillermo Gómez-Peña." http://www. homepage.montana.edu/~linker/minorart.html

Lippard, Lucy R. 1984a. *Get the Message? A Decade of Art for Social Change*. New York: Dutton.

———. 1984b. "Trojan Horses: Activist Art and Power." In *Art after Modernism: Essays on Rethinking Representation*, ed. Brian Wallis. New York: New Museum of Contemporary Art/Godine.

———. 1990. *Mixed Blessings: New Art in a Multicultural America*. New York: Pantheon.

———. 1995. "The Pains and Pleasure of Rebirth: European and American Women's Body Art." In *The Pink Glass Swan: Selected Feminist Essays on Art*. New York: New Press.

Lipsitz, George. 1998. *The Possessive Investment in Whiteness: How White People Profit from Identity Politics*. Philadelphia: Temple University Press.

Lipton, Eric, and Michael Cooper. 2002. "City Faces Challenge to Close Widest Budget Gap since 70's." *New York Times*, 4 January (online edition).

Livingston, Steven. 1997. "Beyond the 'CNN Effect': The Media–Foreign Policy Dynamic." In *Politics and the Press: The News Media and Their Influence*, ed. Pippa Norris. London: Lynne Rienner.

Lobe, Jim. 1995. "U.S.-Mexico: U.S. Executives Chief Nafta Beneficiaries So Far." 29 April. ips-info@igc.apc.org

Lohr, Steve. 2000. "Welcome to the Internet, the First Global Colony." *New York Times*, 9 January 2000 (online edition).

López, Ian F. Haney. 1996. *White by Law: The Legal Construction of Race*. New York: New York University Press.

López, Julio César. 1996. Interview with Subcomandante Marcos. *Proceso* 1002 (15 January).

López, Sebastián. 1992. "Identity: Reality or Fiction." *Third Text* 18 (spring): 15–25.

López Uribe, María Helena. 1994. "El GATT." *Latinoamérica internacional* 15: 39–41.

Luke, Timothy. 1996. Review of Nina Felshin, ed., *But Is It Art? The Spirit of Art as Activism* and Mary Jane Jacob, Michael Brenson, and Eva M. Olson, *Culture in Action: A Public Art Program of Sculpture Chicago. Contemporary Sociology* 25.5.

Lyman, Rick, and Bill Carter. 2001. "In Little Time, Pop Culture Is Almost Back to Normal." *New York Times*, 4 October (online edition).

Mackowski, Maura J. 1994. "How Do You Translate 'Opportunity'? Hundreds of U.S. Companies Soon Will Be Using Bilingual Labels. Guess Who Can Benefit?" *Hispanic Business* (June): 148–150.

Madrick, Jeff. 2000. "Government's Role in the New Economy Is Not a Cheap or Easy One." *New York Times*, 11 May (online edition).

Madsen, Wayne. 2001. "Homeland Security, Homeland Profits." CorpWatch. http://www.corpwatch.org/issues/PID.jsp?articleid=1108. Accessed 21 December 2001.

Magiciens de la Terre. 1989. Special issue of *Third Text*, 6 (spring). Translation of *Les Cahiers du Musée National d'Art Moderne.* Paris: Éditions du Centre Pompidou.

Magnífico: Hispanic Culture Breaks Out of the Barrio. 1988. Special issue of *Time*, 11 July.

"Maia proibe Viva Rio na prefeitura." 1995. *Jornal do Brasil*, 5 December. http://www.jb.com.br/dez0595.html

Manglano-Ovalle, Iñigo. 1999. Comments at "initial residency" for inSITE2000, 11 July.

———. 2000. Interview by George Yúdice. 17 June.

Marable, Manning. 1991. *Race, Reform, and Rebellion: The Second Reconstruction in Black America, 1945–1990.* 2d ed. Jackson: University Press of Mississippi.

Mariátegui, José Carlos. [1928] 1971. *Seven Interpretive Essays on Peruvian Reality.* Austin: University of Texas Press.

Marquis, Alice Goldfarb. 1995. *Art Lessons: Learning from the Rise and Fall of Public Arts Funding.* New York: Basic Books.

Marquis, Christopher. 2000. "Cuban-American Lobby on the Defensive." *New York Times*, 30 June (online edition).

Marshall, T. H. [1950] 1973. "Citizenship and Social Class." In *Class, Citizenship and Social Development: Essays.* Westport, CT: Greenwood Press.

Martin, Jerry L., and Anne D. Neal. 2001. *Defending Civilization: How Our Universities Are Failing America and What Can Be Done about It.* Washington, DC: Defense of Civilization Fund, American Council of Trustees and Alumni. www.goacta.org/Reports/defciv.pdf

Martín, Martín. 1998. "Studio Miami: How Does an Entertainment Capital Rise from the Ground Up? Cash, Connections and Cool." *Miami Herald*, 13 December (online edition): 1I.

Martin, E. 1967. "Why Museum Education in Today's World?" *Museum News* 46:2.

Martín-Barbero, Jesús. 1987. *De los medios a las mediaciones: Comunicación, cultura, hegemonía.* Barcelona: Gustavo Gili.

———. 1992. "Communication: A Strategic Site for the Debate on Modernity." *Border/Lines* 27.

———. 1993. "La comunicación en las transformaciones del campo cultural." Paper presented at the first meeting of the Inter-American Cultural Studies Network, Universidad Autónoma Metropolitana–Iztapalapa, Mexico City, 3–5 May.

Martínez, Draeger. 1998. "Magazines Target Hispanic Readers." *Miami Herald*, 10 November (online edition).

Martínez Estrada, Ezequiel. 1933. *Radiografía de la pampa.* Buenos Aires: Babel.

Marx, Karl. 1959. *Economic and Philosophic Manuscripts of 1844.* London: Lawrence and Wishart.

———. 1977. *Capital.* Volume 1. Trans. Ben Fowkes. New York: Vintage.

———. [1848] 1995. "On the Question of Free Trade." In *The Poverty of Philosophy.* Trans. H. Quelch. Amherst, NY: Prometheus Books.

Marx, Karl, and Friedrich Engels. [1848] 1967. *The Communist Manifesto.* Harmondsworth, England: Penguin.

Mastrini, Guillermo, and César Bolaño, eds. 1999. *Globalización y monopolios en la comunicación en América Latina: Hacia una economía política de la comunicación.* Buenos Aires: Editorial Biblos.

Mato, Daniel. 1995a. "Beyond the Mall: A View of the Culture and Development Program of the 1994 Smithsonian's Festival of American Folklife in the Context of the Globalization Process." Paper presented at the Center for Folklife Programs and Cultural Studies, Smithsonian Institution.

———. 1995b. "Complexes of Brokering and the Global-Local Connections: Considerations Based on Cases in 'Latin' America." Paper presented at the 19th International Congress of the Latin American Studies Association, Washington, DC, 28–30 September.

———. 1998. "Transnational Identities in the Age of Globalization." *Cultural Studies* 12.4: 598–620.

———. 2000. "Miami en la transnacionalización de la industria de la telenovela: Sobre la territorialidad de los procesos de globalización." Paper presented at the panel "Global Cities and Cultural Capitals I: Media and Culture Industries," 22d Congress of the Latin American Studies Association, Miami, 16–18 March.

———. Forthcoming. "Procesos culturales y transformaciones socio-políticas en América 'Latina' en tiempos de globalización." In *América Latina en Tiempos de Globalización,* ed. D. Mato, E. Amodio, and M. Montero. Caracas: UNESCO-CRESALC.

Mawlawi, Farouk. 1992. "New Conflicts, New Challenges: The Evolving Role for Non-Governmental Actors." *Journal of International Affairs* 46 (winter): 391–411.

Mazer, Robyn A. 2001. "From T-shirts to Terrorism: That Fake Nike Swoosh May Be Helping to Fund Bin Laden's Network." *Washington Post,* 30 September (online edition).

Mazziotti, Nora, and Libertad Borda. 1999. "El show de Cristina y la construcción de lo latino." Research essay, Proyecto UBACYT, "Los géneros de la televerdad. Realidad y ficciòn, lo local y lo global," Nora Mazziotti, director, Instituto de Investigaciones Gino Germani de la Facultad de Ciencias Sociales de la UBA, Argentina.

McAdam, Doug. 1994. "Culture and Social Movements." In *New Social Movements: From Ideology to Identity*, ed. Enrique Laraña et al. Philadelphia: Temple University Press.

McCracken, Ellen, and Mario T. García. 1995. *Rearticulations: The Practice of Chicano Cultural Studies*. Durham, NC: Duke University Press.

McDowell, Edwin. 2001. "Occupancy and Rates Sag at New York Hotels. *New York Times*, 23 December (online edition).

McEvilley, Thomas. 1995. "inSITE94." *Artforum* (summer).

McGowan, Chris, and Ricardo Pessanha. 1991. *The Brazilian Sound: Samba, Bossa Nova and the Popular Music of Brazil*. New York: Billboard Books.

McKee, Patricia. 1999. *Producing American Races: Henry James, William Faulkner, Toni Morrison*. Durham, NC: Duke University Press.

McKenna, Barbara. 1995. "Road Shows in the Information Highway: Intellectual Property Rights Take on New Definitions in a Time of Technological Transformation." *On Campus* 14.8 (May–June): 8–9, 13.

McKinley, Jesse. 2001. "Broadway Is in the War All the Way." *New York Times*, 21 September.

McKoy, Sheila Smith. 2001. *When Whites Riot: Writing Race and Violence in American and South African Culture*. Madison: University of Wisconsin Press.

McLuhan, Marshall, and Quentin Fiore. 1967. *The Medium Is the Massage: An Inventory of Effects*. New York: Bantam.

McLuhan, Marshall, and Bruce R. Powers. 1989. *The Global Village: Transformations in World Life and Media in the 21st Century*. New York: Oxford University Press.

Mead, Rebecca. 1993. "The Professor of Hip." *New York Magazine*, 14 November.

Medina, Cuauhtémoc. 1993. "Barcelona: Paradojas del multiculturalismo." *Curare: Espacio Crítico para las Artes*. Art Supplement to *La Jornada*, 21 September: 7.

———. 1995. "A Line is a Central Point with Two Sides." In *inSITE94*.

Menchú, Rigoberta. 1984. *I, Rigoberta Menchú: An Indian Woman in Guatemala*. Ed. and introduction by Elisabeth Burgos-Debray. Trans. Ann Wright. London: Verso.

Mendes, Antônio José. 1993. "População rejeita casas de apoio a menor." *Jornal do Brasil*, 17 January: 25.

Mendosa, Rick. 1994. "The Year Belongs to Univision." *Hispanic Business* (December): 56–60.

Mercer, Kobena. 1994. "Identity and Diversity in Postmodern Politics." In *Welcome to the Jungle: New Positions in Black Cultural Studies*. New York: Routledge.

———. 1999–2000. "Ethnicity and Internationality: New British Art and Diaspora-Based Blackness." *Third Text* 49 (winter): 51–62.

"Mercosul da cultura ensaia primeiros passos." 1994. Caderno 2. Special supplement to *O Estado de S. Paulo*, 14 August: D1–D4.

Merewether, Charles. 1991. "Like a Coarse Thread through the Body: Transformation and Renewal." In *Mito y Magia en América: Los Ochenta*. Catalogue. Miguel Cervantes and Charles Merewether, curators. Monterrey: Museo de Arte Contemporáneo.

Mesquita, Ivo, et al. 2000. "Curatorial Statement: insITE2000: Landscape–Traffic–Syntax." insITE2000: http://www.insite2000.org

Metzger, Gustav. [1965]. "Manifesto World." In *Auto-Destructive Art: Metzger at AA*. Stuttgart: Sohm Archive, Staatsgalerie.

Mexico: The Splendors of Thirty Centuries. 1990. Catalogue. Metropolitan Museum of Art, New York.

"Miami South Florida." 1999. Special section of *Variety*, 1–7 November: M1–M33.

Midani, André. 2002. Personal communication. 26 August.

Mignolo, Walter D. 1994. *The Darker Side of the Renaissance: Literacy, Territoriality, and Colonization*. Ann Arbor: University of Michigan Press.

Miller, Toby. 1993. *The Well-Tempered Self: Citizenship, Culture, and the Postmodern Subject*. Baltimore: Johns Hopkins University Press.

———. 1996. "The Crime of Monsieur Lang: GATT, the Screen and the New International Division of Cultural Labour." In *Film Policy: International, National and Regional Perspectives*, ed. Albert Moran. London: Routledge.

———. 1998. *Technologies of Truth: Cultural Citizenship and the Popular Media*. Minneapolis: University of Minnesota Press.

Miller, Toby, Nitin Govil, John McMurria, and Richard Maxwell. 2001. *Global Hollywood*. London: British Film Institute.

Miller, Toby, and Marie Claire Leger. Forthcoming. "Runaway Production, Runaway Consumption, Runaway Citizenship: The New International Division of Cultural Labor." *Emergences: Journal for the Study of Media and Composite Cultures*.

Miller, Toby, and George Yúdice. 2002. *Cultural Policy*. London: Sage.

Milroy, Sarah. 1997. "Potent Border Show Tears Down Barriers." *Globe and Mail*, 11 October: C14.

Minade, Lorie. 2001. "Branson's Cash Pile Shrinks." *BBC News* 22 June. http://news.bbc.co.uk/hi/english/business/newsid_1402000/1402423.stm

Minayo, Maria Cecília de Souza, et al. 1999. *Fala Galera: Juventude, Violência e Cidadania na Cidade do Rio de Janeiro*. Rio de Janeiro: Garamond/UNESCO.

Minow, Martha. 1988. "We, the Family: Constitutional Rights and American Families." In *The Constitution and American Life*, ed. David Thelen. Ithaca: Cornell University Press.

Mitchell v. United States. 313 U.S. 80 1941, app.

Mito y Magia en América: Los Ochenta. 1991. Catalogue. Miguel Cervantes and Charles Merewether, curators. Monterrey: Museo de Arte Contemporáneo.

Mobil. 1990. "Helping Others Help Themselves." Op-ed advertisement. *New York Times*, 30 September: 17–18.

Molica, Fernando. 1995. "Chuva atrapalha passeata pela Paz." *Folha de São Paulo*, 29 November: section 3, 1.

Monaghan, Peter. 1993. "North American Academic Cooperation Becomes a Higher-Education Goal." *Chronicle of Higher Education* (22 September): A37.

Moncada, Adriana. 1993. "La obra de Ehrenberg es punto de flexión en el arte mexicano y latinoamericano de este siglo: Víctor Muñoz." *Uno Más Uno* (16 May): 22.

Moncrieff Arrarte, Anne. 1998. "Region Emerges as Entertainment Capital." *Miami Herald*, 25 June: 1A.

Monsiváis, Carlos. 1992. "De la cultura mexicana en vísperas del Tratado de Libre Comercio." In *La educación y la cultura ante el Tratado de Libre Comercio*, ed. Gilberto Guevara Niebla and Néstor García Canclini. Mexico City: Nueva Imagen.

Monsiváis, Carlos, and Hermann Bellinghausen. 2001. "Marcos Interview by Carlos Monsiváis and Hermann Bellinghausen." *La Jornada*, 8 January. English trans. by Irlandesa. http://flag.blackened.net/revolt/mexico/ezln/2001/marcos_interview_jan.html

Moore, Michael. 2001. *Stupid White Men and Other Sorry Excuses for the State of the Nation.* New York: Regan Books.

Moraes, Angélica de. 1998. "Fábio Magalhães conta como será a Bienal do Mercosul." *O Estado de São Paulo*, 28 July. http://www.estado.estadao.com.br/edicao/pano/98/07/27/ca2606.html

Morais, Federico. 1997. "Reescrevendo a história da arte latino-americana." In *I Bienal de Artes Visuais do Mercosul /I Bienal de Artes Visuales del Mercosur, de 2 de outubro a 30 de novembro de 1997.* Porto Alegre: Fundação Bienal de Artes Visuais do Mercosul.

Moreno Gonzales, John. 2001. "Mexico President Pledges Assistance, Vows to Aid Fight, Mexican Families." *Newsday*, 5 October.

Mort, Frank. 1990. "The Politics of Consumption." In *New Times: The Changing Face of Politics in the 1990s*, ed. Stuart Hall and Martin Jacques. London: Verso.

" 'Mortos estavam amarrados,' dizem freiras." 1992. *Folha de São Paulo*, 4 October: 1–15.

"Mortos na Detenção podem superar 111." 1992. *Folha de São Paulo*, 5 October: 1–1.

Mosco, Vincent. 1990. "Toward a Transnational World Information Order: The U.S.-Canada Free Trade Agreement." *Canadian Journal of Communication* 15.2 (May): 46–64.

Moskowitz, Daniel B. 1994. "Free Trade Gridlock? What a Republican Congress Will Mean for Foreign Trade Policy." *International Business* (December): 78–79.

Motion Picture Association of America. 1999. "Statement of Jack Valenti, Chairman and CEO, MPA, before the Committee on Ways and Means Subcommittee on Trade, Regarding U.S.-China Trade Relations and the Possible Accession of China to the WTO." Press release. 8 June.

———. 2002. "Study Shows Copyright Industries as Largest Contributor to the U.S. Economy." *Copyright Press Releases*, 22 April.

Mouffe, Chantal. 1992a. "Democratic Citizenship and the Political Community." In *Dimensions of Radical Democracy: Pluralism, Citizenship, Community*, ed. Chantal Mouffe. London: Verso.

———. 1992b. "Feminism, Citizenship, and Radical Democratic Politics." In *Feminists Theorize the Political*, ed. Judith Butler and Joan W. Scott. New York: Routledge.

"Movimento Funk leva desesperança." 1992. *Jornal do Brasil*, 25 October: 32.

Moylan, Tom. 1995. "People or Markets: Some Thoughts on Culture and Corporations in the University of the Twenty-First Century." *Social Text* 44.

Moynihan, Daniel Patrick. 1965. *The Negro Family: The Case for National Action*. Washington, DC: U.S. Department of Labor, Office of Policy Planning and Research.

Mufti, Aamir. 1995. "Minor Questions: German Jew and Indian Muslim as Problem for Modernity." *Social Text* 45.

Muñoz, José Esteban. 1999. *Disidentifications: Queers of Color and the Performance of Politics*. Minneapolis: University of Minnesota Press.

Myerson, Allen R. 1994. "The Booming, Bulging Tex-Mex Border." *New York Times*, 7 August: F1, F6.

———. 1995. "Strategies on Mexico Cast Aside." *New York Times*, 14 February: D1, D7.

Myrdal, Gunnar. 1996. *An American Dilemma: The Negro Problem and Modern Democracy*. New Brunswick, NJ: Transaction Publishers.

Nader, Ralph. 1965. *Unsafe at Any Speed: The Designed-in Dangers of the American Automobile*. New York: Grossman.

———. 1994. "Testimony of Ralph Nader: On the Uruguay Round of the General Agreement on Tariffs and Trade." Senate Foreign Relations Committee. 14 June.

Nader, Ralph, et al. 1993. *The Case against Free Trade*. San Francisco: Earth Island Press.

The Nafta and Educational Policy Symposium. 1993. "Educational Policy Recommendations under the NAFTA." Symposium, University of Arizona, 2–3 April.

NAFTA and Inter-American Trade Monitor. 1994a. 1.1 (30 May).

NAFTA and Inter-American Trade Monitor. 1994b. 1.14 (29 August).

NAFTA and Inter-American Trade Monitor. 1994c. 1.24 (7 November).

NAFTA and Inter-American Trade Monitor. 1994d. 1.31 (26 December).

"NAFTA Notebook." 1993. *Canadian Forum* (January): 9–17.

Naftathoughts: A Newsletter on Nafta. 1993. Washington, DC. 3.4 (October).

Nakayama, Thomas K., and Judith N. Martin, eds. 1999. *Whiteness: The Communication of Social Identity*. Thousand Oaks, CA: Sage.

Nasar, Sylvia. 1993. "GATT's Big Payoff for the U.S.: The Third World Promises to Become a Much Larger Trading Partner." *New York Times*, 19 December: F7.

Nascimento, Abdias do, and Elisa Larkin Nascimento. 2000. "Dança da decepção: Uma leitura das relações raciais no Brasil." In *Beyond Racism: Embracing an Interdependent Future: Brazil, South Africa, the United States*. Atlanta, GA: Comparative Human Relations Initiative, Southern Education Foundation. http://www.beyondracism.org/port_danca.htm

Nascimento, Gilberto. 1992. "Jovens dizem ter sido torturados por policiais." *Folha de São Paulo*, 19 November: 3–5.

Nash, Nathaniel C. 1995. "Benetton Touches a Nerve and Germans Protest." *New York Times*, 3 February: D1.

Natalichio, Oscar F., Marcelo Freyre, and Jaime Fuchs. 2001. "La alegría de la vida." *Página* 12, 11 October. http://www.pagina12.com.ar/2001/01-10/01-10-11/ PAG22.HTM

National Association of Latino Arts and Culture. *Transcript of First Annual Conference*. San Antonio, TX.

Neal, Larry. 1989. *Visions of a Liberated Future: Black Arts Movement Writings*. Ed. Michael Schwartz. New York: Thunder's Mouth Press.

Neff, Jack. 2000. "Benetton Goes from Death Row to Diapers." *Advertising Age* 71.3 (April): 1.

Negri, Toni. 2001. "El terrorismo es una enfermedad del capitalismo globalizado." *Página* 12. 28 October.

Nehru, Jawaharlal. 1954. *Jawaharlal Nehru's Speeches*. New Delhi: Publications Division.

Neto, Antônio Fausto, Paulo César Castro, and Ricardo J. de Lucena Lucas. 1995. "A construção discursiva da violência: O caso do Rio de Janeiro." *1994–95. Comunicação and Política* 1.2 (December–March): 109–140.

Netzer, Dick. 1978. *The Subsidized Muse: Public Support for the Arts in the United States*. London: Cambridge University Press.

Newfield, Christopher. 1995. "Corporate Pleasures for a Corporate Planet." *Social Text* 44.

NGO Forum. 1994. "Guiding Principles for Promoting Effective Public Participation." 19 August. ax:env.summitamer.

Nicholson, Linda, and Steven Seidman, eds. 1995. *Social Postmodernism: Beyond Identity Politics*. Cambridge, England: Cambridge University Press.

Niebuhr, Gustav. 1995a. "The Minister as Marketer: Learning from Business." *New York Times*, 18 April: A1, A20.

———.1995b. "Where Religion Gets a Big Dose of Shopping-Mall Culture." *New York Times*, 16 April: 1, 14.

Niec, Halina. 1998. "Cultural Rights: At the End of the World Decade for Culture Development." Preparatory paper for "The Power of Culture: The Intergovernmental Conference on Cultural Policies for Development," Stockholm, 30 March–2 April. http://www.unesco-sweden.org/Conference/Papers/Paper2.htm

Noble, Barbara Presley. 1993. "The Unfolding of Gay Culture." *New York Times*, 27 June: F23.

Nojeim, Gregory T. 2001. "Threats to Civil Liberties Post-September 11: Secrecy, Erosion of Privacy, Danger of Unchecked Government." Press release. ACLU, 14 December. http://www.aclu.org/news/2001/n121401b.html

Noreiga, Chon. 1992. "U.S. Latinos and Film: El hilo latino. Representation, identity and national culture." *Jump Cut* 38: 1–6.

Norris, Frank. 1901. *The Octopus: A Story of California*. New York: Doubleday.

North American Free Trade Agreement between the Government of the United States of America, the Government of Canada and the Government of the United Mexican States. 1993. Washington, DC: U.S. Government Printing Office.

"Número de mortos na chacina pode crescer." 1992. *Folha de São Paulo*, 5 October: 1–9.

NYC & Company. 2001. "2000 NYC Visitor Counts Demonstrate Tourism's Continued Growth." 30 July. http://www.candyland.citysearch.com/nycny/nycvb/2000_Visitor.html

Ochoa Gautier, Ana María. 2002. "Listening to the State: Power, Culture, and Cultural Policy in Colombia." In *Companion to Cultural Studies*, ed. Toby Miller. Boston: Blackwell.

O'Connor, Justice Sandra Day. 1998. "Excerpts from Ruling to Uphold Decency Tests for Awarding Federal Arts Grants." *New York Times*, 26 June.

Odierna, Judy. 2001. "Hip-hop Organizer Says Event Won't Return: Colleague's Arrest Generates Protest." *Miami Herald*, 25 August.

"Ódio ao branco chega a São Paulo." 1992. *Folha de São Paulo*, 18 October: section 4, 1.

O'Donnel, Guillermo. 1993. "On the State, Democratization and Some Conceptual Problems: A Latin American View with Glances at Some Postcommunist Countries." *World Development* 21.8: 1355–1369.

"OEA 'julga' invasão na penitenciária." 1992. *Folha de São Paulo*, 8 August: 1–13.

Offe, Claus. 1985. *Disorganized Capitalism: Contemporary Transformations of Work and Politics.* Ed. John Keane. Cambridge, MA: MIT Press.

Ojito, Mirta. 2000. "Best of Friends, Worlds Apart: Joel Ruiz Is Black. Achmed Valdés Is White." *New York Times*, 5 June (online edition).

Oliveira, Ronaldo de, Neuza Pereira Borges, and Carlos Bahdur Vieira, eds. 1992. *ABC RAP: Coletânea de poesia rap.* São Bernardo do Campo: Prefeitura do Município.

Oliver, J. A. 1971. *Museums and the Environment: A Handbook for Education.* New York: American Association of Museums, Arkville Press.

Ollman, Leah. 1997. "A New Frame for the Border." *Los Angeles Times*, 21 September: 58.

Omi, Michael, and Howard Winant. 1986. *Racial Formation in the United States: From the 1960s to the 1980s.* New York: Routledge and Kegan Paul.

Organization of Economic Cooperation and Development. 2000. *Economic Survey of Mexico.* July. http://www.worldbank.org/html/extdr/offrep/lac/mx2.htm

Orme, William, Jr. 1994. "What NAFTA Really Means." *Mexico Business* (May–June): 38–46.

Ornelas, Carlos, and Daniel C. Levy. 1991. "Mexico." In *International Higher Education: An Encyclopedia.* Vol 2. Ed. Phillip G. Altbach. New York: Garland.

Oropeza, Mariano. 2001. "Un barrio a la carta: Un ensayo sobre estilos de vida y ciudad en un caso." In *Consumos culturales en una cultura de consumo en la sociedad argentina del ajuste*, compiled by Ana Wortman. Buenos Aires: Editorial Del Punto.

Orsini, Elisabeth. 1992. "Arrastão, estopim do preconceito." *Jornal do Brasil*, 8 November: B2.

Ortiz, Fernando. 1939. "La cubanidad y los negros." *Estudios Afrocubanos* 3: 3–15.

———. [1951] 1981. *Los bailes y el teatro de los negros en el folklore de Cuba.* Havana: Letras Cubanas.

———. [1940] 1995. *Contrapunteo cubano del tabaco y el azúcar.* Havana: Jesús Montero.

English version: *Cuban Counterpoint: Tobacco and Sugar*. Introduction by Bronislaw Malinowski, new introduction by Fernando Coronil. Durham, NC: Duke University Press.

Ortiz, Renato. 1988. *A moderna tradição brasileira*. São Paulo: Brasiliense.

Ottmann, Goetz. Forthcoming. "Cultura é um Bom Negócio." In *The Challenge of Cultural Policy*, ed. George Yúdice. Minneapolis: University of Minnesota Press.

Owens, Craig. 1992. "The Allegorical Impulse: Toward a Theory of Postmodernism, Part 2." In *Beyond Recognition: Representation, Power, and Culture*, ed. Scott Bryson et al. Berkeley: University of California Press.

Pace, General Peter. 2001. "Testimony of Gen. Peter Pace, Commander-in-chief, U.S. Southern Command, Senate Armed Services Committee." Center for International Policy's Colombia Project. 27 March. http://www.ciponline.org/colombia/032701.htm

Padden, Carol, and Tom Humphries. 1988. *Deaf in America: Voices from a Culture*. Cambridge, MA: Harvard University Press.

Padmakshan, M. 2000. "CBEC Trains Guns on Transfer Pricing." *Economic Times*, 16 June. http://216.34.146.179/160600/16econo4.htm

Pankratz, David B. 1993. *Multiculturalism and Public Arts Policy*. Westport, CT: Bergin and Garvey.

Paoli, Maria Celia, and Vera da Silva Telles. 1998. "Social Rights: Conflicts and Negotiations in Contemporary Brazil." In *Cultures of Politics, Politics of Cultures: Re-Visioning Latin American Social Movements*, ed. Sonia E. Alvarez, Evelina Dagnino, and Arturo Escobar. Boulder, CO: Westview Press.

Paredes, Américo. 1958. *"With His Pistol in His Hand": A Border Ballad and Its Hero*. Austin: University of Texas Press.

Parker, Andrew, and Eve Kosofsky Sedgwick. 1995. Introduction to *Performativity and Performance*, ed. Andrew Parker and Eve Kosofsky Sedgwick. New York: Routledge.

Partnoy, Alicia. 1986. *The Little School: Tales of Disappearance and Survival in Argentina*. Pittsburgh: Cleis.

Pasha, Mustapha Kamal, and David L. Blaney. 1998. "Elusive Paradise: The Promise and Peril of Global Civil Society." *Alternatives* 23: 417–450.

"Passeata do Reage Rio, na principal avenida do centro da cidade." 1995. *Folha de São Paulo*, 3 December: 1–6.

Passell, Peter. 1993. "Regional Trade Makes Global Deals Go Round: Wondering Why We Need Little Old Nafta When We Have a Big Fat GATT? Well, Wonder No More." *New York Times*, 19 December: E4.

———. 1994. "Is France's Cultural Protection a Handy-dandy Trade Excuse?" *New York Times*, 6 January: D1.

Patton, Cindy. 1995. "Performativity and Spatial Distinction: The End of Epidemiology." In *Performativity and Performance*, ed. Andrew Parker and Eve Kosofsky Sedgwick. New York: Routledge.

Paz, Octavio. 1950. *El laberinto de la soledad*. Mexico City: Cuadernos Americanos.

————. 1990. "The Power of Ancient Mexican Art." *New York Review of Books* (6 December).

————. 1993. "Why Incite Demagogy?" *New York Times*, 9 November: A17.

Peixoto, Nelson Brissac. 2002. *Intervenções em Megacidades: Brasmitte/Arte Cidade, São Paulo, Zona Leste*. São Paulo: Arte Cidade. http://www.uol.com.br/artecidade/English/2002 frame_ns.htm

Penha, Marcelo Montes. 2000. "The Ford Foundation and the Emergence of Afro-Brazilian Consciousness." Unpublished manuscript.

————. 2001. "African Heritage and National Representation: Two Cases of Brasilidade in New York City." In *Raízes e Rumos: Perspectivas Interdisciplinares em Estudos Americanos*, ed. Sônia Torres. Rio de Janeiro: Editora 7 Letras.

Pérez, Edwin. 2000. "Memo: Etc." *El Nuevo Herald*, 18 February (online edition): 5C.

Pérez, Matilde, and Gaspar Morquecho. 1995. "El diálogo nacional convocado por el EZLN ya empezó: Invitados zapatistas." *La Jornada*, 21 October.

Pérez de Cuéllar, Javier. 1996. "President's Foreword." In *Our Creative Diversity: Report of the World Commission on Culture and Development*. http://www.unesco.org/culture_and _development/ocd/foreword.htm

"Performances and Shrines Express a Collective Grief." 2001. The Artists Network, 18 September. http://www.artistsnetwork.org/news/news14.html

Perlez, Jane. 2000. "Dispute Could Warm U.S.-Cuba Relations." *New York Times*, 25 April (online edition).

"The Peru Business Report." 1993. *New York Times*, 23 November: A14–A15.

Peterson, Iver. 1999. "City's Artists Are Its Pride and Something of a Pain." *New York Times*, 23 May.

Peterson, Jonathan. 1999. "Trade's Image Takes Beating among Public." *Los Angeles Times*, 31 May 1999.

Petras, James. 2001. "The Geopolitics of Plan Colombia." *Monthly Review* 53.1 (May).

The Pew Research Center for the People and the Press. 2001a. "But Military Censorship Backed, Terror Coverage Boosts News Media's Image." 28 November. http://www. people-press.org/11280irpt.htm

————. 2001b. "Post 9-11 Attitudes: Religion More Prominent, Muslim-Americans More Accepted." 6 December. http://www.people-press.org/12060ique.htm

Pharr, Suzanne. 1994. "The Right's Agenda." *Women's Project* (Little Rock, AK). Distributed by can-rw@pencil.cs.missouri.edu

Phelan, Peggy. 1993. *Unmarked: The Politics of Performance*. New York: Routledge.

"The Philanthropy of Financiers." 1993. *Left Business Observer* 6 (15 December). International Global Communications conference, 22 December. igc.trade.library

Phillips, Patricia C. 1995. "Maintenance Activity: Creating a Climate for Change." In *But Is It Art? The Spirit of Art as Activism*, ed. Nina Felshin. Seattle: Bay Press.

"Picket Stockhausen Concert." 1993. In *In the Spirit of Fluxus*, ed. Elizabeth Armstrong and Joan Rothfuss. Minneapolis: Walker Art Center.

Pincus, Robert L. 1993a. " 'Rebate' Gives Good Return for a Minor Investment." *San Diego Union Tribune*, 22 August: E1, E8.

———. 1993b. "Trio Elevates Migrant Tax Rebate Concept to an Art Form." *San Diego Union Tribune*, 2 August: E4.

Pion-Berlin, David, ed. 1989. *The Ideology of State Terror: Economic Doctrine and Political Repression in Argentina and Peru.* Boulder, CO: Lynne Rienner.

Piper, Adrian. 1988. *Cornered.* Videotape installation. Museum of Contemporary Art, Chicago.

Piscitelli, Alejandro. 2001. Editorial. Interlink Headline News, no. 2416. 11 September. http://www.ilhn.com/ediciones/2416.html

Pitts, Delia C. 1993. "Private Universities in Mexico City: New Directions, New Challenges." Paper presented at Wingspread Conference, Racine, WI.

Piven, Frances Fox, and Richard Cloward. 1993. *Regulating the Poor: The Functions of Public Welfare.* Updated ed. New York: Vintage/Random House.

Poder Ejecutivo Federal. 1996a. *Programa de Cultura 1995–2000.* Mexico City: Consejo Nacional para la Cultura y las Artes.

———. 1996b. *Programa de Desarrollo Educativo 1995–2000.* Mexico City: Consejo Nacional para la Cultura y las Artes.

"La política debe ser instrumento de solución de conflictos: Oñate." 1996. *Uno Más Uno*, 15 January: 5.

Polkinhorn, Harry, Rogelio Reyes, Gabriel Trujillo Muñoz, and Tomás Di Bella, eds. 1991. *Visual Arts on the U.S./Mexican Border—Artes Plásticas en la frontera México/Estados Unidos.* Calexico, CA: Binational Press/Editorial Binacional.

Pompeu, Paulo de Tarso. 1994. "O Arte de Negócio." *Problemas Brasileiros* (July/August): 13–18.

Poppi, Cesare. 1991. "From the Suburbs of the Global Village: Afterthoughts on *Magiciens de la terre.*" *Third Text* 14 (spring).

Portantiero, Juan Carlos. 1981. *Los usos de Gramsci.* Mexico City: Folios Ediciones.

Portes, Alejandro, and Alex Stepick. 1993. *City on the Edge: The Transformation of Miami.* Berkeley: University of California Press.

Potts, Jackie. 1999. "Lincoln Road Revitalized." *Variety*, 1–7 November: M25–M26.

Powell, Corey S. 1995. "The Rights Stuff: Buying and Selling Art in a Digital World." *Scientific American* (January): 30–31.

"President's Committee on the Arts and the Humanities Report to the President, December 1992." 1993. JAMLS 23.1 (spring): 7–13.

Press, Bill. 2001. "American Ayatollahs." Tribune Media Services. 27 September. http://www.cnn.com/2001/ALLPOLITICS/09/27/column.billpress/

Preston, Julia. 1996. "Mexico and Insurgent Group Reach Pact on Indian Rights." *New York Times*, 15 February: A12.

The Progressive Policy Institute. 2000. "What's New about the New Economy?" http://www.neweconomyindex.org/

"Proponen una consulta a los trabajadores sobre desempleo." 2001. *Terra*, 21 May. http://www.terra.com.mx/noticias/nota/20010521/119494.htm

"Protesters Support U.S. Stance on Cuban Boy." 2000. *New York Times*, 7 May (online edition).

Puerto Rican/Hispanic Task Force, New York State Assembly. 1993. Annual Report, Arts and Cultural Affairs Program. Héctor L. Díaz, chairman.

Putnam, Robert. 1993. *Making Democracy Work: Civic Traditions in Modern Italy*. Princeton: Princeton University Press.

———. 2001. "A Better Society in a Time of War." *New York Times*, 19 October.

Putney, Michael. 2000. "Sea Escape: As Most Non-Cuban Refugees Discover, There's Just One Thing Missing from Our Immigration Policy: Fairness." *Miami Metro Magazine* (March): 33–35.

"Q&A with Gabriel Abaroa." 1998. *Latin Music Quarterly* 24 (January): 1, 12.

Quadagno, Jill. 1994. *The Color of Welfare*. New York: Oxford University Press.

Quadros, Vasconcelo. 1992. "Crise estimula o crime." *Jornal do Brasil*, 8 November: 16.

Rabinowitz, Jonathan. 1994. "In L.A., Political Activism Beats Out Political Art." *New York Times*, 20 March: H33.

Radway, Janice. 1999. "What's in a Name? Presidential Address to the American Studies Association, 20 November, 1998." *American Quarterly* 51.1 (March): 1–32.

Rama, Angel. 1967. *Los poetas modernistas en el mercado económico*. Montevideo: Facultad de Humanidades y Ciencias, Universidad de la República.

———. 1970. *Rubén Darío y el modernismo (circunstancia socio-económica de un arte americano)*. Caracas: Universidad Central de Venezuela, col. Temas, no. 39.

———. 1985. *Las máscaras democráticas del modernismo*. Montevideo: Fundación Angel Rama.

———. 1996. *The Lettered City*. Trans. John Chasteen. Durham, NC: Duke University Press.

Ramírez, Adam. 2000. "Some in Broward See Elian Matter as a Dade Problem." *Miami Herald*, 24 April (online edition).

Ramírez, Anthony. 1993. "Back to School for GATT and NAFTA." *Special Supplement on Education, New York Times*: 42–44.

Ramírez, Hernando. 2000. "Los haitianos protestan por las deportaciones." *El Nuevo Herald*, 4 January (online edition): 4A.

Ramírez, Mari Carmen. 1995. "Beyond 'the Fantastic': Framing Identity in U.S. Exhibitions of Latin American Art." *Art Journal* (winter): 60–68.

———. 1993. "Between Two Waters: Image and Identity in Latino-American Art." In *American Visions/Visiones de las Américas: Artistic and Cultural Identity in the Western Hemisphere*, ed. Mary Jane Jacob, Noreen Tomassi, and Ivo Mesquita. New York: American Council for the Arts/Alworth Press.

———. 1996. "Brokering Identities: Art Curators and the Politics of Cultural Representation." In *Thinking about Exhibitions*, ed. Reesa Greenberg, Bruce W. Ferguson, and Sandy Nairne. London: Routledge.

Ramos, Samuel. 1934. *El perfil del hombre y la cultura en México*. Mexico City: Imprenta Mundial.

Randall, Kate. 2001. "Military Tribunals, Monitoring of Lawyers: Bush Announces New Police-State Measures." World Socialist, 17 November. http://www.wsws.org/articles/2001/nov2001/trib-n17_prn.shtml

Rao, J. Mohan. 1998. "Culture and Economic Development." In *World Culture Report 1998: Culture, Creativity and Markets*. Paris: UNESCO.

Raphael, Alison. 1980. "Samba and Social Control: Popular Culture and Racial Democracy in Rio de Janeiro." Ph.D. diss., Columbia University.

Rashid, Ahmed. 2001. "Osama Bin Laden: How the U.S. Helped Midwife a Terrorist." Indimedia, 16 September. http://sf.indymedia.org/news/2001/09/104308.php

Rasmussen, Birgit Brander, et al. 2001. *The Making and Unmaking of Whiteness*. Durham, NC: Duke University Press.

Rea, P. M. 1932. *The Museum and the Community*. Lancaster, PA: The Science Press.

Readings, Bill. 1996. *The University in Ruins*. Cambridge: Harvard University Press.

"Rebelião em presídio de SP deixa 108 mortos." 1992. *Folha de São Paulo*, 4 October: 1–14.

Redburn, Tom. 1993. "Arts World: Many Tiny Economic Stars." *New York Times*, 6 October: B6.

Regen, Richard. 1989. "Flinching and Fear: Is the Art World Doing Jesse Helms's Work for Him?" *Village Voice*, 17 October: 29.

Regents of the University of the State of New York. 1972. "Culture and Education: A Statement of Policy and Proposed Action." *Curator* 15.3.

Reinhold, Robert. 1994. "Free Trade Era Begins, Uneventfully, at Border." *New York Times*, 4 January: A6.

Republican National Committee. 2001. "Approval of Bush Presidency at All Time High with Hispanics." GOP Weekly, 12–16 November. http://www.rnc.org/Newsroom/GOPWeekly/November01/gopw111601.htm

"Rethinking Mexican Immigration." 2001. *New York Times*, 24 July.

Rhoades, Gary, and Sheila Slaughter. 1997. "Academic Capitalism, Managed Professionals, and Supply Side Higher Education." *Social Text* 51 (summer).

Rich, Frank. 1994. "Gay Shopping Spree." *New York Times*, 3 April: E11.

———. 1995. "Garth Neuts Newt." *New York Times*, 19 March: E15.

———. 2001a. "Confessions of a Traitor." *New York Times*, 8 December.

———. 2001b. "Wait until Dark." *New York Times*, 24 November.

Richardson, Malcolm. 1993. "Preface to the Report to the President, President's Committee on the Arts and the Humanities." *JAMLS* 23.1 (spring): 5–6.

Ridgeway, James, and Leonard Zeskind. 1995. "Revolution U.S.A.: The Far Right Militias Prepare for Battle." *Village Voice*, 2 May: 26.

Rieff, David. 1987. *Going to Miami: Exiles, Tourists, and Refugees in the New America*. Boston: Little, Brown.

———. 1993. "Multiculturalism's Silent Partner: It's the Newly Globalized Consumer Economy Stupid." *Harper's* (August): 70.

Rifkin, Jeremy. 1995. *The End of Work: The Decline of the Global Labor Force and the Dawn of the Post-Market Era*. New York: Tarcher/Putnam.

———. 2000. *The Age of Access: The New Culture of Hypercapitalism, Where All of Life Is a Paid-for Experience*. New York: Jeremy P. Tarcher/Putnam.

Rimer, Sara. 1995a. "New Medium for the Far Right." *New York Times*, 27 April: A1, A22.

———. 1995b. "With Extremism and Explosives, a Drifting Life Found a Purpose." *New York Times*, 28 May: 20.

"Rio dá uma chance à Paz." 1993. *Jornal do Brasil*, 18 December: 19.

Rio Funk. 1995. Video documentary. C. Marchand, director. Secretariat of Social Development, Rio de Janeiro.

"Risco de 'explosão social' preocupa Itamar" (Risk of "social explosion" preoccupies Itamar). 1992. *Jornal do Brasil*, 22 October: 3.

Rivera-Lyles, Jeannette. 2000. "FIU hacia la elite universitaria de EU." *El Nuevo Herald*, 4 January (online edition).

Riviere, G. A. 1949. "The Museum and Adult Education." In UNESCO, *Adult Education, Current Trends and Practices*. Paris: UNESCO.

Robbins, Bruce. 1993. *The Phantom Public Sphere*. Minneapolis: University of Minnesota Press.

———. 1995. "Some Versions of U.S. Internationalism." *Social Text* 45.

Roberts, Johnnie L. 2001. "Big Media and the Big Story." *Newsweek*, 13 October.

Robles, Frances. 2000. "Elian Saga Awakens Activists to the Cause." *Miami Herald*, 22 May (online edition).

———. 2001. "Families Afraid to Talk about Missing Relatives." *Miami Herald*, 25 September.

The Rockefeller Foundation: A New Course for Action. 1999. New York: The Rockefeller Foundation.

Rockwell, John. 2001. "Peering into the Abyss of the Future." *New York Times*, 23 September.

Roddick, Anita. 1991. *Body and Soul, Profits with Principles: The Amazing Success Story of Anita Roddick and The Body Shop*. New York: Crown.

Rodriguez, Nelson M., and Leila E. Villaverde, eds. 2000. *Dismantling White Privilege: Pedagogy, Politics, and Whiteness*. New York: P. Lang.

Roediger, David R. 1991. *The Wages of Whiteness: Race and the Making of the American Working Class*. London: Verso.

———. 1994. *Towards the Abolition of Whiteness: Essays on Race, Politics, and Working Class History*. London: Verso.

———. 1998. *Black on White: Black Writers on What It Means to Be White*. New York: Schocken.

———. 2002. *Colored White: Transcending the Racial Past*. Berkeley: University of California Press.

Roht-Arriaza, N. 1996. "Of Seeds and Shamans: The Appropriation of the Scientific and Technical Knowledge of Indigenous and Local Communities." *Michigan Journal of International Law* 17 (summer): 1–47.

Rohter, Larry. 1996. "Miami, the Hollywood of Latin America." *New York Times*, 18 August (online edition).

Rojas, Javier. 2000. "Un Museo Guggenheim en Rio de Janeiro." Terra Networks Mexico, 16 November. http://clubs.terra.com.mx/arquitectura/articulos/int/5333/

Rojas, Rosa. 1996. "Tello: Para los indios, política del Estado." *La Jornada*, 10 February.

Rondelli, Elizabeth. 1994–95. "Media, representações sociais da violência, da criminalidade e ações políticas." *Comunicação y Política* 1.2 (December–March): 97–108.

Ronfeldt, David. 1995. "The Battle for the Mind of Mexico." Unpublished paper, Rand Corporation, June.

Roque, Atila. 2000. "Cultura e Cidadania: A experiência do Afro Reggae." Working paper for Project on "Parcerias, Pobreza e Cidadania." Brazil: Fundação Getúlio Vargas-SP. http://200.214.79.73/notitia/leitura/pdf/ afro_reggae.pdf

Rosaldo, Renato. 1989. *Culture and Truth: The Remaking of Social Analysis*. Boston: Beacon.

———. 1997. "Cultural Citizenship, Inequality, and Multiculturalism." In *Latino Cultural Citizenship: Claiming Identity, Space, and Rights*, ed. William V. Flores and Rina Benmayor. Boston: Beacon.

Rosaldo, Renato, and William V. Flores. 1987. "Notes on Cultural Citizenship." Unpublished manuscript. Stanford Center for Chicano Research, Stanford, CA.

Rose, Jacqueline. 1986. "Feminine Sexuality: Jacques Lacan and the école freudienne." In *Sexuality in the Field of Vision*. London: Verso.

Rose, Nikolas. 1999. *Powers of Freedom: Reframing Political Thought*. Cambridge: Cambridge University Press.

Rosen, Jeff. 1993. "Merchandising Multiculturalism: Benetton and the New Cultural Relativism." *New Art Examiner* (November): 18–26.

Rosenberg, Carol. 2000. "Miami Attracting Celebrity Exiles: Famous Flee Colombia for Life in Quieter, Safer South Florida." *Miami Herald*, 3 April (online edition).

Rosler, Martha. 1982. "Notes on Quotes," *Wedge* vol. 3.

Ross, Andrew. 2000. "The Mental Labor Problem." *Social Text* 18.2 (summer) 1–31.

Ross, David A. 1993. "Know Thyself (Know Your Place)." In *Whitney Museum of American Art: 1993 Biennial Exhibition*. Catalogue. Elisabeth Sussman, curator. New York: Harry Abrams.

Ross, Thomas. 2000. "The Richmond Narratives." In *Critical Race Theory: The Cutting Edge*, ed. Richard Delgado and Jean Stefancic. 2d ed. Philadelphia: Temple University Press.

Rossman, Marlene L. 1994. *Multicultural Marketing: Selling to a Diverse America*. New York: American Management Association.

Rothenberg, Paula S., ed. 2001. *White Privilege: A Reader*. New York: Worth.

"Rubem César prefere evitar discussão." 1995. *O Globo*, 26 November.

Said, Edward. 1993. *Culture and Imperialism*. New York: Knopf.

Saldívar, José David. 1995. *The Dialectics of Our America: Genealogy, Cultural Critique, and Literary History*. Durham, NC: Duke University Press.

Salinas de Gortari, Carlos. 1991. "North American Free Trade: Mexico's Route to Upward Mobility." *New Perspectives Quarterly* 8.1 (winter): 4–9.

Sánchez, Alberto Ruy. 1991. "A New Imaginary Geography." In *Mito y Magia en América: Los Ochenta*. Catalogue. Miguel Cervantes and Charles Merewether, curators. Monterrey: Museo de Arte Contemporáneo.

Sandheusen, Richard L. 1994. *Global Marketing*. Hauppauge, NY: Barron's Educational Series.

Sandoval, Ricardo. 2001. "Senators Optimistic on Migrant-worker Pact." *Dallas Morning News*, 18 April.

Sanger, David E. 1995a. "Trying to Help Aid Plan, U.S. Asks Mexico for Border Crackdown." *New York Times*, 26 January: A14.

———. 1995b. "U.S. Bailout of Mexico Verging on Success or Dramatic Failure." *New York Times*, 2 April: 1, 16.

———. 1995c. "U.S. Threatens $2.8 Billion of Tariffs on China Exports." *New York Times*, 1 January: 14.

Santana, Elcior. 1999. Remarks at "Transnationalization of Support for Culture in a Globalizing World," Bellagio Study and Conference Center, Villa Serbelloni, Bellagio, Italy, 6–10 December.

Santiago, Fabiola. 2000. "Satire or Slur? Label Opens Ethnic Wounds in S. Florida." *Miami Herald*, 16 June (online edition).

Santiago, Silviano. 1978. "O entre-lugar do discurso latino-americano." In *Uma literatura nos trópicos*. São Paulo: Perspectiva.

Santos, Boaventura de Sousa. 1995. *Toward a New Common Sense: Law, Science and Politics in the Paradigmatic Transition*. New York: Routledge.

Santos, Rafael dos. 1996. "Movimentos sociais, educação e questões do cotidiano dentro das relações raciais na sociedade brasileira. Estudo de caso: O trabalho do Grupo Cultural Afro Reggae (GCAR)." M.A. thesis, Faculdade de Educação, Universidade Federal Fluminense, Niterói, Rio de Janeiro, Brazil.

"São Paulo organiza frente antinazista." 1992. *Folha de São Paulo*, 26 September: 3–1.

Sapir, Edward. 1924. "Culture, Genuine and Spurious." *American Journal of Sociology* 29: 401–429.

Sarduy, Severo. 1980. "El barroco y el neobarroco." In *Latin America in Its Literature*, ed. César Fernández Moreno. Trans. Mary G. Berg. New York: Holmes and Meier.

———. 1982. *La simulación*. Caracas: Monte Avila Editores.

———. 1987. *Ensayos generales sobre el Barroco*. Mexico City: Fondo de Cultura Económica.

Sartwell, Crispin. 1998. *Act Like You Know: African-American Autobiography and White Identity*. Chicago: University of Chicago Press.

Sassen, Saskia. 1991. *The Global City: New York, London, Tokyo*. Princeton: Princeton University Press.

Saunders, Frances Stonor. 1999. *Cultural Cold War: The CIA and the World of Arts and Letters*. New York: New Press.

Savan, Leslie. 1995. "Error in the Artland: TV News's Graphic Explosion." *Village Voice*, 2 May: 29.

Sayre, Henry M. 1989. *The Object of Performance: The American Avant-Garde since 1970*. Chicago: University of Chicago Press.

Schaeffer, Claudia. 1992. *Tenured Lives: Women, Art and Representation in Modern Mexico*. Tucson: University of Arizona Press.

Scheonung, Michelle M. 1993. "Trade Pact Bad Bargain for Women?" *Atlanta Constitution*.

Schild, Verónica. 1998. "New Subjects of Rights? Women's Movements and the Construction of Citizenship in the 'New Democracies.' " In *Cultures of Politics, Politics of Cultures: Re-visioning Latin American Social Movements*, ed. Sonia E. Alvarez, Evelina Dagnino, and Arturo Escobar. Boulder, CO: Westview.

Schjeldahl, Peter. 1993. "Southern Exposure." *Village Voice*, 22 June: 87.

Schlesinger, Arthur, Jr. 1995. "Back to the Womb? Isolationism's Renewed Threat." *Foreign Affairs* (July/August): 2–8.

Schneemann, Carolee. [1979] 1997. *More Than Meat Joy: Complete Performance Works and Selected Writings*. 2d ed. Ed. Bruce McPherson. Kingston, NY: McPherson.

Schudson, Michael. 1997. "Cultural Studies and the Social Construction of 'Social Construction': Notes on 'Teddy Bear Patriarchy.' " In *From Sociology to Cultural Studies: New Perspectives*, ed. Elizabeth Long. Oxford: Blackwell.

Schwartz, Roberto. 1992. *Misplaced Ideas: Essays on Brazilian Culture*. Ed., trans., and introduction by John Gledson. London: Verso.

Sciolino, Elaine. 1995. "President Imposes Trade Sanctions on Chinese Goods: A Trade Tie That Binds." *New York Times*, 5 February: 1, 12.

Scoffield, Heather. 1999. "Canadians Feel Nafta Does More Harm Than Good, Study Says." *Globe and Mail*, 2 July.

Scott, Bruce R. 2001. "The Great Divide in the Global Village." *Foreign Affairs* (January–February): 160–177.

Scott, David Clark. 1993. "Canada, Mexico Build University Ties." *Christian Science Monitor*, 6 October: 14.

Scott, James C. 1985. *Weapons of the Weak: Everyday Forms of Peasant Resistance*. New Haven: Yale University Press.

———. 1990. *Domination and the Arts of Resistance: Hidden Transcripts*. New Haven: Yale University Press.

Secretaría de Hacienda y Crédito Público. 1994. *The Main Questions on Customs Regarding North American Free Trade Agreement*. Mexico City: Hacienda.

Sedgwick, Eve Kosofsky. 1990. *Epistemology of the Closet*. Berkeley: University of California Press.

———. 1992. *Between Men: English Literature and Male Homosocial Desire*. New York: Columbia University Press.

Seigel, Micol. 2001. "Beyond Compare: The Transnational Construction of Race and Nation in the U.S. and Brazil, 1918–1933." Ph.D. diss., New York University.

Sekula, Allan. 1998. "Dead Letter Office." In insiTE97: *Private Time in Public Space/Tiempo privado en espacio público*, ed. Sally Yard. San Diego: Installation Gallery.

Semati, Mehdi. 2001. "Reflections on the Politics of the Global 'Rolling-News' Television Genre." *Global Journalism*. Special issue of *Archives*, no. 6 (spring/summer). http://www.tbsjournal.com /Archives/Spring01/spr01.html

"Services: Working-Group Discussions." 1997. *October* 80 (spring).

Shanahan, James L. 1993. *United Arts Fundraising in the 1990s: Serving the Community Arts System in an Era of Change*. New York: American Council for the Arts.

Shefrin, Ivan H. 1993. "The North American Free Trade Agreement: Telecommunications in Perspective." *Telecommunications Policy* (January–February): 14–26.

Shenon, Philip. 2002. "Judge Delays Order to Identify Detainees Until Appeals Ruling." *New York Times*, 16 August.

Shorrock, Tim. 1996. "Drop Seen in Real Wages in All Three Nafta Countries." *Journal of Commerce* (29 May).

Sieberg, Daniel. 2001. "War Games: Military Training Goes High-tech." 23 November. http://www. cnn.com/2001/TECH/ptech/11/22/war.games/

Silveira, Evanildo da. 1992. " 'Rap' em São Paulo dá lições de cidadania." *Jornal do Brasil*, 8 November: 16.

Sims, Calvin. 1993. " 'Buying Black' Approach Paying Off in Los Angeles." *New York Times*, 23 May: E5.

Simmons-Lewis, Suzanne. 2000. "Outrage over Refugee Plight: Haitians Slam U.S. Decision to Send Boat People Home." *Village Voice*, 10 January: 15.

Sinclair, Upton. 1906. *The Jungle*. New York: Doubleday, Page and Company.

Singh, Nikhil Pal. 1998. "The Black Panthers and the Undeveloped Country of The Left." In *The Black Panther Party: Reconsidered*, comp. Charles E. Rose. Baltimore: Black Classic Press.

Sinkin, Richard N. 1999. "Mexico's Maquiladora Industry." *InterAmerican Update* 9.4 (April/May). http://www.iahco.com/newsletter.htm

Sisco, Elizabeth, Louis Hock, and David Avalos. 1993. *Arte-Reembolso/Art Rebate*. Part of "La Frontera/The Border" exhibition, cosponsored by the Centro Cultural de la Raza and the Museum of Contemporary Art, San Diego.

Sklair, Leslie. 1991. *Sociology of the Global System*. Baltimore: Johns Hopkins University Press.

———. 1993. "Consumerism Drives the Global Mass Media System." *Media Development* 2: 30–35.

Skowa e a Máfia. 1989. "Dance." *La Famiglia*. Recording. EMI-Odeon 064 792699.

Slater, David, ed. 1994. *Social Movements and Political Change in Latin America: Latin American Perspectives*. London: Sage.

Sloan, Stephen. 2001. "What Future War Looks Like." Interview with Declan McCullagh and Ben Polen. *Wired News*. 18 September. http://www.wired.com/news/conflict/0,2100,46915-2,00.html

Smith, Roberta. 1990. "Waging Guerilla Warfare against the Art World." *New York Times*, 17 June: H1, H31.

Só, Pedro. 1992. "Zunzunzum contra os bailes funk." *Jornal do Brasil*, 30 October: B1.

Soares, Lucila. 1994. "Inegração do Mercosul começa em 95." *Jornal do Brasil, Negócios y Finanças*, 6 August: 1.

Soares, Luiz Eduardo. 1996. "Rio de Janeiro, 1993: A tríplice ferida simbólica e a desordem como espetáculo." In *Violência e Política no Rio de Janeiro*, ed. Luiz Eduardo Soares et al. Rio de Janeiro: ISER/Relume Dumará.

Sodré, Muniz. 1992. *O social irradiado: Violência urbana, neogrotesco e midia*. São Paulo: Cortez Editora.

Solomon-Godeau, Abigail. 1984. "Photography after Art Photography." In *Art after Modernism: Essays on Rethinking Representation*, ed. Brian Wallis. New York: New Museum of Contemporary Art/Godine.

Sontag, Deborah. 1993. "Reshaping New York City's Golden Door." *New York Times*, 13 June: 1, 18.

Souza, Paulo Renato. 1996. Interview. *Exame* (10 June).

Southern Poverty Law Center. 2000. "Neither Left nor Right." *Intelligence Report* (winter). http://www.splcenter.org/intelligenceproject/ip-index.html

"Spanish-language Web Sites Specialize." 1999. *Miami Herald*, 14 September (online edition): 2C.

Spencer, Neville. 1996. "Zapatistas Work to Establish Political Front." Interview with Priscilla Pacheco Castillo of the FZLN. *Green Left Weekly* 241 (7 August).

Staley, Samuel R. 2001. "Manhattan's Urban Future after the Terrorist Attacks: An Interview." Reason Public Policy Institute. 5 October. http://www.rppi.org/wtc/100501staley.pdf

Stam, Robert, and Ella Shohat. 2001. "French Intellectuals and the U.S. Culture Wars." *Black Renaissance Noire* 3.2 (spring).

Staples, Stephen. 2001. "Global Cops: The Corporate Security State's Assault on Democracy." Paper presented at the conference Global Cops: The Corporate Security State's Assault on Democracy. St. Joseph's Parish, Ottawa, 5 October.

Stark, Andrew. 1995. "Gore and Gingrich: Men in a Mirror." *New York Times*, 5 February: E17.

Steiner, Henry, and Philip Alston. 1996. *International Human Rights in Context: Law, Politics, Morals*. Oxford: Clarendon Press.

Stern, Carol Simpson, and Bruce Henderson. 1992. *Performance: Texts and Contexts*. New York: Longman.

Stern, Christopher. 1998. "U.S. Ideas Top Export Biz." *Variety*, 11–17 May.

Stiglitz, Joseph E. 2002a. *Globalization and Its Discontents*. New York: Norton.

———. 2002b. "A Second Chance for Brazil and the I.M.F." *New York Times*, 14 August.

Stiles, Katherine. 1987. "Synopsis of the Destruction in Art Symposium (DIAS) and Its Theoretical Significance." *The Act* 1.2.

————. 1988. "Rafael Montañez Ortiz." In *Rafael Montañez Ortiz: Years of the Warrior, Years of the Psyche, 1960–1988*. Catalogue. New York: El Museo del Barrio.

————. 1992. "Survival Ethos and Destruction Art." *Discourse* 14.2 (spring).

————. 1993. "Between Water and Stone: Fluxus Performance: A Metaphysics of Acts." In *In the Spirit of Fluxus*, ed. Elizabeth Armstrong and Joan Rothfuss. Minneapolis: Walker Art Center.

Stoll, David. 1999. *Rigoberta Menchú and the Story of All Poor Guatemalans*. Boulder, CO: Westview Press.

Stone, Melinda. 1998. "The Popotla and the Movie Maquiladora." *Public Art Review* (spring-summer).

Storper, Michael. 1989. "The Transition to Flexible Specialisation in the U.S. Film Industry: External Economies, the Division of Labour, and the Crossing of Industrial Divides." *Cambridge Journal of Economics* 13: 273–305.

Stout, David. 2002. "Bush Requests $2.1 Billion More for Homeland Security." *New York Times*, 25 January.

Streeter, Thomas. 1996. *Selling the Air: A Critique of the Policy of Commercial Broadcasting in the United States*. Chicago: University of Chicago Press.

"Studio City: A $100 Million Development Debate Complex Proposed at Washington Ave." 1998. *Miami Herald*, 9 August (onlne edition).

Subcomandante Marcos. 1996. "For the Photography Event in Internet." EZLN communiqué posted 8 February.

Il Sud del Mondo: L'Altra Arte Contemporanea. 1991. Catalogue. Marsala: Galeria Civica d'Arte Contemporanea, Palazzo Spano' Burgio, Chiesa del Collegio, 14 February–14 April.

Sullivan, Edward J. 1991. "Paths of Memory: Re-assessment of the Past in Recent Art from Mexico and the Andean Countries." In *Mito y Magia en América: Los Ochenta*. Catalogue. Miguel Cervantes and Charles Merewether, curators. Monterrey: Museo de Arte Contemporáneo.

"Surfista do morro vai lutar." 1992. *Jornal do Brasil*, 21 October: 12.

"Survival of the Arts." 2001. Editorial. *New York Times*, 20 November.

Sussman, Elisabeth. 1993. "Coming Together in Parts: Positive Power in the Art of the Nineties." In *Whitney Museum of American Art: 1993 Biennial Exhibition*. Catalogue. Elisabeth Sussman, curator. New York: Abrams.

Takaki, Ronald. 2000. *Iron Cages: Race and Culture in 19th-Century America*. Rev. ed. New York: Oxford University Press.

Tanner, Marcia. 1994. Preface and Acknowledgments to *Bad Girls*. Catalogue. New Museum of Contemporary Art, New York.

Taussig, Michael. 1987. *Shamanism, Colonialism, and the Wild Man: A Study in Terror and Healing*. Chicago: University of Chicago Press.

Taylor, Diana. 1997. *Disappearing Acts: Spectacles of Gender and Nationalism in Argentina's Dirty War*. Durham, NC: Duke University Press.

Terranova, Tiziana. 2000. "Free Labor: Producing Culture for the Digital Economy." *Social Text* 18.2 (summer): 33–58.

Thandeka. 1999. *Learning to Be White: Money, Race, and God in America*. New York: Continuum.

Thomas, Mike. 1994. "Mid-term Marks for Nafta." *Mexico Insight* (27 August): 19.

Thomas, R. Roosevelt. 1991. *Beyond Race and Gender: Unleashing the Power of Your Total Workforce by Managing Diversity*. New York: American Management Association.

Thompson, E. P. 1963. *The Making of the English Working Class*. London: Victor Gollancz.

Thompson, Ginger. 2001. "Senators Led by Helms Meet with Mexican Leader." *New York Times*, 17 April (online edition).

Tommasini, Anthony. 2001. "Of Necessity, Thoughts Turned to Purpose and Relevance." *New York Times*, 30 December.

Tomorrow, Tom. 2001. "Academic Subversives." *This Modern World*, cartoon. http://salon.com/comics/tomo/2001/12/03/tomo/index.html

Toner, Robin. 1995. "Rifts Emerge inside the G O P." *New York Times*, 16 March: A1, B3.

"Too Many High-Tech Visas Doled Out Last Year." *New York Times*, 7 April (online edition).

Tormollan, Carole. 1995. "Concentric Circles: Interviews with Independent Curator Mary Jane Jacob." *High Performance* 18 (spring/summer).

Torres, Blanca, and Celia Toro. 1992. "The Renewed Centrality of the United States in Inter- American Relations: The Issues and the Actors." Paper presented at the conference "Rethinking Development Theories," Institute of Latin American Studies, University of North Carolina–Chapel Hill, 11–13 March.

Torres, Sônia. 2001. "Roots and Routes of American Studies: Internationalizing the Margins." Paper presented in the special session of the International American Studies Association, British Association for American Studies, Keele University, England, 6–9 April.

———, ed. 2001. *Raízes e Rumos: Perspectivas Interdisciplinares em Estudos Americanos*. Rio de Janeiro: Editora 7 Letras.

Tovar y de Teresa, Rafael. 1994. *Modernización y política cultural: Una visión de la modernización de México*. Mexico City: Fondo de Cultura Económica.

"Trade Talks Could Open Hispanic Floodgates." 1992. *Advertising Age* 63.5 (3 February): 25.

"Treaty on Consumption and Lifestyle." 1992. http://www.igc.org/habitat/treaties/consume.html

"Tres linhas estratégicas." 1995. *Jornal da Cidadania*. (April).

Tricks, Henry. 2001. "Mexico Stocks on the Up." *Financial Times*, 11 April (online edition).

Trippi, Laura, Gina Dent, and Saskia Sassen. 1993. *Trade Routes*. Exhibition brochure. New Museum of Contemporary Art, New York, 10 September–7 November.

Turner, Frederick Jackson. 1920. *The Frontier in American History*. New York: Holt.

Turner, Victor. 1982. *From Ritual to Theatre: The Human Seriousness of Play*. New York: PAJ Publications.

Twomey, Michael J. 1993. *Multinational Corporations and the North American Free Trade Agreement*. Westport, CT: Praeger.

Ulanovsky Sack, Daniel. 1992. "El día en que los marginados tomaron la ciudad." *Clarín*, 25 October: 20.

"Um terço apóia ação da polícia no Carandiru." 1992. *Folha de São Paulo*, 10 August: 1–12.

"Uma Casa da Paz em plena guerra." 1994. *Jornal do Brasil*, 22 November: 12.

UNESCO. 1998. "General Introduction." *World Culture Report 1998: Culture, Creativity and Markets*. Paris: UNESCO.

United Nations, Population Fund. 1999. "U.S. Scorecard." September. http://www.unfpa.org/modules/6billion/ccmc/u.s.scorecard.html

UNwire. 2001. "WTO: Agreement Reached in Doha; January Trade Round Set." 15 November. http://www.unwire.org/unwire/2001/11/15/current.asp#21802

"U.S. Army Goes Hollywood for High-tech Training." 1999. CNN.com. 18 August. http://www.cnn.com/US/9908/18/army.hollywood/

U.S. Commercial Service. 2001. "Brazil Country Commercial Guide FY 2002." http://www.usatrade.gov/Website/CCG.nsf/CCGurl/CCG-BRAZIL2002-CH-1:-0069D575

U.S. Congress. 1988. *United States Code: Congressional and Administrative News*. 100th Congress. Second Session. Vol. 4. St. Paul, MN: Est Publishing.

U.S. Industrial Outlook 1993. 1993. Washington, DC: U.S. Department of Commerce.

U.S. Information Infrastructure Task Force (IITF), Working Group on Intellectual Property Rights. 1995. *Intellectual Property and the National Information Infrastructure: The Report of the Working Group on Intellectual Property Rights*. Bruce A. Lehman, chair. Washington, DC: Office of Legislative and International Affairs, U.S. Patent and Trademark Office, September.

U.S. State Department. 2001a. "President Bush at National Day of Prayer and Remembrance Service." 14 September. http://usinfo.state.gov/usa/islam/s091401.htm

———. 2001b. "Remarks by the President in Honor of Eid Al-Fitr." 17 December. http://usinfo.state.gov/usa/islam/s121701.htm

———. 2001c. "Remarks by the President in Meeting with Muslim Community Leaders." 26 September. http://usinfo.state.gov/usa/islam/s092601.htm

———. 2001d. "Statement from Assistant Attorney General Ralph F. Boyd Jr. Regarding the Treatment of Arab, Muslim Americans or Americans of South Asian Descent." 13 September. http://usinfo.state.gov/usa/islam/s091301.htm

U.S. State Department. Bureau of Educational and Cultural Affairs. 2001. "Proposal Submission Instructions." 27 August. http://e.usia.gov/education/rfps

U.S. Senate. 2001. USA Patriot Act. October 24. http://www.epic.org/privacy/terrorism/hr3162.html

U.S. Supreme Court. 2000. *George W. Bush, et al., Petitioners v. Albert Gore, Jr., et al*. On Writ of Certiorari to the Florida Supreme Court. No. 00-949. 12 December. http://caselaw.lp.findlaw.com/scripts/getcase.pl?court=US&vol=000&invol=00_949

Universal Forum of Cultures–Barcelona. 2002: http://www0.barcelona2004.org/Portades.nsf/public/BCN2004English. Accessed 11 November.

Valenzuela Arce, José Manuel. 1988. *¡A la brava ése! Cholos, punks, chavos banda*. Tijuana: El Colegio de la Frontera Norte.

————. 1993. "Mi barrio es mi cantón: Identidad, acción social y juventud." In *Nuevas identidades culturales en México*, ed. Guillermo Bonfil Batalla. Mexico City: Consejo Nacional para la Cultura y las Artes.

Vargas, Xico. 2001. "Internet para pobre." http://www.no.com.br/servlets/newstorm. notitia.apresentacao.ServletDeNoticia?codigoDaNoticia=24206&dataDoJornal= 994192211000

Vargas Llosa, Mario. 1991. "Mexico: The Perfect Dictatorship." *New Perspectives Quarterly* 8.1 (winter): 23. http://www.npq.org/issues/V81/p23.html

Vega Cánovas, Gustavo. 1993. "México–Estados Unidos–Canadá 1991–1992." *Boletín de El Colegio de México* 51–52 (September–December): 6–14.

Ventura, Zuenir. 1988. *1968. O ano que nunca terminou*. Rio de Janeiro: Editora Nova Fronteira.

————. 1994. *Cidade Partida*. São Paulo: Companhia das Letras.

Verbitsky, Horacio. 2001. "Refutacion a Viñas, Schoklender, Zito Lema y Pastor de Bonafini." *Página 12*, 11 October.

"Vereadores dançam na chuva." 1993. *Jornal do Brasil*, 18 December: 19.

Verhovek, Sam Howe. 1993. "San Antonio's Wild about Free Trade." *New York Times*, 15 November: A14.

————. 1998. "Benefits of Free-Trade Pact Bypass Texas Border Towns." *New York Times*, 23 June.

Vernez, Georges. 1993. "Needed: A Federal Role in Helping Communities Cope with Immigration." Rand Corporation Report. RP-177.

Vianna, Hermano. 1988. *O Mundo Funk Carioca*. Rio de Janeiro: Jorge Zahar.

————. 1999. *The Mystery of Samba: Popular Music and National Identity in Brazil*. Trans. and introduction by John Charles Chasteen. Chapel Hill: University of North Carolina Press.

Viau, Susana. 2000. "Exclusivo: El documento definitivo sobre Moneta, Pou y el Citi." *Página 12*, 25 February: 3. http://www.pagina12.com.ar/2001/01-02/01-02-25/pago3.htm

Vila, Pablo. 2000. *Crossing Borders, Reinforcing Borders: Social Categories, Metaphors, and Narrative Identities on the U.S.-Mexico Frontier. Border Ethnographies. The Limits of Border Theory*. Austin: University of Texas Press.

Viva Rio. 1996. *Ações do Viva Rio*. Brochure.

————. 2001. 20 October. http://www.vivario.org.br/indexN.htm

"Viva Rio é para sempre." 1993. *Jornal do Dia*, 18 December: 1.

Volkerling, Michael. 2001. "From Cool Britannia to Hot Nation: 'Creative Industries' Policies in Europe, Canada and New Zealand." *International Journal of Cultural Policy* 7.2 (spring).

Waisbord, Silvio. 2000. "Media in South America: Between the Rock of the State and the Hard Place of the Market." In *De-Westernizing Media Studies*, ed. James Curran and Myung-Jin Park. London: Routledge.

Wakankar, Milind. 1995. "Body, Crowd, Identity: Axioms of Governmentality in the Postcolony." *Social Text* 45.

Wallach, Arnei. 1994. "Taking It from the Street. Part 2." *New York Newsday*, 7 July: B4–B5.

Walle, Mark van de. 2000. *Magnets for Misery: Trailer Parks and America's Dark Heart of Whiteness.* New York: Juno.

Wallis, Brian. Forthcoming a. "How Folk Art Got Black." In *The Challenge of Cultural Policy*, ed. George Yúdice. Minneapolis: University of Minnesota Press.

———. Forthcoming b. "Public Funding and Alternative Spaces." In *The Challenge of Cultural Policy*, ed. George Yúdice. Minneapolis: University of Minnesota Press.

———, ed. 1984. *Art after Modernism: Essays on Rethinking Representation.* New York: New Museum of Contemporary Art/Godine.

Ware, Vron, and Les Back. 2001. *Out of Whiteness: Color, Politics, and Culture.* Chicago: University of Chicago Press.

Warner, Michael. 1993. Introduction to *Fear of a Queer Planet: Queer Politics and Social Theory*, ed. Michael Warner. Minneapolis: University of Minnesota Press.

———. 2000. "Zones of Privacy." In *What's Left of Theory? New Work on the Politics of Literary Theory*, ed. Judith Butler, John Guillory, and Kendall Thomas. New York: Routledge.

Warnock, John W. 1992. "Marketing Mexico." *Canadian Forum* (June): 10–13.

Waterman, Peter. 1999. "Reflections on the Export and Import of Civil Society in Times of Globalisation." Global Solidarity Dialogue, September. http://www.antenna.nl/~waterman/biekart.html

Waters, Malcolm. 1995. *Globalization.* New York: Routledge.

Weaver, Jay, Jordan Levine, and Don Finefrock. 2000. "Judge Halts Dade Ban on Cuba Arts Link." *Miami Herald*, 17 May (online edition).

Weintraub, Sidney, ed. 1993. *Free Trade in the Western Hemisphere.* Special issue of *Annals of the American Academy of Political and Social Science* 526 (March).

Wellman, Linda. 1999. "The Effects of the Internet on Copyright and Intellectual Property: New Legal Issues for Publishers in the Electronic Marketplace." *Office.com* 30 August. http://www.office.com/global/0,2724,63-286_1,FF.html

Welang, Justo. 1997. "Entrevista: 'Un proyecto ambicioso,' adució el señor Justo Werlang." http:www/joycelarronda.com.br/1bienal.entrev_e.htm

West, Guida. 1981. *The National Welfare Rights Movement: The Social Protest of Poor Women.* New York: Praeger.

Westell, Anthony. 1991. "The Weakening of Canadian Culture." *American Review of Canadian Studies* 21.2–3 (summer/autumn): 263–268.

Wetherell, Margaret, and Jonathan Potter. 1992. *Mapping the Language of Racism: Discourse and the Legitimation of Exploitation.* New York: Columbia University Press.

Whitney Museum of American Art: 1993 Biennial Exhibition. 1993. Catalogue. Elisabeth Sussman, curator. New York: Abrams.

Whittaker, Beajaye. 1993. "The Arts of Social Change: Artistic, Philosophical, and Managerial Issues." *JAMLS* 23.1 (spring): 25–35.

Will, George F. 1993. "Immigration's Cultural Baggage." *News and Observer*, 30 July: A15.

Williams, Raymond. 1958. *Culture and Society: 1780–1950*. New York: Columbia University Press.

———. [1961] 1965. *The Long Revolution*. Harmondsworth, England: Penquin.

———. 1977. *Marxism and Literature*. Oxford: Oxford University Press.

Winant, Howard. 1990. "Postmodern Racial Politics in the U.S.: Difference and Inequality." *Socialist Review* 20.1 (January–March): 121–147.

———. 1992. " 'The Other Side of the Process': Racial Formation in Contemporary Brazil." In *On Edge: The Crisis of Contemporary Latin American Culture*, ed. George Yúdice, Jean Franco, and Juan Flores. Minneapolis: University of Minnesota Press.

———. 1994. "Where Culture Meets Structure: Race in the 1990s." In *Racial Conditions: Politics, Theory, Comparisons*. Minneapolis: University of Minnesota Press.

Wineland, John. 1999. "Rethinking the Philanthropic Ogre: The Privatization of Museums and Exhibitions in Mexico and Brazil." Paper presented at the conference "Representing Latin American/Latino Art in the New Millennium: Curatorial Issues and Propositions." Jack S. Blanton Museum of Art, University of Texas at Austin, 21 October.

Wines, Michael. 1994. "Moderate Republicans Seek an Identity for Gingrich Era." *New York Times*, 26 December: A1, A22.

———. 1995. "Republican Dissidents Want Narrower Family Tax Credit." *New York Times*, 22 March: A1.

Wingspread Conference. "Statement of the Conference on North American Higher Education Cooperation: Identifying the Agenda." Racine, WI, 12–15 September.

Wodiczko, Krzysztof. 2000. Project description. http://www.insite2000.org/testwen/artist_projects/Wodiczko/project-e.html

Wolfensohn, James D. 1998. "Culture and Sustainable Development: Investing in the Promise of Societies." Remarks at conference "Understanding Culture in Sustainable Development: Investing in Cultural and Natural Endowments." Washington, DC: World Bank/UNESCO. http://wbln0018.worldbank.org/Institutional/SPRConferences.nsf/ 547251faccc07412852566b000715b0b/c13d72362c137a9585 2566b2005baccd?Open Document&ExpandSection=2#_Section2

Woodward, Richard B. 1995. "White Mischief: Of Castle and the Blast." *Village Voice*, 2 May: 27.

Working Assets. 1997. "Working Assets Stands for Renewable Energy." *Progressive Populist* 3.8 (August). http://www.populist.com/8.97.letters.html

———. 2001. "Act for Change." http://www.workingforchange.com/activism/about activism.cfm

World Art: An Invitational Exhibition Celebrating Diversity in Art and Artists. 1994. Catalogue. Zigaloe, curator. San Diego Art Institute, 23 March–24 April.

World Bank. 1999a. *Culture and Sustainable Development: A Framework for Action*. Washington, DC. http://lnweb18.worldbank.org/essd/essd.nsf/9b1cfc683a76b671852567cb007 6a25e/fa8a463ac24a48668525684600720ce7?OpenDocument

————. 1999b. *Culture Counts: Financing, Resources, and the Economics of Culture in Sustainable Development. Proceedings of the Conference.* Washington, DC. http://WBLN0018. Worldbank.org/Networks/ESSD/icdb.nsf/D4856F112E805DF4852566 C9007C27A 6/4D4D56F007815BD1852568C800674IDF

————. 2000. *Global Economic Prospects and the Developing Countries 2000.* Washington, DC: World Bank.

World Commission on Culture and Development. 1996. *Our Creative Diversity: Report of the World Commission on Culture and Development.* 2d revised ed. Paris: UNESCO.

Wray, Matt, and Annalee Newitz, eds. 1997. *White Trash: Race and Class in America.* New York: Routledge.

Wright, Robert. 1991. " 'Gimme Shelter': Observations on Cultural Protectionism and the Recording Industry in Canada." *Cultural Studies* 5.3: 306–316.

Wyszomirski, Margaret, and Pat Clubb, eds. 1989. *The Cost of Culture: Patterns and Prospects of Private Arts Patronage.* New York: American Council for the Arts.

Yáñez Chávez, Aníbal. 1999. Participation in "initial residency" for inSITE2000–2001, 11 July.

Yard, Sally, ed. 1998. "Editor's Statement" In *inSITE97: Private Time in Public Space/Tiempo privado en espacio público.* San Diego: Installation Gallery.

Ybarra Frausto, Tomás. 1991. "The Chicano Movement/The Movement of Chicano Art." In *The Poetics and Politics of Museum Display,* ed. Ivan Karp and Steven D. Lavine. Washington, DC: Smithsonian Institution Press.

————. 1992. "Interview with Tomás Ybarra-Frausto: The Chicano Movement in a Multicultural/Multinational Society." In *On Edge: The Crisis of Contemporary Latin American Culture,* ed. George Yúdice, Jean Franco, and Juan Flores. Minneapolis: University of Minnesota Press.

Young, Iris Marion. 2000. *Inclusion and Democracy.* New York: Oxford University Press.

Yúdice, George. 1989. "O sujeito virtual: Agindo na pós-modernidade." Seminar series, Centro Interdisciplinar de Estudos Contemporâneos, Rio de Janeiro, 15–22 September.

————. 1992a. "Postmodernity and Transnational Capitalism in Latin America." In *On Edge: The Crisis of Contemporary Latin American Culture,* ed. George Yúdice, Jean Franco, and Juan Flores. Minneapolis: University of Minnesota Press.

————. 1992b. "We Are Not the World." *Social Text* 31–32: 202–216.

————. 1993a. "For a Practical Aesthetics." In *The Phantom Public Sphere,* ed. Bruce Robbins. Minneapolis: University of Minnesota Press.

————. 1993b. "Postmodernism in the Periphery." *SAQ* 93.3 (summer): 543–556.

————. 1994a. "Consumption and Citizenship?" Revised version of paper presented at the "Globalization and Culture" conference, Duke University, 9–12 November.

————. 1994b. "Estudios culturales y sociedad civil." *Revista de Crítica Cultural* 8.

————. 1994c. "The Funkification of Rio." In *Microphone Fiends: Youth Music and Youth Culture,* ed. Tricia Rose and Andrew Ross. New York: Routledge.

———. 1994d. "Globalización e intermediación cultural." In *Identidad, políticas culturales e integración regional*, ed. Hugo Achugar. Montevideo: FESUR.

———. 1995. "Transnational Cultural Brokering of Art." In *Beyond the Fantastic: Contemporary Art Criticism from Latin America*, ed. Gerardo Mosquera. London: Institute of International Visual Arts, 196–215.

———. 1996a. "Cultural Studies and Civil Society." In *Reading the Shape of the World: Toward an International Cultural Studies*, ed. Henry Schwarz and Richard Dienst. Boulder, CO: Westview Press.

———. 1996b. "El impacto cultural del Tratado de libre comercio norteamericano." In *Culturas en globalización: América Latina-Europa-Estado Unidos: libre comercio e integración*, ed. Néstor García Canclini. Caracas: Nueva Sociedad/Seminario de Estudios de la Cultura (CNCA)/Consejo Latinoamericano de Ciencias Sociales-CLASCO.

———. 1997. "Translating Culture: The U.S-Mexico Fund for Culture." *Voices of Mexico* 39 (April-June): 23–28.

———. 1998. "The Globalization of Culture and the New Civil Society." In *Cultures of Politics/Politics of Cultures: Re-visioning Latin American Social Movements*, ed. Sonia E. Alvarez, Evelina Dagnino, and Arturo Escobar. Boulder, CO: Westview Press.

———. 1999a. "Activism under Neoliberalism in Brazil: Civil Society Networks." *Polygraph: An International Journal of Culture and Politics* 11: 49–64.

———. 1999b. "La industria de la música en el marco de la integración América Latina-Estados Unidos." In *Integración económica e industrias culturales en América Latina*, ed. Nestor García Canclini and Carlos Moneta. Mexico City: Grijalbo.

———. 1999c. "The Privatization of Culture." *Social Text* 17.2: 17–34.

———. 1999d. "Report on the Meeting on the Transnationalization of Support for Culture in a Globalizing World." Rockefeller Foundation, Bellagio, Italy, 6–10 December.

———. 1999e. "Rethinking the Theory of the Avant-Garde from the Periphery." In *Modernism and Its Margins*, ed. José Monleón and Anthony Geist. Minneapolis: University of Minnesota Press.

———. 2000a. "The Development of a U.S. Foreign Relations Cultural Policy: Roosevelt's Good Neighbor Policy as Forerunner of USIA and UNESCO." Paper presented at the panel "Culture and Security: A Neglected Dimension?," Crossroads in Cultural Studies Conference, University of Birmingham, England, 23 June.

———. 2000b. "Para una ecología cultural." Paper prepared for the seminar "Nuevos Retos y Estrategias de las Políticas Culturales Frente a la Globalización," Institut d'Estudis Catalans, Barcelona, 22–25 November.

———. 2000c. "Redes de gestión social y cultural en tiempos de globalización." In *América Latina en tiempos de globalización II: Cultura y transformaciones sociales*, ed. Daniel Mato, Ximena Agudo, and Illia García. Caracas: UNESCO/Instituto Internacional para la Educación Superior en América Latina y el Caribe.

———. 2001a. "From Hybridity to Policy: For a Purposeful Cultural Studies." Introduction to *Consumers and Citizens: Globalization and Multicultural Conflicts*, by Néstor García Canclini. Minneapolis: University of Minnesota Press.

———. 2001b. "Globalización y la nueva división internacional del trabajo cultural." In *La (Indi)Gestión Cultural*, ed. Marcelo Alvarez, Mónica Lacarrieu, and Verónica Pallini. Buenos Aires: CICCUS.

———. 2003a. "La ansiedad ante la hibridez racial y la genealogía de la transculturación." In *Cruce(s) de Culturas: mestizaje y transculturación en América Latina*, ed. Silvia Spitta and Javier Lasarte. Caracas: Monte Avila.

———. 2003b. "Rethinking Area and Ethnic Studies in the Context of Economic and Political Restructuring." In *Rethinking Area and Ethnic Studies*, ed. Juan Poblete. Minneapolis: University of Minnesota Press.

Yúdice, George, Jean Franco, Juan Flores, eds. 1992. *On Edge: The Crisis of Contemporary Latin American Culture*. Minneapolis: University of Minnesota Press.

Zaluar, Alba. 1992. "Arrastão e cultura jovem." *Jornal do Brasil*, 30 October: 11.

Zanetti, Lorenzo. 2000. *A Prática Educativa do Grupo Cultural AfroReggae*. Rio de Janeiro: Grupo Cultural AfroReggae.

Zapatista National Liberation Army (ELZN). 1966. "Fourth Declaration of the Lacandon Jungle." ¡Ya Basta! EZLN site. http://www.ezln.org/documentos/1996/19960101.en.htm. Accessed 12 November 2001.

———. 1994. "Declaration of the Lacandon Jungle." In *Documentos y comunicados: 1° de enero / 8 de agosto de 1994*. Mexico City: Era.

———. [1995] 1999. "Communiqué of the Clandestine Committee." Reproduced in P. J. Elio Faber and Reese Ewing, "Cisneros Goes Online." *LatinCEO* (December 1999): 46–53.

Zate, Maria. 1994. "Looking beyond North America: South America Is Ready for Free Trade. Four Ambassadors Explain Their National Game Plans." *Hispanic Business* (June): 36–42.

Zeitlin, Maurice. 1970. *Revolutionary Politics and the Cuban Working Class*. New York: Harper and Row.

Ziegler, Joseph Esley. 1994. *Arts in Crisis: The National Endowment for the Arts versus America*. Pennington, NJ: A Cappella Books.

Zlotnik, Claudio. 2001. "O'Neill ataca de nuevo: Afirmó que Argentina anda sobre terreno 'muy resbaladizo.'" *Página 12*, 18 August. http://www.pagina12.com.ar/2001/01-08/01-08-18/pag03.htm

Zolberg, Vera L. 1994. "Art Museums and Cultural Policies: Challenges of Privatization, New Publics, and New Arts." *JAMLS* 23.4 (winter): 277–290.

Zukin, Sharon, and Jenn Parker. 1991. "High Culture and Wild Commerce: Redeveloping a Center of the Arts in New York City." Paper presented at conference on New York City, Bremen, Germany, 7–8 June.

INDEX

Abaroa, Gabriel, 204

Acconci, Vito, 298

ACT UP, 37, 52; and Benneton, 171–172

Activism: consumer, 179–181; and corporations, 168–173

Acuña, Rodolfo, 53–54

Adorno, Theodor, 1, 10

Afghanistan: opposition to war in, 349–351, 364 n.3. See also Bush Administration; September 11, 2001

Afro Reggae, 3, 75, 78, 148–159, 152–154, 190, 376 nn.19, 20; lyrics to Capa de Revista, 151; lyrics to Claustrofobia, 109–111; lyrics to Rio 40 Graus, 109–111; lyrics to Som de V.G., 154

The Age of the World Picture, 26–27

Alien Nation, 223, 270

Allen, Terry, 298

Allochtonen, 265–266, 270

Allor, Martin, 224

Alternative art spaces, 333–334

Alvarez, Sonia E., 78, 185

Alÿs, Francis, 298–299

American Canvas (NEA), 11, 26, 318, 335, 345

An American Dilemma, 64

Americans for the Arts, web site of, and September 11th, 345–347

Anti-globalization movement, 361–362, 364 n.2; and culture, 33–37, 193; demonstrations of, 221–222, 231, 236, 344, 351

Anti-immigration, 254

Anzaldúa, Gloria, 252

Appiah, K. Anthony, 57

Arce, Valenzula, 368 n.4

Arfuch, Leonor, 352

Argentina, 70; and the disappeared, 352–353; migrant workers in, 281. See also Latin America

Arquilla, John, 140

Art: alternative spaces, 333–334; binational, 271–284, 288–289; border, 254, 260, 266–271, 268–270, 289, 296–299; community arts programs, 299–316; exhibitions of, 239–241, 264–266, 282–284; expanded role of, 10–13, 27–28; Latin American, 247, 257–258, 264–265, 283–286 (see also Art, Border); maintenance, 384 n.10; and multiculturalism, 261–262, 264, 379 n.7; muralism, 53; parallel market of, 243–247; survey on, 260–262; transnational cultural brokering of, 238–243. See also insITE; and under names of individual artists, artworks, and exhibitions

Art Rebate, 254, 266–271, 268–270

Arte-Reembolso. See Art Rebate

Arte Sem Fronteiras, 274, 283, 284–286

Arthurs, Alberta, 310

Artigas, Gustavo, 382 n.7, 383

Artists. See Art; insITE; and under names of individual artists, artworks, and exhibitions

Arts development, and transformation of cities, 19–21

Arts funding, 52, 266–267; controversy and the NEA, 44–47. See also *American Canvas*; NEA

Ashcroft, John, 65, 234, 341

Asia, financial crisis in, 83

Astarita, Rolando, 357–358

Avalos, David, 266–267, 315

Avant-garde, 27, 335, 386 n.25; and inSITE, 316–327

Avelar, Idelber, 73

Awasinake(On the Other Side), 304, 317

Azcárraga, Emilio, 241

Bakhtin, Mikhail, 3, 32, 38–39, 69, 251

Balfe, Judith Huggins, 239

Barber, Benjamin, 361

Barbosa, Livia, 67–68

Barbrook, Richard, 337

Barnet, Richard, 84, 87

Barry, Judith, 303, 321

Batalla, Guillermo Bonfil, 225, 227

Bateson, Gregory, 33

BAW/TAF (Border Arts Workshop/Taller de Arte Fronterizo), 289, 296, 381 n.4

Beale, Alison, 223

Beaverstock, J.V., 377 n.1

Becker, Carol, 50–51

Bello, Walden, 37

Belmore, Rebecca, 304, 317

Ben & Jerry's, 168–169

Bennet, Tony, 10, 333

Benneton, 171–172, 341

Berland, Jody, 229

The Berlin Wall, compared with U.S.-Mexico border, 297

Bernal, Antonio, 53

Bernays, Edward, 168

Beverley, John, 38

Beyond the Borders: Art by Recent Immigrants, 248

Bilbao, Spain, and cultural tourism, 19–20

Bin Laden, Osama, 343

Biodiversity, 1, 363 n.1

Biopower, 44, 364 n.4

Birmingham Center for Contemporary Cultural Studies, 85

The Black Panthers, 64

Bodies That Matter, 47

The Body Shop, 171

Bolaño, Cèsar, 361–362

Borda, Orlando Fals, 365 n.7

Border, U.S.-Mexico, 251, 255, 256, 259–260, 297–298, 303; and inSITE, 314–315

Border Arts Workshop/Taller de Arte Fronterizo (BAW/TAF), 289, 296, 381 n.4

Border culture, 252–253, 380 n.12

Bourdieu, Pierre, 80–81

Bradley, Jessica, 309

Brazil: and arrastão (looting rampage), 118–121, 128; black and mulatto youth culture of, 112–114, 120–130; and the black movement, 80–81; carnival, 67–69, 71, 130; and civil rights, 179–180; consensus culture of, 112–113; cultural programs of, 277–279; and culture of favor, 67–68; financial crisis in, 83; and funk music, 113, 120–125; and funkeiros, 118–132, 189; impeachment of President Fernando Collor, 115–116; legal system of, 63–64; and massacre in Carandiru, 116–118; and mestiçagem, 114–115, 370 n.9; music and, 120; and national identity, 112–115, 129–132, 369 n.8; and samba, 111–112, 130; social movements in, 75, 134–135, 140–149 (*see also* Afro Reggae; Funkeiros; Viva Rio). *See also* Latin America; Rio de Janeiro

Brenson, Michael, 300, 305

Brimelow, Peter, 222, 223, 270–271

Broad Oppositional Front, 100

Brunner, José Joaquín, 89–90, 92

Buchanan, Pat, 231

Buck-Morss, Susan, 315

Bulmer, Victor Thomas, 368 n.5

Burden, Chris, 318

Bureau of Educational and Cultural Affairs (U.S.), 161

Bürger, Peter, 27, 386 n.25

Bush, George W., 65, 176, 274, 388 n.1

Bush administration, 161, 230, 234, 235; and economic bailouts, 354; and racial profiling, 340–344; and staging of diversity, 339–342, 364 n.3

Butler, Judith, 31–32, 47, 57–62, 316

By the Night Tide/Junto a la marea nocturna (Escobedo), 298

Caldeira, Dulce, 370 n.17

Calibán, 29

Camnitzer, Luis, 282–283, 284

Canada, and effect of free trade on culture, 221–224, 229–230

"Capa de Revista," 151

Capitalism: disorganized, 33–34; effects of transnational on culture, 84

Cárdena, Lázaro, 92–93

Cardoso, Fernando Henrique, 75, 83, 277

Carnival, 67–69, 71, 130

Carpentier, Alejo, 367 n.3

Carvalho, Beth, 112

Castañeda, Jorge, 184–185

Castells, Manuel, 17–21, 156, 167, 192, 196

Cavanagh, John, 84, 87

Cearra, Alfonso Martínez, 20

Central Intelligence Agency (CIA), 84

Century 21, 317

CGC (Cisneros Group of Corporations), 212

Chávez, Aníbal Yáñez, 303

The Christian Coalition, 234

Christo, 254

CIA (Central Intelligence Agency), 84

Cidade Partida, 135, 138–139

Cisneros, Carlos, 212

Cisneros Group of Corporations (CGC), 212

Citizen action initiatives. *See* Social movements

Citizenship, 76, 161–167; and the politics of representations, 162–165; and rights, 164–166. *See also* Global citizenship: and consumer capitalism

Ciudad del Este, U.S. targeting of, 36

Civil rights, 51–52, 65, 66

Civil society, 82, 88, 93, 158; in Latin America, 95–96, 184–186; and neo-liberalism, 95–97; and NGOs, 95–97; and the Zapatistas, 96–108

Clash of Civilizations and the Remaking of World Order, 339

Claustrofobia, 109–111, 113, 369 n.2

Clientelism, 75, 78

Clinton administration: and intellectual property rights, 219; and the Right, 236–237

CMT (Country Music Television), merger of, 223

Coelho, Teixiera, 285

Coffey, Mary K., 334

Collaboration, 287–302, 302–307, 326, 329, 337, 381 n.2

Collins, Sharon, 178

Collor, Fernando, 370 n.10; impeachment of, 115–116

Colombia: and CREA, 15; and Plan Pacífico, 188–189

Common Market of the South. *See* MERCOSUL

Community arts programs, 299–316, 329

CONACULTA (National Council for the Arts and Culture), 276, 307, 310

Consensus culture, of Brazil, 112–113

Consigned to Border: The terror and possibility in things not seen, 303

Consumer capitalism, and citizenship, 161–167

The Consumerist Manifesto, 166

Consumidores y ciudadanos, 92, 186

Consumption: and culture, 166–168; and global citizenship, 181–191; politicized, 168–173

Conversations at the Castle (art exhibition), 300, 306

Cornered, 50

Corporations: and diversity, 174–179, 235–238; effects on Third World, 87–88; and political activism, 168–173

Country Music Television (CMT), 223

The Couple in the Cage, 50

Cross the Razor/Cruzar la navaja, 298

Croucher, Sheila, 198

Cruikshank, Barbara, 162

Cuba: exile community of Miami, 196–198; Revolution of 1959, 72

Cuenca, Carmen, 302, 309

Cultural activism. *See* Social movements

Cultural capital, and inSITE, 307–312

Cultural capitalism, 9, 14–15, 21, 36

Cultural citizenship, 21–25, 165, 217–218; in Rio de Janiero, 133–159

Cultural development, 13–16

Cultural economy, 16–21; and inSITE, 287–337; of Miami, 199–205

Cultural identities, marketing of, 242–243

Cultural imperialism, 28–29, 86–89

Cultural integration, 271–284

Cultural labor: division of, 4, 18–19, 35; in Miami, 211–213

Cultural leftist, 44, 363 n.2

Cultural politics: of inSITE, 312–317

Cultural rights, 21–25

Cultural space, Latin American, 271–284

Cultural studies, and globalization, 84–93

Cultural tourism, and transformation of cities, 19–21

Culturas híbridas, 92

Culture: and community, 22–24; consequences of September 11th on, 344–351; and effect of free trade on, 214–286; and ethical incompleteness, 336; and globalization, 28–29, 82–108; investment in, by MDBS, 13–16; and labor, 330–332, 337; Latin American, under neoliberalism, 93–97; political uses of, 10; protection of, 220; redefinition of, 25, 218–221; as resource, 1, 4, 9–13, 24–38, 279, 334–335; in time of crisis, 338–362; wars, U.S., 12, 36, 44–47, 50; youth, 90–91, 112–114, 120–139

Culture in Action (art exhibition), 300, 305, 306, 320

Curatorship, 239–240, 388 n.35

A Cyborg Manifesto, 40, 42

D' Amato, Alphonse, 232

Da Cunha, Olivia Maria Gomes, 78, 81

Da Silva, Benedita Souza, 120, 136–137, 190

Da Vila, Martinho, 109–112, 369 nn.2, 5

Da Viola, Paulinho, 112

Dagnino, Evelina, 78

DaMatta, Roberto, 66–67, 69, 75, 76, 365 n.9

"Dance" (song), 131

Davidson, Martin, 166

Davies, Hugh, 382 n.4

Dávila, Arlene, 173–174

Day, Jane Stevenson, 248–249

De Bonafini, Hebe Pastor, 356–357, 367 n.13, 389 n.8

De Cuéllar, Javier Pérez, 22

De la Rúa, Fernando, 77

De Léon, Antonio García, 66

De Lima, Roberto Kant, 63
De los medios a los mediaciones, 90
De Mello, Fernando Collor, 76, 277
De Salvo, Roman, 327
De Teresa, Rafael Tovar y, 276
Dead Letter Office, 287–288, 290–295
Debroise, Olivier, 244, 299, 308, 313
*The Decade Show: Frameworks of identity in
    the 80s*, 264
Denny's, discrimination lawsuit of,
    179–180
Dependency theory, 86, 89
Derrida, Jacques, 32
Desmond, Jane, 263, 380 n.14
Devotionalia, 321
Dias, Mauricio, 321, 322, 382 n.7
Dictatorships, in Latin American soci-
    eties, 72–74
DiMaggio, Paul, 45–46, 376 n.1
Diversity: and corporations, 174–179,
    235–238; economic benefits of, 250–
    251
DJ Marlboro, 121
Domínguez, Virginia R., 215, 263, 380
    n.14
Dorf, Michael C., 65
Dorfman, Ariel, 29, 87, 361
Dorland, Michael, 222
Drugs, generic, 37, 359
Duhalde, Eduardo, 76
Duncan, Michael, 297
Durán, Sylvie, 272

El reino de este mundo, 367 n.3
Eliot, T.S., 367 n.2
Empire, 37
Engels, Frederic, 251
Entertainment industries, 4; and free
    trade exemptions, 222–228; in Miami,
    199–213, 377 n.3, 379 n.4; and
    piracy, 36
Entine, John, 171

Epistemes, 29–31
Erre, Marcos Ramírez, 317, 382 n.7
Escobar, Arturo, 78, 188
Escobedo, Helen, 298, 318
ESL: *tonguetied/lenguatrabada* (BAW/TAF),
    317
Esquadrão urbano (rap group), 126
Estrada, Ezequiel Martínez, 43
European Union, 26; and culture as
    resource, 13
Expediency, definition of, 363 n.2
EZLN. *See* Zapatistas

Fernandes, Rubem César, 134–135,
    139–140, 146–147, 190, 372 n.12
Ferraz, Caio, 135, 141, 143, 145, 373 n.16
Film Industry, U.S. *See* Hollywood
Fisk, Robert, 343
FONCA (National Fund for Culture and
    the Arts), 277, 280, 310
Ford Foundation, 3, 79
Foster, Hal, 320, 321
Foucault, Michel, 3, 29–31, 38–39, 60–
    61, 162, 364 n.4
Fox, Claire F., 223, 259–260, 380 n.13
Foxley, Alejandro, 94–95
Franco, Itamar, 113
Fraser, Andrea, 319, 325, 327, 385 n.17
Fraser, Nancy, 54, 76, 165
*The Free Art Agreement/El Tratado de Libre
    Cultura*, 258–259
Free Idea Zone, 258–260
Free trade: and cultural exemptions for
    entertainment, 222–228; effect on cul-
    ture, 214–218; in Canada, 221–224; in
    Mexico, 93–94, 224–228, 231. *See also*
    North American Free Trade Agreement
    (NAFTA)
Freedom of Information Act, 65
Freire, Paulo, 306, 365 n.7
Freyre, Gilberto, 43, 114–115
Frito-Lay, 177

FTA (U.S.-Canada's Free Trade Agreement), 222–223

Fuentes, Carlos, 224–225, 229

Fuller, Colleen, 223

Funk music, Brazilian, 113. *See also* Funkeiros

Funkeiros, 118–132, 189. *See also* Funk music, Brazilian

Fusco, Coco, 50

Gabriel, John, 180

Gagnon, Michelle, 223

García Canclini, Néstor: and identity, 59; call for social change, 92–93; on citizenship, 248; and civil society, 97, 188; on consumption, 186–187; and "cultural reconversion," 130, 249; on *inSITE97*, 314; on public space, 220–221; on U.S. films, 227–228

Gardel, Carlos, 71

Garnham, Nicholas, 220

Garza, Cecilia, 322

GATT. *See* General Agreement on Trade and Tariffs (GATT)

Gautier, Ana María, 388 n.4

Gay culture, and marketing, 173–174

GCAR (Grupo Cultural Afro Reggae). *See* Afro Reggae

Gender Trouble, 58

General Agreement on Trade and Tariffs (GATT), 9, 214, 216; and the cultural economy, 17–18; and cultural goods, 218–221

Getino, Octavio, 272, 274–275, 286

Gevers, Ine, 264–265

Giannotti, José Arthur, 117

Gilmore, Samuel, 246

Gilroy, Paul, 57, 59

Gitlin, Todd, 363–364 n.2

Glazer, Nathan, 22

Global citizenship, and consumption, 181–191

Global Dreams, 84

Globalization, 11, 28, 31, 35, 82, 83; and cities, 192–193; and cultural studies, 84–93; and culture, 28–29, 82–108; and labor, 192–195; and Latin American, 88–93, 188–189; and social movements, 88; and viral metaphor, 83–84

Gohn, Maria da Glória, 158, 286

Goldberg, Bob, 359

Goldman, Shifra, 241

Gómez-Peña, Guillermo, 50, 250–260, 271, 285

Gonzales, Rodolfo "Corky," 54

González, Elián, 197–198, 210, 377 n.4

Goodall, Jane, 41–42

Gordon, Avery, 235, 1175

Governmentality, 27, 52, 54, 107, 162–163, 245, 369 n.9, 386–387 n.29

Govil, Nitin, 18

Gramsci, Antonio, 366 n.10

Grassroots movements. *See* Social movements

Ground Zero, 352–353

Gruner, Silvia, 298, 382 n.7

Grupo Cultural Afro Reggae (GCAR). *See* Afro Reggae

Guggenheim Museum: Bilbao, Spain, and transformation of city, 19–20; New York, and September 11th, 345

Guilbaut, Serge, 12

Hanchard, Michael, 80, 364 n.3

Haraway, Donna, 40–45, 49, 363 nn.1, 2

Hardt, Michael, 34, 37

Heidegger, Martin, 26–27

Helms, Jesse, 47, 163, 236

Hendershot, Heather, 168

Hernández, Sofia, 328, 382 nn.5, 6, 385 n.15

Herscovici, Alain, 359

Het Klimaat, 264–265

Hickey, David, 313
High culture, 4
Hispanics, U.S.: and marketing, 173–174
Hock, Louis, 266, 382 n.7
Hoggart, Richard, 85, 87
Hollywood, 17–18
Homeland security (U.S.), 65
How to Read Donald Duck, 29, 86
Huntington, Samuel, 84, 339
Hybrid Cultures, 249
Hybridity, 92, 252–253, 256, 378 n.7; Latin American, 71, 89, 90–92

IADB (Inter-American Development Bank), 289, 372 n.9; and cultural development, 13–14
IBASE (Instituto Brasileiro de Análises Sociais e Econômicas), 135
Identity, Latin, 206–11
Identity politics: Brazilian, 66–68; and cultural citizenship, 165–166; and indigenous peoples, 101–106; and social movements, 77–81; United States, 47–60, 66–67; Zapatistas, 66–67
IMF (International Monetary Fund), 35, 37, 94, 216, 224; and Argentina, 76; and Latin America, 276; and 1990's financial crisis, 83
Immigrants: and *Art Rebate*, 266–271; and free trade, 233, 237–238, 266; and Miami, 205–213
Inaugural Speech, 325
Indigenous peoples: and identity politics, 101–106; of Mexico, 92–93, 101–103; and the museo comunitario movement, 101–102; and performativity, 105; and the Smithsonian Institute, 102–105. *See also* Zapatistas
InSITE, 254, 287–337, 379–380 n.8, 381 n.3, 382 n.7, 385 n.19; and avant-garde, 316–327; catalogues of, 312–315, 384 n.13; cultural politics of, 312–

317; curation of, 302, 308, 314–315, 327; and the maquiladora, 302–307; organization of, 325–326; precedents to, 299–300; processes of, 326–330
Institute for the Study of Religion (ISER), 133, 139, 372 n.12
Institutional Revolutionary Party (PRI), 67, 100, 107, 225–226
Instituto Brasileiro de Análises Sociais e Econômicas (IBASE), 135
Instituto Nacional Indigenista (Mexico), 101
Intellectual property: and the cultural economy, 2, 17–19; and Latin America, 359–360, 361; and non-Western culture, 2; and pharmaceutical patents, 35–38, 359, 361; and the redefinition of culture, 218–221; and September 11th, 36–37
Inter-American Development Bank (IADB), 289, 372 n.9
Inter-American Foundation, 104–105
International Waters/Aguas internacionales, 382 n.7
ISER (Institute for the Study of Religion), 133, 135, 372 n.12
Island on the Fence/Isla en la muralla, 298

Jaar, Alfredo, 382 n.7
Jabor, Arnoldo, 138
Jacob, Mary Jane, 300, 306, 311, 319, 329, 384 n.14
Jameson, Frederic, 24, 166, 332
Jeitinho, 68, 79
Jelin, Elizabeth, 76, 353, 367 n.12
Julien, Isaac, 57
The Jungle, 167
Júnior, Jóse, 148–149, 154, 156, 376 n.19

Karp, Ivan, 243
Katz-Fishman, Walda, 217
Kester, Grant, 258

Kollman, Raúl, 355
Kreamer, Christine Mullen, 243
Krichman, Michael, 302, 327
Krischke, Paulo, 78
Kristeva, Julia, 316, 386 n.24
Krugman, Paul, 356
Kushner, David, 385 n.16
Kwon, Miwon, 329–330, 384 n.12

La Casita en la Colonia Altamira, 314
La Frontera/The Border (art exhibition), 266, 289
La Vida en un sorbo: El café en México (exhibition), 102
Labatt, Blair, 254
Labor, effect of globalization on, 192–195
Lacan, Jacques, 61
Laclau, Ernesto, 32, 55, 59, 96
Langley, Stephen, 245
Laó, Agustín, 52
Las Reglas del Juego/The Rules of the Game, 382 n.7
Lasch, Christopher, 163
Lash, Scott, 33–34
Latin America. *See also* individual countries: and civil society, 95–96; corporate hijacking of, 358–362; dictatorships in, 72–74, 353; and globalization, 86–93; hybridity of, 71, 89–92; identity politics in, 66–68, 77–81, 367–368 n.3; and intellectual property law, 359–360; performativity of, 70–76; populism in, 69–71; and privatization, 76; and regional federalism, 184–191
Lauredo, Luis, 204
Lavine, Steven, 243
Law, U.S.: and Latin American attitudes towards, 60–81
Leite, Ilka Boaventura, 68
Lema, Vicente Zito, 357

Lewis, George E., 317
Lila Wallace–Reader's Digest Fund, and minority artists, 244–245
Linker, James A., 258–259
Lirtzman, Sidney I., 175
Llosa, Mario Vargas, 225
Lohr, Steve, 9, 195
London, and the creative economy, 16
The Loop, 298–299
López, Sebastián, 265, 266
Los Pasos perdidos, 367 n.3
Los Voluntarios, 54
Lowe, Jean, 313
Luke, Timothy, 329

Magiciens de la Terre, 264
Maia, César, 133–134
Manglano-Ovalle, Iñigo, 320, 321, 327, 382 n.7
Marable, Manning, 57
Mariátegui, José Carlos, 29
Marshall, T.H., 164
Martín-Barbero, Jesús, 90–91, 92
Marx, Karl, 214, 251, 331, 332, 336, 380 n.11
Mato, Daniel, 104, 206
Mattelart, Armand, 29, 87, 361
Maxwell, Richard, 18
Mazer, Robyn, 36–37
McDonald's, 84, 180–181
McEvilley, Thomas, 297
McGowan, Chris, 112
MCI, and diversity, 177
McLuhan, Marshall, 87, 367 n.2
McMurria, John, 18
McVeigh, Timothy, 60
MDBs (Multilateral Development Banks), and cultural development, 14–15
Media, Latin American, 274–275
Medina, Cuauhtémoc, 312–313, 318
Mehri, Ali Khalil, 36
Menchú, Rigoberta, 38

Menem, Carlos, 77, 353

Mercer, Kobena, 57

MERCOSUL (Common Market of the South), 26, 274, 281, 286, 380 n.15; Biennial, 282–284; and culture, 281–282; financial crisis and, 83; and Latin American Cultural Space, 280

Merewether, Charles, 243

Merrill Lynch, and diversity, 177

Mesquita, Ivo, 314

Mestiçagem, 114–115

Mestizaje, 210–211

Mexico, 70, 380 n.9; and art exhibitions, 93, 240–247; artists from, 307–308; effect of free trade on culture of, 93–94, 224–228, 231, 368 n.7; film distribution and viewing in, 227–228; indigenous peoples of, 92–93, 101–102; and museo comunitario movement, 96, 101–103, 334; and NAFTA, 97, 225, 240–243, 310, 368 n.7; and neoliberalism, 93–100; new cultural programs of, 276–277, 308–311; new curatorial process of, 308; and the Zapatistas, 97–108. See also Latin America

Mexico: The Splendors of Thirty Centuries, 93, 240–241, 243, 247

Miami, 273, 379 n.7; as cultural capital of Latin America, 195–213; cultural labor in, 211–213; entertainment industries in, 199–213, 377 n.3, 379 n.4; and immigrants, 205–213; and multiculturalism, 198, 205–213

Microsoft, 177

Midani, André, 157

The Middle of the Road/La mitad del camino, 298

Miller, Toby, 18–19, 61, 211–212

Milroy, Sarah, 304–305

Minow, Martha, 56

Mito y Magia en América: Las Ochenta, 93, 241–242

Mittal, Anuradha, 37

Mobil, 172

Monsiváis, Carlos, 227

Moore, Michael, 365 n.5

Morais, Federico, 282

Mosco, Vincent, 223

The Mothers and Grandmothers of the Plaza de Mayo, 73–74, 351, 352; response to September 11th, 356–357

Mouffe, Chantal, 55, 59, 96

Movement of National Liberation, 100

Moynihan, Daniel Patrick, 22

Multiculturalism, 160–164, 230; and the arts, 261–262, 264; in Miami, 198, 205–213

Multilateral Development Banks (MDBS), 14–15

Muralism, 53

Museo comunitario movement, 96, 101–103, 334

Museo de Arte Contemporáneo de Monterrey, 240–243, 308, 385 n.18

Museums, 19; bourgeois, 333. See also under names of individual museums

Myrdal, Gunnar, 64

Nader, Ralph, 167

NAFTA. See North American Free Trade Agreement (NAFTA)

NARAS (National Association of Recording Artists), 197, 207

National Association of Recording Artists (NARAS), 197, 207

National Coordinating Committee of Coffee Growing Organizations, 102

National Council for the Arts and Culture (CONACULTA), 276, 307, 310

National Endowment for the Arts (NEA), 4, 52, 233, 333, 382 n.8; and American Canvas, 11, 26; and the arts funding controversy, 44–47; and diversity, 245–246

National Fund for Culture and Arts
(FONCA), 277, 280, 310

National Museum of Anthropology
(Mexico), 101

National Museum of the American
Indian, 102–104

National popular will, 69–71, 366 n.11

NEA. See National Endowment for the
Arts (NEA)

Negri, Toni, 34, 37

Neoliberalism, 82, 84, 158; and civil
society, 94–97; and Latin America,
93–97, 186–187; and Mexico, 93–
100

NGOs. See Non-governmental organizations (NGOs)

Nichols, Terry, 60

Nixon, Richard, 52, 115

Non-governmental organizations
(NGOs) 368–369, nn.6–8; and Afro
Reggae, 155–156; and civil society,
95–97; skepticism towards, 34; and
social movements, 77–79, 155–156;
and Working Assets, 170

Norris, Frank, 167

North American Free Trade Agreement
(NAFTA), 94, 214, 216, 286; and art
exhibitions, 240–243; conferences
on, 256–258; and intellectual property
rights, 218–219; and Latin American
cultural space, 280; and Mexico, 97,
225, 240–243, 368 n.7; track record
of, 232–233; and U.S., 231–232; and
U.S.-Mexican border, 253–254. See also
Free trade

Nova Cara (CD), 150–152, 152, 156

Novels, 32

Núñez, Dulce María, 242

The Octopus, 167

The Old People Speak of Sound: Personality,
Empathy, Community, 317

On the Fetish-Character in Music and the
Regression of Listening, 10

Operation Gatekeeper, 254

The Order of Things, 29

The Origin of the Work of Art, 27

Ortiz, Fernando, 43, 211, 378 nn.7, 8

Ortiz, Renato, 379 n.3

Osorio, Pepón, 317

Ostrander, Tobias, 322

Our Grief is not a Cry for War, 350

Panthers of the Night (rap group), 126

Paradise Creek Educational Park Project, 315

Paredes, Americo, 252

Parker, Andrew, 47

Patents, pharmaceutical, 37

Patterson, Patricia, 314

Paz, Octavio, 43, 240–241, 310

Pechman, Clarice, 141

Peekskill (New York), and arts development, 20

Peixoto, Nelson Brissac, 300–301

Penha, Marcelo, 66

Pérez, Rudy, 207

Performance artists, 50–51

Performativity, 3, 28–31, 38, 41–81, 162;
and attitudes towards the law, 60–81;
and culture wars, 44–47; differences
between national societies, 40–44,
60–81; and indigenous peoples, 105;
in Latin American societies, 70–76;
and mourning, 352; in scholarship,
80–81; and social movements, 51–
53, 73–76; in the United States,
44–81

Perón, Juan Domingo, 71

Peru, and cultural development, 14

Pessanha, Ricardo, 112

Petras, James, 356

Pierce, William L., 60

Piper, Adrian, 50

Piracy, of music, 36

Plaza of Three Culture in Tlatelolco, 92

Politics of representations, and citizenship, 162–165

The Popotla Wall (RevArte), 303

Portantiero, Juan Carlos, 70

Pouissant, Alvin, 366 n.9

Poverty, 217–218

PRI (Institutional Revolutionary Party), 67, 100, 107, 225; and NAFTA, 225–226

Primate Visions, 40–41

Privatization, in Latin American, 76, 368 n.5

Proposition 187, 266

Public Hearing, 317

Putnam, Robert, 14, 347

The Question Concerning Technology, 26–27

Racial profiling, 340–344, 365–366 n.9

Rama, Angel, 365 n.7

Ramírez, Mari Carmen, 240, 247, 258

Ramos, Samuel, 43

Rascón, Armando, 318, 320

Regional federalism, 184–191

Reich, Robert, 65

Representations, politics of. See Politics of representations

Retamar, Roberto Fernández, 29, 364 n.3

Ribiero, Manoel, 141

Riedweg, Walter, 321, 322, 382 n.7

Rieff, David, 160–161

Rifkin, Jeremy, 9, 20, 34, 387 n.34

The Right, 230–238; and rhetoric of diversity, 235–238

Rio 40 Graus, 109–111, 113, 369 n.4

Rio de Janiero, 109–159, 370–371 n.18, 371 n.3; and arrastão (looting rampage), 118–121, 128, 130, 370 nn.12, 16; black and mulatto youth culture in, 112–114, 120–139 (see also Funkieros);

and Claustrofobia, 111, 369 n.2; and rap music, 125–127; social movements in, 75, 134–135, 140–149 (see also Afro Reggae; Funkeiros; Viva Rio); violence in, 133–139, 370 n.14, 372 n.7; and Viva Rio, 88, 132–135, 139–140, 142–149, 371 n.1, 372 n.7, 373 nn.17, 18. See also Brazil

Rockefeller Foundation, 376 n.20, 387 n.32; and inSITE, 310; and minority artists, 244–245, 257

Rollof, Ulf, 298

Ronfeldt, David, 95–96, 140

Rosaldo, Renato, 22

Rose, Nikolas, 332

Rossman, Marlene L., 175

Rowing in Eden, 317

Rozenblat, Sergio, 195, 377 n.2

Said, Edward, 61–62

Saldívar, José David, 364 n.3

Salinas, Carlos, 225, 276, 308, 311

Samba, 71; and Brazilian national identity, 111–112

Samba: Rhythm of Life, 112

San Diego–Tijuana region. See Border, U.S.-Mexico

Sánchez, Alberto Ruy, 240–242

Sandheusen, Richard L., 237

Santana, Elcior, 14–15

Santiago, Silviano, 68, 69

Santos, Boaventura de Sousa, 24, 27–28, 61, 68–69, 365 n.7

Santos, Milton, 122

Sarduy, Severo, 69

Sassen, Saskia, 87

Schild, Verónica, 78

Schlokender, Sergio, 357

Schudson, Michael, 42

Schwarz, Roberto, 62

Scott, James C., 157

Scott, Jerome, 217

Seattle, Battle of. *See* Anti-globalization movement

Sedgwick, Eve Kosofsky, 47

Seigel, Micol, 81

Sekula, Allan, 287–288, 290–295

23 *September 1994/23 de septiembre de 1994*, 298

September 11, 2001, 36–37, 83, 338, 388 n.3, 389 n.5; cultural consequences of, 344–351; effect of, on Latin America, 354–358, 389 n.7; and government use of the media, 347–351; and U.S. law, 65. *See also* Afghanistan: opposition to war in

Sims, Calvin, 180

Sinclair, Upton, 167

Sinkin, Richard N., 306–307

Sisco, Elizabeth, 266

Sklair, Leslie, 84, 87

Small, Deborah, 317

Smith, R.G., 377 n.1

The Smithsonian Institute: and indigenous peoples, 102–105; National Museum of the American Indian, 102–104

Soares, Luiz Eduardo, 141–142

Soares, Valeska, 382 n.7

Social movements: anti-globalization, 33–37, 193, 221–222, 231, 236, 344, 351, 361–362; and globalization, 88; and identity politics, 51–60, 77–81; and media coverage, 158; "NGOization of," 77–79, 155–156; and performativity, 51–53, 73–76; and regional federalism, 184–191; in Rio de Janeiro, 134–135, 140–149; in United States, 51–60. *See also* Afro Reggae; Funkeiros; Museo comunitario movement; Zapatistas; Viva Rio

Sodré, Muniz, 185

"Som de V.G." (song), 154

Standing reserve, 9, 26–27

Stavenhagen, Rodolfo, 101

Steps to an Ecology of Mind, 33

Stevens, John Paul, 65

Stoll, David, 38

Stone, Melinda, 303

Streeter, Thomas, 17

Stupid White Men and Other Sorry Excuses for the State of the Nation, 366 n.5

Subcomandante Marcos, 105–106

A Tale of Two Cities, 318

Tarzan among the Apes, 41

Taussig, Michael, 367 n.3

Taylor, Diana, 74

Taylor, P.J., 377 n.1

Teatro Campesino, 53

Televisa, 94, 97, 108, 241

Terrorist networks, 83

Thompson, E.P., 85

Titanic, set of, 287, 303, 311

Torres, García, Joaquín, 283

Torres, Sônia, 263

Toy an Horse, 382 n.7

Trade-related intellectual property rights (TRIPS), 37–38

Transitio, 328, 382 n.6

Transnational cultural brokering, of art, 104, 238–243, 368–369 n.8

Transnationalization, in Latin America, 90–94, 251

Transterritorialization, of entertainment industries in Miami, 213

TRIPS (Trade-related intellectual property rights), 37–38

Turner, Frederick Jackson, 251, 380 n.10

The Turner Diaries, 60

UFW (United Farm Workers), 53

Ukeles, Mierle Laderman, 384 n.10

UNESCO (United Nations Educational,

Scientific and Cultural Organization), 1, 10, 22, 25, 274, 284; and cultural citizenship, 217; and cultural identity, 79

Unilever, 169

United Farms Workers (UFW), 53

United Nations Educational, Scientific and Cultural Organization. *See* UNESCO

United States: and American studies, 262–263, 380 n.14; attitudes towards the law in, 60–61, 64–65; and cultural rights, 22; and culture as resource, 11–13; and culture wars, 12, 36, 44–47, 50; and effect of free trade on culture, 221, 230–238; identity politics in, 47–60, 66; and immigrants, 233, 237–238; performativity in, 44–60; and The Right, 230–238; social movements in, 51–60; and use of appellation "Americans," 364 n.3

The Universal Forum of Cultures, 273–274

Unsafe at Any Speed, 167

Upside-down-map, 283

Urry, John, 33–34

U.S.-Canada Free Trade Agreement. *See* FTA

U.S.-Mexico Fund for Culture, 272, 280, 309, 310, 385 n.20

USA Patriot Act, 341

Utopia Unarmed, 184–185

Velho, Gilberto, 117

Ventura, Zuenir, 135–136, 138–139

Verbitsky, Horacio, 360–361

Vianna, Hermano, 91, 120–121, 124–125, 127, 368 n.4

Videla, Jorge, 72

Vila, Pablo, 253

Villa, Esteban, 53

Viñas, David, 357, 389 n.8

Viva Rio, 18, 88, 132–135, 139–140, 142–149, 371 nn.1, 2, 4, 6, 373 nn.17, 18

The Volunteers, 54

Wacquant, Loïc, 80–81

Wallis, Brian, 245

Warner, Michael, 49–50, 173

Waters, Malcolm, 29

Wechsler, Joanna, 117

West, Richard, 103

Westell, Anthony, 222

Westinghouse Electric Corporation, 223

Whiteness studies, 364 n.5

Will, George F., 267, 270

Williams, Raymond, 85

Wilson, Pete, 266

Winant, Howard, 112, 233, 234

Wineland, John, 278

With His Pistol in His Hand: A Border Ballad and Its Hero, 252

Wodiczko, Krzysztof, 323–325, 323

Wolfensohn, James D., 13

Workers, exploitation of, 35

Working Assets, 169–171

The World Bank, 35, 37, 94, 216; and cultural development, 13–14; and Latin America, 276

World Culture Report 1998: Culture, Creativity and Markets, 28

World Trade Organization (WTO) 9–10, 17, 37, 193, 216, 232; and corporations, 217; and the cultural economy, 17–18; and cultural goods, 218–221; and pharmaceutical patents, 359

WTO. *See* World Trade Organization (WTO)

Yard, Sally, 305, 313

Ybarra-Frausto, Tomás, 53

Young, Iris Marion, 3, 23–24, 376 n.2

Young Lords Party, 52, 86
Youth cultures. *See* Culture: youth

Zaluar, Alba, 123
Zapatista National Liberation Army. *See* Zapatistas

Zapatistas, 34, 66, 88, 286; and civil society, 96–108. *See also* Indigenous peoples
Zolberg, Vera L., 245

George Yúdice is Professor of American Studies

and Spanish and Portuguese at New York University.

He is also the Director of the Center for Latin American

and Caribbean Studies.

Library of Congress Cataloging-in-Publication Data

Yúdice, George.

The expediency of culture : uses of culture in the

global era / George Yúdice.

p. cm. — (Post-contemporary interventions)

Includes bibliographical references and index.

ISBN 0-8223-3180-2 (cloth : alk. paper)

ISBN 0-8223-3168-3 (pbk. : alk. paper)

1. Culture. 2. Cultural policy. 3. Globalization—

Social aspects. 4. Consumption (Economics)—

Social aspects. I. Title. II. Series.

HM621.Y83 2003

306—dc22   2003014768